Historical Archaeologies of Transhumance across Europe

Transhumance is a form of pastoralism that has been practised around the world since animals were first domesticated. Such seasonal movements have formed an important aspect of many European farming systems for several thousand years, although they have declined markedly since the nineteenth century. Ethnographers and geographers have long been involved in recording transhumant practices, and in the last two decades archaeologists have started to add a new material dimension to the subject.

This volume brings together recent advances in the study of European transhumance during historical times, from Sweden to Spain, Romania to Ireland, and beyond that even Newfoundland. While the focus is on the archaeology of seasonal sites used by shepherds and cowherds, the contributions exhibit a high degree of interdisciplinarity. Documentary, cartographic, ethnographic and palaeoecological evidence all play a part in the examination of seasonal movement and settlement in medieval and post-medieval landscapes. Notwithstanding the obvious diversity across Europe in terms of livestock, distances travelled and socio-economic context, an extended introduction to the volume shows that cross-cutting themes are now emerging, including mobility, gendered herding, collective land-use, the agency of non-elite people and competition for grazing and markets.

The book will appeal not only to archaeologists, but to historians, geographers, ethnographers, palaeoecologists and anyone interested in rural lifeways across Europe.

Eugene Costello is a landscape archaeologist with interests in pastoralism, non-elite society and the archaeology of the Reformation. He received his BA (UCC) in 2011, MA (Sheffield) in 2012, and PhD (NUI Galway) in 2016. He was a National Endowment for the Humanities Postdoctoral Fellow at University of Notre Dame, USA, for 2016–2017, and is currently Visiting Lecturer in the School of Geography and Archaeology at NUI Galway.

Eva Svensson is a historical archaeologist and professor in the Department of Life and Environmental Sciences, Karlstad University, Sweden. Her main research interests include social and ecological approaches to forested landscapes in a long-term perspective, and subaltern environment and lifescapes in the eighteenth to twentieth centuries. She has published extensively on both topics in Swedish and English.

Themes in Contemporary Archaeology

Series Editors:

Professor Kristian Kristiansen, *University of Gothenburg, Sweden*
Professor Eszter Bánffy, *German Archaeological Institute, Frankfurt, Germany*
Professor Peter Attema, *University of Groningen, Netherlands*

Series Editorial Assistant:

Claes Uhnér, *German Archaeological Institute, Germany*

Themes in Contemporary Archaeology provides cutting edge summaries of areas of debate in current archaeological enquiry, with a particular emphasis on European archaeology. The series has a broad coverage, encompassing all periods and archaeological disciplines from theoretical debate to statistical analysis and three-dimensional imaging. The multi-author volumes are based on selected sessions from the well-regarded annual conference of the European Association of Archaeologists.

Published Volumes:
Volume 1: Assembling Çatalhöyük
Volume 2: Trypillia Mega-Sites and European Prehistory, 4100–3400 BCE
Volume 3: Going West?
    The Dissemination of Neolithic Innovations between the Bosporus and the Carpathians

E
A European Association
A *of* Archaeologists

The European Association of Archaeologists (EAA) is the association for all professional archaeologists of Europe and beyond. The EAA has around 2,200 members from sixty countries worldwide working in prehistory, classical, medieval, and later archaeology.

The EAA aims

- to promote the development of archaeological research and the exchange of archaeological information
- to promote the management and interpretation of the European archaeological heritage
- to promote proper ethical and scientific standards for archaeological work
- to promote the interests of professional archaeologists in Europe
- to promote co-operation with other organisations with similar aims.

www.routledge.com/Themes-in-Contemporary-Archaeology/book-series/TCA

Historical Archaeologies of Transhumance across Europe

Edited by Eugene Costello and Eva Svensson

LONDON AND NEW YORK

First published 2018
by Routledge
2 Park Square, Milton Park, Abingdon, Oxon OX14 4RN

and by Routledge
711 Third Avenue, New York, NY 10017

Routledge is an imprint of the Taylor & Francis Group, an informa business

© 2018 selection and editorial matter, Eugene Costello and Eva Svensson; individual chapters, the contributors

The right of Eugene Costello and Eva Svensson to be identified as the authors of the editorial material, and of the authors for their individual chapters, has been asserted in accordance with sections 77 and 78 of the Copyright, Designs and Patents Act 1988.

All rights reserved. No part of this book may be reprinted or reproduced or utilised in any form or by any electronic, mechanical, or other means, now known or hereafter invented, including photocopying and recording, or in any information storage or retrieval system, without permission in writing from the publishers.

Trademark notice: Product or corporate names may be trademarks or registered trademarks, and are used only for identification and explanation without intent to infringe.

British Library Cataloguing-in-Publication Data
A catalogue record for this book is available from the British Library

Library of Congress Cataloging-in-Publication Data
A catalog record for this title has been requested

ISBN: 978-0-8153-8032-0 (hbk)
ISBN: 978-1-351-21339-4 (ebk)

Typeset in ACaslon Pro
by Apex CoVantage, LLC

Contents

	List of figures and tables	vii
	List of contributors	xi
CHAPTER 1	Transhumant pastoralism in historic landscapes: beginning a European perspective *Eugene Costello and Eva Svensson*	1
CHAPTER 2	The Scandinavian shieling – between innovation and tradition *Eva Svensson*	15
CHAPTER 3	From written sources to archaeological remains – medieval shielings in central Scandinavia *Susanne Pettersson*	29
CHAPTER 4	Winter housing: archaeological perspectives on Newfoundland's non-pastoral transhumant tradition *Anatolijs Venovcevs and Barry C. Gaulton*	43
CHAPTER 5	What do we really know about transhumance in medieval Scotland? *Piers Dixon*	59
CHAPTER 6	Ethno-geoarchaeological study of seasonal occupation: Bhiliscleitir, the Isle of Lewis *Patrycja Kupiec and Karen Milek*	75
CHAPTER 7	Morphology of transhumant settlements in post-medieval South Connemara: a case study in adaptation *Eugene Costello*	93
CHAPTER 8	The changing character of transhumance in early and later medieval England *Mark Gardiner*	109
CHAPTER 9	Seasonal pastoral settlement in the lower mountains of the Auvergne region (France) during the medieval and modern periods (thirteenth–eighteenth centuries) *Frédéric Surmely, Violaine Nicolas, Jay D. Franklin, Robert Linam, Manon Cabanis and Julien Le Junter*	121
CHAPTER 10	Moving up and down throughout the seasons: winter and summer grazing between Provence and the southern Alps (France) AD 1100–1500 *Sylvain Burri, Vanessa Py-Saragaglia and Roxanne Cesarini*	135
CHAPTER 11	Alpine settlement remains in the Bernese Alps (Switzerland) in medieval and modern times: the visibility of alpine summer farming activities in the archaeological record *Brigitte Andres*	155
CHAPTER 12	Short- and long-distance transhumant systems and the commons in post-classical archaeology: case studies from southern Europe *Anna Maria Stagno*	171
CHAPTER 13	Transhumance in the mountains of northern Tuscany (Italy) *Massimo Dadà*	187
CHAPTER 14	The role of marginal landscapes in understanding transhumance in southern Tuscany (twelfth–twentieth centuries AD): a reverse perspective integrating ethnoarchaeological and historical approaches *Edoardo Vanni and Davide Cristoferi*	197
CHAPTER 15	Transhumant herding systems in Iberia *Margarita Fernández Mier and Catarina Tente*	219

CHAPTER 16	**Transhumance dynamics in the Gredos Range (central Spain) during the last two millennia: environmental and socio-political vectors of change**	233
	José Antonio López-Sáez, Antonio Blanco-González, Daniel Abel-Schaad, Sandra Robles-López, Reyes Luelmo-Lautenschlaeger, Sebastián Pérez-Díaz and Francisca Alba-Sánchez	
CHAPTER 17	**Ovine pastoralism and mobility systems in Romania: an ethnoarchaeological approach**	245
	Robin Brigand, Olivier Weller, Felix Adrian Tencariu, Marius Alexianu, Andrei Asăndulesei	

Index	264

Figures

1.1	Distribution map of study areas and regions dealt with by each chapter	2
2.1	Medieval house foundation, Gammelvallen, Ångersjö	17
2.2	Pollen diagram, Backasätern shieling	19
2.3	The forest farmer's year in Offerdal parish during the mid-eighteenth century	22
2.4	The Backa hamlet and outlands; the outland east of Backasätern shieling has not been surveyed	23
2.5	Occurrence of settlement and impact of different land-use activities over time at the Backa estate	24
3.1	A modern summerhouse at *Herlandsetra*	29
3.2	Modern remains of a timber building at *Herlandsetra Nedre*, Vestfold County, Norway	31
3.3	Map showing the regions mentioned in the article	32
3.4	Possible building at *Melgårdsetern* showing low earthworks surrounding a rectangular hollow	35
3.5	Trench 1 cutting the western wall of the medieval building at *Vesetra*	39
3.6	Results based on radiocarbon dates from the investigated shielings	40
4.1	One of the few winter house drawings	45
4.2	Large open hearth at the Sunnyside 1 site	47
4.3	Distribution of winter houses around Big Mussel Pond in relation to the modern community of O'Donnells	48
4.4	Interior of a European cabin in Labrador	49
4.5	Approximate migration routes between summer communities and their associated winter places in Notre Dame and Bonavista Bays, Newfoundland	53
5.1	Plan and section of beehive hut at Airigh a' Sguir, Uig, Isle of Lewis: stone with turf covering	64
5.2	An example of a dimpled turf shieling mound at Airigh na Stainge, Argyll and Bute	65
5.3	Site plan of shieling hut group at Bidein An Tighearna, Isle of Eigg	66
5.4	Late medieval hut at Camp Shiel Burn, Scottish Borders	69
5.5	Post-medieval stone and turf-walled hut at Lawers Burn, North Lochtayside	70
5.6	Two late medieval turf huts overlying an earlier turf structure at Kiltyrie, North Lochtayside	70
5.7	Medieval turf-walled hut at Kiltyrie, North Lochtayside	71
6.1	Map of the Isle of Lewis showing the location of the Bhiliscleiter shieling settlement and Port of Ness	76
6.2	A student visits a shieling at Filiscleitir, Ness	77
6.3	Three Ness women prepare to leave the shieling	77
6.4	Topographic survey of shielings at Bhiliscleiter	78
6.5	Plan of Structures 10–12 at Bhiliscleiter, showing the location of Test Pits 1–3	79
6.6	Thin section 1, showing clay floor in layer 4.1; clay nodule with temper in layer 4.2; and zone of compaction in layer 4.3	83
6.7	Thin section 2, showing charred peat in layer 4.6; charred peat impregnated with iron in layer 4.4; and horizontally bedded plant tissues in layer 4.7	84
6.8	Thin section 6, showing pottery fragment in layer 4.8; dense matrix of amorphous organic matter in layer 4.9; and charred peat in layer 4.12	86
6.9	Thin section 4, showing grass phytoliths in dense amorphous organic matter matrix; plant tissues; and wood tissues	88
7.1	Carna peninsula, with townland boundaries in green; unenclosed rough grazing shaded red	95
7.2	Distribution of farmhouses (*c.* 1838) in home townlands and sites in connected summer pastures; Glinsce and Seanadh Bhuire sites not shown	96
7.3	Probable booley dwellings of various design, with calf pen to south; Gleannán	97
7.4a	Rectangular type, Gleannán 9	98
7.4b	Example of irregular type, Gleannán 12; possible butter store in north-east	98
7.5	Intact early nineteenth-century farmhouse in Ogúil, Kilannin (east of Carna peninsula)	99
7.6	D-shaped booley dwelling in centre of photograph built up against two boulders sitting next to one another, An Cnoc Buí 4	100
7.7	Booley dwelling in Beitheach Chatha built up against large boulder	101
7.8	Centre of An Aill Mhór group in Gleannán	104
7.9	Farmhouses and fields in home townlands of An Aird Thiar and Thoir	105
8.1	The seventh- to eighth-century sunken building at North Marden (Sussex) on the South Downs	111
8.2	Selected areas of transhumance and other places mentioned in the text	112
9.1	General location of the two study areas	122
9.2	Aerial photograph of the medieval hamlet du Lac-d'En-Haut (La Godivelle, France)	123
9.3	Table of radiocarbon dates obtained on medieval sites of Cantal and Sancy	125
9.4	General map of site n° 54 indicating the areas tested	126
9.5	Plan of site n° 1365 (Lacapelle-Barrès, Cantal)	128
9.6	Pot found in site 335 (seventeenth century; Saint-Clément, Cantal)	128
9.7	Modern hamlet of Pré-Rigot (Compains, France)	130
9.8	Geographical distribution of the aligned structures (*peignes ou tras*) in the Sancy	131
9.9	Aerial view of aligned structures concentration, at Le Roc Blanc (Perpezat, Puy-de-Dôme)	132

viii *Figures*

10.1	Study area	137
10.2	Wintering flows of Alpine herds (AD 1100–1300)	138
10.3	Wintering flows of western and central Alpine herds (AD 1300–1500)	140
10.4	Wintering flows of eastern Alpine and Provencal herds (AD 1300–1500)	141
10.5	Summering flows of western Provencal herds (AD 1300–1500)	142
10.6	Summering flows of central and eastern Provencal herds (AD 1300–1500)	143
10.7	Reconstruction of shepherds' routes (AD 1300–1500)	145
10.8a–b	Distances travelled for wintering and summering (AD 1300–1500)	146
10.8c–h	Assessment of wintering and summering flows	146
10.9a	Site of Coste de Tonis	148
10.9b	Structure of Coste de Tonis 1	148
10.9c	Structure of Fangeas X and IV	148
10.9d	Structure of Col de Barral (Le Lavandou, Var)	148
10.9e	Structure of Roque Fadade 6 (Le Muy, Var)	148
11.1	Map of the Oberhasli region showing the locations of the valleys, passes, sites and places discussed in the text	156
11.2	The building types of the most important categories: building remains, rock-shelter structures and animal pens	158
11.3	Innertkirchen BE, Murläger (aerial view of the structures built into the slope and the remains of the walls)	160
11.4	Innertkirchen BE, Zum See (orthophoto of the alp level)	161
11.5	Brienz BE, Axalp-Litschentellti (north facade, section and ground-plan with fireplace of a sixteenth-century milking hut)	164
12.1	Map of the sites investigated by the 'Archimede' project (circles) which also designates the other sites detailed in the text (triangles)	172
12.2	Commons and municipalities on the eastern Alevese Plain (the round areas correspond to preserved *seles*)	173
12.3	Seasonal movements in eastern Liguria (seventeenth–twentieth c.)	175
12.4	The investigated areas and identified topographic units in Alava and Gipuzkoa	177
12.5	Hamlets involved with rights in the Parzonería General de Gipuzkoa and Alava and the location of the arrival points of a select few transhumance routes	178
12.6	Sites and test-pit locations in Malla	179
12.7	Periods and comparative matrix of the Malla investigations	181
12.8	Beorlatza. a. Charcoal kiln site. b. Ancient pollarded oak	183
13.1	Map of the research area	188
13.2	Pastures on the Apuan Alps: the huts of Sagro	189
13.3	Medieval hospice of Centocroci	192
13.4	Map of the *comunalia* of Vinca that shows fourteenth-century 'versant-transhumance'	194
13.5	Pastoral huts around Monte Sagro	194
14.1	Mediterranean transhumance routes	198
14.2	The study area showing the locations of sites quoted in the text (Tuscany, Italy)	199
14.3	The compound enclosures of barren Monte Labbro	204
14.4	The Pigelleto Reservoir showing the customs road mentioned in the cadastre of AD 1822 (*Doganella*)	207
14.5	Prile Lagoon and other humid environments during the medieval period	209
14.6	Historical photographs representing shepherds' villages (1865) and maps (1680–1699) with huts around Prile Lagoon	210
14.7	Modern huts near Vetulonia	211
14.8	Hut with foundations (site B)	212
15.1	Iberian case-study area: Cantabrian Mountains (northwest Spain) and Estrela Mountain (northern-central Portugal)	220
15.2	*Braña La Mesa* (Asturias, Spain)	223
15.3	Soida (Celorico da Beira). Archaeological site from the tenth century, Estrela Mountain.	225
15.4	Moudreiros (Asturias, Spain)	227
15.5	Medium-scale transhumance from Estrela Mountain (Portugal)	228
15.6	A *chozo* for *Mesta* herds from the Cantabrian Mountains	230
16.1	Location of the Gredos Range in central Iberia	235
16.2	Synthetic pollen diagrams of four well-dated peat bogs from the Gredos Range	236
17.1	High terrace Chalcolithic settlement (*Dealul Pandele*) and sheepfold without a dairy	246
17.2	The study area in Romania (stars): the Moldovan Plain and foothills and the southern Carpathians	249
17.3	Models of the various types of pastoralism (nineteenth–twentieth centuries)	250
17.4	A seasonal sheepfold with facilities for the preparation of milk products	251
17.5	The typical plan of a seasonal sheepfold in the Moldovan foothills	253
17.6	High mountain pastures, North Parâng *zānoaga*	255
17.7	Salt rock exploitation and the supply of salt boulders to private homesteads and local sheepfolds	257
17.8	Salted soils and pastoralism in the Moldavian Plain	258
17.9	Transhumance routes overlap mountain relief and the geology of salt (in blue)	260

Table

6.1 Summary of features observed in thin sections 1–2, 4, and 5–6 at Bhiliscleiter shieling settlement   89

Contributors

Daniel Abel-Schaad is a PhD Researcher and his main interests are related to plant ecology from a palaeoecological perspective and its implications on conservation and management of relict species. He is currently working in the Department of Botany of the University of Granada (Spain) on a project about the evolution of the forests of *Cedrus atlantica* and *Abies pinsapo* at both sides of the Strait of Gibraltar.

Francisca Alba-Sánchez is Associate Professor (civil servant) at the University of Granada. She is interested in palaeoecology, conservation biology, plant–environment relationships and ecological niche modeling. In addition she has focused on *glacial refugia* and postglacial spread for Mediterranean relict plant species. She knows the physical processes involved in the dispersion–deposition mechanisms of pollen grains, a very useful skill to get Quaternary Distribution Models of Western Mediterranean relict species. She has published in journals such as *Diversity and Distributions, Quaternary Science Reviews, Agricultural and Forest Meteorology, Review of Palaeobotany and Palynology, Vegetation History and Archaeobotanany, Journal of Arid Environments, Expert Systems with Applications.*

Marius Alexianu, PhD, is Associate Professor and head of the Ethnoarchaeology section of the Arheoinvest Platform from the "Alexandru Ioan Cuza" University of Iaşi, Romania. He is the main author of the first ethnoarchaeological study in Romania (1992) and of the first book on the ethnoarchaeology of the salt springs from Eastern Romania (2007). He has won two national research projects regarding the ethnoarchaeology of the salt springs and salt mountains from extra-Carpathian areas of Romania (2007–2010 and 2011–2015).

Brigitte Andres works as a Project Manager for archaeological excavations and historic building archaeology at the Department for Urban Construction of the City of Zurich. She has a PhD in Medieval Archaeology from the University of Zurich. Her main interests are urban topography, alpine and landscape archaeology.

Andrei Asăndulesei is currently a Researcher in the Department for Interdisciplinary Research – Field Science – "Alexandru Ioan Cuza" University of Iaşi, Romania. His main research interest is prehistoric archaeology, with special focus on interdisciplinary investigations of prehistoric sites. Since 2014 he has coordinated a research project aimed at elaborating and applying a model of non-intrusive research in prehistoric sites from the region of Moldavia.

Antonio Blanco-González is a Post-Doctoral Researcher with the University of Salamanca, Spain. He has held academic positions at the University of Durham (UK) as a Marie Curie fellow and at the University of Valladolid (Spain). His research interests include social theory and formation theory, mainly applied to later prehistoric Iberia. He has published on these subjects in journals such as *Quaternary Science Reviews, Journal of Archaeological Method and Theory, Journal of Social Archaeology, Antiquity* or *Cambridge Archaeological Journal,* as well as book chapters in peer-reviewed volumes.

Robin Brigand received a PhD in Archaeology from the Universities of Franche-Comté (Besançon, France) and Padua (Italia). He is currently a Post-Doctorate Researcher at UMR 8215 Trajectoires (Paris, France). His studies on the spatial impact of Neolithic societies focus – using various scales – on site systems and their environments, settlement patterns, raw material acquisition and distribution, landscape dynamics. Within this framework, he is involved in an ethnoarchaeological study on territorial practices surrounding salt uses and circulation in Romanian Moldavia.

Sylvain Burri is a French CNRS Researcher from the laboratory LA3M UMR 7298 CNRS, University of Aix-Marseille. He is a medievalist historian and archaeologist. His research focuses on rural crafts, plant resources management and uses, and landscape, especially of forest and uncultivated lands.

Manon Cabanis is an Anthraco-Carpologist with INRAP Rhône-Alpes/Auvergne and UMR 6042 CNRS, Clermont-Ferrand, in France. Her research interests are carpology, anthracology, palaeoenvironment and landscape archaeology.

Roxanne Cesarini is a masters degree student in history and archaeology at the University of Aix-Marseille. She is interested in pastoral economy (regulation and incomes), life on upland pastures (structures and activities) and mobility of herds and herders.

Eugene Costello is a Historical Archaeologist with interests in pastoralism, non-elite landscapes and the archaeology of the Reformation. He received his BA (UCC) in 2011, MA (Sheffield) in 2012, and PhD (NUI Galway) in 2016. He was a National Endowment for the Humanities Postdoctoral Fellow at University of Notre Dame, USA, for 2016–2017.

Davide Cristoferi is Doctor in Medieval History at the University of Siena (2016). Now he is member of the GINI project (Growth, INequality and Institutions) at Ghent University (Belgium). He studies the rural and economic history of Late Medieval–Early Modern Tuscany with a focus on the role of socio-political institutions.

Massimo Dadà graduated at the University of Venice; he obtained his PhD degree at the University of Pisa, where he was also Research Fellow. Currently a freelance archaeologist, his main interests concern monasteries, hospitals, roads and mobility in the Middle Ages. He directs the "Da Canossa a Luni" archaeological project, with excavations and surveys in the Appennine uplands.

Piers Dixon is Deputy Head of Survey and Recording in Historic Environment Scotland, formerly of the Royal Commission on the Ancient and Historical Monuments of Scotland. Piers has research interests in medieval rural settlements and is a committee member of Ruralia (www.ruralia.cz/). His book on lowland Scotland *Puir Labourers and Busy Husbandmen* was published by Birlinn in 2002.

Jay D. Franklin, PhD, is Professor of Anthropology in the Department of Sociology and Anthropology at East Tennessee State University, Johnson City, TN USA. His research interests are upland/highland archaeology, rock shelter and cave archaeology, prehistoric stone tool technologies, pottery technology, Palaeolithic archaeology, French medieval archaeology.

Mark Gardiner is Reader in Medieval Archaeology in the School of History and Heritage at the University of Lincoln in the United Kingdom. He has a long-standing interest in seasonal settlement and has previously published on aspects of the subject in the context of Ireland.

Barry C. Gaulton is an Associate Professor in the Department of Archaeology, Memorial University of Newfoundland. His research interests focus on the historical archaeology of early modern North America with particular reference to extractive industries, vernacular architecture, material culture and seasonal mobility.

Julien Le Junter holds a master 2 from the Blaise Pascal university, France. His master's degree was dedicated to the pastoral huts of the Sancy mountains.

Patrycja Kupiec received her PhD in Archaeology from the University of Aberdeen. She is a Fellow of Society of Antiquaries of Scotland and Associate Fellow of Higher Education Academy. Her research interests include geoarchaeology, Viking and early medieval archaeology, ethnoarchaeology, transhumance and gender studies.

Robert Linam works with Cultural Resource Analysts Inc. as an Archaeological Field Technician in the USA. His research interests are: Western European medieval archaeology, medieval France, rural habitation.

José Antonio López-Sáez is a Tenured Scientist in the Institute of History at the Spanish National Research Council (CSIC), Madrid, Spain. His research interests include palaeopalynology and archaeopalynology (pollen, spores, non-pollen palynomorphs) from different periods (Palaeolithic to Middle Ages) and different sedimentary contexts (lakes, peat bogs, archaeological sites, palaeosoils, etc.), prehistoric agriculture with particular emphasis on the origins and expansion in the Mediterranean and Mesoamerica, and high-mountain environments during the Holocene. He has published on these subjects in journals such as *Nature*, *Journal of Archaeological Science*, *Quaternary International*, *Quaternary Science Reviews*, *Quaternary Research*, *Review of Palaeobotany and Palynology*, *Vegetation History and Archaeobotany*, etc.

Reyes Luelmo-Lautenschlaeger is a PhD Researcher with the Autonomous University of Madrid and Spanish National Research Council, Spain. Her research interests include human and ecological dynamics in mid-mountain and high-mountain ecosystems during the Late Holocene. She has published on these subjects in journals such as *Vegetation History and Archaeobotany*, *Cuaternario y Geomorfología* or *Grana*.

Margarita Fernández Mier is Associate Professor of Medieval History at the University of Oviedo. She specialises on Early Medieval Times in Spain. Her main research focus is on the archaeological and historical study of medieval rural history. In recent years she has implemented a project of agrarian archaeology in the northwest of the Iberian Peninsula.

Karen Milek received her PhD in Archaeology from the University of Cambridge. She is Associate Professor (Reader) in Geoarchaeology at Durham University, and Honorary Research Fellow in the School of Geosciences, University of Aberdeen. Her interests include geoarchaeology, ethno-geoarchaeology and the archaeology of the early medieval and historical periods.

Violaine Nicolas holds a PhD in Archaeology from Université de Caen in France. Her research interests are: Medieval and Modern Age archaeology and history of France.

Sebastián Pérez-Díaz is a Post-Doctoral Researcher in the Institute of History at the Spanish National Research Council (CSIC), Madrid, Spain. He has held academic positions at the University of Basque Country (Spain) as a Juan de la Cierva fellow. His research interests include vegetation history and anthropisation dynamics during the Holocene, mainly applied to later prehistoric of northern Iberia. He has published on these subjects in journals such as *Quaternary International*, *Vegetation History and Archaeobotany*, *Journal of Archaeological Science: Reports*, *Boreas*, as well as book chapters in peer-reviewed volumes.

Susanne Pettersson is an Archaeologist at the Norwegian Maritime Museum. She has participated in research projects on outland archaeology, rural medieval settlements and historical archaeology.

Vanessa Py-Saragaglia is a French CNRS Researcher from the laboratory GEODE in Toulouse. She is an archaeologist and archaeobotanist (anthracologist and dendrologist) and studies anthropisation phenomena and natural resource exploitation modalities in European high mountain areas. Her research focuses on past environmental changes and aims to reconstruct forest cover dynamics and trajectories related to human practices and climate change during the Holocene.

Sandra Robles-López is a Pre-Doctoral Researcher in Autonomous University of Madrid; nowadays she is developing her PhD at the Centre for Human and Social Sciences (CCHS) (Spain). She graduated in Biological Sciences in the Autonomous University of Madrid and focused her professional career in palaeobotany. Recently she studied quaternary vegetation in Central Spain from an ecological and historical point of view. She has published in journals such as *Quaternary International*, *Vegetation History and Archaeobotany*, *Journal of Archaeological Science*, as well as book chapters.

Anna Maria Stagno is Marie Curie IE fellow at the University of the Basque Country. Her research focuses on archaeology of commons, rural archaeology and environmental resources management, crossing field and archival sources. She is a member of the Laboratory of Environmental Archaeology and History of the University of Genoa and coordinates the European Network of the Archaeology of Commons.

Frédéric Surmely, PhD, Hab. Prehistory, is Curator of Archaeology in DRAC Auvergne-Rhône-Alpes and UMR 6042 CNRS, Clermont-Ferrand, France. His research interests are: late palaeolithic archaeology, lithic raw material, upland/highland archaeology, French Medieval and Modern Age archaeology.

Eva Svensson is a Professor in the Department of Life and Environmental Sciences, Karlstad University, Sweden. Eva's main research interests include social and ecological approaches to forested landscapes in a long-term perspective, and subaltern environment and lifescapes in the 18th–20th centuries. She has published extensively on both topics in Swedish and English.

Felix Adrian Tencariu, PhD, is a Senior Researcher at the Interdisciplinary Research Department – Field Science – "Alexandru Ioan Cuza" University of Iași, Romania. He is an archaeologist interested in the prehistory of southeastern Europe, his research being oriented towards integrating ethnoarchaeology, experimental archaeology and archaeometry to enhance the archaeological interpretation and help understanding past behaviours and technologies.

Catarina Tente is a Professor of Medieval Archaeology at Nova Lisbon University and researcher of Institute of Medieval Studies. She has a PhD in Archaeology, and she had published several articles on settlement and social structures in Early Middle Ages. She currently coordinates a team of researchers that aims to study medieval rural societies in central Portugal.

Edoardo Vanni is a Doctor in Archaeology and History at the University of Foggia (2014). At present he has a post-doctoral fellowship at the University of Siena. His topics are archaeological method and theory, ancient landscape studies, salt production and pastoralism in Italy.

Anatolijs Venovcevs is a GIS Technologist for the Town of Happy Valley-Goose Bay, Labrador and an alumnus of the Department of Archaeology, Memorial University of Newfoundland. His thesis research focused on the material culture, seasonal mobility, and spatial distribution of Euro-Newfoundlander winter houses.

Olivier Weller is a Research Fellow at CNRS (UMR 8215, Trajectoires, CNRS-Pantheon-Sorbonne University, Paris, France). His research focuses on the archaeology of salt, specifically the origins of production in terms of exploitation techniques, uses and socio-economic implications during the European Neolithic. The approaches are both technological, ethnoarchaeological and ethnohistorical, as well as palaeoenvironmental, physical-chemical or geomatic. His study area spans from Europe (France, Spain, Germany, Romania) to Oceania (New Guinea).

CHAPTER 1

Transhumant pastoralism in historic landscapes
Beginning a European perspective

EUGENE COSTELLO AND EVA SVENSSON

TRANSHUMANCE – A CONCEPT BETTER TO DISCUSS THAN TO DEFINE?

Pastoralism offers a vast field of study, and within it transhumant practices represent an important range of past and contemporary human mobility strategies. In its widest sense, transhumance may simply be described as the seasonal movement of livestock. The *Oxford English Dictionary* adds some environmental qualification to this by defining transhumance as "the action or practice of moving livestock from one grazing ground to another in a seasonal cycle, typically to lowlands in winter and highlands in summer". The wide-ranging geographic and social implications of such a definition mean, of course, that the study of transhumant practices permits a very wide perspective on human society, touching on themes as diverse as livestock management, economic responsiveness, social mobility and competition for land. Furthermore, use of the relative words 'lowlands' and 'highlands' means that a considerable proportion of the earth's surface may be considered as potential settings for transhumance. There are consequently many ways in which people might conceive of and define the practice, and there has not been *one*, but many transhumant pastoralisms in Europe during historical times.

For ethnographers, who long dominated the field of historical transhumance, it was diversity, not shared experiences and characteristics that were emphasised. The importance of ethnography and ethnographic documentation of transhumant pastoral regimes all over Europe on the eve of their demise cannot be overestimated. These records are now invaluable to historical archaeologists working with transhumant pastoralism, especially as the field is difficult to access with only archaeological methods. They also form narratives of their own, transmitting transhumance as a pre-modern, out-dated mode of production located in the peripheries of mainstream and modern farming, and not as a rational agricultural practice. Another prominent feature of the ethnographic narratives on transhumance is regionalisation, emphasising geographically bounded regional, and even local, characteristics and traditions as structuring principles. These regionalised approaches have often been combined with both nature determinism and the assumption that characteristics of a cultural system are more strongly accentuated in the peripheries than the centres (See below "Transhumance and pastoralism – an overview", with references; Svensson, Chapter 2, this volume with references).

The preconceived notions of transhumant pastoralism as peripheral and regionalised have worked as barriers to approaches to transhumant pastoralism from European or cross-European perspectives. The fact that both the transhumance systems and the seasonal nodes/sites (e.g. shielings, booley huts, *säter*, *brañas*; Collis et al., 2016) have been named differently across Europe means that co-operation between scholars from different countries has been hampered. The lack of inclusive concepts allowing scholars of transhumant pastoralism from different parts of Europe to recognise what they shared long meant that it was common to have different conference sessions for scholars from Scandinavia and north-west Europe and for scholars from southern Europe, including Alpine regions and the Mediterranean. Due to a lack of meeting places, intersections and commonly understood or shared concepts or definitions, parallel discourses developed. Moreover, in countries where transhumance had not survived till the present day, there was very little discourse at all regarding transhumance, the archaeology of such practices being neglected until very recently.

The session organised by the present writers with Mark Gardiner at EAA Glasgow 2015, "Historical Transhumance in Europe: Finding Common Ground in Marginal Landscapes", was very important in uniting European archaeologists who deal specifically with historical transhumance. Two previous EAA sessions, in 2011 and 2012 respectively, had drawn archaeologists together to speak about aspects of summer upland farming, but they took long-term perspectives, from the Neolithic to present day; moreover, the resulting collection of essays focused mainly on Italy and the Alps (Collis et al., 2016). By narrowing the chronological focus to the last 1500 years or so, when documentary sources are common, we aimed in Glasgow

© 2018 European Association of Archaeologists

to foster a more incisive debate on the contribution of archaeology to transhumance studies across the continent. This decision facilitated discussion as we started to broach the questions thrown up by a European-wide perspective. Indeed, the fruitfulness of comparative debate on historical transhumance evident at Glasgow was an important driver for publishing many of the session papers in the present volume (see Figure 1.1 for distribution map).

Part of the progress triggered by the session has been a realisation of the need for appropriate contextualisation, problematisation and theorisation. Even within historical times, this is necessary to understand the various factors and qualities connected to and supporting regional transhumant systems in their European context. Different kinds of transhumance make use of similar natural conditions, such as mountain areas (albeit at a wide variety of altitudes) which are unsuitable for large-scale cereal cultivation, but usable, and used, in different ways, e.g. grazing, diverse resource extraction and hunting. Other shared characteristics are the importance of livestock and herding, but both the livestock and the herders differed. Sheep, goats and cows were herded sometimes by men, often of marginal social positions in society, and sometimes by women, more often members of landholding families. The agents in different transhumance systems could be elite members of society or landholding peasants, or both. Transhumance could serve as a kind of pioneer farming system in non-arable land, or it could succeed permanent settlement in certain areas after year-round farming had been abandoned. It could operate in a specialised proto-capitalistic context, or as part of versatile economy. The primary and secondary products of transhumant livestock could be traded at long distances or consumed entirely or mostly in the local system.

In spite of these differences, all participants in the EAA Glasgow session expressed an understanding of transhumance as a socio-ecological experience (cf. Ingold, 1980). Movements of livestock were embedded in the social and economic structure of communities, but the decision of people to move was in turn always linked to seasonal changes in weather, vegetation and livestock reproductive cycles. Transhumance therefore offers an unusually rich insight into the creation of social practice amongst farming peoples, in that every variant was (quite literally) a navigation of economic opportunity, social situation and environmental circumstance. Transhumant mobility can be seen as an elastic strategy for tackling these diverse and changing conditions. The key to understanding it in a cross-European perspective is therefore the acceptance of it as anything but a unified practice. At the Glasgow session, it was clear that forging concrete definitions would be counter-productive to the ambition of enhancing cross-European understanding. Or, to quote Professor Stig Welinder in summing up the session: "some concepts are better to discuss than to define". For the

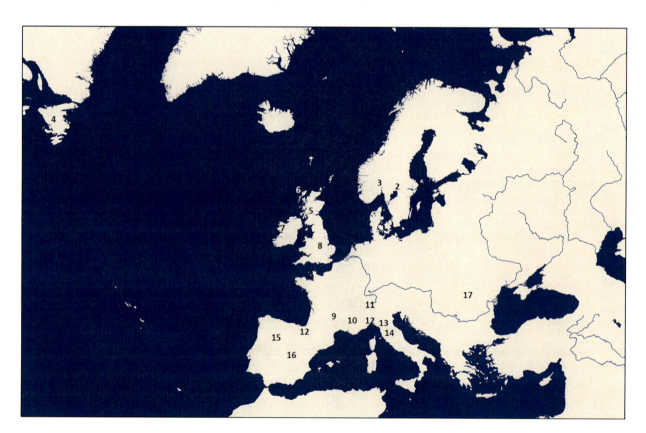

Figure 1.1. Distribution map of study areas and regions dealt with by each chapter

moment, at least, transhumance is one of these concepts. The editors of this volume would therefore like to suggest that it be understood as a *boundary object*, in the Star & Griesemer (1989: 393) definition:

> Boundary objects are objects which are both plastic enough to adapt to local needs and the constraints of the several parties employing them, yet robust enough to maintain a common identity across sites. They are weakly structured in common use, and become strongly structured in individual site use. They may be abstract or concrete. They have different meanings in different social worlds but their structure is common enough to more than one world to make them recognizable, a means of translation. The creation and management of boundary objects is a key process in developing and maintaining coherence across intersecting social worlds.

After an overview is presented of transhumance in its pastoral context, the present writers then go on to discuss it as a boundary object in historical Europe, under a few select themes.

TRANSHUMANCE AND PASTORALISM – AN OVERVIEW

It is certainly convenient to think of transhumance as a plastic 'boundary object' rather than a well-defined phenomenon. Nonetheless, in order to create a better understanding of how it has been addressed, and to position the importance of this volume in the research history of transhumance, an overview of previous work is needed.

First of all, it is of essence to distinguish participants in transhumance from other kinds of pastoralists, that is to say, anyone "whose livelihood comes from tending grazing animals" (Gefu & Gilles, 1990: 35). Anatoly Khazanov's (1994) attempt to classify various types of pastoralism is of much relevance here. Nomadic pastoralism, in its purest form, is characterised by a complete lack of agriculture (in the sense of arable farming), and in modern times is recorded only in North Eurasia, High Inner Asia, the Eurasian steppes, Arabia and the Sahara (Khazanov, 1994: 19). Moreover, people involved in full nomadic pastoralism lack a fixed base, so confusion with transhumance should not arise in this case. Less clear-cut, however, are the differences between the latter and what Khazanov (1994: 19) calls 'semi-nomadic pastoralism'. This is much more widespread around the globe and involves some element of agriculture along with the periodic changing of pastures

throughout most or all of the year. Other variations of pastoralism have been identified too. In 'semi-sedentary pastoralism' and 'distant-pastures husbandry', arable farming constitutes a more important element in the economy and as a consequence not everyone in the community moves with the stock under these systems (Khazanov, 1994: 21–23). In Central Asia, for instance, the Kirghiz are described as semi-sedentary in the late nineteenth century because their migrations with livestock took place over only three to three and a half months every year, with most family members remaining behind due to agricultural commitments (Simakov, 1978: 24). Both Johnson (1969: 18–19) and Khazanov (1994: 23) complain that scholars are too liberal in what they label 'transhumance', pointing to some vertical (lowland–upland) livestock movements in Europe which might better be described as semi-nomadic. This seems unduly fastidious, however. When talking about pastoralism, researchers really have in mind a broad spectrum of livestock management. That spectrum ranges from, on the one extreme, a community having no arable at all and continually re-locating over the course of a year to, on the other, full sedentism with a dependence on arable, and livestock being kept year-round on the one farm supplemented by fodder. If one considers that transhumant strategies occupy what is roughly the middle of this pastoral world, it is unsurprising that a close definition is impossible.

All the same, even if transhumance encompasses a range of practices, some 'fine-tuning' ought to be attempted. Barth (1962: 342), usefully, frames it as a form of pastoralism which allows people engaged in agriculture in specific ecological zones to use seasonally productive pastures in other areas. This quite rightly emphasises the agro-pastoral nature of transhumance and the role of the environment in encouraging movement. Where common areas of pasture are available, it is in the interests of farmers to make use of them since it frees up land for crops at home and allows them to keep more livestock using the extra grazing. Seasonality becomes a factor when these common pastures are located on poor or environmentally extreme land that only has a plentiful vegetation cover for half the year or slightly less. This is the case in much of Europe, where farmers based in the most fertile, crop-producing areas have traditionally exploited high-altitude and other extensive pastures during the summer (e.g. Bladé, 1892; Klein, 1920; Arbos, 1923; Davies, 1941; Braudel, 1972: 85–102). The fixed nature of these winter and summer zones introduces a regularity to transhumance that nomadic and semi-nomadic pastoralism do not exhibit to the same degree.

The maximisation of arable and pastoral land through seasonal exploitation of land in a different environmental context is therefore a pillar of transhumant movements. However, this still leaves room for debate. Scholars working on the Continent have tried to separate out what they see as different types of transhumance. The geographer Davies (1941: 155–56) makes a useful, if overly simplistic, distinction between two types that could still be observed in his time: the first being 'Mediterranean' transhumance, driven by the need to get livestock out of parched lowlands over the summer; and the second, 'Alpine' transhumance, which he argues is based on the need to free up land in the lowlands for crops. This second type is, or was, practised in the valleys and slopes of the Pyrenees, Alps, Carpathians, and also western Britain and Norway (Davies, 1941: 155–56). Davies bases his classification on his perception of Mediterranean and Alpine transhumance as practices which performed different functions in response to different physical environments. In reality, however, these functions are not mutually exclusive, and operational details such as livestock management and social organisation form equally important determinants in the classification of transhumance.

Braudel (1972: 85–87) outlines two kinds of transhumance relevant to the Mediterranean world for the end of the sixteenth century. The first – 'normal' transhumance – involved lowland sheep farmers and shepherds moving large flocks to the mountains for the summer, simply because the lowlands were unsuitable for stock raising at that time of year (akin to Davies's simplified 'Mediterranean' transhumance). The second – 'inverse' transhumance – involved people who were based in the high mountains bringing flocks down to over-winter at more clement altitudes. It is important to add that the large-scale transhumance of sheep which took place in Braudel's Mediterranean world, and the seventeenth and eighteenth centuries especially, was strongly linked to the growth of agrarian capitalism; wool sheared from the sheep was sold *en masse* to the market by speculative herd owners, some of whom became very powerful and organised, as in *La Mesta* of Spain (Klein, 1920). In his review of seasonal pastoralism in southern Germany, Luick (2004) also associates 'transhumance' with large-scale sheep movements. In eighteenth- and nineteenth-century Swabian–Franconian transhumance, large flocks of sheep were moved from lowlands to the summer pastures of the Jura Mountains, a journey which for some lasted several hundred kilometres and several weeks (Luick, 2004: 140–41). This is what Luick considers transhumance proper, that is to say, where livestock are brought long horizontal distances "by herders only – the owners . . . and the families of the herdsmen usually stay[ing] at their residential places" (Luick, 2004: 138). For him, the movement of family members with cows over shorter horizontal distances – but longer vertical distances – to high-altitude summer pastures forms part of a different 'alp-system' (Luick, 2004: 138). While echoing Davies's earlier dichotomy, he dispenses with the idea that vertical Alpine movements actually amount to 'transhumance'.

Our examination of transhumance so far has relied upon the contemporary or near-contemporary viewpoints of historians, geographers and others. However, *past* societies which engaged in pastoralism are not as open to neat classification. The difficulty, for example, of tracing pastoral nomadic peoples in the archaeological record has been discussed by Cribb (1991) and Barnard and Wendrich (2008), all of whom employ modern ethnographic data in order to understand prehistoric or ahistorical contexts. Detailed analysis of the socio-economic basis for pastoralism, as Galaty and Johnson (1990) present using case studies from the contemporary world, is simply not possible for pre-modern times due to a lack or scarcity of comprehensive data on land, labour and livestock ratios. This is especially true of prehistoric transhumance in Europe, with archaeologists proposing various models as to how it emerged and operated (e.g. Halstead, 1996; Greenfield, 1999; Kienlin & Valde-Nowak, 2004; Bentley & Knipper, 2005; Arnold & Greenfield, 2006; Nicolis et al., 2016; Pearce, 2016; Shishlina & Larionova, 2016; Walsh & Mocci, 2016). That said, recent isotopic studies of animal bone have shown that firm conclusions regarding the *existence* of seasonal livestock movements in certain periods and regions are attainable (Balasse et al., 2013; Tornero et al., 2013; Valenzuela-Lamas et al., 2016). Similar challenges face the historical archaeologist, albeit they are less extreme because of the availability of historical records which, in some parts of Europe, provide fairly detailed information on grazing rights and disputes. These provide an opportunity to better scrutinise pastoral systems, and to differentiate between different kinds of movement. However, the archaeological evidence should not be treated simply as an illustration of the historical record. It offers its own narrative of (agro-)pastoral communities insofar as it contains details that are often unobtainable in texts written from an elite perspective. The morphology of seasonal sites and upland enclosures can, for example, be used to deduce local aspects of herder organisation and livestock management that would never have been recorded officially and are only partially remembered for recent times in oral history.

THEORETICAL PERSPECTIVES ON HISTORICAL TRANSHUMANCE IN EUROPE

Regarding transhumance as a boundary object rather than a definition, the contexts of similarities and differences become crucial. The presentations at the EAA formed a journey to beautiful landscapes in high places, through time as well as space. Not only were there different histories of transhumant pastoralism, staged in various natural settings and material worlds, but each of these histories changed as they were played out with different kinds of livestock and different groups of people under shifting economic regimes. It also became clear from the presentations and subsequent discussions that similarities, differences, shared experiences and comparative perspectives were often strongly linked to the question of scale – geographically, socially and analytically. Furthermore, contrasting factors like cattle versus sheep/goats, male herders versus female herders, cheese/butter versus wool and elite versus peasants could, when raising the analytical focus to market forces and power structures instead of local or regional prerequisites, turn out to be responses and strategies to what happened in the outside world. Rather than pigeon-holing the various forms of transhumance as exponents of particular regional cultures, our discussions at EAA Glasgow showed that transhumant pastoralism was embedded in different contexts for more complex reasons and could be used as an important vehicle for breaking new economic directions and for adaptation or response to changing internal and external conditions.

It really needs to be emphasised that local and regional systems of transhumance were created in a flux of natural conditions, agrarian practices, historical path dependence, economic regimes, power structures and social contexts. This explains a lot of the diversity in historical archaeologies of European transhumance. In order to discuss all of it with a genuinely cross-European perspective, however, theoretical frameworks must be employed. Few papers in this volume have elaborated on theoretical approaches, and granted, within particular study areas, transhumant systems and their chronological development might appear understandable without the explicit use of theory. Nevertheless, for the international level which this book sets out to capture, it is much more difficult to explain diversity without a conceptual framework.

Two theoretical concepts in particular stand out as fruitful for a more elaborate framing of transhumance in cross-European perspective: post-colonialism, and intersectionality[1] (not least of gender). In all papers, transhumance is played out in so-called marginal areas, mostly different kinds of upland. Previously, transhumance had been located on the margins of archaeological research. The post-colonial turn in the discipline of archaeology has been vital in opening up transhumance and so-called marginal landscapes in general as a research field in which larger field projects might be staged, some of which are presented in this volume. What is more, due to the post-colonial turn, previously marginalised landscapes are now acknowledged to have had greater importance and influence on past societal conditions than was once thought by archaeologists.

For its part, the importance of intersectionality is visible in the division between southern and northern Europe regarding the herding of transhumant livestock.

Southern European systems were dominated by male herders, often of relatively low social status, whereas female herders belonging to landholding families tend to dominate in Scandinavia, as well as in western Ireland and Scotland at a late date. The gendered nature of herding and the social status it implied were connected to particular local and regional contexts. In many cases, male herders seem to have been employed in a professional sense as part of large-scale and sometimes elite-controlled transhumance, i.e. in south-eastern France (Burri et al., this volume), northern Italy (Carrer, 2016: 102–3; Dadà, this volume; Stagno, this volume; Vanni & Cristoferi, this volume), Castilian Spain (Fernández Mier & Tente, this volume; López-Sáez et al., this volume) and Romania (Brigand et al., this volume). In northern Europe, by contrast, female herding was integrated into local agrarian systems, as seen in nineteenth-century western Ireland (Costello, this volume), early twentieth-century Hebridean Scotland (Kupiec & Milek, this volume) and Sweden from at least the seventeenth century (Svensson, this volume). In each case, the gendered nature of herding and its social status had a bearing on how society was organised; indeed, it even played a role in the evolution of gender statuses. For example, a connection has been made in Scandinavia between the relatively high independence of females and their role as herders at shielings or *säter/fäbod*. Having said all that, it must be cautioned that there are also instances in each of the above southern European countries, along with Switzerland (Andres, this volume), where males from within local communities could act as herders in situations that were not very different from the community-based pastoral movements of northern Europe. Thus, one cannot make an exclusive correlation between female herding and small-scale transhumant systems.

Drawing from other theoretical concepts to contextualise and understand transhumant systems across Europe as a whole, it is argued that both practice theory and actor network theory offer solid potential frameworks. Theories of social practice give primacy to neither the agent nor the structure; instead, they are thought to work together in an on-going reproduction of the world (Bourdieu, 1977, 1990; Kosík, 1976; Giddens, 1979, 1984). Although several strands of 'praxeology' have emerged, not least Giddens's structuration theory, they all, at their core, hold that "social practices are routines: routines of moving the body, of understanding and wanting, of using things, interconnected in a practice" (Reckwitz, 2002: 255). The importance of things, or the material world in general, including landscapes, is emphasised more strongly in actor network theories (ANT). This is a more recent school of thought which forwards hybrid perspectives on human/material interaction, providing for the non-human agency of objects, occasionally called actants (e.g. Barad, 2003; Barad, 2007; Latour, 2005; Whatmore, 2002).

Regardless of whether we acknowledge both human and non-human agency or stress the importance of the material world in human agency, the two frameworks may be cited as interpretative tools for archaeologists studying historical transhumance. Some of the 'things' which transhumant people dealt with in their everyday lives include the permanent and seasonal sites they occupied, the routes they used to travel between them, the boundaries separating them, the livestock bred and herded, farming tools, the commodities they produced – arguably the entire physical landscape and the climate which helped shape it and contribute to the necessity of transhumance. Reckwitz (2002: 255) says that a social structure is formed by the routine actions of people in their handling of such 'things'. If, therefore, one sees a system of transhumance as a social structure which is produced and reproduced by many individual farmers and herders working and making decisions in a landscape that contains a unique set of cultural and natural conditions, or as a network forged by these actors and actants, one can begin to consider how different conditions in another area might involve agents *there* practising another form of transhumance. In this regard, it is crucial to add that every social structure or network is temporal and must be broken or shifted "in everyday crises of routines" (Reckwitz, 2002: 255). This might easily be translated to the world of transhumant pastoralism in medieval and modern Europe, where transhumant systems were not static and could be altered over short or long periods of time through the agency of their participants. Such shifts in operation might be a response to relatively quick disruptions from above or from outside, political governance for example, or they might be adaptations to slow external change like climate patterns. Furthermore, changes might also be caused either partly or entirely by reproduction of the transhumant structure *within* a region over several generations. Change of the latter sort would fall into three main interdependent categories: social, economic and environmental – prime examples of each being population growth or decline, increasing or decreasing production for market, the improvement/ clearance or desertion of land.

New Methodological Approaches – New Encounters with Transhumance

It is not only new theoretical approaches in archaeology that are opening up possibilities for researching transhumance – the topic itself can also aid the development of more sophisticated methodological practice. The complexity of transhumance as a phenomenon, and particularly of the sites, creates challenges that render the subject a kind of methodological laboratory. That is

to say, its novelty and complexity for historical archaeologists means that it offers more than a linear pursuit of new knowledge on the human past. It can equally be used to develop better interdisciplinary approaches to bigger archaeological problems, such as mobility, non-elite settlement, marginality and human/livestock interdependency. While it is clear that ethnography and historical documents remain important sources, both for empirical investigation and interpretation, they have been accompanied in this volume by several other methods. Much new information has been retrieved with archaeology, palaeobotany, place names, historical maps and geoarchaeology, and new conclusions have been drawn by comparing these results with narratives based on the traditional sources. Rather than dismiss them, however, most authors show a strong understanding of historical and ethnographical narratives and have used it to discuss new archaeological data. For instance, Brigand et al. use ethnographic information to tease out the archaeological imprint of various types of pastoral movements, Vanni and Cristoferi elaborate further on ethnoarchaeology, Andres uses ethnographic and historical information to interpret surveyed remains, and Burri et al. are able to picture complex grazing patterns using historical documents. A special case is offered by Kupiec and Milek, who in order to obtain a more refined history of a single shieling house, compare detailed ethnographic information from a single site with the results of advanced geoarchaeological analyses of different layers in an excavated horizon.

That said, another common methodology is to combine archaeology and palaeobotany. These results are partly in harmony with and partly challenging of ethnographic and historical narratives, sometimes revealing hitherto unknown landscape histories. The strength of palaeobotanical investigations is clearly stated in several papers (Dixon, this volume; López-Sáez et al., this volume; Pettersson, this volume; Stagno, this volume; Surmely et al., this volume; Svensson, this volume; see also Walsh & Mocci, 2016). Palaeobotanical data provide insights into the time depth and changing nature of land-use around seasonal sites, including the opening of forests for grazing, burning events (evidenced by charcoal), cereal cultivation (sometimes as part of year-round occupation) and abandonment. By themselves, archaeological excavations can allow more detailed encounters with daily life in seasonal settlements, as displayed by Kupiec and Milek, and also Venovcevs and Gaulton (this volume). In many cases, however, geoarchaeological analysis is not possible, nor is the material culture of seasonal sites always very rich, especially when found in peaty acidic soils. The integration of (radiocarbon-dated) palaeobotanical evidence into archaeological projects can therefore help to trace different chronological layers in the environs of seasonal sites. This is of essence to the study of transhumance given the interdependence of herders, their animals and landscape ecology (see further discussion below on "The landscape palimpsest").

If archaeology and palaeobotany are best used on recorded sites, or for surveys of limited areas, historical maps and place names offer entry points for larger-scale distribution mapping of transhumance pastures and seasonal sites. Together with historical documents and ethnographical sources, historical maps and place names are useful for identifying pastures and seasonal sites, especially when their use has changed or they have been deserted in later times (e.g. Stagno, 2016; Costello, this volume; Dixon, this volume; Fernández Mier & Tente, this volume; Gardiner, this volume; Pettersson, this volume). Relict place names are sometimes the only clues to transhumant practices and seasonal sites which have been overlain by subsequent activities. They are also useful when trying to reconstruct transhumant movements that are unaccounted for in other sources.

Mobility and its Meaning

One cross-European theme which emerged at the EAA session, and which stands out even more clearly now, is mobility. This is perhaps unsurprising – its role in transhumance is obvious. All the same, the present writers would like to stress an aspect of mobility in transhumance that needs further consideration, i.e. that domesticated livestock are not *moved* by themselves, but by humans who travel with them and bring along aspects of their culture. It almost goes without saying that humans (aided sometimes by their dogs) carry out the task of herding; nonetheless, it is of essence to include their participation more explicitly. People make the movement of livestock a 'practice', and the extent of their movement reflects the amount of labour needed at seasonal pastures in terms of herding, dairying and small-scale cultivation, as well as at home for intensive cultivation, fishing and/or industry. What is more, in parts of the world where transhumance has ceased or (as is inevitable) been altered, the archaeological remains of seasonal settlements are now the only obvious physical evidence of the practice. Archaeologists therefore have it in their power to examine how human mobility to and from such sites formed part of a social strategy at the same time that it served a farming system.

Depending on these factors and contemporary perceptions of social roles, mobility may also be gendered. As outlined above, there seems to have been a clear predominance of young female dairymaids at sites associated with summer pasturing of cows in post-medieval Scandinavia, and later still in western Ireland and Scotland. Elsewhere in Europe, it is generally assumed that

male herdsmen alone would have had mobility. These assumptions need to be tested more rigorously, however. The present volume provides two interesting cases of whole families moving, that is, the *vaqueiros de alzada* in northern Spain and European settlers' winter housing system in Newfoundland. The *vaqueiro* families moved twice a year over short distances between their summer and winter housings, taking their animals and belongings with them, while in Newfoundland winter housing was used by families as well as male collectives (Fernández Mier & Tente, this volume; Venovcevs & Gaulton, this volume). Both of these practices are attested in the post-medieval period, for which historical and ethnographic evidence is fairly plentiful; earlier in the historical period, though, where we rely to a greater extent on archaeological and palaeoenvironmental evidence, it is possible that our methods have underestimated the seasonal movement of whole families in some parts of Europe, at least over short distances. For example, a few seventeenth-century historical sources in Ireland hint at the abandonment of lowland settlements and their crops entirely for the summer (e.g. O'Sullivan, 1971: 46), while Dixon (this volume) works on the assumption that whole communities moved seasonally in the central Highlands of Scotland in the middle of the second millennium AD. Whether or not isotopic studies of ancient human bone could help to detect the seasonal movement of either whole or partial communities remains to be fully evaluated, and is always subject to the quality of preservation and the ethical approval of people today (but see McGlynn, 2007, for an encouraging early attempt).

This brings us to another key point of comparison within mobility, i.e. scale, which is far from even in historical times. In Europe, the question of scale has had an influence on what historical archaeologists call transhumance. Each region and country has its own tradition of research, with a multitude of publications in several different languages as well as academic disciplines stretching back to the early twentieth century. In one way, it is for good reason that separate traditions of research exist, since there are very real differences in climate, topography and governance across Europe during medieval and modern times. At any rate, it means that there are various conceptions of transhumance amongst the present volume's contributions, and these conceptions are based, at least in part, on how far and how many livestock were moved. With regard to seasonal movements in the medieval south-east of France, Burri et al. argue that movements within the same territory did not amount to transhumance. Indeed, citing Rendu (2006: 9), they point out that the term 'transhumance' only gained popularity after the emergence of large-scale movements of sheep in the second half of the second millennium, i.e. the 'normal' and 'inverse' types which Braudel proposes. Similarly, for Romania,

Brigand et al. distinguish between local/agricultural pastoralism, mountain pastoralism and transhumance – the latter involving tens of thousands of sheep being herded, in some cases, beyond the borders of Romania in the late eighteenth and early nineteenth centuries. Surmely et al. choose not to use the term 'transhumance' at all when discussing relatively local pastoral movements to mountainous summer pastures in medieval and early modern Auvergne, south-central France. Neither is it commonly used in the Alpine region or Scandinavia. At the same time, Fernández Mier and Tente are happy to employ 'transhumance' for a range of seasonal pastoral movements in medieval and modern Iberia, simply qualifying it with the prefixes short-, middle- and long-distance. Stagno, too, describes both local and long-distance movements in post-classical Mediterranean contexts as transhumance, although she points out that distinct terms are used for each type in the languages of Italy, southern France and the Basque Country.

Furthermore, the clear-cut distinctions that are made in mainland Europe between different types of transhumance, and between transhumance and shorter seasonal movements, is not easy to relate to some northern European contexts. In Ireland and Britain, for example, there is a less well-developed understanding of the various kinds of seasonal movements which took place in the historical period. To some extent, this may be due to the fact that transhumant practices started to decline earlier in north-west Europe, and so folk memories which might have aided interpretation of the archaeological record are fewer and less detailed. Compare this to the diversity of pastoral movements attested ethnographically in southern European countries, which has made attempts at classification almost inevitable. In addition, there may simply *not* have been the same diversity of pastoral systems at work in much of northern Europe, including Scandinavia and the Alpine region. For instance, it is highly doubtful if there was ever transhumance on the scale of what emerged in France, Spain, Italy and the Balkans after the end of the medieval period – geographical constraints and social structures may have favoured the seasonal management of livestock in less diverse ways in northern Europe. Yet this has not stopped scholars in Ireland, Scotland and England using the term 'transhumance'. In the post-medieval period, booleying in Ireland and shieling practices in northern Britain may have only involved seasonal movements of dairy cattle over distances of 2–20km, usually by families or their younger (female) members, but they have been labelled as forms of transhumance by academics since the 1950s, a usage which continues to this day (e.g. Graham, 1954; MacSween, 1959; McDonnell, 1988; Bil, 1990; Gardiner, this volume; Costello, this volume; Dixon, this volume; also for Iceland, Kupiec et al., 2016). Controversially, Venovcevs

and Gaulton (this volume) even employ the concept of transhumance where very few if any livestock moved with people to the inland winter settlements of European settlers in Newfoundland, Canada.

THE SOCIAL STRUCTURES OF TRANSHUMANCE – COMMONS AND COLLECTIVE PRACTICES

As discussed above, people and livestock did not move around haphazardly, even if the mobility pattern in many cases may appear random to us now. The movement was guided by a number of reasons such as the quality of pastures, ownership of land and rights to grazing, social relations and the scale of arable farming commitments. In all cases, though, transhumant movements are characterised by a reliance on commons or collective organisation of one form or another.

The concept of commons is complex and involves great variation in terms of history, geographic scale, the resources at stake, along with associated institutions and decision-making arrangements. Nevertheless, commons may be described as community landscapes to which user rights are attached either in the form of ownership or through customary tenure involving a high degree of negotiation between individuals, households, task groups, etc. Commons arrangements could solve situations encountered by small agrarian populations involved in the extensive exploitation of surrounding forests or uplands, where long distances sometimes had to be covered in order to hunt, find pasture for livestock and source craft materials. Commons were important drivers for shaping local social relations, administrative patterns, co-operation and identity. Commons can be seen as the unifying and tenacious socio-ecological adhesive which constitutes communities. By understanding how commons are reproduced contextually over time, in relation to broader societal changes, one can gain an understanding of not only resource dilemmas but also how specific places and identities are constructed. Commons have also been important platforms for regional and interregional contact and interaction.[2]

Current research, following Elinor Ostrom (Ostrom, 1990), highlights that commons are effective co-operative platforms for shaping innovative strategies in facing unforeseen futures and meeting and shaping change. Transhumant herding involved teamwork, sometimes by groups of professional herders, and sometimes by co-operative organisations rooted in their respective rural communities. The collective work form was an important identity shaper of transhumant practices, producing and reproducing identity and skill management among professional herders, respectively strengthening local communities through joint engagement in co-operatives where people had very similar goals. Such co-operation was also reproduced in other contexts, and helped expand the capacities of individual farming households.

Commons, co-operation and collective practices are often visible in the landscape through the same archaeological features that are connected to transhumance, i.e. farmsteads, villages, the seasonal dwellings of herders and the boundaries (natural or anthropogenic) associated with pasture rights. In southern Europe, long-distance transhumance, often characterised by elite or commercial interests, appears strongly connected to mountain commons, with pasture rights not necessarily located at the closest possible distance from the settlements of herd owners, thus creating crossing mobility patterns. Clustering of herders' huts, sometimes amounting to small villages, and occasionally also large pens and enclosures located by or on the pastures, bear witness to the existence of co-operation in herder communities. In many regions there also appear, concurrently, to have been shorter transhumance systems that were more integrated with village agrarian practices and which used common pastures restricted to those villages or parishes. These systems, if very short distances were involved, sometimes operated on more of a daily basis with only common milk sheds being used. Or they could involve fuller transhumant movements to multi-functional seasonal sites for both livestock and herders (Andres, this volume; Brigand et al., this volume; Burri et al., this volume; Dadà, this volume; Fernández Mier & Tente, this volume; Stagno, this volume, Surmely et al., this volume; Vanni & Cristoferi, this volume).

In northern Europe and the Alpine region, dominated by relatively short-distance transhumant systems integrated into local communities' agrarian practices, the remains of seasonal dwellings form the main physical vestiges of transhumance. The herders who occupied them usually formed groups of people from different families that were based in the same village or area of permanent settlement; these groups could be either loose or tight, as deduced from the density of surviving seasonal dwellings and their arrangement relative to one another. Here, again, the livestock could be grazed in a variety of ways depending on livestock numbers and the amount of common pasture available in a given period. In some cases, they were brought to land that was common to specific villages or communities, in others, to larger commons shared by many transhumant herders (Andres, this volume; Costello, this volume; Dixon, this volume; Gardiner, this volume; Pettersson, this volume; Svensson, this volume).

During late medieval and post-medieval times, common rights were increasingly challenged by elite peoples in most parts of Europe. For instance, in Scotland, commons were increasingly restricted due to takeovers by elite landowners with commercial interests, either

for market-orientated livestock production or other purposes (Dixon, this volume). The existence of parallel transhumance systems within many parts of southern Europe bears witness to competition for grazing rights on common pastures between local communities and the larger herds of elites or commercial interests that were driven from hundreds of kilometres away. Such competition emerged in the central French Pyrenees and in parts of Spain where *La Mesta* operated (Lévêque, 2013: 98; Fernández Mier & Tente, this volume). The process of competition over common land and grazing rights poses an interesting challenge for future research on historical transhumance.

THE LANDSCAPE PALIMPSEST

As Blache (1934: 22) pointed out a long time ago, transhumance implies so many environmental and social conditions as to make strict classification impossible. This is certainly the case when one conceives of European transhumance and its material legacy over the last 1500 years. It is impossible to impose a strict definition on a set of practices that have endured so long and been re-invented in a bewildering variety of contexts. Indeed, a strict definition for all of Europe would be downright inadvisable given that archaeologists have yet to understand so much about seasonal land-use and settlement. Transhumant activities form part of a rural palimpsest, where the landscape contains many overlapping chronological features and layers. The routine decision-making or 'path dependence' (Mahoney, 2000) of people in transhumance was influenced by that palimpsest. They had to choose whether to follow particular traditions or break them in changed circumstances. The resulting layered creation, which, in composition, was both cultural and material, is evident in several of the studies in this book. Gardiner, for example, traces through historical, archaeological and place-name evidence the development and decline of transhumance in medieval England as permanent settlement expanded into upland hills formerly reserved for summer pasture. Andres, relying on historical and ethnographic sources on shifting production focuses, teases out layers in surveyed material in the Swiss Alps. Using palaeoenvironmental data from central Spain, López-Sáez et al. record increasing human impact on mountain forest vegetation as a result of transhumance in the second millennium AD, albeit in this case as a result of the growth of long-distance transhumance. In Southern Tuscany, Vanni and Cristoferi also refer to increased environmental impact on forests in later medieval times, while citing the interchangeable occupation of mountain sites between charcoal producers and shepherds. Multiple uses of forested areas are evident in archaeological, palaeoenvironmental and ethnographic sources from mid-Sweden over the medieval and modern periods – an 'innovation package' which included elk hunting, charcoal production and, increasingly, iron bloomeries, not simply shieling use (Pettersson, this volume; Svensson, this volume). Clearly, then, there are numerous activities and environmental impacts associated with transhumance over time, and each of these has left a layer for us to trace in Europe's varied landscapes.

Of course, the notion of palimpsest means that even within closely defined study areas there is no one archaeology of transhumance. The summer sites used by herders, which usually attract the most attention, were constructed, altered and abandoned in concert with evolving land-use. A number of contributions to the present volume bear this out, particularly those incorporating the results of excavation and environmental sampling. In the central Scottish Highlands, Dixon (this volume) shows that surviving shieling sites are located on relatively high pastures which do not seem to have been used for transhumance until the late medieval period, this being reflected in occupation dates which generally only start in the fourteenth century and relatively small amounts of midden material compared to shieling sites elsewhere in Scotland. Working in Norway and Sweden, Pettersson has shown that each site had a complicated history from the late first millennium AD up to the present, with some shielings established on former farmsteads after a period of forest regrowth, some growing out of existing shielings, and others still being established at roughly the same time as the farmsteads several kilometres away to which they were linked. Furthermore, Surmely et al. present a convincing case of a layered landscape around upland sites in the Auvergne of France, where small year-round farming settlements gave way entirely to seasonal herding associated with specialised cattle breeding in the thirteenth century, followed by further changes in the architecture of seasonal settlements thereafter.

The Heritage of Transhumance in Europe: from The Past for The Future?

Transhumance is a declining practice in modern farming, meaning that its value is increasingly being seen in the context of the environment, as cultural and natural heritage, rather than an economically essential practice. When demonstrating the value of transhumance, it is generally aspects of its final phases that are easiest to preserve and manage for the future. Transhumance has an element of 'otherness' and 'the exotic' which make it attractive to both heritage management and tourism. Its perception as different is somewhat inevitable given

how unusual the seasonal mobility of humans and animals now is in European society.

Transhumance, however, is not viewed as a cultural asset in quite the same way across Europe. In some regions, its importance lives on in the collective memory of communities, whereas in others it has been forgotten. Furthermore, the strength and funding behind heritage management varies from country to country, both inside and especially outside the European Union. In the EU, traditional farming practices are not always high on the list of priorities for funding bodies because of the payments which farmers already receive as part of the Common Agricultural Policy (CAP).

Often considered by authorities to be more important than cultural heritage is the biological diversity which has been created through grazing and haymaking associated with transhumance. The cessation of transhumance regimes thus causes threats to 'nature'. A special challenge for heritage management is that transhumance is located somewhere in between the wild and the cultivated, being staged in, and transforming, the uplands. How can the past be managed while making things grow?

Managing the heritage of transhumance thus demands a combination of cultural heritage management and nature conservation. But we would like to add yet another component, namely rural development. With the increasing urbanization and decrease of rural life in modern Europe, the former 'homes' of transhumance are suffering and appear to be among the most vulnerable areas in Europe. The desertion of the uplands is the greatest threat to the transhumance heritage, both cultural and natural (e.g. Fischer et al., 2008; Speed et al., 2012).

Regulations on environmentally friendly farming have, together with optional 'green' schemes, formed part of CAP for many years now, but there continues to be a failure to recognise the role of cultural heritage in facilitating protection of the natural environment. Older farming practices like transhumance will never be replicated exactly in today's world or the future; nor should they, having declined for various economic and social reasons. Instead we should be open to new forms of transhumance and reuse of transhumance adapted to current contexts. The intimate knowledge of land, livestock and the seasons which transhumant communities developed over time still contains important lessons regarding human–environment interaction which archaeologists are in a position to retrieve. This knowledge is especially valuable in the conversion towards more sustainable agriculture.

The contributions to this book all emphasise the importance of transhumance to rural economies in past times. Transhumance has not only been a major means of making a living in harsh environments such as the uplands, but also been a source of wealth and a way of spreading risk. From the contributions it is clear that transhumance was an adaptable force, adjusting to the different challenges posed to rural societies in Europe.

We would like to put forward the suggestion that transhumance, even as a practice which has been largely abandoned, still has capacity to contribute to more sustainable futures for the vulnerable European uplands today. Just as transhumance is a boundary object for scholars from different parts of Europe, as expressed in the EAA session and in this book, it can be a boundary object also for people who are working for sustainable futures in the uplands all over Europe and thus a means of understanding cross-European challenges and creating cross-European responses to the desertion of the uplands.

The best way of managing the heritage of transhumance is to regard transhumance as a living heritage, able to adjust to today's demands and challenges. For instance, by keeping livestock at transhumance sites the biological diversity can be promoted and new products delivered to a market increasingly demanding environmentally friendly products. Three examples close to the editors can be mentioned. First, in the limestone karst of the Burren, County Clare, in Ireland, the Burren Beo Trust is working with local farmers to encourage the continuation of winter grazing by cattle so as to ensure that hazel scrub does not take over the landscape and cause serious habitat loss for many rare wildflowers. Second, at the reopened Viking Age shieling Ransbysätern, Värmland, Sweden cattle are kept inside the fenced areas, instead of outside the fences as in older times. This non-historical practice has helped maintain the meadows inside the fences and its rich biodiversity at the same time that the cattle are available to visitors. Another example from the central Scottish Highlands does not actually prioritise farming, but draws on the country's former tradition of shieling to educate young people and their teachers in sustainability and the value of the outdoors (theshielingproject.org).

These examples of neo-transhumance and their obvious appropriation of the past typify how communities might integrate a living (or dead) tradition of seasonal grazing with attempts to maintain biodiversity. With local co-operation and governmental support, the meat, dairy and crops produced in such sustainable farming systems can be marketed to the growing niche of consumers who do not want food that is produced at the cost of environmental and social values. At the same time, these operations could draw further interest and participation from the public as part of an educational process for the many urbanised Europeans who now – some of them – want to know more about rural life and why it can still involve such a distinctive seasonal rhythm of people and animals.

A Few Final Words . . .

The discussion of 'transhumance' is taking on new life across Europe as historical archaeologists reconcile the material culture of pastoralism with existing historical accounts, (near-) contemporary ethnography and palaeoenvironmental data. A plurality of different but related meanings is healthy for a topic that appeals to so many and which is currently experiencing a steep upward curve in scholarship (as reflected in the very enthusiastic attendance and number of speakers at the very conference session which gave rise to this book!). The local and regional meanings which transhumance has been given are not for the present writers to quibble with. It is hard to deny, however, that it offers an eminently suitable umbrella term for historical archaeologists seeking to create an international dialogue. At the end of the day, students of seasonal human–livestock movements between fixed areas in the landscape have more in common with one another than they do apart – regardless of the endlessly variable distances and scales which that way of life permits.

It should also be remembered that transhumance was never restricted to Europe, but is a global phenomenon, as was briefly presented above in the section "Transhumance and pastoralism – an overview". So far, however, historical archaeologies of transhumance have largely been restricted to Europe. Furthermore, there are clearly prehistoric roots to seasonal pastoralism, though admittedly this has received increasing attention. These issues are beyond the chronological and geographical scope of the present volume for good reason, but that is not to say they are without relevance. It is hoped that as the historical archaeology of European transhumance now starts to come of age, other aspects of world pastoralism will too be unlocked from the archaeological record – creating a global dialogue on what has been a widespread practice since humans first started to follow and domesticate ungulates in the ancient Near East.

Acknowledgements

We would like to acknowledge the support of an Irish Research Council New Foundations grant (EAA-TRANS) in facilitating the three organisers' planning for and participation in the original session at EAA Glasgow 2015 (Eugene Costello, Mark Gardiner and Eva Svensson). Moreover, we would like to thank the European Association of Archaeologists for making its subsequent publication possible and for including it in their new peer-reviewed book series, *Themes in Contemporary Archaeology*. Series editor Kristian Kristiansen kindly encouraged us to publish the proceedings having listened to our session, and editorial assistant

Claes Uhnér provided unfailing assistance and advice during the publication process. Last but not least, we would like to thank two anonymous reviewers for their comments on this introductory chapter as well as the rest of the manuscript.

NOTES

1 Intersectionality is the study of overlapping or intersecting social identities and related systems of oppression, domination or discrimination.
2 The definition of commons here follows the LoRE-project (Living on the Rural Edge: The Emergence and Transmission of Europe's Biocultural Heritage of Commons and Communal Livelihoods) headed by Associate Professor Karl-Johan Lindholm, Department of Archaeology and Ancient History, Uppsala University, Sweden. See also Lindholm et al., 2013 and Sandström et al., 2017. Compare Oosthuizen, 2013.

REFERENCES

Oral communication
Stig Welinder, Professor emeritus, Mid-Sweden University. Concluding comments, the session "Historical Transhumance in Europe: finding common ground in marginal landscapes", EAA Glasgow, September 2015.

Bibliography
Arbos, P. 1923. The geography of pastoral life: illustrated with European examples. *Geographical Review*, 13:559–75.
Arnold, E. & Greenfield, H. 2006. *The Origins of Transhumant Pastoralism in Temperate South Eastern Europe: A Zooarchaeological Perspective from the Central Balkans*. BAR International Series 1538. Oxford: BAR Publishing.
Balasse, M., Bălășescu, A., Janzen, A., Ughetto-Monfrin, J., Mirea, P. & Andreescu, R. 2013. Early herding at măgură boldul lui Moş ivănus (early 6th millennium BC, Romania): general settings and annual rhythm of the husbandry, from stable isotope analysis of faunal remains. *European Journal of Archaeology*, 16:221–46.
Barad, K. 2003. Posthumanist performativity: toward an understanding of how matter comes to matter. *Signs: Journal of Women in Culture and Society*, 28(3):801–31.
Barad, K. 2007. *Meeting the Universe Halfway: Quantum Physics and the Entanglement of Matter and Meaning*. Durham & London: Duke University Press.
Barnard, H. & Wendrich, W. eds. 2008. *The Archaeology of Mobility: Old World and New World Nomadism*. Los Angeles: Cotsen Institute of Archaeology Press.
Barth, F. 1962. Nomadism in the mountain and plateau areas of south west Asia. *The Problems of the Arid Zone. UNESCO Arid Zone Research*, 18:341–55.
Bentley, R.A. & Knipper, C. 2005. Transhumance at the early Neolithic settlement at Vaihingen, Germany. *Antiquity*, 79:306.
Bil, A. 1990. *The Shieling, 1600–1840: The Case of the Central Scottish Highlands*. Edinburgh: John Donald.
Blache, J. 1934. *L'Homme et la Montagne*. Paris: Librairie Gallimard.

Bladé, J.F. 1892. Essai sur l'histoire de la transhumance dans les Pyrénées françaises. *Bullétin de Géographie Historique et Descriptive*, 7:301–15.
Bourdieu, P. 1977. *Outline of a Theory of Social Practice (translated edition)*. Cambridge: Cambridge University Press.
Bourdieu, P. 1990. *The Logic of Practice (translated edition)*. Stanford: Stanford University Press.
Braudel, F. 1972. *The Mediterranean and the Mediterranean World in the Age of Philip II. Volume I (translated edition)*. London: Collins.
CAP. The Common Agricultural Policy: a partnership between Europe and farmers. http://ec.europa.eu/agriculture/cap-overview/2012_en.pdf (accessed 18 May 2016).
Carrer, F. 2016. The 'invisible' shepherd and the 'visible' dairyman: ethnoarchaeology of Alpine pastoral sites in the Val di Fiemme (eastern Italian Alps). In: J.R. Collis, M. Pearce & F. Nicolis, eds. 2016. *Summer Farms: Seasonal Exploitation of the Uplands from Prehistory to the Present*. Sheffield Archaeological Monographs 16. Sheffield: J.R. Collis Publications, pp. 97–108.
Collis, J.R., Pearce, M. & Nicolis, F. eds. 2016. *Summer Farms: Seasonal Exploitation of the Uplands from Prehistory to the Present*. Sheffield Archaeological Monographs 16. Sheffield: J.R. Collis Publications.
Cribb, R. 1991. *Nomads in Archaeology*. Cambridge: Cambridge University Press.
Davies, E. 1941. The patterns of transhumance in Europe. *Geography*, 26:155–68.
Fischer, M., Rudmann-Maurer, K., Weyand, A. & Stöcklin, J. 2008. Agricultural land use and biodiversity in the Alps: how cultural tradition and socioeconomically motivated changes are shaping grassland biodiversity in the Swiss Alps. *Mountain Research and Development*, 28:148–55.
Galaty, J.G. & Johnson, D.L. eds. 1990. *The World of Pastoralism: Herding Systems in Comparative Perspective*. New York: Guilford Press.
Gefu, J.O. & Gilles, J.L. 1990. Pastoralists, ranchers and the state in Nigeria and North America: a comparative analysis. *Nomadic Peoples*, 25(7):34–50.
Giddens, A. 1979. *Central Problems in Social Theory: Action, Structure and Contradiction in Social Analysis*. London: Palgrave Macmillan.
Giddens, A. 1984. *The Constitution of Society: Outline of the Theory of Structuration*. Cambridge: Polity Press.
Graham, J.M. 1954. Transhumance in Ireland, with special reference to its bearing on the evolution of rural communities in the west. Unpublished PhD Thesis, Department of Geography, Queen's University Belfast.
Greenfield, H.J. 1999. The advent of transhumant pastoralism in temperate Southeast Europe: a zooarchaeological perspective from the Central Balkans. In: L. Bartosiewicz & H.J. Greenfield, eds. *Transhumant Pastoralism in Southeastern Europe: Recent Perspectives from Archaeology, History and Ethnology*. Archaeolingua, Budapest, pp. 15–36.
Halstead, P. 1996. Pastoralism or household herding? Problems of scale and specialisation in early Greek animal husbandry. *World Archaeology*, 28:20–42.
Ingold, T. 1980. *Hunters, Pastoralists and Ranchers. Reindeer Economies and Their Transformations*. London: Cambridge University Press.
Johnson, D.L. 1969. *The Nature of Nomadism: A Comparative Study of Pastoral Migrations in Southwestern Asia and Northern Africa*. Chicago: University of Chicago.
Khazanov, A. 1994. *Nomads and the Outside World*. Second edition. Madison: University of Wisconsin Press.

Kienlin, T.L. & Valde-Nowak, P. 2004. Neolithic transhumance in the Black Forest Mountains, SW Germany. *Journal of Field Archaeology*, 29:29–44.

Klein, J. 1920. *The Mesta: A Study in Spanish Economic History, 1273–1836*. Cambridge, MA: Harvard University Press.

Kosík, K. 1976 (1963). *Dialectics of the Concrete: A Study on Problems of Man and World*. Dordrecht: Reidel.

Kupiec, P., Milek, K., Gísladóttir, A.G. & Woollett, J. 2016. Elusive *sel* sites: the geoarchaeological quest for Icelandic shielings and the case of Þorvaldsstaðasel, in northeast Iceland. In: J.R. Collis, M. Pearce & F. Nicolis, eds. *Summer Farms: Seasonal Exploitation of the Uplands from Prehistory to the Present*. Sheffield Archaeological Monographs 16. Sheffield: J.R. Collis Publications, pp. 221–36.

Latour, B. 2005. *Reassembling the Social: An Introduction to Actor-Network-Theory*. Oxford: Oxford University Press.

Lévêque, S. 2013. Mountain summer shelters in the Haut Adour Region of the Central French Pyrenees: examples from the Campan and Lesponne Valleys (Hautes-Pyrénées). In: L.R. Lozny, ed. *Continuity and Change in Cultural Adaptation to Mountain Environments: From Prehistory to Contemporary Threats*. New York: Springer, pp. 97–122.

Lindholm, K.J., Sandström, E. & Ekman, A.K. 2013. The archaeology of the commons. *The Journal of Archaeology and Ancient History*, 10:1–49.

Luick, R. 2004. Transhumance in Germany. In: R.G.H. Bunce, M. Pérez Soba, R.H.G. Jongman, A. Gómez Sal, F. Herzog & I. Austad, eds. *Transhumance and Biodiversity in European Mountains, Report of the EU-FP5 project TRANSHUMOUNT (EVK2-CT-2002–80017)*, IALE publication series (1). Wagingen: Alterra, pp. 137–54.

MacSween, M.D. 1959. Transhumance in North Skye. *Scottish Geographical Magazine*, 75:75–88.

Mahoney, J. 2000. Path dependence in historical sociology. *Theory and Society*, 29:507–48.

McDonnell, J. 1988. The role of transhumance in northern England. *Northern History*, 24:1–17.

McGlynn, G. 2007. Using $\delta^{13}C$, $\delta^{15}N$, $\delta^{18}O$ stable isotope analysis of human bone tissue to identify transhumance, high altitude habitation and reconstruct palaeodiet for the early medieval Alpine population at Volders, Austria. Unpublished PhD Thesis, Faculty of Biology, LMU München.

Nicolis, F., Mottes, E., Bassetti, M., Castiglioni, E., Rottoli, M., & Ziggiotti, S. 2016. Going up the mountain! Exploitation of the Trentino Highlands as summer farms during the Bronze Age: the Dosso Rotondo site at Storo (northern Italy). In: J.R. Collis, M. Pearce & F. Nicolis, eds. *Summer Farms: Seasonal Exploitation of the Uplands from Prehistory to the Present*. Sheffield Archaeological Monographs 16. Sheffield: J.R. Collis Publications, pp. 109–38.

Oosthuizen, S. 2013. *Tradition and Transformation in Anglo-Saxon England: Archaeology, Common Rights and Landscape*. London: Bloomsbury Academic.

Ostrom, E. 1990. *Governing the Commons: The Evolution of Institutions for Collective Action*. Cambridge: Cambridge University Press.

O'Sullivan, W. 1971. William Molyneux's geographical collections for Kerry. *Journal of the Kerry Archaeological and Historical Society*, 4:28–47.

Pearce, M. 2016. Hard cheese: upland pastoralism in the Italian Bronze and Iron Ages. In: J.R. Collis, M. Pearce & F. Nicolis, eds. *Summer Farms: Seasonal Exploitation of the Uplands from Prehistory to the Present*. Sheffield Archaeological Monographs 16. Sheffield: J.R. Collis Publications, pp. 47–56.

Reckwitz, A. 2002. Toward a theory of social practices: a development in culturalist theorizing. *European Journal of Social Theory*, 5:243–63.

Rendu, C. 2006. Transhumance: prélude à l'histoire d'un mot voyageur. In: P.Y. Laffont, ed. *Transhumance et Estivage en Occident des Origines aux Enjeux Actuels*. Toulouse: Presses Universitaires du Mirail, pp. 7–29.

Sandström, E., Ekman, A.K. & Lindholm, K.J. 2017. Commoning in the periphery – the role of the commons for understanding rural continuities and change. *International Journal of Commons*, 11(1):508–31.

Shishlina, N.I. & Larionova, Y.O. 2016. Pastoral exploitation of the Caspian and Don Steppes and the North Caucasus during the Bronze Age: seasonality and isotopes. In: J.R. Collis, M. Pearce & F. Nicolis, eds. *Summer Farms: Seasonal Exploitation of the Uplands from Prehistory to the Present*. Sheffield Archaeological Monographs 16. Sheffield: J.R. Collis Publications, pp. 21–32.

Simakov, G.N. 1978. Opyt tipologizatsii skotovodcheskogo khoziaistva u kirgizov. (Konets XlX-nachalo XX v.). *Sovetskaya Etnografiya*, 6:14–27.

Speed, J., Austrheim, G., Birks, H.J.B., Johnson, S., Kvamme, M., Nagy, L., Sjögren, P., Skar, B., Stone, D., Svensson, E. & Thompson, D.B.A. 2012. Natural and cultural heritage in mountain landscapes: towards an integrated valuation. *International Journal of Biodiversity Science, Ecosystem Services & Management*, 8:313–20.

Stagno, A.M. 2016. Seasonal settlements and husbandry resources in the Ligurian Apennines (17th–20th centuries). In: J.R. Collis, M. Pearce & F. Nicolis, eds. 2016. *Summer Farms: Seasonal Exploitation of the Uplands from Prehistory to the Present*. Sheffield Archaeological Monographs 16. Sheffield: J.R. Collis Publications, pp. 73–96.

Star, S.L. & Griesemer, J.R. 1989. Institutional ecology, 'translations' and boundary objects: amateurs and professionals in Berkeley's Museum of vertebrate zoology, 1907–39. *Social Studies of Science*, 19:387–420.

Tornero, C., Bălăşescu, A., Ughetto-Monfrin, J., Voinea, V. & Balasse, M. 2013. Seasonality and season of birth in early Eneolithic sheep from Cheia (Romania): methodological advances and implications for animal economy. *Journal of Archaeological Science*, 40:4039–55.

Valenzuela-Lamas, S., Jiménez-Manchón, S., Evans, J., López, D., Jornet, R. & Albarella, U. 2016. Analysis of seasonal mobility of sheep in Iron Age Catalonia (north-eastern Spain) based on strontium and oxygen isotope analysis from tooth enamel: first results. *Journal of Archaeological Science: Reports*, 6:828–36.

Walsh, K. & Mocci, F. 2016. An historical ecology of the Neolithic to medieval periods in the southern French Alps: a reassessment of 'driving forces'. In: J.R. Collis, M. Pearce & F. Nicolis, eds. *Summer Farms: Seasonal Exploitation of the Uplands from Prehistory to the Present*. Sheffield Archaeological Monographs 16. Sheffield: J.R. Collis Publications, pp. 183–202.

Whatmore, S. 2002. *Hybrid Geographies: Natures, Cultures, Spaces*. London: Sage Publications.

CHAPTER 2

The Scandinavian shieling – between innovation and tradition

Eva Svensson

Shielings (Sw. *fäbod* or *säter*, No. *seter*) functioned as a means for expanding agrarian enterprises (mainly the grazing of cattle) from the farmstead or hamlet to areas lying outside those fields that were currently being worked. Shielings were used mainly in regions whose climatic conditions were difficult or who had limited acreage. The classic Scandinavian shieling consisted of a fenced site in outlying lands which included structures for dwelling, stabling cattle, processing milk and meadows for haymaking. The cattle were grazed in the forests surrounding shielings and guarded by female herders.

Shielings were only used seasonally (most often in the summer), although there are examples of winter shielings in the high mountainous areas of Norway. The distance between shielings and their mother farmsteads/hamlets varied, not least due to natural conditions. However, a distance of about 10 kilometres was quite common. Shielings were normally situated at higher altitudes. Often there were well-marked paths (shieling paths were known as *fäbodstig* or *säterstig* in Swedish) which included resting places between the hamlet and the shieling. Most shielings went out of use during the first half of the twentieth century, although there was a period of increased usage during the Second World War. Today, there are very few shielings which are still active and several of those are operated mainly as museums or tourist attractions.

This paper will argue, in contrast to earlier research, that shielings were important, flexible innovations which appeared on the forested or mountainous edges of the agrarian economy and that the innovative character of the shielings should be taken into account as part of today's heritage management.

Mapping a Relict – the Ethnographic Shieling in Scandinavia

The shielings interested both the ethnographers and geographers who mapped traditional folk culture in the early twentieth century when the system was already in decline and considered to be a relic of pre-industrial

agrarian practices (e.g. Erixon, 1918; Erixon, 1956; Frödin, 1925). Advocates of modern agriculture argued against the use of shielings as they believed them to be obstacles to rational cattle breeding; cattle of both sexes were believed to run around mixing as freely as they liked (Hellström, 1917: 544). In addition, shielings came into conflict with the increasingly important forestry industry, as grazing damaged the tree growth (Björkbom, 1907).

Ethnographers placed shielings within a north Scandinavian cultural bundle of phenomena which mainly occurred north of the Limes Norrlandicus, a climatic border sometimes also referred to as the 'shieling border'. Areas north of the Limes Norrlandicus were home to self-possessive and egalitarian peasants who touted female inheritance rights, freedom, sour milk and sledges. Those lands south of the Limes Norrlandicus were filled with noblemen, oak trees and wagons. However, the simplified dichotomy between north and south Scandinavia was continuously challenged as folk culture was not as easily restricted as geography; there were many examples of exceptions to the division. The clarity of such divisions were also complicated by the particular period under discussion as many of the aforementioned phenomena (as well as the shielings themselves) appeared to have expanded and retracted geographically over time (Berg, 1983; Erixon, 1918; Erixon, 1956; Frödin, 1925; Nyman, 1952). The main reason for the ethnographers' attraction to shielings was the assumption that shielings were ancient relics. As such, they were exotic examples of peripheral otherness in an increasingly industrial, modern and urban society. Shielings were considered more as symbols of north Scandinavian particularity than as constructions for cattle breeding.

There were two major challenges which faced early shieling scholars. First, it was viewed as necessary that shielings be divided into different typological and geographical groups based on their different characteristics. Second, the age of the shieling system needed to be assessed. As relics of an exotic form of pre-industrial agrarian system, the shieling system was presumed to have had a long pedigree, although exactly how long

© 2018 European Association of Archaeologists

that pedigree stretched back was debatable. Questions surrounding the age of the shieling system also came to be intertwined with typological issues as well as with concerns of what a shieling really was.

Typology was interlinked with function and form. The hamlets in some areas had several shielings, of which a few were located closer to the inner pastures and fields. These became known as short-distance shielings (Sw. *närfäbod*). Others were located at longer distances from the hamlets and were referred to as long-distance shielings (Sw. *längfäbod*). In most cases, the shielings located in the distant outlands were 'real' shielings, insofar as they were larger and more multifunctional. The short-distance shielings mostly functioned as short-term stopping points when moving the cattle between the hamlet and the long-distance shielings. Systems with several shielings were labelled as multi-shieling systems, whereas systems with only a main shieling were labelled single-shieling systems. In northern Sweden, yet another form of organizing the use of shieling (the half-shieling) was also common. At the half-shieling, cattle were grazed during the summer season and (female) herders only stayed at the shielings during the night. Lastly, a distinction between eastern and western shielings was made. The eastern type of shielings was used only for cattle grazing, whereas, both grazing and haymaking were performed at the western shielings. However, the cultivation of cereals was not supposed to have been pursued at any 'real' shieling (Montelius, 1977: 10–12, with references).

The Norwegian archaeologist, Bjørn Hougen, posited the presence of transhumance and the seasonal movements of people and cattle between coastal and inland areas in early prehistory. He based this on the observation that Stone Age artefacts had a considerably wider spatial distribution (including mountainous areas) than did artefacts from later periods. According to Hougen, transhumance and shielings preceded the establishment of permanent farmsteads in the Norwegian inland river valleys in the Roman Iron Age, that is, in the early centuries AD (Hougen, 1947).

A very different hypothesis was put forward by Norwegian historian Jørn Sandnes. Although shielings had been mentioned in medieval law documents, Sandnes suggested that 'real' shielings were a modern phenomenon. The principle impetus behind their establishment was, he argued, the need for winter fodder for cattle. In the twelfth and thirteenth centuries, haymaking was initially practiced in the outlands. This practice was abandoned during the Late Medieval Agrarian Crisis when deserted farmsteads offered opportunities for haymaking closer to the settlement. Shielings, often on locations previously used for haymaking, came into use in the sixteenth and seventeenth centuries as a response to increased population pressure on agrarian resources (Sandnes, 1989; Sandnes, 1991: 219–20).

A somewhat intermediate position which emphasized the development of shielings over time was presented by geographer Michel Cabouret. Using three commonly used names for shielings in Norway and some Swedish areas (*stöl*, *säl* and *säter*), Cabouret suggested a relative chronology for three different evolutionary stages. *Stöl* designated temporary (but regularly used) localities in the outlands and was presumably the oldest form. The next phase (*säl*) referred to sites which were used more regularly and included one-room houses for the longer stays during which milk was processed into various dairy products. *Säter* represented the most complex and could, thus, be assumed to be the youngest type of shielings known from the historic period. In order to determine the dating of the different stages of the shieling system, Cabouret used the Scandinavian colonization of Iceland in the Viking Age as a chronological baseline. As the words *stöl* and *säl* appeared in Iceland, he suggested that these shieling stages likely evolved before or during the Scandinavian colonization. The subsequent appearance of *säter*, absent on Iceland, could be considered a younger form which presumably developed during the high medieval period of growth. In any case, shielings were always secondary to permanent farmsteads (Cabouret, 1989).

NEW METHODS – AND THE EMERGENCE OF A NEW HISTORY OF SHIELING ORIGIN

The use of proxy data, such as stray finds, place names and indirect historical records has its limitations and can only offer tentative answers to the questions of age and function. Investigations into specific shieling sites and a more thorough engagement with chronology had to wait until the later part of the twentieth century due to lack of interest from archaeologists. Shielings were not readily associated with prehistoric or early historic periods; they were considered exponents of peripheral and marginal practices and landscapes and their locations rarely (if ever) made them the subjects of rescue excavations. Mainstream archaeology and antiquarians were simply more interested in chieftains in great halls than in women and cattle in distant forests and mountains.

Another discouraging problem was the complexity of shieling sites. The earliest investigations involving surveying and mapping campaigns showed that shieling sites were spread over large areas and included several dispersed house foundations of apparently indeterminable age; they also gave the impression of having included many features that were difficult (or perhaps even impossible) for the archaeological eye to identify. There was no easy way of determining the oldest feature for excavation or of finding an alternative means of dating the establishment phase. This conundrum was compounded by the possibility that the first construction of houses on a shieling site was preceded by land-use, as suggested by Cabouret (1989).

The first modern excavations of shielings were unsystematic, such as the near-accidental excavation of a shieling house at Gammelvallen, Ängersjö, in Sweden (inspired by strong local community interest and fuelled by interactions with archaeologists). Nonetheless, the high medieval date of the house foundation triggered large-scale excavations of both Gammelvallen and similar shielings nearby (Magnusson, 1989). The slightly sunken, stone-lined nature of its house foundation (Figure 2.1) was considered to be typical of medieval shieling house foundations, and was sought out by archaeologists prospecting for sites that might contain the oldest shieling phases. However, other investigations would soon show that this 'house foundation' might actually represent a milk cellar (placed underneath the house), which was a common feature well into modern times. Scholars concluded, moreover, that houses on shielings could be far older and have a wide variety of different appearances (Emanuelsson et al., 2003: 121–24, with references).

The excavations at Gammelvallen, Ängersjö, became the starting point for a large-scale interdisciplinary project on the economies and lifestyles of a north Scandinavian village over a long period of time. While shielings were among the most commonly investigated objects, palaeobotany, and pollen analysis in particular, were key to unlocking methodological problems which archaeology was not able to address, i.e. the dating of shielings and changes in shieling land-use over time (Emanuelsson, 2001). Palaeobotany also helped to problematize the concept of a shieling insofar as it detected the presence not only of haymaking, but also of cereal cultivation. In other words, they could exhibit the same land-use characteristics as farmsteads.

Pollen analysis had already been responsible for some major breakthroughs in shieling chronology for western Norway. In combination with archaeological investigation, it indicated sporadic grazing as early as the Bronze Age/Early Iron Age on a couple of historically known shieling sites. A number of cooking pits but no house foundations were found, and burial finds contemporary with the sporadic grazing have been documented at the farm historically connected to the shieling. These results indicate that farmstead and transhumant grazing together formed a package which facilitated the establishment of settlement in mountain areas. That said, the first establishment of shielings in their historically known form (i.e. with intense seasonal grazing and buildings) was not until the Viking Age

Figure 2.1. Medieval house foundation, Gammelvallen, Ängersjö
Photo: Eva Svensson

or early medieval period in western Norway (Kvamme, 1988; Magnus, 1986).

Similar results were produced by pollen analysis on shielings in several areas of western Sweden, such as Ängersjö, Dalarna and northern Värmland (Emanuelsson, 2001; Emanuelsson et al., 2003; Olsson, 1998). Sporadic grazing (and sometimes haymaking) appear to have taken place at a number of shieling sites prior to the establishment of the historically known shieling mode. Dates were slightly later than in western Norway: the early land-use more often dating to the middle or second half of the first millennium AD and the historically known mode of shielings to the Viking Age and medieval period (e.g. Figure 2.2).

Although it shall not be further explored here, it is tempting to connect the changing forms of land-use on shieling sites with the evolutionary scheme connected to the *stöl, säl* and *säter* as proposed by Cabouret (1989). The more sporadic forms of grazing could be represented by *stöl* or even *säl*, whereas *säter* would correspond with the historically known shieling mode which appeared in the Viking Age and early medieval period. Support for such an assumption could be found in the investigations of shieling sites in the Scandinavian Viking Age colonies of Iceland and the Faroe Islands. The sites investigated on Iceland and the Faroe Islands show that, in contrast to Cabouret's assumption, the Scandinavians brought with them fully developed shielings as part of their Viking Age settlement strategies (Mahler, 2007; Sveinbjarnardóttir, 1991).

The re-interpretation of the shielings as more flexible elements in an agrarian system did not go unchallenged; the question was raised as to whether sites with flexible functions (or rather the historical phases at shieling sites which showed a variety of functions) should be considered shielings at all. The Swedish agrarian historian Jesper Larsson (Larsson, 2009) pointed out that this very flexibility and variety hampered analytical studies which craved clear definitions. A return to the ethnographic definitions of shielings was, thus, a necessity to making certain that it was a shieling and nothing else that was under study. A 'real' shieling should be restricted to a site on which grazing, haymaking and dairy production were practiced and which operated within the self-subsistent economy of the farms. If these conditions were not met, the site could not be considered a shieling. Moreover, earlier phases at 'real' shielings with more complex functions should be omitted. Using such a strict definition, shielings again became a relatively late historical phenomenon secondary to farms. This was further emphasized as Larsson ruled out the Viking Age and early medieval shielings in spite of the fact that the features from the historically known shielings were in place. According to Larsson, 'real' shielings were not established until after the Late Medieval Agrarian Crisis, at which point they played a major role in the restructuring of agriculture with increased cattle breeding.

An analysis of the historical role of shielings in agrarian practices and economies (as well as in society in general) is of course dependent on the definition of a shieling. Sticking to a rigid definition makes shielings throughout the late medieval to early modern period a fairly unchangeable complement to peripheral farms. Apparently, a shieling scholar has to choose between sticking to a normative definition or trying to understand the narratives offered by the material culture of pollen, house foundations, clearance cairns, artefacts and the other historic and prehistoric objects present at shieling sites. Whether or not these sites should be labelled as shielings is of lesser importance. However, I will both stick with the concept of shieling and follow the second option in that I wish to try and understand the meanings of the material culture remains. I will do so by starting from the beginning: the innovative farm-shieling package.

AN INNOVATION PACKAGE: SHIELING, FARM AND OUTLAND USE

The aforementioned investigations in western Norway indicate that the farm-shieling association originated as a package. Having investigated shielings and settlements in different parts of western Sweden, the palaeobotanist, Marie Emanuelsson (2001), concluded that the combination of farm and shieling made feasible the expansion of settlement into rough terrain, such as dense forests or mountainous areas where land for cereal cultivation, grazing and haymaking was scarce and scattered over great distances. Earlier assumptions of successive relationships with either the farm or the shieling as the place of origin could, thus, be challenged with the superiority of dating tools offered by pollen analyses compared to proxy data.

Emanuelsson suggests that shielings (or, rather, the farm-shieling combination) should be considered an innovation. Innovation in this context should not be viewed in the older, rather strict technological sense, but rather as a concept which has been developed to include social and cultural processes, agency and decision-making. It has been argued that it is important to understand that the seeds of innovation are embedded in situational rationalism as well as in cultural contexts. Of importance for productive innovative environments are combinations of previous thinking and new ideas and the socialization of innovation with reciprocity creating socially solid organizational relationships (Styhre, 2013; Svensson, 2015). Such a description applies well to the innovative farm-shieling package.

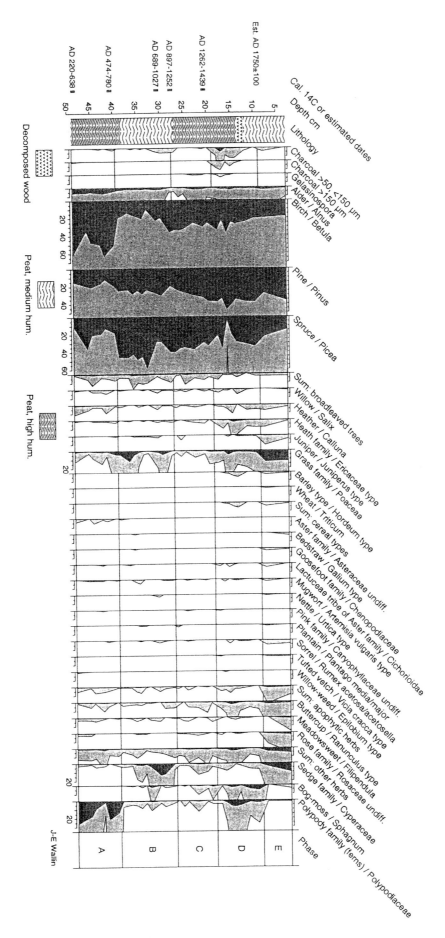

Figure 2.2. Pollen diagram, Backasätern shieling
Source: Marie Emanuelsson after Emanuelsson et al. (2003: fig. 43)

The model of a farm-shieling package appears not to have been straightforward. Pollen analyses as well as archaeological investigations (e.g. Amundsen, 2007; Emanuelsson, 2001; Emanuelsson et al., 2003; Olsson, 1998; Risbøl et al., 2011) have shown that there were discrepancies and variations within this theme at a number of sites. In reality, it is not always easy to tell the difference between a farm and a shieling. Ethnographically, a shieling was used for haymaking, grazing and dairy production, whereas a farm was the centre of a more complex economy which also engaged in cereal cultivation. However, investigations often discover indications of cereal cultivation at shielings (e.g. clearance cairns, fossil fields and cereal pollen), at least on a periodic basis. The actual relationship between farm and shieling was clearly both more strategic and flexible than implied by ethnographic models. It is likely that land-use at shielings could be expanded in relation to the needs of farms (for example, changing market conditions or those periods when there were many children in the home who required more food). There are also some indications that shielings (or parts thereof) could have been used on a temporary basis as farms, especially by young couples who were waiting for a farm of their own (Svensson, 1998: 104).

The farm-shieling package – as a means for making possible the settlement of difficult areas – should not be viewed in isolation and the apparent variations in shieling practice require contextualization. First, the package was not introduced in virgin land. Second, the package was accompanied by a number of other uses of the outlying landscapes. Bjørn Hougen (Hougen, 1947) connected the distribution of stone artefacts in mountainous areas to early transhumance. Prehistoric, Neolithic and Bronze Age use of the outlying areas are visible in most parts of Scandinavia, not only through stone artefacts but also through solitary graves, seasonal settlements and other sites (such as pitfalls for elk and reindeer). It has been argued that long-distance pastoralism (perhaps in concert with the Secondary Products Revolution) was an important part in an expansive (but temporal and not institutionalized) exploitation of outlying areas (Indrelid, 1994; Prescott, 1995; Svensson, 1998: 165–67). Like Hougen, I argue that prehistoric land-use (or rather the new landscapes that were created) functioned as a means of introducing shielings and agrarian settlements.

Prehistoric land-use initiated interactive transformations and transition processes which shaped hybrid landscapes both by means of and with regards to a variety of natural conditions, material culture, human strategies and traditions. Hybridity and non-human agency must be considered key words for understanding the ongoing processes, including the innovation and development of shielings, processes in which the hybrid landscapes themselves were major actors or actants

(e.g. Barad, 2003; Latour, 2005; Whatmore, 2002). The hybridity of the landscape had an active role not only for the making of shielings, but also for the fundamental organizational strategies, versatility and flexibility which characterized the eventual rural ways of making a livelihood in mountainous and forested areas (Svensson, 1998).

The package which enabled the establishment of permanent farmsteads and fields in the mountain river valleys and forested areas included not only shielings, but also a variety of other kinds of resource utilization methods, called outland use (Sw. and No. *utmarksbruk*; Svensson, 1998). Although outland use varied between different areas, some of the more common non-agrarian activities included the hunting of game and fur-bearing animals, the production of iron and tar and the quarrying of different stone materials. The products from these activities were often intended for sale (if only in part) and so were sensitive to demand and market competition.

Naturally, many of the outland activities which people engaged in served to increase the (often insufficient) acreage of the farm and so included the more familiar and traditionally agrarian activities of cattle grazing, cereal cultivation and haymaking relocated to the outland. Shielings were the most elaborate sites for accommodating the agrarian usage of outland areas. But hay was also made on natural or semi-natural meadows on both solid ground and mires. The north Scandinavian sedge mires produced a nutritious hay, and were often dammed to increase the growth of sedges. Minor fields for outland cereal cultivation in the forest have also been detected, not least by means of pollen analyses (Amundsen, 2007; Emanuelsson, 2001; Emanuelsson et al., 2003; Olsson, 1998; Risbøl et al., 2011).

Taken together, the diversified uses of the outland offered a substantial economic base for making a living. Versatility and the provision of multiple sources of income was also an efficient strategy for risk-management. Insufficient yields in one branch could be compensated by increasing production in another. However, this strategy of versatility posed challenges as it required elaborate ways of combining practices and organizing work.

ORGANIZING DIVERSITY – ENTER THE SHIELING MAID

This versatile outland economy faced several challenges: 1) making relatively few people cover large areas with geographically dispersed resources, 2) the organization of processing tasks which required people to stay away from the farm during longer or shorter periods of time and 3) the large skill sets required for operating sometimes quite technologically demanding procedures. These challenges were met with organization strategies, including communality, seasonality – and women, the shieling maids.

Collectives were key to managing the many things in agrarian life that required cooperation, mutual assistance, the pooling of different skills and common decision-making, with shieling management being among the most demanding of these practices (see Lindholm et al., 2013 for discussions on commons in the landscape). According to written documents from medieval and post-medieval times, shielings were divided by a number of farms which were either located within the same hamlet or were spread out over several. Through an inheritance system in which all children had inheritance rights, a shieling share could follow an heir/heiress who married into a farm in another hamlet. The property pattern at a shieling could, thus, be very complex (Wennersten, 2002). The maintenance and operation of the shielings (including haymaking) was carried out by a special co-operative which included joint owners and was called the shieling collective (Sw. *fäbodlag*). By contrast, the herding, milking and dairy work was assigned to female members of the households in the co-operative or to persons hired by the co-operative (Larsson, 2009: 95–99).

The complex combination of joint ownership and collective management required regulations, monitoring and sanctions prohibiting the unsustainable and unfair use or abuse of the shielings. There were local regulations (or mutual agreements) on how many cattle each partner could send to the shieling for summer grazing. The departure and return dates from the shielings were regulated through local customs and were surrounded by festivities which marked the dates. As the festivities included the public appearance of the shieling maids going to specific church services, local communities could also ensure that these regulated departure and return dates were not violated. There were also forms of sanctions which treated overstaying the agreed duration of the shieling season or the sending of too many cattle as a criminal offence of grass theft (Sw. *gräsrån*) (Svensson, 1998: 102).

Relying on work co-operatives solved the problem of raising sufficient work forces and the need for different skill sets according to the specific assignments needed. However, it did not resolve the issue of having enough people carrying out the many tasks which needed tending in the versatile outland economy. This challenge was met by spreading chores over the year and seasonal planning was an important tool in pre-industrial rural organization. While some work had to take place during certain seasons (e.g. ploughing, sowing, harvesting and haymaking), others were more flexible and were, therefore, performed during other parts of the year (Figure 2.3). While the shielings proper were nearly always operated during the summer season, the houses at the shieling could be used in connection with other outland tasks during other seasons. Maintenance and sometimes also the expansion of shielings were preferably carried out after they were cleared of cattle and herders.

Lastly, Scandinavia had a particular response to the issue of worker numbers: it was principally females who worked as herders at the shielings (see also Costello, this volume). In most parts of Europe as well as southern Scandinavia, herding cattle was a male task. The emergence of shieling maids (as they were often young women) instead of male herders has been discussed. A Swedish royal ordinance from 1686, recommending the use of female instead of male herders in order to avoid the sexual abuse of cattle, has been cited. However, according to written sources, shieling maids were common in the medieval period and well before 1686. Whether cattle sodomy was more of a problem in Scandinavia than the other parts of Europe which practiced transhumance is debatable. According to seventeenth-century court rolls from two court districts in western Sweden, cases of animal sodomy were rare. When brought to court the abused animal was always a horse. Perhaps the 1686 royal ordinance was an attempt to make female herders more common outside shielings as well, as Sweden was almost constantly at war in the seventeenth century and needed men as soldiers (Svensson, 1998: 103 with references).[1]

The most likely explanation for Scandinavian shieling maid traditions is to be found in the need for many hands working in those societies that made use of their outlands and dairy production at the shielings. In mountainous and forested Scandinavia, the number of tasks located in outlying landscapes was high and could not be managed by men alone. Women commonly participated in a wide range of activities otherwise reserved for men, a situation which both attracted and repelled foreign visitors. If gender labour division could be turned on its head in the sense that women took over male chores, there was one task traditionally assigned to women that was impossible for men to perform: dairy work. A man caught milking would be stigmatized. It could only be excused in life-threatening situations (Löfgren, 1982: 10). The presence of women tending the cattle at the shielings was, therefore, a simple solution to the workforce challenge and the demands of cultural practice.

MOVING ON – SHIELINGS IN MEDIEVAL AND MODERN TIMES

The evolution of Scandinavian shielings was interwoven with changes in agrarian economy and society, and was strongly regional in character. For instance, in

22 *Eva Svensson*

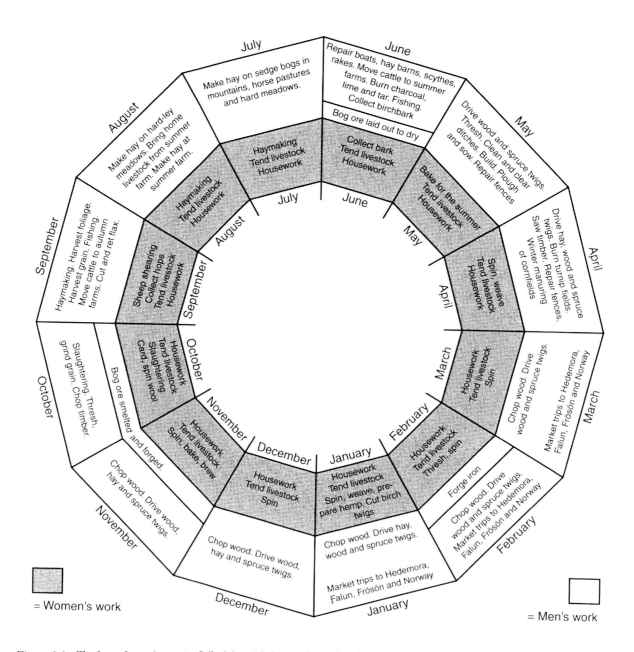

Figure 2.3. The forest farmer's year in Offerdal parish during the mid-eighteenth century
Source: After Svensson (2008: fig. 3), based on Magnusson (1986: fig. 130)

the Faroe Islands, the use of shielings was abandoned in the twelfth and thirteenth centuries and replaced with large-scale sheep breeding. The closing down of shielings in the Faroe Islands was a result of the introduction of a new agrarian economy and the arrival of Norwegian royal power in the islands (Mahler, 2007).

Although comparatively more stable, shielings in mainland Scandinavia still changed over time. Palaeobotanical and archaeological investigations in western Sweden and eastern Norway have come up with fairly similar chronological trends in shieling dynamics. During the Viking Age and high medieval period, they were used on a fairly small scale and most likely only hosted small flocks of goats and a few cows. Starting with the Late Medieval Agrarian Crisis, shieling use intensified continuously until it reached a climax in the nineteenth century. In the twentieth century, shieling use began to decline and most were deserted or abandoned by the middle of century (Amundsen, 2007; Emanuelsson, 2001; Emanuelsson et al., 2003; Olsson, 1998; Risbøl et al., 2011). The increased use of shielings during the Late Medieval Agrarian Crisis stands out as an anomaly, especially in Norway with a dominant meta-historical narrative of great devastation and the abandonment of agrarian life after the Black Death (see Pettersson, this volume).

Nonetheless, the trend over time is fairly clear. I argue that it followed its own logic or, rather that the logic of the trend was embedded in the interaction of hybrid landscapes of outland use and wider social context. In order to shed light on the process, the detailed, interdisciplinary case study, with several parallels, of the Backa hamlet and its shieling and outland use will be presented. The hamlet Backa is located on a narrow strip of sediment in the Klarälven River Valley. It was, in this context, a fairly large hamlet with extensive forested and hilly outlands. The hamlet also included fields for cereal cultivation, meadows and a secondary unit known as Skinnerud which was settled on agrarian land outside the confines of the hamlet for a short period of time. In the outlands bloomery iron production sites with charcoal pits, pitfalls for elk, meadows (both on solid ground and on dammed sedge mires), minor fields for cereal cultivation and a shieling, Backasätern (Figures 2.2 and 2.4) have been documented. The hamlet (especially Skinnerud, which was deserted and available for excavation) and different features of the outland were investigated using a variety of methods, such as analyses of pollen, historical maps, field surveys and excavations (Emanuelsson et al., 2003).

The investigations showed that permanent settlement, fields and meadows in the hamlet of Backa originated in a time somewhere in the middle of the Iron Age, although there were traces of previous use of the site which dated to the Neolithic and Bronze Age. During the Viking Age, settlement expanded in the hamlet including at the settlement of Skinnerud in the tenth century. However, using prime arable land for settlement meant a reduction in the hamlet's overall cereal cultivation. The excavations at Skinnerud unearthed a fairly wealthy farmstead which had a smithy as well as space for leather work.

In the outlands, there was bloomery iron production, pitfall hunting and haymaking. The Backasätern shieling was in use from the middle of the Iron Age and demonstrated an extensive increase in iron production and pitfall hunting in the tenth century. The agrarian outland use, however, did not increase during this period, and cereal cultivation on the infields diminished. In fact, Backasätern was deserted from around AD 1000 until the fourteenth century. Apparently, the Backa peasants had chosen to intensify iron production and elk hunting and to reduce the production of cereals and cattle breeding, the latter probably as a way of pooling labour resources to support the former activities. As bloomery iron and elk antler and skins were lucrative commodities, they also offered financial opportunities, as exemplified in the

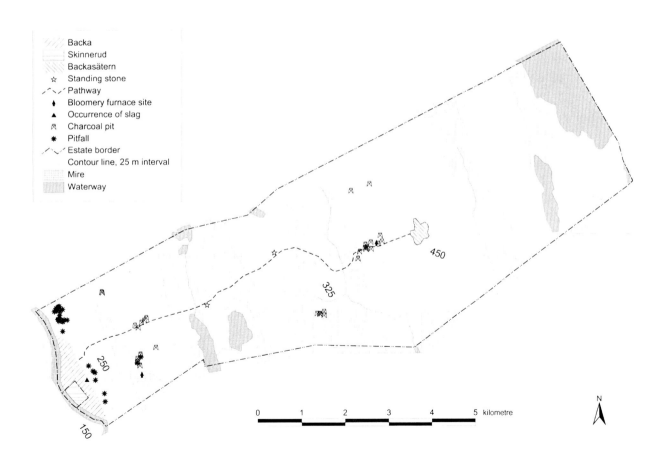

Figure 2.4. The Backa hamlet and outlands; the outland east of Backasätern shieling has not been surveyed
Source: Stefan Nilsson and Eva Svensson. After Svensson (2008: fig. 12)

imported beads and other artefacts found at the Skinnerud excavations.

However, being dependent on the market could be risky, a lesson learned the hard way by Backa peasants in the early thirteenth century. First, bloomery iron production and then pitfall hunting fell out of practice due to a number of external factors. Growing royal power concentrated trade in the new towns in the realm and comb-makers and other artisans who had previously worked in antler switched to the more readily available cattle bones and the Swedish Mining District's large-scale, high-quality blast furnace iron production took over the iron market.

These developments spelled a crisis for the hamlet of Backa and its peasants, calling for active solutions that were offered by the versatile economy. Bloomery iron production and pitfall hunting were reduced to meet domestic needs. These actions were accompanied by an increase in arable production, both at the fields near the hamlet and in the outlands. Around 1250, Skinnerud was deserted and replaced by a field, and outland cereal cultivation and haymaking increased. In the late fourteenth century, Backasätern was reopened (Figure 2.5). The seemingly anomalous increase in cereal cultivation and cattle breeding contemporary with the Late Medieval Agrarian Crisis was thus the

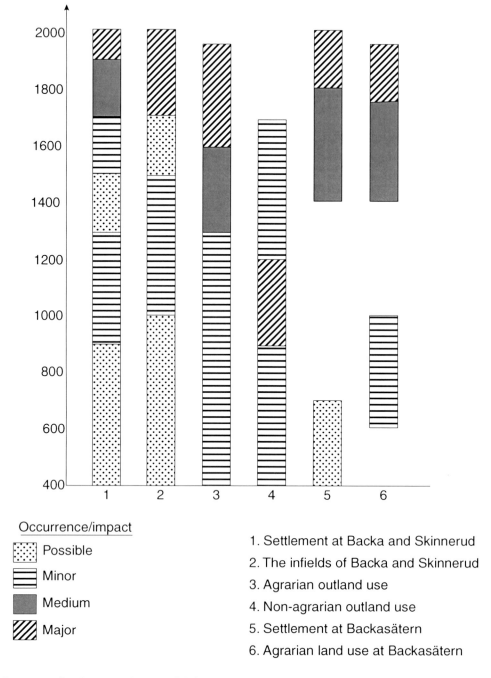

Figure 2.5. Occurrence of settlement and impact of different land-use activities over time at the Backa estate
Source: Marie Emanuelsson, Annie Johansson, Susanne Pettersson, Eva Svensson and Pontus Ullgren. After Emanuelsson et al. (2003: fig. 50)

response of a versatile farming community to another kind of crisis.

However, the wealth gained from the open market had not been forgotten as deserted bloomery iron production sites, charcoal pits and pitfalls for elk formed material reminders in the landscape. New opportunities arrived at the end of the medieval period. The rapid expansion of the Swedish Mining District offered a new market with its high demand for cattle for food, ropes and other things. By expanding and intensifying land-use at the shieling and haymaking facilities, more cattle could be bred at Backa for trade with the Mining District.

With the coming of industrialism, urbanization, modernity and the welfare state, shielings were faced with a new challenge. They could not keep pace with modern, improved farming, nor compete with well-paid year-round industrial jobs which offered both social security and summer holiday. Judging from the depopulation and closing down of agrarian enterprises in the mountainous and forested areas of Scandinavia, this crisis could not be surmounted by a change of focus in the versatile shieling-farmstead economy.

MUSEUMS OR RETRO-INNOVATIONS AND NEO-TRADITIONAL ORGANIZATIONS? IS THERE A NEW FUTURE FOR SHIELINGS?

But perhaps this crisis, too, might pass. It should be remembered that it took the peasants about a hundred years to come around when the crisis hit in the early thirteenth century. There are cracks in today's neoliberal hegemony in which alternatives are geminating, alternatives that may offer a new birth to both shielings and the versatile agrarian economy in which they took part. However, active heritage management and nature conservation strategies are essential for any potential rebirth of shielings and these must be less concerned with conserving a few remaining shieling skeletons and more involved in the pursuit of the true heritage of shielings, namely with regards to their strategic, active and flexible roles in making local economies resilient.

Today, both heritage management and nature conservation hope to conserve a few ethnographic model shielings (with the help of funding from the European Union). A lot of energy and resources have been poured into the preservation of a few buildings with old-fashioned exteriors and artificially scythe-mown meadows which have no real use today. While heritage managers and nature conservationists are seeking solutions for preserving a handful of shielings, there are new rural movements opening up new markets and opportunities for shielings (Berglund, 2015). Pictures from the chicken industry, mad cow disease and the horsemeat scandal as well as nostalgic assumptions about the green and traditional countryside have triggered new markets for 'safe' locally and traditionally produced eco-friendly foods (Marsden & Smith, 2005).

Interestingly, these new ruralism movements for alternative food production are often characterized by a package, combining what can be labelled retro-innovations and neo-traditional organizations. The new products are often inspired by local tradition and are tied together with small-scale, eco-friendly modes of production. Cattle, poultry and other meat producers graze beside old-fashioned farm buildings, far from pesticides and fertilizers. Tradition and references to past agrarian ways is also an increasingly important asset for brand development in the form of what is called 'history marketing' (Schug, 2010). The producers in the new ruralism movement often organize themselves in neo-traditional ways, relying on collective and versatile qualities. Numerous new production co-operatives are starting up in which former rural industries have moved out and new forms for collective, grassroots economical structures (such as crowdfunding) are emerging. It is also common to rely on combined income sources, such as small-scale food production and tourism.[2]

Shielings could be integrated into the new ruralism movement as they fit very well into the package of retro-innovations and neo-traditional organization. A new future for shielings within the new ruralism movement would also be well in line with the historically and contextually dependent character of shielings. However, as both the shieling sites and the modes for operating shielings would need to be adapted to fit the new production conditions, such strategies would come into conflict with the preservation ambitions of heritage management and nature conservation. Thus, the future of shielings depends on our decision about the nature of their heritage. Are they traditions or are they innovations?

BETWEEN TRADITION AND INNOVATION – SOME CONCLUSIONS

Since the first early ethnographic studies, Scandinavian shielings have been associated with past traditions and have been hampered by the preconceived notion that they are outdated relics which belong to peripheral contexts. For ethnographers, their very charm lay in their exotic otherness in relation to modern industrial society. However, their association with geographical and social peripheries and the fact that they were managed by women meant that they were of little interest to archaeology.

The major breakthrough for the study of shielings came with the introduction of interdisciplinary landscape studies which, when they involved shielings, were often conducted by scholars who had personal relations with forested or mountainous areas. Through interdisciplinary studies (especially the use of pollen analysis) shielings were acknowledged as part of hybrid landscapes which had a longer history and which could be interpreted as part of an innovation package which made possible the establishment of permanent agrarian settlement in the mountainous and forested areas of Scandinavia. These studies also showed that shielings had been used strategically by farming communities and had been expanded and contracted in relation to other kinds of outland use and the demands of different markets.

Still, in the world of today's heritage management and nature conservation, it is the traditional aspect of shielings that is emphasized rather than their innovative past. By focusing conservation of shielings on a model of how they were managed shortly before they were closed down in the first half of the twentieth century, the dynamic characteristics of shielings are swept under the carpet. An alternative and more sustainable future for shielings could involve their incorporation in new ruralism movements involving alternative food production. However, this would demand an abandonment of the focus on shielings as relics of an outdated agrarian system and an acknowledgement of shielings as dynamic and strategic entities.

ACKNOWLEDGEMENTS

I am grateful to Marie Emanuelsson, Annie Johansson, Stefan Nilsson and Susanne Pettersson for working with me in the *Settlement, Shieling and Landscape* project in which 'everything' was discovered. Thanks also to Camilla Berglund for discussions on local food. Last, but not least, many thanks to Mark Gardiner for correcting my English in the initial draft.

NOTES

1 Even if she was not implicated with sodomy, the shieling maid was associated with sexual liberty in pre-industrial agrarian society to some degree. Young men could visit the shieling without chaperons. She also made an appearance in early pornographic movies.
2 This will be further investigated by Camilla Berglund and Eva Svensson.

REFERENCES

Amundsen, T., ed. 2007. *Elgfangst og bosetning i Gråfjellområdet*. Varia 64. Bind II. Oslo.
Barad, K. 2003. Posthumanist performativity: toward an understanding of how matter comes to matter. *Signs: Journal of Women in Culture and Society*, 28(3):801–31.

Berg, G. 1983. Limes norrlandicus and the formation of ethnological theory: a contribution to a discussion. *Ethnologica Scandinavica, A Journal for Nordic Ethnology*: 7–14.
Berglund, C. 2015. *Närheter och avstånd i ett nordvärmländskt skogslandskap: praktiker och betydelser i nya tidsrumsliga sammanhang*. Karlstad: Karlstad University.
Björkbom, C. 1907. Om skogsbetet. *Skogsvårdsföreningens folkskrifter*, 1905–1907(9):1–32.
Cabouret, M. 1989. Esquisse d'une chronologie des etapes de la formation de la vie pastorale en Norvège. *(Norsk) Historisk tidskrift*, 1989(1):28–37.
Emanuelsson, M. 2001. *Settlement and Land-Use History in the Central Swedish Forest Region: The Use of Pollen Analysis in Interdisciplinary Studies*. Diss. Umeå: Swedish University of Agricultural Sciences.
Emanuelsson, M., Johansson, A., Nilsson, S., Pettersson, S. & Svensson, E. 2003. *Settlement, Shieling and Landscape: The Local History of a Forest Hamlet*. Stockholm: Almqvist & Wiksell International.
Erixon, S. 1918. Bebyggelseundersökningar. Öfversikt. Periodiska bebyggelsetyper. Fäbodväsen. *Fataburen. Kulturhistorisk Tidskrift*, 1918:21–57.
Erixon, S. 1956. Betesvandringar och flyttsystem. *Folk-liv* 19/20:39–55.
Frödin, J. 1925. *Siljansområdets fäbodbygd*. Lund: Gleerups.
Hellström, P. 1917. *Norrlands jordbruk*. Uppsala: Almqvist & Wiksell.
Hougen, B. 1947. *Fra seter til gård: studier i norsk bosetningshistorie*. Oslo: Norsk Arkeologisk Selskap.
Indrelid, S. 1994. *Fangstfolk og bønder i fjellet. Bidrag till Hardangerviddas førhistorie 8500–2500 år før nåtid*. Oslo: Universitets Oldsaksamling.
Kvamme, M. 1988. Pollen analytical studies of mountain summer-farming in western Norway. In: H.H. Birks, H.J.B. Birks, P.E. Kaland & D. Moe, eds. *The Cultural Landscape: Past, Present and Future*. Cambridge: Cambridge University Press, pp. 349–67.
Larsson, J. 2009. *Fäbodväsendet 1550–1920: ett centralt element i Nordsveriges jordbrukssystem*. Uppsala: Sveriges Lantbruksuniversitet.
Latour, B. 2005. *Reassembling the Social: An Introduction to Actor-Network-Theory*. Oxford: Oxford University Press.
Lindholm, K-J., Sandström, E. & Ekman, A-K. 2013. The archaeology of the commons. *Journal of Archaeology and Ancient History*, 10:2–49.
Löfgren, O. 1982. Kvinnfolksgöra – om arbetsdelning i bondesamhället. *Kvinnovetenskaplig tidskrift*, 1982(3):6–14.
Mahler, D.L. 2007. *Sæteren ved Argisbrekka: økonomiske forandringer på Færøerne i vikingetid og tidlig middelalder*. København: Københavns Universitet.
Magnus, B. 1986. Iron Age exploitation of high mountain resources in Sogn. *Norwegian Archaeological Review*, 19(1):44–50.
Magnusson, G. 1986. *Lågteknisk järnhantering i Jämtlands län*. Stockholm: Stockholm University.
Magnusson, G. 1989. Medeltida fäbodlämningar i Ängersjö. In: O. Hemmendorff, ed. *Arkeologi i fjäll, skog och bygd. 2. Järnålder – medeltid*. Östersund: Jämtlands läns museum, pp. 167–74.
Marsden, T. & Smith, E. 2005. Ecological entrepreneurship: sustainable development in local communities through quality food production and local branding. *Geoforum*, 36:440–51.
Montelius, S. 1977. *Fäbodväsendet i övre Dalarna*. Stockholm: Akademilitteratur and Institutet för Folklivsforskning.
Nyman, A. 1952. Det svenska fäbodväsendets sydgräns. *Folkliv 1952. Acta Ethnologica et folklorisica Europea*, 90–96.

Olsson, M. 1998. Pollenanalytiska undersökningar av säter-miljöer i Dalby och Gunnarskog socknar, Värmland. LUDQUA uppdrag. Unpublished report. Lund.

Prescott, C. 1995. Aspects of early pastoralism in Sogn, Norway. *Acta Archaeologica*, 66:163–89.

Risbøl, O., Stene, K. & Sætren, A., eds. 2011. *Kultur och natur i Grimsdalen landskapsvernområde: sluttrapport fra DYLAN-prosjektet.* NIKU Tema 38. www.niku.no/filestore/Publikasjoner/NIKUTema38.pdf (accessed 25 November 2015).

Sandnes, J. 1989. Ljåen og krøttermulen. Om opphav og alder til det norske seterbruket. *(Norsk) Historisk tidskrift*, 1989(3):351–57.

Sandnes J. 1991. Utmarksdrift og ressursutnyttelse i Norge i eldre tid. In: S. Gissel, E. Österberg & S. Göransson, eds. *Plov og pen. Festskrift til Svend Gissel 4. Januar 1991.* København: Det kongelige Bibliotek, pp. 213–21.

Schug, A. 2010. *History Marketing: använd företagets historia i kommunikation och marknadsföring.* Stockholm: Ekerlid.

Styhre, A. 2013. *A Social Theory of Innovation.* Malmö: Liber.

Sveinbjarnardóttir, G. 1991. Shielings in Iceland: an archaeological and historical survey. *Acta Archaeologica*, 61:73–96.

Svensson, E. 1998. *Människor i utmark.* Stockholm: Almqvist & Wiksell International.

Svensson, E. 2008. *The Medieval Household: Daily Life in Castles and Farmsteads: Scandinavian Examples in their European context.* Turnhout: Brepols.

Svensson, E. 2015. Innovations in the rural edge. Inventions and smart organizations in the Scandinavian outland use. In: P. Gaidukov, et al., eds. *Towns and Villages in Medieval Rus: Archaeology, History, Culture. To mark the 60th birthday of the Academician Nikolai Makarov.* Moscow: Russian Academy of Sciences, pp. 69–77.

Wennersten, E. 2002. *Släktens territorier: en jämförande studie av sociala regelverk i det förindustriella bondesamhället i Dalarna och Hälsingland 1734–1826.* Stockholm: Stockholm University.

Whatmore, S. 2002. *Hybrid Geographies: Natures, Cultures, Spaces.* London: Sage Publications.

CHAPTER 3

From written sources to archaeological remains – medieval shielings in central Scandinavia

Susanne Pettersson

Although Scandinavian shielings (Sw. *fäbod* or *säter*, No. *seter*) remained in use well into the middle of the twentieth century, by then they were considered the old-fashioned relics of a pre-industrial agrarian system. As such a system, shielings have been the subject of many academic studies over the past century, first by ethnologists and historians and then later by archaeologists and paleo-botanists. The traditional shieling as described by ethnologists (e.g. Erixon, 1918; Erixon, 1956; Frödin, 1925) was a seasonal settlement in the outlying lands of a farm which had houses and facilities for people, cattle and milk processing and was additionally under the control of female herders. The cultivation of cereals was not supposed to have taken place at any 'real' shieling (Montelius, 1977: 10–12).

Age, Origin and Content

Old Norwegian laws, such as the *Gulatingslov*, the *Frostatingslov* (before AD 1100) and the *Magnus Lagabøters landslov* (AD 1274) provide details about legal rights and obligations for shieling systems (Reinton, 1969: 12). However, the linguistic content, age and origin of shielings have been discussed since the beginning of the twentieth century. Some scholars suggest that shielings were secondary to the main farmstead and that the traditional shieling developed from the sixteenth century (Sandnes, 1989, 1991) or that transhumance and shielings preceded the establishment of permanent farmsteads, perhaps even in the first century AD (Hougen, 1947).

Figure 3.1. A modern summerhouse at Herlandsetra
Photo: Susanne Pettersson

© 2018 European Association of Archaeologists

Later investigations based on pollen analysis and the results of archaeological excavations in Sweden and Norway have confirmed grazing activity on a couple of historically known shielings as early as Late Bronze Age or Early Iron Age (1100 BC–AD 400). These results allow us to suggest that the combination of farmstead together with transhumance and grazing formed a package which facilitated the establishment of settlements in barren terrain. Shielings with intense seasonal grazing and buildings were established during the Viking Age (AD 800–1050) or later (Emanuelsson, 2001; Kvamme, 1988; Magnus, 1986). Fully developed shielings could form a part of settlement strategies during the Viking Age and are even known from investigations of the Scandinavian colonization of Iceland and the Faroe Islands (Mahler, 2007; Sveinbjarnardóttir, 1991). The innovative shieling-farm package was also supplemented by non-agrarian outland use, such as hunting and iron production. These last can be identified by features such as pitfalls for elk and bloomery furnaces and their associated charcoal pits (Svensson, 1998; Emanuelsson, 2001; Amundsen, 2007).

Archaeology and paleo-botany have not only confirmed prehistoric or medieval use of shielings, but have also shown periodic use or alterations in intensity of shieling exploitation over time; occasionally, this even developed into permanent occupation (Myrdal & Söderberg, 1991; Svensson, 1998; Emanuelsson, 2001, Emanuelsson et al., 2003). Another alternative was exactly the reverse: deserted farmsteads were turned into shielings, especially during the Late Medieval Agrarian Crisis (Antonson, 2004; Hansson et al., 2005).

With his focus on deserted farmsteads in Jämtland County, human geographer Hans Antonson (2004) examined landscape changes before, during and after the Medieval Agrarian Crisis in the fourteenth century. Twelve deserted farmsteads were chosen for further study, all of which were identifiable by the written sources, archaeological remains and extant traces of medieval buildings. The visible remains of modern shielings were identified at six of these study sites (Antonson, 2004; 140–60). One of Antonson's conclusions involved defining the development of the landscape as part of the fluctuation in the settlements (from shieling to farmstead followed by desertion and re-colonization) within a cyclic system (e.g. Antonson, 2004: 214).

A common problem within archaeological study, on the other hand, involved the identification of early medieval settlements. Archaeologists have discussed the subject at several occasions (e.g. Martens et al., 2009; Beronius Jörpeland, 2010) and Lena Beronius Jörpeland based her study on archaeological investigations of medieval sites in eastern Sweden (*Mälardalen* in Figure 3.3). Three of her conclusions are of significant interest to this article. First, settlements did move around within the principle fields of the farm. Second, buildings were often hard to interpret since they were fragmented and incomplete (even without the damage from subsequent activities). Third, an unfamiliar construction method could have been used during the early medieval period (Beronius Jörpeland, 2010).

With its aim of using archaeology as the basis for discussion, this article will focus on the medieval period at some shielings as seen from a long-term perspective. Age and origin are examined by place name, written sources, pollen analyses and radiocarbon dates. Clearing, grazing, cereal cultivation and accommodation patterns will be discussed in relation to 'real' shielings as defined by ethnographers as well as to flexibility and the transhumance and grazing package which facilitated the establishment of settlement in inhospitable terrain. Finally, the impact of the central Scandinavian convention of building houses in timber and the effects of modern practices at most shielings will be addressed with regards to how to identify a medieval or prehistoric shieling from among modern sites and remnants when all timber has disappeared (Figure 3.2).

For more information about Scandinavian shielings, their research history and theoretical perspectives, the reader may refer to Eva Svensson's article in the present volume.

THREE CASE STUDIES

Personal involvement and sites known to have had long-lasting occupation periods determine the selection of three case studies. At the same time, the chosen studies comprise one rescue excavation and two research projects and benefit from the comparisons of two different kinds of investigative results. The following presentation will follow a chronological order according to date of investigation, followed by discussion prior to the next project.

The first case examined here is based on a pilot study and the *Settlement, Shieling and Landscape* project which investigated four shielings in the northern part of Värmland County, western Sweden. The second case study consists of three shielings which were included in the *Gråfjellprosjektet* in Hedmark County, eastern Norway. The last study is based on the *Seterbruket i Vestfold – alder, form og utbredelse* (the use of shielings in Vestfold – age, shape/sort and distribution/spreading) project which focused on four shielings in Vestfold County, southeast Norway (Figure 3.3).

FOUR SHIELINGS IN DALBY PARISH, VÄRMLAND COUNTY, SWEDEN

The first case study is located to Dalby parish in the northern part of Värmland, Sweden. The forest and

Figure 3.2. Modern remains of a timber building at Herlandsetra Nedre, *Vestfold County, Norway*
Photo: Susanne Pettersson

mires which span both sides of the Klarälven River dominate the landscape of the parish. Most settlements are situated within the Klarälven River's narrow valleys at altitudes between 150–200 metres above sea level. The associated shielings are located in the surrounding forest area and appear at distances of between 1 to 10 kilometres at altitudes of 400–500 metres above sea level. As arable land is limited, there are no prehistoric burial sites known within miles, although most of the farmsteads have prehistoric place names and the forested areas contain many archaeological features, such as pitfalls for elk and bloomery iron sites. Both feature categories can mainly be dated to c. AD 900–1250 (Svensson, 1998; Emanuelsson et al., 2003: 10).

A research project, initialized by a pilot study in 1995 aimed to locate and investigate one of the oldest shielings in Dalby parish through a study of four farmsteads and their related shielings (*säter*). The sources on which the selection was based included medieval documents, the prehistoric or medieval place names for the farms and shielings and/or a name which referred to an older shieling (Sw. *Gammelvallen*). All four farmsteads (*Bänteby, Likenäs, Persby* and *Backa*) were classified as medieval (pre-AD 1520) and were listed for taxation in 1503. Landscape survey and the mapping of the visual remains at all four shielings were carried out in 1995–1996. Pollen analysis was executed at three of the sites (Johansson et al., 1997; Olsson, 1998).

Bänteby (the farmstead) and *Bäntebysätern* (its shieling) were categorized as medieval because they refer to a variant of the Christian name Benedictus, combined with '-*by*' (meaning settlement). Eight timber buildings were found at the shieling along with forty-seven house foundations, five areas with cairns resulting from the clearance of agricultural fields (hereafter clearance cairns) and various extant paths and fences were registered and mapped at the site (Johansson et al., 1997). Pollen analysis from a mire close to the shieling revealed evidence for forest clearance and increased amounts of grass, indicating a forest grazing activity during the fourteenth century; more intense use including grazing and cereal cultivation occurred from the eighteenth century on (Olsson, 1998).

Likenäs/Gammelsätern's topographic name for the farmstead indicates a possible prehistoric settlement – the name of the shieling translating as 'the older shieling'. Four timber buildings at the site have been converted to modern summerhouses with four standing buildings representing the ruins of the shieling. The survey registered eighteen house foundations, some clearance cairns and some stone walls/fences (Johansson et al., 1997). Pollen analysis from the site indicated forest clearance and increased grass quantities during the Late Iron Age

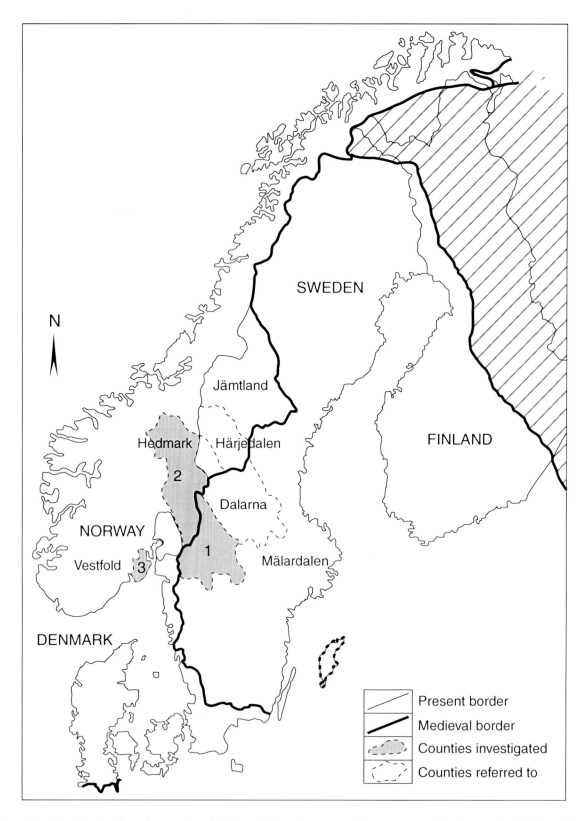

Figure 3.3. Map showing the regions mentioned in the article. The three case studies are numerated in the following fashion: 1) Settlement, Shieling and Landscape *(Emanuelsson et al., 2003)*, 2) Elgfangst og bosetning i Gråfjellområdet *(Amundsen, 2007)* and 3) Seterbruket i Vestfold – alder, form og utbredelse *(Pettersson, 2011)*

Source: Susanne Pettersson

(AD 680–900). This last provides a possible settlement date and was accompanied by the addition of cereal cultivation in modern times (Olsson, 1998).

The third selection (*Ransby/Ransbysätern*) derives from the Old Norse name '*Ramn*' combined with '*-by*' indicating a Viking Age/early medieval date (AD 800–1200). The shieling is divided into three areas with a single timber building still standing. Fifty-one house foundations, one well, one milk-cooler, five clearance cairn areas and some stone walls/fences were surveyed and mapped (Johansson et al., 1997), with pollen analysis indicating forest clearance and increased grass quantities during Late Iron Age/early medieval period (AD 1000–1210). Grazing activity and a general increase in activity, with some cereal cultivation, were noted for the sixteenth century (Olsson, 1998).

Backa/Backasätern was chosen because of its place name – '*backa*' being an old word for a slope or hilly site, commonly found at prehistoric settlements. At the shieling *Backasätern*, ten timber buildings, forty house foundations, ten possible house foundations and several clearance cairns were identified and mapped (Johansson et al., 1997). One pollen analysis was performed here during the main project in 1998, indicating haymaking and possible grazing activities from the seventh to the eleventh centuries AD. This was followed by a period of abandonment and then a reopening of the site in the fifteenth century (Emanuelsson et al., 2003: 110). The pollen evidence suggests that haymaking/grazing could have formed a package for establishing a prehistoric settlement at *Backa* and meshes well with the presumed prehistoric ages of the farmsteads in *Backa*.

Further exploration around the farmsteads even revealed a possible prehistoric or medieval settlement while a concentration of fire-cracked stones, flint fragments and iron slag from a bloomery site were found in an open field south of the hamlet of *Backa*, in an area called *Skinnerud*. An initial excavation took place here in 1996, followed by other excavations as part of the main project in 1998–1999. Three house foundations were excavated, all of which were dated to the late tenth century. One cultural layer in the courtyard was dated to AD 420–600, suggesting *Skinnerud* to be a secondary unit to the hamlet of *Backa*, established on a site which was already in use during the sixth century (Johansson et al., 1997; Emanuelsson et al., 2003: 46).

The investigation at *Backasätern*

Encouraged by the results from the early medieval settlement and evidence for prehistoric activity at *Backa/Skinnerud*, an excavation was undertaken at *Backasätern* in 1998–1999. Although most of the visible structures were modern, five house foundations with low, square hearths and a square, recessed structure with small embankments on two sides seemed to be older. Two buildings with low, square hearths, the same sort of recessed structure and one house foundation with a square cellar pit were selected for small-scale excavation. None of the seven trenches at the shieling exceeded 2 square metres.

Further examination of the structure and artefacts recovered from one of the house foundations with a square hearth was shown to be modern. It was excluded from further analysis. Two buildings with hearths and the house with the cellar pit were all radiocarbon dated to the fifteenth and sixteenth centuries. The presumed dwelling house with its recessed structure and embankments on two sides did also include a hearth and a bench. A particular activity layer within the building gave a sixteenth-century date while the hearth was dated to AD 409–688 (Emanuelsson et al., 2003: 115–21). The older activity is roughly contemporary with the possible clearing of woody vegetation at *Skinnerud* and seems close to the grazing/haymaking impact noted in the pollen analysis of *Backasätern*. The sixteenth-century date coincides with the reestablishment of the shieling and the appearance of *Skinnerud* in written sources (Emanuelsson et al., 2003: 46, 109f, 116).

The investigation at *Backasätern* revealed some of the problems of dealing with modern activities at older sites as well as some of the difficulties involved with the remains of timber buildings which do not have wall foundations with stone sills. A hearth in a low recessed structure with two faintly visible earth banks was the only structure that corresponded to the first grazing phase at *Backasätern*. The quantities of artefacts collected from the excavations were very limited; most items included undated or modern finds, including nails, pieces of flint for making fire, knives, window glass and modern earthenware (Emanuelsson et al., 2003: 117–21). Given that it was a small-scale survey, the combination of archaeology, human geography and paleoecology garnered a lot of knowledge. The following case study includes more analyses, structures and, most of all, a large investigation area.

THREE SHIELINGS WITHIN *GRÅFJELLPROSJEKTET*, HEDMARK COUNTY, NORWAY

As the *Gråfjellprosjektet* was concerned with a rescue excavation prior to the construction of a military exercise field, most of the excavation was performed by mechanical excavator. Following the conclusions drawn from an archaeological evaluation performed by the Norwegian Institute for Cultural Heritage Research (NIKU) in 2000–2001 (Risbøl et al., 2000, 2001, 2002), the Museum of Cultural History, University of Oslo, executed the project in 2003–2005. Three out of thirteen shielings located within the space earmarked for the exercise field were selected for archaeological excavation: *Melgårdsetern*, *Sørgårdsvollen* and *Rødseter*.

Hedmark County has a consistent undulating topography and, in addition to limited arable land, also has a selection of archaeological features similar to those of northern Värmland. The investigation area included wooded outlying fields with extensive bog areas. The Rena River flows along the west side of the exercise field. Most farm settlements were positioned in the river valley at an altitude of 290 metres above sea level with their associated shielings located less than 6 kilometres away at an altitude of 430–650 metres above sea level.

Deset Østseter acts as an overarching name for two of the shielings (*Melgårdsetern* and *Sørgårdsvollen*) which were used by various farmsteads in the hamlet of *Deset*. The latter place name is known to be prehistoric. The shielings were situated on different sides of a small river called the Deia. A total of eleven timber buildings were still standing, some of which were still being used for recreation and hunting. Three house foundations and a few clearance cairns were recorded during the evaluation at *Melgårdsetern*, while one house foundation and some clearance cairns were noted at *Sørgårdsvollen* (Risbøl, et al., 2001).

Pieces of coal culled from a pollen sample from *Melgårdsetern* indicate an activity which involved a fire, probably a slash-and-burn clearing technique which was already present at the site during the first century AD (Amundsen, 2007: 239). An iron bloomery site and some charcoal pits investigated in the eastern part of *Melgårdsetern* in 2003 were dated to AD 1025–1275 (Rundberget, 2007: 86).

(Figure 3.4) and a door handle in another suggested that both structures were fragmented and incomplete building remains. All traces of buildings and the eleven structures will be handled as house foundations in the following.

Thirty-one charcoal samples were analyzed from the yard plot at *Melgårdsetern*, of which nine post-dated AD 1650 and two were prehistoric, covering the timespan from AD 650–775. This left sixteen medieval and one early modern date from ten buildings for further analysis. Based on four samples within the AD 1030–1285 timespan, three buildings were older than the Medieval Agrarian Crisis. The five structures dated by nine samples to AD 1305–1485 could date from periods either before or after the crisis. Two buildings were more recent, one dated to AD 1414–1440 and the other one to AD 1435–1655 (Amundsen, 2007: 272). More than 700 finds were collected from *Melgårdsetern* of which the majority were found by metal detector. In addition to some pieces of iron slag, one medieval horseshoe nail and three pieces of flint for fire setting were the modern artefacts, such as window glass, industrially produced nails, steel wire, clay pipes and lead bullets (Amundsen, 2007: 274).

Since most clearance cairns were reinterpreted as hearths and only a small amount of cereal cultivation was known from modern times (Amundsen, 2007: 239), there was no evidence for earlier cultivation at the site. The oldest activity at the site seemed to be slash-and-burn clearing prior to grazing activity which dated from the first century AD, followed by iron production and two buildings during the twelfth century. One building was added during the thirteenth century, five more were completed during the fourteenth century and at least one more was erected during the sixteenth century.

Melgårdsetern

The excavation at *Melgårdsetern* formed the first large-scale investigation of a shieling in the region and highlighted problems in locating medieval house foundations. A total of 6,759 square metres of space were investigated at the shieling during the 2003 and 2004 campaigns. During the excavation, the number of identified buildings increased from the three identified over the course of the archaeological evaluation to seven house foundations and eleven building traces. Three clearance cairns were reinterpreted as hearths in different buildings, which also include activity layers, floors, wall foundations and postholes (Amundsen, 2007: 235ff).

Some low earthworks and stones from a hypothetical wall foundation indicated the traces of buildings. The two keys found inside one of these structures

Sørgårdsvollen

The excavation at *Sørgårdsvollen* involved two structures, a house foundation and traces of another one within a total excavated area of 907 square metres. An almost square stone structure with a height of 0.1 metres was visible in the high grass, although it was not included in the archaeological evaluation. Later excavation in this area confirmed it as a hearth. The western wall could be identified by a stone foundation sill wall and the eastern wall by a 0.1 metre deep foundation cut. The presence of both a small road to the north and a later structure to the south had damaged the building (Amundsen, 2007: 267).

The later structure was identifiable as a building due to the presence of low earthworks and some stones (0.04–0.1 metres high) which surrounded a dark

Figure 3.4. Possible building at Melgårdsetern *showing low earthworks surrounding a rectangular hollow partly filled with the stones placed there as part of later activities at the site*
Photo: Susanne Pettersson

cultural layer which was later interpreted as an internal floor. Given that it cut and affected the first building, this structure was shown to be later than the building which contained a hearth. Four charcoal samples (two from each of the structures) turned out to have similar date ranges (AD 1307–1465), suggesting a close succession (Amundsen, 2007). A date in the fourteenth or early fifteenth century could represent clearance and likely also the presence of the first building. The other building seems to have been dated by charcoal related to the clearance. One of the samples had a shorter timespan associated with it and narrowed down the date to AD 1400–1430, suggesting that the activity was later than the Agrarian Crisis and that the shieling was likely an extension of *Melgårdsetern*. Forty-two artefacts were collected from the building area, although all of them were undatable or were modern as iron slag, nails, horseshoe nails, mountings or clay pipes.

Rødseter

The third shieling excavated within *Gråfjellprosjektet* exhibited a topographic place name taken from the farmstead/hamlet of *Rød*. The shieling was situated in hilly woodlands and lay 6 kilometres from the hamlet in the Rena River Valley at an altitude of 435 metres over sea level. In 1822, one of the farmsteads from *Rød* was relocated and established at *Rødseter*, which at that time consisted of five shielings along with one crofter (Amundsen, 2007: 149). Pollen analyses performed close to the shieling indicate grazing from the first century AD (Amundsen, 2007: 148).

The *Rødseter* investigation took place in 2004–2005 based on an archaeological evaluation of fifty-two clearance cairns and four house foundations close to a system of hunting pits and one iron bloomery production site (Amundsen, 2007). Approximately twenty clearance cairns and field terraces within the settlement were included in the excavation. According to the sixty-three radiocarbon dates from stratigraphic layers confirmed by pollen and macrofossil analysis, slash-and-burn clearing events followed by cereal cultivation took place at the site during the ninth century and were ongoing until the late eighteenth century (Amundsen, 2007: 190ff).

Once again, the estimated number of buildings was raised by the results of the excavation. In this case, the four house foundations known from the archaeological evaluation became eight buildings. Three clearance cairns were reinterpreted as hearths as they were also associated with other building structures, such as floor layers and wall foundations. Two unregistered low stone heaps forming two hearths in another building resulted in a total of five buildings with at least one hearth, an indication of accommodation or cooking. The remaining three buildings represented outhouses (Amundsen, 2007).

Forty charcoal samples were analyzed from the yard plot at *Rødseter*. Fourteen samples produced dates after the middle of the seventeenth century and five samples were considered to represent activities which predated the buildings. The older activities were represented by two Late Iron Age samples (AD 720–1025) and three early medieval samples (AD 1070 to 1370) (Amundsen, 2007: 231). These samples would have been contemporary with the agricultural activities at the site and all of them predated the Agrarian Crisis during the middle of the fourteenth century. Two samples were taken from a well close to the foundations of the house. The bottom layer was dated to AD 1185–1250, indicating the time at which it was dug. The date gleaned from the upper layer (1470–1635) suggests its final use was during the sixteenth century.

This leaves nineteen radiocarbon dates to determine the establishment of the buildings. The oldest dates connected to four of the buildings suggest an establishment during the fourteenth century, dispersed across the whole century from 1305 to 1405. Two houses could be dated to the fifteenth century (1400–1445). One building was dated to the sixteenth century (1530–1655). Most of the buildings remained in use into the eighteenth century (Amundsen, 2007: 193–235). More than 700 finds were gathered from the buildings' vicinity. Most of them were of modern date and indicate activities such as cooking, handicraft production, agriculture and hunting along with preserved fragments of clothing (Amundsen, 2007: 235). Two ring brooches, a double-sided comb, one candleholder, one miniature jar, two horseshoes, one plough coulter, two knives and one iron tool for fire setting were dated to the medieval period. Three of these could be given specific dates: the ring brooches to 1270–1350 and 1350–1400, respectively and the miniature jar to 1350–1450 (Amundsen, 2007: 195, 210). In contrast to previous investigations, this site included a few medieval artefacts; although none of them could confirm use before the Agrarian Crisis, more than one generation could have made use of the ring brooches.

Cereal cultivation which was established during the ninth century and continued into modern times dominated the site. Written sources from 1822 describe the settlement as a shieling which was inhabited by at least one crofter when one of the farmsteads from *Rød* moved closer to the shieling. In addition to the still extant farmstead south of the shieling, and the six medieval to early modern buildings located during excavation, four were established around the time of the Agrarian Crisis in the fourteenth century.

Intense agricultural activities as well as the presence of buildings with stronger wall foundations and medieval artefacts indicate that *Rødseter* was a medieval farmstead. Since the radiocarbon dates give a wide timespan, is it difficult to say when the grazing activity known from the first century made the changeover to a farmstead and when it became a shieling. In relation to the agricultural activity, a permanent settlement could have already been established during the Late Iron Age, although the buildings supporting this theory remain to be found.

The shieling (or the farmstead, as it were) cannot be analyzed without some of the other archaeological features excavated within *Gråfjellprosjektet*. A system of pitfalls for elk ran across the shieling. Twenty-five of thirty-eight of these pitfalls were excavated. Fifty-eight charcoal samples from different contexts in the pits were analyzed, showing a maximum use from 600 to 1600. Two of the pitfalls were removed from the system and were later reused as charcoal pits in the medieval period (1220–1280 and 1300–1425) (Amundsen, 2007: 122ff), giving a potential hint at the timespan during which the system was not exploited to the same degree. An iron bloomery site excavated south of the shieling dated to 1050–1280 or slightly earlier (Rundberget, 2007: 149). Both activities seemed to be contemporary with the agricultural activity at the shieling/farmstead and mainly earlier than the identified buildings.

FOUR SHIELINGS IN VESTFOLD COUNTY, NORWAY

The third case study is based on the *Seterbruket i Vestfold – alder, form og utbredelse* project which was organized by *Kulturarv* at Vestfold County Council. The project was divided in two parts: a survey of all known shielings in the county and archaeological investigations at four of what were presumed to represent the older shielings (Pettersson, 2011). Vestfold is the second smallest county in Norway, the inland portion of which is covered by forest with settlements located in the river valleys and the coastal area of which is dominated by small cities, hamlets and open fields. Most of the settlements are located at altitudes of 10–100 metres above sea level with their associated shielings some 1–5 kilometres further away at altitudes of 100–500 metres (Pettersson, 2011).

Three hundred and sixty-nine shielings were known by name, cartographic evidence and/or oral tradition as having been connected to c. two hundred farmsteads or hamlets of which all had at least one shieling. Most of the farms had prehistoric place names. Of these, half are known from medieval documents or archaeological features on their properties. If one would assume that the farm-shieling formed a standard package, it would be possible to propose a prehistoric or medieval origin for most of the shielings in Vestfold. The survey has even proven that shielings could be flexible, that they could change location, split, merge, be abandoned or even in modern times be transformed into permanent settlements (Pettersson, 2011).

Two sites with two shielings each were selected for further investigation: the inland shielings of *Herland*, while *Vesetra/Søndre Veseterstulen* were examples from the coastal area.

Herlandsetra (øvre) and *Herlandsetra Nedre* in Lardal municipality

Two farmsteads from *Herland* hamlet had their shielings on a mountain 4 kilometres distant at an altitude of 500 metres above sea level. A prehistoric place name with the suffix '-*land(a)*' indicates periods of agricultural expansion which have been documented at 200–550 and 650–1000 (Wahlberg, 2003: 185). The hamlet of *Herland* is also listed in medieval documents from 1409 and 1425 in three parts: north, south and middle (Rygh, 1907: 26–27). In 1934, five users were listed at the shieling of which three were located at *Herlandsetra (øvre)* and two at *Herlandsetra Nedre*. In addition to the three timber buildings currently used as holiday cottages (Figure 3.1), twenty-three visible structures were identified at *Herlandsetra (øvre)*: four house foundations, one stone-paved pit, one well, five clearance cairns and twelve stone walls/fences.

Limited excavation was undertaken at three of these structures: the stone-paved pit, one small clearance cairn and one stone structure identified as a possible house foundation. Two activity layers were identified in the stone-paved pit; the bottom layer was dated to 1410–1490 and the upper layer to 1470–1650. One low earthwork close to the pit could represent the wall foundation of a building, thereby making the pit a possible cellar (Pettersson, 2011). Trench 2 included some stones which formed a possible clearance cairn. A small assemblage of stones indicated clearance cairns but without traces of agricultural activities. Two activity layers were located: one dug beneath the stones and another which surrounded the stones. Both layers were dated to the Roman period; the pit layer to AD 130–330 and the upper layer to AD 250–430. The lack of grains and other plants in the macrofossil samples suggests that the area was cleared for grazing and harvesting (Pettersson, 2011). Trench 3 included the stone structure recognized as a possible house foundation which turned out to be a section of a longer stone wall. Two phases were identified in the trench, one with a date of AD 410–550 and another to the post-medieval period, 1640–1800. The older activity which dated to

the Migration period was marginally later than the clearance cairn.

One timber building was still standing at *Herlandsetra Nedre* as were twelve house foundations, two wells, nine clearance cairns and three short stone walls. The latter were surveyed and mapped. Since all visible remains had modern surfaces, the first trench was placed over a low bank which had been interpreted as the outer edge of a field. It turned out to be a natural feature without signs of cultivation or activity layers. The next trench included a stone wall in the lower part of what might possibly have been a field. Two layers were visible in the trench, but none of the four samples taken contained any charcoal or macrofossils to confirm human activities or their date. Once again, this was interpreted as clearance for grazing and harvesting with natural soil accumulation. No activities at *Herlandsetra Nedre* could be dated by the archaeological investigations and there were no signs of ploughing. Unfortunately, this site can only be interpreted via the written sources with the complementary examination of modern structures as a possible expansion of *Herlandsetra (øvre)*.

The results of the archaeological survey of *Herlandsetra (øvre)* suggest that the area was cleared by the slash-and-burn method on several occasions, the oldest of which was contemporary with the first agricultural expansion suggested by the place name *Herland* (AD 200–550). A second fire in the fifth century and a third in the seventeenth century or later could represent expansions or reestablishment at the site. By adding a medieval date from the investigated stone-paved pit, the site seems to have been in use from the third century to the modern day, although it has most likely been occasionally deserted during this time period, thereby requiring the setting of new fires to clear the site.

Investigations at medieval shielings in *Ängersjö* (Härjedalen County) involved recessed stone-lined structures which turned out to be the milk cellars below the houses (Emanuelsson et al., 2003: 121–24, with references). The stone-paved pit at *Herlandsetra (øvre)* could represent a similar area. The presence of a potential milk cellar and no signs of cereals or ploughing intimate that this site could fit into the concept of a 'real' shieling insofar as activities were restricted to grazing, haymaking and dairy production. A slash-and-burn clearing event contemporary with the date of the place name suggests that the site formed part of the farm-shieling package which facilitated the establishment of the settlement.

Vesetra and *Søndre Veseterstulen* in the municipality of Sande

The farmstead/hamlet of *Ve* is located in the coastal area in the northern part of *Sandebukta* bay. It is comprised of four farmsteads: *Ve Søndre, Mellem, Nordre* and *Lille* (south, middle, north and the little one). The place name *Ve/Vi* is used to describe prehistoric places of worship or holy places. *Ve Nordre* is mentioned in a medieval tax roll from c. AD 1400 and is described as being next to *Kleppen* farmstead. The latter was abandoned prior to 1668 when it was mentioned as *Ve Søndre* with *Kleppen* (Rygh, 1907: 27).

Vesetra and *Søndre Veseterstulen* are situated on a mountain about 2 kilometres away from the hamlet at altitudes of 180–240 metres above sea level. Both shielings were still in use at the start of the twentieth century with one occupant at *Vesetra* and three at *Søndre Veseterstulen* (Pettersson, 2011). Seven house foundations, one possible building, two wells, a hollow-way and close to forty clearance cairns were surveyed and mapped at *Vesetra*, most of which were clearly modern. The concentration of remains divided the shieling into two areas: one to the north and one to the south. In deference to their construction and topographical location, two clearance cairns in the north and another in the south were reinterpreted as prehistoric burial mounds during subsequent investigations. The rest of the clearance cairns accumulated at different times, from small, low heaps of stone to larger ones made by mechanical gathering (Pettersson, 2011).

Since most structures in the south had been clearly impacted by later activities, the northern part was chosen for archaeological investigation. The partial excavation of two structures was undertaken: the possible building and a low terrace (which was thought to form a field boundary). The first trench was situated in relation to the foundations of what was thought to have been a house: a structure which was only visible by a low wall and some stones next to a flat area. After the clearing of branches and spruce needles from the structure, the north and west walls could be identified as low stone foundation sill walls. The trench which cut the western wall revealed more stones in the sill wall and the presence of an activity layer inside the building (Figure 3.5). Samples taken from the activity layer close to the sill wall were radiocarbon dated to 1220–1300 AD, although the macrofossil sample produced only charcoal and spruce needles (Pettersson, 2011).

The second trench was located across the low terrace which was presumed to have been a field boundary. The investigation revealed a natural formation of stones and soils over a bedrock edge. Following this discovery, no samples were taken.

Søndre Veseterstulen is situated in a slightly lower area about 100 metres to the south of *Vesetra*. Two buildings, three house foundations, four possible buildings, ten clearance cairns, and possible field terraces were surveyed and mapped at the shieling. All house foundations were considered modern and were identifiable in maps which dated from the late nineteenth and early twentieth century, which left one possible house foundation and the remaining agrarian structures for further investigation.

The first trench which cut the pit was interpreted as a possible cellar. Some stones on the side may have represented a wall foundation and a heap of stones a possible hearth. None of the stone accumulations seemed to form part of a construction (though a few stones and a possible activity layer in the pit might have been parts of a structure). A macrofossil sample was found to consist of spruce needles, hazelnuts and a high quantity of charcoal. The latter was given a (calibrated) date of AD 1020–1190, and suggested a fire event associated with forest clearance. The second trench cut the possible field boundary. Two cultivation layers were identified in the profile. Large fragments of charcoal were visible in the bottom layer and some smaller pieces were noted in the upper layer. However, two samples, one from each produced the same Migration-period timespan, AD 436 to 600. It is likely that the charcoal was created by slash-and-burn clearance and then moved through the soil as a result of ploughing Pettersson, 2011).

The oldest activity at the shielings connected to the hamlet of *Ve* was cultivation at *Søndre Veseterstulen*. Although it was older than the establishment of the building at *Vesetra*, it may have been contemporary to the prehistoric burial mounds described at the same site. There were two phases of medieval activity detected at the two shielings, one building at *Vesetra* and a layer in a stone-paved pit at *Søndre Veseterstulen* which were older than the Medieval Agrarian Crisis in the fourteenth century. Agricultural activities during the sixth century at *Søndre Veseterstulen* together with three prehistoric burial mounds and a medieval building at *Vesetra* might indicate something more than seasonal use. It is possible that the shielings were reestablished at the medieval farmstead of *Kleppen* which was known from *Biskop Eysteins jordebog* in AD 1390/1400 and was added to *Wæe søndre* before 1668. As the name *Kleppen* refers to a height or a small mountain (No. *klepp*; Rygh, 1907; 27), it would have been well suited to the topography of shieling.

FLEXIBLE SHIELINGS AND LONG-TERM USE

Using archaeological evidence as our means of addressing the flexibility of shielings, this article has discussed 'real' shielings, their age and origin and has presented three cases studies with eleven shielings. Maps from the nineteenth and twentieth century show all the shielings and their connected farmsteads, of which all are known by either medieval documents or prehistoric or medieval place names. In one way or another, they

Figure 3.5. Trench 1 cutting the western wall of the medieval building at Vesetra, *the northwest corner marked by a larger stone to the left*
Photo: Susanne Pettersson

could also be connected to other categories of archaeological features. All eleven shielings had been used in recent times; timber buildings or ruins were still standing at nine of them. House foundations and clearance cairns were located at all eleven, although most of them exhibited a modern surface. To reiterate, the concept of a 'real' shieling allowed for the presence of buildings for people, cattle and diary production, but not cereal cultivation.

Clearing is known from all sites, six of which were cleared up during the Iron Age and three during the medieval period. Cereal cultivation was also discovered at six sites, of which two were already engaging in this activity during the Iron Age, one in medieval times and the last few only in the modern era. Only three sites (the shielings at *Herland*, *Melgårdsetern* and *Sørgårdsvollen*) could fit into the ethnological definition of a 'real' shieling. They most likely formed part of the farm-shieling package which facilitated the establishment of the settlements.

Cereal cultivation at the historically known shielings at *Rødseter* and *Vesetra/Søndre Veseterstulen* could be explained by their location as a prehistoric/medieval farmstead. Clearance cairns and historic fields at *Rødseter* were dated to the Late Iron Age while most of the buildings and some of the artefacts came from the late medieval period. Although a permanent settlement could have been established at the site during the Late Iron Age, this could not be verified before the fourteenth century with the advent of the first identified building (Figure 3.6). There were no clear signs of a desertion at the site, so it is difficult to determine when the farmstead became the shieling known from the historical records.

The shielings at *Vesetra/Søndre Veseterstulen* had a clear connection to a deserted farmstead which practiced cereal cultivation established during the fifth century and of which one building was dated to the thirteenth century. Known from the written sources, *Kleppen* farmstead was still listed on the tax rolls in AD 1400. By AD 1688, it had probably been deserted when it was incorporated with *Ve Søndre*. How far back in time the shieling goes could not be determined by excavation. However, according to written sources, the farmstead seemed to have survived the Agrarian Crisis in the fourteenth century.

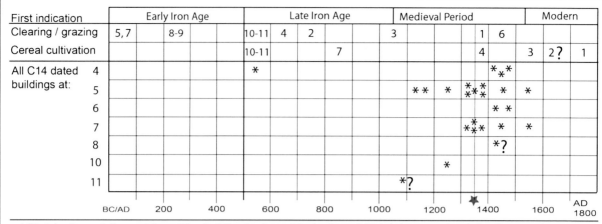

Figure 3.6. Results based on radiocarbon dates from the investigated shielings

An abandonment phase could be identified at *Backasätern*, by contrast. Grazing activities during the Late Iron Age were followed by a medieval desertion and renewed grazing and cultivation in the late fifteenth century. Periodic abandonments might even explain some slash-and-burn events at *Herlandsetra (øvre)*, so far dated by its first such fire event to the third century, a second to the fifth century and a third to the seventeenth century or later.

The only early medieval buildings identified in this study are the three buildings at *Melgårdsetern* and the one at *Vesetra/Søndre Veseterstulen*. The last one was recognized as part of a medieval farmstead and the building identified as traditionally built timber frame on stone sills. Two of the early medieval buildings at *Melgårdsetern* were fragmented and incomplete as described by Beronius Jörpeland in her study from *Mälardalen* (2010). The fragmented buildings were first identified during the dig when a mechanical excavator had removed the top soil; the remains were not likely to have been found by small-scale investigations and hand-dug trenches.

Even though large areas were investigated with the help of an excavator at *Rødseter*, no prehistoric or early medieval buildings could be found at the site. Although agricultural activities ought to have been connected to some kind of settlement, whether the lack of buildings could be explained by the relocation of the settlement within the site or by the use of an unfamiliar construction method must remain an open question.

The chosen sites were attested in written sources, maps with site names which could clearly be linked to a shieling or which had long histories going back to prehistoric or medieval times. Some shielings were established on former farmsteads (*Rødseter, Vesetra/Søndre Veseterstulen*) while others (*Bänteby, Gammelsätern Likenäs, Ransby, Herlandsetern (øvre)* and *Melgårdsetern*) probably were part of the farm-shieling package as they all exhibited dates similar to the presumed age of the place names at the farmsteads. Two shielings could be seen as expansions of an older shieling (*Herlandsetra Nedre* and *Sørgårdsvollen*), the latter having been established after the Agrarian Crisis.

In contrast to the ethnographic model presented by Montelius and others, shielings were more than just places for grazing, haymaking and processing milk. Cereal cultivation was also identified at six of the sites. Excluding the two farmsteads at *Rødseter* and *Vesetra/Søndre Veseterstulen*, cereal cultivation was added to *Backasätern* in the fifteenth century and to most of the other sites during modern times. Although a cursory examination of all the shielings would suggest that they were modern, it was possible to find the long-time perspective beneath the modern structures and artefacts that were found there. This was previously suggested by limited surveys in the *Settlement, Shieling and Landscape* and *Seterbruket i Vestfold* projects; however, large-scale excavations like in *Gråfjellprosjektet* can reveal more. Age, origin and content have all been interpreted in slightly different ways and all the investigated sites had flexible histories in their individual trajectories from grazing to shieling, from farmstead to shieling and in the ongoing cycle of desertion and new clearance.

Acknowledgements

I am glad to have had the opportunity to be a part of all three case studies. Many thanks to the teams behind *Settlement, Shieling and Landscape*, *Gråfjellprosjektet* at the Museum of Cultural History, University of Oslo and *Seterbruket i Vestfold* at *Kulturarv* at Vestfold County Council for involving me in the investigations.

Finally, I extend many thanks to Tom Davies for his comments on the content and language in the initial draft of this article.

REFERENCES

Amundsen, T. ed. 2007. *Elgfangst og bosetning i Gråfjellområ-det.* Oslo: Kulturhistorisk museum, University of Oslo.

Antonson, H. 2004. *Landskap och ödesbölen: Jämtland före, under och efter den medeltida agrarkrisen.* Stockholm: University of Stockholm.

Beronius Jörpeland, L. 2010. *Medeltida landsbygdsbebyggelse i Stockholms län: FoU-projekt: dnr 420–4250–2005.* http://kulturarvsdata.se/raa/samla/html/4968 (accessed 10 December 2016).

Emanuelsson, M. 2001. *Settlement and Land-Use History in the Central Swedish Forest Region: The Use of Pollen Analysis in Interdisciplinary Studies.* Umeå: Swedish University of Agricultural Sciences.

Emanuelsson, M., Johansson, A., Nilsson, S., Pettersson, S. & Svensson, E. 2003. *Settlement, Shieling and Landscape: The Local History of a Forest Hamlet.* Stockholm: Almqvist & Wiksell International.

Erixon, S. 1918. Bebyggelseundersökningar. Öfversikt. Periodiska bebyggelsetyper. Fäbodväsen. *Fataburen. Kulturhistorisk Tidskrift*, 1918:21–57.

Erixon, S. 1956. Betesvandringar och flyttsystem. *Folk-liv*, 19/20:39–55.

Frödin, J. 1925. *Siljansområdets fäbodbygd.* Lund: Gleerups.

Hansson, A., Olsson, C., Storå, J., Welinder, S. & Zetterström, Å. 2005. *Agrarkris och gårdar i Jämtland.* Östersund: Jamtli.

Hougen, B. 1947. *Fra seter til gård: studier i norsk bosetningshistorie.* Oslo: Norsk arkeologisk selskap.

Johansson, A., Nilsson, S., Pettersson, S. & Svensson, E. 1997. *Bebyggelse och säterdrift i norra Värmland 1995–1996. En förstudie. Rapport över arkeologiska undersökningarna vid Backa-Skinnerud, RAÄ 776, Dalby socken och över karteringar av Backasätern, Bäntebysätern, Gammelsätern (Likenäs) och Ransbysätern i Dalby socken samt Ingersbysätern, Sätra och Gammelsätern (Treskog) i Gunnarskogs socken. Arbetsrapport 97:17.* Karlstad: Samhällsvetenskap. Högskolan i Karlstad.

Kvamme, M. 1988. Pollen analytical studies of mountain summer-farming in western Norway. In: H.H. Birks, H.J.B. Birks, P.E. Kaland & D. Moe, eds. *The Cultural Landscape: Past, Present and Future.* Cambridge: Cambridge University Press, pp. 349–67.

Magnus, B. 1986. Iron Age exploitation of high mountain resources in Sogn. *Norwegian Archaeological Review*, 19(1):44–50.

Mahler, D.L. 2007. *Sæteren ved Argisbrekka: økonomiske forandringer på Færøerne i vikingetid og tidlig middelalder: Economic Development During the Viking Age and Early Middle Ages on the Faroe Islands.* København: Københavns Universitet.

Martens, J., Martens, V.V. & Stene, K. eds. 2009. *Den tapte middelalder? Middelalderens sentrale landbebyggelse.* Oslo: Kulturhistorisk museum, University of Oslo.

Montelius, S. 1977. *Fäbodväsendet i övre Dalarna.* Stockholm: Akademilitteratur and Institutet för folklivsforskning.

Myrdal, J. & Söderberg, J. 1991. *Kontinuitetens dynamik: Agrar ekonomi i 1500-talets Sverige.* Stockholm: Almqvist & Wiksell International.

Olsson, M. 1998. *Pollenanalytiska undersökningar av sätermiljöer i Dalby och Gunnarskog socknar, Värmland. LUDQUA uppdrag.* Lund: Unpublished report.

Pettersson, S. 2011. *Seterbruket i Vestfold – alder, form og utbredelse.* Tønsberg: Unpublished report. www.vfk.no/Tema-og-tjenester/Kulturarv/Prosjekter/Avsluttede-prosjekter/Seterbruket-i-Vestfold-2007 (accessed 10 December 2016).

Reinton L. 1969. *Til seters: Norsk seterbruk og seterstell.* Oslo: Det Norske Samlaget.

Risbøl, O., Fretheim, S., Narmo, L.E., Rønne, O., Myrvoll, E.R., Nesholen, B. & Vaage, J. 2001. *Kulturminner og kulturmiljø i Gråfjell, Regionfelt Østlandet, Åmot kommune i Hedmark. Arkeologiske registreringer 2000, fase 2.* www.niku.no/filestore/Publikasjoner/NIKUPublikasjoner102.pdf (accessed 10 December 2016).

Risbøl, O., Ramstad, M., Narmo, L.E., Høgseth, H.B., Bjune, A. & Vaage, J. 2000. *Kulturminner og kulturmiljø i Gråfjell, Regionfelt Østlandet, Åmot kommune i Hedmark. Arkeologiske registreringer 1999, fase 1.* NIKU Oppdragsmelding 93. www.niku.no/filestore/Publikasjoner/NIKUOppdragsmelding93.pdf (accessed 10 December 2016).

Risbøl, O., Risan, T., Bugge Kræmer, M., Paulsen, I., Sønsterud, K.E., Swensen, G. & Solem, T. 2002. *Kulturminner og kulturmiljø i Gråfjell, Regionfelt Østlandet, Åmot kommune i Hedmark. Undertittel Arkeologiske registreringer 2001, fase 3.* www.niku.no/filestore/Publikasjoner/NIKUPublikasjoner116.pdf (accessed 10 December 2016).

Rundberget, B. ed. 2007. *Jernvinna i Gråfjellområdet.* Oslo: Kulturhistorisk museum, University of Oslo.

Rygh, O. 1907. *Norske Gaardnavne: Oplysninger samlede til Brug ved Matrikelens Revision. Bd 6, Gaardnavne i Jarlsberg og Larviks Amt.* Kristiania: Cammermeyer.

Sandnes, J. 1989. Ljåen og krøttermulen. Om opphav og alder til det norske seterbruket. *(Norsk) Historisk tidskrift*, 1989(3):351–57.

Sandnes J. 1991. Utmarksdrift og ressursutnyttelse i Norge i eldre tid. In: S. Gissel, E. Österberg & S. Göransson, eds. *Plov og pen. Festskrift til Svend Gissel 4. Januar 1991.* København: Det kongelige Bibliotek, pp. 213–21.

Sveinbjarnardóttir, G. 1991. Shielings in Iceland: an archaeological and historical survey. *Acta Archaeologica*, 61:73–96.

Svensson, E. 1998. *Människor i utmark.* Stockholm: Almqvist & Wiksell International.

Wahlberg, M. ed. 2003. *Svenskt ortnamnslexikon.* Uppsala: Språk- och folkminnesinstitutet (SOFI).

CHAPTER 4

Winter housing
Archaeological perspectives on Newfoundland's non-pastoral transhumant tradition

ANATOLIJS VENOVCEVS AND BARRY C. GAULTON

INTRODUCTION

In 1987, Philip E.L. Smith, an archaeologist from Université de Montréal, published two seminal articles on European life on the island of Newfoundland (Smith, 1987a, 1987b; see also Smith, 1995). While it took two decades for other academics to follow up on his ideas, Smith's work transformed the way scholars thought about historic Newfoundland. Before Smith, it was often assumed that life in rural Newfoundland relied primarily on the exploitation of cod and other marine resources as is often celebrated in songs, stories, and folklore around the island.

Smith turned that assumption on its head by arguing that, until recently, life for most rural Europeans on the island of Newfoundland was dualistic in nature. Instead of subsisting entirely from the sea, until the 1950s most rural Euro-Newfoundlanders rotated their settlements between two environmental loci: exposed coastal fishing villages, their 'primary' homes where they caught and cured fish in the summers; and sheltered cabins called winter houses in *the country*, the local vernacular word for the island's interior. From their winter homes, Euro-Newfoundlanders utilized terrestrial resources during the long fishing offseason in a tradition colloquially known as 'winter housing' before returning to their summer homes to fish. Smith defined this tradition as non-pastoral transhumance.

The arguments for this nomenclature are best expressed by their original author but the crux of Smith's argument for using the word transhumance to describe Newfoundland winter housing is its dualistic nature that seasonally exploited two distinct environmental zones with strongly contrasting seasonal conditions (Smith, 1987b: 3–4). While it is not the goal here to use Smith's work to redefine what is commonly meant by that term in Europe, the authors will use Smith's expanded definition for the proceeding discussion. In doing so, this paper will present a supplementary view to post-medieval European migratory traditions by exploring the architectural forms, spatial organization, and material culture of winter houses and discuss how this is leading toward a new understanding of the periphery in rural Newfoundland communities. Despite the lack of pastoral animals, this seasonal migration within Newfoundland's maritime culture offers valuable lessons to transhumant practices within European agrarian societies in the study of decentralized seasonal rural migration, transhumant material culture, and the pluralistic extra-capitalist economies that were often necessary for the successful utilization of peripheral environments in the post-medieval period.

A BRIEF INTRODUCTION TO NEWFOUNDLAND

The island of Newfoundland is situated at the easternmost point of North America, jutting out into the cold North Atlantic. Aboriginal groups populated the island starting around 5000 years ago following the last glaciation (Tuck, 1976). The Maritime Archaic, Palaeoeskimo, and ancestral Inuit and Beothuk utilized the island's marine and terrestrial resources for millennia; however the sometimes precarious resource base and harsh climate are believed to have contributed to episodes of abandonment, extinction, or dramatic adaptation (Renouf, 1999; Tuck & Pastore, 1985). In the late 1400s Europeans 'discovered' the New-found-land and its seemingly boundless cod stocks. This was followed by more than a century of seasonal visitation by fishers from France, Portugal, the Basque Country, Spain, and England, most of whom established shore stations for the landing, processing, and curing of cod for shipment to overseas markets (Pope, 1997). The wharfs, stages, flakes, and cook rooms associated with these shore-based facilities required a great deal of wood from the nearby forests and took weeks or months to complete (Yonge, 1663, in Poynter, 1963: 56–8).

In 1610, the English established the first permanent colony at Cupids in Conception Bay. A handful of other colonies were started in the decades following, all of which were located around the Avalon Peninsula and focused on the cod fishery. Although none of these early settlements were considered a financial success by their investors and many were short lived, year-round residents came to better understand both the island's

© 2018 European Association of Archaeologists

potential as well as its limitations. The cool summer months, for example, were ideal for catching and drying inshore cod but the thin, acidic soils, damp climate, and short growing season limited agricultural endeavours (Cadigan, 2009: 3–11; Head, 1976: 41–8). Settlers also became familiar with flora and fauna, particularly during excursions inland to chop wood, hunt, trap, and fish. In 1622, Nicolas Hoskins remarked on the deer (caribou), wolves, bears, foxes, and other fur-bearing animals, as well as the 'Fowles and Birds of the Land . . . all very fat, sweet and wholesome' and many 'wilde fruit and Berries' and 'faire Flowers' (Hoskins, 1622, in Cell, 1982: 205–6).

Newfoundland winters were another story altogether. Contemporaries living in colonies along the outer coasts described it as 'bleak' or 'extremely cold and sterile' (Wynne, 1630, in Gaulton & Miller, 2009; Stock, 1631, in Codignola, 1988). Sir George Calvert, the first Lord Baltimore, was so dismayed after spending one winter at his Ferryland colony in 1628–29 that his entire family and many settlers departed the following summer despite having invested tens of thousands of pounds. His now famous quote about Newfoundland winters still rings true 'from the middest of October to the middest of May there is a sadd face of wynter vpon all this land, both sea and land so frozen for the greatest part of the tyme as they are not penetrable' (Calvert, 1629, in Cell, 1982: 295–96).

The residual settlers from former colonies along with migratory fishers who were tasked to stay behind after the fishing season to protect and maintain shore stations, together formed the nucleus of the early European population of Newfoundland (Pope, 2004). Over the course of the seventeenth and eighteenth centuries large mercantile centres developed including St. John's, Ferryland, Placentia, Carbonear, Harbour Grace, and Trinity but the nature of the cod fishery was such that small villages were dispersed along much of the island's coastline.

The proximity to inshore cod stocks and suitable locations to dry fish were primary factors for settlement whereas shelter, agricultural pursuits, and access to governmental, religious, and commercial institutions were often secondary considerations. Within this context of environmental and socio-economic marginality, most Euro-Newfoundland residents turned their attention inland as a means to shelter themselves from the long, harsh winters and to diversify their subsistence strategies.

HISTORICAL EVIDENCE FOR TRANSHUMANCE

The seasonal nature of the cod-based fishery predicated the development of seasonal economies for those Europeans who chose to winter on the island. As early as the 1660s, cutting wood and sawing boards was considered an important part of the winter activities (Yonge, 1663, in Poynter, 1963: 60). At the same time wealthier members of early Newfoundland society hired men to go hunting and furring over long distances (Pope, 2004: 306–11).

However, life was hard for anybody who overwintered at the fishing stations. Not only did they have to store enough provisions to last them through the season but they also had to build adequate shelter and develop the skills needed to survive in almost complete isolation for up to seven months at a time (Nemec, 2006: 172–73). Employment was scarce and even in the nineteenth century an able-bodied man could be hired for the entire winter for just his room and board (Wilson, 1866: 214). To make matters worse, many of the best fishing operations were located on exposed beaches, islands, and points of land where the winter conditions were inhospitable and exacerbated by the wood-intensive cod fishery and the slow growth of trees that quickly led to deforestation around the settlements (Head, 1976: 18–19).

This, combined with a lack of land titles and government authority, made it more sensible for the English and French settlers of Newfoundland to migrate into *the country* for the winter. There they built their winter houses and lived in them for between four and seven months at a time until the spring. In the shelter of the forests, they hunted, trapped, caught freshwater fish, and procured lumber for firewood, boats, barrels, staves, and other items (Smith, 1987a, 1987b, 1995).

Despite representing what most of Newfoundland's European population was doing for half of the year for close to three centuries, most accounts come from nineteenth-century sources (i.e. de Boilieu, 1861; Bonnycastle, 1842; Cormack, 1928; Jukes, 1842; Lloyd, 1886; Moreton, 1863; Mountain, 1857; Wilson, 1866; Wix, 1836). These accounts describe winter houses as small rectangular structures that ranged from 1.8 by 2.4 to 4.6 by 6.1 m in size and built from wooden posts stuck vertically into the ground, sometimes incorporating live trees for the house corners (Figure 4.1). The walls were chinked with moss or clay and the roof was made from bark or branches. While windows were sometimes present, it was more common for the only natural light to come through the same hole in the roof that allowed smoke to escape; fireplaces were made of low-lying stone or clay-lined wood (de Boilieu, 1861: 52–3; Jukes, 1842: 69; Mills, 1977: 81; Smith, 1987a: 11, 1987b: 243). Many of these houses were not permanent but rather they were abandoned and rebuilt in a different area after one or a few winters (Oldmixon, 1708: 9–10). It was not uncommon for entire extended families to reside in a single house in close quarters; personal space did not exist in the modern sense of the word (Wix, 1836: 53).

Figure 4.1. One of the few winter house drawings
Source: J. Moreton (1863). *Life and Works in Newfoundland: Reminiscences of Thirteen Years Spent There*

While the start date of this tradition is not known, archival references to it appear by the late seventeenth century (Brouillan, 1693; MacPherson, 1977: 108; Smith, 1987a: 14). It was fully established by 1708 (Oldmixon, 1708: 9–10). The reason for this rapid adaptation is uncertain though it is unlikely that it resulted from interactions between European fishers and Newfoundland's native Beothuk given the policy of avoidance and confrontation by both parties (Smith, 1987a: 20, 1987b: 246).

Nor does it seem likely that the transhumant tradition came to Newfoundland with the Europeans. Most Europeans who first settled Newfoundland came from Devon in the English West Country and La Rochelle in the southwest of France. Lesser numbers originated from Wales, southern Ireland, and Brittany. While they may have been aware of transhumant traditions taking place in Devon, western France, or southern Ireland, early settlers probably did not practice it themselves. Rather, it is more likely that winter housing grew from the seasonal nature of the transatlantic migratory fishery which saw seventeenth-century fishers alternate between summers spent fishing in Newfoundland and agricultural pursuits like late harvests, hedging, or animal husbandry in the winters in Europe. In fact, the fishers themselves may have seen the parallels between the transatlantic migratory fishery and transhumant pastoralism; the Basque name for their whaling station in Red Bay, Labrador was the name given to a migratory bird, 'Buitres,' which was considered a companion to men and herds migrating to the summer pastures in the Basque highlands (Pope, 2004: 250–52).

Regardless of how it started, winter housing grew as the population of Newfoundland increased. Eighteenth- and nineteenth-century letters and reports by merchants, military officers, and members of the clergy, some of the few people who could afford to stay in the 'primary' seaside settlements for the winter, are full of references to this tradition taking place throughout Newfoundland (Smith, 1987a: 12–13). The mid-1800s saw the winter housing tradition hit its peak with references to it being recorded all over Newfoundland, southern Labrador, and the neighbouring Canadian provinces.

Winter housing started to decline in the second half of the nineteenth century with the diversification of the winter economy, the proliferation of churches and church-based education, the construction of better-insulated homes, and the introduction of fuel-efficient metal stoves. In spite of this, winter migration survived well into the 1950s through the adaptation of motor boats, sawmilling, and, at times, the railroad system

(Cuff, 1983; Smith, 1987a: 23–25). Today the tradition lives on for many Newfoundlanders through an active cabin culture that, on occasion, impacts the remains of earlier winter houses (Bob Cuff, personal communication, November 19, 2014; King, 2012; Mills, 2012).

ARCHAEOLOGICAL EVIDENCE FOR TRANSHUMANCE

Notwithstanding its long history on the island, the ephemeral nature of winter houses has made archaeological investigation difficult. As of right now, only nine European winter house sites are known from Newfoundland and southern Labrador. Of these, only four have been systematically researched – Sunnyside 1 and Big Mussel Pond 1, 2, and 3. The proceeding discussion is the first time that the authors discussed the results of their primary research at the sites. While this investigation cannot capture the scope of a 300-year tradition, it offers a tantalizing glimpse into how winter housing was practiced.

Sunnyside 1

The earliest archaeological evidence for winter housing comes from the Sunnyside 1 site (ChAl-05), in Trinity Bay, Newfoundland which has been investigated by Barry Gaulton and Steve Mills since 2010 (Gaulton & Mills, 2011, 2014a, 2014b). Nestled in a sheltered cove at the westernmost end of a salt-water channel known as Bull Arm are the remnants of a seventeenth-century winter house and root cellar. Here, Old World vernacular traditions intersect with adaptations predicated upon the environmental and economic realities of life in Canada's easternmost province.

The main archaeological feature at Sunnyside 1 is a massive chimney collapse of angular stones spanning 4.7 by 4.5 m, approximately 1 m high and an overall volume of approximately 6.9 m³ (Figure 4.2). Directly west of the chimney collapse are the low earthen walls of a root cellar, measuring 5.8 by 6.6 m. In spite of their size, both features were unrecognizable from the nearby shoreline only 28 m away due to over 300 years of overgrowth. Partial excavation of the chimney collapse revealed a large fireplace built of angular sandstone/siltstone acquired from several nearby outcrops along the shoreline 87 m away (See King, 1980 for local geology). The exact size and shape of the fireplace remains uncertain pending further excavation; however it appears to be at least 2.4 m wide and 1.5 m deep.

Interestingly, the stratigraphy within the hearth reveals a tapered deposit of sterile clay and small pebbles sandwiched between two occupation layers. This is suggestive of either multiple winter occupations at Sunnyside 1 and/or an attempt to raise up the hearth floor, particularly toward the east end, in an effort to mitigate against problems associated with water runoff and standing water which still occur in the spring and fall. Limited trenching inside the root cellar indicates an interior space of 1.2 by 2.4 m, while its positioning immediately west of the fireplace would have provided easy access as well as some radiant heat to keep provisions from freezing (Gaulton & Mills, 2014b: 11).

The substantial masonry fireplace is clearly at odds with nineteenth-century accounts of heat sources associated with winter housing in Newfoundland. The same can be said for the 854 iron nails and spikes associated with the construction of the wooden superstructure and the presence of window glass fragments along the east side of the building. This was not a tiny wooden cabin built using vertical logs chinked with mud and heated by a chimney of the same. Rather, its appearance was likely that of a modest timber-framed dwelling clad with rough boards and a walk-in fireplace at the gable end. Given the early date for the site (c. 1650–80), it is argued that this winter house was built with permanency in mind because its occupants were still adapting to the environmental, economic, and social conditions of overwintering in Newfoundland. A substantial investment in time and energy demonstrates that its builders planned for a long-term seasonal occupation. Over time, European overwinterers came to understand that the island's marginal resource base required short-term occupation and frequent resettlement.

The material culture from Sunnyside 1 shows that Europeans were actively employed in the forests cutting and sawing wood not only for the construction of this winter house but for the building of small boats and other items necessary for the summer fishery. Woodworking tools include a pit saw fragment, a gouge, and a carpenter's or shipwright's adze (Sloane, 1964). Fishery-related artifacts, by comparison, are poorly represented by a single fish hook.

Evidence for subsistence practices and diet also has a terrestrial focus. Two hundred and forty pieces of lead shot of various sizes along with lead stock, waste, and sprue are associated with the manufacture of ammunition for hunting mammals and birds. Faunal remains reflect the same pattern: 95 per cent is mammal, 1 per cent bird, and 2 per cent fish (2 per cent indeterminate). Identified species include caribou (*Rangifer tarandus*), beaver (*Castor canadensis*), hare/rabbit (Leporidae), cod (*Gadus morhua*), and domesticated pig (*Sus scrofa*) (Elliott, 2014, 2015a).

A large quantity of flint debitage (1240) representing all stages of manufacture, 20 crudely made gunflints, and 15 tinder flints demonstrate that these occupants transported European ballast flint to their winter residence and frequently utilized this resource for the manufacture of fire starters and for spall-type gunflints for

Figure 4.2. Large open hearth at the Sunnyside 1 site
Photo: Barry Gaulton

use in flintlock muskets. None of the gunflints from this site are of the well-made variety produced in European workshops (see Kent, 1983; Kenmotzu, 1990 for nomenclature). This is anomalous with respect to evidence found in contemporaneous domestic assemblages from permanent settlements such as Ferryland, Renews, and Placentia as the pattern is reversed; most gunflints are mass-produced spall or blade-types and there is limited evidence for flint knapping at the household level (Crompton, 2001, 2012; Leskovec, 2007; Mills, 2000; Nixon, 1999).

The ceramic and glass assemblages from this site are very different, in both quantity and variety, compared to that seen on migratory fishery sites and permanent dwellings associated with fishing families. Three short field seasons at Sunnyside 1 have uncovered the remnants of a paltry five ceramic and glass storage vessels, three small tin-glazed bowls or porringers for individual food service, and one glass pharmaceutical bottle. By comparison, fishery-related sites on the outer coasts of Newfoundland contain dozens if not hundreds of storage, cooking, and food/beverage service vessels, the contents of which were used to sustain fishers during the hectic months of the cod fishery (St. John, 2011; Williams, 2006). This divergence can best be explained by the subsistence practices and daily activities associated with summer and winter occupations, as well as practical limitations relating to the transportation of provisions and supplies.

Outside of the large urban centres, most Newfoundland residents had limited opportunities to purchase or otherwise acquire tools, provisions, and supplies beyond that which was available during the fishing season when both local and foreign merchants were eager to trade for salted cod. The movement inland to sheltered locations during the winter months saw many rural residents gather up the *necessities* required for offseason activities and transport them by boat, sled, or cart to their winter abode. Returning to their summer fishing residence in the dead of winter was likely attempted only if absolutely necessary and weather permitting. Under such restrictive, yet potentially liberating conditions, adaptability and ingenuity was paramount.

Cooking, for example, is represented by fragments of a large iron pot and a copper kettle; however the kettle fragments exhibit extensive evidence for repair in the form of riveted patches to extend its use life. A significant quantity of clay tobacco pipe fragments (729) likewise demonstrates that smoking was an important part of daily life but some pieces show signs of curation, having been modified after breakage to accommodate the attachment of a new (wooden?) stem. Finally, one fragment from a broken tin-glazed bowl was repurposed and shaped into a gaming piece. These practices, in addition to the above-mentioned evidence for frequent flint knapping and tool production, show a group of resourceful individuals engaging in a precarious, albeit viable, lifestyle on the edge of the North Atlantic world.

Big Mussel Pond

The other thoroughly investigated winter house sites are located in St. Mary's Bay, Newfoundland behind the small community of O'Donnells which Anatolijs Venovcevs investigated in the summer of 2015. They all date from approximately the 1820s to 1840s and hug the southern shore of a tidal pool called Big Mussel Pond. The sites, labelled as Big Mussel Pond 1 (CgAj-03), 2 (CgAj-05), and 3 (CgAj-06), start about 500 m east of the present-day community and continue at approximately 750 m intervals around the south shore of the pond. All of the sites are located between 50 and 80 m away from the pond and within a few metres of freshwater streams (Figure 4.3).

Despite the 150-year gap between Sunnyside 1 and the Big Mussel Pond sites, the need for warmth and food security is universal. Big Mussel Pond 1 most closely resembles Sunnyside 1 as it contains a rock mound and a cellar. On the surface, the rock collapse extended 3 m north–south and 2 m east–west. When the subsequent excavations revealed that the vertical extent of the collapse was 70 cm tall, the volume was calculated to approximately 2.1 m^3.

The rock mound did not represent a chimney collapse as it did in Sunnyside 1. Rather, it appeared to have served as a crude dry-laid stone backing that was built to protect the wooden house from the open fireplace whose remains were found adjacent to it. The interior of the structure would have looked similar to the summer house photographed in Labrador by Dr. Eliot Curwen in 1893 (Figure 4.4). Excavations around the hearth recovered hundreds of nails of various sizes from the rafters as well as a large, flat hook similar to the one that is seen holding up the kettle over the fire in the photograph. While the current work did not fully expose the hearth at Big Mussel Pond 1, a sondage into the deposit identified two distinct charcoal deposits

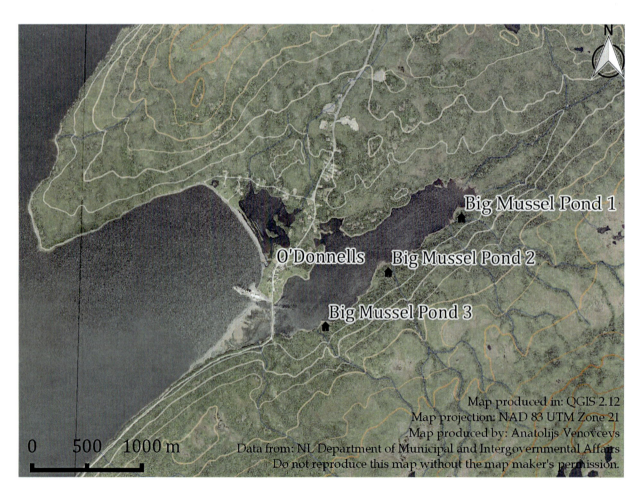

Figure 4.3. Distribution of winter houses around Big Mussel Pond in relation to the modern community of O'Donnells
Source: Anatolijs Venovcevs

Figure 4.4. Interior of a European cabin in Labrador
Source: Reproduced with the permission of The Rooms Provincial Archives Division. VA 152–04, Interior of Goss tilt, Inner Sandy Islands, July 1893/Eliot Curwen, Eliot Curwen fonds

separated by inorganic sandy fill suggesting that the site was occupied for more than just a single winter.

The cellar at Big Mussel Pond 1 is different from Sunnyside 1 as well. Instead of being an earthen structure, it is represented by a simple dry-laid stone foundation. The foundation abuts the rock collapse, is semi-circular, and covers an area of approximately 18 m². Its orientation suggests that it was accessed through a door next to the hearth. A small excavation trench through this feature recovered nails around the periphery of the rock foundation, a possible support post in the centre, and inorganic sandy fill inside. This suggests that the cellar might have been similar to one of the field root pits that were used in Ireland and Great Britain to store vegetables since the eighteenth century (Gage, 2012: 41–50).

Overall, the artifact scatter was approximately 155 m² and, given the orientation of the cellar and the rock collapse, the house was oriented northwest to southeast with the hearth located along the southeast wall of the building. Nails and spikes comprise a quarter of all material recovered from the site suggesting the presence of a significant wooden superstructure. Four pieces of window glass may suggest that a small window was present in the house.

Big Mussel Pond 2 is the smallest of all known winter house sites. The artifact scatter is approximately 54 m² in size. No window glass was recovered and only 15 per cent of the artifact assemblage consisted of nails and spikes. However, a great deal of effort was put into constructing the stone features in this house. While the site lacks a visible cellar and on the surface is only defined by a low rock collapse, the collapse is larger than the one at Big Mussel Pond 1 as it extends 5 m north–south and 2.5 m east–west. The collapse is 50 cm high and its volume is approximately 2.9 m³.

Additionally, work at Big Mussel Pond 2 revealed the presence of an artificial platform of which 5 m² was exposed. It was constructed from dry-laid stone to level the land in front of the hearth on which the winter house stood. From this, it can be surmised that the house was oriented southwest to northeast with the hearth located along the southwest wall. The site displayed no evidence of reoccupation and could have been occupied for just a single winter.

Finally, Big Mussel Pond 3 is unique out of all known winter house sites in Newfoundland as it lacked visible above-ground features beyond the flat surface where the house once stood. Subsequent test pitting over the site revealed evidence of charcoal, fire-reddened soils, and a squat dry-laid foundation which proves that a hearth was present. The limited survey was able to ascertain that the Big Mussel Pond 3 site is approximately 64 m^2 in size and, given the topography and the distribution of artifacts, the house was oriented east to west with the hearth being located on the eastern side of the house.

Regardless of the differences in design, there are many similarities between Sunnyside 1 and the Big Mussel Pond sites when it comes to the artifact assemblages, suggesting a continuity of wintering culture and tradition. For one, Big Mussel Pond 1 showed evidence of lead ammunition production in the form a single clipped musket ball sprue, 23 pieces of lead scrap, 13 pieces of complete lead shot, and 1 old lead cod fishing line weight that was brought to the site as raw material. Big Mussel Pond 2 and 3 also contained lead shot and musket balls but the limited amount of fieldwork failed to produce direct evidence of their manufacture. Forestry was well represented by a saw blade from Big Mussel Pond 1 and a pair of axes, an adze, and a boat hook from Big Mussel Pond 3.

European-made gunflints are also well represented in the Big Mussel Pond assemblages. Three gunflints were recovered from Big Mussel Pond 1, one from Big Mussel Pond 2, and two from Big Mussel Pond 3. All of the gunflints were well worn and some show evidence of reuse as fire strikers. While the Big Mussel Pond sites lack the extensive evidence of ballast flint recycling seen at Sunnyside 1, two flint fragments from Big Mussel Pond 1 and three flint fragments and a crude gunflint from ballast flint from Big Mussel Pond 3 suggest that some recycling was taking place even in the presence of commercial sources.

Recycling is further evinced through pieces of cut, perforated, and cold-hammered copper and metal scrap recovered from two out of the three Big Mussel Pond sites and a mend hole on a small transfer-printed bowl sherd. The constant repurposing of basic consumer goods is not something that was discussed in the recorded instances on the tradition. However, this is not unexpected for a people completely isolated over the winter season.

Subsistence practices were a mix of wild animals and stored provisions. Wild game remains consist of caribou, eider duck (*Somateria mollissima*), and double breasted cormorant (*Phalacrorax auritus*) while stored provisions include pig and cod (Elliott, 2015b–d). The presence of stored provisions is also highlighted by a few barrel hoop fragments and three storage vessels recovered from the Big Mussel Pond sites.

Cooking could have consisted of stews and other wet foods as can be seen by a large iron pot fragment. However, some dry foods could also have been consumed. Out of 16 unique non-storage vessels identified from all three sites, five are teaware, five are flatware, two are hollowware, two are mugs, and two vessels are indeterminate.

Overall the ceramics were much more plentiful than at the seventeenth-century site, probably as a result of the expanded consumer market and the growth of accessibility to these goods in Newfoundland. However, most ceramics from the Big Mussel Pond sites were undecorated in contrast to the year-round or summer fishery sites from the nineteenth century that had a mix of cheap and expensive ceramics (Burke, 1991; Hatcher, 2013; Jones, 2009). Given the isolation of these winter houses, it is possible that more utilitarian ceramic pieces were chosen to serve the family's needs over the winter.

Meanwhile, smoking pipes were common but not as ubiquitous as those at Sunnyside 1 and only three unique liquor containers were identified – one from each of the three sites.

Discussion

Winter houses

Despite the fact that this seasonal movement was practiced by the majority of the Euro-Newfoundland population for approximately 300 years, it has been given little scholarly attention. The notable exception is the seminal works of Philip Smith, who not only drew attention to the anomalous practice of non-pastoral transhumance in a New World context but also critically analyzed the environmental, economic, political, and cultural reasons for its development and persistence (1987a–b, 1995). Important contributions followed by Pope (2004: 248–54) and Nemec (2006), theorizing this tradition as a logical extension of the established pattern of movement by European migratory fishers as well as reorienting our nomenclature to better describe the participants as 'forager-fishers'. In 2005, Smith utilized toponymy to shed further light on the geographic scope of winter house locations throughout the province (2005).

This limited body of research has raised a number of interesting questions, some of which may be answerable archaeologically. The first pertains to the earliest origins and development of the practice. Historical evidence for winter housing dates back to the late seventeenth century and it seems to have been firmly established by the early decades of the eighteenth. Datable artifacts from Sunnyside 1 place this winter occupation to the period 1650–80 (Gaulton & Mills, 2011, 2014a–b). A single C14 date from charcoal in the fireplace (cal AD 1553–1599), though seemingly contradictory, raises the possibility that occupants even utilized old and broken furnishings for fuel. This is further supported by the presence of a chest hinge, small tacks, and many clinched nails in the hearth. The *c.* 1650–80 date for Sunnyside 1 not only pushes back the date for the practice of winter housing but also demonstrates the speed with which European settlers (both single males and nuclear families) were able to transition from a traditional sedentary lifestyle to one of residential dualism. On this final point it is worth noting that many of these early European overwinterers were migratory fishers who were familiar with and comfortable in a setting of patterned movement (see Pope, 2004: 248–54 for discussion).

The adoption of residential mobility within this island setting – as opposed to a seasonal movement across the Atlantic – and the hard-earned lessons that came from it, eventually brought about an evolution or simplification in the construction of winter houses. The timing of this evolution, and variations in the size and permanence of these dwellings can be disentangled with further archaeological investigation. For now it is sufficient to say that the remains at Sunnyside 1 are a hybrid form of architecture whose builders were trying to reproduce some semblance of a permanent dwelling in the context of acquiring the accumulated knowledge for survival and sustainability during Newfoundland's harsh winter. Based on the interior dimensions of the hearth, projected width of the full fireplace, secondary refuse patterns, and other considerations, the building is estimated to have measured between 3.6–4.2 m (12–14 ft) wide and 4.8–6.0 m (16–20 ft) long not including the adjacent root cellar. This is comparable to a permanently occupied planter's house found in Renews dating from the same period and measuring 3.6 by 6.0 m (12 by 20 ft) (Mills, 2000: 47).

Move forward 150 years and we begin to see an architectural tradition that is less labour-intensive and more ephemeral. Due to heavy reliance of timber for fuel and construction, the slow growth of forests, and the natural fluctuations in terrestrial food sources like caribou and migratory birds, Euro-Newfoundlanders learned to make minimal investments in their winter homes, knowing full well that they would need to relocate within a few years' time.

However, these ephemeral structures show quite a bit of variability. For example, the fireplace at Big Mussel Pond 1 has a dry-laid stone backing and the adjacent root cellar was set on a simple stone foundation, whereas Big Mussel Pond 2 is represented structurally by a larger fireplace collapse as well as evidence for the creation of an artificial platform upon which to elevate the house from the surrounding bog. Big Mussel Pond 3, while not well explored, shows an altogether different construction with a relatively small fireplace. Together, these sites portray a small but important sample of winter houses, showing not only a range of architectural forms over time but also the agency and ingenuity of its builders when faced with environmental challenges.

This variation is also seen in the few historic references to the tradition. While the general pattern of residential mobility for shelter and greater access to terrestrial resources is universal, major differences exist on how the tradition was practiced indicating that there were many winter housing traditions instead of just one.

References to winter house architecture describe them as being anything from small shacks to substantially larger houses, often subdivided into separate rooms (Jukes, 1842: 69; Mountain, 1857: 5; Packard, 1891). Most houses are rectangular but there is a reference of square winter houses in mid-nineteenth-century southern Labrador (de Boilieu, 1861: 52). Finally, while many winter houses in eastern Newfoundland were temporary structures built to last for no more than a few winters, preliminary research from western Newfoundland, where land is more suitable for limited agricultural activity, suggests that winter houses there were more permanent. Some houses had a second storey and winter barns were built next to winter houses when fisher-farmers started bringing their herd animals with them on their seasonal migration (Emmanuel House, personal communication, July 28, 2015; Gerald Humber & Sandy House, personal communication, July 27, 2015; Lloyd, 1886: 66; Reynolds et. al., 2014: 146–47).

The household composition of a winter cabin differed as well. While Smith tried to argue that families were the defining feature of Newfoundland transhumance, this was not always the case (Smith, 1987a: 21, 1987b: 246). On occasion, winter houses were occupied by one or two men (Cormack, 1928: 105; Wix, 1836: 29). In other situations, small groups of men would travel into more remote recesses of harbours and bays, though this was often associated with intensive trapping, boat building, or other explicitly commercial activities (Jukes, 1842: 69; Wix, 1836: 83). Identifying the gender and socio-economic backgrounds of winter house residents is an important consideration as more archaeological information on winter housing becomes available.

Spatial organization

Another question relates to the spatial organization of winter communities. What were the distances between houses in a winter 'community' and how far did settlers go when re-establishing new communities after the surrounding resources were depleted? While it appears that most winter houses were built in isolation, with one source from southern Labrador noting that they were spaced 3.2 km (2 miles) apart, it was possible for two to four families to winter together in a small enclave (de Boilieu, 1861: 52; Jukes, 1842: 96, 107; Moreton, 1863: 82; Wix, 1836: 43). In rare instances, 20 families or more were recorded as wintering together, forming entire winter villages (Cuff, 1983; Wilson, 1866: 216).

Smith postulated that the ratio between population and wood supply was of great importance in regard to settlement spacing (1987b: 244). Evidence from Sunnyside 1 and Big Mussel Pond 1, 2, and 3 provides some preliminary archaeological data to shed light on this matter. On the opposite side of the small cove from Sunnyside 1 is a contemporaneous occupation at Frenchman's Island just 300 m away. Quantitative and qualitative similarities in the artifact assemblages from both sites tentatively suggest that Frenchman's Island was another winter occupation although no *in situ* structural remains were found (Evans, 1980, 1981; Gaulton, 2014; Graham, 2012). Two hypotheses can therefore be put forth to explain the proximity of these two contemporaneous sites: 1) they were occupied simultaneously by two groups of similar cultural background or; 2) they were occupied by one group who returned to the same area and built in a slightly different location. Given the immediacy of these two sites, and the fact that provisions such as clay tobacco pipes are identical in form and decoration, the most parsimonious explanation is that this represents two separate domestic units who in all likelihood cooperated in their wintering activities. If correct, then it affords some indication of the spacing between winter houses in a co-inhabited community.

Big Mussel Pond offers a complementary dataset. As stated previously, the sites are spaced 750 m apart yet they could still represent either of the scenarios presented above. All three date from the first half of the nineteenth century, a time when census records indicate that O'Donnells was inhabited by one extended family, the Coombs (Ryan & Ryan, 2000). Spacing between the sites may demonstrate a long-term pattern of winter residency by the same family who moved a short distance to other parts of the pond after adjacent timber stands were exhausted. Alternatively, it is possible that fishers from the nearby community of St. Mary's travelled by boat to overwinter in this less crowded location; therefore, Big Mussel Pond 1, 2, and 3 may represent a shorter period of occupation by multiple families who lived in separate winter quarters but who may have also interacted, shared, and cooperated in daily tasks. Unfortunately the datable artifacts are mute regarding either theory.

Wintering areas had complicated life histories on an island guided by fickle economic and environmental forces. Some places, like the forests around Big Mussel Pond, were always used for seasonal exploitation by the fishers of St. Mary's Bay while some other places, like Sunnyside in the late nineteenth century, were eventually recognized as suitable for year-round occupation. Other locations, like the English colony at Cupids, had more complicated histories; it started off as a permanent settlement, abandoned and reused for wintering, abandoned altogether, and finally reoccupied as a permanent community (Gilbert, 2013; Smith, 1995: 85; Venovcevs, 2015). These fluctuations in permanence are a common trait of other peripheral landscapes whose use has constantly evolved over time (Burri, 2014; Svensson & Gardiner, 2007; Svensson, 2015: 291). This expansion, contraction, and reoccupation in rural Newfoundland helped to organically expand the European frontier and shape the modern human geography of the island. Out of 243 wintering sites whose settlement history is known, 52 are rural communities today; a number which was as high as 137 before many were relocated as part of government-sponsored resettlement programs in the second half of the twentieth century (Venovcevs, 2015: 8–9).

The agency behind winter migration is poorly understood. The limited amount of research that has been done studying the migration patterns between the summer and winter homes have shown a great deal of variation (Venovcevs, 2015). People travelled to their winter dwellings by foot, boat, and, in the twentieth century, even by train car (Cuff, 1983). The distances were usually short. By foot, travel was usually limited to less than 5 km and hardly ever more than 10. By water, distances were farther with most falling within 30 km but some extending for well over 100 (Venovcevs, 2015: 7–9).

Mapping some of the known travel routes reveals a complex web of movements from exposed ocean-side promontories into inner bays, inlets, and harbours (Figure 4.5). While the reasons for this movement might never be fleshed out as most Euro-Newfoundlanders did not leave any written records, work that has been done on better-recorded transhumant traditions in Europe provides a framework for this interpretation. In places like Scotland, the Pyrenees, the French Alps, and Spain seasonal migrations were guided by formal and informal contracts between landlords, tenants, farmers, and communities that saw transhumant farmers broadly disperse across the landscape without always travelling to the closest available seasonal pasture (Bil, 1990; Burri, 2014; Carrer, 2013: 55; Svensson, 2015: 296). While the specific decision-making process that guided each community's behaviour during Newfoundland's winter migration is not known, it was most likely driven by a similar set of formal and informal contracts based on kinship, community, or economic contracts (also see Smith, 1995: 84–85).

Winter housing 53

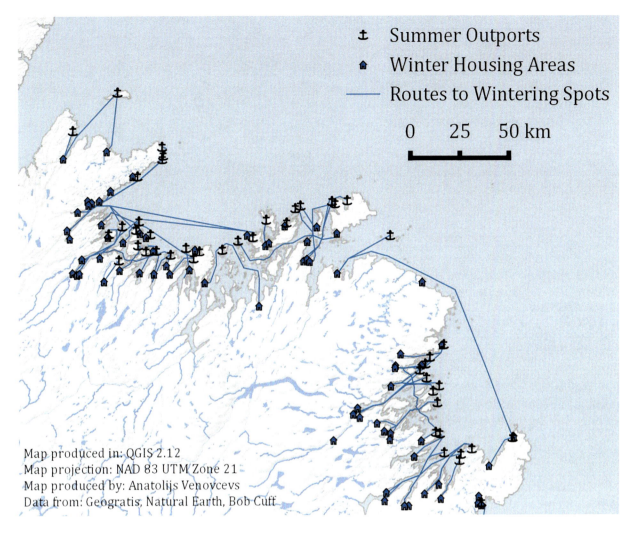

Figure 4.5. Approximate migration routes between summer communities and their associated winter places in Notre Dame and Bonavista Bays, Newfoundland
Source: Anatolijs Venovcevs

Material culture

The provisions, tools, and other items required during these long winter months in the woods is another interesting avenue of inquiry which can supplement similar work that is being undertaken in Europe (Carrer, 2015; Carrer & Angelucci, 2013; Emanuelsson et. al., 2003: 114–24). What was deemed 'necessary' to these transhumant Euro-Newfoundlanders and how are these necessities represented in the archaeological record? As discussed in an earlier section, the necessities transported to winter houses were influenced by a variety of factors including mode of travel and distance from summer residences, as well as the time period in question, changing consumer behaviour, and one's ability to acquire goods from local or foreign merchants during the fishing season. Hunting and forestry are amply represented in the material culture of winter house sites in the form of ammunition, gunflints, gunflint production, faunal remains, axes and saw fragments, and therefore represent primary economic activities. To a lesser extent, woodworking and trapping are signified by specialized iron tools and faunal remains respectively, although an iron trap part was also identified at Frenchman's Island (Graham, 2012). Given the evidence for hunting it is little surprise that few ceramic storage vessels are present at these sites, though this could also be influenced by the fact that some provisions were stored in wooden barrels which leave little to no trace in the archaeological record.

Much like their summer counterparts, winter houses contain artifacts associated with smoking and drinking. Clay tobacco pipes, in particular, represent a significant proportion of the artifact assemblages from Sunnyside 1 and Frenchman's Island but lesser amounts from the nineteenth-century sites at Big Mussel Pond. The presence of clay pipes also implies the availability and 'necessity' of tobacco, stored and transported in barrels. Alcoholic beverages were typically stored and shipped in barrels as well but are frequently represented on post-medieval sites by storage/service containers in the form of glass and ceramic bottles and jugs (Jeffries et al., 2014). Few examples are found on winter house sites in comparison to year-round residences on the coast, many of which also operated as tippling houses. This discrepancy may have everything to do with the more isolated, dispersed, even calm nature of winter occupation, and the frequency with which strong alcoholic beverages were consumed during the frenetic summer months when a large influx of male fishermen with disposable income came to fishing stations and permanent settlements.

Excavated winter house assemblages are likewise notable for what they do not contain: a variety of tools and implements relating to the cod fishery, or coins and tokens for the purchase of goods. Neither is unexpected. Procurement strategies relating to fishing would be limited to salmon and trout in rivers and ponds, while opportunities to purchase goods and services from merchants during the winter season were nonexistent. Fish hooks, prongs, splitting knives, lead line weights, and net weights mostly remained at summer homes while any hard currency may have been cached and left behind along with anything too cumbersome or delicate to include in the winter commute. It is worth mentioning however that occasional lead items related to the fishery were brought to winter abodes and recycled into ammunition for hunting.

In light of the economic and social activities of residents during the winter season, and the resulting differences in the quantity and/or variety of certain artifact types incorporated into the archaeological record, we may be at a point to suggest that material assemblages from winter occupations form a consistent, albeit variable, pattern. Theoretically, this 'winter house pattern' would mirror the primary economic foci of hunting, forestry, and woodworking, exhibit a material assemblage limited in quantity, diversity, and quality, and demonstrate an active strategy of repair, reuse, and recycling born of isolation and necessity. Further research will provide the data to further develop and refine this nascent idea and if proven correct, would be a useful tool in the future identification of winter house sites in this part of North America.

WINTER HOUSING AND EUROPEAN TRANSHUMANCE

With the authors' preliminary results on winter housing, the discussion needs to be drawn back to the original choice to retain the use of the term 'transhumance' and the earlier assertion that the study of this tradition can enrich the study of medieval and post-medieval European transhumance. As discussed above, the

seasonal use of *the country* for winter housing parallels the seasonal uses of the outlands or uplands seen in many parts of Europe.

While the winter housing system was generally more basic than many of the European transhumant traditions, migration into *the country*, an area peripheral to the commercial fishing settlements, played an important role in the yearly survival rounds of rural Newfoundlanders. Much like in certain parts of Europe, Newfoundland transhumance was practiced by people who lived on the social and commercial edge of the European world system, and outside of a few, rare population centres Newfoundland's human geography was dominated by small, tight-knit fishing hamlets, each separated by dozens of kilometres of rugged, uninhabited coastline. The economic survival of these communities depended almost exclusively on the exploitation of cod, the island's aquatic monocrop, which was prone to boom-and-bust cycles. Seasonal migration was often an economic necessity for fishers to minimize the cost of their provisions by living in close proximity to firewood and natural shelter, hunting and trapping their own food, and building boats, barrels, and other equipment needed for the summer fishery. This migratory seasonal expansion of subsistence activities parallels the European farmers who expanded the range of their pasture into areas allotted to them by changes in the season (Bil, 1990; Carrer & Angelucci, 2013; Daugstad et. al., 2014; Emanuelsson et. al., 2003; Svensson, 2015).

Winter housing is also a reminder that transhumant traditions, either in Newfoundland or elsewhere, were dynamic systems. The variations seen in winter houses speak to the organic and evolving nature of this tradition; the distances travelled, the household composition of the winterers, the houses built, and the activities carried out around the winter houses were tailored to individual needs. Similarly, there is a great spectrum both between and within each historic transhumant tradition in Europe that reveals that life ways in the uplands and outlands were not fixed but rather parts of flexible, fluid, and constantly evolving systems that saw 'the periphery' defined and redefined through succeeding generations (Bil, 1990; Burri, 2014; Costello, 2015; Daugstad et. al., 2014; Gardiner, 2008, 2012; Svensson, 2015; Svensson & Gardiner, 2007).

This can be expanded further to the broader cultures that all of these post-medieval rural Europeans were a part. Transhumance does not exist by itself but rather is often engrained into pluralistic economies that rely on other activities like mixed farming, forestry, hunting, iron working, charcoal production, haymaking, honey harvesting, and other seasonal economic pursuits (Bil, 1990: 115–22; Burri, 2014; Costello, 2015; Svensson, 2015; Svensson & Gardiner, 2007; Svensson et. al., 2008). Similarly, winter houses and the activities discussed in this paper are just one side of a larger pluralistic system where Newfoundlanders annually exploited certain seasonal and economically marginal resources, like cod, salmon, and seals as well as participated in commercial logging, berry picking, and small-scale labour-intensive subsistence gardening (Cadigan, 1992, 2002; Porter, 1985; Ryan, 1994). While each of these economies could be relied on for a fleeting amount of time during the yearly cycle and at times produced marginal returns for the labour invested, together they worked in concert to sustain isolated rural Euro-Newfoundlander families for over 300 years into the present day as they balanced their livelihoods between the demands of a precarious market economy and the needs of household-level subsistence.

CONCLUSIONS

This article represents the first serious attempt in 20 years to refine the current understanding of an esoteric European adaptation to the challenges presented by their settlement of a new and often inhospitable continent. While 20 years of historical and theoretical research provide a new perspective on this winter housing tradition, it is the last five years of archaeological study that have supplied a more holistic understanding of Newfoundland culture and history.

In addition, the authors aspired to a new challenge – to employ Philip Smith's term of 'non-pastoral transhumance' as a supplement to the archaeology of traditional transhumance and show that North American research on adaptations to the rural periphery should be incorporated into the discussion taking place in Europe. Though winter housing cannot speak to pastoral cycles and other agricultural pursuits, it does supply information on attitudes towards transience and permanence, the periphery, and the material culture of seasonal migration. While, as originally stated, the goal of this paper was not to redefine 'transhumance,' the variation seen both between and within each European transhumant tradition leads to a reconsideration of what is actually meant by the term. Are pastoral animals a necessity to understand life in a marginal environment or is it more fruitful to consider all of the pluralistic, migratory lifeways that allowed for the successful utilization of these landscapes?

In their introduction to the proceedings from the seventh Ruralia conference, Svensson and Gardiner put forth an argument that terms like marginality and periphery are not inherent elements of either landscapes or people, but rather are relative terms that come from the perspective of the observer (Svensson & Gardiner, 2007). All of the elements of their argument are just as applicable to winter housing as they are to European modes of transhumance. Rather than being a natural,

unoccupied, impassable backwoods of the interior, *the country* is a cultural landscape. While it lay peripheral to suitable cod fishing ground, and thus ignored by Newfoundland scholars until very recently, *the country* played a central role in the lives of rural fisherfolk.

The ongoing research on winter housing faces similar difficulties to those looking at the European transhumant tradition, ephemeral sites, little material culture, work in isolated, rugged locations, and the constant waves of blackflies and mosquitoes. Even though transhumant traditions differ in time and space, this work is important as it allows for a redefinition of landscapes and traditions which have historically been ignored by researchers. The inclusion of winter housing as a non-pastoral cousin of the transhumant family allows the discussion to achieve a greater level of understanding through transatlantic synthesis.

ACKNOWLEDGEMENTS

The authors would like to acknowledge the field and lab volunteers as well as the community members from Sunnyside and O'Donnells who assisted with the excavations and artifact processing from the sites discussed in this paper. This research could not have been done without them. Donna Teasdale deserves gratitude for artifact conservation.

REFERENCES

Bil, A. 1990. *The Shieling 1600–1840*. Edinburgh: John Donald Publishers Ltd.

Boilieu, L. de. 1861. *Recollections of Labrador Life*. T.F. Bredin ed. Toronto: Ryerson Press.

Bonnycastle, R.H. 1842. *Newfoundland in 1842*. London: H. Colburn.

Brouillan, J.F. de M. de. 1693. 1693, décembre, 14 / Plaisance. Correspondance générale; Amérique du Nord. MG1-C11C, Volume 1, fol. 276–79, Library and Archives Canada.

Burke, C.A. 1991. Nineteenth century ceramic artifacts from a seasonally occupied fishing station on Saddle Island, Red Bay, Labrador. MA thesis, Memorial University of Newfoundland.

Burri, S. 2014. Reflections on the concept of marginal landscape through a study of late medieval *incultum* in Provence (South-eastern France). *European Journal of Post-Classical Archaeologies*, 4:7–38.

Cadigan, S. 1992. The staple model reconsidered: the case of agricultural policy in Northeast Newfoundland, 1785–1855. *Acadiensis: Journal of the History of the Atlantic Region*, 21(2):48–71.

Cadigan, S. 2002. The role of agriculture in outport self-sufficiency. In: R.E. Ommer, ed. *The Resilient Outport: Ecology, Economy, and Society in Rural Newfoundland*. Memorial University of Newfoundland: Institute of Social and Economic Research, pp. 241–62.

Cadigan, S. 2009. *Newfoundland & Labrador: A History*. Toronto: University of Toronto Press.

Carrer, F. 2013. An ethnoarchaeological inductive model for predicting archaeological site location: a case-study of pastoral settlement patterns in the Val di Fiemme and Val di Sole (Trentino, Italian Alps). *Journal of Anthropological Archaeology*, 32:54–62.

Carrer, F. 2015. Interpreting intra-site spatial patterns in seasonal contexts: an ethnoarchaeological case study from the Western Alps. *Journal of Archaeological Method and Theory*, 22(4):1–25.

Carrer, F. & Angelucci, D.E. 2013. First archaeological data from an Alpine pastoral enclosure at Val Poré (Val di Sole, Trentino, Italy). *Debates de Arqueología Medieval*, 3:149–65.

Cell, G.T. 1982. *Newfoundland Discovered: English Attempts at Colonisation, 1610–1630*. London: The Hakluyt Society.

Codignola, L. 1988. *The Coldest Harbour in the Land: Simon Stock and Lord Baltimore's Colony in Newfoundland, 1621–1649*. Montreal: McGill-Queen's University Press.

Cormack, W.E. 1928. *Narrative of a Journey Across the Island of Newfoundland in 1822*. F.A. Bruton ed. London: Longmans.

Costello, E. 2015. Post-medieval upland settlement and the decline of transhumance: a case-study from the Galtee Mountains, Ireland. *Landscape History*, 36(1):47–69.

Crompton A.J. 2001. A seventeenth-century planter's house at Ferryland, Newfoundland (CgAf-2, Area D). MA thesis, Memorial University of Newfoundland.

Crompton, A.J. 2012. The historical archaeology of a French fortification in the colony of Plaisance: the vieux fort site (ChAl-04), Placentia, Newfoundland. PhD dissertation, Memorial University of Newfoundland.

Cuff, R. 1983. On the cars: winter logging on the Bonavista Peninsula (1911–1949). *The Newfoundland Quarterly*, 79(2):12–17.

Daugstad, K., Fernández Mier, M. & Peña-Chocarro, L. 2014. Landscapes of transhumance in Norway and Spain: farmers' practices, perceptions, and value orientations. *Norsk Geografisk Tidsskrift – Norwegian Journal of Geography*, 2014:1–11.

Elliott, D. 2014. Sunnyside 1 (ClAl-5) Faunal Analysis. Unpublished report in the authors' possession.

Elliott, D. 2015a. Sunnyside 1 (ClAl-5) Faunal Analysis – Updated Report. Unpublished report in the authors' possession.

Elliott, D. 2015b. Big Mussel Pond 1 (CgAj-3) Faunal Analysis. Unpublished report in the authors' possession.

Elliott, D. 2015c. Big Mussel Pond 2 (CgAj-5) Faunal Analysis. Unpublished report in the authors' possession.

Elliott, D. 2015d. Big Mussel Pond 3 (CgAj-6) Faunal Analysis. Unpublished report in the authors' possession.

Emanuelsson, M., Johansson, A., Nilsson, S., Pettersson, S. & Svensson, E. 2003. *Settlement, Shieling and Landscape: The Local History of a Forest Hamlet*. Lund Studies in Medieval Archaeology 32.

Evans, C.O. 1980. Field report of Frenchmen's Island project. In: C. Thomson & J.S. Thomson, eds. *Archaeology in Newfoundland and Labrador 1980*. St. John's: Government of Newfoundland & Labrador, pp. 88–94.

Evans, C.O. 1981. Frenchmen's Island Site (ClAl-1) 1981 Preliminary Field Report. In: C. Thomson & J.S. Thomson, eds. *Archaeology in Newfoundland and Labrador 1981*. St. John's: Government of Newfoundland & Labrador, pp. 210–25.

Gage, J.E. 2012. *Root Cellars in America: Their History, Design, and Construction 1609–1920*. Amesbury: Powwow River Books.

Gardiner, M. 2008. A preliminary list of booley huts in the Mourne Mountains, County Down. *Ulster Journal of Archaeology*, 67:142–52.

Gardiner, M. 2012. Time regained: Booley huts and seasonal settlement in the Mourne Mountains, County Down, Ireland. In: S. Turner & B. Silvester, eds. *Life in Medieval Landscapes. People and Places in the Middle Ages: Papers in Memory of H.S.A. Fox*. Oxford: Windgather Press, pp. 106–24.

Gaulton, B. 2014. Final Report for Sunnyside 1 (ClAl-05), Permit 13.07. Report on file at the Provincial Archaeology Office, St. John's: Government of Newfoundland & Labrador.

Gaulton, B. & Miller, A.F. 2009. Edward Wynne's The Brittish India or a compendious discourse tending to advancement (circa 1630/31). *Newfoundland and Labrador Studies*, 24(1):111–37.

Gaulton, B. & Mills, S. 2011. A seventeenth-century 'winter house' in Sunnyside, Newfoundland? In: S. Hull & D. Mercer, eds. *Provincial Archaeology Office 2010 Archaeology Review*, Vol. 9. St. John's: Provincial Archaeology Office, pp. 51–6.

Gaulton, B. & Mills, S. 2014a. Further Investigations at Sunnyside 1 (ClAl-05). In: S. Hull, ed. *Provincial Archaeology Office 2013 Archaeology Review*, Vol. 12. St. John's: Provincial Archaeology Office, pp. 56–60.

Gaulton, B. & Mills, S. 2014b. Final Report for Sunnyside 1 (ClAl-05), Permit 13.07. Unpublished report on file Provincial Archaeology Office, St. John's.

Gilbert, W. 2013. 'Dwelling there still': historical archaeology at Cupids and changing perspectives on early modern Newfoundland. In: P.E. Pope & S. Lewis-Simpson, eds. *Exploring Atlantic Transitions: Archaeologies of Transience and Permanence in New Found Lands*. Woodbridge: The Boydell Press, pp. 215–23.

Graham, D. 2012. Where once they stood . . . and dropped things: answering questions about Frenchman's Island (ClAl-1) through artifact analysis. Honours Essay, Memorial University of Newfoundland.

Hatcher, H. 2013. Exploring an anglophone presence at the French Fishing Room, Champ Paya, at Dos de Cheval (EfAx-09) in Cap Rouge Harbour, Newfoundland. MA thesis, Memorial University of Newfoundland.

Head, C.G. 1976. *Eighteenth Century Newfoundland*. Toronto: McClelland & Stewart Limited.

Jeffries, N., Featherby, R. & Wroe-Brown, R. 2014. 'Would I were in an alehouse in London!': a finds assemblage sealed by the Great Fire from Rood Lane, City of London. *Post-medieval Archaeology*, 48(2):261–84.

Jones, J. 2009. *Pécheurs, Pâturages, et Petit Jardins*: A nineteenth-century *Gardien* homestead in the Petit Nord, Newfoundland. MA thesis, Memorial University of Newfoundland.

Jukes, J.B. 1842. *Excursions In and About Newfoundland, During the Years 1839 and 1840*. London: John Murray.

Kenmotzu, N. 1990. Gunflints: a study. *Historical Archaeology*, 24(2):92–124.

Kent, B.C. 1983. More on Gunflints. *Historical Archaeology*, 17(2):27–40.

King, A.F. 1980. Geology of the Avalon Peninsula, Newfoundland. Map 88–001. Government of Newfoundland and Labrador, Department of Mines and Energy, Mineral Development Division. GS#NFLD/1680.

King, H. 2012. Remote wilderness cabins on the Avalon Peninsula: male spaces and culture. MA thesis, Memorial University of Newfoundland.

Leskovec, B. 2007. A rural drinking establishment in Ferryland: life in eighteenth-century Newfoundland. MA thesis, Memorial University of Newfoundland.

Lloyd, F.E.J. 1886. *Two Years in the Region of Icebergs, and What I Saw There*. London: Society for the Propagation of Christian Knowledge.

MacPherson, A.G. 1977. A modal sequence in the peopling of Central Bonavista Bay, 1676–1857. In: J.J. Mannion, ed. *The Peopling of Newfoundland: Essays in Historical Geography*. St. John's: Institute for Social and Economic Research, pp. 102–35.

Mills, D.B. 1977. The development of Folk Architecture in Trinity Bay. In: J.J. Mannion, ed. *The Peopling of Newfoundland: Essays in Historical Geography*. St. John's: Institute for Social and Economic Research, pp. 77–101.

Mills, S.F. 2000. Seventeenth-century life in Renews, Newfoundland: archaeological analysis of an English West Country planter's house. MA thesis, Memorial University of Newfoundland.

Mills, S.F. 2012. 'Going to the cabin, 17th-century style': transhumance in the Newfoundland subsistence economy. October. [paper] St. John's: Council for Northeast Historical Archaeology, St. John's.

Moreton, J. 1863. *Life and Works in Newfoundland: Reminiscences of Thirteen Years Spent There*. London: Rivingtons.

Mountain, J.G. 1857. *Some Account of a Sowing Time on the Rugged Shores of Newfoundland*. London: Society for the Propagation of the Gospel.

Nemec, T.F. 2006. Historic Adaptive Strategies of Euro-Newfoundland Forager-Fishers. In: X.S.R. Campos & X.M.S. Solla, eds. *Galicia & Terranova & Labrador: Comparative Studies on Economic, Political, and Social-cultural Processes*. Santiago: Universidade de Santiago de Compostela, pp. 169–79.

Nixon, D.A. 1999. A seventeenth-century house at Ferryland, Newfoundland (CgAf-2, area B). MA thesis, Memorial University of Newfoundland.

Oldmixon, J. 1708. *The British Empire in America, containing the history of the discovery, settlement, progress and present state of all the British colonies on the continent and islands of America*. London: Nicholson, Tooke, Parker, and Smith.

Packard, A.S. 1891. *The Labrador Coast: A Journal of Two Summer Cruises to That Region*. New York: N.D.C. Hodges.

Pope, P.E. 1997. The 16th-century fishing voyage. In: J. Candow & C. Corbin, eds. *How Deep Is The Ocean? Historical Essays on Canada's Atlantic Fishery*. Sydney: University College of Cape Breton Press, pp. 15–30.

Pope, P.E. 2004. *Fish into Wine: The Newfoundland Plantation in the Seventeenth Century*. Oakland: University of California Press.

Porter, M. 1985. 'She Was Skipper of the Shore-Crew:' notes on the history of the sexual division of labour in Newfoundland. *Labour/Le Travail*, 15:105–23.

Poynter, F.N.L. 1963. *The Journal of James Yonge (1647–1721) Plymouth Surgeon*. Hamden: Archon Books.

Renouf, M.A.P. 1999. Prehistory of Newfoundland hunter-gatherers: extinctions or adaptations? *World Archaeology*, 30(3):403–20.

Reynolds, K., Hull, S. & Mercer, D. 2014. Provincial archaeology office 2013. In: S. Hull, ed. *Provincial Archaeology Office 2013 Archaeology Review*, Vol. 12. St. John's: Provincial Archaeology Office, pp. 145–54.

Ryan, K. & Ryan, J. 2000. History of O'Donnell's, St. Mary's Bay. *Newfoundland's Grand Banks*. http://ngb.chebucto.org/Articles/odonnell-psm.shtml (accessed 1 October 2014).

Ryan, S. 1994. *The Ice Hunters: A History of Newfoundland Sealing to 1914*. St. John's: Breakwater.

Sloane, E. 1964. *A Museum of Early American Tools*. New York: W. Funk.

Smith, P. 1987a. In winter quarters. *Newfoundland Studies*, 3(1):1–36.

Smith, P. 1987b. Transhumant Europeans overseas: the Newfoundland case. *Current Anthropology*, 28(2):241–50.

Smith, P. 1995. Transhumance among European settlers in Atlantic Canada. *The Geographic Journal*, 161(1):79–86.

Smith, P. 2005. Toponymy and winter migrations. *RLS (Regional Language Studies . . . Newfoundland)*, 18:1–7.

St. John, A. 2011. An interpretation of French ceramics from a migratory fishing station, Dos de Cheval, Newfoundland (EfAx-09). MA thesis, Memorial University of Newfoundland.

Svensson, E. 2015. Upland living. The Scandinavian shielings and their European sisters. In: I. Baug, J. Larsen & S.S. Mygland, eds. *Nordic Middle Ages – Artefacts, Landscapes, and Society. Essays in Honour of Ingvild Øye on her 70th Birthday*. Bergen: University of Bergen, pp. 289–300.

Svensson, E., Emanuelsson, M., Johansson, A., Nilsson, S. & Pettersson, S. 2008. The periphery and the market. In: M. Emanuelsson, E. Johansson & A.-K. Ekman, eds. *Peripheral Communities: Crisis, Continuity, and Long-Term Survival*. Reports Department of Urban and Rural Development, pp. 131–42.

Svensson, E. & Gardiner, M. 2007. Introduction: marginality in the preindustrial European countryside. *Ruralia*, 7:21–25.

Tuck, J.A. 1976. *Newfoundland and Labrador Prehistory*. Hull: Canadian Museum of Civilization.

Tuck, J.A. & Pastore, R.T. 1985. A nice place to visit, but . . . prehistoric human extinctions on the island of Newfoundland. *Canadian Journal of Archaeology*, 9(1):69–80.

Venovcevs, A. 2015. Test to sites: challenges and hidden potentials of test-derived spatial analysis. *North Atlantic Archaeology*, 4:1–16.

Williams, J.C. 2006. An analysis of the seventeenth century artifact assemblage for Clear Cove, CfAf-23. Honours Essay, Memorial University of Newfoundland.

Wilson, W. 1866. *Newfoundland and Its Missionaries*. Cambridge: Dakin & Metcalfe.

Wix, E. 1836. *Six Months of a Newfoundland Missionary's Journal*. London: Smith, Elder.

CHAPTER 5

What do we really know about transhumance in medieval Scotland?

Piers Dixon

Introduction

Across Europe, transhumance is a common element of medieval settlement and land-use systems, generally dying out during the seventeenth to nineteenth centuries. In Scotland, for example, the form of transhumance that was practised involved whole communities moving relatively short distances with their cattle and sheep to the summer grazing for the production of butter and cheese, at the same time building shelters called shielings while they were there. This practice ceased in the Lowlands in the seventeenth century, if not before, but carried on in the Highlands until the Clearances of the nineteenth century replaced settlement systems that included transhumance with all-year-round sheep farms. Uniquely in Britain, summer shieling was still practised on Lewis in the Western Isles in the early twentieth century. The shelters or huts that were built to house the people who conducted the animals to the summer grazing are the most visible sign of this practice and the subject of this paper. The dating from recent excavations (Atkinson, 2016; Durham, 2017), which places their occupation in the late and post-medieval periods (*c.*1350–1560 and *c.*1560–1850 respectively), shows a discrepancy with the documented medieval activity (*c.*1100–1560) that suggests some form of transhumance in the high medieval period (*c.*1100–1350) in both highland and lowland areas. To explore the meaning of this apparent gap in the record, various strands of evidence will be reviewed, including the documentary record, place-names, the physical remains of the huts as recorded by field survey and excavation, and the wider landscape evidence provided by palaeoenvironmental analysis.

Documentation

The documentary record for the medieval period is often cryptic and opaque. For shielings this is usually limited to references in the context of listing rights to pasture and other resources. From the later twelfth century shielings are referred to in charters as *scalingas* in Latin, but this tells us little of transhumance as such since the term is specifically applied to the building of temporary huts for seasonal activities, but not as Oram states 'to the activities *per se*, which we are left to guess at' (Oram, 2011: 258). The *scalingas* references in the twelfth century Acts of William I, for example, are mainly restricted to lowland and coastal estates in Perthshire and Angus, which do not necessarily suggest upland pasture, but might encompass lowland bog or salt marsh (Barrow, 1971: 136, 185, 197, 413, 481).[1] Indeed, the shieling huts referred to here could be shelters built by shepherds or herdsmen grazing large herds of stock or flocks of sheep for their meat and wool rather than transhumance as defined above. Winchester, writing about southern Scotland has suggested that the large values or acreages of *scalingas* grants might indicate they should be interpreted as meaning a shieling ground or summer pasture rather than huts as such (Winchester, 2011: 132).

Another strand of evidence which might suggest transhumance comes from analysis of the 'davochs' of Moray by Alasdair Ross (2003, 2011). This has shown that these are territorial units that included settlement, farmland and grazing resources, which in highland regions like Stratha'an in the Cairngorms, included access to upland summer pasture that was often spatially detached from the core settlement area. Davochs have been shown to be pre-twelfth century in date and, that they were a creation of the Kingdom of Alba, possibly as early as the tenth century (Ross, 2011). They appear fully fledged in the twelfth and thirteenth centuries as the building blocks of parishes, with summer grazing patterns already well established. The memory of this was recorded in the eighteenth century by the minister of the lowland parish of Tarland, who noted that Glenernan in Strathdon, Aberdeenshire, itself a davoch, was once used by the inhabitants of Tarland for summer grazing (Dixon & Fraser, 2007: 183) more than 15 km away.

Some support for the existence of a pastoral economy, if not transhumance, comes from the Bishop of Moray's records in the Central Highlands of Badenoch and Stratha'an as well as the Exchequer Rolls for Glamis and Forfar in the early thirteenth century (Innes,

© 2018 European Association of Archaeologists

1837: nos. 16, 76; Burnett & Stuart, 1878: 6–7). In these cases a significant part of the rent was paid in cheese, which is a key product in the transhumance economy as defined above. However, these are topographically two very different areas, and they may not necessarily tell us about transhumance, though it does tell us about the importance of the pastoral economy to both lowland and upland areas. It might be argued that the building of shieling huts was more likely in an upland context because of the distances involved in getting there from the permanent settlement, but this could also occur in a lowland context to gain access to lowland pasture. As has already been suggested, an area of pasture might not be used for transhumance that required staying overnight. Although the record is post-medieval, the touns of Coldinghamshire fringing Coldingham Moor, for example, were allowed to pasture on the moor, but not to stay overnight (Callander, 1987). This limitation may have been because the Priory of Coldingham had been granted rights of warren by Malcolm IV, thus giving the prior powers to restrict access in the interests of preserving the game. Forest laws limited access to pasture, and it was not until the late medieval period that building shieling huts was permitted in Ettrick Forest in the south of Scotland, for example (Gilbert, 1979: 178).

Indeed, it is not until the post-medieval period, and particularly the seventeenth century, that the documentary evidence becomes sufficiently detailed for transhumance practices to be studied, as Albert Bil has done for Highland Perthshire. By this date, however, summer grazing was being replaced by large-scale herding in the Lowlands, with, for example, hirsels of the landowner's sheep being established on selected farms on the Buccleuch estates in the Southern Uplands (e.g. at seven farms in Liddesdale out of 59 in the dale at the time), and drover's leases in common areas of the Ochils replacing summer grazing by farm tenants that included building of shieling huts (Harrison, unpublished a, b). The former appears to be creating all-year-round sheep farms, whereas drovers were using the hill ground to fatten cattle for market in summer, having driven the cattle south from the Highlands and Islands of Scotland in the spring. Neither is transhumance as defined earlier.

A case study from the Ochils may be outlined to illustrate this. John Harrison has conducted documentary research on grazing in the Ochils in the seventeenth century. The changing face of grazing in these lowland hills is illustrated by a report from the minister of Tillicoultry in May 1671. On returning from a fishing expedition with two friends at Broich in Glen Devon, he met two Highlanders who told them they had a lease of the land around from the laird of Abercairney, and warned if any Tillicoultry beasts came north of the heights they would cut their 'houghs',

i.e. hamstrings (National Record of Scotland [NRS], General Deposit 24 1/319). The resultant dispute left a trail of records that includes descriptions of the former shieling grounds but does not indicate that any were upstanding. Witnesses to inquiries in the 1690s could remember going to the shielings a long time ago, staying all summer and making cheese and butter. By the end of the century the main reason to build a shieling hut was to mark ownership of territory (Harrison, unpublished a). This role for shielings was also true of Highland Perthshire at this period, but there, transhumance continued throughout the seventeenth and eighteenth centuries – increasingly in competition it would seem with graziers engaged in livestock rearing for meat (Bil, 1990).

What we know about shieling practice from estate documentation comes mainly from the work of Albert Bil in Perthshire, which is by far the most comprehensive study yet, which focused on the post-medieval period (Bil, 1990). He demonstrated an upland–lowland divide, with few lowland farms being involved in the practice, which confirms the archaeological evidence for their distribution, but contradicts the documentary record cited above for the medieval period.

Bil has examined all aspects of the practice from the documentary sources, and shown that transhumance was an integral part of the farming cycle. Most rural settlement depended on access to good arable land as well as pasture. In an upland context where arable land was limited by geographical factors, the summer grass on the hill was an essential complementary resource. While the fields were under crop from May through to August, the cattle and sheep were removed, particularly where there was only one small infield in continuous use. In an infield-outfield system the outfield was partially cropped on rotations that could be in cycles of up to eleven years in Aberdeenshire, for example (Keith, 1811: 236), so there was always a good portion of fallow ground to be grazed. This was most highly developed in lowland areas of south-east Scotland, but in many parts of the Highlands the outfield was more limited or non-existent. Here the hill grazing comes into its own, providing the new growth of grass that the animals require, just when it becomes unavailable within the township fields. This is also the period at which the hay crop grows on the spaces between the fields, and this is itself a vital adjunct to the cycle, providing winter feed. A second key element in the process of transhumance is the production of cheese and butter. Bil, building on the work of Robert Dodgshon (1981: 190), has shown how this cycle works, whether there is an outfield or not. He has also shown that there were two types of herd, the milk cows or ewes and the geldings or male animals valued as meat and hides to pay rent, known as malls. Where there is outfield the milk herd may be grazed there in the spring, and particularly the tathed land at night, which is temporarily enclosed when it is due to be cultivated the next year. Meanwhile the male herd is taken onto the common rough grazing beyond the outfield and the head-dyke that separates it from the farmland, and then up to the high shielings prior to the milk herd.

Bil has also shown from the documentation that the shielings grounds could be a considerable distance from the farm, although from half a mile to 3 miles (0.8 km to 4.8 km) was the most common, distances of more than 10 miles (16 km) were not unknown. Even longer distances are known in the Cairngorms, for example, in Donside, where the inhabitants of Monymusk sent their beasts to the Cabrach in the Cairngorms, a distance of 30 miles (Dixon & Fraser, 2007: 204–5). Whilst sheep and cattle were the main constituent of the herd taken to the shieling grounds, horses, goats, pigs and poultry were also taken to prevent damage to crops. The system began to break down under commercial pressure from leases of the grazing by strangers during the eighteenth century (Bil, 1990; Harrison, 2016).

Place-Names

Place-names provide another strand of evidence. Winchester (2011) has shown that there are varying forms of place-name that refer to summer bothies or huts, depending on language on the one hand and on usage on the other. Thus in English, bothies are sheals or shiels, in Gaelic *airigh* or *ruidh* (Bil, 1992), while in Scandinavian they are *skali* (Old Norse). While the English and Gaelic names are common in many parts of Scotland, Scandinavian place-names for the practice are found in Dumfriesshire, revealing a phase of Norse settlement among the modern farm names, but these names are also known in the Norse areas of the far north. However, in Orkney, the traditional explanation of *skali* names (*skaill* in Orkney) is that they are the halls of elite settlements (Thompson, 2012). This may be a local usage, but it is a reminder that the place-name may not only refer to transhumance as Winchester indicates, but also to other activities, which could even include fishing and mining (Winchester, 2011: 132). The overall distribution of these various place-names, excluding *skali* names, is interesting, whether or not they are generic or specific, reflecting the location where the summer huts were built and where summer grazing took place. The distribution is confined mainly to upland locations and is not common in low-lying areas (RCAHMS, 2002: 30). However, the shieling place-names that do occur in Fife and other lowland areas suggest the practice of transhumance was practised there, as has been suggested for the Scottish Borders by Winchester (Winchester, 2011; Taylor & Markus, 2012), but few huts have been recorded in Fife to confirm this except for seven sites in upland locations like Craigluscar and the Lomond Hills (Canmore, 2016: ids 49668, 72532, 72537, 72531, 29820, 29899, 29918).

Furthermore, Winchester has shown that 'shiel' place-name usage tells a story too – as a generic name or suffix it may be telling us about a farm that has grown out of a summer grazing site, such as Greenshiels or Foulshiels in the Scottish Borders (Dixon, 2009; Winchester, 2011), but as a prefix it is specific and more topographically descriptive of an area where summer grazing was practised, as in Shieldhill. If, as I suggest from an examination of the locations of the place-names, it is an upland name, it appears to indicate that transhumance was little practised in a low-lying environment. Although we know that animals were being grazed in these areas, it may be that it was practised on a daily basis, such as that recorded on Coldingham Common by the surrounding touns referred to above (Callander, 1987). Or, alternatively, flocks and herds were taken to summer grazing by sheep or cattle herdsman, but not as a practice involving the whole farming community for the production of cheese and butter. Melrose Abbey possessed an extensive sheep run in Ettrick Forest at the top of the Yarrow Valley that ran over to the Ettrick Valley (Fawcett & Oram, 2004: 209–42), but this has left no, as yet, recognisable trace of structures that might have been used by the herdsmen. They also possessed granges in the Lammermuir hills and estates based on Mauchline in Ayrshire from which to exploit upland grazing for cattle and sheep. This type of large-scale summer herding of cattle or sheep and the involvement of monasteries and the Crown in this activity is certainly not part of transhumance practice as described above, but may well have involved a summer movement of large flocks and herds of stock, maintained for their wool, woolfells and hides.

Archaeological Field Definition and Data

To turn to archaeological data, how do we recognise shieling practice and shieling huts? If one compares the location of huts with the place-name evidence, it is evident that the two are related. To an extent this is an exercise in circularity. Huts found at places called *Airigh* (Gaelic) or Shiel are by inference likely to be shieling huts. Moreover, if huts found at these locations are compared with those found in places with unspecific names, the interpretation may be extended.

The first archaeological recording of the field remains of potential shieling huts was mostly carried out by the Ordnance Survey (OS) archaeological teams until their demise in the 1980s. In Scotland, the level of recording outside the OS was limited to the selective recording by the Royal Commission on the Ancient Historical Monuments of Scotland (RCAHMS) Inventory programme (e.g. RCAHMS, 1992), or the more comprehensive recording by Roger Mercer's University of Edinburgh's field survey teams in northern Scotland (Mercer, 1980). Occasional but important studies were made by geographers, such as MacSween on the Isle of Skye or Miller on north Lochtayside (MacSween, 1959; Miller, 1967). This lack of interest is reflected in the annual publication of field work activities in Scotland, *Discovery and Excavation in Scotland* (*DES*), in which the recording of shielings remained almost at zero until 1989. In that year there was a change in afforestation policy by the government that recognised the importance of archaeological sites and other environmental concerns. Recording of all archaeology increased dramatically on two levels – tactical emergency response survey ahead of a forestry proposal, and the strategic mapping of archaeological sites in areas where afforestation was likely. The impact of this change in policy saw shieling huts being recorded by both arms of survey, as is evident in the number recorded in the pages of *DES*. The Afforestable Land Survey (ALS) was established in late 1989 at RCAHMS to carry out strategic survey in consultation with the Forestry Commission and Historic Scotland, a programme it pursued until 2000. It established a methodology which recorded and mapped everything of archaeological interest regardless of date. The ALS programme and the subsequent First Edition Survey Project (FESP), 1995–2001, increased the recording of shieling huts exponentially, more than doubling the recorded shieling hut sites in the national record (55% of 5737 sites in Canmore in 2002); the resultant distribution being mainly in upland areas throughout Scotland, except for Orkney and Shetland (RCAHMS, 2002: 30; Dixon, 2009: 30).

When the ALS was established, it was considered that shieling huts were not immediately recognisable as such without confirmation from other sources such as place-names. Huts could be used for other purposes, such as hunting lodges, illegal distilleries (usually distinguished by closeness to a burn, a hidden location and the presence of a lade), fisherman's bothies, watchman's huts and peat stands (examples of narrow open-ended structures on Ben Lawers were misidentified by Miller [1967] as shieling huts [Boyle, 2003]). Also it was not immediately clear that they were necessarily different *per se* from permanent habitations. For much of the 1990s the ALS recorded small buildings in the field as 'huts' and determined their function from topographic context, place-names and association with other features.

So what are the features that have been used to distinguish shieling huts from other types of site? The approach taken by RCAHMS applied an arbitrary size cut-off to the recording of a hut or small

building, as opposed to one designated as a 'building' – by definition more likely to be a permanent structure (RCAHMS, 1990: 12). As defined by ALS, a 'building' was more than 3 m in internal breadth and 6 m in internal length. In this context, a structure with a 7 m internal length and narrow breadth of 2 m was considered to be a 'hut', though those that were longer tended also to be sub-divided. This limitation of definition was remedied with a blanket change in classification that the FESP project did much to ensure in its desk-based study. It classified as 'shieling hut' all structures where the site was recorded by the OS as shieling hut. In addition, those that were too small to be farm buildings and lacked enclosures or any evidence of cultivation were classified as 'Shieling hut possible'. FESP also included those where the place-name indicated a shieling ground.

The presence of mounds of earth beside the huts, which could be shown by spade testing to contain charcoal and occasional artefacts, provided further support for a 'shieling hut' interpretation, since this could be explained as the midden – there being no need to spread a midden on cultivated land at a shieling (but see below this paragraph). This was brought into particular focus by the Ben Lawers Historic Landscape Project, where it proved difficult to separate structure and midden if turf was used in the walls (see 'Excavation of shieling huts' below). The absence of cultivation proved not to be absolutely watertight as a definition of a 'shieling hut', since it has been shown that 'lazy-bed' rigs were to be found in Assynt, for example, at places recorded on eighteenth-century estate maps as shielings (National Library of Scotland [NLS], Survey of Assynt), possibly the result of shifting patterns of settlement as shieling sites were converted to outfield. Similarly, potato cultivation reportedly took place at some Irish booley sites (Costello, this volume). The use of the land around a shieling settlement for cultivation is a logical step since the annual summer grazing improves the soil. Bil in his study of Perthshire showed that this was the case in the late seventeenth and early eighteenth centuries, and there is the evidence in southern Scotland and northern England of -shiel place-names for permanent settlements that were once, presumably, shieling sites (Bil, 1990; Winchester, 2011). It was further argued that shieling sites could be distinguished from those of other functions because there are several huts in one group. This is based on the argument that a shieling ground was grazed by the inhabitants of a toun, or hamlet, composed of several small tenants, or sub-tenants where there was a tacksman, ranging from two to five in number – the size of a typical Scots toun – each of whom would need a shelter at the summer grazing. In addition, long-term use of the site required constant rebuilding, that left its mark in the archaeological remains with evidence of rebuilding.

A case study of this approach is that of upper Strathdon. Here the land was managed in the medieval period as a forest reserve known as Corcarff. Groups of shieling huts are to be found in side valleys short of the forest reserve and at Fae Vaet on the watershed with Strath Avon, a disputed grazing, on the outer edge of the reserve. Within the forest reserve, a scatter of small individual huts was located, which it was argued could be ascribed to some of the other activities listed above. This is supported by documentary records that tell us the tenants of post-medieval farms that colonised the forest reserve from the fifteenth century had to go to shieling grounds outside the reserve. It is also supported by the groups of huts at the shieling sites themselves, such as Meikle Fleuchat (Canmore, 2016: id 130976), as opposed to singleton huts found within the forest reserve (Dixon & Fraser, 2007: 205–6).

Although, by definition shieling huts are smaller than permanent houses, there were instances where structures have been recorded that defy ready interpretations. Usually these are larger huts that stand out in size if not in architecture from the standard huts. One such example was the large turf hut at Black Bothy at the top of Glen Geldie, which may be the mapped Bothan Geldie on the 1703 plan of the forest of Mar in the Cairngorms (RCAHMS, 1995: 6), which it was suggested may have been used as a hunting lodge or to guard the estate from encroachment by graziers from over the watershed in Glen Feshie.

Architecture of shieling huts

Most huts were subrectangular structures, but on the west coast, especially on the Hebridean islands, what are known as figure-of-eight huts are common, comprising a main structure with a low passage to a smaller chamber leading off it, and also on occasion there may be a second subsidiary cell. The cells may be corbelled with stone as has been recorded on the isles of Eigg, Rum and Skye in the Inner Hebrides. Corbelled beehive-shaped huts are characteristic of Uig parish in the south-west of Lewis, and Harris its neighbour, where suitable stone is easily available and timber scarce (Figure 5.1; DES, 2013: 195–6). These appear to be unique to the Outer Hebrides. But here as is often the case elsewhere the weatherproof covering was turf. Not all circular huts were roofed in this way. Pennant, who observed transhumance while touring the Western Isles in the late eighteenth century, included a description and depiction of huts on the isle of Jura, some of which were conical and roofed with branches and a covering of turf (Pennant, 1776: 205). A description of this technique is recorded by the *Scotsman* newspaper in 1900 as having been used on the Isle of Lewis where it was

reported that three poles were tied together with the feet spread and secured by a stone footing, and the rest covered with branches and turf. Shieling huts in Strathdon, Aberdeenshire, were described in the sixteenth century as being constructed with 'feal and divot', feal being thick brick-like turves for the walls, with plenty of earth, and divots, thin mostly matted grass turves for the roof covering (Dixon & Fraser, 2007: 206). At Riol, as elsewhere on the slopes of Ben Lawers, a few of the huts were stone walled, cruck roofed, with gabled ends, linteled entrances and aumbries. These may either be late examples of shielings huts, or perhaps shepherds bothies (Costello, 2015). A similar progression has been noted in Uig parish on the Isle of Lewis where the late nineteenth-century huts, dated by their appearance on the second edition OS map, are rectangular instead of round, with raised floors and shelving away from the entrance passage that ran across one end of the hut.

Size of huts

The ALS recorded 1129 huts in upland areas of Scotland in the six years from 1990 to 1995 that were presumed to date to the medieval or post-medieval periods (RCAHMS, 1990–95). The mean size was 3.98 m (+/- 1.65 m) by 2 m (+/- 0.7 m) in breadth within walls usually of stone, 0.9 m in thickness, with proportions of two to one, broad enough in which to lie transversely. Most of these huts were stone walled, but 20% of them were recorded as turf or earthen. In addition there was also a separate class of turf-covered earthen mounds, often dimpled, suggesting a collapsed turf-walled and covered hut, of which 728 were recorded, giving a total of 51% that were built of turf (Figure 5.2). These mounds had an average external size of 6.9 m in length by 3.2 m in breadth overall which compares well with the huts that could be measured internally, but some on Skye had developed into large mounds that were as much as 25 m across, suggesting many successive phases of use and reuse, or perhaps multiple huts placed close together. The mounds are, it is argued, huts that have collapsed in on themselves following abandonment, and were built up year on year as they were repaired. Indeed, Malcolm MacSween, who excavated a mound on Trotternish, Isle of Skye, argued they are in effect 'tells' that are mixtures of stone used in the footings, turf in the walls and peat ash from the fires maintained in them during use (Gailey & MacSween, 1961). One area of Scotland bucked the trend, with larger turf huts. Liddesdale, which is situated on the border with England, had huts with a mean internal length of 5.1 m and breadth of 2.3 m, casting doubt on their interpretation as shieling huts, especially where no midden was present (Dixon, 2009: 36).

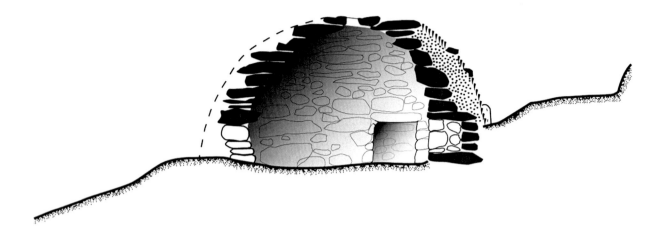

Section x-x¹

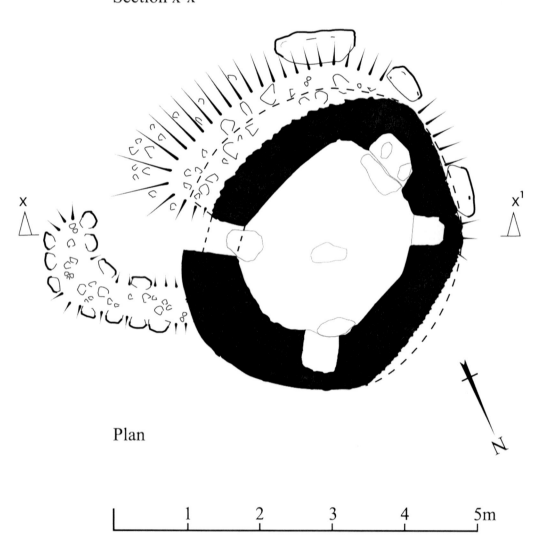

Plan

Figure 5.1. Plan and section of beehive hut at Airigh a' Sguir, Uig, Isle of Lewis: stone with turf covering
Source: © Crown Copyright Historic Environment Scotland: DP196313

Figure 5.2. An example of a dimpled turf shieling mound at Airigh na Stainge, Argyll and Bute
Source: © Crown Copyright Historic Environment Scotland: DP102615

Evidence of function

On the mainland by far the greater number of huts had a single compartment, but extensions to one end or other occur often enough, providing for separations of function. Architecturally, the stone-built huts provide the most information about their internal use. In the Central Highlands, features include stone hearth backs, often placed just inside the entrance, and aumbries, or stone shelving for storage. The beehive huts of the Western Isles have particularly good shelving, probably for milk products (e.g. Figure 5.1, Canmore, 2016: id 72083). A frequent arrangement in the Central Highlands was for the hut to be accompanied by a small round or squarish hut about 1 m across internally, too small for anything but storage. It has been suggested that this was the dairy and it may be a variant on the stone shelving found in many other huts in the area. Outshots or extensions to the main structure may be another method of achieving this, while in the case of figure-of-eight huts the cell off the main chamber could have served the same purpose.

Size of groups

Shieling huts are generally found in groups. The size of the groups varies considerably, but groups are the norm. In the forest of Mar, Aberdeenshire, the groups of huts ranged from two or three up to 40 huts, as at one extensive group on the Allt Connie burn. At Auchingaich in Dumbartonshire there is a group of 55 huts, which have been immortalised by the paintings of William Donnelly at the end of the nineteenth century (Donnelly, 1900a, b). At the Riol in a side valley of Glen Lyon to the north of Ben Lawers, this number is exceeded in a large group of some 80–90 huts. These sites are at the larger end of the scale. Small groupings of some 3–12 huts are more normal (Figure 5.3), which may be seen wherever shieling sites occur, be they on the Isles of Lewis, Skye and Eigg in the west (RCAHMS, 1993a, 2003); in the Strath of Kildonan, Sutherland, in the north (RCAHMS, 1993b); on the slopes of Ben Lawers, Perthshire (Boyle, 2003), in upper Strathdon and the forest of Mar, Aberdeenshire, in the Central Highlands (RCAHMS, 1995; Dixon & Fraser, 2007); Menstrie Glen, Stirlingshire, in the Central Lowlands

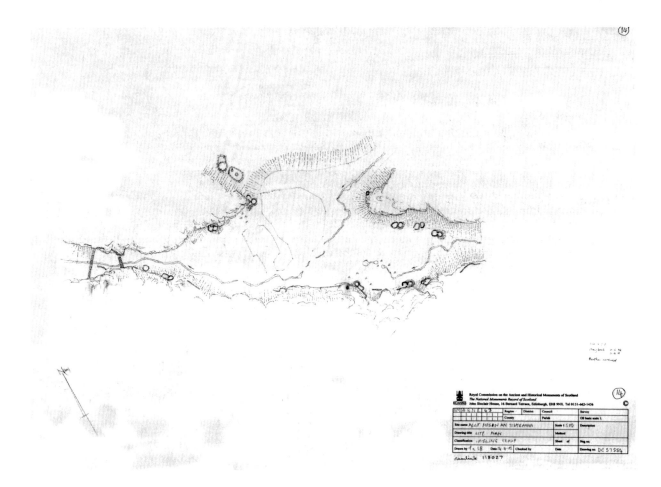

Figure 5.3. Site plan of shieling hut group at Bidein An Tighearna, Isle of Eigg (note the figure-of-eight huts and the dispersed layout)
Source: © Copyright Historic Environment Scotland: GV006076

(RCAHMS, 2008); or in Liddesdale, Roxburghshire, bordering England (Dixon, 2009). Larger groups may be the result of additional townships gaining access to a grazing, adding to the community of summer inhabitants; the reallocation of grazings leading to new huts being built, or even estate policy such as that on North Lochtayside requiring tenants to move to new sites every five years to improve the growth of the grass. All of these policies were found by Harrison working on the summer grazing practised by the North Lochtayside tenants in the seventeenth and eighteenth centuries (Harrison, 2016).

Morphology of groups

What is striking about shieling groups is the dispersed distribution of the huts. There is usually a discrete distance of *c.* 20–30 m between the huts. Indeed, the clustered array of multi-cellular stone huts depicted by Captain Thomas on the Isle of Lewis is quite exceptional (Thomas, 1862–63, 1870), and best paralleled by structures on Hirta (Gannon & Geddes, 2015: 59–63).

The normal spacing of huts may be seen wherever they are found, as in the range of places listed the paragraph above. It is also invariable that they are situated beside a burn, near to a source of water, on outwash fans of tributary burns, or spread along the banks and terraces of a burn. They still frequently reveal themselves by the rich green grass beside them. The enrichment of the soil around the huts was a well-known benefit, encouraging the idea of cultivation adjacent to the huts (Bil, 1990).

Paleo-Environmental Proxy Evidence

One of the more difficult issues relating to shielings and transhumance is how to assess the effects of summer grazing practices on the local flora. Tipping (2010: 192) has tried to define what transhumance is in floral terms as 'landscape elements that were reserved exclusively for pasture', but this definition does not indicate that shieling huts were built, only that there was no evidence of those species related to cultivation in the catchment area. Pollen analysis is a proxy tool rather than a direct one. However, it is possible to target pollen-bearing bogs and to measure the quantity of different species that grow in the vicinity of shieling huts or shieling pastures at dates when the practice is documented. Two rather different vegetational histories have been outlined through pollen analysis. These may be described broadly as highland and upland (the latter being the hilly areas of the Lowlands). The two main exponents of this approach are Richard Tipping and Althea Davies. Tipping worked on Ben Lawers in the Central Highlands and in the Bowmont Valley of the Cheviots on the Scottish border. Davies has worked on a site at Leadour on the south side of Loch Tay, opposite Ben Lawers, and in the Breamish Valley of the Cheviots, which although in Northumberland, encapsulates many of the same issues that are present in the north Cheviots (Davies & Dixon, 2007; Davies & Hamilton, 2007; Tipping, 2010; Tipping et al., in prep.).

The Ben Lawers data (Tipping et al., in prep.) has been presented from two cores at the top edge of the furthest extent of cultivation where there were some turf huts, Leacann Ghlas (*c.* 320 m a.s.l.), and a core at the high shielings, Tarmachan (*c.* 540 m.a.s.l.). The key finding here is that there was still extensive woodland cover in the early medieval period (*c.* 400–1100), possibly with a wood pasture management, well suited to maintaining the woodland and providing summer grazing. This regime began to break down at the end of the medieval period, with an increase in heather and the clearance of the woodland habitat in the fifteenth and sixteenth centuries, suggesting that grazing pressures increased and there were traces of occasional cultivation, possibly by occupants of shieling huts. Tipping has argued that this heather increase is related to selective summer grazing and shieling occupation in particular. However, slightly later than this in the seventeenth century, the droving of cattle to lowland markets is documented and the leasing of highland grazing that conflicted with that of shieling practice. Since the floral environment changes before the documented events described here, Tipping concludes that it is an intensification of shieling practice as population pressures increased from mid-sixteenth century onwards that is the cause of the vegetational change not droving. Althea Davies's work at Leadour has recorded similar late- and post-medieval changes (Davies & Hamilton, 2007).

The model from Bowmont Valley in the Cheviot Hills of the English/Scottish Borders in particular is rather different in that it starts from a different base, one that is already cleared of any significant woodland cover in later prehistory. The medieval period saw a growth in evidence for cultivation in the high medieval period from about AD 1100 to 1300, in what is essentially a grassland environment. In the late medieval period the higher grazings changed to a heather and grass environment, as heathland increased through increased precipitation and impeded drainage leading to peat formation rather than increasing grass cover, and increased *calluna* heath. It is further argued that muir burn was a standard practice in managing the heather. This was presumably intended to improve grass growth. However, the summer-grazing regime, whether through ranching by monastic stock or transhumance by villagers, gave the heather more opportunity to recover at the expense of grass, since sheep prefer grass and did not eat the heather (Tipping, 2010). Tipping suggested that this grazing regime also increased soil acidification. Modern all-year-round grazing tends to have a different result, with grass replacing heather through prolonged preferential sheep grazing. Davies and Dixon, working in the Breamish Valley, Northumberland, have interpreted a similar vegetational history and have argued for a similar summer-grazing regime, giving way to intensive sheep grazing in the modern period (Davies & Dixon, 2007).

EXCAVATIONS OF SHIELING HUTS

While it might be thought the poverty of the material culture of excavated shieling huts precludes any useful archaeological benefits in excavating them, the presence of midden heaps provides an excellent potential source of evidence for material culture and dating, as well as modern techniques of environmental analyses. To date, only the recent work by the Ben Lawers Historic Landscape Project has explored this potential (see below).

Huts were dug by antiquarians at the end of the nineteenth century at Auchingaich (MacRitchie, 1900: 277–8), where it would seem from the drawings they hit upon a corn-drying kiln rather than a hut, or else it was the base of a corbelled cell of a figure-of-eight stone hut, which would be unusual on the mainland – possible corn-drying kilns have been recorded at shieling sites, such as in Glen Derry in the Cairngorms (RCAHMS, 1995). In the 1920s, Fairbairn, a local antiquarian enthusiast, excavated some huts at Slackshaw Burn, near Muirkirk, once part of a hunting forest belonging to the Stewarts. These produced late medieval pottery and little else, providing a rough date for the shieling huts that were built with turf and stone (Fairbairn, 1927). Malcolm MacSween's excavation of a turf hut on the Isle of Skye, which was carried out as part of his study of rural settlement on Trotternish, was not materially productive and undated, and it is his contribution to understanding the tell-like build-up over time of turf huts that was his most significant legacy (Gailey & MacSween, 1961). From then until the last 25 years little interest was shown in excavating shielings, while the focus of rural settlement studies, if there was any, was on clearance townships and the lack of identifiable medieval buildings in the Highlands.

In the 1990s, this began to change quite dramatically with the small-scale excavations at Torrin on the Isle of Skye (Canmore, 2016: id 11454). Here Martin Wildgoose, who had been recording shieling huts as part of his landscape surveys in advance of afforestation, decided to sample the huts. He partly excavated two huts, one of which was radiocarbon dated to the late medieval period (AD1430 +/- 70), while the other one also produced evidence under the floor of an earlier phase of turf structure of early medieval date and a pit underneath it which indicated Iron Age activity on the site (AD1020 +/- 50 and 269BC +/- 60 respectively). The possibility of earlier origins to transhumance was now brought into focus, although the settlement context for the earlier phases of occupation remains questionable in such a small-scale excavation. The later huts were figure-of-eight type, and one of the two cells in the hut excavated in 1991 had traces of burning which the excavator suggested was an indication of a kiln for smoking fish or cheese (Wildgoose, 1991; Canmore, 2016: id 11454). Materially it has to be said the sites were not productive.

At the other end of the country in 2009, the Peebles Archaeology Society that had been engaged in an exploration of illicit whisky still sites stumbled on a shieling hut at Camp Shiel, near Traquair in the Southern Uplands – itself a generic shiel place-name (Winchester, 2011). This site lies in the forest of Traquair, a royal forest based on the nearby castle. The Society recorded several still sites on the burn, as well as retting ponds for flax production, and excavated one. Nearby there was what appeared to be a hut that was expected to be for the workers of the whisky still. Instead it proved to be a late medieval hut with interleaved stone and turf walls, dated by three radiocarbon determinations ranging from AD 1290–1400. It was a slightly irregular rectangle on plan, some 4 by 2 m internally, with a hearth in the middle of one side, with flat stones against the wall for a fireback, and, unusually, an entrance in one end. Materially it was once again lacking in any artefacts (Durham, 2017; Figure 5.4).

In the Central Highlands, following pilot excavations at Edramucky on Ben Lawers from 1996–99, the Ben Lawers Historic Landscape Project, a multidisciplinary field project that ran from 2001–2005, provided an excellent chance to explore shieling huts and other rural settlement structures scientifically. Huts at three different sites were excavated: Edramucky Burn, Lawers Burn and Kiltyrie. The first two were high-level shieling groups at over 600 m above sea level, while those at Kiltyrie were turf buildings and huts on the edge of a cultivated area, shown by the presence of rig and furrow at an altitude of 350 m. These excavations are by far the most productive exploration of shieling huts to date. Five huts at Edramucky, two at Lawers

Burn and three huts and two larger buildings at Kiltyrie were dug, covering a range of structural types, both turf and stone-based (Atkinson, 2016).

At the Edramucky site, huts were distributed on both sides of the Edramucky Burn and four different types were sampled: oval turf huts, a rectangular stone hut, a small round stone hut 1.8 m across, and what appeared to be a figure-of-eight hut (Canmore, 2016: id 24495). Three huts were excavated on the north of the burn. One was a turf-walled hut measuring 3.4 m by 2.5 m within banks 1 m in thickness that produced a late medieval date of cal AD 1453–1651 and displayed traces of compacted turves. A rectangular stone-walled hut which produced similar dates, cal AD 1470–1650, measuring 5.5 m by 1.6 m with a drystone inner face and turf outer face, was extended, probably in the eighteenth century. Three sherds of late medieval redware pottery were recovered from a trackway next to an oval stone structure that was modified in the seventeenth century with the addition of a second rectangular chamber to the south south-east composed of a turf wall faced with stones, making the figure-of-eight shape, which was itself then enlarged and turned into an enclosure in the eighteenth century. Of a group of three turf huts on a moraine bank on the south of the burn, comprising two beside a smaller one, both the larger huts were radiocarbon dated from the late fifteenth to the mid-seventeenth centuries, and overlay mesolithic deposits. Five sherds of unglazed sandy textured pottery were recovered from one of the turf huts, similar to sherds found in the excavations at Kiltyrie that were dated to the twelfth century – much earlier than the radiocarbon date. A horseshoe and a prong from a rake or fork were also recovered.

At the Lawers Burn site, two huts were investigated in a group of 60 situated on a terrace on the north of the burn: one a rectangular hut with turf mounds either side of the entrance, the other an amorphous turf and stone structure (Canmore, 2016: id 24546). The walls of the better preserved hut were stone faced on the inside and clad with turf on the outside. It was dated to after the fifteenth century by a radiocarbon date from the old ground surface under the walls. The hut had a later phase of reuse with a fire pit that was dated by radiocarbon to the eighteenth century (cal AD 1720–1890) and by post-medieval reduced-ware pottery of a later eighteenth century date, but radiocarbon determinations from the floor of the hut suggest the main phase of occupation dated from the fifteenth to the seventeenth centuries. The external banks of earth outside the hut may have been built up from carbonised material from midden deposits and rakings from the fire pit (Figure 5.5). A division into a sleeping area in the west end and a living area in the east was suggested. There was a fire pit and upright slabs

Figure 5.4. Late medieval hut at Camp Shiel Burn, Scottish Borders; excavated by Peebles Archaeology Society
Source: © Copyright Joyce Durham

that acted as a fireback just inside the entrance at the east end, with an adjacent smooring pit for keeping the fire going overnight. Stone discs measuring 0.18 m in diameter that had been heated were recovered; they may have been for baking bannocks (flat unleavened bread), which the six-row barley grain from the site suggests could have been made from bere barley. Alternatively it has been suggested the unheated discs may be cheese presses, although roof weights have also been proposed. The author suggested a lean-to roofing structure in the absence of post settings (Atkinson, 2016).

At the Kiltyrie site, which lay just beyond the head-dyke of Kiltyrie township, two turf huts, one overlying an earlier rectangular turf structure were excavated (Canmore, 2106: id 283820). These huts were oval on plan while the earlier structure was an open-ended peat store which itself overlay an earlier subrectangular turf building of medieval date. The excavator argued that the two huts were wig-wam structures with turf and stone walls based around three splayed poles (Atkinson, 2016; Figure 5.6). While one of the oval huts is probably post-AD1300 in date, the other has radiocarbon determinations that give a date of c.1400–1450. A larger subrectangular turf-walled building a short distance to the west produced radiocarbon dates of c.1150–1300 (Figure 5.7); it has been argued that this was a permanent turf-walled building with a central stone hearth like the early medieval buildings excavated at Lair (Strachan & Sneddon, 2014) and Pitcarmick, also in Perthshire. Indeed, the structure is comparable in date and size with the medieval Phase 4 building constructed over the west end of the Pictish long house in Area E at Pitcarmick, with a radiocarbon date of c.1040–1220 (Carver et al., 2012).

In summary, shieling huts and shieling activity in this part of the Central Highlands of Perthshire around Lochtayside date to the late and post-medieval periods, c.1450–1775, post-dating a short-lived medieval phase of permanent occupation at the lower-lying Kiltyrie site, where larger subrectangular turf-walled buildings were uncovered (Atkinson, 2016). There was no chronological difference between the turf huts and the turf and stone huts, but the earlier medieval structures at Kiltyrie, whether permanent or not, were turf-walled.

Figure 5.5. Post-medieval stone and turf-walled hut at Lawers Burn, North Lochtayside, under excavation by GUARD
Source: © Copyright Piers Dixon

Figure 5.6. Two late medieval turf huts overlying an earlier turf structure at Kiltyrie, North Lochtayside, under excavation by GUARD
Source: © Crown Copyright Historic Environment Scotland. DP215336

Figure 5.7. Medieval turf-walled hut at Kiltyrie, North Lochtayside, excavated by GUARD
Source: © Crown Copyright Historic Environment Scotland: DP215134

Conclusions and Discussion

First of all there seems little doubt that the thousands of shieling hut groups documented by field observation are the summer shelters of people practising transhumance. However, as with permanent settlement, identifying sites that are high medieval (AD 1100–1350) in date as opposed to late- and post-medieval, has not been very successful. Second, the documentary sources, although tricky to interpret, suggest that there is a well-established exploitation of summer pastures and transhumance throughout Scotland in the medieval period that carries on into the better documented post-medieval period in the Highlands, while becoming extinct in the Lowlands in the seventeenth century. Third, medieval references to shielings may refer to other activities that may require temporary shelters, not just transhumance as defined here. And fourth, the upland bias in the distribution of shieling huts may be the result of the draining and conversion to arable of lowland bogs and pasture during the agricultural improvements, removing perhaps the remains of low-lying shieling huts that are suggested above by the medieval documentation.

Alternatively, the summer movement of cattle and sheep hinted at by the monastic records of Melrose Abbey and other monasteries may be the explanation of some of the *scalingas* in the medieval documents that Winchester argues are about summer grazings not shelters (Winchester, 2011: 132), and not just by the monasteries but by royal and lay estates too. The use of coastal grazings in summer may be seen in this light as preparing cattle and sheep for market and export in the growing medieval burghs like Perth, Roxburgh, Berwick and Aberdeen, as hides, woolfells and wool. This still leaves the large-scale production of cheese to be explained and the detached grazings belonging to davochs in the heart of the Cairngorms. It would seem to me that this would require shelters and we should be finding structures dating to the high medieval period.

There is at least a *prima facie* case for earlier medieval sites to be found under later huts – a possibility suggested by the evident longevity of the tell-like turf mounds found at many highland sites and by the eleventh-century turf hut under the later shieling hut at Torrin, Isle of Skye. However, the Ben Lawers experience does not indicate that locating this early evidence will be readily successful in the central Highlands, where most of the summer grazing is high level. On North Lochtayside, the evidence suggests that the exploitation of the high shielings did not develop until the late and post-medieval period, probably under increased grazing pressures. The turf building at the lower, Kiltyre, site that is interpreted as a permanent building on grounds of size could be an early shieling hut despite its larger size. Indeed, this is one of the options suggested for the medieval reuse of one end of the early medieval long house site at Pitcarmick. What this and the other medieval turf huts at that site indicate is that the settlement pattern in Highland Perthshire was changing at the beginning of the second millennium AD. Indeed, it should not be expected that grazing patterns and transhumance were part of a static system that did not evolve in response to external factors such as the new burgh markets in the twelfth century.

This changing settlement pattern, particularly in the high shielings, is supported by the palaeoenvironmental data from the Central Highlands of Perthshire described by Tipping and Davies (Davies & Hamilton, 2007; Tipping et al., in prep). That from the Cheviots in the Scottish Borders which suggests summer grazing made its impact on the landscape from the fifteenth century, is less well supported by the archaeological evidence since few shieling huts have been located or excavated in the Bowmont Valley. Indeed, the interpretation depends as much on summer herding regimes by the monasteries as it does on transhumance.

The discrepancy between the documentary and excavated evidence for the medieval period is based upon a rather random sample of excavated sites, except for the campaign on Ben Lawers. Until more huts in a variety of locations have been excavated and further complementary pollen analysis has been done, Ben Lawers should not be seen as the model for the Highlands let alone the Lowlands which appears to have had its own trajectory in the dynamics of transhumance.

Different trajectories of periods of use should be expected in different areas. Our research designs need to take into account that transhumance could develop and change at different times in different places. Techniques of excavation need to employ scientific methods that can address the question of the functionality of the huts. Only at Ben Lawers has there been a body of material culture assembled from the totality of huts excavated to provide any depth of analysis relating to the economy of transhumance, and this was as much from the artefactual evidence as the environmental data. Finally, the Shieling Project opens up an immediate prospect of further exploration of this relatively neglected topic (The Shieling Project, 2016).

NOTE

1 Arbroath Abbey, unspecified lands in Angus, AD 1178; unspecified lands of the earl of Strathearn in Perthshire, AD 1172–3; Walter de Berkeley, Inverkeilor, Angus, AD 1173–1180; Walter Gifford, Tealing and Powgavie, Angus, AD 1196–c.1201; Humphrey Berkeley, Balfeith, Kincardineshire, AD 1198–9.

REFERENCES

Atkinson, J. ed. 2016. Ben Lawers: an archaeological landscape in time. *Scottish Archaeological Internet Reports*, 62. Available at: http://archaeologydataservice.ac.uk/archives/view/sair/contents.cfm?vol=62 (accessed 2016).

Barrow, G.W.S. ed. 1971. *Regesta Regi Scottorum, ii: The Acts of William I, 1165–1214.* Edinburgh: Edinburgh University.

Bil, A. 1990. *The Shieling 1600–1840: The Case of the Central Scottish Highlands.* Edinburgh: John Donald.

Bil, A. 1992. Transhumance place-names in Perthshire. *Proceedings of the Society of Antiquaries of Scotland*, 122:383–402.

Boyle, S. 2003. Ben Lawers: an improvement period landscape on Lochtayside, Perthshire. In: S. Govan, ed. *Medieval or Later Rural Settlement: Ten Years On.* Edinburgh: Historic Scotland, pp. 17–30.

Burnett, G. & Stuart, J. eds. 1878. *The Exchequer Rolls of Scotland*, 1. Edinburgh: H. M. General Register House.

Callander, R. 1987. *Patterns of Landownership in Scotland with Special Reference to Aberdeenshire.* Finzean: Haughend.

Canmore. 2016. The National Record of the Historic Environment of Scotland. Available at: https://canmore.org.uk/.

Carver, M., Barrett, J., Downes, J. & Hooper, J. 2012. Pictish byre-houses at Pitcarmick and their landscape: investigations 1993–5. *Proceedings of the Society of Antiquaries of Scotland*, 142:145–99.

Costello, E. 2015. Post-medieval upland settlement and the decline of transhumance: a case-study from the Galtee Mountains, Ireland. *Landscape History*, 36:47–69.

Davies, A.L. & Dixon, P.J. 2007. Reading the pastoral landscape: palynological and historical evidence for the impacts of long-term grazing on Wether Hill, Ingram, Northumberland. *Landscape History*, 29:35–45.

Davies, A. & Hamilton, A. 2007. 'Written in the hills': an environmental history project in the Scottish uplands. *History Scotland*, 7(3):25–32.

DES, 2013. *Discovery and Excavation in Scotland*, New Ser. 13 (2012). Edinburgh: Archaeology Scotland.

Dixon, P.J. 2009. Hunting, summer grazing and settlement: competing land use in the uplands of Scotland. In: J. Klapste, ed. *Medieval Rural Settlement in Marginal Landscapes, Ruralia VII.* Turnhout: Brepols, pp. 27–46.

Dixon, P.J. & Fraser, I. 2007. Chapter 8: the medieval and later landscape. In: RCAHMS, *In the Shadow of Bennachie: A Field Archaeology of Donside.* Edinburgh: Society of Antiquaries of Scotland Monograph, pp. 137–214.

Dodgshon, R.A. 1981. *Land and Society in Medieval Scotland.* Oxford: Clarendon Press.

Donnelly, W.A. 1900a. The mound dwellings of Auchingaich. *Journal of the British Archaeological Association*, New ser. 6:363–67.

Donnelly, W.A. 1900b. Scene of the newly discovered mound dwellings Auchingaich Glen. *Illustrated London News*, 13 October 1900.

Durham, J. 2017. Camp Shiel Burn, Traquair: Report on Survey and Excavations 2007–2010. http://www.peeblesarchsoc.org.uk/Reports/Camp_Sheil_Report.pdf (accessed 2017).

Fairbairn, A. 1927. Notes on excavation of prehistoric and later sites at Muirkirk, Ayrshire, 1913–1927. *Proceedings of the Society of Antiquaries of Scotland*, 61:283–84.

Fawcett, R. & Oram, R. 2004. *Melrose Abbey.* Batsford: London.

Gailey, A. & MacSween, M.D. 1961. Some Shielings in North Skye. *Scottish Studies* 5:77–84.

Gannon, A. & Geddes, G. 2015. *Hirta*. Edinburgh: Royal Commission on the Ancient and Historical Monuments of Scotland.

Gilbert, J. 1979. *Hunting Reserves in Scotland*. Edinburgh: John Donald.

Harrison, J. Unpublished a. Glen Devon: A report for Royal Commission on the Ancient and Historical Monuments of Scotland. National Record of Historic Environment Scotland, MS 1155/2.

Harrison, J. Unpublished b. Liddesdale: A Report for Royal Commission on the Ancient and Historical Monuments of Scotland. National Record of Historic Environment Scotland, MS 1155/3.

Harrison, J. 2016. Post-medieval Loch Tay: Exploiting the margins. The documentary evidence. In: J. Atkinson, ed. *Scottish Archaeological Internet Reports*, 62:210–13.

Innes, C. ed. 1837. *Registrum Episcopatus Moraviensis, e pluribus codicibus consarcinatum circa A.D.MCCCC. Cum continuatione diplomatum recentiorum usque ad A.D.MD-CXXIII*. Edinburgh: Bannatyne Club.

Keith, G.S. 1811. *A General View of the Agriculture of Aberdeenshire*. Aberdeen: Board of Agriculture.

MacRitchie, D. 1900. Hut-circles at Auchingaich Glen, Dunbartonshire. *The Antiquary*, 36:377–78.

MacSween, M.D. 1959. Transhumance in North Skye. *Scottish Geographical Magazine*, 75:75–88.

Mercer, R.J. 1980. *Archaeological Field Survey in Northern Scotland, 1976–79*. Occasional Paper no. 4. Edinburgh: University of Edinburgh.

Miller, R. 1967. Land use by summer shielings. *Scottish Studies*, 11:193–221.

NLS, Survey of Assynt. Survey of Assynt by John Hume in 1774 deposited in the National Library of Scotland. Available online at: http://maps.nls.uk/estates/assynt/ (accessed 2016).

NRS, GD 24. Papers of the Family of Stirling Home Drummond Moray of Abercairny deposited at the National Records of Scotland, Edinburgh.

Oram, R. 2011. *Domination and Lordship: Scotland 1070–1230*. Edinburgh: Edinburgh University Press.

Pennant, J. 1776. *A Tour in Scotland and a Voyage to the Hebrides, 1772*. Chester: John Monk.

RCAHMS. 1990–95. Unpublished Field Databases of the Afforestable Land Survey of the Royal Commission on the Ancient and Historical Monuments of Scotland, National Record of the Historic Environment of Scotland, MS 731/1–14, 16–18.

RCAHMS. 1990. *North-East Perth: An Archaeological Landscape*. Edinburgh: Royal Commission on the Ancient and Historical Monuments of Scotland.

RCAHMS. 1992. *An Inventory of the Ancient Monuments of Argyll*, 7. Edinburgh: Royal Commission on the Ancient and Historical Monuments of Scotland.

RCAHMS. 1993a. *Waternish: An Archaeological Survey*. Edinburgh: Royal Commission on the Ancient and Historical Monuments of Scotland.

RCAHMS. 1993b. *Strath of Kildonan: An Archaeological Survey*. Edinburgh: Royal Commission on the Ancient and Historical Monuments of Scotland.

RCAHMS. 1995. *Mar Lodge Estate: An Archaeological Survey*. Edinburgh: Royal Commission on the Ancient and Historical Monuments of Scotland.

RCAHMS. 2002. *But the Walls Remain'd: the First Edition Survey Project, 1995–2001*. Edinburgh: Royal Commission on the Ancient and Historical Monuments of Scotland.

RCAHMS. 2003. *Eigg: The Archaeology of a Hebridean Landscape*. Broadsheet 12, Edinburgh: Royal Commission on the Ancient and Historical Monuments of Scotland.

RCAHMS. 2008. *'Well Shelterd & Watered': Menstrie Glen, a farming landscape near Stirling*. Edinburgh: Royal Commission on the Ancient and historical Monuments of Scotland.

Ross, A. 2003. The Province of Moray, c.1000–1230. Unpublished PhD, University of Aberdeen.

Ross, A. 2011. *Kingdom of Alba c.1000–1130*. Edinburgh: John Donald.

Strachan, D. & Sneddon, D. 2014. Lair Excavations. *Discovery and Excavation in Scotland*, New Series 14:157.

Taylor, S. & Markus, G. 2012. *The Place-Names of Fife, 5, Discussions, Glossaries and Edited Texts*. Donington: Shaun Tyas.

The Shieling Project: An Airigh. www.theshielingproject.org/ (accessed 2016).

Thomas, F.W.L. 1862–63. Notice of beehive houses in Harris and Lewis. *Proceedings of the Society of Antiquaries of Scotland*, 3:127–44.

Thomas, F.W.L. 1870. On the primitive dwellings and hypogea of the Outer Hebrides. *Proceedings of the Society of Antiquaries of Scotland*, 7:193–95.

Thompson, W. 2012. Skaill names in Orkney. *Northern Scotland*, 3(1):1–15.

Tipping, R. 2010. *Bowmont: An Environmental History of the Bowmont Valley and the Northern Cheviot Hills, 10000 BC–AD 2000*. Edinburgh: Society of Antiquaries of Scotland.

Tipping, R., McCulloch, R., McEwan, A., Tisdall, E. & Tyler, A. In prep. Medieval and post-Medieval summer transhumance in the central Scottish Highlands and its impacts on upland landscapes. Unpublished paper in preparation, Stirling University.

Wildgoose, M. 1991. Torrin, Isle of Skye. *Discovery and Excavation in Scotland 1991*. Edinburgh, pp. 45–46.

Winchester, A. 2011. Seasonal settlement in Northern England: Shieling place-names revisited. In: R. Silvester & S. Turner, eds. *Life in Medieval Landscapes: People and Places in the Middle Ages*. Macclesfield: Windgather Press, pp. 125–49.

CHAPTER 6

Ethno-geoarchaeological study of seasonal occupation
Bhiliscleitir, the Isle of Lewis

PATRYCJA KUPIEC AND KAREN MILEK

INTRODUCTION

Despite being amongst some of the most visible field remains seen within upland locations in Scotland, shielings as a subject of archaeological investigation have received relatively scant attention, and the focus of research has been mainly on their broader role as a part of economic or folk studies in the post-medieval period (Raven, 2012). Limited work was undertaken in the late 1950s and '60s (Gaffney, 1959; Gaffney, 1967; MacSween, 1959; MacSween & Gailey, 1961), and this interest was kept alive by ethnographic work by Fenton (1978, 1980), and the historical study of shielings in Perthshire by Bil (1989, 1990a, 1990b).

Recent archaeological surveys by Raven (2012) on South Uist and by Branigan (2002) and Branigan and Foster (2002) on Barra and Bishop's Isles recorded numerous putative shieling sites with different shapes, sizes, and numbers of the structures visible on the ground, and different materials utilized to construct them, which all hint at different functions and chronologies of the sites. The earliest phase of one of the sites targeted for test-pit excavation on Barra was dated to the Viking Age on the basis of the artefactual assemblage, which was comparable to that of the Viking-Age farm of Kilpheder on South Uist (Branigan & Foster, 2002). The site was interpreted as a shieling due its marginal location, small size, and a shieling place-name, Gunnary, the shieling (Gaelic *airigh*) of Gunnar (Norse male name). However, since this is the only putative early medieval shieling site identified in the whole of the Outer Hebrides to date, we lack the wider picture of the importance of the shieling economy, the lengths and nature of occupation, or the developments, changes, and transitions the tradition underwent through time.

The decline of the shieling system in the Outer Hebrides coincided with a period of reorganization of the highland and island farming society, which involved the clearance of townships to form consolidated sheep farms, and the subsequent emigration of large numbers of crofters. As a result of these socio-agrarian changes the practice of summer transhumance was largely abandoned in the Western Isles by the nineteenth century, with the exception of the Isle of Lewis, where it survived until the early 1950s. The long survival of the shieling tradition on the Isle of Lewis, with ethnographic sources detailing the use of local shieling sites, provides an excellent opportunity for archaeological investigation of historically known shielings to broaden the repertoire of possible interpretations of the archaeological record, and improve the identification and interpretation of past shieling sites.

The criteria used to identify shielings in Scotland and the North Atlantic region vary significantly, and are often quite arbitrary, and based only on their presumed marginal location, place-names of unknown date and provenance, and atypical structural remains or artefactual assemblages (Love, 1981; MacSween & Gailey, 1961; Mahler, 2007; Matras et al., 2004). The unchanging function of putative shieling sites is also often assumed, with no consideration made for possible shifts in the type and duration of occupation in response to changing economic, social, and cultural conditions, both on local and regional scales. This paper argues for the need for a more rigorous approach to shieling identification, using high-resolution geoarchaeological methods, which have the potential to identify punctuated occupation at archaeological sites (Kupiec et al., 2016). To establish an analytical and interpretive framework that would be suited to investigate occupation surfaces at seasonally occupied sites, this paper presents the results of an ethnoarchaeological study of floor deposits at the nineteenth- to mid-twentieth-century shieling site at Bhiliscleitir on the Isle of Lewis, and compares them to floor formation processes, site maintenance practices, and activity areas described by an informant who stayed at the site.

THE SITE OF BHILISCLEITIR

The Bhiliscleitir shieling settlement is situated 4 km from the road end at Skigersta on the east coast of Ness, Isle of Lewis, in north-west Scotland (Figure 6.1). The site consists of a group of eight structures, which are arranged in close proximity and in a circular pattern (Figure 6.4). In total, 14 ruins of structures/ rooms are still visible on the ground. The presence of a

© 2018 European Association of Archaeologists

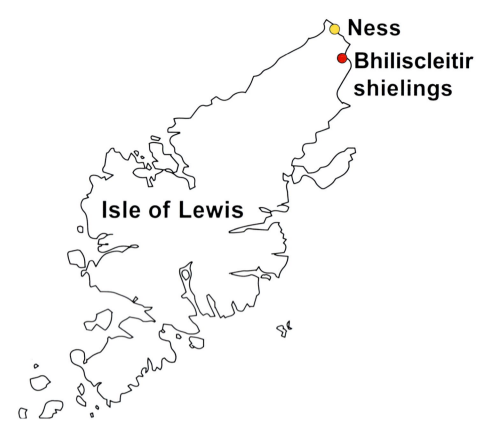

Figure 6.1. Map of the Isle of Lewis showing the location of the Bhiliscleitir shieling settlement and Port of Ness

slight mound underlying the ruins suggests that the site went through multiple phases of use, which resulted in a build-up of occupation deposits, and/or earlier ruins.

The site functioned as a shieling settlement until the 1950s, and at least since the mid-1800s, as it is marked on the first edition OS map (1853), but little is known about its chronology beyond that. The collapse deposit overlying the final occupation deposit in Structure 10 captured two bottle stoppers with a stamp and logo of W.M. Younger's Brewery in Edinburgh, and a bottle stopper of the same type was excavated from the collapse deposit in Structure 11. These bottle stoppers can be dated to pre-1960, when W.M. Younger's Brewery merged with Newcastle's Tyne Brewery to form Scottish & Newcastle Ltd. According to Anne Macleod of *Comunn Eachdraidh Nis* (Ness Historical Society), even after the site ceased to be used as a shieling settlement it remained a popular summer camping destination, especially for local teenagers (Anne Macleod pers. comm.). The site was visited by the photographer Dan Morrison in 1936, and his two published photographs depict the inside of one of the shielings (Figure 6.2), and two women standing in the front of a shieling hut (Figure 6.3). The first photograph captures the internal features and furnishings of the shieling in the final years of its use: a side bench, a wardrobe placed on what appears to be a bed of moss, a small table with milking utensils placed underneath and next to it, a central fire with a kettle over it, plates and mugs, a bed platform in the background, and walls covered with wallpaper. The latter photograph shows the stone foundation of the walls, and the roof construction, with the multiple strips of turf piled one on top of the other.

In 2012, Catriona Macdonald interviewed Mary Campbell, who spent three summers at Bhiliscleitir as a young girl. Her recollections record the internal organization of the shieling in detail:

> It was the old traditional house on a smaller scale. And when you came in on the door and you brought the cattle in at night . . . they would go down to the right, one in his own, and the other in his own, and you went up to the living quarters to the left, in our house. . . . The bed . . . was made out of blocks of turf with a stone front. . . . And then the mattress . . . the heather . . . and you could change the heather as often . . . if the heather got flat and uncomfortable you could put fresh heather in. . . . And there was also lawn turf on benches, the grass side up . . . like cushions. There was a cupboard for the basins, for the milk storage, the milk that turned sour to make the cream and the cheese and things. There was a cupboard for the milk at the end of the bench, . . . and there were shelves on top with the crockery.

Figure 6.2. A student visits a shieling at Filiscleitir, Ness
Source: Dan Morrison (1936)

Figure 6.3. Three Ness women prepare to leave the shieling
Source: Dan Morrison (1936)

In 2007 Chris Barrowman surveyed the site for the Ness Archaeological Landscape Survey. The survey recorded the dimensions, internal organization, and the state of preservation of the shieling ruins. A topographic survey was also undertaken, and its results clearly show the extent of the mound on which the site is located (Figure 6.4, from Barrowman, 2015: 99).

Methodology

The archaeological work at the site presented here was undertaken in 2013. Two c. 0.7 x 1.5 m assessment trenches (TP1 and TP2) were opened in Structure 10, and one smaller, c. 0.7 x 1.2 m assessment trench (TP3) was opened in Structure 11 (Figure 6.5). Based on the visible internal features in Structure 10 (a possible side bench and bed platform), and in Structure 11 (possible side troughs), the functions of these structures were tentatively interpreted as a dwelling and a byre respectively. After the removal of the overlying turf and stone collapse layers, the test trenches were excavated to the bottom of the uppermost occupation deposits to expose the floor layers resulting from the last phase(s) of the structures' use. Due to time constraints, TP2 was only excavated down to the layer of stone collapse, which exposed and permitted recording of a side bench.

The uppermost deposits in TP1 contained debris from the collapse of the structural elements, including window pane glass and pieces of corrugated iron. The deposits directly underlying the turf and root mat in both structures were also rich in finds, mainly glass bottles and fragments of other vessels. These probably represent the post-abandonment use of the shieling huts as temporary shelters.

Two floor deposits were exposed in TP1, both of which were compact and contained small quantities of charcoal flecks. However, the lowermost deposit was sandier, suggesting that it may represent a short

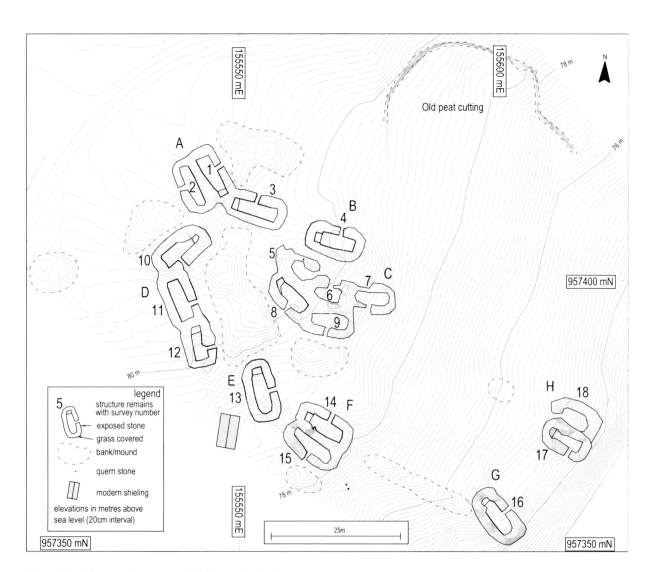

Figure 6.4. Topographic survey of shielings at Bhiliscleitir
Source: After Barrowman (2015: 99)

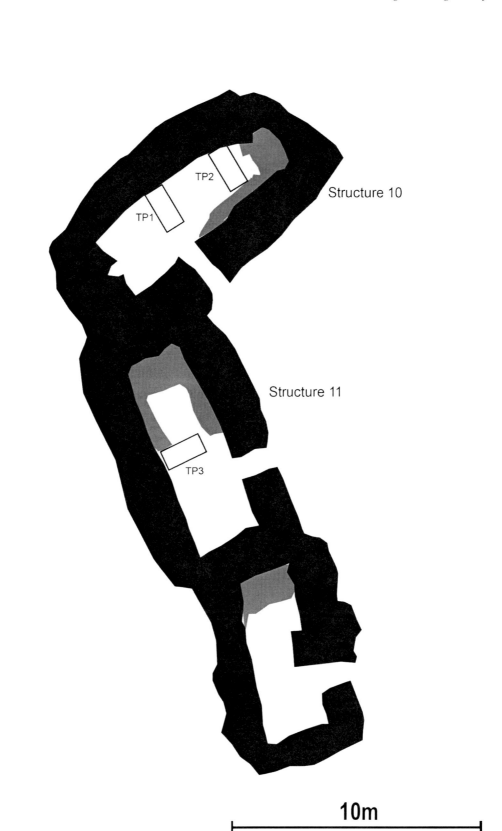

Figure 6.5. Plan of Structures 10–12 at Bhiliscleitir, showing the location of Test Pits 1–3; internal features are highlighted in grey

abandonment phase when windblown sand could accumulate in the structure. Both deposits formed above a cobbled surface constructed with small rounded pebbles. In Structure 11, a very humic layer was deposited on the cobbled surface. The texture and the composition of this deposit suggested a very high organic content, which was interpreted in the field as a possible dung layer, in line with the preliminary interpretation of the structure's main function as that of an animal shelter. The cobbled surface exposed in this building was different from that excavated in TP1. It appears that in Structure 11 less care was taken to select cobbles of uniform size, roundness, and smoothness, and the cobbles were not arranged in any particular pattern. It is possible that the cobbled surface in Structure 10 had more of an aesthetic function, creating a nice, even floor surface, and in Structure 11 it was inserted to aid drainage and improve the maintenance, and perhaps even a seasonal removal, of very organic floor deposits. The cobbled surface in Structure 11 was thick, and consisted of at least two distinct cobbling phases, with the older phase resting on a sterile yellow sandy loam, which can be interpreted as the natural soil underlying the site.

Excellent preservation of the ruins, and the well-documented last phase of their use, makes the Bhiliscleitir shielings settlement an excellent case study to explore the nature of summer transhumance on the Isle of Lewis, and to test the potential of microscopic investigation to detect seasonal occupation. Undisturbed block samples for micromorphological analysis were taken through the stratified sequence of occupation deposits by pressing aluminum sampling tins into the sections cutting through the uppermost occupation deposits in TP1 and TP3. One sample was taken from the NE section of the assessment trench in Structure 10 (sample 6), and one sample from the N section of the assessment trench in Structure 11 (sample 4). Two more samples were taken from the top of the floor layer, context 004, exposed in Structure 10 (samples 1–3). Sample 3 was kept for sub-sampling, and was not thin sectioned. The thin sections were made following the procedures outlined in French (2015: 97–100), and micromorphology descriptions followed the terminology in Bullock et al. (1985) and Stoops (2003). The results of the ethno-geo-archaeological study of the floor sediments in two structures at Bhiliscleitir are presented below.

The ultimate composition of any archaeological floor deposits is determined by a complex set of interactions between a wide range of processes, including intentional and accidental anthropogenic impacts, which are idiosyncratic in nature and do not follow a set of known rules. With the passage of time a range of natural physical, chemical, and biological post-depositional processes, such as bioturbation, the decomposition of organic matter, and the diagenesis of anthropogenic materials also alter the composition of floor deposits (Courty et al., 1989; FitzPatrick, 1993; Rolfsen, 1980; Schiffer, 1996). Since many different human-induced and natural processes can result in similar microfabrics and pedofeatures, a rigorous framework for analyzing the composition of floor deposits is essential to separate cultural and natural floor formation processes, and to investigate the nature and duration of activities that had originally taken place at shieling sites.

Numerous ethnoarchaeological and experimental studies of floor formation processes address the problem of equifinality (e.g. Boivin, 2000; Macphail et al., 2004; Milek, 2012), but no such research had been previously conducted at seasonally occupied pastoral settlements. Shielings would have been subjected to a unique set of cultural practices associated with their temporary occupation and pastoral function, which could have had an effect on the formation and preservation of the archaeological floor deposits at these sites. For example, according to historical and ethnographic sources on shieling structures in the Hebrides, it was once common for a turf roof of a shieling hut to be repaired or re-erected on an annual basis, usually shortly before the start of a shieling season (Campbell, 1896; MacKenzie, 1904). This could have involved either maintenance work on the roof, which would have disintegrated substantially during the cold season in the unheated shieling hut, or occasionally erecting a new roof. If similar practices were used in earlier centuries, the periodically roofless shieling structures could have acted as wind-blown sediment traps, which would have significantly altered the composition of their floor deposits, resulting in accumulation of aeolian sand during the periods of seasonal disuse. Temporary abandonment could have also resulted in weathering and partial disintegration of organic structural elements, such as turf walls and wooden roof supports, with organic material contained within them accumulating on the floors. Moreover, features that are considered characteristic for trampled occupation surfaces, such as increased compaction, a platy microstructure with characteristic horizontal cracks (planar voids), and the horizontal orientation of occupation debris such as bone, ash, plant tissues, small artefacts, etc. (Davidson et al., 1992), might be less pronounced in floor deposits of seasonally occupied structures, where trampling would have been significantly less than in permanently occupied structures.

RESULTS

The micromorphological description will begin with a general overview of the main characteristics of the deposits captured in thin section, while more detailed descriptions of the separate samples, and tables summarizing the most important micromorphological characteristics, are presented in the following sections. The basic mineral composition of the occupation deposits captured in thin sections from the Bhiliscleitir shielings settlement was dominated by very fine-coarse sand (63–2000 μm in size). The fine fraction (<50 μm) was mainly composed of amorphous organic matter; that is, organic matter that had decomposed to such an extent that it no longer had any visible cell structures and could not be identified optically. Two deposits (layers 4.1 and 4.4) were dominated by clay. The layers that were interpreted as occupation deposits tended to be associated with very fine-fine sand grains (63–100 μm in size), which most likely represent the dominant grain size of the underlying substrate. Due to reworking by soil fauna some layers appeared to be composed of two or more distinctive fabrics. In these mixed, heterogeneous deposits fine sand grains dominated more compact and organic-matter-rich areas, which may be indicative of disturbed floor deposits. The fine sands in the floors at Bhiliscleitir could have made their way into the buildings through a number of routes, including the trampling and reworking of the substrate underlying the floors, trampling soil in from outside the buildings, and the gradual disaggregation of the turves in the roof.

Some deposits captured in thin section had compositions dominated by larger-sized, medium-coarse sands (250–1000 μm), with few anthropogenic inclusions. Two possible explanations for the formation of these deposits were considered: 1) intentional spreading of sand on the floors as a maintenance practice to keep them level and clean, and 2) wind deposition during the periods of the structures' disuse/abandonment. The practice of spreading sand on the earthen floors was reported in some nineteenth- and early twentieth-century travel accounts from the Outer Hebrides (e.g. Gordon, 1937), and it was suggested for archaeological sites such as the Iron Age wheelhouse at Cnip, on Lewis, and the wheelhouse at Sollas, on South Uist (Armit, 1996: 144–46). The ethnographic accounts, however, suggest that the intentional spreading of ash or dry powdered peat was more common than clean sand alone (see Kissling, 1943: 86 and MacKenzie, 1905: 402 for floor maintenance practices in the Outer Hebrides, and Milek, 2012: 134–35 for comparable practices in Iceland). Furthermore, these floor maintenance practices were reported for permanently occupied farms, and not for shieling settlements. Mary Campbell also does not mention the practice of spreading sand on the floors in her interview, and instead she states that 'the floor was earth, compressed, . . . and some clay' (Campbell in Macdonald, 2012: 79). Her recollection was corroborated by microscopic analysis of thin sections from Structure 10, which captured a distinctive clay floor. A natural windblown accumulation of medium-coarse sand is therefore a more plausible explanation for the formation of these deposits. The transport and deposition of coarser sand particles would require high wind velocity and/or a close sand source, as material coarser than 500 μm in diameter is normally transported over the ground surface by saltation and creep. Mean monthly wind speeds on the Isle of Lewis in December/January are about 16 knots (18 mph), though daily mean wind speeds over 30 knots (35 mph) with gusts in excess of 50 knots (58 mph) are not uncommon. The highest gust recorded at Stornoway in recent years was 98 knots (113 mph) in

February 1962 (Comhairle nan Eilean Siar Contaminated Land Inspection Strategy, n.d.). The Bhiliscleitir shielings settlement was exposed to the elements, and close to a sandy beach, which would have made these medium and coarse sand accumulations possible.

These deposits could be classified as 'loamy sands'; that is, deposits composed of 70–85% sand grains. Due to the high degree of bioturbation their dominant microstructure (the size, shape, and arrangement of grains, aggregates, and voids) was a channel microstructure, in which earthworm channels were the most frequent type of void. An intergrain microaggregate microstructure, in which the solid components of the sediments are a mixture of single grain particles such as sand grains and small aggregates of amorphous organic matter, was also present in these sand deposits, but it was never recorded for floor deposits (described below). Since all sand layers were embedded in a fine compact matrix of amorphous organic matter, the distribution of individual particles in relation to finer material (the coarse/fine related distribution) was such that the finer material filled all the spaces between the coarser constituents, a so-called porphyric or embedded coarse/fine related distribution. There was also a localized enaulic coarse/fine related distribution, in which small aggregates of fine material (in this case mostly amorphous organic matter and soil fauna excrements) were present in the interstitial spaces between sand grains. These sand layers were captured between floor deposits, and they may be indicative of periods when the site was temporarily abandoned, and windblown sand could accumulate on their floors. Some of these deposits contained higher quantities of amorphous organic matter, which might be associated with the weathering of the turf-built structural elements in the unheated buildings during abandonment phases.

Since all deposits captured in thin section were subjected to reworking by soil fauna, which resulted in relatively high quantities of granular soil fauna excrement in the form of minute aggregates of fine material, and numerous channels and vughs (irregularly shaped voids), floor layers could not be recognized only on the basis of the characteristics considered typical for trampled floors: increased compaction, a dominant platy microstructure, the presence of horizontal planar voids, and/or the horizontal orientation of occupation debris (Courty et al., 1989; Davidson et al., 1992). The high organic matter content noted in these occupation surfaces made them highly palatable to soil fauna, which probably encouraged post-depositional bioturbation. While pockets of the original fabric showed the characteristic horizontal orientation of components, in most areas the original organization of the sediment had been significantly altered. In the case of heavily bioturbated sediments like these, it would be difficult to distinguish horizontal bedding in the field, and high-resolution techniques, such as micromorphological analysis, might be the only way to identify the original organization and composition of the deposits. Only two floor layers captured in thin sections from Structure 10 at Bhiliscleitir, layers 4.8 and 5.13, preserved a localized platy microstructure, with horizontal planar voids indicative of downward compaction by trampling. The occupation surfaces were therefore recognized on the basis of increased quantities of amorphous organic matter and plant and wood tissues, and inclusions of charred organic remains. Increased quantities of wood and plant tissues may be interpreted as waste products from food processing and consumption, fuel storage, weathering of the turf and wood built roof, animal fodder, craft activities, or the wide variety of plant- and wood-made artefacts and furnishings, while charred organics may be indicative of accidental or intentional spreading of hearth waste on the floors.

Layers 4.2, 4.8, 4.10, and 5.11 also captured small fragments of pottery, including an unfired nodule of clay with fine sand temper, which suggests that small-scale ceramics manufacture could have taken place at Bhiliscleitir. According to Mary Campbell there was a source of clay near the site (Campbell in Macdonald, 2012: 79). Interestingly, according to oral tradition, Hebridean crogan pots cradled in moss were used to carry milk back from the shielings to the townships (Cheape, 1992–93, 2010). Crogan manufacture was carried almost exclusively by women who historically were also the keepers of shielings. The pots were glazed with milk and fired on the hearth, which would have made it possible to produce these during the annual stay at the shieling. Sample 6 also captured a fine layer composed of amorphous organic matter, fragmented grass phytoliths and grass pollen, and phosphatic nodules, which could be interpreted as a deposit of herbivore dung. TP1, from which this sample was taken, was located in the central part of Structure 10, and away from the bed platform, so it might have been an area where cows were kept overnight, as pointed out by Mary Campbell.

In less bioturbated areas the components in floor deposits were horizontally/sub-horizontally oriented, which suggests that they accumulated on a gradually accruing occupation surface. In contrast to the wind-blown sand deposits they had a low degree of sorting of their components. The thickness of floor deposits varied from 3 mm to 25 mm, and their composition was dominated by sandy silt loams, and silt loams (with the quantity of sand varying between 10% and 40%). Finer sand grains were also more abundant in these deposits. Where floor layers were less affected by soil fauna reworking, they were compacted, and displayed a porphyric coarse/fine related distribution, which is often associated with trampled occupation surfaces (Davidson et al., 1992).

STRUCTURE 10

Sample 1

Sample 1 was taken from context 004 exposed in TP1. Context 004 was described in the field as a very organic, dark reddish brown silt loam deposit, which contained small quantities of charcoal flecks. It was interpreted as a floor surface that formed during the last occupation phase of Structure 10. During the microscopic analysis this final occupation phase could be subdivided into three distinctive floor surfaces (Table 6.1).

The uppermost floor deposit, layer 4.1, was a thin and compact layer composed almost entirely of clay and fine- to medium-sized sand grains (Figure 6.6). The so-called birefringence fabric of this layer was different to that of other deposits captured in thin section at Bhiliscleitir. The birefringence fabric describes the interference colours of the fine material observed between crossed polarizers. While the majority of the deposits had an undifferentiated b-fabric, with no observable interference colours, this layer displayed a stipple-speckled b-fabric, with randomly oriented and isolated striations of clay. In contrast to some clay features studied on other archaeological sites, in which the clay created a mono-striated (single orientation) b-fabric (e.g. hearth constructions in Milek & French, 2007), the orientation of the clay striations in the upper floor layer of Structure 10 suggests that clay was applied to the floor in a random fashion, without any dominant direction. The layer was very clean and it contained very few inclusions, with 2–5% amorphous organic matter, and trace quantities of minute fragments of charred organics. These were rounded, and since the sample was taken close to the wall they may relate to maintenance practices, such as sweeping, which can result in accumulations of fragmented and rounded inclusions by the wall. Mary Campbell does not mention any specific floor maintenance practices ('we hadn't any cleaning to do, just your bed'), but it is possible that older women performed these. The inclusions tended to cluster towards the surface of the clay floor, with some found deeper in the layer, suggesting downward movement by trampling. The presence of a clay floor in Structure 10 confirms that pride was taken in maintaining an aesthetically pleasing shieling structure, and it corroborates well with the photographic record, which attests to well-maintained internal spaces at the Bhiliscleitir shieling settlement.

The underlying layer, 4.2, was composed of 40–50% amorphous organic matter, 10–20% plant tissues, 10–20% wood tissues, 2–5% charred peat, 2–5% charred amorphous organic matter, and trace quantities of charcoal, charred plant, and grass phytoliths (Table 6.1). Mary Campbell mentions a range of plant and wood furnishings used at Bhiliscleitir, such as heather bedding, a wooden bedstead, turf 'cushions' for side benches, and driftwood for shelves and for the roof construction: 'they had to have driftwood, as much as they could afford, to stop the turf from falling in'. The layer also contained trace quantities of fungal sclerotia, which are typical for topsoils, and are also frequently found in areas with increased organic matter content (FitzPatrick, 1993: 221). It could have derived from the roof turves, or it could be associated with high quantities of organic inclusions captured in the layer.

Charred organic remains, which originated in a hearth, may have been spread across the occupation surface by trampling, or sweeping across the floor. The deposit also captured a poorly fired clay fragment, with a fine- to medium-sized sand temper (Figure 6.6). It had a sharp boundary typical of fired ceramics, but it did not display isotropism, which is characteristic for ceramics fired at a temperature of 800–850°C for sustained periods of time. Localized darkened rims around the pore spaces instead suggest a firing temperature of around 500°C or less (Gregor, 2014), which is consistent with the temperature range of a domestic hearth. The chaotic structure of the matrix and temper suggests a hand-modelled vessel rather than a wheel-thrown one. The presence of low-temperature fired ceramic fragment in the hearth deposits may be indicative of small-scale pottery manufacture in Structure 10. This is supported by the presence of an unfired clay nodule with a similar sand temper.

The lowermost floor layer captured in sample 1, 4.3, was a fine layer of charred organic material in an amorphous organic matter matrix. The layer contained 10–20% charred peat, 5–10% charcoal, 2–5% charred amorphous organic matter, and trace quantities of charred plant tissues, which attest to a variety of fuel sources utilized by the inhabitants of this shieling hut. The deposit also captured 2–5% plant tissues, and 5–10% wood tissues, some of which contained phlobaphene (a reddish coloured phenolic substance), and probably represent wood bark. This layer can be interpreted as intentional or accidental spreading of the hearth waste on the floor. No calcareous ash accumulations were preserved in the layer, but they could have been leached down the profile with percolating rainwater.

Sample 1 did not capture an abandonment phase between layers 4.2 and 4.3, and they most likely belong to the same occupation phase. Layer 4.1 may represent a separate occupation phase, during which a clay floor was constructed in Structure 10. Fine-medium

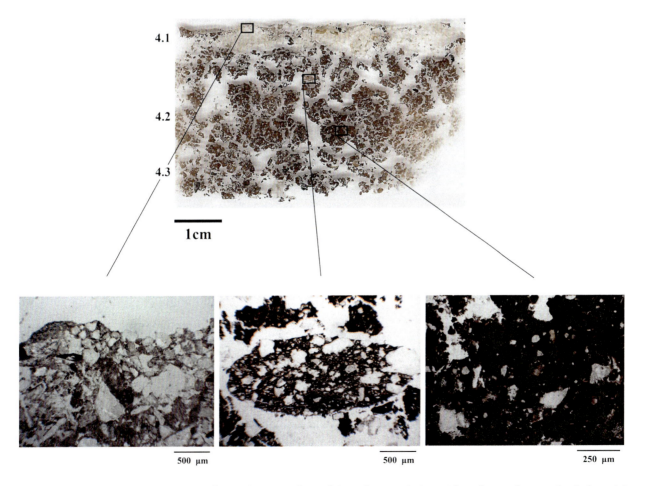

Figure 6.6. Thin section 1, showing clay floor in layer 4.1; clay nodule with temper in layer 4.2; and zone of compaction in layer 4.3

sand grains captured in this layer might derive from the clay source, as it is unlikely that clay would have been processed extensively prior to applying it to the floor. Mitchell notes in his 1880 description of crogan pottery manufacture by one Mrs. Macleod: 'the clay she used underwent no careful or special preparation. She chose the best she could get, and picked out of it the larger stones, leaving the sand and the finer gravel which it contained'. It is likely that a similar low degree of processing would be applied to clay used to construct a floor of a seasonally occupied dwelling. It is also possible that the medium-sized sand grains represent a fine windblown layer, which had originally been deposited between the two occupation phases, but which was re-mixed by bioturbation.

Sample 2

Sample 2 was taken to the east of sample 1, and it captured a sequence of occupation deposits associated with context 004. Layers 4.4–4.6 corresponded well with layers 4.1–4.3, which were captured in sample 1, and they can be interpreted as representing the same phase of occupation, with no pronounced differences in the composition of floor deposits, which would point to distinctive activity areas in Structure 10 (see Table 6.1).

The lowermost deposit captured in sample 2, layer 4.7, was significantly enriched in amorphous organic matter (40–50%), and it contained 5–10% wood tissues, 2–5% fungal sclerotia, and trace quantities of plant tissues and grass phytoliths. The layer also captured accumulations of charred peat and charcoal, but all of these inclusions were more fragmented than the charred organic matter captured in the layer above. Layer 4.7 also contained one fragment of uncharred peat, which may be indicative of fuel storage inside the structure. This deposit can be interpreted as a disturbed floor layer, which is likely to have formed during the same occupation phase as the overlying deposits.

Sample 6

Sample 6 was taken from the NE section of TP1, close to the wall of Structure 10. It captured a sequence of

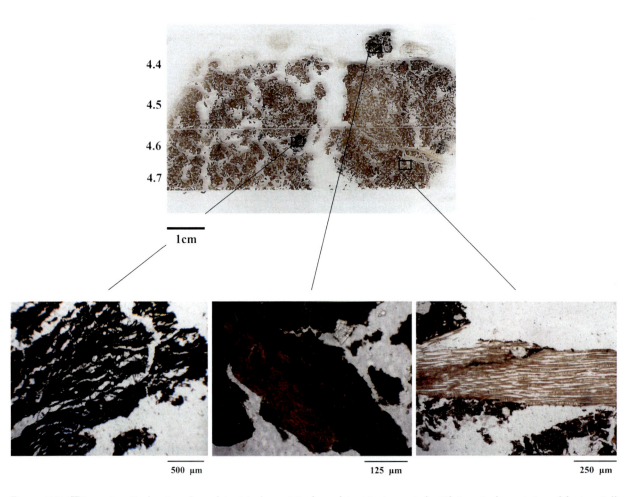

Figure 6.7. Thin section 2, showing charred peat in layer 4.6; charred peat impregnated with iron in layer 4.4; and horizontally bedded plant tissues in layer 4.7

occupation surfaces alternating with sand deposits, and mixed deposits composed of at least two distinctive fabrics. These deposits corresponded with the two contexts described in the field: context 004, and context 005 (Table 6.1). Context 005 was described in the field as a very dark brown, compact, organic silt loam deposit. It was sandier than context 004, and it also appeared to contain smaller quantities of charcoal flecks. It was provisionally interpreted as an occupation surface mixed with a deposit of windblown sand indicative of a short abandonment phase. The deposits captured in sample 6 could be subdivided into distinctive sub-phases: layers 4.8, 4.10, and 5.15 (mixed deposits), layers 4.9, 4.12, 5.9, 5.11, and 5.13 (occupation surfaces), and layers 4.11, 5.8, 5.10, 5.12, and 5.14 (sand accumulations).

The uppermost layer captured in this sequence, layer 4.8, was a disturbed sandy silt loam deposit, which appeared to be composed of two distinctive fabrics. The dominant fabric was associated with very fine-fine sand grains, and it was enriched in amorphous organic matter (40–50%). It also contained inclusions of 10–20% charred peat, 10–20% charcoal, 2–5% charred amorphous organic matter, 2–5% wood tissues, and trace quantities of phytoliths, diatoms, and plant tissues. The quantities of charred organic remains increased towards the top of the layer, and in places they were horizontally bedded, perhaps hinting at a very disturbed lensing. It appears likely that this lens formed when hearth waste was spread onto the floor. 2–5% rubified ferrous nodules and trace quantities of diatoms may be residues of this peat ash deposit. This fabric also captured a fragment of low-fired ceramic (Figure 6.8). The chaotic character of its matrix and temper suggests a hand-modelled vessel, perhaps of crogan tradition. This organic-rich fabric was associated with a range of anthropogenic inclusions, and it preserved zones of compaction with localized planar voids. Based on these characteristics it can be interpreted as a disturbed floor surface. The second fabric was composed of medium-coarse sand grains, which accumulated towards the bottom of the layer. This accumulation of well-sorted sand grains might be indicative of a lens of aeolian sand deposited during a short abandonment phase.

The lower mixed deposit was also classified as a sandy silt loam, and its composition was similar to layer 4.8. The dominant fabric of layer 4.10 was also enriched with 40–50% amorphous organic matter, and it captured significant quantities of charred organics, including 20–30% charred peat and 5–10% charcoal. The layer also contained trace quantities of plant tissues, phytoliths, diatoms, ferrous nodules, and phosphatic nodules. High quantities of charred peat towards the top of the layer suggest the presence of a disturbed lens composed of hearth waste material. A fragment of a low-fired ceramic was captured in an earthworm channel cutting through this layer, and it is likely that it was translocated

from it. Despite reworking by soil fauna, which resulted in a dominant channel microstructure, the layer preserved zones of compaction, and its overall porosity was relatively low at 20–30%. The second fabric was associated with accumulations of medium-coarse sand with few inclusions. The two fabrics can be interpreted as indicative of a disturbed occupation surface mixed with a lens (or lenses) of windblown sand, possibly related to a short abandonment phase.

Sample 6 captured two other occupation surfaces, which alternated with mixed deposits and sand layers. Layer 4.9 was a fine deposit composed of a dense matrix of amorphous organic matter (50–60%), with inclusions of 5–10% fragmented phytoliths, 2–5% wood tissues, and trace quantities of diatoms and plant tissues (Figure 6.8). The layer also contained 5–10% phosphatic nodules. Its composition is indicative of a deposit composed almost entirely of herbivore dung. Its degree of compaction, low porosity (10–20%), and a localized massive microstructure suggest compaction by trampling. TP1 was opened in the central part of Structure 10, and it appears that in this phase of occupation it was the location of the boundary between the part of the building used to house livestock and the main residential space. The deposit also captured inclusions of fragmented charred organic remains embedded in this compacted organic matrix at random angles, which suggest that they could have been trampled into the layer, probably by the inhabitants moving between different parts of the structure. This 3 mm thick layer of herbivore dung may relate to a short episode when cattle were kept in the central space, and the layer had no equivalents in other samples taken from Structure 10. One might speculate that sample 6 captured a slight change in the use of the internal space in Structure 10, which involved the byre end encroaching on the central part of the structure.

The final occupation surface captured in sample 6, layer 4.12, was composed of 40–50% amorphous organic matter, with significant quantities of charred organics: 10–20% charred peat, 2–5% charred amorphous organics, and trace amounts of charred plant and charcoal. Most components were horizontally oriented, which suggest that they accumulated on a gradually accruing surface; however, the layer also experienced some disturbance by soil fauna, with the largest fragment of charred peat vertically oriented due to bioturbation.

Layer 4.11, which separated the final occupation surface, 4.12, from mixed deposit 4.10, was a very fine lens of moderately sorted medium-coarse sand. It contained 10–20% amorphous organic matter, 2–5% minute fragments of charred amorphous organics, and trace quantities of fragmented charred peat and phytoliths. This layer may be indicative of a short abandonment phase, but its poor sorting, and the presence of relatively high quantities of amorphous organic matter, charred

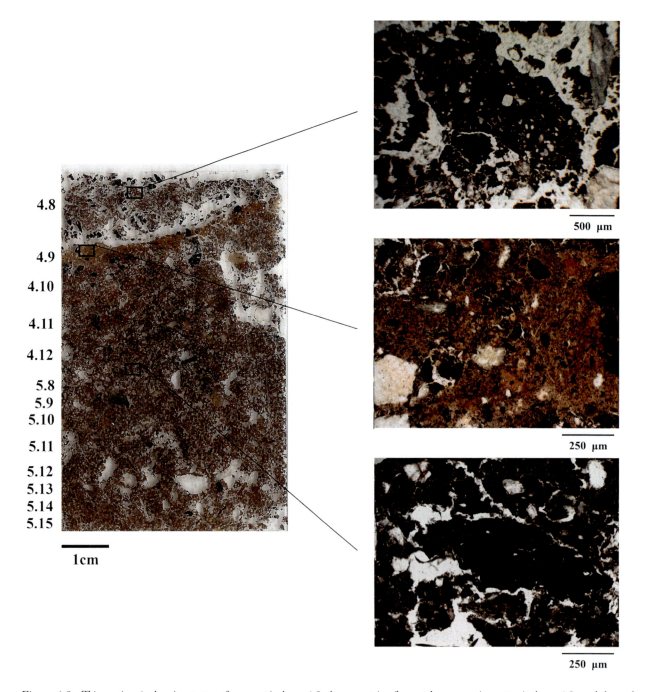

Figure 6.8. Thin section 6, showing pottery fragment in layer 4.8; dense matrix of amorphous organic matter in layer 4.9; and charred peat in layer 4.12

organic matter, and other organic inclusions, suggest that it might have formed as a result of the weathering of structural turves in the unheated shieling structure, with possible additions of aeolian sand.

Context 005 was also captured in this thin section as a sequence of sand layers alternating with occupation deposits, but it was less disturbed than context 004, and it contained only one mixed layer composed of more than one fabric. The uppermost layer in this sequence, 5.8, was a fine lens of moderately sorted medium-coarse sand. It contained 20–30% amorphous organic matter, 2–5% charred peat, 2–5% charred amorphous organic matter, and trace quantities of charcoal, plant tissues, and phytoliths. Charred organic remains captured in the layer were very fragmented, and minute in size. The sandy loam deposit was quite compact with an overall porosity of 10–20%, and it appeared embedded in a fine organic matrix, which suggests that it was subjected to post-depositional trampling. This sand deposit may be indicative of a short abandonment phase, with inclusions derived from the weathering of structural turves.

Sample 6 captured three more sand deposits, layers 5.10, 5.12, and 5.14, which were similar in composition to layer 5.8, but contained lower quantities of amorphous organic matter. These sand lenses were thin (with the maximum thickness of 4–7 mm), and only partially preserved. They were composed of 70% moderately sorted medium-coarse sand, and 10–20% amorphous organic matter. The lowermost lens, layer 5.14, also contained small quantities of very fine gravel. In all three deposits the sands that dominated the layers were embedded in a fine organic matrix, and displayed a localized single-spaced porphyric coarse/fine related distribution, which suggests that they might have been subjected to trampling. All lenses contained up to 2–5% very fragmented charred amorphous organic matter and charred peat, and trace quantities of plant tissues and phytoliths. Layers 5.10, 5.12, and 5.14 can be interpreted as abandonment phases between three distinctive occupation phases. These deposits were composed of windblown medium-coarse sand grains, mixed with the material associated with the weathering of the turf-built walls and roof (organic matter, sand grains of different sizes, plant tissues, and phytoliths). The minute charred organics might be also windblown in origin, or they could be associated with soot weathered from the ceiling and walls.

Between these sand accumulations sample 6 captured three distinctive occupation surfaces, layers 5.9, 5.11, and 5.13. These varied in thickness from 5–8 mm, and were classified as sandy silt loam deposits, with the coarse fraction dominated by fine-medium sand grains. They contained higher quantities of sand grains than occupation deposits associated with context 004, an observation also made in the field due to the 'sandier' feel of this layer during hand texturing. All three deposits were very similar in composition, and they contained 40–50% amorphous organic matter, up to 2–5% plant tissues, and trace quantities of phytoliths. The quantities of charred organic matter varied slightly between the layers, with 10–20% charred peat, 2–5% charcoal, 2–5% charred amorphous, and trace quantities of charred plant tissues in 5.9, 5–10% charred peat, 5–10% charcoal, 2–5% charred amorphous organic matter, and trace quantities of charred plant tissues in 5.11, and 10–20%, 2–5% charcoal, and 2–5% charred amorphous organic matter in 5.13. Peat appeared to be the main source of fuel during all of these occupation phases, supplemented by low quantities of wood. Layer 5.11 and 5.13 also captured small fragments of pottery, with the appearance typical of low-temperature fired ceramics (non-isotropic between crossed polarizers, with some charring around pore spaces). These two ceramic fragments also displayed a poorly oriented matrix and temper ranging from very fine-medium sand, which, together with a firing temperature range of a domestic hearth, suggest that they represent handmade vessels. The bioturbation of all three layers resulted in dominant channel and vughy microstructures, and a porosity of 20–30%. However, all deposits also contained localized zones of compaction in which there was a dominant single-spaced porphyric coarse/fine related distribution. Layer 5.13 also captured localized planar voids, which suggest downward compaction by trampling. In some places the horizontal orientation of components was preserved, but generally they were randomly oriented due to reworking by soil fauna. Layers 5.9, 5.11, and 5.13 can be interpreted as relatively short-lived occupation deposits. Their relatively uniform composition suggests that there was no major change in internal organization of activities (at least in the central space) during these three occupation phases, which might relate to three shieling seasons.

The final deposit captured in this thin section was a very disturbed layer, which appeared to be mixed with the overlying sand lens 5.14. When areas dominated by medium-coarse sand grains were excluded from the visual estimates, the main fabric was similar to other floor deposits captured as a part of this context. Layer 5.15 was composed of 40–50% amorphous organic matter, and it contained inclusions of 10–20% charred peat, 2–5% charcoal, 2–5% charred amorphous organic matter, and 2–5% wood tissues. Horizontal orientation of components was preserved in zones of compaction, which also displayed a single-spaced porphyric coarse/fine related distribution. However, outside of these compacted areas, the layer was affected by intensive bioturbation, which resulted in the random orientation of inclusions, a porosity of 30–40%, and channel and vughy microstructures. Layer 5.15 can be interpreted as a disturbed occupation surface, locally mixed with material from windblown sand lenses.

STRUCTURE 11

Sample 4

Sample 4 captured context 008, which was described in the field as a very humic deposit, which formed on top of a cobbled surface. Its texture and composition suggested a very high organic content, and it was noted that the layer was very similar in appearance to dung-rich layers typical of animal byres. The cobbled surface in this assessment trench was very thick, and consisted of at least two distinctive layers. A cobbled surface is often, though not exclusively, associated with buildings that housed animals, as it improves drainage and makes it easier to remove animal waste.

To an extent this preliminary interpretation was corroborated by thin section analysis. Sample 4 captured a thick deposit, which was dominated by amorphous organic matter at 50–60%. It also captured 5–10% plant tissues, 5–10% wood tissues, and 2–5% grass phytoliths (Figure 6.9). The quantities of the latter are probably

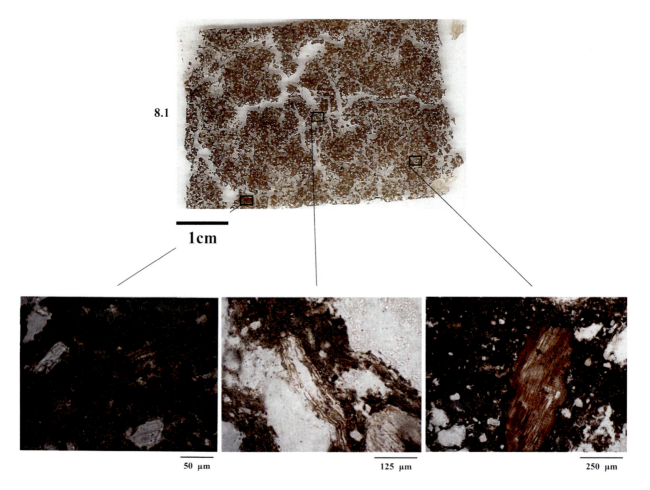

Figure 6.9. Thin section 4, showing grass phytoliths in dense amorphous organic matter matrix; plant tissues; and wood tissues

underestimated as in places they appeared obscured by the dense organic matrix, and were therefore difficult to identify. The layer also contained 2–5% fungal sclerotia, which are commonly found in organic soils. The deposit also captured very fragmented charred organic remains, including 2–5% charred peat, and 2–5% charred amorphous organic matter. These were randomly oriented and minute in size, and could have been wind-deposited. Layer 8.1 can be interpreted as a turf-collapse layer, most likely representing the collapse of the turf roof. This corroborates well with Mary Campbell's account, which noted that roofs were not seasonally removed at the Bhiliscleitir shieling settlement during the last years of its use. Elongated grass phytoliths, plant tissues, and amorphous organic matter are indicative of the decomposed grassy component of turf, while fungal sclerotia and the sandy component of layer 8.1 are most likely derived from the soil held by grass roots. Trace quantities of woody tissues captured in the layer may be the remains of wooden structural elements that collapsed with the roof. The layer also contained small amounts of charred organic matter, which could be indicative of soot accumulation in the roof turf. This collapse deposit accumulated directly on the cobbled surface, and there was no evidence for floor layers below it. It is possible that these were removed during the last season of occupation, which would support the interpretation of this part of Structure 11 as an animal shelter, with dung deposits frequently cleaned out of the cobbled floor.

Discussion

The sequences of ephemeral occupation surfaces alternating with thin windblown deposits, which were identified in thin sections 1, 2, 4, and 6, could not be identified in the field with the naked eye; however, slight differences in textures were recognized during excavation, and fine lensing was suspected. It would not be possible to identify these layers without the aid of high-resolution microscopic analysis. While the occupation deposits could be recognized on the basis of high quantities of anthropogenic inclusions, horizontal bedding of these components, and increased compaction, they were very ephemeral, especially in comparison to floor sediments studied micromorphologically at permanently occupied settlements (e.g. Milek, 2005; Milek, 2012). They also lacked well-developed platy

Table 6.1 Summary of features observed in thin sections 1–2, 4, and 5–6 at Bhiliscleiter shieling settlement

Sample	Layer and microstratigraphic unit	Maximum thickness in thin section (mm)	Structure				Groundmass					Organic and biomineral inclusions													Pedofeatures			
			Porosity	Microstructure	Horizontal orientation	Degree of sorting	Birefringence fabric	Nature of fine material	Soil texture	C/F related distribution	C/F(50 μm) ratio	Charred amorphous organic matter	Charcoal	Charred plant tissues	Charred peat	Amorphous organic matter	Plant tissues	Wood tissues	Phytoliths	Diatoms	Fungal sclerotia	Bone	Burnt bone	Pottery	Fe nodules	Fe replaced organic matter	Phosphatic nodules	Excremental pedofeatures
1	4.1	6	••••	C, G		P	STS	YB, S	SC	SPR	50:50	+				••			+	+					+			+.
1	4.2	25	•••••••	C, G	+	P	U	B, LB, D	SIL	DPR-OPR	10:90	••	•	+	••	•••••••	••••	••••	+		+			••	+			•••
1	4.3	7	••••••	C, (L)G	+	P	U	YB, B-DB, D	SIL	DPR-OPR, (L) CE	10:90	••	•••	+	••••	•••••••	••	•••	+		+				+		•	••••
2	4.4	4	•••••••	C, G		P	STS	YB, GR, S	SC	SPR	50:50	+				••			+	+					+			••
2	4.5	16	•••••	C, V, (L) G	+	P	U	LB-DB, D	SIL	DPR-OPR	10:90	••	+	+		•••••	•••		+	••		•			•		•	•••
2	4.6	7	•••••	C	+	P	U	LB-DB, D	SIL	OPR, (L) CE	10:90	•	••			••••	•••		+	••					+		•	••
2	4.7	7	••••••	C, V	+	P	U	LB, DB, D	SIL	OPR, (L) CE	10:90	•	••			•••••••	•	••••	+	••							+	••
4	8.1	35	•••••	C, V	+	P	U	LB-B, D	SIL	DPR-OPR	20:80	••	••			••••••••	•••	•••		+	••						••	••
6	4.8	15	••••••	V, C	+	P	U	YB, B-DB, D	SSL	SPR-DPR, EE-CE	40:60	••	••••		••••	•••••••	+	••	•	+	+				••		+	•••
6	4.9	3	••••	MS, V		P	U	Y-YB, D	SSL	SPR	30:70	•••	••		•••	•••••••	+	••	•••	+					••		•••	+

' trace amounts, · <2%, ·· 2–5%, ··· 5–10%, ···· 10–20%, ····· 20–30%, ······ 30–40%, ······· 40–50%, ········ 50–60%, ········· 60–70%

(L): localized; horizontal orientation: + (present), +++ (dominant)

(Continued)

Table 6.1 (Continued)

Sample	Layer and microstratigraphic unit	Maximum thickness in thin section (mm)	Structure				Groundmass					Organic and biomineral inclusions													Pedofeatures			
			Porosity	Microstructure	Horizontal orientation	Degree of sorting	Birefringence fabric	Nature of fine material	Soil texture	C/F related distribution	$C/F_{(50\,\mu m)}$ ratio	Charred amorphous organic matter	Charcoal	Charred plant tissues	Charred peat	Amorphous organic matter	Plant tissues	Wood tissues	Phytoliths	Diatoms	Fungal sclerotia	Bone	Burnt bone	Pottery	Fe nodules	Fe replaced organic matter	Phosphatic nodules	Excremental pedofeatures
6	4.10	12	•••••	C	+	P	U	B, D	SSL	SPR	40:60	•	•••		•••••	••••••••	•		•	+				••	+		+	+
6	4.11	2	••••	C, (L)I		MSR-P	U	B-DB, D	LS	SPR, EE-CE	70:30	••			•	••••			+		+							+	•
6	4.12	5	••••	V, C	+	P	U	B-DB, D	SSL	SPR	30:70	••	+	+	••••	••••••••	•		+	+					+		+	•
6	5.8	4	••••	C, (L)I		P-MSR	U	B, D	SL	SPR, CE	60:40	••	•		••	••••••	•		+	+					•			•
6	5.9	5	•••••	V, C	+	P	U	B-DB, YB, D	SSL	SPR	30:70	••	••	+	••	••••••	••		+		•				+		+	•
6	5.10	4	•••••	C		MSR-P	U	B, D	LS	SPR, (L)CE	70:30	••			••	••••••	+								••			•
6	5.11	8	•••••	V	+	P	U	B-DB, D	SSL	SPR	30:70	••	•••	+	•••	••••••••			+						••	+	••	•
6	5.12	7	••••	C, (L)I		MSR-P	U	B-DB, D	LS	SPR, FE-CE	70:30	••			•	••••••	••								+		+	••
6	5.13	8	•••••	C, (L) PL	+	P	U	B-DB, D	SSL	SPR	30:70	••	••		••••	••••••	•		+					•	+			
6	5.14	6	••••••	C, I		P-MSR	U	B, D	LS	EE-CE, SPR	70:30	•			••	••••••			+						•			
6	5.15	9	••••••	C, V	+	P	U	B, D	SSL	SPR, FE-CE	40:60	••	••		••••	••••••••				••					••		••	

' *trace amounts,* ˮ *2–5%,* ˮˮ *5–10%,* ˮˮˮ *10–20%,* ˮˮˮˮ *20–30%,* ˮˮˮˮˮ *30–40%,* ˮˮˮˮˮˮ *40–50%,* ˮˮˮˮˮˮˮ *50–60%,* ˮˮˮˮˮˮˮˮ *60–70%*

(L): localized; horizontal orientation: + (present), +++ (dominant)

Microstructure:	Degree of sorting:	Soil texture:	C/F related distribution:	Fine material:	Limpidity:	Birefringence:
G: granular	P: poorly sorted	LS: loamy sand	SPR: single spaced porphyric	B: brown	S: speckled	STS: stipple-speckled
V: vughy	MSR: moderately sorted	SL: sandy loam	DPR: double spaced porphyric	DB: dark brown	D: dotted	U: undifferentiated
C: channel	W: well sorted	SSL: sandy silt loam	OPR: open porphyric	LB: light brown		
MS: massive		SIL: silt loam	CE: coarse enaulic	YB: yellowish brown		
PL: platy		SC: sandy clay	EE: equal enaulic	Y: yellow		
I: intergrain microaggregate			FE: fine enaulic	GR: grey		

microstructures and planar voids, which reflects the temporary nature of occupation of the structures, with less intensive foot traffic within them. Micromorphological analysis was also essential for the identification of microscopic residues that could not be identified in the field, such as plant and wood tissues, dung, residues of ash, and, in some cases, minute fragments of artefacts. These residues relate to a wide range of activities, maintenance practices, and internal furnishings in the two studied structures, and they corroborate well with the descriptions of these provided by Mary Campbell. The microscopic study attests to the presence of livestock in the residential structures, the sources of fuel utilized by the inhabitants of the site, which included both wood and peat, and small-scale craft activities, such as domestic pottery production. It also provided additional information about possible maintenance practices, such as the sweeping of floors and constructing clay floors. Micromorphological analysis also enabled the identification of aeolian sand deposits, which were recognized on the basis of their high degree of sorting and low quantities of inclusions. These uncompacted and 'clean' deposits are likely to have accumulated during periods when the structures were seasonally abandoned.

The formation of the clean sandy deposits associated with seasonal abandonment phases would have been affected by site maintenance practices. The practice of the seasonal removal of the roofs reported for the Hebridean shielings could have contributed to a more pronounced accumulation of aeolian sand during periods of disuse, which might be characteristic of shieling settlements that were maintained in this way. The layers of aeolian sand at Bhiliscleitir were quite ephemeral, which might be related to the abandonment of this maintenance practice in the last phases of the site's use. Temporary abandonment could also result in weathering, a more pronounced disintegration, and sometimes even a partial collapse of structural elements such as turf walls and wooden roof supports, which were reported as the dominant building materials for Scottish shielings. The organic matter within these building materials could accumulate on the floors of disused structures, a process that is likely to explain the composition of some of the abandonment deposits identified at Bhiliscleitir.

One of the main goals of this study was to improve techniques for the identification of punctuated occupation at suspected shieling settlements, and to gain a better understanding of activities associated with summer transhumance. The analytical framework developed for this study enabled the identification of shifts in the type and the duration of occupation at the Bhiliscleitir shieling settlement; however, a more systematic geoarchaeological sampling strategy, which was beyond the scope of this study, could potentially allow for an even better understanding of the spatial organization of activities within the shieling structures, and could enable the

identification of activity areas outside of them, where many day-to-day tasks are likely to have taken place during the summer months. This analytical framework has been successfully applied to the identification of punctuated occupation at two putative shielings in the Outer Hebrides with origins in the early medieval period: Morsgail on the Isle of Lewis, and Kildonan on South Uist (Kupiec & Milek, forthcoming).

The ethno-geoarchaeological study at Bhiliscleitir proved invaluable on several fronts. The stratigraphic sequence captured in thin section attests to the punctuated nature of occupation at the site, and it demonstrates that micromorphological analysis of floor sediments can be applied to detect periods of punctuated occupation and abandonment at other putative shieling sites. The study also broadens our understanding of the range of possible floor formation processes, including everyday activities and maintenance practices, which could have been taking place at seasonally occupied pastoral settlements in both the recent and the more distant past. While it is not possible to draw a direct analogy between cultural practices at this twentieth-century shieling site and shielings used in the distant past, this ethno-geoarchaeological research extends the repertoire of possible interpretations, and it demonstrates the potential of micromorphological analysis to detect seasonal occupation and the activities associated with it.

REFERENCES

Armit, I. 1996. *The Archaeology of Skye and the Western Isles*. Edinburgh: Edinburgh University Press.

Barrowman, C. 2015. *The Archaeology of Ness, Results of the Ness Archaeological Landscape Survey*. Stornoway: Acair Ltd.

Bil, A. 1989. Transhumance economy, setting and settlement in highland Perthshire. *Scottish Geographical Magazine*, 105:156–67.

Bil, A. 1990a. The decline of shieling tradition in Perthshire. *Review of Scottish Culture*, 6:61–66.

Bil, A. 1990b. *The Shieling: 1600–1840: The Case of the Central Scottish Highlands*. Edinburgh: John Donald.

Boivin, N. 2000. Life rhythms and floor sequences: excavating time in rural Rajasthan and Neolithic Çatalhöyük. *World Archaeology*, 31:367–88.

Branigan, K. 2002. *Barra and the Bishop's Isles: Living on the Margin*. Stroud: Tempus.

Branigan, K. & Foster, P. 2002. *From Barra to Berneray: Archaeological Survey and Excavation in the Southern Isles of the Outer Hebrides*. Sheffield: Sheffield Academic Press.

Bullock, P., Fedoroff, N., Jongerius, A., Stoops, G., Tursina, T. & Babel, U. 1985. *Handbook for Thin Section Description*. Wolverhampton: Waine Research Publications.

Campbell, D. 1896. Highland Shieling in the olden time. *Transactions of the Inverness Scientific Society and Field Club*, 5:62–69.

Cheape, H. 1992–93. Crogans and Barvas Ware: handmade pottery in the Hebrides. *Scottish Studies*, 31:109–27.

Cheape, H. 2010. 'A cup fit for the king': literary and forensic analysis of crogan pottery. A paper presented at Ceramic Views of Scotland and Northern England from the Neolithic to the 20th century: Issues of Method, Practice and Theory. University of Glasgow, July 1–2, 2010.

Comhairle nan Eilean Siar Contaminated Land Inspection Strategy. n.d. Chapter 3: characteristics of Comhairle nan Eilean Siar's area. www.cnesiar.gov.uk/contaminatedland/documents/inspectionstrategy.pdf (accessed 4 September 2014).

Courty, M.A., Golderberg, P. & MacPhail, R. 1989. *Soils and Micromorphology in Archaeology*. Cambridge Manuals in Archaeology. Cambridge: Cambridge University Press.

Davidson, D.A., Carter, S.P. & Quine, T.A. 1992. An evaluation of micromorphology as an aid to archaeological interpretation. *Geoarchaeology*, 7:55–65.

Fenton, A. 1978. *The Island Blackhouse (And a Guide to 'The Blackhouse')*. No. 42. Arnol. Edinburgh: H.M.S.O.

Fenton, A. 1980. The traditional pastoral economy. In: M.L. Parry & T.R. Slater, eds. *The Making of Scottish Countryside*. London: Croom Helm, pp. 93–113.

FitzPatrick, E.A. 1993. *Soil Microscopy and Micromorphology*. New York: John Wiley & Sons.

French, C. 2015. *A Handbook of Geoarchaeological Approaches for Investigating Landscapes and Settlement Sites*. Oxford: Oxbow Books.

Gaffney, V. 1959. Summer shealings. *Scottish Historical Review*, 38:20–35.

Gaffney, V. 1967. The shielings of Drumochter, *Scottish Studies*, 11:91–99.

Gordon, S. 1937. *Afoot in Wild Places*. London: Cassella.

Gregor, M. 2014. Thin section analyses in the study of the ancient ceramic materials. In: L. Lisá, ed. *Soil Micromorphology in General and Archaeological Context*. Brno: Mendel University in Brno, pp. 80–85.

Kissling, W. 1943. The character and purpose of the Hebridean black house. *Journal of the Royal Anthropological Institute*, 46:78–99.

Kupiec, P., Milek, K., Gísladóttir, Guðrún Alda & Woollett, J. 2016. Elusive sel sites: the geoarchaeological quest for Icelandic shielings and the case of Þorvaldsstaðasel, in northeast Iceland. In: J. Collis, M. Pearce & F. Nicolis eds. *Summer Farms: Seasonal Exploitation of the Uplands from Prehistory to the Present*. Sheffield: J.R. Collis Publications, pp. 221–36.

Love, J.A. 1981. Shielings of the Isle of Rum. *Scottish Studies*, 25:39–63.

Macdonald, C.M. 2012. The shielings of Cuidhsiadar and Filiscleitir: chronicling the tradition of annual migration to the moors as it was then; investigating the death of transhumance in the area; and examining what exactly the shielings mean now. Unpublished BSc dissertation. University of Strathclyde.

MacKenzie, J.B. 1905. Antiquities and old customs of St. Kilda, compiled from notes made by Rev. Neil MacKenzie, minister of St. Kilda 1829–43. *Proceedings of the Society of Antiquaries of Scotland*, 39:97–402.

MacKenzie, W.M. 1904. Notice on certain structures of archaic type in the Island of Lewis-Beehive Houses, Duns and Stone Circles. *Proceedings of Society of Antiquaries of Scotland*, 38:173–204.

MacPhail, R.I., Cruise, G.M., Allen, M.J., Linderholm, J. & Reynolds, P. 2004. Archaeological soil and pollen analysis of experimental floor deposits; with special reference to Butser Ancient Farm, Hampshire, UK. *Journal of Archaeological Science*, 31:175–91.

MacSween, M. 1959. Transhumance in north Skye. *Scottish Geographical Magazine*, 75:75–88.

MacSween, M. & Gailey, A. 1961. Some shielings in northern Skye. *Scottish Studies*, 5:77–84.

Mahler, D.L. 2007. *Sæteren ved Argisbrekka. Økonomiske forandringer på Færøerne I Vikingetid og Tidlig Middelalder*. Tórshavn, Fróðskapur: Faroe University Press.

Matras, A.K., Stummann Hansen, S. & Andreasen, H. 2004. A Viking Age shieling in Skarðsvík, Fugloy, Faroe Islands. *Fróðskaparrit*, 51: 200–211.

Milek, K.B. 2005. Soil Micromorphology. In: N. Sharples, ed. *A Norse Farmstead in the Outer Hebrides, Excavation at Mound 3, Bornais, South Uist*. Oxford: Oxbow Books, pp. 35–36.

Milek, K.B. 2012. Floor formation processes and the interpretation of activity areas: an ethnoarchaeological study of turf buildings at Thverá, northeast Iceland. *Journal of Anthropological Archaeology*, 31:119–37.

Milek, K.B. & French, C.A.I. 2007. Soils and Sediments in the Settlement and Harbour at Kaupang. In: D. Skre, ed. *Kaupang in Skiringssal*, Kaupang. Excavation Project Publication Series, Volume 1. Aarhus: Aarhus University Press, pp. 321–60.

Morrison, D. 1997. *The Photographs of Dan Morrison*. Stornoway: Acair Ltd.

Raven, J. 2012. The shielings survey: South Uist. In: M. Parker Pearson (ed.) *From Machair to Mountains: Archaeological Survey and Excavation on South Uist*. Oxford: Oxbow, pp. 160–78.

Rolfsen, P. 1980. Disturbance of archaeological layers by processes in the soils. *Norwegian Archaeological Review*, 13:110–18.

Schiffer, M.B. 1996. *Formation Processes of the Archaeological Record*. Salt Lake City: University of Utah Press.

Stoops, G. 2003. *Guidelines for Analysis and Description of Soil and Regolith Thin Sections*. Madison: Soil Science Society of America.

CHAPTER 7

Morphology of transhumant settlements in post-medieval South Connemara
A case study in adaptation

EUGENE COSTELLO

INTRODUCTION

As recently as the early twentieth century, and especially during the nineteenth century and earlier, a type of small-scale transhumance known as booleying prevailed in many parts of Ireland. This was a strategy whereby farmers took their livestock – usually dairy cows – to rough grazing in marginal areas for the summer and lived with them there in what are referred to as 'booley' huts or houses. The cattle were then brought back to the home farm in late autumn and overwintered there. The term 'booleying' is derived from the Irish word *buaile*, which signifies a milking-place in summer pasturage, a fold or a dung-yard (Ó Dónaill, 1977: 152–53).

The last two instances of booleying died out in Achill Island in the 1940s (Ó Moghráin, 1943; Graham, 1954; McDonald, 2014) and in South Connemara in the 1910s. By that time, and in the previous century too, booleying had become a small-scale non-elite practice undertaken by tenant farmers and their families who would move their cattle no more than a few kilometres to rough pastures. Livestock numbers are not recorded but few tenants are likely to have had more than twenty cattle, based on the size of their home farms and the amount of commonage they had access to. A significant body of ethnographic evidence relating to this last phase of transhumance exists in the National Folklore Collection and in other published accounts – thanks, largely, to the work of the Irish Folklore Commission during the 1930s and 1940s. The geographic spread of these accounts is unsurprisingly biased towards the areas where booleying survived longest, that is, along the western and north-western Atlantic coast – particularly western County Galway, western County Mayo and County Donegal. Compared to the rest of Ireland, these areas contained high densities of small tenant farmers on small amounts of good land by the coast or at the bottom of sheltered valleys; much larger tracts of less productive peaty soils occupied the low hills and mountains further inland. The latter was where tenant farmers sent their dairy cows to graze for the summer and early autumn. Transhumance died out between the seventeenth and early nineteenth centuries in the rest of the country due to a complex mix of economic and demographic pressures (Costello, 2015; 2016a; 2016b; 2016c). The possibility should be noted, however, that communities in some parts of Ireland may never have relied on transhumance, employing a largely sedentary mode of livestock rearing. For example, in the extensive fertile lowlands of east Galway, much of the Midlands and parts of central Munster, farmers – regardless of time period – have only had access to very small tracts of rough pasture. Transhumance cannot be regarded as the natural reflex of farmers who have livestock: their need to move always depended on the physical environment and how intensively other people around them were making use of the land.

A lot of archaeological evidence possibly relating to seasonal transhumant settlement is now coming to light in Ireland's hills and mountains. It takes the form of structures that were used as summer dwellings by herders who stayed with and milked dairy cows at rough pasture, as well as other subtle features associated with them. When their remains are interrogated with the help of ethnographic and historical data, the archaeology of seasonal transhumant settlement becomes a rich source of information. It is not without its complications, however, particularly when trying to build a chronology.

This paper focuses on transhumance in the Carna peninsula of South Connemara during the post-medieval period. It examines the material culture of transhumant settlements in the period, *c.* 1700–1910, and – with the help of ethnographic and historical sources – seeks to demonstrate how recent seasonal land-use manifested itself in the archaeology of marginal landscapes. It is a timely study in this regard, as no serious fieldwork has hitherto been undertaken on transhumance in Connemara. Indeed, in the whole of Ireland, archaeologists have generally shied away from tackling the subject – the Mourne Mountains, Co. Down, Achill, Co. Mayo, and the writer's own work in the Galtee Mountains of Limerick and Tipperary forming recent exceptions (Gardiner, 2012; McDonald, 2014; Costello, 2015). Overall, researchers still have a very patchy idea of the morphology of booley dwellings, the features, if any, associated with them and the various social and environmental factors

© 2018 European Association of Archaeologists

influencing their design. This has had the effect of stymying attempts to explain how transhumant farmers and their livestock altered marginal landscapes through time – a great shame considering that transhumant movements are attested in documentary sources as far back as the early medieval period (Neilson Hancock, 1865: 132; Plummer, 1922: 157; O'Rahilly, 1962: 24; Lucas, 1989: 58–67). For example, a farmer of one hundred cows named Dima from modern-day Meath/Westmeath is said, in an eleventh-century saint's life, to have brought his animals on a grazing tour (*ar cuairt bhuailteachuis*) to the Glendalough area of the Wicklow Mountains, where the cows grazed in woodland and were milked by herdsmen (Plummer, 1922: 153–54). Dima's grazing tour is highly likely to have taken place during the summer and is the first instance in the documentary record of the word *buailteachas* – the standard word in Modern Irish for booleying (Ó Dónaill, 1977: 153). Interestingly, the relatively large number of cows owned by Dima and the long distance which they were taken – at least 50 or 60 km – suggests that Irish transhumance was not always as small-scale and local as twentieth-century ethnographic accounts of 'booleying' would lead us to believe.

In spite of this reference and a few others besides, along with the encouraging archaeological evidence now being revealed, transhumance is confined to brief mentions (or not mentioned at all) in the main historical and archaeological textbooks that deal with medieval and post-medieval Ireland (Barry, 1987; Edwards, 1990: 46, 53, 57; Ó Cróinín, 1995: 101; O'Keeffe, 2000: 68–69). The extent of this oversight becomes alarming if it is considered that pre-industrial Irish society, no less than the rest of Europe, had a mix of arable and pastoral farming as the ultimate basis for its existence. In an effort to improve our understanding of one important aspect of past Irish farming, therefore, the present paper gives the stage to the seasonal settlements of transhumant farmers. In doing so, it poses two specific questions. First, what factors are evident in the morphology of booley sites, and how were they influenced by the geographic marginality of herders using them? Second, what is the archaeological evidence for management of both people and livestock at these sites, and what, in turn, might that say about the social complexity of transhumant communities in South Connemara during the eighteenth and nineteenth centuries?

The Study-Area and Ethnographic Evidence for Transhumance

The Carna peninsula is known in Irish as *Iorras Aithneach*, which translates suitably as 'The Stormy Peninsula' (Hogan, 1910: 472). It constitutes the major part of the civil parish of Moyrus in the barony of Ballynahinch, County Galway, on Ireland's western seaboard (Figure 7.1). The Carna peninsula is a fairly constrained space in terms of farming and possibilities for sustaining a substantial population. It extends *c.* 14 km to the south-west from the main landmass and is 12 km across at its widest point. Most of the west of the peninsula is flat with a number of rises and small hills. The east of the peninsula is higher, being dominated by the hilly spine of Cnoc Mordáin. This rocky ridge is the only part of the peninsula to exceed 150 m a.s.l. – its peak reaching 354 m. However, rough pasture stops well short of this altitude. Thus, there was not much *vertical* mobility in the Carna peninsula. Rather, its geography means that it transhumance was largely a *horizontal* movement. This is somewhat unlike other surviving instances of post-medieval transhumance in Ireland; for example, the rough summer pastures of the Galtee Mountains and the Mourne Mountains were both used in the seventeenth and eighteenth centuries by people based in the surrounding lowlands. However, even these upland pastures (200–700 m) are relatively low by comparison with the tracts of summer grazing used in transhumant systems of France and Italy (Burri, this volume; Vanni & Cristoferi, this volume).

Furthermore, most of the study-area is quite poor in terms of soil quality. The interior, particularly its flatter expanses, is largely characterised by blanket peat and scattered lakes. Slightly more productive in agricultural terms are small patches of peaty podzols found on the drier and rockier rises and hills. Unsurprisingly, these locations are where likely booley dwellings tend to be found, as shown below. Peaty podzols are more extensive on the peninsula's southern coast and its nearby islands, along with pockets of acid brown earths, lithosols and undifferentiated alluvium (EPA Envision, 2015). The coastal fringe that harbours these arable soils is where permanent settlement has historically been concentrated. Indeed, the existence of better soils here is likely to be partly a consequence of gradual anthropogenic soil enrichment – through the digging in of seaweed and sand. This process was at its most intense during a period of extreme population growth that affected all of Ireland during the eighteenth and early nineteenth centuries (see Smyth, 2012). In the Carna peninsula, a marginal environment where population densities had been very low previously, the expansion of permanent settlement did not lead to the loss of much rough pasture. By 1838, when the Ordnance Survey produced the first detailed 6" maps of the area, there were still approximately 10,641 hectares of unenclosed rough grazing in the peninsula, as illustrated by Figure 7.1. The attractiveness of the coast and the resources which the sea could offer are therefore major features in the recent settlement history of Carna. Nonetheless, it is also true that the interior was relied upon by its coastal inhabitants as part of a local transhumant system.

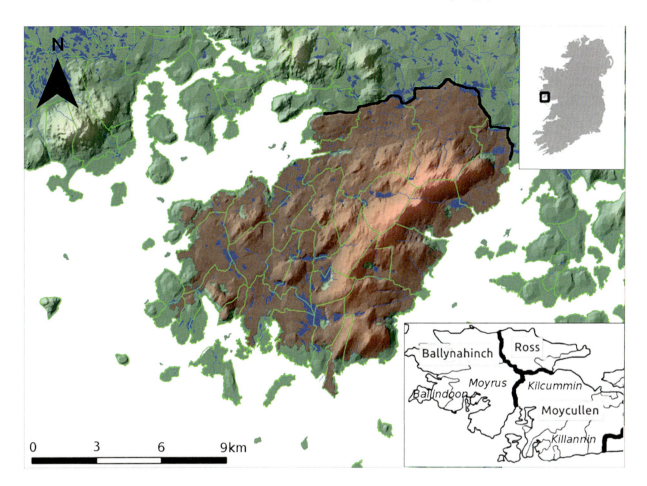

Figure 7.1. Carna peninsula, with townland boundaries in light green; unenclosed rough grazing shaded red
Source: Digitised from 1838 6" map by Eugene Costello; Ordnance Survey Ireland (2015)

Ethnographic accounts are a crucial source of information on the transhumance which they practised, at least as observed in its last phase. At the beginning of the twentieth century, Browne (1902: 520) describes how small tenant farmers on Maínis and Máisean islands, as well as parts of the coast of Carna, sent dairy cows 8–9.5 km inland every summer and autumn, where they were looked after by watchers who sheltered in "boolies". Oral tradition collected by fieldworkers of the National Folklore Commission and others makes clear that the herders were usually unmarried daughters of the tenant farmers, and sometimes their wives and young sons; the summer huts in which they stayed were known locally as *brácaí* (singular: *bráca*) and went out of use gradually between 1880 and 1920. Milk produced at these sites was either taken home each day or churned into butter on-site (National Folklore Collection, n.d., Ms.155: 50–57; Ms.156: 54–57; Ms.157: 434–42; Mac Giollarnáth, 1941, 277–80; Ó Cathasaigh, 1943: 159–60; Graham, 1954: 22–24; Gibbons, 1991: 45; Ó Héalaí & Ó Tuairisg, 2007: 21). Most of these accounts name out areas where booley sites could be found, and a few even mention the names of their occupants and what part of the coast or islands they came from (though in respect of the latter the accounts are sometimes contradictory).

Local information, moreover, mentions the conditions that made transhumance necessary in the Carna peninsula. One reason was the occurrence of deficiency diseases in cattle when they grazed for too long either by the coast or in the interior. Thus, *galar trua* tended to afflict them on cobalt-poor sandy soils, while another disease, known as *brios brún*, could affect cattle when on hill pasture, probably due to a lack of phosphorous (Doherty, 2001: 62). Both were cured by giving cattle a change of pasture for at least six weeks (Beartla King, Carna, pers. comm.; Ó Cathasaigh, 1943: 160). The other main principle behind transhumance, locally, was the need to conserve grass at home that would be needed as winterage; this was particularly important given that more ground was taken up by oats and potato cultivation prior to the twentieth century (Costello, 2016b; Ó Gaora, 1937: 164; Ó Cathasaigh, 1943: 159–60; Beartla King, Carna, pers. comm.).

Transhumant Settlement in the Carna Peninsula

The remains of structures likely to have been used each summer by transhumant herders are fairly common on rough pasture in the peninsula's interior. This was suggested first of all by examination of satellite imagery, and confirmed by fieldwork. None of the structures had previously been recorded on Ordnance Survey maps or in the Record of Monuments and Places (Archaeological Survey of Ireland, 2014). Walk-over survey, followed by selective detailed survey, has been carried out in two townlands in the centre of the study-area, i.e. An Cnoc Buí and Gleannán. Adjoining parts of Glinsce and Seanadh Bhuire townlands were also covered. All of those areas covered by fieldwork are now totally uninhabited. Out of the whole study-area, An Cnoc Buí and Glinsce were given the most attention because mid-nineteenth-century rentals record that they, respectively, were "in the occupation of the tenants of" An Más and An Aird Thiar, two densely settled townlands on the south-western coast of the peninsula (Martin rentals, 1837–52; Encumbered Estates' Court, O'Brien, 1852; Figure 7.2). This is valuable historical evidence as it pins down the origins of transhumant movements to the areas of rough pasture in question, allowing for a more penetrating discussion of seasonal settlement (at least for the nineteenth century).

All told, fieldwork in the above areas has recorded a total of sixty-four structures, the simplest of which are small shelters. Ten of these have been identified with a fair degree of confidence, with another four tentative. Shelters are generally not large enough for a person to lie down in comfortably and in some cases may not even have been roofed, their purpose simply to provide herders with a temporary respite from the elements. Most are quite crude, being found beside or between boulders and rock outcrops where short rubble walls sufficed to close off a small patch of ground approximately 1.4 m or less in internal length. Others still have little or no masonry and are effectively natural shelters. Overall, shelters are more common in the western townlands of An Cnoc Buí and Glinsce than in Gleannán and Seanadh Bhuire, which is probably due to the more exposed and windswept nature of much of the former townlands. A further thirteen structures are classified as rubble-walled enclosures or partly enclosed areas for livestock. Although one of these measures 16 m by 8 m, and may have been used as a general sort of enclosure for sorting livestock, the rest are between 5 m and 12 m in maximum width (Figure 7.3). These

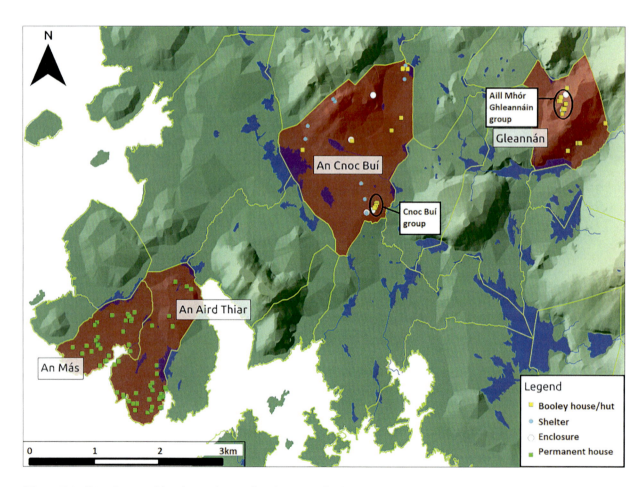

Figure 7.2. Distribution of farmhouses (c. 1838) in home townlands and sites in connected summer pastures; Glinsce and Seanadh Bhuire sites not shown
Source: Drawn by Eugene Costello

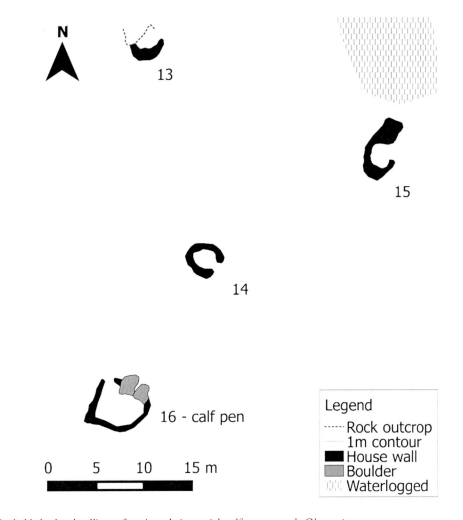

Figure 7.3. Probable booley dwellings of various design, with calf pen to south; Gleannán
Source: Drawn by Eugene Costello

are better described as 'pens', and were probably used to enclose calves. They were also brought up to rough grazing at the start of summer but were kept in at night (Mac Giollarnáth, 1941: 280). Interestingly, a survey of farming in Co. Galway in 1824 says that it was common practice for a calf to "empty two teats, whilst the dairy-maid is milking the other two" (Dutton, 1824: 142). Pens may therefore have helped to regulate the amount of time that calves spent with cows prior to being weaned fully.

Then there are slightly more substantial dwellings – the remains, probably, of booley huts or *brácaí*. These vary in size, shape and method of construction, but all are at least large enough to accommodate two adults while sleeping, or more if they were children. This size tallies reasonably well with ethnographic information which says four to five girls would sleep in a *bráca* (Graham, 1954: 23). In total, thirty-six of these were identified, including nine somewhat tentative examples (due to collapse). Only two out of all these have an internal division, which is unsurprising given their relatively small dimensions.

The Morphology of Summer Dwellings: Adaptation and Human Agency

In terms of morphology, only four out of the thirty-six former booley dwellings could be assigned to a discrete category. The four in question are rectangular in shape and have drystone walls constructed mostly of coursed masonry. Three of the four contain the remains of a gable at one end. Externally, the four structures measure an average of 3.7 m x 3.2 m (11.8 m^2) externally and 2.4 m by 1.8 m (4.3 m^2) internally (Figure 7.4a). Their rectangular coursed walls are somewhat reminiscent of the farmhouses in which tenant families were based, that is, in areas of permanent settlement by the coast. As depicted on the Ordnance Survey maps of 1838, and as they survive on the ground today, these farmhouses were long, rectangular and constructed mostly of coursed masonry (Figure 7.5). The basic similarity in form between them and the four booley dwellings mentioned is suggestive of a similar date of construction for both, i.e. sometime during the eighteenth or nineteenth centuries. Such a model has been

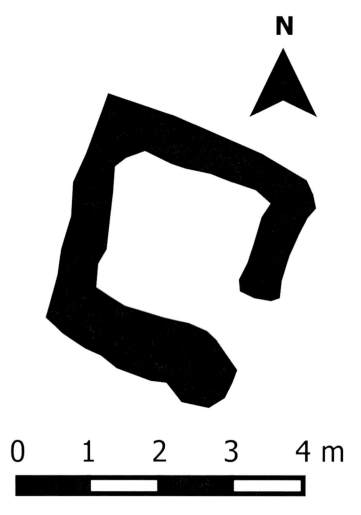

Figure 7.4a. Rectangular type, Gleannán 9
Source: Drawn by Eugene Costello

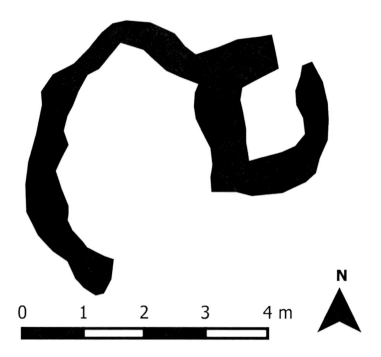

Figure 7.4b. Example of irregular structure, Gleannán 12; possible butter store in north-east
Source: Drawn by Eugene Costello

Figure 7.5. Intact early nineteenth-century farmhouse in Ogúil, Killannin (east of Carna peninsula)
Photo: Eugene Costello

proposed for seasonal settlement in the Galtee Mountains, in the south of Ireland, where a similar but larger type of booley dwelling predominates; its style seems to be derived from rectangular farmhouses built in the late eighteenth and early nineteenth centuries on the Galtees' lower slopes (Costello, 2015: 64). The Galtee Mountains, however, have a particular landscape history which makes it easier to assign construction dates to both farmhouses and booley dwellings. Furthermore, in the Carna peninsula, there is a greater discrepancy in size between farmhouses and booley dwellings – the four rectangular examples discussed here being only a third the length of farmhouses (which generally measure 10–14 m by 4.5–6 m externally). Thus, the present writer's attempts to date these booley dwellings to the later post-medieval period must remain quite tentative.

In any case, the rest of the booley dwellings – some thirty-two – display much less uniformity in terms of morphology. They are poorly constructed (or collapsed) rubble-walled huts, often built against a rocky outcrop or incorporating a boulder in one or more of their walls. Their shape is usually roughly rectangular but circular and irregular examples exist as well (Figures 7.3 and 7.4b).

There is variation in terms of size too. Some structures measure approximately 5.5 m by 3 m externally, and others as little as 2.3 m by 2 m. On average, they measure 3.4 m by 2.7 m (9.2 m^2) externally and 2.6 m by 1.7 m (4.4 m^2) internally. The apparent unpredictability of these – the vast majority of booley dwellings – makes it difficult to divide them into neat morphological categories. Why, then, is the morphology of summer pastoral dwellings in the Carna peninsula so varied? One explanation lies in the physical environment in which they are found. South Connemara has a very uneven land surface with rocks and rocky outcrops poking out from its boggy landscape almost everywhere. Those who had to build here would therefore have found it convenient to adapt the form of their structures to the landscape. For example, the northern side of An Cnoc Buí 4 – a roughly D-shaped house – is formed by two natural in-situ boulders (Figure 7.6). Just outside Gleannán's north-western boundary, a single site in Beitheach Chatha encapsulates the adaptive nature of construction even better (Figure 7.7). Here, a rubble-walled booley dwelling which would otherwise have been oval is truncated by a massive boulder. Thus, the structure itself is roughly C-shaped while the boulder blocks its open end. Other booley dwellings again are partially dug out of slopes for shelter. None of this construction was fortuitous. It was a consequence of deliberate actions by individuals working on their own or in small groups who wanted to construct a sufficiently weather-proof summer habitation without unnecessary effort. In order to strike that balance in the rocky landscape of South Connemara, the archaeological evidence shows that people frequently employed features in the natural topography as a building tool.

The reliance of transhumant people on the landscape's unpredictable rockiness has both straightforward and complex implications. First of all, it confirms that standard shapes and dimensions could not be maintained in the design of booley dwellings because herders were making different strategic decisions at each new location. The construction style of every booley dwelling was altered slightly every time, depending on how uneven the surface, the size and location of boulders and how much shelter was offered by nearby hillocks and rises. Second, and perhaps more importantly, it shows that herders did not have to build with reference to socially acceptable forms, but could use their own capacity for innovation to adapt to the physical realities of the environment in which seasonal settlement took place. In this regard, the construction of booley dwellings in the Carna peninsula offers an insight into the relationship between two opposing factors in the make-up of social practice, namely, agents and structures. The relationship between these two is a well-known pillar of theoretical debate in the social sciences. A formative influence on the matter has been the sociologist Anthony Giddens (1981; 1984), who developed the idea that agents (individuals with the capacity for independent action) and structures are *united* in the creation of social practice. Structuration theory, as it is known, has since been taken up and discussed extensively in archaeological contexts, mainly to help interpret prehistoric societies (Hodder, 1982; Barrett, 1994; Barrett & Fewster, 2000; Dobres & Robb, 2000; Barrett, 2001).

However, it is no less valuable for the historical period; and it may even provide a framework for the interpretation of the archaeology of post-medieval transhumant settlements. With transhumance as a social practice receiving virtually no theorisation in

Figure 7.6. D-shaped booley dwelling in centre of photograph built up against two boulders sitting next to one another, An Cnoc Buí 4
Photo: Eugene Costello

Figure 7.7. Booley dwelling in Beitheach Chatha built up against large boulder
Photo: Eugene Costello

Ireland up to now, the current paper's application of structuration theory is intended only as a preliminary assessment of its potential. Regarding the above unpredictability of rubble-walled booley dwellings, an initial obvious question may be posited: what does their morphology say about the relationship of herders, as agents, with the wider structures of their world, and how we define those structures? For the Carna peninsula, the present writer would argue that the terrain of summer pasture represented an important *physical* structure. It could also be argued that since the shape and size of most booley dwellings is intimately associated with the nuances of topography, the people who built them were agents who mediated with the physical structure of the landscape. In other words, they used their individual agency to make choices about construction which befitted the unique micro-topography of each new site.

Resistance to Social Structure?

If we accept that people built booley dwellings in the Carna peninsula with reference – mainly – to the physical structure of the landscape, it must then be asked how they adapted to other structures in their world. As participants in a seasonal movement, transhumant people were never totally detached from home settlements: even during the summer season, regular journeys with butter and milk were necessary in both directions. Through these products, herders remained integral to the economic structure of home. Family members based by the coast relied on them for part of their diet and also sold some of the butter to market in the early nineteenth century (Dutton, 1824: 140, 353). The issue of transhumant communities' integration into a market economy in the post-medieval period is a wide one, however, and lies beyond the scope of the current paper. More relevant here is the question of transhumant herders' connection to the contemporary *social* structure of home settlements.

The morphology of the vast majority of booley dwellings in Carna is so varied as to suggest very little effort was made to implement a set design, much less recreate the long rectangular form of permanent dwellings at home. The physical environment seems to have been a more important factor in their design. Of course, since none of the booley dwellings here have been excavated, there is still a great deal of uncertainty as to when each site was constructed and how long it was in use. The relative abundance of local ethnographic data relating to the use of booley dwellings (or *brácaí*) in transhumance makes it probable that most of them were at least *occupied* during the period, 1750–1910. That said, the occupation of some probably stretches back before 1750, while others may even have been abandoned by that date. With recent fieldwork in Ireland concentrating (rightly) on the identification and survey of booley dwellings, uncertainty about chronology is a problem for archaeologists across the country. To date, it is only in the north-east of the island of Ireland, specifically the uplands of Antrim and Down, that a handful of trial excavations at possible booley sites have taken place (Evans & Proudfoot, 1958; Williams & Robinson, 1983; Williams, 1984; McSparron, 2002). One excavation was also recently undertaken at the clustered booley settlement of Annagh on Achill Island, in the north-west of the country (McDonald, 2014: 206–19). Pottery and glass finds at Annagh demonstrate that two of its drystone booley dwellings, rectangular on the inside but more curved on the outside, were occupied in the late eighteenth and nineteenth centuries. Their size – *c.* 5 m x 3.5 m externally – is very similar to those surveyed in the Carna peninsula. Generally speaking, though, it is difficult to obtain solid dating evidence from excavations of booley dwellings, especially when trying to pin down their construction. The peaty acidic soils of Ireland's uplands are not conducive to the survival of small metal finds, macro plant remains or bone, while valuable roof timbers would probably have been removed after abandonment. Furthermore, the designs of individual booley dwellings are likely to have changed slightly every year as winter damage to walls or roofs was repaired. Dating such minute alterations would be virtually impossible in the mostly drystone booley dwellings of the Carna peninsula.

Nonetheless, existing field evidence makes it clear that houses in transhumant settlements do not fit into the same architectural tradition as late eighteenth- and nineteenth-century farmhouses in permanent settlements. If transhumant herders could construct and certainly occupy dwellings so visibly at odds with contemporary farmhouses as well as with one another, what does that say about the strength of their community's social structure? Did herders have greater agency to reject aspects of wider society because of their marginal situation, several kilometres from home? Of relevance here is an idea which has emerged in archaeological debates about agency (Hodder & Hutson, 2003: 96–99). The idea of resistance recognises that agents sometimes reject aspects of a social or cultural structure if another competing structure has to be reckoned with. The writer believes that its application in

the interpretation of transhumant settlements offers a major avenue for future archaeological research in Ireland and elsewhere. In the present study-area, the physical structure of marginal landscapes and the raw materials which they provided made it difficult for people to implement a set design that was considered necessary in wider society. The resistance of people in this regard was facilitated by the relative weakness of social structures in hills that lay well beyond core areas of settlement. Arguably, their marginality in terms of location meant that they were not subject to the same intensity of social scrutiny that people living in densely settled areas had to deal with, be it from senior family members or political and religious elites.

This idea is supported by the fact that life was less restrictive at summer pasture, as borne out by a preliminary investigation of early twentieth-century ethnography. The young females who looked after and milked the cows at booley sites had, it is said, "plenty of time for singing, dancing and knitting" (Graham, 1954: 24), while another account recalls that the singing, dancing and fun would occasionally attract local young men to the summer pastures (National Folklore Collection, n.d., Ms.156; 55). The Irish saying, "Thug sí an damhsa ó bhuaile léi/She brought the dance from the booley" (Ó Dónaill, 1977: 152–53) also alludes to the general sense of gaiety which life at transhumant settlements entailed. Social practice in communities of transhumant herders is discussed in more detail by Costello (2017).

BRINGING IT BACK HOME – DIVISION OF SPACE AT TRANSHUMANT SETTLEMENTS

Yet people at summer pastures were not totally free of outside influence. Beyond the actual booley dwellings, the morphology of their transhumant settlements betray the mark of wider society to a limited extent. In two locations, transhumant settlement reached a level of complexity not normally seen at booley sites; indeed, they incorporate elements of enclosure. The first is An Aill Mhór ('The Big Cliff'), in the centre of Gleannán, where thirteen structures are found along an undulating stretch of rocky pasture roughly 500 m in length. The group contains three well-built houses, several irregular house forms and three livestock pens. However, as Figure 7.8 illustrates, there is also a series of curvilinear walls running through the settlement, and making use of natural outcrops and ridges where possible; they appear to divide its central area in two, between a higher terrace on the east and a lower terrace on the west – the latter being particularly busy in archaeological terms. The second complex booley settlement is located on a similar, but less elevated patch of rocky pasture in the south of An Cnoc Buí. It contains five rubble-walled houses of various shapes and one pen. Again, curvilinear walls (incorporating several rocky outcrops) outline much of the settlement and divide it roughly into two areas, the southern of which contains little evidence of habitation. In both Gleannán and An Cnoc Buí, the walls in question rarely exceed 0.5 m in height. Given that there are few tumbled stones lying around, sods of peat would have been required to make the walls stock-proof.

These booley settlements are intriguing for two reasons. First, they contain a greater density of structures than any other part of the peninsula surveyed by the writer. With individual structures generally sited 20–60 m apart, the south of An Cnoc Buí and Aill Mhór are not clustered settlements. However, they do form loose groups and that is not seen elsewhere. In the rest of their respective townlands, as well in neighbouring Seanadh Bhuire and Glinsce, structures are more isolated, i.e. they tend to be more than a hundred metres apart, if not several hundred (Figure 7.2). The occurrence of structures in greater densities at these two locations may be explained by the fact that they occupy advantageous positions, both in terms of soil quality – drier and supporting more palatable grasses and sedges – and because they offer fairly expansive views of much of the surrounding landscape. The group at Aill Mhór, especially, occupies a desirable niche between wet bog in the flatlands to the west and exposed rock on the hills east of it. The second notable factor about these settlements is, of course, the presence of low stone walls running around and through them. This complexity has not been observed around any other booley dwellings in fieldwork areas in the Carna peninsula, nor has it, for that matter, been seen in any other archaeological surveys of seasonal sites in Ireland to date (Gardiner, 2012; McDonald, 2014; Costello, 2015).

On one level, the presence of low stone walls is a product of clearance, an activity which improved the quality of herbage around booley dwellings. Stone clearance was facilitated at the sites in question by the presence of a sizeable labour force relative to isolated booley dwellings. However, clearance did not have to lead to the building of walls – in the Aill Mhór group, numerous cairns are visible where people simply deposited stone in a heap (Figure 7.8). No one interpretation of the walls provides a complete answer. The main sticking-point is whether they were meant to keep livestock in, or out. One possibility is that cows were brought into the enclosures at night for protection against wolves, a predator that was common up to the start of the eighteenth century and is said in local folklore to have approached booley sites (National Folklore Collection, n.d., Ms.155: 54–57; Hardiman, 1846: 9). This scenario would allow for the milking of cows each morning and evening within the enclosures. Furthermore, gradual accumulation of dung would, in both cases, have improved the quality and quantity of grass in the vicinity.

Alternatively, the enclosures may have been designed to exclude cattle. In the Aill Mhór group, small patches of cultivation ridges are visible next to several of the booley dwellings, particularly in the lower western area. These were almost certainly for potatoes, a crop known to have been cultivated at seasonal sites in Ireland during the nineteenth century (Ó hEochaidh, 1943: 139; Ó Danachair, 1945: 250; McDonald, 2014: 193; Costello, 2015: 52). Enclosing walls may have helped to deter cattle from entering and causing damage. Be that as it may, the Cnoc Buí group has no evidence of cultivation, so the walls cannot have been for this purpose alone. The second scenario in which cattle would have been excluded is if small-scale haymaking took place within the enclosures. Herders may have used the latter as small meadows from which hay was saved late in the grazing season, probably August. The saving of hay on mountainous land is attested in 1756 for the Limerick/Kerry/Cork border area of south-western Ireland (Smith, 1756, 88, footnote 9), and also in the Uíbh Ráthach peninsula of South Kerry up to the early twentieth century (O'Sullivan & Sheehan, 1992). Relatively small amounts of *fionnán* or purple-moor grass cut and dried on the hills could have supplemented the diet of cows while they over-wintered on coastal farms. If livestock were indeed excluded from the enclosures, herders would have had to milk cows where they stood in summer pasture, which is not as impractical as it sounds. Milking in the field was common on Irish farms during the summer months before the advent of modern milking machines, and was the experience of the present writer's grandparents in counties Limerick and Kerry. Moreover, cows that receive regular close attention from people tend to become very quiet and can often be milked without tethering.

There may also be an implicit social meaning in these enclosures. This is brought out by a comparison with permanently settled land, where, in the very farms that depended on transhumance, enclosure of space was intrinsic to how contemporary tenant farmers managed the landscape. As a map from 1838 shows, farmhouses were distributed in a complicated network of irregular fields (Figure 7.9). The development of similar enclosures at Aill Mhór in Gleannán and in the south of An Cnoc Buí raises the possibility that post-medieval farmers in Carna valued the idea of divided space and tried to reproduce it at booley settlements. It is telling that this only happened at seasonal sites which contained several houses, in other words, sites which approached the social complexity of home. By contrast, division of space does not feature at booley settlements in Achill, even though they are larger (McDonald, 2014: Appendix 1). During the later eighteenth and nineteenth centuries, tenant farmers in Achill were typically based in large nucleated settlements, outside which lay communal infields

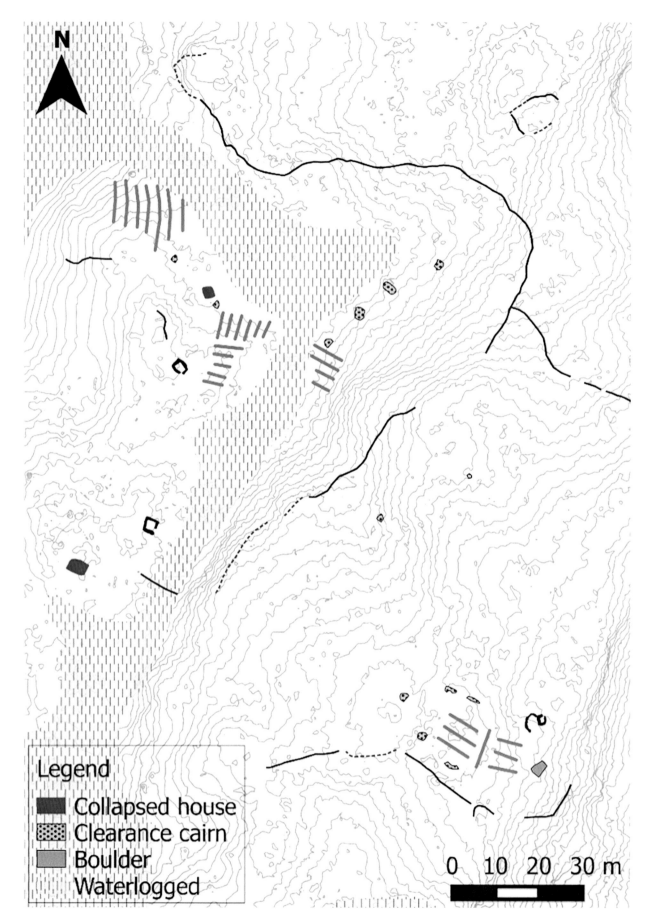

Figure 7.8. Centre of An Aill Mhór group in Gleannán
Source: Eugene Costello; contours generated from photography taken by Dr. Paul Naessens, Western Aerial Survey Ltd.

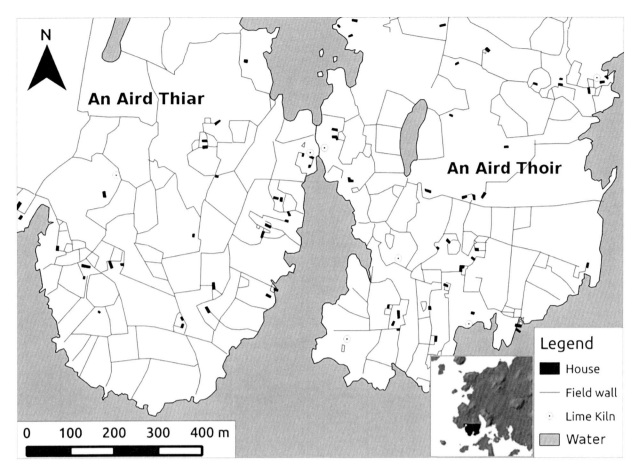

Figure 7.9. Farmhouses and fields in home townlands of An Aird Thiar and Thoir
Source: Digitised by Eugene Costello from 1838 6" map; Ordnance Survey Ireland, 2015

of tillage. Thus, permanently enclosed farmland did not exist to be replicated in Achill.

That said, even if tenants in Carna maintained separate holdings at home, they still accessed their respective summer pastures on a communal basis with neighbours (Martin rentals, 1837–52). In the peninsula's interior, there were no boundaries to separate the cattle of various tenants – they simply grazed together. Indeed, there were not even boundaries between the rough pastures of one townland and another; rather, the boundaries of An Cnoc Buí, Gleannán and other inland pastures were defined by natural features in the landscape which, it can only be assumed, were respected by traditions of mutual understanding. It is significant for future studies of Irish transhumance that the notion of commonage did not preclude herders from enclosing small patches of ground in the immediate vicinity of booley settlements, and recreating, as it were, a little piece of home while away on transhumance.

Conclusion

This paper has outlined the results of interdisciplinary research into small-scale transhumance in the Carna peninsula of South Connemara, as practised during its last phase in the eighteenth and nineteenth centuries. Particular attention has been paid to the archaeological evidence for transhumant settlements on rough hill pastures, the function of which ethnographic and historical sources have helped to elucidate. The material culture of this aspect of transhumance contains a duality of influences. On the one hand, people drew from their own innovative capacities to adapt construction styles to an extremely varied micro-topography. This is evident in the unpredictable form of most booley dwellings and also in the use of rock outcrops and ridges when enclosing space. The marginal position occupied by transhumant herders in society seems to have facilitated a degree of license in this regard. On the other hand, elements of enclosure at two complex transhumant settlements suggests that they were not entirely independent of the social structure of their community – the notion of divided space being derived from home settlements.

As fieldwork continues, our understanding of the material culture of Irish transhumance will evolve further. The present paper has demonstrated, as a preliminary stage, that structuration theory is a useful tool in the interpretation of this data. This is important given current difficulties in finding absolute dates for booley dwellings. The expansion of fieldwork across the Carna peninsula and other areas, followed by systematic small-scale excavation at both seasonal and permanent sites will provide a much richer and chronologically informed source of data for the archaeologist. Use of structuration theory and other conceptual frameworks in order to keep pace with the production of this evidence can eventually help bring the complicated and poorly documented world of pastoralism out of the margins of Irish archaeological debate. For the moment, it is concluded that people who looked after cows seasonally in South Connemara during the late eighteenth and nineteenth centuries saw summer pasture both as a microcosm of home *and* as a place where slightly different rules applied.

REFERENCES

Archaeological Survey of Ireland, 2014. Record of monuments and places. http://webgis.archaeology.ie/National-Monuments/FlexViewer (accessed 1 April 2015).

Barrett, J.C. 1994. *Fragments from Antiquity: An Archaeology of Social Life in Britain, 2900–1200 BC.* Oxford: Blackwell.

Barrett, J.C. 2001. Agency, the duality of structure, and the problem of the archaeological record. In: I. Hodder, ed. *Archaeological Theory Today.* Cambridge: Polity Press, pp. 141–64.

Barrett, J.C. & Fewster, K.J. 2000. Intimacy and structural transformation: Giddens and archaeology. In: C. Holtorf & H. Karlsson, ed. *Philosophy and Archaeological Practice: Perspectives for the 21st Century.* Göteborg: Bricoleur Press, pp. 25–33.

Barry, T.B. 1987. *The Archaeology of Medieval Ireland.* London: Routledge.

Browne, C.R. 1902. The ethnography of Carna and Mweenish, in the parish of Moyruss, Connemara. *Proceedings of the Royal Irish Academy,* C 6:503–34.

Costello, E. 2015. Post-medieval upland settlement and the decline of transhumance: a case-study from the Galtee Mountains, Ireland. *Landscape History,* 36(1):47–69.

Costello, E. 2016a. Feirmeoirí faoi cheilt: dul chun cinn agus dúshláin sa taighde faois ghnás an bhuailteachais [The hidden farmers: progress and difficulties in the study of transhumance]. *Béaloideas: Journal of the Folklore Society of Ireland,* 84:191–210.

Costello, E. 2016b. Seasonal management of cattle in the booleying system: new insights from South Connemara, western Ireland. In: M. O'Connell, F. Kelly & J.H. McAdam, eds. *Cattle in Ancient and Modern Ireland: Farming Practices, Environment and Economy.* Newcastle: Cambridge Scholars Publishing, pp. 66–74.

Costello, E. 2016c. Seasonal settlement and the interpretation of upland archaeology in the Galtee Mountains, Ireland. *Landscape History,* 37(1):87–98.Costello, E. 2017. Liminal learning: social practice in seasonal settlements of western Ireland. *Journal of Social Archaeology,* 17:188–209.

Dobres, M.A. & Robb, J.E. eds. 2000. *Agency in Archaeology.* London: Routledge.

Doherty, M.L. 2001. The folklore of cattle diseases: a veterinary perspective. *Béaloideas,* 69:41–75.

Dutton, H. 1824. *A Statistical and Agricultural Survey of the County of Galway.* Dublin: Royal Dublin Society.

Edwards, N. 1990. *The Archaeology of Early Medieval Ireland.* London: Routledge.

Encumbered Estates' Court, O'Brien, 1852. *Rental and particulars of the Martin estate,* 14 July 1852, Volume 17. MRGS 39/008, National Archives of Ireland.

EPA Envision, 2015. National Soils Database. http://gis.epa.ie/Envision/ (accessed 7 August 2015).

Evans, E.E. & Proudfoot, B. 1958. Excavations at the Deer's Meadow. *Ulster Journal of Archaeology,* 21:127–31.

Gardiner, M. 2012. Time regained: booley huts and seasonal settlement in the Mourne mountains, Co. Down, Ireland. In: S. Turner & R. Silvester, eds. *Life in Medieval Landscapes: People and Places in Medieval Britain.* Macclesfield: Windgather Press, pp. 106–124.

Gibbons, E. ed. 1991. *Conamara faoi cheilt/hidden Conamara.* Letterfrack: Connemara West Press.

Giddens, A. 1981. *A Contemporary Critique of Historical Materialism: Volume 1. Power, Property and the State.* London: MacMillan.

Giddens, A. 1984. *The Constitution of Society: Outline of the Theory of Structuration.* Cambridge: Polity Press.

Graham, J.M. 1954. Transhumance in Ireland, with special reference to its bearing on the evolution of rural communities in the west. Unpublished PhD thesis, Queen's University Belfast.

Hardiman, J. ed. 1846. *A Chorographical Description of West or h-Iar Connaught, Written A.D.1684 by Roderic O'Flaherty.* Dublin: Irish Archaeological Society.

Hodder, I. ed. 1982. *Symbolic and Structural Archaeology.* Cambridge: Cambridge University Press.

Hodder, I. & Hutson, S. 2003. *Reading the Past: Current Approaches to Interpretation in Archaeology.* Cambridge: Cambridge University Press.

Hogan, E. 1910. *Onomasticon goedelicum locorum et tribuum Hiberniae et Scottiae: An Index, with Identification, to the Gaelic Names of Places and Tribes.* Dublin: Royal Irish Academy.

Hole, F. 1996. The context of caprine domestication in the Zagros region. In: D. Harris, ed. *The Origins and Spread of Agriculture and Pastoralism in Eurasia.* London: University College London Press, pp. 263–81.

Lucas, A.T. 1989. *Cattle in Ancient Ireland.* Kilkenny: Boethius Press.

Mac Giollarnáth, S. 1941. *Annála beaga ó Iorrus Aithneach.* Baile Átha Cliath: Oifig an tSoláthair.

Martin rentals, 1837–52. M. 2429–31, 3440–01, 3443, National Archives of Ireland.

McDonald, B.T. 2014. Booleying in Achill, Achillbeg and Corraun: survey, excavation and analysis of booley settlements in the civil parish of Achill. Unpublished PhD thesis, National University of Ireland, Galway.

McSparron, C. 2002. A note on the discovery of two probable booley dwellings at Ballyutoag, County Antrim. *Ulster Journal of Archaeology,* 61:154–55.

National Folklore Collection, n.d., Newman Building, University College Dublin, Ireland.

Neilson Hancock, W., ed. 1865. *Ancient Laws of Ireland, Volume 1.* Dublin: Alexander Thom.

Ó Cathasaigh, S. 1943. Buailíochaí in iarthar Chonamara. *Béaloideas,* 13:159–60.

Ó Cróinín, D. 1995. *Early Medieval Ireland, 400–1200.* London: Routledge.

Ó Danachair, C. 1945. Traces of the Buaile in the Galtee Mountains. *Journal of the Royal Society of Antiquaries of Ireland,* 75:248–52.

Ó Dónaill, N. 1977. *Foclóir Gaeilge-Béarla*. Baile Átha Cliath: Oifig an tSoláthair,

Ó Gaora, C. 1937. *Obair is luadhainn nó saoghal sa ngaedhaltacht*. Baile Átha Cliath: Oifig Díolta Foilseacháin Rialtais.

Ó Héalaí, P. & Ó Tuairisg, L., eds. 2007. *Tobar an dúchais: béaloideas as Conamara agus Corca Dhuibhne*. An Daingean: An Sagart.

Ó hEochaidh, S. 1943. Buailteachas i dTír Chonaill. *Béaloideas*, 13:130–58.

O'Keeffe, T. 2000. *Medieval Ireland: An Archaeology*. Stroud: Tempus.

Ó Moghráin, P. 1943. Some Mayo traditions of the Buaile. *Béaloideas*, 13:161–72.

O'Rahilly, C. 1962. *Cath Finntrágha (edited ms. Rawlinson B 487)*. Dublin: Dublin Institute for Advanced Studies.

Ordnance Survey Ireland, 2015. Historic First Edition 6"maps. http://maps.osi.ie/publicviewer/ (accessed 7 May 2015).

O'Sullivan, A. and Sheehan, J. 1992. Fionnán enclosures: aspects of traditional land use in South Kerry. *Journal of the Kerry Archaeological and Historical Society*, 25:5–19.

Plummer, C. 1922. *Bethada Náem nÉrenn (Lives of Irish Saints), Volume 1*. Oxford: Clarendon Press.

Smyth, W.J. 2012. 'Mapping the people': the growth and distribution of the population. In: J. Crowley, W.J. Smyth & M. Murphy, eds. *Atlas of the Great Irish Famine, 1845–52*. Cork: Cork University Press, pp. 13–22.

Smith, C. 1756. *The Ancient and Present State of the County of Kerry*. Dublin: Self-published.

Williams, B.B. 1984. Excavations at Ballyutoag, County Antrim. *Ulster Journal of Archaeology*, 47:37–49.

Williams, B.B. & Robinson, P. 1983. The excavation of Bronze Age cists and a medieval booley dwelling at Glenmakeeran, County Antrim, and a discussion of booleying in north Antrim. *Ulster Journal of Archaeology*, 46:29–40.

CHAPTER 8

The changing character of transhumance in early and later medieval England

Mark Gardiner

Most studies of transhumance in England have examined particular places and particular periods. There have been few attempts at broader analyses to situate individual examples within a larger framework of changing responses to the exploitation of the English countryside over an extended period (Fox, 2012 is a notable exception). Fundamental to any such perspective is a need to recognize that transhumance in England was one strategy of land-use, and the areas grazed on a seasonal basis were not necessarily fundamentally different from other land. In contrast to some regions of transhumance in Scandinavia or many parts of continental Europe, the summer pastures in England were not all bleak moorlands or uplands which were otherwise unusable. The difference in elevation between the 'uplands' of England and the home settlements was often only a matter of a hundred metres or less. This leads to the second point considered here, which was that transhumance in England was a transformative practice which affected the ground that was grazed and often served as a means of preparing the land for cultivation and permanent settlement. Grazing concentrated nutrients in places where the animals were corralled for the night and suppressed woodland. The third point to be discussed is that transhumance was not merely as an economic practice but also a social one which led to the definition of boundaries and so shaped the territorial structure of England. In undefined or poorly defined territories, usage and occupation was a mark of possession, and the maintenance of the practice preserved a claim on the land. This paper seeks to look at the shifting character of transhumance which, over an extended period, was an important influence in shaping the countryside of England – the settlements, boundaries and indeed the landscape as a whole.

Discussions of transhumance often begin with an attempt to seek a close definition of the practice, to identify a feature which separates the true aspect from the less 'authentic' forms (Fox, 1996: 2–6). This is illusory, since no form was more pure, more true or more authentic than any other. Transhumance was a range of practices, which at one end included the seasonal movement of various livestock – cattle, sheep and sometimes pigs – on an annual basis to distant summer pastures, but at the other takes in seasonal grazing on open land not very far distant from the farmstead. What defines transhumance in England was a significant movement of animals according to a seasonal cycle in a recurring manner. We must exclude from this definition the practice of removing animals from pasture fields adjoining the farm during the winter months to prevent poaching (that is, damage to the grass sward). The underlying purpose of transhumance was to utilize more remote and often less productive lands during the summer when the forage was abundant, so that the livestock could be kept upon the proximal pasture, either grazing on the cut hay or upon the standing grass during the winter-time when animals had to be kept within or close to shelter.

Transhumance as a Developing Practice

This paper examines the changing patterns of transhumance over the millennium from AD 500 to 1500. By the sixteenth century, and indeed much earlier, the practice had largely ceased except in a few remote places. One of the limitations of a number of earlier studies is that they have tended to assume that the seasonal movement was an age-old practice which if recorded in, say the thirteenth century, must have had its roots many hundreds of years earlier. The argument here rejects that perspective and instead starts from the point of view that transhumance was a changing practice which was continuously adapted to shifts in economy and land use. The implications of this view need to be briefly considered, since they conflict with a number of assumptions about the development of the English landscape.

Since at least the early 1980s, it has generally been argued that while settlements may move in location, the essential framework of boundaries stayed largely the same (Michelmore, 1979: 1–2). The most thorough expression of this idea is the concept of the multiple estate proposed by Glanville Jones on the basis of late medieval Welsh documents. He argued that in both Wales and England pieces of upland were annexed to

© 2018 European Association of Archaeologists

regions of lowland in a regular, almost formal structure, and that the origin of such fixed units dates back in essence to the Iron Age. He sought to assemble fragments of evidence, some of it very late in date, showing detached lands of parishes or manors, which were the remaining evidence of former links between home lands and summer pastures (Barnwell & Roberts, 2011). Although aspects of Jones's argument have been much criticized (Gregson, 1985; Hadley, 1996), the idea of persistent links between upland pasture, lowland marsh and central settlement core has been fundamental to much of the work on the reconstruction of landscapes of the early medieval period. For example, in Surrey, John Blair (1991: 15–21) has sought to reconstruct the estate structure on the evidence of the links between home estates and outlying pastures. The view that boundaries endure, even though much else might change, has also been fundamental to the interpretation of the structure of England.

The second problem with the assumption that transhumance was a persistent practice concerns the late-recorded examples, particularly the grazing of the uplands on the moors of northern England and the South-West. It has been argued that these must be the last vestiges of the long-lasting custom and they preserved evidence of much earlier usage and behaviour. Such an approach is, to give one example, fundamental to the approach of K.P. Witney (1976: 211–75) who has sought to trace the late medieval denns or animal pastures in the Weald of Kent back to Domesday Book and to grants made in the ninth and tenth centuries.

The approach which regards seasonal settlement as a changing and developing practice is therefore a significant departure from most earlier scholarship. It has, however, been anticipated in a number of studies, particularly Stuart Wrathmell's interpretation of the development of Wharram Percy which stressed the way in which seasonal settlement was replaced by permanent occupation, leaving only slight traces in the landscape (Wrathmell, 2012: 87, 172–73). Wrathmell's analysis itself builds on an influential paper by Alan Everitt (1977) which argued that many of the early medieval summer pastures were not in areas of dense woodland or in bleak uplands, but in relatively low lands known as 'wolds'. Subsequent work has modified Everitt's initial conclusions and other scholars have argued that the use of wold for open land was a secondary meaning. The root of the word is the Old English *wald/weald*, meaning woodland. The term 'wold' was applied to areas which had been wooded early in the medieval period, but within a few centuries had been cleared to become open country (Hooke, 2013: 43; cf. Fox, 1989: 83). Everitt's work led others to look at the various wolds in England and consider how many had once been used as summer pasture – the Cotswolds, the Lincolnshire wolds and the wolds in Leicestershire and Nottinghamshire

(Hooke, 1978; Everitt, 1979; Fox, 1989: 85–89; Slater, 1979). Not only did it direct the attention of scholars to consider the way in which settlement had developed in these places, it also drew attention to the fact that transhumance was a major factor in the development of early medieval landscape across England. Before Everitt's paper discussions of transhumance had been largely confined to areas of dense woodland and to the tree-less moorlands. The possibility that transhumance might have taken place over a wider range of landscapes began to interest scholars.

With these preliminary remarks, it is possible now to turn to the detail of the changing character of transhumance. In order to provide a chronological perspective on transhumance, it is useful to distinguish an Early and Middle Anglo-Saxon phase of activity (*c.* 500–900) from later activity, covering the period 900–1200, which is better recorded in documents and has left greater trace in the landscape. That in turn can be separated from a third phase from 1200 onwards when transhumance was largely restricted to upland wastes. These divisions, though somewhat arbitrary, allow the changing character of transhumance to be traced.

The first phase of medieval transhumance (AD 500–900)

Transhumance formed an important element of the Anglo-Saxon economy, but it is nevertheless remarkable that there are references to it in one of the earliest surviving prose texts from England. *The Anonymous Life of St Cuthbert* mentions that in his youth Cuthbert spent time tending flocks on the hills with other shepherds on Leader Water on the Scottish borders where he apparently spent the night. It is recorded that the future saint was subsequently travelling in winter near Chester-le-Street (Co. Durham) when he took shelter from the rain in dwellings used only in the spring and summer, which seem very likely to have been shielings (Colgrave, 1940: 68–71, also 168–71). *The Life*, written in the years close to 700, but supposedly referring to events half a century earlier, suggests that such situations would have been familiar to contemporary readers.

The archaeological evidence for this early phase of transhumance is more difficult to identify. Settlement evidence from this period is slight and that for seasonal occupation is particularly difficult to locate. The most thorough archaeological investigation of a transhumance landscape has been undertaken in the area around Wharram Percy. The excavations of the late medieval deserted village are very well known but, as the project developed, the study embraced other periods, and in the final volume Stuart Wrathmell sought to interpret the evidence of settlement within the 'wolds model'. He argued that in the Early Anglo-Saxon period the Yorkshire Wolds were used as seasonal grazing pastures and suggested the excavated sixth- to seventh-century sunken buildings were temporary shelters for the shepherds (Wrathmell, 2012: 95). Wrathmell identified a change in the character of settlement in the mid- to late seventh century when the Wolds were reoccupied on a permanent basis. Curvilinear enclosures were constructed, known as Butterwick-type settlements, often associated with sunken buildings, some of which have been dated to the seventh to ninth century. The interpretation of these is disputed. Wrathmell sees them as evidence of permanent occupation, while Stocker and Everson argue that they are a further phase of seasonal settlement. Both groups agree that permanent settlement had certainly been established in the Wharram area by the second half of the ninth century when crop-processing waste was recorded and a mill site had been established at Wharram (Everson & Stocker, 2012: 204).

The importance of the Wharram study is that it records the progression from seasonal to permanent occupation in a wolds landscape. While the timing of the transition is disputed, the sequence is not, and it provides a clear model for the sort of archaeological remains we might expect to characterize temporary settlements. Sunken buildings are common enough when found in conjunction with post-built above-ground houses, but where they are found in isolation, it has been argued that they may have served as temporary accommodation for summer shepherds or cowherds (Gardiner, 2011: 211–13; Fox, 2012: 141–44). The sunken house discovered at North Marden on the Sussex Downs cut into the silted-up ditch of a prehistoric oval barrow, was identified as a summer settlement for a shepherd. That identification was reinforced when subsequent stripping of the adjoining land found no evidence for further, larger buildings in the vicinity (Figure 8.1; Drewett et al., 1986; Down & Welch, 1990: 221). In that case, the seasonal settlement was not the precursor of permanent buildings, as it was at Wharram. The sunken buildings found beneath thirteenth- and fourteenth-century farmsteads at Hound Tor on Dartmoor certainly did precede permanent occupation, but whether there was a gap between the periods of seasonal and full-time settlement is unclear (Beresford, 1979: 110–12).

These examples raise the question whether it is possible to identify other isolated sunken buildings which either developed into larger settlements, or alternatively were later abandoned. The chalk downland is rarely cited as an area of transhumance, but the North Marden shepherd's house suggests it might have served in that way. Environmental work done on the Sussex Downs and

Figure 8.1. *The seventh- to eighth-century sunken building at North Marden (Sussex) on the South Downs, probably used as for accommodation while grazing during the summer (scale length: 2m)*
Photo: Peter Drewett

adjoining area in Hampshire indicated that arable cultivation ceased after the Roman period and in the early medieval period settlement seems to have been largely confined to the valleys (Gardiner, 2003: 152). One of the few excavated settlements on the upper slopes of the chalk downland was located at Church Down, Chalton (Hampshire; Figure 8.2). The seventh-century settlement comprised 57 post-built structures and four

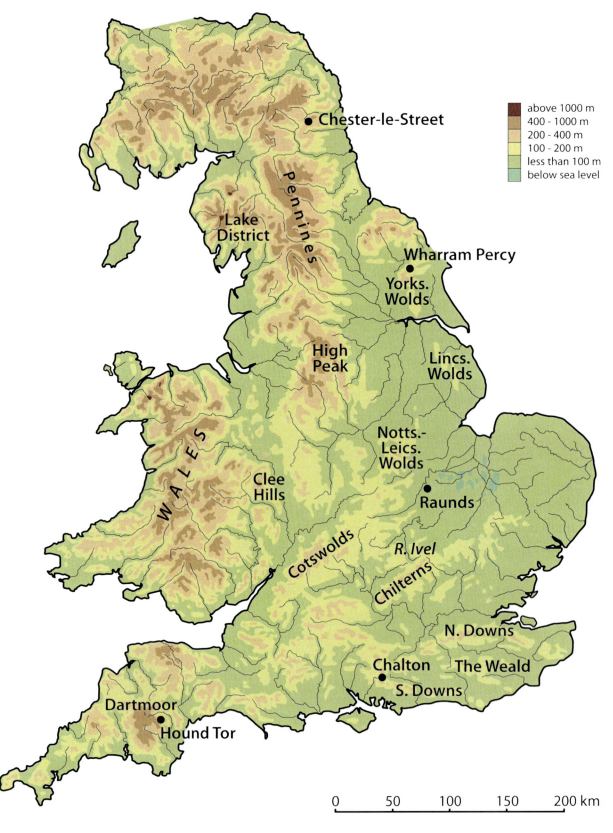

Figure 8.2. Selected areas of transhumance and other places mentioned in the text

sunken buildings. One of these was exceptionally large and from the range of finds appears to have belonged to the main period of settlement, but the others could have been transhumance huts which preceded the main period of occupation (Champion, 1977). However, the chronological relationship of the above- and below-ground buildings is uncertain and until further work is done on the publication it is not possible to do more than speculate on the origins of the site.

An important, but less influential aspect of Everitt's paper was his discussion of the territories occupied by the home farms of those settlements practising transhumance. He argued that these were largely situated in river valleys where the soils were more suitable for cultivation. The valleys were the core of natural units or 'river estates' often named after the river itself. The estates included land on the uplands used for grazing. Archaeological survey in the Raunds area has provided some support for this interpretation because it showed that all the early medieval farmsteads were situated close to rivers or streams (Parry, 2006: 92–96). Further south, the River Ivel around Biggleswade which appears to have formed the centre of a distinct unit from an early date. The people known as *Gifle* are listed amongst the tributary groups in Tribal Hidage, an enigmatic document attributed to a date within the period 670 to 690 (Davies & Vierck, 1974: 227). Their name is taken from the River Ivel and is also remembered in the parishes of Northill (*Nortgiuele*) and Southill (*Sudgiuele*) which adjoin the river to the west, while an outlying branch of the people is reflected by the place-name Yielden some 25km to the north-west. Excavations to the west of Biggleswade found a pair of excavated ditches, apparently flanking a drove road up to 90m wide and perhaps dating to the eighth or ninth century the road provides a material expression of one link between the river valley and the 'upland' – little of it rising above 90m above sea level) – to the west. A second drove road to the south though traced for a shorter distance, provided further evidence for the movement of animals to the upland (Edgeworth, 2008).

The second phase of medieval transhumance (AD 900–1200)

The second phase of transhumance is better recorded in historical sources, because of their greater number from the tenth century onwards. We can also be more confident in using evidence from the landscape, including patterns of drove roads and boundaries. Traces of the road system from around the turn of the millennium seem to have persisted in the landscape, while the pattern of boundaries seems to have become increasingly fixed around this time. One of the best known

illustrations of using later evidence to identify patterns of transhumance is the study by Ford of Warwickshire, which employed a combination of early charters and late medieval records of detached property (Ford, 1979: 150–51). The pattern of droveways in part of this area recorded by Hooke (1998: 160–61) reflect a similar orientation and she noted that one of these tracks was described in a charter of 963 as 'the way to the shire wood' (Sawyer, 1968: no. 1307).

A similar approach has been adopted by Fox who notes that there were linkages between estates some distance from Dartmoor and lands on its periphery. One example he cites is the connection between Cockington on Tor Bay and a virgate (conventionally about 30 acres [12ha] of land) at Dewdon on the western edge of the moor recorded in Domesday Book. Fox (2012: 108–38) argues, that because of their distance from the home settlement, the lands adjoining Dartmoor must have been used on a seasonal basis. He seems to hesitate when trying to explain the way in which these moor-edge settlements might have been used, suggesting that they were intended to serve as a place of seasonal habitation for the herdsmen (Fox, 2006: 97). However, they were simply too large for that purpose. A charter of 956 granted an estate, which included moor-edge lands of one hide at Bittleford and another hide at Brimley (Sawyer, 1968: no. 601; Fox, 2012: 111–14). A hide was an extensive area, nominally around 120 acres (*c*. 50ha) but varying considerably in size, and clearly much too large for a house alone. A more probable interpretation is that these had been areas of the summer grazing. Later, and certainly by the tenth and the eleventh centuries in those cases mentioned, the moor-edge land was occupied all year-round and the summer grazing was moved on to the higher land of the moor itself.

Similar arguments have been made by Ian Whyte for the Lake District, an area for which, however, there are few early documentary sources. He notes that place-names formed from Old Norse *sætr* occurred at a lower altitude in the main dales, than those formed from *skáli* which were in tributary valleys or on the slopes of the fells. Both words refer to shielings and so the difference suggests that the former were the earliest occupied transhumance huts, while later ones on poorer ground were given *skáli* names. In dating the use of the elements, it is notable that it was *skáli* rather than *sætr* that entered Middle English to form *shāle, schēle* which is the base of the modern word 'shieling', a building at a seasonal settlement. Whyte interprets the change in location as an indication that the earlier shieling sites were subsequently occupied by the later eleventh and early twelfth centuries, and later sites had to be established higher in the hills. But this was not the end of the process. By the early thirteenth century, Scalthwait-erigg and Skelsmergh – both *skáli* place-names – were permanently occupied (Whyte, 1985: 105–10).

The same was probably happening in Kent, but there it is obscured by the continuing use of the Old English word, *denn*. Although usually translated as swine pasture, at some stage it began to be applied to any distant settlement in the Weald, whether seasonal or not, and whether used by pigs. For example, *Hwetonstede* (Whetsted in Capel, Kent), was described as a swine pasture (*denbær*) of Snodland in a charter of AD 838 (Sawyer, 1968: no. 280). However, the place-name means the 'wheat place', which seems to suggest that conditions then had progressed well beyond a hut in the woods occupied only when the acorns and beech nuts were falling. It is from hints such as these that the replacement of seasonal by permanent settlement has to be traced, but the extraordinary advance in settlement is clarified a few centuries later from the lists of churches in the Weald recorded in Textus Roffensis and Domesday Monachorum of *c.* 1100 which imply a substantial and permanent population (Sawyer, 1978: 136–37).

In this phase too the areas once used for common seasonal grazing were increasingly being broken up between individual estates. For example, chalk downland in Oxfordshire had by the tenth century been divided into discrete areas for the use of specific estates (Hooke, 1987: 133–37). The same pattern can be seen in the pattern of estates and later manors to the north of the Thames in Buckinghamshire. Here settlements, some of which have been excavated close to the river, had grazing and farmsteads some 10km to the north in the Chiltern Hills (Foreman et al., 2002; Chenevix-Trench, 1973: 242–43). Often the division must have been made in the manner described in *c.* 1210 for Brockham and Betchwork in Surrey, where the boundary was established along hedges and other landmarks (Blair, 1991: 94).

The third phase of medieval transhumance (AD 1200–1500)

The rising pressure of population in England in the thirteenth century put increasing pressure on commonland. Much of the land suitable for cultivation as pasture or as arable had been already been enclosed from the woodland or moorland. Some sense of the scale of enclosure of commonland is apparent from a study of County Durham which included substantial areas of moorland at the fringes of the Pennines. Figures here suggest that the acreage of arable increased 34% between the late twelfth or early thirteenth century and the mid-fourteenth century (Dunsford & Harris, 2003: 49). Where commonlands remained, the rights to graze and take wood were more precisely defined to manage their usage. This is unusually well documented

in Wyfold (Oxfordshire) on the Chiltern hills where around 1200 the land was covered with trees and heath. A grange was established there by the monks of Thame Abbey and as a consequence the lord of Rotherfield gave up his rights in the common pasture adjoining the grange. The monks' pasture was then enclosed by a hedge and the tenants' rights to take timber and have grazing were limited to the common wood beyond, but even that had to be shared with the monks (Roden, 1968: 61). A similar process of woodland division can be followed in Sussex where the history of a dispute between John de Tregoz and the abbot of Fécamp was narrated in a charter of 1195. The woods of *Dureshurst* had been divided between the two in 1164 so that John had a three-quarters share and the abbot a one-quarter part. The division of rights to the timber, pannage and pasture was done on this proportionate basis, so that when John cut three trees, the abbot was entitled to cut one other. Thirty years later this arrangement had broken down, and it was agreed to divide the wood up with a boundary so that the rights were more precisely defined (Round, 1899: no. 142).

The establishment of upland livestock farms or granges was an important factor in both the decline of transhumance and the restriction of commonland. The term 'grange' is sometimes applied only to monastic cattle or sheep farms, but there were similar lay establishments. These large livestock farmsteads provided year-round accommodation for livestock so that it was not necessary to drive them off the hills in the winter. During the coldest months, most of the animals were housed inside and fed on hay (Aitkin, 1994: 17). Granges expanded sharply in number in the thirteenth century to exploit the upland pastures. In Wyresdale (Lancashire) alone there were 20 cattle farms in 1297 situated at intervals of between 0.5 and 1km along the valley, at least one of which replaced a former seasonal settlement (Higham, 2004: 115–18). The result of this intensified use was that the great common wastes of the moorlands were divided between the lords and the tenants of individual lordships and their boundaries marked with walls or hedges, such as that constructed in Cumberland in 1266 between the lands of Sir Roger de Lancaster and Henry, lord of Tirril (Ragg, 1910: 447–50). Pressure on the common wastes were being felt even in these areas and their use for shielings was also in decline. By the early thirteenth century much of the seasonal movement to the summer pastures was over relatively short distances and the cutting of grass for hay in Allendale in 1421–22 suggests that the shielings there had become permanently occupied (Winchester, 1987: 95; Winchester, 2000: 93).

One of the last areas where seasonal movement of livestock is claimed to have been widespread in southeast England, was the Weald but here too it is apparent that it was very much reduced. There is some evidence for it on the archbishop's Kent manors where the customs regulating the grazing of pigs in the Wealden woodlands are noted in *c.* 1285. However, it may have been only the lord's pigs which were still driven into the woods; it is unclear whether it was still a practice of his tenants (Witney, 1976: 155; Witney, 2000: xxxvi–xxxviii). In the adjoining area of Sussex by the late thirteenth century the tenants of the archbishop of Canterbury seem to have had the right of common only on the waste adjoining their tenement. In the northern part of the archbishop's manor of South Malling the townships were based upon areas of local common woodland (Gardiner, 1996: 128). The impression is that here, as elsewhere, the long-distance movement of herders with their livestock had largely disappeared.

Throughout England by the thirteenth century, and possibly well before, common rights had been substantially restricted with priority given to local people. At the same time new practices by which livestock on the summer pastures were overseen by local paid supervisors, who replaced the herders who had formerly travelled with the flocks and dwelt for the summer in the uplands. Fox (2012: 46) describes this as impersonal transhumance because, although the animals moved, the people did not. The local people took in animals from more distant settlers and were paid to look after them on the commonland. While Fox has documented this on Dartmoor, we may suspect that the practice elsewhere was similar. In the Weald too there was a distinction between the rights of those living by the commonland and those sending livestock from a distance, perhaps to be looked after by others. On Ashdown Forest in Sussex, the inhabitants bordering the common were charged *2d.* per pig, but those of 'outsiders' (*extranei*) were charged *3d.* (Legge, 1907: 314). A similar distinction was made at Otford in the Kent Weald and probably elsewhere on the archbishop's estate. Tenants paid *2d.* for pannage (grazing of pigs in woodland), while the outsiders (*forinseci*) paid twice that (Du Boulay, 1961: 81).

Summary of the development of transhumance

Three phases of transhumance have been identified and it is possible now to summarize their main features. The seasonal movement of livestock appears to have been a very early feature of the Anglo-Saxon economy, yet the first stages remain hard to trace because the remains are slight and the documentary references to the activity comparatively few. The early phase of transhumance included movement of animals from the valley bottoms on to higher land, and it seems to have been widespread, perhaps even ubiquitous. During the second phase permanent farmsteads were established in many of the places which had been initially used as summer settlements and the seasonal grazing grounds were pushed upwards into more remote and often more barren areas of upland. Continued links between the lowland and upland areas are often marked by detached portions of estates and parishes, and also by well-established system of drove roads. In the final phase common rights were increasingly circumscribed, which meant that long-distance movement of animals was more difficult. A system of 'impersonal transhumance' developed by which herders living close to upland commons took in and looked after the livestock from tenants settled at a distance. Gradually, granges replaced shielings and the scope for transhumance was greatly reduced as rights over the common wastes were limited. By the thirteenth century transhumance in England was in sharp decline.

TRANSHUMANCE AS A TRANSFORMATIVE PRACTICE

Historians, discussing the term 'wolds', have suggested that there was a change in those areas from woodland to open land. The Old English word *wald/weald* was applied in Warwickshire before 800 to areas which had been wooded (Wager, 1998: 160). The subsequently almost tree-less state of the wolds shows that large-scale clearance took place, probably within the early Middle Ages. Sarah Wager has suggested that the areas in which this took place were wood pasture, that is, open land with a few trees and used for grazing (Wager, 1998: 140; Fleming, 2012). The clearance of the woods on such land would have required much less labour than for areas of coppice, or more dense woodland. Indeed, it is possible that heavy grazing over a period of time may have prevented the growth of saplings and led to the disappearance of the woodland without any active intervention to clear it (Wager, 1998: 139–40). The Dutch ecologist, Frans Vera (2000) has argued that intense grazing by ungulates is sufficient to prevent the regrowth of trees and that the woodland will eventually become open land as the elderly trees die. However, that view has not been met with uncritical acceptance (Mitchell, 2005). On the other hand, work on the impact of wild boar on the woodland, which were not far removed in their behaviour from medieval domesticated pigs, has suggested that its impact would have been significant. Even at the very modest density of 2 pigs/km^2, boar significantly reduced tree seedling regeneration in oak woodland and autumn pannage by herds of pigs may have acted similarly (Sweitzer & Van Vuren, 2002).

There are numerous historical examples of the transformation of grazed woodland commons to open land. Oliver Rackham notes the example of Thorpe Wood

(Norfolk) which was transformed from woodland in the early twelfth century to areas of heath with some woods by 1236, apparently due to heavy grazing (Rackham, 1976: 136–38). The outwoods at Havering (Essex) which in 1086 had provided pannage for 500 swine was subsequently divided up and by 1306 it was said that one of these, Romford Wood, was devastated (Powell, 1978: 19). In the Sussex Weald areas of upland were turned into open heath in the thirteenth and fourteenth centuries, partially by grazing and partly by firing the heather to encourage new growth which is more palatable to livestock. When, however, the pressure of grazing was reduced in the later fourteenth and fifteenth century, woodland was able to re-establish itself on the heaths (Gardiner, 1996: 127).

Grazing at sufficient intensities, unless carefully regulated, did have the effect of reducing the number of trees on commonland. Another impact of grazing was that it concentrated nutrients around the sites of the shielings where the livestock was milked or kept overnight and dung was dropped. This led to the growth of better pasture which in turn encouraged more intense grazing and so to further manuring of the soil. This prepared the soil around the shielings for cultivation. Permanent farms with their surrounding fields of pasture and arable were able to be developed out of sites of shielings as the pressure of population drove the expansion of settlement. This seems to have been what happened at Hound Tor where the area around the shielings was converted into field in the thirteenth and early fourteenth centuries (Beresford, 1979: 150–52).

Transhumance as a social practice

Links between home farms and summer pastures have been identified in some areas of the England from the network of parallel drove roads. Perhaps surprisingly, there has been very little discussion of why such a network of tracks should arise and what its implications are. There is no fundamental reason why the seasonal movement of livestock should lead to the formation of such an orderly pattern. For example, roads, although tending in the same general direction from the valleys to the hills, might cross each other. The reality is that this tends not to happen, but instead the pattern is overwhelmingly parallel, though routes do occasionally converge. In one of the few discussions of the pattern, Fox (2012: 195–96) has suggested two reasons for the large number of tracks. He argues, first, that this was to prevent congestion on the drove roads when many animals were being moved. Second, he notes that numerous tracks meant the pasture along the way would not have been consumed by earlier flocks or herds. He adds a further point about the pattern of roads: straight

routes were preferred because they allowed livestock, often weak in the springtime, to reach the grazing lands as promptly as possible. He draws attention to a charter of 1031 which mentions the road to Dartmoor used by the men of Buckland (Sawyer, 1968: no. 963) suggesting that some routes were associated with particular estates.

Whatever the reason for this recurrent pattern of droveways, the result was the same: the system of parallel tracks meant that settlements tended to have the same neighbours in both the valleys and in the summer pastures. In effect, the social communities in the valleys were reproduced in the uplands. The nature of such early medieval communities is poorly understood, but in many of the discussions of such groups the role of geography is underplayed. Instead of seeing such groups arising out of the role of river valleys in providing a common centre and unifying core, the emphasis has tended to be on the importance of extended families and kings in bringing together these communities (Yorke, 2000: 82–85). However, some recent studies have stressed the importance of communities based around river valleys or other geographical areas (Faith, 2009: 28–29; Lloyd, 2013: 93–94). The management of common grazing in the uplands was a problem which necessarily concerned whole communities, since the use of the land had to be regulated and animals from different herds or flocks which had become intermixed had to be separated. Oosthuizen (2011: 162–67, 180) goes beyond this and argues that common grazing played an active part in community building. The network of droveways reflects the importance of neighbours in the working together at the local level in the summer pastures, and also reflects the wider community's involvement in the overall management of the commonland.

A further aspect of the pattern of drove roads is the distance between the home farms and summer pastures. Why was it necessary for herders in the early medieval period to travel so far, and why were areas of woodland nearer to hand were not used instead? One possible explanation is that summer grazing was a way of staking a claim on a territory. Medieval society saw land in terms of rights over areas, rather than ownership. In order to make a claim on land, it had to be shown that it was used and had been used in the past. Transhumance was a practical way of asserting claims over a wider area. This is not to say that the sole reason for moving livestock to the uplands was to claim common rights there, but rather that by moving over and through territory and by settling, even for the summer alone, on an area of pasture, the land could be annexed by a community. There was a strategic interest in moving animals large distances, even if it was not strictly necessary for economic purposes. It is impossible to know the origin of such rights of usage and how communities gained new rights to distant pasture lands, though Oosthuizen (2011: 179–81) is inclined to place their origins in prehistory. She does not argue, along with Glanville Jones, that such territories were fixed and unchanging. Yet, while recognizing the possible fluidity of common rights, we should balance it with a realization that usage was not entirely transitory: tradition conferred rights which were not swept away by the lapse of a single year or two. Even in areas of transhumance where the boundaries may not have been sharply defined, it was in everyone's interest to establish the nature of rights and remember these.

TOWARDS A LONG-TERM PERSPECTIVE

It has already been noted that implicit in most discussions of transhumance in England has been a view that the late surviving evidence was an attenuated survival of earlier practices. Equally, it has been indicated that this is an inadequate and, indeed, a misleading interpretation. Transhumance was not an unvarying practice which gradually faded away over the centuries, but one which was adapted, often quite radically, to different circumstances. Projecting late evidence backwards does not therefore provide an accurate guide to the earlier situation. We must begin the critique of the view of the attenuation of transhumance with consideration of the model of the wolds. As an hypothesis, for it is no more than that, the wolds model has proved to have a powerful explanatory value for both the place-names and features of the landscape. For example, when applied at Wharram Percy, it provided a valuable means of interpreting the archaeological discoveries which were otherwise difficult to put in an explanatory framework. The implications of the view that the wolds had been formerly wooded areas of seasonal grazing have been inadequately explored and two aspects, in particular, need further consideration here.

First, the interpretation points to a stratum of transhumance which is otherwise very poorly attested because it had almost ceased before significant numbers of documentary sources were compiled. It has also left rather limited traces in the landscape. The droveways which linked the parent settlement to the wold pastures are less apparent in the landscape, something that Fox (1989: 87) attributed to the early severance of connections between the two. Equally, the presence of detached portions of manors or parishes, often a mark of transhumance are less common in the wold regions for the same reason (Fox, 1989: 87–9).

The second aspect of the 'wold interpretation' is the implication that transhumance was much more widespread than had been assumed. The seasonal movement of livestock was well recorded in some areas, including the Weald and the Warwickshire Arden, but little

suspected in the Cotswolds and the Nottinghamshire and Leicester Wolds, areas which were cleared of woodland at an early date. Once it was recognized in such places, the argument that it might also have been found in the Cambridgeshire and Lincolnshire Wolds could also be made, though there remains little work on the subject in these areas. Moreover, there seems no reason to assume that transhumance was limited to those areas described as 'wolds' or where it was recorded in later documents. Peter Warner (1996: 48–49) has, for example, suggested that the pattern of roads in north Suffolk and south Norfolk suggests a pattern of transhumance to the interfluves either side of the Waveney valley. Almost any area of early medieval woodland may have been used for seasonal grazing, and as evidence has grown for its widespread nature, it increasingly appears that it was a general practice for early medieval settlements throughout England.

It follows from these two points that many early medieval shieling sites were either later abandoned or, as at Wharram Percy, developed into year-round settlements. Transhumance, if it persisted, must have moved to other areas where permanent occupation had not been established. So what we see in the tenth- and eleventh-century records of the practice is evidence of places which had not yet been permanently settled, either because the soils were unattractive, or because the rising pressure of population in that area was insufficient to lead to the occupation of such sites. Moreover, the places in which transhumance still occurred in the twelfth and thirteenth centuries were the least attractive places of all, areas which because of the density of woodland or the nature of the soils remained unsuitable for the establishment of farmsteads. It is therefore a mistake to argue that such places provide evidence for earlier transhumance; they were areas which were so undesirable that permanent settlement had yet to be established. It is hardly surprising to find, when we look at the evidence, that late medieval transhumance remained only in the high uplands and the dense woodlands, places which continued to be unattractive for farmers. Further research is required to establish whether such difficult areas had been used at all for early medieval transhumance or in that period were simply 'wild', open land.

A further aspect of transhumance which had been identified is that the rights of common over land were increasingly restricted to the surrounding communities. More distant settlements had largely lost their claims. Tenterden in Kent (the denn or animal pasture of the people of Thanet) was 60km away from the parent settlement, and charters of the period and other place-names indicate that this was not exceptional. By the time of Domesday Book (1086), the use of distant animal pastures in Kent was already in decline and transhumance was being reoriented towards places closer to hand. The manors in that county with the highest swine renders, and presumably those grazing the greatest number of livestock in the Weald, were those closest to the periphery of the woodland and with closest access to the resource (Witney, 1976: 97–100). When we get to the better documented thirteenth and fourteenth century, a consistent pattern has emerged with lands closest to the common having greater rights than those further away. So, the farms adjoining Dartmoor had 'venville' rights which gave their tenants to graze animals on the upland for a small fixed fee. In Derbyshire lands adjoining the Forest of the High Peak called 'wenlands' (a term clearly related to the 'venville', and here contrasted with 'widelands' which lay further away) had similar rights, and settlements in Shropshire around Clee Forest had rights to graze that area of the Clee Hills (Cox, 1905: 408; Winchester, 2004: 22).

CONCLUSION

The discussion of transhumance above is a further stage in the critical re-examination of the ideas which have underpinned our interpretation of the medieval landscape of England. In an earlier study we sought to take a more nuanced examination of a single area of woodland (Chatwin & Gardiner, 2005). The common theme of both this paper and that previous one is a critical scepticism of a number of assumptions underlying the interpretation of the medieval landscape. It is argued here that while they are not necessarily incorrect, it must be recognized that the evidential basis on which they are based is often insubstantial. Too often, assumption has been added to assumption and neither the foundations of the interpretation, nor the implications have been re-examined. Transhumance was undoubtedly an important factor in the formation of the English landscape but, by failing to understanding the changing character of the practice over time, it has not been possible to appreciate the nature of its contribution.

ACKNOWLEDGEMENT

I am grateful to Libby Mulqueeny for preparing Figure 8.2.

REFERENCES

Aitkin, M.A. 1994. Land use and management in the upland demesne of the De Lacy estate of Blackburnshire *c.* 1300. *Agricultural History Review*, 42(1):1–19.

Barnwell, P.S. & Roberts, B.K. 2011. *Britons, Saxons and Scandinavians: The Historical Geography of Glanville R.J. Jones.* Turnhout, Brepols.

Beresford, G. 1979. Three deserted medieval settlements on Dartmoor: a report on the late E. Marie Minter's excavations. *Medieval Archaeology*, 23:98–158.

Blair, J. 1991. *Early Medieval Surrey: Landholding, Church and Settlement.* Stroud, Alan Sutton.

Champion, T. 1977. Chalton. *Current Archaeology*, 5(12):364–69.

Chatwin, D. & Gardiner, M.F. 2005. Rethinking the early medieval settlement of woodlands: evidence from the western Sussex Weald. *Landscape History*, 27:31–49.

Chenevix-Trench, J. 1973. Coleshill and the settlements of the Chilterns. *Records of Buckinghamshire*, 19(3):241–58.

Colgrave, B. 1940. *Two Lives of Saint Cuthbert: A Life by an Anonymous Monk of Lindisfarne and Bede's Prose life.* Cambridge: Cambridge University Press.

Cox, J.C. 1905. Forestry. In: W. Page, ed. *The Victoria History of the County of Derby: Volume 1.* London: Archibald Constable, pp. 397–425.

Davies, W. & Vierck, H. 1974. The contexts of Tribal Hidage: social aggregates and settlement patterns. *Frühmittelalterliche Studien*, 8:223–93.

Down, A. & Welch, M.G. 1990. *Chichester Excavations VII: Apple Down and the Mardens.* Chichester: Chichester District Council.

Drewett, P.L., Holgate, B., Foster, S. & Ellerby, H. 1986. The excavation of a Saxon sunken building at North Marden, West Sussex. *Sussex Archaeological Collections*, 124:109–18.

Du Boulay, F.R.H. 1961. Denns, droving and danger. *Archaeologia Cantiana*, 76:75–87.

Dunsford, H.M. & Harris, S.J. 2003. Colonization of the wasteland in County Durham, 1100–1400. *Economic History Review*, 56(1):34–56.

Edgeworth, M. 2008. Linking urban townscape with rural landscape: evidence of animal transhumance in the River Ivel Valley, Bedfordshire. *Medieval Settlement Research*, 23:22–27.

Everitt, A. 1977. River and wold: reflections on the historical origin of regions and pays. *Journal of Historical Geography*, 3(1):1–19.

Everitt, A. 1979. The wolds once more. *Journal of Historical Geography*, 5(1):67–71.

Everson, P. & Stocker, D. 2012. Wharram before the village moment. In: S. Wrathmell, ed. *A History of Wharram Percy and its Neighbours (Wharram: A Study of Settlement on the Yorkshire Wolds, XIII)*. York: York University Archaeological Publications, pp. 164–72.

Fleming, A. 2012. Working with wood-pasture. In: S. Turner & B. Silvester, eds. *Life in Medieval Landscapes: People and Places in the Middle Ages.* Oxford: Windgather, pp. 15–31.

Faith, R. 2009. Forces and relations of production in early Medieval England. *Journal of Agrarian Change*, 9(1):23–41.

Ford, W.J. 1979. Some settlement patterns in the central region of the Warwickshire Avon. In: P.H. Sawyer, ed. *English Medieval Settlement.* London: Edward Arnold, pp. 143–63.

Foreman, S., Hillar, S. & Petts, D. 2002. *Gathering the People, Settling the Land. The Archaeology of a Middle Thames Landscape: Anglo-Saxon to Medieval.* Oxford: Oxford Archaeology.

Fox, H.S.A. 1989. The people of the wolds in English settlement history. In: M. Aston, D. Austin & C. Dyer, eds. *The Rural Settlements of Medieval England: Studies Dedicated to Maurice Beresford and John Hurst.* Oxford: Blackwell, pp. 77–101.

Fox, H.S.A. 1996. Introduction: transhumance and seasonal settlement. In: H.S.A. Fox, ed. *Seasonal Settlement*. Leicester: Department of Adult Education, University of Leicester, pp. 1–23.

Fox, H.S.A. 2006. Fragmented manors and the customs of the Anglo-Saxons. In: S. Keynes & A.P. Smyth, eds. *Anglo-Saxons: Studies Presented to Cyril Roy Hart*. Dublin: Four Courts Press, pp. 78–97.

Fox, H.S.A. 2012. *Dartmoor's Alluring Uplands: Transhumance and Pastoral Management in the Middle Ages*. Exeter: University of Exeter Press.

Gardiner, M.F. 1996. The geography and peasant rural economy of the eastern Sussex High Weald, 1300–1420. *Sussex Archaeological Collections*, 134:123–39.

Gardiner, M.F. 2003. Economy and landscape change in post-Roman and early medieval Sussex, 450–1175. In: D.R. Rudling, ed. *The Archaeology of Sussex to AD 2000*. King's Lynn: Heritage, pp. 151–60.

Gardiner, M.F. 2011. Late Saxon Settlement. In: H. Hamerow, S. Crawford & D. Hinton, eds. *A Handbook of Anglo-Saxon Archaeology*. Oxford: Oxford University Press, pp. 198–217.

Gregson, N. 1985. The multiple estate model: some critical questions. *Journal of Historical Geography*, 11(4):339–51.

Hadley, D.M. 1996. Multiple estates and the origins of the manorial structure of the northern Danelaw. *Journal of Historical Geography*, 22(1):3–15.

Higham, N.J. 2004. *A Frontier Landscape: The North West in the Middle Ages*. Macclesfield: Windgather Press.

Hooke, D. 1978. Early Cotswolds woodland. *Journal of Historical Geography*, 4(4):333–41.

Hooke, D. 1987. Anglo-Saxon estates in the Vale of the White Horse. *Oxoniensia*, 52:129–43.

Hooke, D. 1998. *The Landscape of Anglo-Saxon England*. London: Leicester University Press.

Hooke, D. 2013. Old English *wald, weald* in place-names. *Landscape History*, 34(1):33–49.

Legge, W.H. 1907. Forestry. In: W. Page, ed. *The Victoria History of the County of Sussex: Volume 2*. London: Archibald Constable, pp. 291–325.

Lloyd, J. 2013. The origins of the lathes of East Kent. *Archaeologia Cantiana*, 133:83–113.

Michelmore, D.J.H. 1979. The reconstruction of the early tenurial and territorial divisions of the landscape of northern England. *Landscape History*, 1:1–9.

Mitchell F.J.G. 2005. How open were European primeval forests? Hypothesis testing using palaeoecological data. *Journal of Ecology*, 93:168–77.

Oosthuizen, S. 2011. Archaeology, common rights and the origins of Anglo-Saxon identity. *Early Medieval Europe*, 19(2):153–81.

Parry 2006. *Raunds Areas Survey: An Archaeological Study of the Landscape of Raunds, Northamptonshire 1985–94*. Oxford: Oxbow Books.

Powell, W.R. 1978. *A History of the County of Essex: Volume 7*. Oxford: Published for the Institute of Historical Research by Oxford University Press.

Rackham, O. 1976. *Trees and Woodland in the British Landscape*. London: Dent.

Ragg, F.W. 1910. De Lancaster. *Transactions of the Cumberland and Westmorland Antiquarian and Archaeological Society*, new series, 10:395–494.

Roden, D. 1968. Woodland and its management in the medieval Chilterns. *Forestry*, 41(1):59–71.

Round, J.H. 1899. *Calendar of Documents Preserved in France*, 1. London: Her Majesty's Stationery Office.

Sawyer, P.H. 1968. *Anglo-Saxon Charters: An Annotated List and Bibliography*. London: Royal Historical Society.

Sawyer, P.H. 1978. *From Roman Britain to Norman England*. London: Methuen.

Slater, T. 1979. More on the wolds. *Journal of Historical Geography*, 5(2):213–18.

Sweitzer, R.A. & Van Vuren, D.H. 2002. Rooting and foraging effects of wild pigs on tree regeneration and acorn survival in California's oak woodland ecosystems. In: R.B. Standiford, D. McCreary & K.L. Purcel, eds. *Proceedings of the Fifth Symposium on Oak Woodlands: Oaks in California's Changing Landscape*. Berkeley, California: United States Department of Agriculture, Forest Service, Pacific Southwest Research Station, pp. 219–31.

Vera, F.W.M. 2000. *Grazing Ecology and Forest History*. Wallingford: CABI.

Wager, S.J. 1998. *Woods, Wolds and Groves: The Woodland of Medieval Warwickshire*. Oxford: British Archaeological Reports.

Warner, P. 1996. *The Origins of Suffolk*. Manchester: Manchester University Press.

Whyte, I.D. 1985. Shielings and the upland pastoral economy of the Lake District in medieval and early modern times. In: J.R. Baldwin & I.D. Whyte, eds. *The Scandinavians in Cumbria*. Edinburgh: Scottish Society for Northern Studies, pp. 103–17.

Winchester, A.J.L. 1987. *Landscape and Society in Medieval Cumbria*. Edinburgh: John Donald.

Winchester, A.J.L. 2000. *The Harvest of the Hills: Rural Life in Northern England and the Scottish Borders, 1400–1700*. Edinburgh: Edinburgh University Press.

Winchester, A.J.L. 2004. Moorland forests of medieval England. In: I.D. Whyte & A.J.L. Winchester, eds. *Society, Landscape and Environment in Upland Britain*. Birmingham: Society for Landscape Studies, pp. 21–34.

Witney, K.P. 1976. *The Jutish Forest: A Study of the Weald of Kent from 450 to 1350 AD*. London: Athlone Press.

Witney, K.P. 2000. *A Survey of the Archbishop Pecham's Kentish Manors, 1283–1285*. Maidstone: Kent Archaeological Society.

Wrathmell, S. 2012. *A History of Wharram Percy and its Neighbours (Wharram: A Study of Settlement on the Yorkshire Wolds, XIII)*. York: York University Archaeological Publications.

Yorke, B. 2000. Political and ethnic identity: a case study of Anglo-Saxon practice. In: W.O. Frazer & A. Tyrrell, eds. *Social Identity in Early Medieval Britain*. London: Leicester University Press, pp. 69–89.

CHAPTER 9

Seasonal pastoral settlement in the lower mountains of the Auvergne region (France) during the medieval and modern periods (thirteenth–eighteenth centuries)

FRÉDÉRIC SURMELY, VIOLAINE NICOLAS, JAY D. FRANKLIN, ROBERT LINAM, MANON CABANIS AND JULIEN LE JUNTER

INTRODUCTION

Since 2000, a multidisciplinary research project has been undertaken in the lower mountains of the Auvergne region (France) with the goal of better understanding the human occupation of this rugged landscape from the late Mesolithic to the twentieth century. This paper focusses on the modern period (AD 1453–1789) and the shifting habitation and landscape usage that signalled an economic shift at the end of the medieval period. Between 2000 and 2011, a 70 km² area of the southern Cantal Mountains was the focus of examination, but since 2012, research has primarily concentrated on a few municipalities, particularly Compains (in the Sancy Mountains of the Puy d'Dôme). Prior to this project, no intensive study of human occupation or changes in landscape usage during the modern period in these regions had ever been done.

While both areas appear broadly similar, they are in fact two very distinct geographic areas of the lower mountain ranges of Auvergne (Figure 9.1). The 70 km² investigated in the Cantal was located on a *planèze* (a type of basaltic plateau specific to the Cantal) just to the south of the 'Plomb du Cantal', a vast triangular plateau originating from the last active phases of Cantal's strata volcanos which occurred approximately 3.5 million years ago. A strong, relatively regular, north-to-south declivity with an altitude of 1600 m at the northern end and 1000 m at the southern end can be observed. In a general sense this large *planèze* (plateau) exhibits an irregular surface and is deeply rent by valleys. The research area specifically targeted the mountain territory of five main municipalities: Pailherols, Saint-Clément, Lacapelle-Barrès, Malbo and Brezons, with a few incursions into the municipalities of Saint-Jacques-des-Blats, Cézens, Thiézac and Paulhac. The climate is particularly harsh in this area; it exhibits both lower-than-average temperatures and abundant precipitation (above 2 m a year on average). The water supply, therefore, is plentiful, as is exemplified by the numerous small rivers, brooks and peat bogs which are scattered throughout the region. The average annual temperature is 4°C (measured at 6 a.m.) at an altitude of 1100 m and 2.5°C at 1350 m. Quarried

stone blocks used for construction are the main natural resource of note in the area as no large-scale mineral or exploitable ore supplies are present. In spite of the harsh climate, the lower part of the area is fertile and appropriate for cultivation. It is important to emphasize that, even if it is an undeniable geological entity, the sud du Plomb *planèze* is by no means environmentally homogenous. The north-to-south slope, numerous valleys and variable sun exposure allow for a great variety of localized biotopes. Human activity has a long history there, although some particularities of this trajectory have been erased by more recent human activity.

We began our research in the Sancy range and concentrated on a few areas situated in different parts of the mountain range (the Mont-Dore, Saulzet-le-Froid and Compains municipalities). The relief of the terrain is more pronounced in the Sancy Mountains primarily due to its more recent volcanic activity. In Compains, for example, the Montchal/Pavin/Montcineyre eruptions occurred relatively recently at 7000 BP (Juvigné, 1992) and caused an accumulation of volcanic fallout. However, the climate is identical to that in the Cantal insofar as it is both cold and damp.

Finally it has to be said that the environment of the lower mountain range engenders specific preservation conditions. The absence of major rearrangements or profound changes due to intensive ploughing following the medieval period has allowed for the preservation of archaeological sites and, on occasion, the integrity of even plot shapes themselves. Unfortunately, the lower mountain range of the Auvergne area is also known for the severity of its erosion as well as some physical and chemical factors which have altered many sites. These factors often lead to the destruction of the majority of any organic remains (with the exception of charcoal and burned seeds). Bone or ligneous remains have been recovered only rarely, if ever.

METHODOLOGY

As stated above, research on the modern period was carried out within the framework of a broader study of

© 2018 European Association of Archaeologists

122 *Frédéric Surmely et al.*

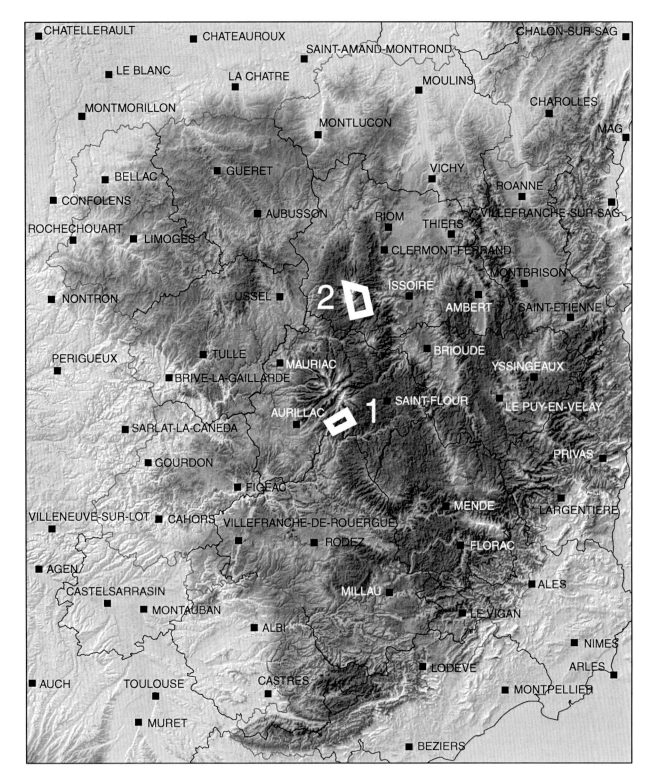

Figure 9.1. *General location of the two study areas*
Source: © E. Langlois

the general history of populations living in the lower mountains as well as the evolution of the landscape of the regions since late prehistory (late Mesolithic; Surmely et al., 2009). This research was a collective and multidisciplinary scheme which combined several different chronological specialists, historians, geologists and paleo-environmental specialists (palynologists, anthracologists and carpologists).

Our work began by conducting systematic pedestrian surveys throughout the research area and was complemented by aerial surveys to detect relief abnormalities from human activity. We also conducted general surface collections. Relief abnormalities and confirmed archaeological sites were marked via GPS. The entirety of the marked sites was recorded in a file which included all of the available descriptive information. This file was then uploaded and processed in a geographic information systems (GIS) program.

More than 1400 unique sites dating from as far back as the late Mesolithic were recorded during the initial surveys. Following this, those sites which were deemed the most likely to offer the most data were excavated. Seven sites dating to the modern period were excavated: six in the Cantal survey area and one in the Sancy area. These excavations were carried out over large surfaces (on average, they measured 35 m²) wherever possible in order to establish a more complete understanding of the layout of any structures that were present. Archival research (particularly for the Cantal area) was carried out, although surviving records for the area were limited almost exclusively to contemporary times (AD 1789–1880).

Permanent Settlement During the Medieval Period

Our research revealed a polymorphic pattern of human habitation with isolated houses and crofts gathered into small hamlets and which often share the same territory (Nicolas et al., 2012; Surmely, 2015). These settlements are situated below the altitude of 1285 m, which appears to be the cultivation limit. The structures are often surrounded by developments linked to agricultural activity such as paths, terraces, gardens and ditches. In most cases, one notices that the inhabitants looked for spots sheltered from the wind on plots with little slope which also gave an overall view of their surroundings (Figure 9.2). In this rainy environment, water seems to have been of secondary importance (at least in everyday domestic activities). In one case, however, the presence of a nearby well was unmistakable. Many of these clustered structures were known individually in advance of the start of our project through studies carried out in different parts of Auvergne in the twentieth century (Fournier & Fournier, 1983; Lapeyre, 2004; Moulier, 2007; Sermet & Raymond, 1998). They were also referred to as 'deserted villages' after the Anglo-Saxon model (Dyer & Jones, 2010). In accordance with modern British researchers, we prefer to qualify them as hamlets, due to the small concentrations of buildings they contain (a maximum of 15 units) and the lack of any identifiable building representing a place of power or religion. In both of our study areas, none of the clusters were fortified or enclosed by walls. However, these fortified clusters did exist in other areas. Sadly, they have not been studied as yet, so the differentiation between simple fortified hamlets and real fortified mounds remains uncertain. Our work also revealed the existence of isolated crofts with one or two buildings, which were unknown in the region prior to this research.

Figure 9.2. Aerial photograph of the medieval hamlet du Lac-d'En-Haut (La Godivelle, France)
Source: © F. Surmely

Buildings that date from medieval times show shared characteristics in two areas: they are partially constructed below ground level, and they are surrounded by an external earthen wall. The foundation of the structures was deeply excavated on average (1–1.5 m), thereby removing superficial deposits and levelling the rocky substratum. Perhaps most importantly, this method both improved insulation and reinforced the structure. Rubble from the foundation excavation was stacked lengthways outside the structure to form an earthwork bank which leaned against the building in order to strengthen the main wall and to further improve the building's insulation. One has to note that the creation of these earthwork banks appears to be a unique phenomenon of buildings in the Massif Central. Partially sunken structures are found in other areas of France in various environments, but none of these structures appears to have the additional surrounding earthen embankment (Cattedu, 2009; Colin et al., 1996; Peytremann, 2005; Poirot, 2012).

The walls of the structures were built of drystone and assembled with clay rather than mortar. They are generally thick with an average of 0.8 m and solidly constructed. Some of the stones used weigh more than 300 kg. The builders had no difficulties finding material on these volcanic soils. One can be led to think that the use of stones for building also helped with clearing the fields. The shape of the buildings also varied; although 'L' shaped buildings with side extensions can also be found, the most frequently observed layout involved an elongated quadrilateral shape (similar in style to a longhouse). Most of the seemingly isolated structures are limited to one building. However, more complex groups comprising two or more distinct areas of structures and open areas or yards have also been found. Structure 1 at the site of 'Les Yvérats', in the Sancy, is comprised of a large structure with two other units joining it whose purposes are still to be determined. This structure is in the centre of a group of five other isolated buildings (of which one is 'L' shaped). Our research showed no evidence for internal partitions within the buildings. However, the use of a separation wall was found on the Cantal site of Cotteuges (Moulier, 2007).

All buildings had a limited amount of openings (typically one or two at the most). The main access is always opened in a gutter wall. The entrance was sometimes preceded by a long corridor (either straight or curved) whose length sometimes exceeded 7 m (Surmely, 2015). The presence of such corridors in continental Europe is, thus far, unique to the Massif Central in France; some similar arrangements have been recorded in Greenland and northern Canada (Park, 1988; Murphy, 2012).

In the vast majority of cases, a form of vegetation was used as roofing material, rye straw, reeds or gorse. However, at the site of Malbo (site n° 699; Surmely, 2009), the roof was consolidated using large stone slabs found nearby on a mixed roofing pattern. The floor of most buildings was covered with large, flat tiles which were laid out in a haphazard fashion. A wooden floor may have covered this fixture in order to keep the occupants away from dampness and to facilitate their comings and goings. One or two stone slabs were placed for hearths in each of the excavated buildings.

The simplicity of the artefact assemblages found at these sites is typical for other similar sites from the same period (Cattedu, 2009). Metal items are rare and are limited to knives, nails and horse equipment (shoes and harness rings, etc.). No coins have been discovered as yet. Ceramic furnishings are found in larger quantities, though they are limited to various domestic vessels.

Palynological, carpological and anthracological analysis was carried out in isolated farms as well as the grouped hamlets. The palynological results show a weak taxon frequency due to the presence of cattle in all buildings under study (with one exception). The study of burnt grain recovered from several of the sites showed the same result, namely, the only cereal present in any significant quantity is rye. The predominance of rye is surely due to its resistance to frost and to acidic soils, making it an ideal choice for the harsh mountain climate. Local cereal cultivation is characterized by the presence of taxons typical of rye agriculture: corn-cockle (*Agrostemma githago*), yellow bugle (*Ajuga chamaepitys*), rye brome (*Bromus secalinus*), cornflower (*Centaurea cyanus*), wild buckwheat (*Fallopia convolvulus*) and field sorrel (*Rumex acetosella*). Other cultivated plants were found, such as: oats (*Avena sativa*), peas (*Pisum sativum*), wheat (*triticum sp*) and barley (*Hordeum vulgare*). These additional cultivated plants were for consumption by the farm or hamlet rather than for sale. The practice of general mixed farming was, therefore, present in the area. Barley would have been harvested in autumn and is viable in a wide variety of soils, resisting both drought and frost up to a point. The nutritional value of barley makes it very popular for both human and animal consumption. We also found morsels of carbonized flat barley cakes at two sites, which seem to indicate local consumption.

Most buildings excavated were thought to have been used for human occupation or activities (as dwellings or workshops). This conclusion was reached by the presence of the following criteria: hearth stone(s), varied furniture, carbonized grain flat cakes, stairs or long corridors. In two cases, it was determined that the space was used for animal stabling, due to the lack of furniture as well as (in one instance) the existence of a drain.

THE END OF THE MEDIEVAL PERIOD AND THE BEGINNING OF SPECIALIZED BREEDING

We were able to physically date the rectangular stone houses in all excavated structures. By the use of C_{14}

dating (Figure 9.3), we concluded that their occupation and subsequent abandonment took place prior to the thirteenth century in both areas. We did not notice any discrepancy between hamlets or isolated buildings, although our analysis remains limited due to the lack of precision in the carbon dating. Therefore, we cannot link their desertion to the Hundred Years War or to the plague of 1348, as has been suggested by researchers in the past. British historians and archaeologists have arrived at similar conclusions regarding similar structures (Dyer & Jones, 2010). None of the buildings gave indications that they were used by more than one generation, nor were there any subsequent alterations to the structures. One must believe, therefore, that the occupation period of these structures was relatively short. This appears to have been the case for many medieval buildings throughout Europe (Dyer & Jones, 2010).

The most plausible hypothesis for this brief period of occupation is the wholesale economic transformation of the region at the end of the medieval period. The diversified farming model was replaced with a more specialized summer pasturing system within a speculative farming framework. Archives from the Cantal (Bouyssou, 1972–1974) and the Sancy (Fournier & Fournier, 1983) corroborate this phenomenon. This shift in land usage is also visible through pollen analyses of core drillings from local peat bogs. In the Cantal area, we were able to complete nine core drillings from five peat bogs ranging in altitude from 1000 m to 1450 m. We deem the intrinsic variety and the gradient of these marshy areas as a reliable way of characterizing the evolution of the countryside in the research areas. As a general rule, deforestation became more important between the third and fourth centuries AD. The Vèze site shows a new period of environmental clearance at the end of the twelfth century (Nicolas et al., 2012; Surmely et al., 2009). The pollen markers show diversified agricultural and pastoral activity for that period as well as evidence for cereal farming in the lower part of lowlands and grazing in the highland zone. This shift in landscape usage may be linked to a period of climatic deterioration which seems to have begun around that period in France (Carozza, 2009).

A speculative farming strategy replaced the previous system of subsistence agriculture; summer cattle grazed in mountain pastures and their husbandry was oriented towards a system of commercial cheese production. The consequences of this economic transformation would have involved the retraction of permanent dwellings, the desertion of farms and hamlets and the construction of shelters specifically designed as dwellings for shepherds and cheese manufacturing. This change is described in a few documents examined by L. Bouyssou and G. Fournier. It is the beginning of the '*Montagnes*' (high-altitude pastures), the huge stretches of land belonging to religious officials or other powerful landowners and farmed by modest tenants who lived on the mountain with their cattle during the summer months.

We have identified the buildings constructed as shelters under this new system throughout the areas surveyed. These are small simply built standard sized cabins (4 x 4 m, internal). The ground was only slightly excavated (from 0.5 to 0.70 m in depth) and the rubble stacked in a much smaller earthwork bank than the one found in the medieval buildings. There are no stones present. Wooden separations upheld a framework made

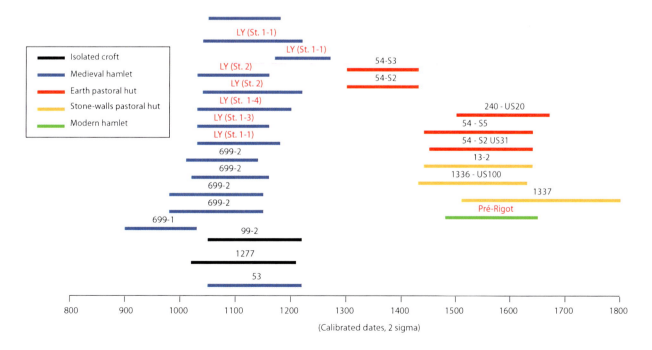

Figure 9.3. Table of radiocarbon dates obtained on medieval sites of Cantal and Sancy
Source: © F. Surmely

of perishable material (thatch or squares of turf) with a pillar hole being found in some buildings whose probable purpose was the central roof support. The absence of stone flooring or drainage was also noted. On site 54, a hearth stone was found in one of the structures. In all other structures of this site, no fittings of any sort were discovered.

These structures can be isolated or found in groups of two or more (the largest recorded to date included 13 buildings; Nicolas et al., 2012: fig. 4). The geographic distribution of these buildings is more diverse than the oblong housing of the previous period; some structures were even discovered at 1515 m. Interestingly, site 54 (which represents the only group of small square buildings tested) included two different layouts (Figure 9.4). One of the dwellings (n° 2) contained abundant ceramic furnishings which were mainly composed of fragments of closed cooking and serving receptacles (pots, pitchers). This building also contained an 80 cm^2 basalt slab used as a hearth stone. In the three other buildings we tested, no improvements were found and ceramic furnishings, totally absent in two of the structures, were limited to only a few fragments in the last structure.

Determining the exact nature of these structures is a complex issue. Some completely lack remnants of tools or ceramics as well as any form of permanent fixtures. One must surmise, therefore, that they served as animal shelters or for the storage of fodder and/ or tools. Modern-day sources mention the systematic existence of buildings designed to protect young calves from bad weather and wolves (Moriceau, 2011) which bear a resemblance to these structures. A few buildings contained both artefacts and fixtures (hearth stones) indicating their use as human dwellings. Their small size, the nature of furnishings found and the extreme

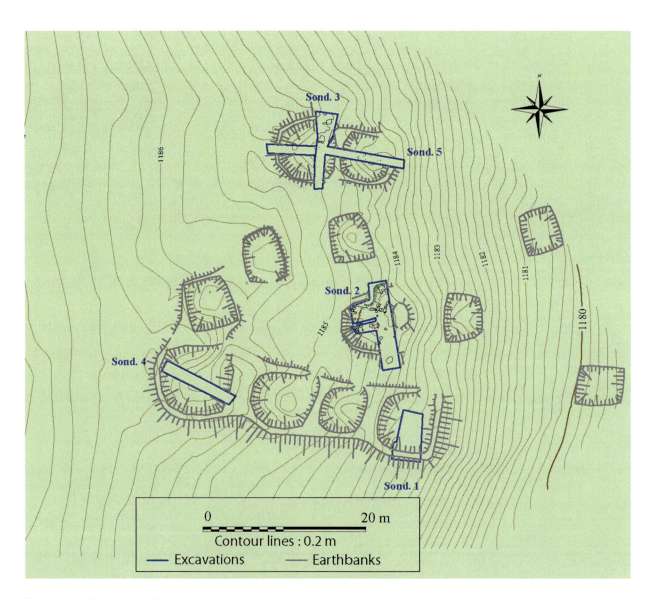

Figure 9.4. General map of site n° 54 indicating the areas tested
Source: © P. Boudon and F. Surmely

simplicity of their architecture corroborate their use as seasonal shelters frequented by a limited number of individuals.

The shelters referred to in texts as *cabanes* (Fournier & Fournier, 1983) assuredly match the square buildings described above. They were inhabited only during the summer period (i.e. between May and October) and were linked with farms which were located in the surrounding villages in the valleys, approximately within a 5 km range. The guarding of cattle at these places was an exclusively male activity. Their construction as well as their use started at the beginning of the fourteenth century and survived well into the early modern period. These structures would later be replaced in the sixteenth century by larger and more solid buildings that incorporated stone walls. The palynological analyses show the spread of pastureland between the fourteenth and sixteenth centuries in a completely open environment with small islands of woodland (Nicolas et al., 2012).

The Mid-Fifteenth Through Nineteenth Centuries: The Golden Age of The Shepherd

At the beginning of the seventeenth century, the amount of land given over to the summer grazing of cattle and other livestock continued to increase. New stone buildings appeared in increasing numbers and some of the stone and earth houses of the medieval period were reoccupied. The newer stone structures of the early modern period returned to a 'heavier' type of construction that resembled the longhouse-like structure of the eleventh and twelfth centuries. During this period, the site of village 54 was reoccupied, as was site 240 (La Montagne du Buel, Malbo) in the Cantal. Site 240 was arranged in the same linear fashion as was common in the medieval period. These large stone structures were more costly in terms of the amount of labour and time required for their construction. Their appearance speaks to the success of cattle breeding specifically for the production of cheese and the desire to invest further in its growth. These larger stone structures appeared in both the Cantal and Sancy during this time. However, none of these structures in the Sancy has yet been excavated. The chronological overlap of the radiocarbon dates obtained from both the smaller and the larger stone structures gives no indication that the larger stone structures supplanted the smaller ones. It is more likely that both types of construction coexisted over a period of time and were dependent on the finances of the land manager.

Structure 13.2 on the Montagne de la Vèze (Paillerols) is an example of the larger stone construction type. It is similar to the quadrangular medieval farms insofar as it had a small access passage and a thatched roof. These new buildings are very similar to the former medieval farms, so it is difficult to date the buildings by simple visual examination during surveying. What distinguishing criteria can be used to differentiate between these structures? The wide diversity of plans and dimensions (especially lengths) prohibit the use of the shape of the buildings as a true discriminating criterion. According to L. Fau (2006), the key to differentiating between the structure types is in the placement of the accesses to the buildings. We believe this conclusion to be misleading. Pastoral edifices prior to the sixteenth to eighteenth centuries were mainly built with an entrance in a gutter wall (buildings n° 1335, 1336, 1337, 1338, 335 and 1365), whereas entrances on gable walls were more rare (buildings n° 13–2) (Nicolas et al., 2012). There are cases of structures which showed double accesses in both the gutter wall and the gable wall (building n° 1799). At least one of the medieval structures included two entrances (one in the gable wall and the other on the frontage). Let us finally add that determining the entrance location is sometimes impossible due to erosion or the refilling of a large number of sites.

However, one distinguishing characteristic of the more modern stone-wall huts is that their foundations are shallower than those of the medieval crofts. They also have no curved entrance corridors. Perhaps most importantly, we noticed that the majority of them were divided internally into two parts and exhibited a difference in the elevation of the floor in both areas. This feature has only been found on pastoral buildings dated to the sixteenth and seventeenth centuries. The two parts were linked by stone stairs. In the Cantal, excavations showed that the inferior room, dug in the earth, was used as a cellar and that it had neither access to the outside nor any fittings.

We found several of these structures in different places in the Cantal survey area. They were almost identical, with an average length of 10 to 15 m and a width of 5 m. Structures at the Lacapelle-Barrès Mountains (site 1365; Figure 9.5) as well as at St. Clément (site 335; Figure 9.6) and Pailherols (site 1335–1338) were all partially excavated. Structure 1365 of the Montagne de Peyre was almost totally excavated. Remains of the shepherds' activities and lives, such as knives, scissors and earthenware bowls with small handles for the consumption of soup were found in the living room on the western end of the structure. The other room, connected to a closed door via a staircase, was probably a cellar for the storage of cheese. Nearby we found an area lined with stone slabs (site 1366) which likely served as a yard in which animals were kept overnight. The Montagne de Bane site consisted of a cluster of four similar buildings, three of which were excavated by test pits. In all of them, the cellar is situated within the slope as to be well sheltered from the outside. It likely represents

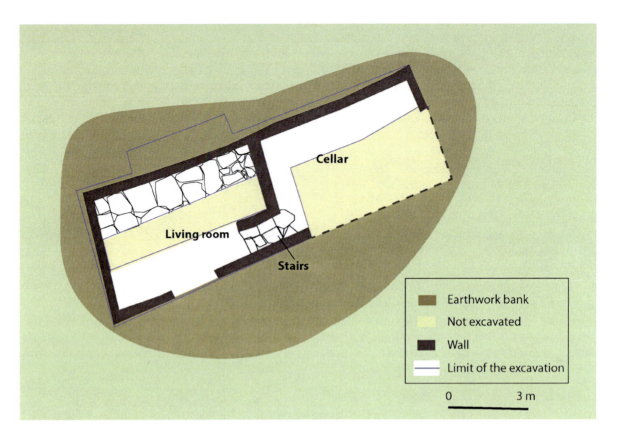

Figure 9.5. Plan of site n° 1365 (Lacapelle-Barrès, Cantal)
Source: © F. Surmely

Figure 9.6. Pot found in site 335 (seventeenth century; Saint-Clément, Cantal)
Source: © F. Surmely

a group of shepherds farming the pasture together and sharing the structures.

Further examination of the archives in the Cantal confirmed our ground findings. Farming activities centred on the commercial use of cattle for cheese making. In addition, the average travelling distance of the cattle to the summer pastures from the wintering sheds could reach up to 15 km (a day's walk). Almost every morsel of land was grazed by milk cows. The pastures used to fatten the cattle played only a minor role (Durand, 1946: 268). The farmland was divided into hayfields up to an altitude of 1150 m. The land above the pastures was carefully distributed between the *fumades* (the land surrounding the croft) and the *aygades* (the large expanses of roaming land which stretched across the plateau (Nicolas, 2012). Mountain grazing land belonged to large landowners (aristocrats and noblemen) and was leased out to locals. V. Nicolas examined hundreds of leases which ranged from the early seventeenth century to the end of the eighteenth century (Nicolas, 2014). On the eve of the French Revolution, the marquis of Miramon owned 475 hectares of mountain grazing land in our survey area alone.

The archives disclosed a disparity in the value of the *montagnes*. Altitude had no influence; the most sought-after sites were those with a water supply and good grazing. The farms were consolidated by land sales, marriages and inheritance and which all affected the distribution and size of the farmsteads. As the grazing of cattle was a very lucrative enterprise, investment in farmsteads and grazing land increased (Nicolas, 2014).

Beginning in the eighteenth century a new architectural evolution arrived which involved the dualization of pastoral buildings. Next to the construction used as living area and cheese making (called a *buron*), another – often larger – structure (called the *védélat* or *bédélat*) was added. These were intended to house young herd animals at night. Both human habitation and livestock sheds still had thatched roofs, as seen in the two neighbouring buildings (n° 338 and 1799) from the Montagne du Clos (Saint-Clément) site excavated in 2009.

The best-documented step in the evolution of the stone buildings is also the last. The *burons* were eventually covered by a stone vault. These were made from spring stone or were built of small worked stones which were liberally applied with mortar and were covered on the outside by large stone slabs. A stone vault was the advantage of the stronger and longer-lasting materials and enabled the additional benefit of a chimney, if desired. The addition of a chimney would have created a more inviting environment for the farmer during cheese making or other activities. Changes were also made to the cellar. Rather than being dug into the ground they were instead simply placed upslope and partially buried. The *bédélats*, however, remained thatched. These often restored vaulted *burons* sheltered shepherds through the nineteenth and into the first half

of the twentieth century. Technological advances (such as motorized vehicles, electric and barbed wire fencing) as well as the development of beef livestock farming have brought a halt to this long history and have also emptied the mountains of what was once an intensive human presence.

Was Husbandry The Only Activity in The Mountains?

Animal husbandry, especially of cattle, played an important role in the mountains of the Cantal and Sancy. Pollinic diagrams show the extent of the grazing pasturage. Archives also demonstrate the importance of breeding through sales and leasing data. The structures which dotted the landscape stand testament to these investments in the livestock economy. However, some discoveries led us to believe that breeding was not the only economic activity which took place. In the Cantal, pollen diagrams indicate the existence of cereal crops throughout the modern period. Moreover, a map from 1782 mentions a 'ruined mill'. In the municipality of Compains in the Sancy, our survey revealed that seasonal huts as well as permanent hamlets were built in the highlands during the modern period (seventeenth century). Upon examination, the hamlet of Pré-Rigot was found to have been occupied for a short time and then abandoned before the beginning of the eighteenth century. One explanation for this relatively brief occupation could be the great famine which plagued the French countryside at the end of the reign of Louis XIVth (Figure 9.7).

Differences Between The Cantal and The Sancy Mountains

An extraordinary concentration of one particular type of structure was found only in the Sancy Mountains. While the exact purpose of these structures is unknown to this day, they could represent pastoral structures from the modern period (Figure 9.8). One finds only very few such structures in the Cantal Mountains (there was only one in our study area) and only sparsely in the Mont-Dômes and Forez mountains. They are locally known as *tras* or *peignes* (lit. 'combs') due to their particular shape when seen from above. An evident standardization seems to characterize them. They appear as a vertical alignment of individual cells or huts which are partially buried and sit close together. Each cell has an opening to the outside through an access corridor. On most occasions one finds an isolated, large cell above this alignment (Figure 9.9). The relation between these rows and the larger, isolated cells is evident. The cell's demarcations appear to have been made of earth or

Figure 9.7. Modern hamlet of Pré-Rigot (Compains, France)
Source: © F. Surmely

perishable components and are virtually identical to the first mud pastoral structures. In some cases, however, they were built of stone cants.

While the layout is uniform, variation does exist in the number of huts found in a row (referred to as *tra*). If one considers that a *tra* consists of a minimum of four cells (Surmely, 2012), this number can range from four to twenty-one with the average being seven. In single area, structures of differing sizes can be found without any apparent explanation. Aside from these long and regular rows of adjoining cells (*peignes véritables* or 'real combs'), what is most apparent are the simpler structures of rows of two or three huts (which we call double or triple huts) or rows of non-adjoining huts (clusters) or even isolated cells. All the structures which cannot be qualified as 'combs' and which are, nonetheless, interspersed with long rows should most likely be grouped together into the same category.

These structures are mainly found on plateaus at altitudes between 1100 m and 1470 m. They are typically dug down into the ground in areas with little slope. Where the grade of the slope is high, they are placed in the slope itself. These structures are very common in some areas and non-existent in others. We have noted their presence around lakes and marshy areas and their geographical distribution resembles the location of the nineteenth-century stone *burons*. Their density varies from one area to the next. The variation ranges from seven structures (all kinds of isolated or grouped cells) per hectare on the Chantauzet au Mont-Dore plateau and ten in the Bois de la Védrine (Saulzet-le-Froid) to an average of three and a half in the mountains around Compains.

Aside from the physical counts carried out following different methods, actual archaeological fieldwork was very limited in both survey areas. Since 1945, only two field surveys were carried out (Allios, 2012; Paul, 1972). Although a few texts concerning the 1619–1835 period were published by G. Fournier (1983), the information they presented is limited. This data is insufficient to allow for a chronological, let alone functional characterization of these structures which can be found by the thousands in the Sancy and Cézallier mountains. In the absence of the requisite fieldwork, one is left, therefore, to draw inferences from the region's history. The construction and use of these structures is probably

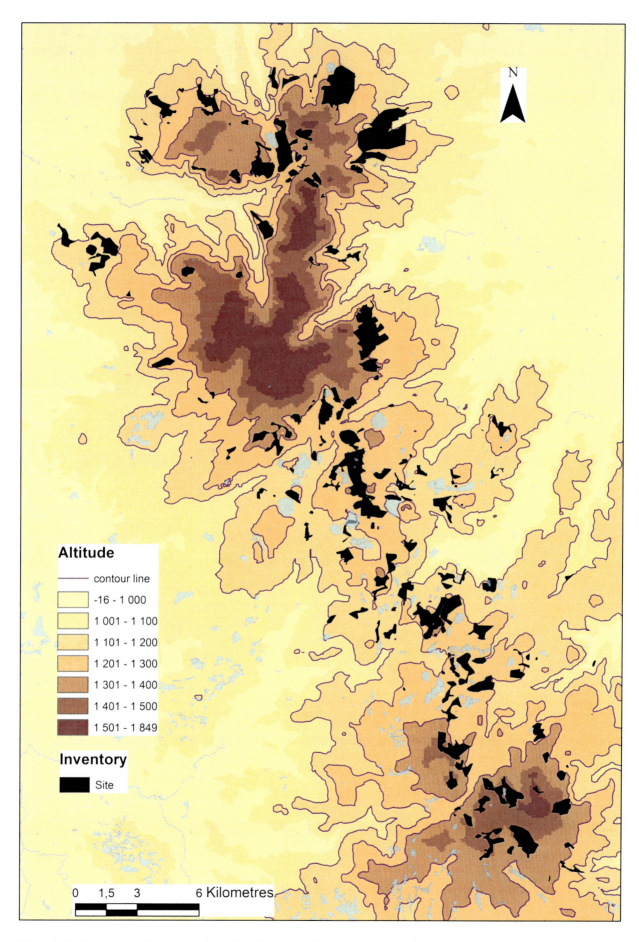

Figure 9.8. *Geographical distribution of the aligned structures (*peignes ou tras*) in the Sancy*
Source: *J. Le Junter*

Figure 9.9. Aerial view of aligned structures concentration, at Le Roc Blanc (Perpezat, Puy-de-Dôme)
Source: F. Surmely

spread out over a long period of time. Though impossible to prove today, their disparity in shape is most surely due to a chronological evolution. It is also difficult to determine their exact function. Granted, if one refers to the few texts that are known as well as their geographical placement, the importance of these structures to pastoral grazing is undeniable. Finally, the different kinds of animal farming surely played a role in determining the shape of these structures. A coexistence of cattle herds (for beef or dairy farming) and sheep herds (Arbos, 1923; Fournier & Fournier, 1983) was indeed found in the Sancy Mountains during the modern and contemporary periods. Working the *montagnes à lait* (lit. 'milk mountains') for the production of cheese evidently required different and more intricate buildings than did animal husbandry at the *montagnes à graisse* (fat mountains) used for raising beef even if one does not take the importance of sheep farming into account. Although more complex with regards to quantification, the latter was undeniably existent in the Brion animal sale registers.

However, questions regarding the very large numbers of these structures in some areas also remain. There are a few texts (Fournier & Fournier, 1983) which reference the possibility of an annual creation of new structures; however no clear conclusions can be drawn. Organizing an annual re-excavation from season to season or year to year would be problematic at best (Allios, 2012; Nicolas et al., 2012; Surmely and Le Junter, 2017). Refurbishment and restoration without complete re-excavation seems a more logical conclusion. One might posit that collective farming in these mountains created a need to rapidly build more structures. Although rarely seen in the south of the Cantal due to expansive land-ownership, this way of farming appears to have reached its peak in the Sancy at the end of the modern and the beginning of the contemporary periods (Lhéritier, 1937).

Conclusion

There is an interruption in the history of the Auvergne Mountains. Prior to the thirteenth century, the land below 1280 m was utilized and populated year-round in the form of small clusters of hamlets and isolated farms linked to the villages in the valleys. The mountainous dwellings were well adapted to the harsh climate faced by their inhabitants. The surge of commercial seasonal cattle breeding supplanted the system of permanent habitation by dramatically lowering the human population as well as reshaping the structures and landscape to better suit a seasonal pastoral lifestyle. Prior to our studies, this phenomenon was unknown. Through a multidisciplinary approach and archaeological excavation, we have been able to create a chronology of the architectural changes in structures linked to the shifting economy of the Auvergne Mountains. However, much remains to be done to in order to build a deeper understanding of the Auvergne Mountains' pastoral history, particularly with regards to the study of the thousands of mysterious *peignes* which are scattered throughout the mountains of the Auvergne.

ACKNOWLEDGEMENTS

Many thanks to Claire Sneeden who translated this paper. The authors would also like to thank Yannick Miras and F. Blondel (UMR 6042), as well as all the landowners who have allowed and continue to allow us to conduct research on their properties.

REFERENCES

Allios, D. 2012. Recherches archéologiques sur la commune de Murol. In: *Bilan d'activité 2010–2011 du service régional de l'archéologie d'Auvergne*. Clermont-Ferrand: Direction Régionale des Affaires Culturelles, pp. 118–19.

Arbos, P. 1923. The geography of pastoral life illustrated with European examples. *Geographical Review*, 13:559–75.

Bouyssou, L. 1972–1974. Les montagnes cantaliennes du XIIIème au XVIIIème siècles. *Revue de la Haute-Auvergne*, 43:143–64, 44:36–78.

Carozza J-M. 2009. Introduction: entre changement global et effets locaux: quel Petit Âge Glaciaire dans le sud de la France? *Archéologie du Midi médiéval*, 27(1):139–42.

Cattedu, I. 2009. *Archéologie médiévale en France. Le premier Moyen-Âge*. Paris: la Découverte.

Colin, G., Darnas, I., Pousthomis, N. & Schneider, L. 1996. *La maison du castrum de la bordure méridionale du Massif Central*. Archéologie du Midi Médiéval, Supplément, 1(1).

Durand, A. 1946. *La vie rurale dans les massifs volcaniques des Dores, du Cézallier, du Cantal et de l'Aubrac*. Thèse de l'université de Clermont-Fd.

Dyer, C. & Jones, R. 2010. *Deserted Villages Revisited*. Hatfield: University of Hertfordshire Press.

Fau, L. 2006. *Les monts d'Aubrac au Moyen Âge. Genèse d'un Monde Agropastoral*. Paris: Editions de la Maison des Sciences de l'Homme (DAF).

Fournier, G. & P.-F. 1983. La vie pastorale dans les montagnes du centre de la France. *Bulletin Historique et Scientifique de l'Auvergne*, 91, n° 676:199–538.

Juvigné, É. 1992. Distribution of widespread late glacial and Holocene tephra beds in the French Central Massif. *Quaternary International*, 14:181–85.

Lapeyre, O. 2004. *Un village médiéval déserté: Espinasse de Collandres (Cantal)*. Bulletin du GRHAVS, 64.

Lhéritier, J. 1937. La région des Monts-Dores: essai sur l'habitat. *Revue de Géographie Alpine*, 25(4):619–61.

Moriceau, J.-M. 2011. *L'homme contre le loup. Une guerre de 2000 ans*. Paris: Fayard.

Moulier, J.-C. 2007. Cotteuges, un village de l'an mil. *Revue de la Haute-Auvergne*, 69:7–57.

Murphy, P. 2012. *Identifying the Inuit Communal House Phase in Southern Labrador*. Occasional Papers in Northeastern Archaeology 19. St. John's: Copetown Press.

Nicolas, V. 2012. La fourme de Cantal, "reine des fromages" de Haute-Auvergne. Evolution des modes de production au XVIIᵉ et XVIIIᵉ siècles. *Revue de la Haute-Auvergne*, 75(4):439–56.

Nicolas, V. 2014. Les montagnes d'estive vendues comme bien nationaux sous la Révolution. L'exemple des communes de la périphérie méridionale du Plomb du Cantal. *Revue de la Haute-Auvergne*, 76(2):145–61.

Nicolas, V., Surmely, F., Miras, Y. & Lllergo-Lopez, Y. 2012. L'évolution des paysages et des architectures sur la planèze sud du Plomb du Cantal, du XIᵉ au XIXᵉ siècle: apport des données archéologiques, archivistiques et paléoenvironnementales. In: C. Guilleré, ed. *Le paysage rural au Moyen-Âge*. Paris: Éditions du CTHS (Actes des congrès des sociétés historiques et scientifiques), pp. 79–105.

Park R.-W. 1988. Winter houses and qarmat in Thule and Historic Inuit settlement patterns: some implications for Thule studies. *Canadian Journal of Archaeology*, 12:163–75.

Paul, S. 1972. Le site archéologique de la Montagne de Razat à Laqueuille. In: Collectif, *Congrès préhistorique de France. Compte-rendu de la XIXè session Auvergne, 6–14 juillet 1969*. Paris: Société Préhistorique Française, pp. 302–19.

Peytremann, E. 2005. L'architecture rurale dans l'Ouest de la France entre le VIe et le XIIe siècle, d'après les données de l'archéologie. In: A. Antoine, ed. *La maison rurale en pays d'habitat dispersé, de l'Antiquité au XIXe siècle*. Rennes: Presses Universitaires de Rennes, pp. 77–98.

Poirot, A. 2012. *Contournement sud-ouest de Vichy (Allier). Rapport final d'opération*. Moulins: SAPDA.

Surmely, F. 2009. *Rapport de sondage du site 699 (Rissergues, Malbo)*. Clermont-Ferrand: Service régional de l'archéologie d'Auvergne.

Surmely, F. 2012. *Prospection inventaire sur les communes de Compains, le Mont-Dore et Saulzet-le-Froid. Rapport 2012*. Clermont-Ferrand: Service régional de l'archéologie d'Auvergne.

Surmely, F. 2015. *Le site médiéval des Yvérats (Compains, Puy-de-Dôme). Rapport de sondage*. Clermont-Ferrand: Service régional de l'archéologie d'Auvergne.

Surmely, F. & Le Junter, J. 2017. Les structures présumées pastorales du massif du Sancy. *Revue Archéologique du Centre de la France*.

Surmely, F., Miras, Y., Guenet, P., Nicolas, V., Savignat, A., Vannière, B., Walter-Simonnet, A.V., Servera, G. & Tzortzis, S. 2009. Occupation and land-use history of a medium mountain from the Mid-Holocene: a multidisciplinary study performed in the South Cantal (French Massif Central). *Comptes Rendus Palevol*, 8(8):737–48.

CHAPTER 10

Moving up and down throughout the seasons
Winter and summer grazing between Provence and the southern Alps (France) AD 1100–1500

Sylvain Burri, Vanessa Py-Saragaglia and Roxanne Cesarini

Introduction

'Transhumance' is a key component of the cultural identity of south-eastern France, as evidenced by the organisation of just such a movement as a celebration of Marseille's nomination as 2013's European Capital of Culture. Today transhumance is considered more as a timeless and fixed phenomenon or an ancient and perpetual activity. The 'Great Transhumance' occurred between eighteenth and mid-twentieth centuries and was routed between the plains of western Provence (especially the Crau) and the southern French Alps and Italian Piedmont (Clapier, 1838; Fournier, 1900; Guillaume, 1908; Rouquette, 1913; Truchot, 1936; Fabre, 1997; Musset, 2006; Pichard, 2006; Lebaudy, 2000, 2006, 2011; Lebaudy & Albera, 2001). However, the origins of this phenomenon are usually assigned to medieval and ancient times and applied to all the Provencal territory, thereby creating a real historical, geographic and cultural paradigm. For these reasons, it is critical to define transhumance. In the Mediterranean area, 'transhumance' refers to the seasonal migration of animal herds between different (but complementary) ecological and climatic regions with various availabilities of grass according to the season. This is especially true in the Provencal lowlands and the Alpine uplands. Seasonal migration is not only an adaptation to environmental constraints, but also an economic strategy used to optimise animal husbandry and whose character, extent and magnitude also depend on social, economic and institutional conditions. Seasonal migration becomes necessary only when the number and the size of herds exceed the fodder capacities of the area in which they are kept, i.e. when animal husbandry becomes speculative (Coulet, 1986, 1996; Moriceau, 2005: 325–71).

The transhumance history must be written step by step. In order to begin to overcome the Great Transhumance paradigm, we use the term 'transhumance' with caution and only when we feel genuinely justified. Since it is associated with modern scholarly classification (Rendu, 2006), we prefer medieval terminologies of summering (migration for summer grazing) and wintering (migration for winter grazing)

rather than 'transhumance normale' (a practice in which livestock from the plains and hills of Provence summer in the Alps) and 'transhumance inverse' (a practice in which Alpine flocks winter in the plains and hills of Provence). Other expressions one finds in the literature which further muddy the waters include "Mediterranean transhumance" and "Alpine transhumance" (Davis, 1941). Indeed, the latter refers to seasonal vertical mobility between valley and upland pastures in a single territory or neighbouring territories regulated by common rights or compascuité agreements. The livestock which graze in the high mountains in summer are kept in stables in nearby valleys during the winter. "Alpine transhumance" therefore does not refer to a mid-to-long-distance migration between complementary grazing areas (a movement which would not have to involve vertical mobility). Geographers have studied pastoral migration between the southern Alps and Provence since the early twentieth century (Arbos, 1915, 1922; Blanchard, 1950; Artaud, 1961–1962; Gardelle, 1965). T. Sclafert pioneered the historical study of animal husbandry in southern France (Sclafert, 1926, 1934, 1939, 1959). While some historians dealt with this topic in broader rural studies (Février, 1959; Durbec, 1967; Paillard, 1968; Malausséna, 1969; Stouff, 1986; Struyf, 1977), specific research was completed by P. Coste (1972, 1977; Coste & Coulet, 1994) and N. Coulet (1978, 1986, 1988, 1990, 1996, 1998, 2001a, 2001b) in Provence and later by H. Falque-Vert (1997, 2006) in Dauphiné. There are relatively few further studies (Kaiser-Guyot, 1974; Besson, 1977; Leydet, 1982; Boyer, 1990; Venturini, 1997; Lassalle, 1997, 2001, 2006; Lassalle & Palmero, 2010; Mouthon, 2007; Carrier & Mouthon, 2010). By contrast, archaeologists started to study pastoral settlements in the mountainous environments of the Pyrenees in the 1980s (Rendu, 1998, 2000, 2003; Rendu et al., 2016). In the French southern Alps, research started in the Ecrins Massif in the 1990s (Mocci et al., 2005; Walsh, 2005; Walsh et al., 2003, 2011; Walsh et al., 2010) and then continued, albeit to a lesser extent, in other areas: Vercors and Dévoluy-Buëch (Morin & Picavet, 2006; Morin et al., 2010), Champsaur and Ubaye Valley (Palet-Martinez et al., 2003; Garcia et al., 2007)

© 2018 European Association of Archaeologists

and Mercantour (Geist, 2006; Suméra & Geist, 2010). Despite the diachronic nature of these investigations, the majority focused on human occupation and upland pasture uses during prehistory and how those phenomena evolved up to Roman times (Jospin & Favrie, 2008). Specific attention was paid to the environmental impact of human activities in those areas (Court-Picon et al., 2007; Walsh et al., 2007, 2014; Brisset, et al., 2012; Segard, 2009). Those studies which focused on the medieval period centred around the exploitation of natural resources (mainly woodlands) and mining activities (Py et al., 2014; Py-Saragaglia, et al., 2015). Although archaeoenvironmental and archaeological studies demonstrate the continuity of human activities in upper mountain areas already from the Bronze Age and their strong intensification during the medieval period, very few focused on medieval pastoral structures. Moreover, in direct contrast with high mountain archaeology, lowland pastoral archaeology is almost non-existent. The only data available were derived from excavations in the Crau plain (Badan et al., 1995; Henry et al., 2010) and central Provence (Burri, 2012, 2014).

Despite the fact that archaeologists have demonstrated the prehistoric origin of Alpine vertical mobility in the French southern Alps, the origin of the mid- and long-distance seasonal migration of flocks is still a hot topic. Since the discovery of several large Roman sheep pens in the Crau Plain in western Provence (Badan, et al., 1995, 2006; Leveau & Segard, 2004; Leveau, 2006a, 2006b), discussion of this topic has increased exponentially. Archaeozoological studies have shown that these sheep pens were occupied in winter (Congès & Leguilloux, 2012). After consultation with the ancient records (Strabon, Pliny the Elder), Italian models of Roman transhumance and the organisation of the modern Great Transhumance, scholars concluded that the seasonal long-distance migration of flocks from the Crau to the southern Alps existed during the Roman era. However, archaeological and archaeoenvironmental data from the southern Alps did not show important human occupation evidence in upland pastures during this period. To the contrary, they even suggested their abandonment in some areas (Mocci et al., 2005, 2010; Walsh, 2005; Walsh & Mocci, 2011; Walsh et al., 2013; Walsh et al., 2010, 2016; Palet-Martinez et al., 2003; Garcia et al., 2007; Segard, 2009). Historical studies demonstrated that even in the late medieval period (fourteenth–fifteenth centuries), only the largest flocks from the Arles-Crau area (more than 500 animals) migrated to Alpine valleys during summer, while the others stayed in the Crau or were moved to the neighbouring wetland pastures of the Camargue and the surroundings marshes and hills of Alpilles and Luberon (Stouff, 1986: 450–51; Coste & Coulet, 1994). Both elements

either mitigate or bring into question the existence of a Roman summering migration to the Alps (Badan et al., 2006; Leveau & Segard, 2004; Leveau, 2006a, 2006b). Recent inferences from ethno-archaeological studies have caused the reinterpretation of the lack of Roman pastoral remains as a result of an economic "shift from a dairyingfocused Alpine pastoralism to a wool/meatfocused transhumance" (Carrer, 2015:16). However, the dichotomy between wool- and meat-focused and dairying-focused husbandry has not been proven in antiquity and did not exist during the medieval period: long-distance migrant herds were also exploited for dairy products and local Alpine flocks were also bred for their meat, wool and skins (Arnaud d'Agnel, 1908; Sclafert, 1926, 1959; Paillard, 1968; Kaiser-Guyot, 1974: 64–66; Struyf, 1977; Leydet, 1982; Coulet, 1988a; Carrier & Mouthon, 2010). Data are still insufficient to prove the existence of an ascending animal migration from Provence to the Alps during the Roman period. Obviously, this does not mean that pastoral husbandry was not largely practised during Roman and early medieval periods. Whereas the use of the Crau sheep pens ended in the fifth century AD, five upland pastoral sites (huts and enclosures) attest to Alpine pastoral activities during the early medieval period (Palet-Martinez et al., 2003; Segard, 2009; Mocci et al., 2005). The few early medieval written sources which address this topic also confirm the use of Alpine upland pastures (Geary, 1985: 52; Carrier & Mouthon, 2010: 59–61; Durand, 2014, 2016) but do not reference an actual seasonal migration of herds from another region. This paper focuses on the period from AD 1100 to 1500, which is characterised by the first evidence of seasonal migration, its development, structuring and globalisation. In particular, it aims to create a better understanding of medieval mid- and long-distance herding between the Provence and the southern Alps. Furthermore, it proposes the first synthesis of previous and current historical and archaeological investigations (which are unpublished, at least in part) as a milestone for future research (Figure 10.1). This is addressed with the caveat that this paper deals only with the seasonal migration of sheep and goats as they represent the majority of animal husbandry in late medieval Provence. The mobile herding of cattle, horses and swine were more or less significant across different areas (Sclafert, 1928, 1959; Stouff, 1966; Malausséna, 1969; Coulet, 1978; Struyf, 1977). Moreover, this paper highlights the chronology and geography of both wintering and summering migration systems and their gradual fusion. It also explores their economic, social and logistical organisation (schedules, structure, actors and routes). Finally, by blending historical and archaeological data, it examines the daily life of the shepherds on summer and winter pastures.

Doubts and The First Evidence of Seasonal Pastoral Migration Between Provence and The Southern Alps AD 1100–1300

The winter grazing of Alpine herds in Provence: a customary practice

Before the thirteenth century, the documentary records (which are almost exclusively produced by monastic communities) deal with monastic herds. From the mid-twelfth century onwards, the livestock of the chartreuse of Durbon was moved down either to Forcalquier or Vienne and Albon counties near the Rhône Valley. The abbeys of Vercors (Leoncel and Les Ecouges) took their animals to the north (Wullschleger, 1994). At the same time, the abbey of Boscodon had the right to send its flocks to Provence and to Forcalquier counties, although no further details can be gleaned from the archives (Figure 10.2). The abbeys of Lure and Cruis on Lure Mountain had some grazing rights in Mouriès on the Crau Plain (Nicollet, 1925; Sclafert, 1959). However, the downwards migration of herds for the winter did not concern monastic herds alone. Indeed, flocks from the high Roya Valley over-wintered in the Ligurian lowlands in the mid-eleventh century and on the Provence coast during the late twelfth century (Février, 1959; Coulet, 1978; Lassalle, 2001). In contrast, Alpine herds from the Queyras usually went down to the Po Valley in winter (Falque-Vert, 1997; 2006). Fiscal documents from the mid-thirteenth century relating to tax collection on migrating herds (*pasquerium*) define a spatial boundary between upper and lower Provence. This boundary fits well with the limits of summer and winter pastures (Guichard, 1846; Durbec, 1967; Baratier, 1969; Coste, 1972; Coste & Coulet, 1994; Venturini, 1997). These documents not only prove the antiquity, but also the customary nature of the downward migration of upland flocks in Provence. The customary nature of this wintering is confirmed by the first preserved accounting registers which date from 1299. These documents concern the *baillies* of Brignoles, Saint-Maximin and (to a lesser extent) Barcelonnette and record the number and size of wintering flocks coming from the Bléone, Asse, Ubaye, Var and Verdon Valleys (Sclafert, 1959; Coulet, 1978).

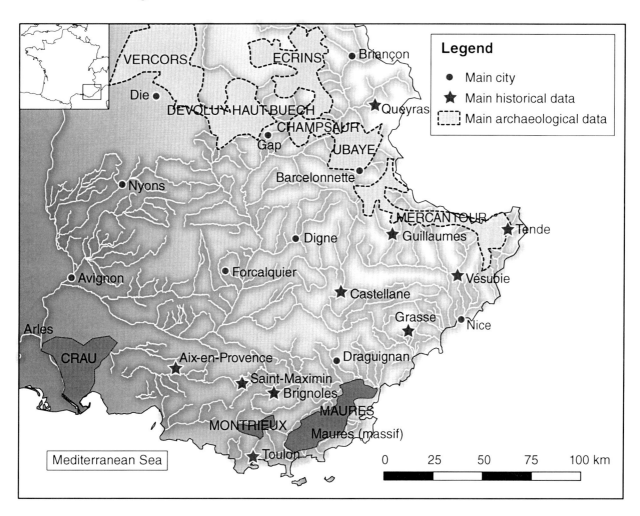

Figure 10.1. Study area
Source: R. Cesarini

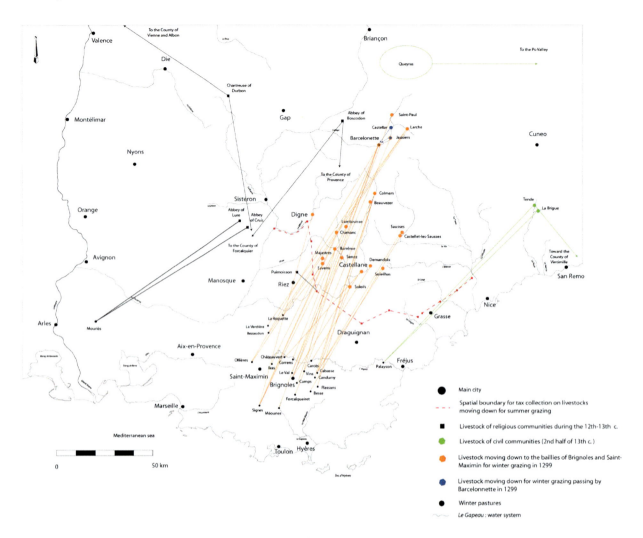

Figure 10.2. Wintering flows of Alpine herds (AD 1100–1300)
Source: S. Burri

Summer ascending migration of flocks from Provence to the southern Alps

From the eleventh century onwards, Provencal monasteries acquired pastures both in the mountains and lowlands, suggesting the establishment of complementary pastoral areas composed of winter and summer pastures. That being said, the possession of these pastures did not necessarily imply the migration of flocks from one to the other. For example, during the eleventh century, the abbey of Saint-Victor de Marseille acquired pastures in the middle and upper Verdon Valley in the Saint-Geniez-Dromon Massif as well as in the Var Valley and the Pre-Alps of Riez. While T. Sclafert (1939, 1959) interpreted the formation of this vast pastoral domain as evidence of the herds' summer migration, H. Bresc (Abbé et al., 1996: 6) is more cautious and warns us against the absence of concrete evidence for migration. The first concrete documentary evidence of summer migration describes the presence of flocks from the abbey of Saint-Pons de Nice which grazed in the Valdeblore during the mid-eleventh century (Boyer, 1990: 60–1). Things became clearer during the twelfth and thirteenth centuries through the acquisition of grazing and passage rights by several monasteries. The abbey of Le Thoronet obtained pasture rights in Saint-Auban (1146) and in Soleilhas (1184). During the first part of the thirteenth century, monks extended their pastoral area to the middle Verdon Valley (Aiguines, Bagarry, Bauduen, La Palud and Rougon), the Pre-Alps of Digne (Levens and Creisset), the north of the *viguerie* of Draguignan (Châteauvieux and La Martre) and to the plateaus of the Grasse hinterlands (Séranon and Gourdon). In addition, their pastoral activity was supported by their exemption to the *pasquerium* granted by the Count (Barbier, 1994). During the thirteenth century, the Carthusians of Montrieux obtained grazing rights over the territory of Castellane and in the Durance Valley (Oraison). Over time, they became gradually exempt from toll payments in Castellane, La Roquette, Oraison,

Gaubert and Barjols. The Castellane toll road led to the pastures of the upper Verdon Valley and to the middle and upper Var Valley, while those in Barjols and Quinson gave access to the lower and middle Verdon Valley. The Gaubert toll station opened the way to the Digne Pre-Alps and, finally, through Oraison, the herds travelled up the Durance Valley. During the same period (1244), the chartreuse of La Verne obtained grazing rights to the entirety of Castellane territory and was then exempted from all grazing taxes and toll payments therein (1328). The grazing area of the Valbonne abbey's livestock was smaller and was confined to the Grasse hinterlands: La Malle, Gourdon and Caussols (Coulet, 2001a). Finally, the sheep of the Hospitallers of Puimoisson were moved up over a very small distance to Aiguines (Maurel, 1897; Sclafert, 1959: 23). In legal documentation, conflicts related to the presence of Provence herds in pastures belonging to Boscodon-Les Crottes and Saint-Paul-sur-Ubaye demonstrate that peasant communities' flocks already shifted between the Provencal lowlands and Alpine uplands during the late thirteenth century (Sclafert, 1959; Coulet, 1978). The accounting register of Barcelonette (1299) confirm the summer migration of flocks coming from La Verdière and Castellane to Ubaye Valley via Barcelonnette (Coulet, 1978).

Wintering and Summering Migration Flows from AD 1300 to 1500

In the fourteenth century, written documents (deeds, accounting registers and other legal documentation) increased. Their preservation allows us to shed some light on mid- and long-distance mobile herding. A gradual increase in Provencal sheep husbandry occurred from the mid-fourteenth century onwards. It intensified during the second quarter of the fifteenth century with the rise of free upland pasture areas due to a decline in Alpine demography. This was compounded by the development of the wool market and a rise in meat consumption[1] (Stouff, 1970; Coulet, 1986, 1988a; Carrier & Mouthon, 2010). This economic dynamism was accompanied by an increase in herd size; large herds of several thousands of animals exceeded the summer fodder capacity of Provencal pastures. This change in the scale of animal husbandry required increased mid- and long-distance migration in order to obtain adequate fodder for the animals. From 1430 onwards, summer ascending migration seems to have become more prominent at the expense of inverse movements. However, the growing complexity of the pastoral economy is reflected by the use of a herding contract – called a '*mégerie*' – between Alpine and Provence herders. Through this, they bring together their respective livestock. This led to the fusion of wintering and summering

systems as was recorded in the Castellane accounts from the early sixteenth century (Besson, 1977; Coulet; 1978; Burri, 2012: 291–307, 351–62). Despite being incomplete, fourteenth and fifteenth-century written sources provide enough information for seasonal flows to be mapped relatively accurately (Capus, 1681; Guichard, 1846; Arbos, 1915; Nicollet, 1925; Sclafert, 1926, 1934, 1939, 1959; Février, 1959; Durbec, 1967; Paillard, 1968; Birrell, 1968; Baratier, 1969; Malausséna, 1969; Coste, 1972, 1977; Stouff, 1966, 1986; Struyf, 1977; Leydet, 1982; Royer, 1988; Coste & Coulet, 1994; Coulet, 1978, 1986, 1988a, 1988b, 1990, 1996, 2001a, 2001b; Boyer, 1990; Falque-Vert, 1997, 2006; Barbier, 1994; Wullschleger, 1994; Venturini, 1997; Lassalle, 2001; Lassalle & Palmero, 2010; Ghersi, 2004; Musset, 2006; Burri, 2012, 2014; Blanc, 2014).[2] The distribution of both summering and wintering areas resulted from gradual competition between herding areas as well as between herders themselves (Coulet, 1978, 1988a: 373–84). What is presented here is only the general trend.

Wintering flows

Winter grazing flows can be mapped for all areas other than western Provence.[3] Sheep coming from the Bleone and Asse valleys mainly moved down to the *baillies* of Saint-Maximin and Brignoles (Figure 10.3). Flocks from the Ubaye Valley grazed only on small area west of Brignoles, while those from the Verdon and Var valleys wintered in the whole of central Provence from Saint-Maximin in the west to Fréjus in the east. In eastern Provence, sheep from the Grasse hinterlands and the Roya Valley were moved either within the Grasse hinterlands or to central Provence. On the contrary, livestock from the high Vésubie Valley seemed to have stayed in the base of valley and around Nice (Figure 10.4). The movements of flock from the *viguerie* of Draguignan were characterised by the short distances they covered within the *viguerie*. Here, it is very interesting to highlight the existence of winter pastoral migration conducted by lowland communities. However, this practice was recorded neither in common rights nor in *compascuité* agreements. Instead, it was the subject of wintering contracts. The distance travelled ranged from less than 10 km to more than 140 km (Figure 10.8a). N. Coulet (1978) has defined three scales of migratory flows for wintering: small scale from 1 to 40 km, medium scale from 40 km to 80 km and large scale over 80 km.[4] Using this classification, we can characterise the scale of migratory flows from each area of origin: small-scale migration for flocks from the Vésubie Valley and upper and lower Provence; medium-scale mobility for those from the high plateaus and the Asse Valley and large-scale migration from the Verdon, Var, Bleone

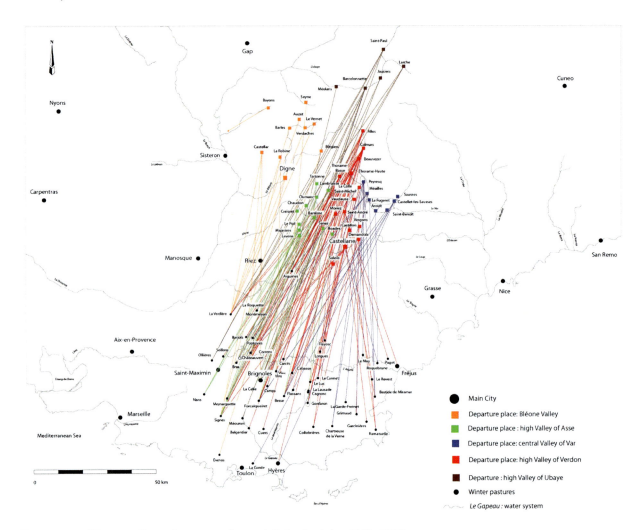

Figure 10.3. Wintering flows of western and central Alpine herds (AD 1300–1500)
Source: S. Burri

and Roya valleys. A fourth scale may be suggested here: very large-scale migration for movements over 120 km, as was the case for flocks from the Ubaye Valley. Obviously, these categories show a general trend and do not express the idiosyncratic variability of each case.

Summering flows

Sheep and goats from Provence moved up to various summering areas depending on their place of origin. First, the flocks from western Provence moved up to a wide area situated between the mountains of the Vercors and the Tinée Valley (Figure 10.5). Within this group, there was competition between herds from Arles, Salon-Berre and Aix in the Vercors, Diois, Lure Mountain and the Asse and Bléone valleys. On the contrary, flocks from Aix seemed to be the only Provencal ones in the Champsaur, Valgaudemar and Devoluy (Dauphiné). Some of them (Aix and Salon) even crossed the border into Piedmont. In contrast, some herds from Arles crossed the Rhône River to go to Mont Lozère, in the Kingdom of France. The short-distance migration of herds from upper Provence was probably due to the closeness of the lowlands to the uplands. The flocks which migrated from central Provence to an area between the Digne region and Tinée Valley or to the Ubaye Valley were in competition with those from western Provence (Figure 10.6). There was no significant difference in the destinations of flocks from lower and central Provence. In eastern Provence, the closeness of the coast and the mountains explains the short distances travelled. Excluding the Var and Tinée valleys and the high plateaus of Grasse hinterlands, flocks from eastern Provence were not in competition with other Provencal herds. By contrast, livestock from Provence, Liguria and Piedmont competed in the Roya Valley.

In all, there were considerable differences in the distances travelled (Figure 10.8b), ranging from less than 10 km to more than 180 km. In short, the present writers characterise four migration scales from textual

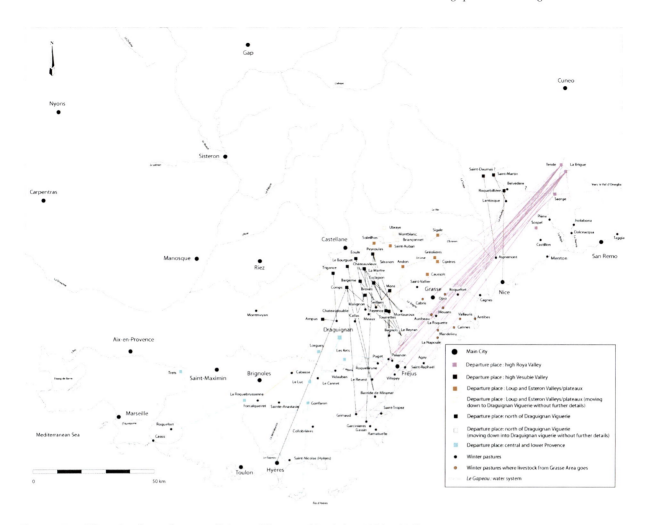

Figure 10.4. Wintering flows of eastern Alpine and Provencal herds (AD 1300–1500)
Source: S. Burri

data: the small-scale migration of flocks coming from eastern Provence; a medium scale for those from central and northern Provence; a large-scale for those from western Provence and a very large scale for those from Arles, Marseille and Salon. Once again, these general trends hide significant variability, which we cannot explore in more detail here.

The road and Daily Life on Summer and Winter Pastures

Forms of seasonal pastoral migration organisation

Moving herds of more than one hundred animals up and down over long distances and crossing various environmental and political entities required a specific kind organisation (Arnaud d'Agnel, 1908; Paillard, 1968; Kaiser-Guyot, 1974: 56–60; Coulet, 1986, 1988a, 1988b, 1996, 2001b; Royer, 1988, 2003; Blanc, 2014). This is largely unknown before the fourteenth century, as the available sources only provide information about tax collection on the passage of herds and grazing rights. During the fourteenth and most of the fifteenth century, the intensification and generalisation of sheep husbandry resulted in a very structured business (Paillard, 1968; Malausséna, 1969; Sclafert, 1959; Coulet, 1986, 1988a, 1988b, 1996, 2001b; Royer, 1988, 2003; Blanc, 2014). Deeds (herding contracts, pasture rental agreements, etc.) reveal different kinds of more or less complex organisation that could be classified into five different categories. Categories 1, 2 and 3 concern both summer and winter grazing systems, while categories 4 and 5 deal exclusively with summering systems. In category 1, the herder (alone or in association with another party) leased his flock to another herder for a determined period. Profits were often divided equally. In the second category, the herder entered into a herding agreement with a shepherd for one season in return for wages. Both types of contracts sometimes

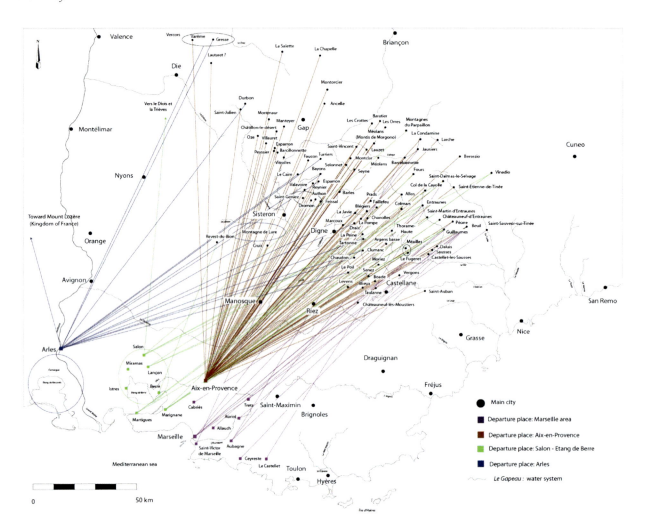

Figure 10.5. Summering flows of western Provencal herds (AD 1300–1500)
Source: S. Burri

contained a clause regarding animal summering migration but, unfortunately provided no further information. In the third case, the herder contracted a rental agreement with the pasture owner (either an individual or a community). The contract specified the duration of the rental duration, the date of entry and exit and the maximum number and type of livestock (sheep, goats, cattle or mixed herds). The owner was expected to provide enough grass, salt and sometimes medicinal ointment (juniper tar) for the animals. In addition, he was expected to furnish the dogs' food supplies and to ensure the safety of the animals on his pasture. These clauses were usually more detailed for summer pastures than for winter pastures. A higher level of structuring characterises the fourth and fifth cases. They show the professionalisation of stakeholders and the intervention of specialised intermediaries, i.e. pasture dealers and flock drivers. Pasture dealers could rent and resell pastures to herders, whereas flock drivers worked as middlemen between owners or pasture dealers and herders. While not a shepherd, the flock driver drove flocks from one point to another. In order to optimise his activity, he could often gather flocks from different herders into a single herd. The pasture dealer was often also a flock driver. The legal terms of a sub-rental agreement did not change compared to a 'direct' rental agreement. Driving agreements specified the respective obligations of the parties, such as the payment of tolls and passages, to ensure the safety of the animals on the road to and from the mountains and to compensate the herder in the case of an animal's loss. The reality behind this general overview was much more complex, as evidenced by the rare accounting registers of the 'transhumance entrepreneur'. The Noé de Barras notebook shows the whole complexity of the organisation of flock driving through the relationships between the flock driver, his shepherds and the lords and landowners along the road. The notebook reports the payment of a multitude of passage rights, the negotiation of places to stay for the night, grazing relays, watering places and conflict management related to damage caused by animals (Royer, 1988; Blanc, 2014). Some communities of the Roya Valley had a specific way of directly managing their

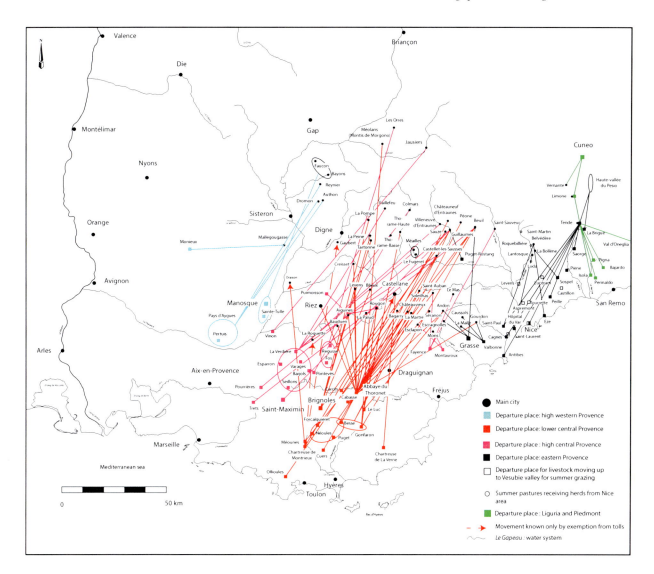

Figure 10.6. Summering flows of central and eastern Provencal herds (AD 1300–1500)
Source: S. Burri

common pastures, which were divided into large parcels called *bandites*. Every year, the municipal council leased these *bandites* to herders. Their use was clearly regulated: certain parcels were reserved for local or external herders, cattle or sheep and goats and for spring or summer grazing (Struyf, 1977).

On the road

Some accurate documents provide key milestones to reconstruct medieval routes from Provence to the southern Alps (Paillard, 1968; Coulet, 1988a: 368–73; Royer, 1988, 2003; Musset, 2006; Burri, 2012: 362–5; Blanc, 2014). We assume that shepherds used the same routes in both directions, thus, that wintering and summering routes were the same (Figure 10.7). In most cases, only a few stops are known: the place where livestock came into the driver's care, toll stations and sometimes salt supply places. The flock drivers' and herders' notebooks allow us to precisely reconstruct the routes and their crossing points, such as in the case of the road from western Provence to Ubaye Valley. It should be noted that the multiplicity of roads leads to the same point. Therefore, it is almost impossible to accurately assess journey times which depended on the routes chosen as well as on the nature and size of the flock, weather conditions and the relief of the landscape. These aspects are known and documented only from the eighteenth century (Clapier, 1838; Fournier, 1900; Guillaume, 1908; Rouquette, 1913; Compan, 1961; Pichard, 2006). It is impossible to model medieval shepherds' mobility on the road to pastures as well as on the pasture itself.[5]

The calendar of summering and wintering was mainly defined by environmental and weather conditions (drought, snow) and their effects on the availability of grass (Schippers, 1986a, 1986b). The start and end dates determined the dates of the trade fairs at which shepherds sold a part of their products (animals, wool, hides and dairy products). According to pasture rental agreements and the accounts of the Castellane tolls from the early sixteenth century, herds' entry into summer pastures occurred from the beginning of May to the end of June. While most exit dates ranged from early to late September, some were even later (October 24th) or earlier (August 24th), depending on the areas and years concerned. The duration of summer grazing can sometimes be assessed and shows a great variability of practice. It could range from 69 to 205 days. In contrast, the winter grazing season usually began during September. Some pastures were opened later (October to January). Similarly, May was the most common month for departure away. That being said, some herds left in April, while others waited until June (Burri, 2012: 290–313).

It is impossible to reconstruct the whole density of winter and summer grazing flows and their development during the late medieval period. However, some documents allow us to assess the number of transhumant flocks for a particular period and place. Winter grazing flows are well documented thanks to the *pasquerium* account registers of the Count of Provence and the Bishop of Fréjus (Sclafert, 1959; Février, 1959; Coste, 1972; Coulet, 1978; Burri, 2012: 370–407). The overall evolution of the pattern of wintering flows in the *baillies* of Saint-Maximin and Brignoles does not reflect the complexity of the evolution of each flow (Figure 10.8c–e). There are significant differences concerning their origin, amplitude and evolution. As regards the period prior the sixteenth century, the absence of Alpine accounting registers makes the assessment of summering flows rather difficult. Based on deeds, N. Coulet (1986) suggested that *c.* 40,000–50,000 sheep from the Aix area summered annually in the Alps during the mid-fifteenth century. The accounts of Castellane's toll station show the increase of the transhumant flow by tens thousands of animals per year from 1504 to 1510 (Besson, 1977; Coulet, 1978; Burri, 2012: 352–61) (Figure 10.8f–h). For the second part of the sixteenth century, similar information is available on the flows of herds passing through the village of Guillaumes in eastern Provence (Gourdon & Gourdon, 2014). Different scales of analysis show the complexity of the flows. These fluctuations are difficult to interpret consistently as a result of the lack of data concerning other areas and time spans. P. Coste (1972) interpreted the significant decrease of the number of wintering animals in the *viguerie* of Draguignan between 1346 and 1374 (from 60,000 to less than 23,000) as a consequence of the general insecurity of the period. This conclusion is confirmed by the absence of the passage of summering animals through Barcelonnette in 1358 (Coulet, 1978).

Shepherds' lifestyle and activities on pastures

Medieval shepherds' daily life on pastures is still an unknown aspect (Kaiser-Guyot, 1974; Le Roy Ladurie, 1975). Texts provide specific but inadequate information about the mobile shepherd's lifestyle on summer Alpine pastures (Arnaud d'Agnel, 1908; Canestrier, 1952; Lombard, 1962; Leydet, 1982; Kaiser-Guyot, 1974; Royer, 1988, 2003; Burri, 2012: 449–53). Often the pasture owner had to provide a good and sufficient hut (*cabanna*) for shepherds during the summer grazing season. Sometimes, shepherds used only half of a hut. The rent was either paid in cash or in kind (with cheese). If the hut was not in good condition, the pasture owner was obliged to repair it before the shepherd's arrival. Such huts were built of stone with timber frames and wooden roofing (wood shingles). Sometimes specialised craftsmen (such as masons or carpenters) built this type of structure (Royer, 1988, 2003). Usually, the pasture owner supplied the shepherds' bread (*apanagium*) and, sometimes, the dressing (*calciamentum*). The shepherd's hut may be accompanied by other structures, i.e. an enclosure, sorting enclosure, cellar for the shepherds' equipment (*cellerio pro negotia*) or dairy (*cella or frederius*). Sometimes, the shepherds used a common *cella* which was owned by the village community and which they were allowed to access only upon payment of a special tax on dairy products called *cellagium*. In return, the community maintained the building. Notebooks and accounting registers provide some accurate information on shepherds' *instrumentum*: the tools of daily life as well as the items required for cheese-making and other paraphernalia (dog collars, flock bells, etc.) (Arnaud d'Agnel, 1908; Royer, 1988, 2003).

Archaeology also documents material aspects of the shepherd's life in mountain pastures. In accordance with a published dataset, we have identified five late antique-early medieval pastoral occupation centres (four in Vercors, four in Champsaur and two in Ecrins), thirteen from the eleventh to the thirteenth century (four in Champsaur, four in Ecrins and five in Mercantour) and six late medieval sites (one in Champsaur, four in Ecrins and one in Mercantour) (Mocci et al., 2005; Walsh, 2005; Walsh, et al., 2003, 2010, 2016; Palet-Martinez et al., 2003; Garcia et al., 2007; Segard, 2009; Py & Durand, 2010; Py-Saragaglia et al., 2015; Geist, 2006; Suméra & Geist, 2010; Morin & Picavet, 2006; Morin et al., 2010). However, this inventory reflects mostly the state of research rather than the extent of medieval settlement. On the basis of morphological and size criteria, archaeological structures are usually classified into two main types: huts and pens.[6] Those structures may be insulated. This is particularly the case for small huts whether or not they were associated with a pen. They

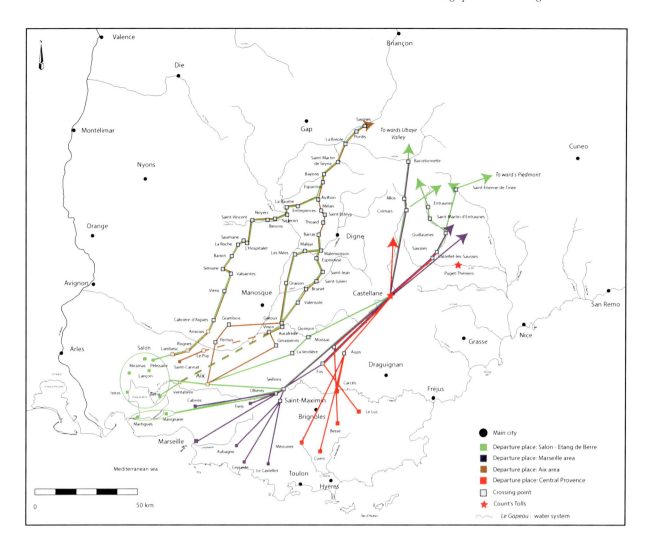

Figure 10.7. Reconstruction of shepherds' routes (AD 1300–1500)
Source: S. Burri

can be also grouped into hamlets with few or several huts with or without other arrangements (pens, irrigation canals, terraces, etc.) (Figure 10.9a). Most of the structures were entirely built of stone or were at least constructed with stone substructures (Figure 10.9b). Perishable materials were used for elevations. The roofs were covered with lauze or shake.[7] The scarcity of archaeological material found in these sites provides little information on the shepherd's daily life (Figure 10.9c). The main challenges are to recognise archaeological evidence of wooden structures (i.e. mobile enclosures) and to discriminate the function of different structures (e.g. principal dwelling, shelter, dairy, etc.). In spite of a narrow spectrum of human activities in the high mountain environment, several other activities could create similar temporary dwellings and structures (such as mining in the Ecrins Massif or in the upper Roya Valley, forestry and haymaking (see Py-Saragaglia et al., 2015; Burri, 2014). At the site of Fangeas X (Freissinières, Hautes-Alpes), a two-room structure (48 m²) first occupied during the thirteenth century and reused in the fifteenth and sixteenth centuries seems to be related to haymaking and storage as evidenced by two scythe stones (stones sharped at both ends) (Figure 10.9c). Charcoal analyses reinforced this hypothesis insofar as they also indicated summer occupation (Py-Saragaglia et al., 2015). Hay production was closely tied to local animals' winter housing in sheds located in the valley and not to long-distance mobile herding (Falque-Vert, 1997; Carrier & Mouthon, 2010: 250–56).

The main archaeological research took place on areas located on the margins or away from Provencal summer grazing areas. Thereby it is difficult to cross textual and archaeological data related to summering migrations of flocks from Provence. Moreover, a concentration on the archaeological evidence of migrant livestock requires discriminating structures related to the simple vertical mobility of Alpine flocks from those of mid- or long-distance mobile flocks in order to assess its real place. F. Carrer (2015, 2016) attempted to distinguish these two types of temporary settlements by suggesting

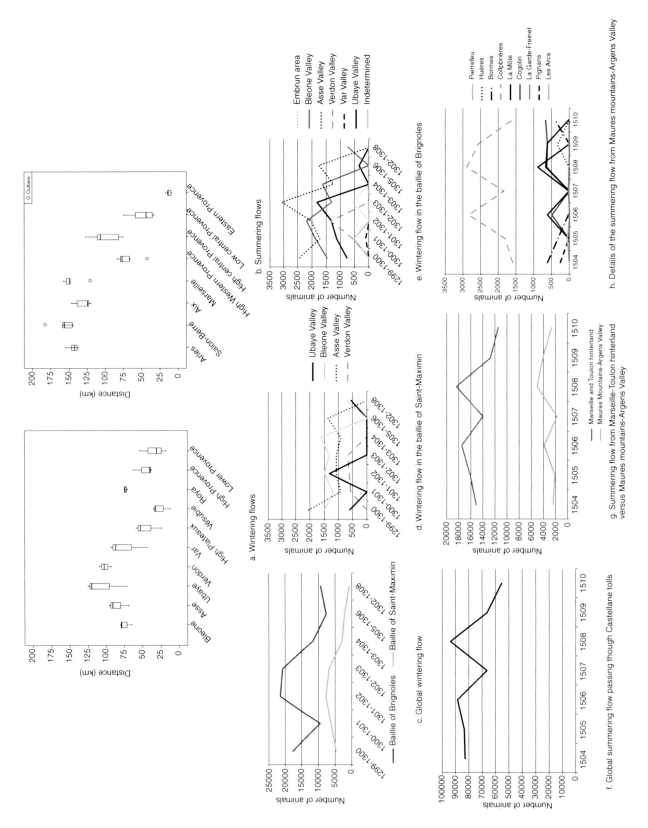

Figures 10.8a–b. *Distances travelled for wintering and summering (AD 1300–1500)*
Source S. Burri

Figures 10.8c–h. *Assessment of wintering and summering flows*
Source: S. Burri

that local Alpine dairy-oriented herding structures were more complex and permanent than 'transhumant' wool- and meat-oriented herding sites. As mentioned above, these arguments cannot easily be transposed to medieval herding practices in southern France without a specialised herding system. Both local and migrant herding produced secondary products. We believe that it is clearly impossible to prove the presence of mid- and long-distance animal populations based on the shape of archaeological structures as the current knowledge base stands at present.

The same issues apply to shepherds' lifestyles during winters in the lowlands. Texts are also of little help, probably due to a lack of structure in the descending migration system. Winter pasture rental agreements never mention the fact that pasture owners had an obligation to provide housing for annuitants or their shepherds. Sometimes, they stipulate the right to cut some wood for the construction of pens and animal shelters (Burri, 2012: 453).[8] The only reference to wintering housing concerns the right of the shepherds of the abbey of Léoncel, in Vercors to cut wood for the construction of their dwellings in Châteauneuf near the banks of the Isère (Sclafert, 1926). The pastoral use of caves for goat kids is documented at Dégoutaux cave (Belgentier, Var) in 1288 (Boyer, 1980: charter 381) but the local or foreign origin of the goats is not specified. Medieval pastoral sites in the Provencal lowlands are rare in the archaeological literature. Although a few open-air sites have been reported in unpublished field survey reports, none have yet been excavated. One of them, the Col de Barral site (Le Lavandou, Var), included a hut (c. 3.6 m^2) connected to a large stone enclosure (c. 105 m^2) which may date from the thirteenth or fourteenth century (Borréani, 1991)[9] (Figure 10.9d). Medieval cave occupations are also known but have long been neglected in favour of prehistoric ones (Raynaud, 2001). For the thirteenth and fourteenth centuries, pastoral activities have been demonstrated in the Vieux Mounoï Cave (Signes, Var) by burnt manure layers and rock polishing (Acovitsioti-Hameau et al., 1993). However, most commonly, the characterisation of the type of activity which is carried out is impossible due to the lack of discriminating structures, artefacts and/or specific micromorphological patterns, such as was the case at the sites of Roque Fadade and Castel Diol 2 (Le Muy, Var) (Figure 10.9e). These sites hosted temporary and repeated occupations which echoed the tempo of the occupancies of summering huts. Moreover, a very large spectrum of woodland activities (i.e. timber cutting, charcoal production, tar making, harvesting of bark and leaves and shifting cultivation) could have led to the construction of similar temporary settlements. Indeed, when space (distance travelled from the producer's residence to its place of production), time (duration of the operating season) and technical (operational time and monitoring)

constraints were too high, these activities led to the construction of temporary dwellings (Burri, 2012, 2014).

In all cases, even if the pastoral use of certain sites can be demonstrated, it is currently strictly impossible to discriminate archaeological sites related to mid- and long-distance mobile herding and/or to sedentary and short-distance vertical mobile herding in both lowland and upland environments.

CONCLUSION

The seasonal migration of flocks between summer and winter pastures was not only a response to environmental constraints but also a part of a complex socio-economic process that evolved in complementary territories. This synthesis shows the multi-faceted reality of the animal migration in both temporal and spatial dimensions. It flies in the face of the conventional and fixed picture painted by the Great Transhumance paradigm. We have highlighted the main chronological milestones of the medieval history of the seasonal shift of flocks between Provence and the southern Alps. This chronology must be specified through new historical survey in disregarded areas, especially in Alpine contexts. To analyse and characterise migration patterns, four levels of seasonal migration have been defined: close range (up to 40 km), medium-distance (up to 80 km), large distance (from 80 km to 120 km) and very large distance (over 120 km). We have observed a significant difference between the distances travelled for wintering (from Provence to the Alpine uplands) and summering (from the Alps to the Provencal lowlands). The relationship between the distances travelled and the size of the herds evidenced by N. Coulet (1978) must be studied further. The distribution of grazing area could result from a gradual competition between herding centres and herders themselves. The same variability can be observed in the duration of summering, which ranges from c. 70 to 210 days. Some medieval shepherds' routes can be reconstructed more or less accurately. The amplitude of wintering and summering animal flows can be assessed for only a select few areas during this period. This issue requires further investigation to better understand the fluctuations across space and time. From the fifteenth century onwards and following on the intensification and generalisation of sheep herding, seasonal migration became a real business led by specialised persons. The historical study of its social and economic structure must be continued at a regional scale. One of the less-known aspects involves the daily life of shepherds. Summer life is more documented by both historical and archaeological data. Notwithstanding the difficulties faced by pastoral archaeology, i.e. the bad preservation and invisibility of wooden structures

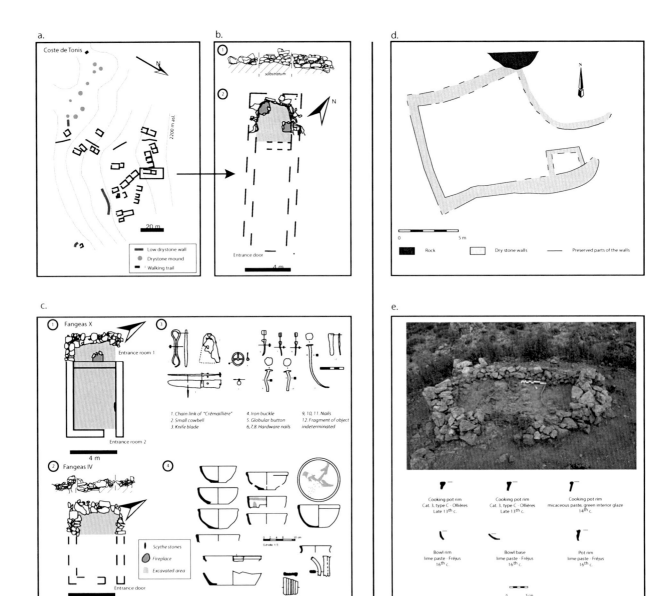

Figure 10.9a. Site of Coste de Tonis (Ecrins Massif), 2200 m a.s.l. Topographic survey of noticeable remains of a large group of several agro-pastoral structures (2180–2200 m.a.s.l.)
Source: B. Ancel (Service culturel municipal de l'Argentière-la Bessée) and V. Py-Saragaglia

Figure 10.9b. Structure of Coste de Tonis 1 (fifteenth c.), 2200 m.a.s.l.: 1) Elevation of interior walls in the excavated area and 2) General plan of the structure comprised of two parts
Source: E. Dantec, V. Py-Saragaglia)

Figure 10.9c. Structure of Fangeas X and IV (twelfth–thirteenth c. and fifteenth–sixteenth c.) – 2000–2010 m.a.s.l.: 1) General plan of Fangeas X comprising two rooms with independent entrances, 2) Elevation of interior walls in the excavated area of Fangeas IV and general plan of the structure, 3) Archaeological metal material from the two Fangeas X and IV and dated from thirteenth–sixteenth c., 4) Archaeological ceramic material from Fangeas X dating from thirteenth–sixteenth c. (Guionova in press)
Source: V. Py-Saragaglia, O. Thuaudet (LA3M, UMR 7298 CNRS), G. Guionova (LA3M, UMR 7298 CNRS)

Figure 10.9d. Structure of Col de Barral (Le Lavandou, Var) (thirteenth–fourteenth c.) – plan
Source: M. Borréani (Centre Archéologique du Var)

Figure 10.9e. Structure of Roque Fadade 6 (Le Muy, Var) (twelfth–seventeenth c.) – picture and ceramic material
Source: S. Burri

or their functional characterisation, this approach is the only way to reconstruct shepherds' daily life. Moreover, the application of biosciences to archaeology can offer a variety of new research perspectives, i.e. the chemical analysis of residues and sediments (Dudd & Evershed, 1998, 2008; Craig, 2002), micro-morphology, and mineralogical examinations of mineral residues from manure[10] (Brochier, 1991; Brochier et al., 2002; Goren, 1999).

To conclude, archaeology's current challenge is to develop new methods in order to discriminate structures related to long-distance mobile and local herding. Isotopic analysis is one of the most promising methods, especially the characterisation of strontium isotopes (87Sr/86Sr), which can provide excellent evidence for geographic mobility (Balasse et al., 2002; Balasse & Ambrose, 2005; Meiggs, 2007). Vertical mobility can be also documented by archaeozoology, archaeobotany (Martin, 2014; Py-Saragaglia et al., 2015) and by lake sediment DNA (Giguet-Covex et al., 2014). Late medieval and post-medieval sites could be a great testing ground for such improvements in the future. This implies a closer collaboration between historians and archaeologists. The relative richness and diversity of medieval and post-medieval historical and archaeological data allows us to test and assess the reliability of these new approaches in order to improve them, e.g. to cross data from strontium isotopic analysis with the detailed study of the standard practice of mixing Provence and Alpine flocks and the synchronic practice of wintering and summering.

NOTES

1 Mutton was the most requested and appreciated meat in late medieval Provence (Stouff, 1970, 180–81).
2 All maps are qualitative and do not reflect the amplitude of the flows. They were all made by Sylvain Burri according to previous research as well as our unpublished work.
3 For example, no data is available on the winter grazing of herds coming from mountainous areas in the Crau and Camargue before the sixteenth century (Stouff, 1986: 451; Merle-Comby, 1983).
4 All distances are calculated as the crow flies.
5 For current pastoral mobility modeling, see Cheylan et al., 1990; Le Couédic, 2010, 2012, 2016.
6 This paper does not discuss the issue of differentiating between sheepfolds and cattle corrals.
7 A thin section split from a bolt and used for roofing or weatherboarding.
8 As a general rule, according to common rights, every shepherd had the right to cut wood for his own use (i.e. the building of huts, enclosures and sheepfolds).
9 We thank Marc Borréani for his authorisation to publish the archaeological plan of this site.
10 E.g. spherulite and druzes (spherical fibrous crystal and star-shaped carbonate concentrations produced by animals' intestines) and phytoliths (opal skeletons of vegetal tissues).

REFERENCES

Abbé, A., Bresc, H. & Ollivier, J.-P. 1996. *Bergers de Provence et du pays niçois.* Nice: Serre Editeur.

Acovitsioti-Hameau, A., Cazenave, A. & Hameau, Ph. 1993. La Grotte du Vieux-Mounoï (Signes): les niveaux historiques. *Cahier de l'ASER*, 8:11–26.

Arbos, Ph. 1915. Les moines pasteurs de Durbon. *Recueil des travaux de l'institut de géographie Alpine*, 3 (2–3):145–61.

Arbos, Ph. 1922. *La vie pastorale dans les Alpes françaises: étude de géographie humaine.* Paris: Armand Colin.

Arnaud d'Agnel, G. (abbé) 1908. *Les comptes du Roi René publiés d'après les originaux conservés aux archives des Bouches-du-Rhône*, Paris: Librairie Alphonse Picard et fils.

Artaud, A., 1961–1962. La transhumance dans les Basses-Alpes. *Bulletin de la société scientifique et littéraire des Basses-Alpes*, 36(227–28):263–87; 37(227):18–35; 37(230):79–90; 37(231–32):121–40.

Badan, O., Brun, J.-P. & Congès, G. 2006. Les bergeries romaines de la Crau d'Arles. In Jourdain-Annequin, C. and J.-C. Duclos, eds. *Aux origines de la transhumance. Les Alpes et la vie pastorale d'hier à aujourd'hui.* Paris: Picard, pp. 159–72.

Badan, O., Congès, G. & Brun, J.-P. 1995. Les bergeries romaines de la Crau d'Arles. Les origines de la transhumance en Provence. *Gallia*, 52:263–310.

Balasse, M. & Ambrose, S.H. 2005. Mobilité altitudinale des pasteurs néolithiques dans la vallée du Rift (Kenya): premiers indices de l'analyse du δ13C de l'émail dentaire du cheptel domestique. *Anthropozoologica*, 40(1):147–66.

Balasse, M., Ambrose, S.H., Smith, A. & Price, T.D. 2002. The seasonal mobility model for prehistoric herders in the South-western cape of South Africa assessed by isotopic analysis of sheep tooth enamel. *Journal of archaeological science*, 29(9):917–32.

Baratier, E. 1969. *Enquêtes sur les droits et revenus de Charles d'Anjou en Provence (1252 et 1278) avec une étude sur le domaine comtal et les seigneuries de Provence au XIIIe siècle.* Paris: Bibliothèque Nationale.

Barbier, E. 1994. *L'abbaye cistercienne du Thoronet au Moyen Âge. Son origine, son territoire, ses possessions.* Marguerittes: Editions Equinoxe.

Besson, S. 1977. La transhumance en Provence au début du XVIe siècle d'après les registres de péage de Castellane (unpublished master thesis, Université de Provence).

Birrell, J.R. 1968. La ville de Berre à la fin du Moyen Âge. In *Cahiers du centre d'études des sociétés méditerranéennes*, Aix-en-Provence: Publications des Annales de la faculté des lettres d'Aix-en-Provence, 59, pp. 109–68.

Blanc, W. 2014. Le carnet de Noé de Barras. Radioscopie de la transhumance provençale. *Histoire et sociétés rurales*, 42: 5–41.

Blanchard, R. 1950. *Les Alpes Occidentales V. Les Grandes Alpes françaises du Sud.* Grenoble, France: B. Arthaud.

Borréani M. 1991. Carte archéologique du Lavandou et de Bormes-les-Mimosas (Unpublished report. Toulon: Centre Archéologique du Var).

Boyer, J.-P. 1990. *Hommes et communautés du haut pays niçois médiéval: La Vésubie (XIIIe–XVe siècles).* Nice: Centre d'études médiévales.

Boyer, R. ed. 1980. *La Chartreuse de Montrieux aux XIIe et XIIIe siècles.* Marseille: J. Laffite.

Brisset, E., Guiter, F., Miramont, C., Delhon, C., Arnaud, F., Disnard, F., Poulenard, J., Anthony, E., Menier, J.-D., Wilhem, B. & Pilles, C. 2012. Approche multidisciplinaire d'une séquence lacustre holocène dans les

Alpes du Sud au lac Petit (Mercantour, alt. 2200 m., France): histoire d'un géosystème dégradé. *Quaternaire*, 23(4):309–19.

Brochier, J.-E. 1991. Géoarchéologie du monde agropastoral. In: J. Guilaine, ed., *Pour une archéologie agraire. A la croisée des sciences de l'Homme et de la nature*. Paris: Armand Colin, pp. 303–22.

Brochier, J.-E., Villa, P. & Giacomarra, M. 2002. Shepherds and sediments: geo-ethnoarchaeology of pastoral sites. *Journal of Anthropological Archaeology*, 11:47–102.

Burri, S. 2012. Vivre de l'inculte, vivre dans l'inculte en basse Provence centrale à la fin du Moyen Âge: histoire, archéologie et ethnoarchéologie d'un mode de vie itinérant (unpublished doctoral thesis, Aix Marseille University).

Burri, S. 2014. Reflections on the concept of marginal landscape through a study of late medieval *incultum* in Provence (South-eastern France). *European Journal of Post-Classical Archaeologies*, 4:7–38. www.postclassical.it/vol.4_files/PCA%204_Burri_YOUNG%20RESEARCHER%20AWARD_2014.pdf.

Canestrier, P. 1952. La transhumance dans la haute vallée du Var au XVIe siècle. Documents dialectaux. *Nice historique*, 45:45–9.

Capus, J. (Don). 1681. *Fundationes et dispositiones Cartusiarum Provinciae*.

Carrer, F. 2015. Herding strategies, dairy economy and seasonal sites in the Southern Alps: ethnoarchaeological inferences and archaeological implications. *Journal of Mediterranean Archaeology*, 28(1):3–22.

Carrer, F. 2016. The 'invisible' shepherd and the 'visible' dairyman: ethnoarchaeology of Alpine pastoral sites in the Val di Fiemme (eastern Italian Alps). In: Collis J., Pearce M. and Nicolis F., eds. *Summer Farms. Seasonal Exploitation of the Uplands from Prehistory to the Present.* Sheffield: Sheffield Archaeological Monograph 16, pp. 97–107.

Carrier, N. & Mouthon, F. 2010. *Paysans des Alpes: les communautés montagnardes au Moyen Âge, Rennes*. Rennes: Presses universitaires de Rennes.

Cheylan, J.-P., Deffontaines, J.-P., Lardon, S., Savini, I. 1990. Les pratiques pastorales d'un berger sur l'alpage de Vieille Selle: un modèle reproductible, *Mappemonde*, 4, www.mgm.fr/PUB/Mappemonde/M490/BERGER.pdf.

Clapier, A. 1838. Des troupeaux de Crau et de la transhumance. *Annales provençales d'Agriculture pratique, d'économie rurale et d'horticulture*, 11(132), 1838, pp. 549–88.

Compan, A. 1961. Transhumance et douane aux confins des Basses-Alpes et du Haut Comté de Nice (1814–1840). *Provence historique*, 11(46):343–53.

Congès, P. & Leguilloux M. 2012. La gestion des troupeaux transhumants dans la Crau d'Arles (Bouches-du-Rhône, France) à l'époque romaine. Données archéologiques et archéozoologiques. In: M.S. Busana & P. Basso, eds. *La lana nella Cisalpina romana. Economia e società. Studi in onore di Stefania Pesavento Mattioli*. Padova: Padova University Press, pp. 311–22.

Coste, P. 1972. La vie pastorale en Provence au milieu du XIVᵉ siècle. *Etudes rurales*, 46:61–75.

Coste, P. 1977. L'origine de la transhumance en Provence: enseignements d'une enquête sur les pâturages comtaux de 1345. In: Institut de recherches méditerranéennes, *L'élevage en méditerranée occidentale*. Paris: Editions du CNRS, pp. 113–19.

Coste, P. & Coulet N. 1994. Que sait-on des origines de la transhumance en Provence? In: A. Pitte and J.-C.

Duclos, eds. *L'homme et le mouton dans l'espace de la transhumance*. Grenoble: Glénat, pp. 65–70.

Coulet, N. 1978. Sources et aspects de l'histoire de la transhumance des ovins en Provence au bas Moyen Âge. *Le monde alpin et rhodanien*, 6 (3–4):213–47.

Coulet, N. 1986. Du XIIIᵉ au XVᵉ siècle. Mise en place d'un système, Histoire et actualité de la transhumance en Provence. *Les Alpes de lumière*, 95/96:50–55.

Coulet N. 1988. *Aix-en-Provence. Espace et relations d'une capitale* (milieu XIVe s.–milieu XVe s.). Aix-en-Provence: Publications de l'université de Provence.

Coulet, N. 1990. Notes sur l'élevage en Haute-Provence (XIVᵉ–XVᵉ s.). *Provence Historique*, 40(161):257–66.

Coulet, N. 1996. Une entreprise: la transhumance en Provence au Moyen Âge. In: R. Comba, A. Dal Verme and I. Naso, eds. *Greggi mandrie e pastori nelle Alpi occidentali (secoli XII–XX)*. Cuneo: Rocca de' Baldi, pp. 43–49.

Coulet, N. 1998. Relations de transhumance entre Aix et Barcelonnette au milieu du XVe siècle. *Provence historique*, 43(191):100–106.

Coulet N. 2001a. L'économie de l'abbaye de Valbonne et la transhumance en Provence au XIIIᵉ siècle. *Provence historique*, 51(205):327–35.

Coulet, N. 2001b. Vom 13. bis 15. jahrhundert: die etablierung der provenzalischen transhumanz. *Histoire des Alpes*, 6:147–58.

Court-Picon, M., Walsh, K., Mocci, F., Segard, M., Palet-Martinez, J., 2007. Occupation de la montagne et transformation des milieux dans les Alpes méridionales au cours de l'âge du Bronze: approche croisée des données palynologiques et archéologiques en Champsaur et Argentiérois (Hautes-Alpes, France). In: C. Mordant, H. Richard and M. Magny, eds. *Environnements et cultures à l'âge du Bronze en Europe occidentale*. Paris: CTHS, pp. 89–106.

Craig, O.E. 2002. The development of dairying in Europe: potential evidence from food residues on ceramics. *Documenta Praehistorica*, 29:97–107.

Davis, E. 1941. The patterns of transhumance in Europe. *Geography*, 26(4):155–68.

Dudd, S., Evershed, R. P. 1998. Direct demonstration of milk as an element of archaeological economies. *Science*, 282 (5393): 1478–1481.

Durand, A. 2014. Notes sur la signification du terme "alpes" dans la documentation diplomatique des Alpes du Sud (VIIIᵉ–XIIIᵉ s.). *Provence historique*, 64(256):363–70.

Durand, A. 2016. Medieval Southern Alpine Mountains, perceptions and interweaving diverse sources. In: P.C. Anderson, L. Peña-Chocarro and A. Heiss, eds. *Agricultural and Pastoral Landscapes in Preindustrial Society*. Oxford: Oxbow, EARTH monograph series, 3, pp. 250–70.

Durbec, J.-A. 1967. L'élevage dans la région de Grasse avant 1610. *Bulletin philologique et historique*: 61–119.

Evershed, R.P., Payne, S., Sherratt, A.G., Copley, M.S., Coolidge, J., Urem-Kotsu, D., Kotsakis, K., Özdogan, M., Özdogan, A.E., Nieuwenhuyse, O., Akkermans, P.M., Bailey, D., Andeescu, R.-R., Campbell, S., Farid, S., Hodder, I., Yalman, N., Özbasaran, M., Bicakci, R., Garfinkel, Y., Levy, T. & Burton, M.M. 2008. Earliest date for milk use in the Near East and southeastern Europe linked to cattle herding. *Nature*, 455:528–31.

Fabre, P. 1997. *Hommes de la Crau: des coussouls aux alpages*. Les Angles: Cheminements.

Falque-Vert, H. 1997. *Les hommes et la montagne en Dauphiné au XIIIᵉ siècle*. Grenoble: Presses universitaires de Grenoble.

Falque-Vert, H. 2006. Aspects de la transhumance dans le Dauphiné alpestre au Moyen Âge. In: C. Jourdain-Annequin and J.-C. Duclos, eds. *Aux origines de la transhumance. Les Alpes et la vie pastorale d'hier à aujourd'hui.* Paris: Picard, pp. 67–75.

Février, P.-A. 1959. La Basse Vallée de l'Argens. Quelques aspects de la vie économique de la Provence orientale aux XVe et XVIe siècles. *Provence Historique*, 9(35):39–61.

Fournier, J. 1900. Les chemins de la transhumance en Provence et en Dauphiné d'après les journaux des conducteurs de troupeaux au XVIIIe siècle. *Bulletin de géographie historique et descriptive*, 1–2, pp. 237–63.

Garcia D., Mocci F., Tzortzis S., Walsh, K. & Dumas, V. 2007. Archéologie de la vallée de l'Ubaye (Alpes-de-Haute-Provence, France): premiers résultats d'un projet collectif de recherche, *Preistoria Alpina*, 42:23–48.

Gardelle, C. 1965. La transhumance ovine entre les régions méditerranéennes et les Alpes en 1964. *Revue de géographie Alpine*, 53(3):449–77.

Geary, P. J. 1985. Aristocracy in Provence: The Rhône Basin at the Dawn of the Carolingian Age. Stuttgart: A. Hiersemann.

Geist, H. 2006. Les enclos d'altitude dans le Mercantour. In: C. Jourdain-Annequin and J.-C. Duclos, eds. *Aux origines de la transhumance. Les Alpes et la vie pastorale d'hier à aujourd'hui.* Paris: Picard, pp. 173–85.

Ghersi, N. 2004. *Le pays mentonnais à travers les actes notariés à la fin du Moyen Âge.* Menton: Société d'art et d'histoire du Mentonnais.

Giguet-Covex, C., Pansu, J., Arnaud, F., Rey, P.-J., Griggo, C., Gielly, L., Domaizon, I., Coissac, E., David, F., Choler, P., Poulenard, J. & Taberlet, P. 2014. Long livestock farming history and human landscape shaping revealed by lake sediment DNA. *Nature Communications*, 5:321.

Goren, Y. 1999. On determining use of pastoral cave sites: a critical assessment of spherulites in archaeology. *Journal of the Israël Prehistoric Society*, 29:123–28.

Gourdon, M. & Gourdon, M.-L. 2014. *Nos bergers. Histoire du pastoralisme dans les Alpes-Maritimes*, Breil-sur-Roya: Les Editions du Cabri.

Guichard, F. 1846. *Essai sur le cominalat dans la ville de Digne, institution municipale des XIIIe et XIVe siècles.* Digne: Guichard imprimeurs.

Guillaume, P. (abbé) 1908. Un troupeau de Provence dans les Alpes de 1781 à 1794. *Annales des Alpes*, 8:101–19; 159–63; 178–89.

Guionova, G. in press. La céramique de la cabane de Fangeas X (Freissinières, 05). Archéologie du midi médiéval, 33.

Henry, F., Talon, B. & Dutoit, T. 2010. The age and history of the French Mediterranean steppe revisited by soil wood charcoal analysis. *The Holocene*, 20(1):25–34.

Jospin, J.P. & L. Favrie (eds.) 2008 *Premiers Bergers des Alpes: De la préhistoire à l'Antiquité.* Isère, France.

Kaiser-Guyot, M.-T. 1974. *Le berger en France aux XIVe et XVe siècles.* Paris: Edition Klincksieck.

Lassalle, J. 1997. Quelques données sur les pratiques pastorales dans la vallée de la Roya aux XV–XVIe siècles. In: *L'élevage en Provence.* Mouans-Sartoux: Publication du Centre Régional de Documentation Occitane, pp. 135–51.

Lassalle, J. 2001. Terres communes et délimitations de territoires à partir des litiges sur la transhumance (XIIIe–XVe siècles). *Provence historique*, 51(206):445–65.

Lassalle, J. 2006. Aux confins de la Provence orientale, l'exercice de quelques droits d'usages au milieu du XVe siècle. In: P. Jansen, ed., *Entre monts et rivages: les contacts entre la Provence orientale et les régions voisines au Moyen Âge.* Antibes: Publications de l'APDCA, pp. 35–53.

Lassalle, J. & Palmero B. 2010. L'exploitation pastorale des territoires de confins de la haute vallée de la Roya à travers les sources écrites (XIIe–XVIIIe s.). Contribution à une approche pluridisciplinaire. In: S. Tzortzis and X. Delestre, eds. *Archéologie de la montagne européenne.* Aix-en-Provence: Errance, pp. 85–95.

Lebaudy, G. 2000. Dans les pas des bergers piémontais en Provence. Traces, parcours et appartenances, Migrance, marge et métiers. *Le monde alpin et rhodanien*, 1–3, pp. 151–74.

Lebaudy, G. 2006. Des "gens de moutons". Sur les traces des bergers piémontais dans l'espace de la grande transhumance provençale-Alpine. In: P.Y. Laffont, ed. *Transhumance et estivage en Occident, des origines aux enjeux actuels, Actes des XXVIe Journées Internationales d'Histoire de l'Abbaye de Flaran (9–11 septembre 2004)*, Toulouse: Presses universitaires du Mirail, pp. 341–53.

Lebaudy, G. 2011. Les bergers du Piémont à saute-frontière. Transhumance ovine et migrations transfrontalières dans les Alpes sud-occidentales (XVe–XXIe siècles). In: E. Gili and B. Palmero, eds. *La culture de l'échange sur les Alpes sud-occidentales. La Cultura dello scambio sulle alpi sud-occidentali*, Genova: Brigati, pp. 207–24.

Lebaudy, G. & Albera, D. eds. 2001. *La routo. Sur les chemins de la transhumance entre les Alpes et la mer, Cuneo: Nerosubianco Ecomuseo della pastorizia-Maison de la Transhumance-Maison du berger.*

Le Couédic M., 2010. *Les pratiques pastorales d'altitude dans une perspective ethnoarchéologique; Cabanes, troupeaux et territoires pastoraux pyrénéens dans la longue durée*, (unpublished doctoral thesis, University François-Rabelais of Tours).

Le Couédic, M. 2012. Modéliser les pratiques pastorales d'altitude dans la longue durée. *Cybergeo: European Journal of Geography [On line], Systèmes, Modélisation, Géostatistiques*, article 590, mis en ligne le 09 février 2012. http://cybergeo.revues.org/25123 (consulté le 15 février 2012).

Le Couédic, M. 2016. Cabanes, cheminement et *cujalas*: parcours de troupeaux à l'estive. In: C. Rendu, C. Calastrenc, M. Le Couédic and A. Berdoy, eds. *Estives d'Ossau. 7000 ans de pastoralisme dans les Pyrénées.* Toulouse: Le Pas d'oiseau, pp. 53–57.

Le Roy Ladurie, E. 1975. *Montaillou, village occitan de 1294 à 1324.* Paris: Editions Gallimard.

Leveau, P. 2006a. Entre la plaine de la Crau et le massif des Ecrins, la question du pastoralisme romain. In: C. Jourdain-Annequin and J.-C. Duclos, eds. *Aux origines de la transhumance. Les Alpes et la vie pastorale d'hier à aujourd'hui.* Paris: Picard, pp. 205–21.

Leveau, P. 2006b. Entre le delta du Rhône, la Crau et les Alpes, les séquentiations du temps pastoral et les mouvements des troupeaux à l'époque romaine. In: P.Y. Laffont, ed. *Transhumance et estivage en Occident, des origines aux enjeux actuels, Actes des XXVIe Journées Internationales d'Histoire de l'Abbaye de Flaran (9–11 septembre 2004)*, Toulouse: Presses universitaires du Mirail, pp. 83–96.

Leveau, P. & Segard, M. 2004. Le pastoralisme en Gaule du Sud entre plaine et montagne: de la Crau aux Alpes du Sud. *Pallas*, 64: 99–113.

Leydet, J.-L. 1982. La transhumance dans le pays d'Aix d'après les registres de notaires aixois de la deuxième moitié du XVe siècle (unpublished master thesis, Université de Provence).

Lombard, M. 1962. Étude sur la transhumance des troupeaux en Provence entre 1513 et 1536, d'après les actes notariés d'Arbaud Gombaud, notaire de Saint-Maximin. *Bulletin* de la société d'études scientifiques et archéologiques de Draguignan et du Var, 7:62–71.

Malausséna, P.-L. 1969. *La vie en Provence orientale aux XIVe et XVe siècles. Un exemple: Grasse à travers les actes notariés*, Paris: Pichon et Durand-Augias.

Martin, L. 2014. *Premiers paysans des Alpes. Alimentation végétale et agriculture au Néolithique*. Rennes, Presses universitaires de Rennes.

Maurel, J.-J. 1897. *Histoire de Puimoisson et de la commanderie de chevaliers de Malte*. Paris: Alphonse Picard & fils éditeurs.

Meiggs, D.C. 2007. Visualizing the seasonal round: a theorical experiment with strontium isotope profiles in ovicaprine teeth. *Anthropozoologica*, 42(2):107–27.

Merle-Comby, M.-Ch. 1983. Quand les moutons de l'Hôtel-Dieu du Puy hivernaient en Provence: trois comptes de transhumance sous François Ier. *Cahiers de la Haute-Loire*: 113–36.

Mocci, F., Palet-Martinez, J., Segard, M., Tzortzis, S. & Walsh, K. 2005. Peuplement, pastoralisme et modes d'exploitation de la moyenne et haute montagne depuis la préhistoire dans le Parc national des Ecrins. In: A. Bouet and F. Verdin, eds. *Territoires et paysages de l'âge du Fer au Moyen Âge. Mélanges offerts à Philippe Leveau*. Bordeaux: Ausonius Editions, pp. 45–61.

Mocci, F., Segard, M., Walsh, K. & Golosetti, R. 2010. Données récentes sur l'occupation humaine dans les Alpes méridionales durant l'Antiquité. In: S. Tzortzis and X. Delestre, eds. *Archéologie de la montagne européenne*. Aix-en-Provence: Errance, pp. 309–23.

Moriceau, J.-M. 2005, *Histoire et géographie de l'élevage français. Du Moyen Âge à la Révolution*. Paris: Fayard.

Morin, A. & Picavet R. 2006. Archéologie et pastoralisme d'altitude (Vercors, Dévoluy, haute vallée du Buëch). In: C. Jourdain-Annequin and J.-C. Duclos, eds. *Aux origines de la transhumance. Les Alpes et la vie pastorale d'hier à aujourd'hui*. Paris: Picard, pp. 187–203.

Morin, A., Serrières, L. & Picavet, R., avec la collaboration de Carron, P.-Y., Jospin, J.-P., Teyssonneyre, Y., Griggo, C., Mouthon, F. 2010. Structures pastorales sur les Hauts Plateaux du Vercors et les Hauts de Chartreuse, In: S. Tzortzis and X. Delestre, eds. *Archéologie de la montagne européenne*. Aix-en-Provence: Errance, pp. 227–34.

Mouthon, F. 2007. L'inventaire du bétail dans une communauté Alpine à la fin du XIVe siècle. *Histoire et Sociétés Rurales*, 27:91–120.

Musset, D. 2006. Parcours de transhumance. In: C. Jourdain-Annequin and J.-C. Duclos, eds. *Aux origines de la transhumance. Les Alpes et la vie pastorale d'hier à aujourd'hui*. Paris: Picard, pp. 123–27.

Nicollet, F.-N. 1925. La transhumance: troupeaux de Bertaud, Durbon et Boscodon (Hautes-Alpes) hivernant dans la Crau au XIIIe siècle. *Annales de Provence*, 22:139–45.

Paillard, P. 1968. L'élevage à Salon-de-Provence de 1470 à 1550. *Bulletin philologique et historique*, 1:319–30.

Palet-Martinez, J., Ricou, F. & Segard, M. 2003. Prospection et sondage sur les sites d'altitude en Champsaur (Alpes du Sud). In: C. Rendu, ed. *Habitats et systèmes pastoraux d'altitude (Pyrénées, Massif Central, Alpes), Archéologie du Midi médiéval*, 21, pp. 199–210.

Pichard, G. 2006. Les comptes d'une "société de bêtes à laine" pour la transhumance et l'hivernage (1750–1761). À propos d'un livre de raison arlésien. *Histoire et sociétés rurales*, 25:115–29.

Py, V. & Durand A. 2010. Évolution des écosystèmes et des pratiques agrosylvopastorales et minière pour la production de bois de feu dans le Haut-Champsaur et la Haute-Durance (France) de l'âge du Bronze ancien au XVIe siècle, In: S. Tzortzis and X. Delestre, eds. *Archéologie de la montagne européenne*. Aix-en-Provence: Errance, pp. 283–92.

Py, V., Véron, A., Edouard, J.-L., Beaulieu (de), J.-L., Ancel, B., Segard, M., Durand, A., Leveau, P., 2014. Interdisciplinary characterisation and environmental imprints of mining and forestry in the upper Durance valley (France) during the Holocene. *Quaternary International*, 353:74–97.

Py-Saragaglia, V., Durand, A., Ancel, B., Walsh, K., Edouard, J.-L. & Mocci, F., 2015. Les dynamiques de la végétation et des anthroposystèmes d'altitude cernées par l'anthracologie pastorale et minière à l'échelle d'un haut vallon alpestre (Freissinières, France). *Archéosciences, revue d'Archéométrie*, 39:69–92.

Raynaud, C. 2001. L'occupation des grottes en Gaule méditerranéenne à la fin de l'Antiquité. In: P. Ouzoulias, C. Pellecuer, C. Raynaud, P. Van Ossel and P. Garmy, eds. *Les campagnes de la Gaule à la fin de l'Antiquité*. Antibes: Editions APDCA, pp. 449–71.

Rendu, C. 1998. La question des *orris* à partir des fouilles archéologiques de la montagne d'Enveig (Cerdagne). État des recherches et éléments de réflexion. In: A. Rousselle et M.-C. Marandet, eds. *Le paysage rural et ses acteurs*. Journée d'étude du 25 nov. 1995 du Centre de recherches historiques sur les sociétés méditerranéennes, Perpignan: Université de Perpignan, pp. 245–77.

Rendu, C. 2000. *Fouiller des cabanes de bergers: pour quoi faire?* Etudes rurales, 153–54:151–76.

Rendu, C. 2003. *La Montagne d'Enveig. Une estive pyrénéenne dans la longue durée*. Perpignan: Trabucaire.

Rendu, C. 2006. Transhumance: prélude à l'histoire d'un mot voyageur. In: P.-Y. Laffont, ed. *Transhumance et estivage en Occident des origines aux enjeux actuels*. Toulouse: Presses universitaires du Mirail, pp. 7–29.

Rendu C., Calastrenc C., Le Couédic M., Berdoy A., eds. 2016. *Estives d'Ossau. 7000 ans de pastoralisme dans les Pyrénées*. Toulouse: Le Pas d'oiseau.

Rouquette, P. 1913. *La transhumance des troupeaux en Provence et bas Languedoc*. Montpellier: imprimerie Firmin et Montane.

Royer, J.-Y. ed. 1988. Le journal de Noé de Barras, un entrepreneur de transhumance au XVe siècle. Texte provençal inédit de 1480, *Alpes de lumière*, 98.

Royer, J.-Y. 2003. Les transhumants du Roi René. *Verdons*, 11:13–23.

Schippers, T. 1986a. Le cycle annuel d'un berger transhumant. In: D. Musset and F.-X. Emery, eds. *Histoire et actualité de la transhumance en Provence*, Mane: Les Alpes de lumière, 95/96, pp. 63–68.

Schippers, Th. 1986b. *Temps vécus, temps perçus. Au fil des saisons en Provence intérieure*, Paris: Éditions du CNRS.

Sclafert, T. 1926. *Le Haut-Dauphiné au Moyen Âge*. Paris: Société anonyme du Recueil Sirey.

Sclafert, T. 1928. Sisteron au début du XVIe siècle (d'après un cadastre). *Annales de Géographie*, 37(206):167–73.

Sclafert, T. 1934. A propos du déboisement des Alpes du sud – le rôle des Troupeaux. *Annales de Géographie*, 43(242):126–45.

Sclafert, T. 1939. Un aspect de la vie économique dans les hautes vallées des Alpes du Sud: la surcharge pastorale. *Bulletin de l'Association des géographes français*, 120:58–66.

Sclafert, T. 1959. *Cultures en Haute-Provence: déboisements et pâturages au Moyen Âge*. Paris: SEVPEN.

Segard, M. 2009. *Les Alpes occidentales romaines: développement urbain et exploitation des ressources des régions de montagne (Gaule narbonnaise, Italie, provinces Alpines)*. Aix-en-Provence: Errance.

Stouff, L. 1966. Peuplement, économie et société de quelques villages de la montagne de Lure 1250–1450. *Cahiers du centre d'études des sociétés méditerranéennes*, 1. Aix-en-Provence: Publications de la faculté des lettres et sciences humaines, pp. 35–109.

Stouff, L. 1970. *Ravitaillement et alimentation en Provence aux XIVe et XVe siècle*. Paris-La Haye: Mouton et CO.

Stouff, L. 1986. *Arles à la fin du Moyen Âge*, Aix-en-Provence: Publications de l'Université de Provence.

Struyf, P. 1977. La vie économique à Tende au XVe siècle. *Recherches régionales Alpes-Maritimes*, 17:29–50.

Suméra, F. & Geist, H. 2010. Exploitation de la haute montagne du Mercantour et impact sur l'environnement depuis l'âge du Fer. Etude de cas: l'exemple du vallon de Millefonts, commune de Valdebore (Alpes-Maritimes), In: S. Tzortzis and X. Delestre, eds. *Archéologie de la montagne européenne*. Aix-en-Provence: Errance, pp. 45–55.

Truchot, H. 1936. Les troupeaux transhumant du sud-est de la France. *Bulletin de la société scientifique et littéraire des Basses-Alpes*, 26(171):161–93.

Venturini, A. 1997. L'élevage dans la viguerie de Nice (XIIIe–XIVe siècles). In: *L'élevage en Provence*. Mouans-Sartoux: Publication du Centre Régional de Documentation Occitane, pp. 101–33.

Walsh, K. 2005. Risk and marginality at high altitudes: new interpretations from fieldwork on the Faravel Plateau, Hautes-Alpes. *Antiquity*, 79:289–305.

Walsh, K., Court-Picon, M., de Beaulieu, J.-L., Guiter, F., Mocci, F., Richer, S., Sinet, R., Talon, B. & Tzortzis, S. 2014. A historical ecology of the Ecrins (Southern French Alps): archaeology and palaeoecology of the Mesolithic to the Medieval period. *Quaternary International*, 353:52–73.

Walsh, K. & Mocci, F. 2011. Mobility in the mountains: late third and second millennia Alpine societies' engagements with the high-altitude zones in the Southern French Alps. *European Journal of Archaeology*, 14(1–2):88–115.

Walsh K., Mocci, F., Court-Picon, M., de Beaulieu, J.-L., Guiter, F., Richer, S., Talon, B., 2016. Driving forces and variability in the exploitation of a high-altitude landscape from the Neolithic to Medieval Periods in the southern French Alps. In: J. Collis, M. Pearce and F. Nicolis, eds. *Summer Farms. Seasonal Exploitation of the Uplands from Prehistory to the Present*. Sheffield: Sheffield Archaeological Monograph 16, pp. 181–201.

Walsh, K., Mocci, F., Dumas V., Durand A., Talon B. & Tzortis S. 2003. 9000 ans d'occupation du sol en moyenne et haute montagne: la vallée de Freissinières dans le Parc national des Ecrins (Freissinières, Hautes-Alpes). In: C. Rendu, ed. *Habitats et systèmes pastoraux d'altitude (Pyrénées, Massif Central, Alpes)*, *Archéologie du Midi médiéval*, 21, pp. 185–98.

Walsh, K., Mocci, F. & Palet-Martinez, J. 2007. Nine thousand years of human/landscape dynamics in a high altitude zone in the southern French Alps (Parc National des Ecrins, Hautes-Alpes). *Preistoria Alpina*, 42:9–22.

Walsh, K., Mocci, F., Tzortzis, S., Bressy, C., Talon, B., Richer, S., Court-Picon, M., Dumas, V. & Palet-Martinez, J. 2010. Les Ecrins, un territoire d'altitude dans le contexte des Alpes occidentales de la Préhistoire récente à l'âge du Bronze (Hautes-Alpes, France), In: S. Tzortzis and X. Delestre, eds. *Archéologie de la montagne européenne*. Aix-en-Provence: Errance, pp. 211–25.

Wullschleger, M. 1994. Les moines du Vercors et le mouton. In: A. Pitte and J.-C. Duclos, eds. *L'homme et le mouton dans l'espace de la transhumance*. Grenoble: Glénat, pp. 71–82.

CHAPTER 11

Alpine settlement remains in the Bernese Alps (Switzerland) in medieval and modern times
The visibility of alpine summer farming activities in the archaeological record

BRIGITTE ANDRES

INTRODUCTION

Due to the construction of a new public transport system connecting three wintersport destinations in the Oberhasli region of Switzerland, entitled the "Hasliberg-Frutt-Titlis Snow Paradise", the Archaeological Service of the Canton of Bern organized a large-scale project.[1] Given that the Bernese Alps generally forms a blank spot on the archaeological map (particularly so in the case of Oberhasli), the Archaeological Service decided to arrange for extensive prospections along the perimeters of the project's target area in order to assess the region's archaeological potential.

The campaign results from Gadmen Valley, Gen Valley and the Hasliberg produced the unexpectedly high quantity of nearly 400 new sites (all of which were documented and inventoried according to site location). As recent research on deserted alpine settlements has been primarily limited to central Switzerland and Valais, this was an opportune occasion to evaluate archaeological sites from the Bernese Alps.[2] The majority of the known structures in this region are related to the *Alpwirtschaft* (alpine summer farming or seasonal alpine animal husbandry) of the medieval period as well as to its modern descendent (which the written sources claim is a local evolution of what was practiced in that earlier time period). Due to its advantageous position near to several passes, Oberhasli traded both cattle and cheese with regions to the south.

Given that *Alpwirtschaft* is still practiced in the study area, the consideration of archaeological sites in isolation would be nonsensical. The local continuity of this type of farming allowed for the comparison of archaeological remains from past centuries with their chronologically younger counterparts. With regards to the comparative investigation of farmhouse features such as location, design and size, extant research and excavation results from other regions can act as an excellent corollary.

This paper will first present the most important site categories which were documented over the course of the above-mentioned prospection campaigns. Their subsequent cultural and historical classification allows for the determination of those comparisons which are the best means of interpreting unexcavated prospection sites as well as the degree to which the various alpine farming activities are visible within the archaeological record.

TRANSPORT TOPOGRAPHY AND LAND EXPANSION IN OBERHASLI

The region of Oberhasli lies in the east of the Bernese Alps on the northern side of the Aare-Gotthard massif and includes the Aare catchment area from its origin at Grimsel Pass almost to the shores of Lake Brienz (Figure 11.1). Due to their unique position at the geological crossroads between limestone and granite mountains, the landscapes within this region are very diverse (Hess, 1921). Both the sheer mountain faces and the swampy valley floor played important roles in the colonization of Oberhasli; settlements tended to be built at slight elevations into the scree of streambeds rather than directly on the valley floor (Vischer, 2003: 143). Although it is located in what is today a peripheral region of the Canton of Bern, the numerous mountain passes which pass through Oberhasli would have easily facilitated trade and exchange in earlier times.

Bronze Age and Roman-era finds at Grimsel and Brünig passes underscore the early use of Alpine passes (Nagy & Schwarz, 2013, 2014, 2015; Schaer & Martin-Kilcher, 2009: 264–65). Roman finds were recovered from Wyler in Innertkirchen in 1964 and include ceramics, brick fragments and wall tiles.[3] With its convenient location within easy access to the Joch, Susten and Grimsel passes, it seems as if Wyler was already acting as a kind of transportation hub in the Roman period.

First mentioned in AD 1234, Meiringen's Michaelskirche (St. Michael's Church) can best be understood within the context of national transport policy. Due to the fact that the church was repeatedly buried in mudslides, the remains of several previous buildings have been preserved underneath the standing structure (Brülisauer, 1984: 1; Gutscher, 2008). Of these, the oldest visible remains date from the ninth or tenth century. The founding of a church during this period

© 2018 European Association of Archaeologists

156 Brigitte Andres

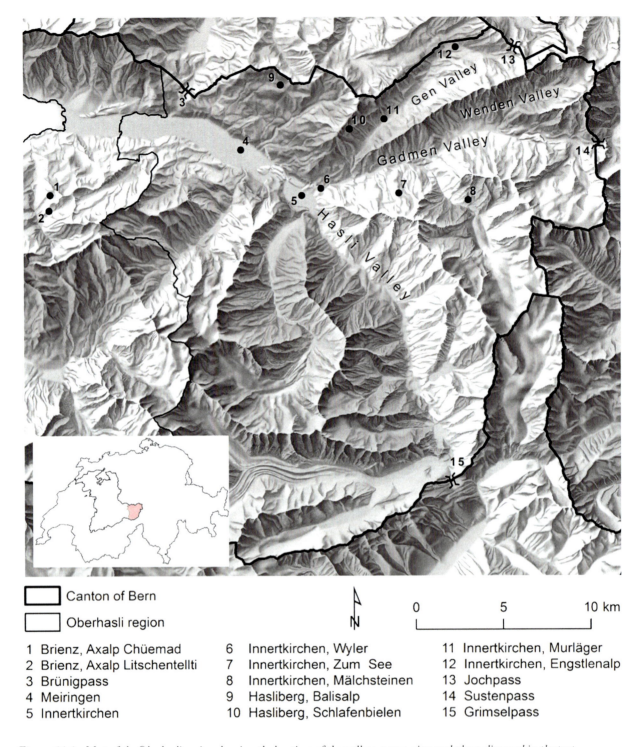

Figure 11.1. Map of the Oberhasli region showing the locations of the valleys, passes, sites and places discussed in the text
Source: Swisstopo (JA100012)/Geodatabase of the Canton of Bern as prepared by Brigitte Andres, Archaeological Service of the Canton of Bern

1 Brienz, Axalp Chüemad
2 Brienz, Axalp Litschentellti
3 Brünigpass
4 Meiringen
5 Innertkirchen
6 Innertkirchen, Wyler
7 Innertkirchen, Zum See
8 Innertkirchen, Mälchsteinen
9 Hasliberg, Balisalp
10 Hasliberg, Schlafenbielen
11 Innertkirchen, Murläger
12 Innertkirchen, Engstlenalp
13 Jochpass
14 Sustenpass
15 Grimselpass

would coincide with the extension of the dominion of the northern alpine kings into Italy in the eighth century and would act as further proof of the importance of mountain passes in the early medieval period (Winckler, 2012: 118–19).

The rise in grass pollen in the eighth century can be linked to the intense clearing activities which resulted in the opening of the alpine landscape (Heiri et al., 2003; Lotter et al., 2006; Wick et al., 2003). In many cases, monasteries were involved in such actions, as they had held economic interest in the development of alpine pasturage which dated from the early medieval period. In the late medieval period, a sharp rise in the use of high-altitude grazing land came along with the shift from simple self-sufficiency to an economic specialization in livestock and dairying (Sablonier, 1990;

Sauerländer, 2015; Sieber & Bretscher-Gisiger, 2012). Because of this, the region contributed greatly to the cheese and cattle trade.

The most important alpine transport route for Oberhasli stretched from Obwalden in the western part of central Switzerland through Hasli Valley and Wallis to Domodossola in northern Italy. However, as said route traversed the Brünig, Grimsel *and* Gries passes, its indirectness may have been the cause for it never having been as frequented as were other and more direct transalpine routes over the Grisons passes, Great St. Bernard or even Gotthard pass (Von Rütte, 1990: 1–2).

In addition to agriculture, other economic activities such as iron mining, tourism or the use of hydropower have also influenced the formation of the landscape over the centuries.

ALPWIRTSCHAFT AS PART OF MULTISTAGE AGRICULTURAL SYSTEMS

In contrast to pastoral nomadism or transhumance, the *Alpwirtschaft*, temporarily practiced during the summer months, entailed a close working relationship with a base in the valley. Indeed, the supply system which threaded through the Swiss Alps (of which traditional *Alpwirtschaft* was an important part) utilized the landscape of different elevations (i.e. the valley, mountainous zone and the upper pasturage) according to the season (Stebler, 1903: 3–5; Weiss, 1941: 25–29). During the three- to four-month summer stay on the alp, the economic focus was on the livestock and the production of dairy products. The cattle were kept at the alps so that the hay supplies so important in the winter months could be laid in from the valley meadows. In the early summer, the pasture terraces were successively grazed according to the seasonal development of vegetation from the bottom up. The same actions were repeated in reverse order in the autumn. In Oberhasli, a modernized form of *Alpwirtschaft* is still part of local agriculture today.

ARCHAEOLOGICAL SITES

Deserted medieval settlements (DMSs) and modern settlement structures both tend to be mentioned in the agricultural, commercial and industrial sectors. Naturally, the activities therein involved impacted their surrounding environment to varying degrees. For this reason, a working knowledge of the processes involved in the founding and abandonment of settlements contributes to a better understanding of cultural landscapes (Haupt, 2012: 133).

Although the naturalist Johann Jakob Scheuchzer had already described alpine DMSs in the eighteenth century, archaeological research on this subject only began to flourish in Switzerland in 1971 following Werner Meyer's excavation of the deserted village of Glarus Süd, Bergeten (Canton of Glarus) (Meyer et al., 1998). As a discipline, researching deserted villages lies at the intersection of archaeology, history, ethnography and farmhouse studies. Unfortunately, within the Swiss Alps, this body of research is not complete; archaeological excavations of alpine DMSs have generally focussed on central Switzerland and the Wallis. However a bevy of recent prospection campaigns have examined medieval and recent *Alpwirtschaft* installations, located in almost all of the Swiss mountain cantons (e.g. Auf der Maur et al., 2005; Degelo, 2011; Sauter, 2009; Taramarcaz & Curdy, 2013; Zappa, 2008).

The prospection results

The Oberhasli prospection project completed systematic surveys in 2003, 2004 and 2006 in the Gadmen and Gen valleys as well as above the treeline in the alpine pasturage at Hasliberg. The object of these prospection campaigns was primarily the creation of a site inventory for those alpine regions that would have been affected by the construction of new ski lifts. Accordingly, the majority of the new sites made by the project were some 1600–2000 m above sea level. The focus was on those features which were still visible to the naked eye within the landscape (e.g. standing walls; Ebersbach & Gutscher, 2008).

In the course of documentation, archaeological sites were freed from vegetation and then subsequently drawn, photographed and described. The carefully measured and scaled sketches produced thereby constituted an important basis for later comparison and evaluation.

Despite the large area prospected and the high number of sites made therein, there were some restrictions in the dating and interpretation of the results as the prospection sites were not excavated. Thus, although they could have provided important information on function, the interior areas of the various structures remain largely unknown. While it is not impossible that some prehistoric structures must have been included in these sites, comparisons with excavated DMSs suggest that the majority of the ground-plans were more likely medieval and modern remains.

In consequence, the cultural and historical evaluation of the material was accomplished not only by comparison with excavation data from other regions, but also by bringing various non-archaeological resources from the region into the mix. The latter included historical and ethnographic documents and photographic evidence as well as direct comparisons with extant alpine buildings.

158 Brigitte Andres

Building remains

The 185 structures classified as building remains mostly consist of jagged pieces of drystone wall at various heights, many of which included only bases or even merely a few aligned stones (Andres, 2014: 96–114). Their shapes were generally approximately square or rectangular and can be reconstructed to a building without a great many further structural details (Figure 11.2). Whether a building was free-standing or whether it was built into or against a rock wall or boulder, (thereby allowing for a natural wall or roof) is unimportant. In many instances, the rear parts of the buildings' foundations were dug into the slope. As is evidenced by the alpine structures still visible in the landscape, wall plinths were often complemented by a timber superstructure; some buildings were nonetheless entirely built of stone. The inside floor of the structures

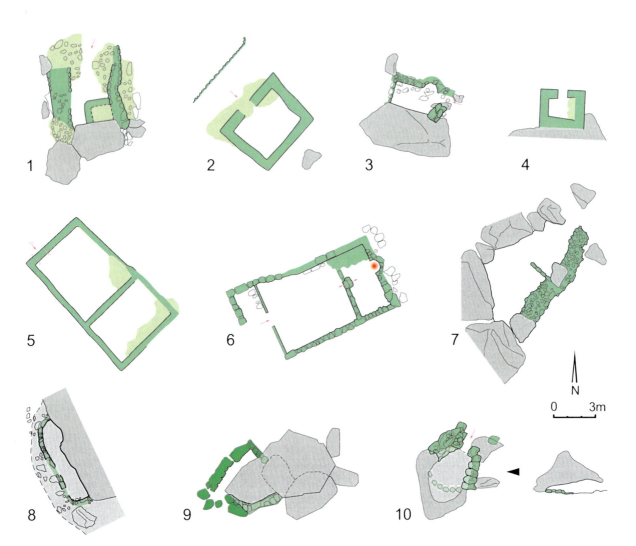

Legend
dark green: wall remains
light green: fallen wall
grey: rock
red: hearth

One-roomed building
1. Innertkirchen, Zum See 13
2. Innertkirchen, Unter dem schwarzen Berg 1
3. Innertkirchen, Zum See 1
4. Innertkirchen, Spycherberg/Under Seck

Two-roomed building
5. Innertkirchen, Unter dem schwarzen Berg 1
6. Innertkirchen, Mettlenberg

Animal pen
7. Innertkirchen, Drosi

Rock-shelter structure
8. Hasliberg, Hinder Tschuggi 14: group 1
9. Innertkirchen, Steingletscher 1: group 2
10. Innertkirchen, Zum See 3: group 3

Figure 11.2. The building types of the most important categories: building remains, rock-shelter structures and animal pens
Source: Marc Müller, Archaeological Service of the Canton of Bern

measured between 1 and 82 m². A spare majority (53%) of these ruins exhibited modest inner surface areas of 1–15 m².

As the ruins discussed here were not excavated, their layouts often lack information regarding their indoor facilities (e.g. fireplaces, flooring and benches, etc.). However, structures in the outdoor area (such as terraced courtyards and annexes or sheds) were more easily identified.

Due to these facts, the categorization of the structures according to plan was particularly reliant on formal and topographical criteria. In terms of the building remains, one can distinguish between single and multi-room ground-plans. The lion's share of the data seems to be from simple, one-room structures. Interestingly, while the multi-room ground-plans were usually more uniform in their exterior structures, there are some singular exceptions to that rule.

Rock-shelter structures

The 35 structures which utilize natural rock within the landscape include rooms that abut a boulder or rock wall, or are sheltered to some degree by a natural rock formation (Andres, 2014: 114–18). Living space which utilized native rock would often very carefully and consciously alter that stone to suit the builders' purposes, an occurrence which often gave rise to the irregular ground-plans. The spectrum of anthropogenic alterations includes everything from stacked stones and simple dry walls to elaborate installations.

A clear delineation between ground-plans and rock-shelter structures is not always an easy undertaking due to the fact that the structures can be built against a rock wall or boulder or, as described, can occasionally even be roofed by stone. An important criterion for the classification within the category of rock-shelter structures is, therefore, the dominance of natural elements. This was usually accompanied by a more irregular shape and a lower ceiling.

Nonetheless, three kinds of natural rock constructions emerged, including structures which were: 1) built against a rock wall with a mostly semi-circular wall shape, 2) built against a boulder with a partially covered, irregular shape and 3) built against a boulder and completely covered by rock with an irregular shape.

Animal pens

Pens served as a means to both protect and to corral cattle and small livestock and can be differentiated from building structures because of the shape and the style of their construction. The 15 structures interpreted as pens

are irregular in shape and were constructed from larger dry wall than was utilized in the construction of other kinds of structures (Andres, 2014: 119–21). Once again, topography and the available naturally deposited stone had an impact on configuration and design. Larger stones and boulders were almost always incorporated into the structure of the pens; as a result, they made up a proportionately greater amount of the building materials involved in pen construction than were used in the erection of farmsteads. A natural result of this practicality in pen construction is the manifold forms of the constructions used to this end. Due to their heavily worn walls and indistinct shapes an interpretation of such structures as animal pens is debatable.

In spite of these challenges, animal pens were classified into three groups according to their arrangement and combination with other structures. Group 1 includes those pens associated with a single ruin. The second category (Group 2) groups together those pens which were part of a combination of several buildings and rock-shelter structures (the structures' chronological or functional context is often unclear). Group 3 includes only a single case, as said example concerns the only large installation within the research area. The large inner surface of the structure with its small, peripheral subdivisions and an in-built building construction are reminiscent of the enclosure system in Pontresina GR, Val Languard (Meyer, 1998: 302), in Brienz BE, Axalp-Chüemad (Gutscher, 2004) and in Elm GL, Ämpächli (Obrecht, 1998: 107).

Pasture walls

Pasture walls functioned as markers delimiting pastures from each other. Although to some degree a side effect of the collection of stones found in the pasture, such constructions also made pasture borders visible.

Pasture walls were not systematically recorded or documented in the prospection project (Andres, 2014: 121–22). As far as their masonry was concerned, the general construction seems to involve the setting of smaller stone material before the later addition of larger blocks. When the pastures were near mountain brooks, rounded stones were utilized in the wall masonry.

In Oberhasli, three functional pasture wall groups could be distinguished: 1) a border wall which separated two alps, 2) a middle wall which demarcated two neighbouring pastures on the same alp and 3) a retaining wall which kept animals away from a dangerous drop.

Some of these pasture walls are noted on modern topographic maps and remain in use. In some places, these structures have fallen over or been subject to stone robbing.

Settlement structure

Examination of the structure of the deserted settlements shows that it was closely linked to the local topography. While the site selection process was heavily influenced by factors such as the availability of shelter and water, the internal structure of the settlements themselves seems to have been dictated by economic and operational requirements (Andres, 2014: 126–41). The size of the earthworks at the DMS at Innertkirchen BE, Murläger clearly demonstrates that the inhabitants of the region did not simply make do with the easiest means of constructing a bunker. Instead, they intentionally designed their settlement in such a way so as to facilitate the easy access of both humans and their animal charges. However, this concern with accessibility sometimes necessitated that large quantities of earth be displaced and that several meters of support walls be erected.

The following case studies describe the arrangement and association of various buildings within two abandoned settlements. As dating information is missing, these comparisons must necessarily be limited to the formal level.

Innertkirchen, Murläger

The deserted village of Innertkirchen BE, Murläger is located at a slight elevation on the western edge of the Gen Valley (Figure 11.3). Slightly above the route of a modern road are a series of terraces on which the remains of a minimum of seven buildings as well as a smattering of unclassifiable walls are located. The

Figure 11.3. Innertkirchen BE, Murläger (aerial view of the structures built into the slope and the remains of the walls [photo taken from the southeast])
Source: Andri Spinas, Archaeological Service of the Canton of Bern

visible remains of the buildings are situated on four to five subsequent levels.

The structures include three rectangular and four square ground-plans of various sizes, of which five enclose inner surfaces measuring less than 10 m² (nos. 3, 5, 7, 8 and 9). The preservation conditions of the walls vary depending on the degree to which they were built into the slope. While the standing heights of the walls were measured at 1 m (no. 1) or even 1.8 m (no. 3) and the retaining walls of the slope are still clearly visible, it seems that the northeastern part of the DMS suffered greater erosion. That being the case, the visible parts of the walls are heavily overgrown everywhere. The fact that the side walls' heights of nos. 1 and 3 decline from uphill to downhill side suggests a log construction onto a stepped wall foundation.

The wall sections in the range of nos. 4 and 6 might conceal the remains of buildings. However, the terraces which created a flat surface by no. 4 are apparent. No. 6's semi-circular wall could have served as a retaining wall supporting a path leading from the lower terraces to their middle-level compatriots. Alternatively, it is possible that this structure served as an enclosure or animal pen.

The Gen Valley alp was first mentioned by the written sources in 1323 (Brülisauer, 1984: 13; no. 15). In the early modern period, it was used by several cooperatives which kept horses as well as cattle and cows. The passage through the Gen Valley and the area of the alp formed the route to Engstlenalp in the far part of the valley as well as to Joch Pass and to the access point for the ore fields. In 1817, 310 head of cattle were kept on the alp (Zybach, 2008: 27).

Innertkirchen BE, Zum See

On the shores of a small mountain lake near Spycherberg alp lay the remains of twelve buildings built onto boulders and two animal pens (Figure 11.4). Because

Figure 11.4. Innertkirchen BE, Zum See (orthophoto of the alp level: the building remains are scattered around the lake within the marked area)
Source: Swisstopo (JA100012)/Geodatabase of Bern Canton as prepared by Marc Müller, Archaeological Service of the Canton of Bern

of the difficult terrain, it is impossible to rule out the presence of other (potentially more heavily decayed) structures. The examples below demonstrate the variety of configurations present at the site. It is conceivable that combinations of buildings were in simultaneous use, albeit for different functions.

Four rectangular buildings are comparable in both size and shape, but suffer from different degrees of preservation. The remainders of the foundations of building nos. 4 and 9 each include a pen. East of the lake are the remains of structures 13 and 14. The latter are situated next to a small stream. This particular arrangement was probably intentional, as the water was needed in alpine dairies. The corner of the wall in the southeast of building 13 could have served as a hearth.

The rock-shelter structures (nos. 7 and 11) as well as the remains of structure 1 are comparable in terms of their narrow and deep construction shapes. The construction of building 6 under a rock wall as well as the foundation remains of nos. 2 and 12 were each located between several rocks and boulders and are similar in size.

The rock-shelter constructions of structures 3 and 8 exhibit a unique shape. Although they were completely roofed by natural rock (and were probably also artificially enlarged in the interior), these two chambers also included carefully bricked entrances. It is possible that they were used as storerooms.

Some of the alpine buildings still in use today are protected by large boulders. One might surmise, therefore, that these modern structures had earlier predecessors. According to legal sources, there was a conflict in pasture level Zum See in 1630 when a herd of goats was driven over the cattle alp to pasture on the *Hochberg*, the highest pastures where only sheep and goats were driven to (Brülisauer, 1984: 244–46; no. 152). Whether some of the building remains date from this period remains unknown.

Non-Archaeological Sources

The examination of non-archaeological data allows for the study of the development of the alpine economy in Oberhasli in medieval and modern times. That being said, the focus thus far has been on architectural data or on the infrastructure surrounding the various activities involved in *Alpwirtschaft*. In this section, the principle focus was placed on describing the main activities involved in *Alpwirtschaft* (dairy farming, the care of livestock and the production of wild alpine hay). To this end, this article concentrated primarily on texts from the Oberhasli region. The information gleaned therefrom was supported by additional sources from other regions of the Swiss Alps or general texts on *Alpwirtschaft*. The most important of these are briefly presented below.

Historical written sources

Due to the fact that the author is not a trained historian, this text has purposefully limited its historical investigations to published texts from the period from about 1300 to 1900. These include legal documents, topographical descriptions, travelogues and statistical investigations.

As far as medieval texts from the Oberhasli region are concerned, the majority can be classed as legal resources (Brülisauer, 1984; Kurz & Lerch, 1979). The papers belonging to the monastery of Interlaken (which provided information about alp land rights and ownership in the medieval period) were lost after the Reformation in the Canton of Bern 1528. Interestingly, the same kind of documents (i.e. materials relating to the law) were available for the sixteenth and seventeenth centuries. Early modern travel reports (e.g. Stumpf, 1548; Scheuchzer, 1746) dealt more with the geology and history of the Alps in general; descriptions of alpine huts or the alpine economy were only very rarely included. In the eighteenth and nineteenth centuries, the number of scientific texts (e.g. Gerber-Visser, 2012; Gruber, 1783; Kasthofer, 1818; Schatzmann, 1862; Sprüngli, 1760; Sprüngli, 1762), statistical studies about the alps and their usage (Bernisches Statistisches Bureau, 1902; Statistisches Bureau, 1868) and travel reports (e.g. Storr, 1784; Storr, 1786; Wyss, 1816; Wyss, 1817) rose sharply.

In summary, it can be said that alpine architecture was barely mentioned in the written sources. Information on the practice of *Alpwirtschaft* and the conditions under which it was undertaken were often only indirectly addressed within the legal material. Moreover, there are no reports written by the persons who engaged in *Alpwirtschaft* on the subject of their own activities, although some reports written by outsiders are present.

Historical pictorial sources

Images of alpine buildings may provide clues to their construction and interior design. The images which were analyzed to this end all date from the period after 1500. However, before 1800 such examples are quite rare. As a whole, the material is vague and provides little temporal or regional evidence regarding the appearance of the buildings. However, at the very least, different kinds of constructions can be discerned (i.e. stone and wood buildings; e.g. Roth, 1993: colour plate IV; Scheuchzer, 1746: plate 2; Stumpf, 1548: 265; Zybach, 2008: 49).

Interiors were usually described and depicted in a similar fashion. Wooden material and furniture tended to dominate a simple décor with tables or benches as work surfaces. In most cases, the material included the idealized images that make regional structural differences difficult to recognize.

Ethnographic sources

The folkloric and ethnographic sources include descriptions and pictures of traditional alpine economy until the age of the engine kicked into gear. They describe conditions in the nineteenth century and the first half of the twentieth century (Stebler, 1903; Weiss, 1941; Zahler, 1909).

Unfortunately, there were no such examples from the region of Oberhasli; to date, the region has not been the subject of historical research. To this end, other works about the Alps in general and other regions were used.

Extant alpine huts

Extant alpine huts provide important information on the types of construction and interior furnishings that might have been utilized in earlier time periods. For the most part, they seem to have been erected via a combined construction method in which stone foundations and bases were supplemented by wooden superstructures. Because of the fact that the only remains of such wooden buildings would be their rectangular, drystone bases or supports, comparisons within this area are often limited to ground-plans alone.

In the Oberhasli region, existing alpine huts show designs which rarely date back further than 1800. The exception to this rule is the *Melkhütte* (milking hut), a typical design that has been handed down only in the eastern Bernese Alps (Figure 11.5; Affolter et al., 1990: 169). Such log house structures have a characteristic porch used as a milking stall. The oldest known *Melkhütten* date from the sixteenth century (Gutscher, 2002). The survival of the *Melkhütte* design is evidenced by pictorial and written documents from the period around 1800 (Roth, 1993: colour plate IV; Wyss, 1817: 551–61).

CULTURAL AND HISTORICAL CONTEXT OF ALPINE SUMMER FARMING INFRASTRUCTURE

Medieval and modern alpine summer farming developments

It was only after the fourteenth century that the keeping of large livestock took hold in the Alps. Following the opening of Schöllenen Gorge and the Gotthard route in 1200, the growing demand for livestock from Lombardi (I) shifted the erstwhile homesteading and self-sufficiency which characterized the northern Alps to the commercial retention of livestock (Bundi, 1982: 188; Glauser, 1988: 158; Sablonier, 1990). With the regulation of grain farming in the fifteenth century, specialization continued to increase; wheat farming became more common in the Swiss Plateau and pastures were enlarged in the rainy alpine foothills and in the alpine valleys.

Starting in the fourteenth century, the management of public lands, forests and alps in the Oberhasli region was jointly managed by cooperatives. The deciding factor with regards to membership in one of these cooperatives was possession of one's own household (Dubler, 2002). In the eastern Bernese Alps, people organized themselves into small *Sennten* (farming and shepherding communities). Apparently, larger associations did not exist (Schatzmann, 1862: 9).

Proof of the importance of *Alpwirtschaft* in Oberhasli is evidenced by the fact that, even in the fourteenth century, texts were written which addressed the problems caused by increased grazing (Brülisauer, 1984). The intensification of cattle raising gradually led alp grazing rights to be more oriented towards bovines. The dairy cow became the standard from which grazing rights were calculated. After the fifteenth century, sheep and goat pasturing was moved to the *Hochberg* (high mountains which were difficult for the larger, less agile cattle to access). Despite the intensification of cattle raising, it seems as if sour milk cheese made from cow's and goat's milk remained the region's main dairy product. Although butter was also produced, only small amounts of it ever reached the cities. Leftovers from the cheese-making process were fed to the pigs which were kept with the cows on the alp occasionally. The increased amount of dairy cows produced a concomitantly greater amount of milk. In order for the cheese produced thereby to be stored for longer periods, in the sixteenth century, the Oberhasli region converted to a rennet-based cheese-making process (*Labkäserei*).

During the 1600s, rennet cheese replaced sour milk cheese in Oberhasli (as well as in most parts of the Swiss Alps). The advantage of that particular kind of cheese lay in the length of its shelf life and its stability gained by storage. In addition, such cheeses were well suited to transport with pack animals over long distances. While there was evidence for trade contacts with northern Italy in the medieval period, around 1600, written materials detail the export of full-fat cheeses from Oberhasli to northern Italy (Crenna, 1989: 474–76). This led to a renewal of complaints by the Bernese authorities about the butter shortage, as the supplies from the Bernese Alps were too low to meet the needs of the cities (Bircher, 1979: 100–101; Rennefahrt, 1966: 38; no. 23; Schatzmann, 1862: 32–34). This situation lasted until the end of the eighteenth century.

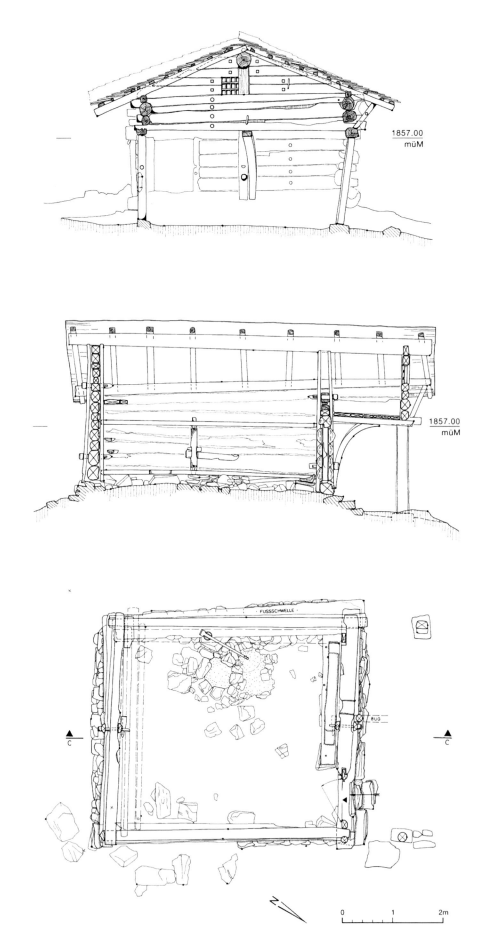

Figure 11.5. Brienz BE, Axalp-Litschentellti (north facade, section and ground-plan with fireplace of a sixteenth-century milking hut)
Source: Eliane Schranz, Archaeological Service of the Canton of Bern

The advent of rennet cheese and its resulting export opportunities led to a rise of *Alpwirtschaft* in the seventeenth and eighteenth centuries (Bircher, 1979: 100–103). Archaeological finds suggest that the transition to the rennet-based process brought about a move to newer and larger buildings. However, in order for this to be confirmed, both excavation and dating would be required.

Delimitation of the alpine regions

With the advent of written records in the thirteenth century, came the first written description of alps and alpine subjects in Oberhasli. All of the alps on which are found DMSs were mentioned in the fourteenth and fifteenth centuries in the legal documents; these descriptions were usually within the context of changes in ownership or boundary disputes. While the rules about grazing rights and the use of the alps had previously been orally transmitted, in the fourteenth century, that framework was formalized and written down. It was within these texts that the term "alp" was defined as a clear area with an organized programme of use. Which persons had use of an alp were clearly regulated as were the type and kind of animals that might be pastured there (Brülisauer, 1984). However, little is known about the emergence of the alps as specific territories treated in this fashion. Whether or not the alps were originally sought out by wandering shepherds whose continual usage made pasture boundaries and grazing rights into some sort of *de facto* law must remain unclear (Sablonier, 1990: 51–52, 83–85).

Pasture boundaries were usually created along existing topographical formations, such as rock ledges and high points in the landscape. Cliffs and streams serve as natural boundaries. This orientation towards features within the surrounding terrain must have originated in a time in which field borders were not fixed by wooden fences, walls or ditches, but were rather regulated by those very topographic elements. It may have been that the only indications of where a shepherd might graze his herd were marks scratched into stone (Brülisauer, 1984: 108; no. 77).

Many of the borders of today's municipalities and cantons were once pasture boundaries. The far-reaching boundaries of Innertkirchen and Hasliberg (i.e. they stretch into other valleys) indicate how important even distant pasturage was.

Raising livestock

Both large and small cattle herds leave different signatures within the archaeological record than the raising of cattle for the dairy industry. Some of these visible traces include the specific means by which fields were divided, the remains of the accommodations of shepherds or animal pens, stables and/or milking sheds. In Oberhasli, animal pens differ from building structures only in terms of their shape and design. Animal pens usually consist of significantly coarser masonry than was used in the erection of buildings.

Larger animal pen systems such as those known from Central Switzerland, Grisons and Valais are not known from Oberhasli. The only example which approaches these categories is that of the animal pen at Innertkirchen BE, Mälchsteinen in the Triftgebiet which measures some 200 m². The closest large pen system lies further west of the Oberhasli region in Brienz BE, Axalp-Chüemad. It consists of eight large pens into which small sheds were constructed. It was dated by C14-analysis and a few small finds to the thirteenth and fifteenth centuries (Gutscher, 2004).

At the end of Oberhasli's Gen and Wenden valleys as well as on the terraces of Hasliberg alp are a variety of different place names which hint at the earlier presence of animal pens. Their particular locations at the end of the valleys suggest that these places might have been used to sort the animals following the beasts' descent from the alps (Weiss, 1941: 119). The numerous compartments within the animal pen system at Axalp seem indicative of the same function.

The cow-sheds on the alps had several functions: they were forms of protection, provided space for quiet rumination, milking and the collection and the selective use of manure (Affolter et al., 1990: 159). It was only with the changes brought about by the agricultural revolution in 1800 and the economic improvements which followed thereafter that the first stables were built in Oberhasli. They were constructed in the nineteenth century (Kasthofer, 1818: 168; Sprüngli, 1760: 875–77) and served as shelter for livestock and are most often recognizable by the middle aisle with cow stalls on both side. This sort of a structural development arc is known from farmhouse research: first, extant structures added a stable area; it was only later that multi-room buildings were erected (Affolter et al., 1990: 169). This arrangement of a small dairy area and a larger stable can be found in Oberhasli both in existing buildings as well as in documented archaeological building remains. The statistical examinations from the late nineteenth century mention that stable structures were still rare in Oberhasli at that point in time (Bernisches Statistisches Bureau, 1902: 60).

From the sixteenth century onwards, pigs were kept on the alp alongside the cattle (Brülisauer, 1984: 178–81; no. 113). Even today, on the alps of Oberhasli numerous free-standing stables are visible in which the animals were housed. Often unused, these pigsties resemble building structures insofar as they are composed of a foundation trench and were often executed via block construction with wooden superstructure. It is quite possible that some of the smaller structures documented as buildings should actually have been classed as pigsties.

Milk processing

In addition to the location of those fields or pastures which were utilized, the system by which they were worked and the topographical layout of the area in total, the kind of cheese produced by a specific concern had a major impact on infrastructure and shape of those buildings erected therefore. The dairy was the central part of a cheese producer's base as it contained all the equipment required for the processing of milk. If a dairy had not been directly incorporated into a building, supplementary cellars and storage space were often added separately.

In the beginning of the nineteenth century, no separate cool storage rooms were reported at Oberhasli (Wyss, 1817: 556–59). Raw milk was stored in a hut until it was heated in a cauldron hung over a wood fire and processed into cheese by the addition of rennet. The resultant curd was then placed in round wooden molds and pressed with stones. The work space consisted often of stone or wooden benches. Stone benches were found during excavations in Central Switzerland[4] and were also sporadically found in Oberhasli. Wooden benches and shelves have survived in existing alpine buildings and are often seen in the pictorial records. Unfortunately, most of the containers and equipment used in this process were made of wood and have not survived (Zahler, 1909). It is also likely that most utensils, (or at least the more valuable of these) were brought down to the valley for the winter months.

The subsequent storage and aging of cheese was carried out in free-standing structures. These wooden structures were lined with a single layer of stone and had raised floors, thereby allowing for the circulation of the climate's dry air. Such drying racks have been used in the eastern Bernese Alps since the fifteenth century (Affolter et al., 1990: 171).

It is difficult to attribute different functions to the diverse buildings which were part of cheese production without excavation. Those which were used for the cooling and processing of milk as well as the storage of the cheese should all have square or rectangular layouts and should mostly differ only in size. Since one might assume that cheese production mostly took place indoors, it seems logical that those buildings in which its processing was undertaken should contain a combination of specific elements, including hearths, shelves and workbenches.

Wild hay production

One activity which was very important for *Alpwirtschaft* but is also hardly recognizable within the archaeological record is the production of wild hay. As one of the main products of alpine economy, hay was principally produced as feed stock for the winter months in the valleys, although it was also used on the mountain in case of need (i.e. if an animal was ill or if it snowed during the summer). In this context, wild hay fields are comprised of small grass fields on slopes too steep for them to be accessed by the cattle herds. This wild hay was often stacked into conical piles called *Tristen*. A *Triste* consists of a base (such as a bed of stones or branches) and a wooden rod rammed into the middle of the haystack (Stebler, 1903: 228).

Some important wild hay areas can be identified within the Oberhasli region on the basis of the written records (Gruber, 1783: 12–13; Statistisches Bureau, 1868: 396–97). One such example was recovered from the Gen Valley where a stone pile and a sickle fragment were discovered from a terrace of Hasliberg BE, Schlafenbielen above a steep incline. This stone pile could have easily served as the underlying basis for a *Triste*. In Hasliberg BE, Balisalp two semi-circular terraces supported by drystone walls were also documented which are reminiscent of the traditional *Tristen* locations from Grisons (Giovanoli, 2003: 411, 428). According to a local informant, remnants of wire cable found on the surface of one of the terraces were part of a "hay cable", a gravity-transport system for sending hay from the harvest area down to the barn or the valley.

CONCLUSION: THE VISIBILITY OF ALPINE SUMMER FARMING ACTIVITIES

The activities of *Alpwirtschaft* described above may be variably recognized in different archaeological sites. The animal husbandry left more easily recognizable features, including pens, stables and pasture boundaries, than the milk processing which took place in the interior space. According to tradition, one must assume that *Alpwirtschaft* in Oberhasli was focussed mainly on the production of dairy products and only secondarily on cattle raising. Without excavation, the classification of building remnants as dairies remains problematic because characteristic findings (such as hearths and workbenches) were rarely documented. This also means that it is difficult to tell whether those hearths which can be recognized were used within the context of a dwelling or as part of the work involved in dairying. Moreover, the kind of cheese storage practiced in Oberhasli is not easily recognizable, as the wooden structures were lined only with a single layer of stones (which, also, leave almost no archaeological trace).

Although a case-by-case analysis of the use and function of each individual building remain and rock-shelter structure is outside the scope of this paper, functional analysis can be achieved on the basis of some building types. Partly based on a process of elimination, the determination of function can be accomplished through an examination of the buildings' sizes. For example, a structure measuring some 50 m^2 can hardly represent the space required for a storage cellar. The larger ruins and foundations often represent stables. In some cases, this category included multipurpose buildings which served as both stables and dairy.

A large number of the building remains may have served as one-roomed dairies which combined living and working areas under a single roof. The interior space of dairy huts from Brienz BE, Axalp-Litschentellti and two of the dairies examined from Bellwald VS, Richinen covered some 14–18 m^2 (Bitterli-Waldvogel, 1998). This size range also includes the spaces measured for 18 of the structures recorded in Oberhasli.

Even some of the more frequent smaller foundations (measuring up to 15 m^2) seem to have been used as dairies as well. However, studying their smaller foundations and construction is difficult; some options for comparison include the excavated remains of buildings from the DMSs of Hospental UR, Blumenhütte, Glarus Süd GL, Braunwald-Bergeten and Kippel VS, Hockenalp-Altstafel (Meyer et al., 1998).

Those very small structures which measured less than 5 m^2 of interior space seem to be less well suited for work and were instead most likely utilized for storage, cooling rooms, pigsties or shepherd accommodations. As some of these very small buildings were somewhat removed from the other buildings, it seems less likely that they served as storage structures or pigsties, making their use as dwellings a good alternative. That being said, some of the pigsties which are still standing have been documented with interiors which would fit within this size range.

The determination of groups of buildings whose functions complemented each other is difficult and must be based here almost exclusively on their inner surfaces. That being said, different examples of combinations of cool storage, dairying and storeroom structures which resemble each other in terms of shape and size are recognizable within the finds from the DMS Innertkirchen BE, Zum See. Naturally, the needs of the shepherds must necessarily have also required the re-organization and re-purposing of some of the buildings, such as was exemplified at Valais; structures originally intended for dairies were then later used as stables (Bitterli-Waldvogel, 1998: 273–74).

Interestingly, it seems as if the pens and pen systems presumably dating to the medieval period were lacking in Oberhasli when that region is compared to the data from Central and Southeastern Switzerland. However, what we do not know is whether these differences are more related to topography or economics. The questions surrounding the exact function of each animal pen and the workflow of activity on the alp must be examined, as it is assumed that the various pen types served different functions. Small pens might have contained a small flock of sheep overnight, quarantined sick animals, or perhaps even served as pig pens. Larger pens were likely to have been used for the shearing of sheep or the separation of the herd following their decent in the autumn.

As a result of various other factors, from the sixteenth century on the construction of alpine buildings seems to have moved more towards multi-room structures in the western Bernese Alps, Canton of Uri and Grisons. By contrast, the private alps in the Simmen and Saanen Valley meant that entire families went to the alp; in such cases, buildings tended to be larger and to contain more living space. In Oberhasli, rather than immediately building new multi-roomed structures, the locals reworked extant buildings via the same principle. In this way, while the switch to more modern structures did occur, it did so at a later date (Affolter et al., 1990: 159). On the other hand, the production of butter as well as specific types of cheese was decisive in terms of the integration of refrigeration and storage rooms to alpine buildings. According to written sources, the production of full-fat cheese, that was stored in separate storehouses, was widespread in Oberhasli. By contrast, the production of butter was not practiced to a large extent, making the installation of cool storage areas superfluous in the region. Both inspectors as well as travellers within Oberhasli reported that, even in the 1900s, the majority of structures were still simple single-roomed constructions.

Various sources were available for the assessment of the different categories of sites and the types of activities practiced on the Alps. The comparison of existing buildings and archaeological discoveries was supplemented by descriptions obtained from the written sources and traditions regarding method and use. That being said, these diverse materials were not always utilized to the same degree; sometimes the written sources were more useful, sometimes it was more the study of the construction that brought more information to the figurative table. In any case, it is only after 1800 that a good quantity of non-archaeological sources becomes available. Therefore, archaeological conclusions drawn from these sites should be taken with a degree of caution. Nonetheless, it is mostly through such analyses that the more inconspicuous of alpine summer farming activities (such as the production of wild hay) were made known. At the same time, it is dangerous to equate function because of formal similarities. Although much of the material discussed within this paper gives some indications of the use and intent of the structures under examination, due to the lack of solid dates associated with it, that data has yet to be confirmed.

NOTES

1 Many thanks to Samantha Reiter, who translated the paper.
2 The analysis of these sites was part of the author's dissertation project (Andres, 2014).
3 Archive and magazine of the Archaeological Service of the Canton of Bern (344.001.).
4 Elm, Ämpächli GL: Obrecht 1998a, 113, 116; Glarus Süd, Bergeten GL: Geiser 1973, 19; Hospen Valley, Blumenhütte UR: Obrecht 1998b, 79.

REFERENCES

Affolter, H.C., von Känel, A. & Egli, H.-R. 1990. *Die Bauernhäuser des Kantons Bern. Vol. 2: Das Berner Oberland.* Die Bauernhäuser der Schweiz 27. Basel: Schweizerische Gesellschaft für Volkskunde.

Andres, B. 2014. Vil mehr feys khässen – Wüstungsforschung und Alpwirtschaft in der Region Oberhasli: Eine archäologisch-historische Einordnung. Unpublished PhD thesis, University of Zurich.

Auf der Maur, F., Imhof, W. & Obrecht, J. eds. 2005. *Alpine Wüstungsforschung, Archäozoologie und Speläologie auf den Alpen Saum bis Silberen, Muotatal SZ: Mit Beiträgen von Heidemarie Hüster-Plogmann, Jörg Schibler und Flavio Zappa.* Mitteilungen des Historischen Vereins des Kantons Schwyz 97.

Bernisches Statistisches Bureau. 1902. *Ergebnisse der Alpstatistik im Kanton Bern pro 1891–1902.* Mitteilungen des Bernischen statistischen Bureaus. Bern: K.J. Wyss.

Bircher, R. 1979. *Wirtschaft und Lebenshaltung im schweizerischen "Hirtenland" bis Ende des 18. Jahrhunderts.* Bern: K.J. Wyss.

Bitterli-Waldvogel, T. 1998. Alp Richinen, Bellwald VS 1984. In: W. Meyer, F. Auf der Maur, W. Bellwald, T. Bitterli-Waldvogel, Ph. Morel & J. Obrecht, eds. *"Heidenhüttli". 25 Jahre archäologische Wüstungsforschung im schweizerischen Alpenraum.* Schweizer Beiträge zur Kulturgeschichte und Archäologie des Mittelalters 23/24. Basel: Schweizerischer Burgenverein, pp. 270–93.

Brülisauer, J. ed. 1984. *SSRQ BE II/7. Das Recht des Amtes Oberhasli.* Aarau: Sauerländer.

Bundi, M. 1982. *Zur Besiedlungs- und Wirtschaftsgeschichte Graubündens im Mittelalter.* Chur: Calven-Verlag.

Crenna, M. 1989. I modi inquisitoriali nel Novarese. *Bollettino storico per la Provincia di Novara*, LXXX(1):455–91.

Degelo, L. 2011. Zeugen früher Alpwirtschaft: Alpwüstungen in Giswil. In: Kanton Obwalden, ed. *Kultur- und Denkmalpflege in Obwalden 2008–2009*, pp. 68–77.

Dubler, A.-M. 2002. Bäuert. In: *Historisches Lexikon der Schweiz (HLS)*, version from 7 February 2002. www.hls-dhs-dss.ch/textes/d/D10405.php (accessed 6 March 2016).

Ebersbach, R. & Gutscher, D. 2008. Alpine Prospektion im Oberhasli. Vorbericht 2003–2006. In: Erziehungsdirektion des Kantons Bern, ed. *Archäologie Bern 2008. Jahrbuch des Archäologischen Dienstes des Kantons Bern.* Bern: RubMedia, pp. 189–96.

Gerber-Visser, G. 2012. *Die Ressourcen des Landes. Der ökonomisch-patriotische Blick in den Topographischen Beschreibungen der Oekonomischen Gesellschaft Bern (1759–1855).* Archiv des Historischen Vereins des Kantons Bern 89. Baden: Hier + Jetzt.

Giovanoli, D. 2003. *Alpschermen und Maiensäss in Graubünden. Bäuerliche Bauten, Betriebsstufen und Siedlungsstrukturen ausserhalb der Dörfer Graubündens von der frühen Neuzeit bis 1960*, 1st ed. Bern: Haupt.

Glauser, F. 1988. Von alpiner Landwirtschaft beidseits des St. Gotthards 1000–1350. Aspekte der mittelalterlichen Gross- und Kleinviehhaltung sowie des Ackerbaus der Alpenregionen Innerschweiz, Glarus, Blenio und Leventina. *Der Geschichtsfreund*, 141:5–173.

Gruber, Samuel T. 1783. *Physisch topographische Beschreibung der Landschaft Oberhasle. Manuskript Burgerbibliothek Bern GA Oek. Ges. 123 (9), transkribiert von Gerrendina Gerber-Visser.*

Gutscher, D. 2002. Axalp, Litschentellti. *Jahrbuch der Schweizerischen Gesellschaft für Ur- und Frühgeschichte*, 85:341.

Gutscher, D. 2004. Axalp, Bärengehege. *Jahrbuch der Schweizerischen Gesellschaft für Ur- und Frühgeschichte*, 87:407–8.

Gutscher, D. 2008. Die Michaelskirche von Meiringen als archäologischer Zeuge früherer Naturkatastrophen. Reste von acht Vorgängerbauten zugänglich. In: Erziehungsdirektion des Kantons Bern, ed. *Archäologie Bern 2008. Jahrbuch des Archäologischen Dienstes des Kantons Bern.* Bern: RubMedia, pp. 133–48.

Haupt, P. 2012. *Landschaftsarchäologie. Eine Einführung.* Darmstadt: WBG.

Heiri, O., Wick, L., van Leeuwen, J.F.N., van der Knaap, W.O. & Lotter, A.F. 2003. Holocene tree immigration and the chironomid fauna of a small Swiss subalpine lake (Hinterburgsee, 1515 m asl). *Palaeogeography, Palaeoclimatology, Palaeoecology*, 189(1–2):35–53.

Hess, E. 1921. *Forstbotanische Monographie des Oberhasli von Interlaken bis zur Grimsel.* Bern: Büchler.

Kasthofer, K. 1818. *Bemerkungen über die Wälder und Alpen des Bernerischen Hochgebirges. Ein Beitrag zur Bestimmung der Vegetationsgrenze schweizerischer Holzarten, des Einflusses der Waldungen auf die Kultur des Hochgebirgs, des Verhältnisses der Forstwirthschaft zur Landwirthschaft und der Bedinge für Verbesserung der Alpenwirthschaft*, 2nd ed. Aarau: Heinrich Remigius Sauerländer.

Kurz, G. & Lerch, C. 1979. *Geschichte der Landschaft Hasli. Bearbeitet von Andreas Würgler.* Meiringen: Brügger.

Lotter, A.F., Heiri, O., Hofmann, W., van der Knaap, W.O., van Leeuwen, J.F.N., Walker, I.R. & Wick, L. 2006. Holocene timber-line dynamics at Bachalpsee, a lake at 2265 m a.s.l. in the northern Swiss Alps. *Vegetation History and Archaeobotany*, 15(4):295–307.

Meyer, W. 1998. Kleinere Prospektionen. In: W. Meyer, F. Auf der Maur, W. Bellwald, T. Bitterli-Waldvogel, Ph. Morel & J. Obrecht, eds. *"Heidenhüttli". 25 Jahre archäologische Wüstungsforschung im schweizerischen Alpenraum.* Schweizer Beiträge zur Kulturgeschichte und Archäologie des Mittelalters 23/24. Basel: Schweizerischer Burgenverein, pp. 294–308.

Meyer, W., Auf der Maur, F., Bellwald, W., Bitterli-Waldvogel, T., Morel, Ph. & Obrecht, J., eds. 1998. *"Heidenhüttli". 25 Jahre archäologische Wüstungsforschung im schweizerischen Alpenraum.* Schweizer Beiträge zur Kulturgeschichte und Archäologie des Mittelalters 23/24. Basel: Schweizerischer Burgenverein.

Nagy, P. & Schwarz, P.-A. 2013. Archäologische Prospektionen im Kanton Obwalden. Vorbericht zur Kampagne 2012. *Jahrbuch Archäologie Schweiz*, 96:152–64.

Nagy, P. & Schwarz, P.-A. 2014. Archäologische Prospektionen im Kanton Obwalden. Vorbericht zur Kampagne 2013. *Jahrbuch Archäologie Schweiz*, 97:180–94.

Nagy, P. & Schwarz, P.-A. 2015. Archäologische Prospektionen im Brüniggebiet. Vorbericht zur Prospektionskampagne 2014 in Lungern OW und Meiringen BE. *Jahrbuch Archäologie Schweiz*, 98:154–74.

Obrecht, J. 1998. "Ämpächli", Elm GL 1984. Archäologische Untersuchung einer hochmittelalterlichen Alpsiedlung. In: W. Meyer, F. Auf der Maur, W. Bellwald, T. Bitterli-Waldvogel, Ph. Morel & J. Obrecht, eds. "*Heidenhüttli*". *25 Jahre archäologische Wüstungsforschung im schweizerischen Alpenraum*. Schweizer Beiträge zur Kulturgeschichte und Archäologie des Mittelalters 23/24. Basel: Schweizerischer Burgenverein, pp. 105–23.

Rennefahrt, H. ed. 1966. *SSRQ I/8.1. Das Stadtrecht von Bern*. Aarau: Sauerländer.

Roth, A.G. 1993. *Der Sbrinz und die verwandten Bergkäse der Schweiz*. Burgdorf: Schweizerische Käseunion.

Sablonier, R. 1990. Innerschweizer Gesellschaft im 14. Jahrhundert. Sozialstruktur und Wirtschaft. In: Historischer Verein der Fünf Orte ed. *Innerschweiz und frühe Eidgenossenschaft. Jubiläumsschrift 700 Jahre Eidgenossenschaft. Band 2: Gesellschaft, Alltag, Geschichtsbild*. Olten: Walter-Verlag, pp. 11–233.

Sauerländer, D. 2015. Viehwirtschaft, Kap. 2: Hochmittelalter bis frühe Neuzeit. In: *Historisches Lexikon der Schweiz (HLS)*, version from 1 April 2015. www.hls-dhs-dss.ch/textes/d/D26236.php (accessed 6 March 2016).

Sauter, M. 2009. *Wüstungsforschung im Kanton Uri. Ergebnisse der hochalpinen Prospektion im Brunni- und Schächental, auf Haldi und dem Surenenpass*. Altdorf: Gamma.

Schaer, A. & Martin-Kilcher, S. 2009. Das Heiligtum und sein Umland. In: S. Martin-Kilcher & R. Schatzmann, eds. *Das römische Heiligtum von Thun-Allmendingen, die Regio Lindensis und die Alpen*. Schriften des Bernischen Historischen Museums 9. Bern: Bernisches Historisches Museum, pp. 257–83.

Schatzmann, R. 1862. *Die Milchwirthschaft im Kanton Bern in historischer, technischer und statistischer Beziehung. Separat-Abdruck aus dem 3. Heft der "Schweizerischen Alpenwirthschaft"*. Aarau: J.J. Christen.

Scheuchzer, J.J. 1746. *Natur-Geschichte des Schweitzerlandes samt seinen Reisen über die Schweizerischen Gebürge: aufs neue herausgegeben, und mit einigen Anmerkungen versehen von Joh. Georg Sulzern*. Zürich: David Gessner.

Sieber, C. & Bretscher-Gisiger, C. 2012. *Acta Murensia. Die Akten des Klosters Muri mit der Genealogie der frühen Habsburger*. Basel: Schwabe.

Sprüngli, J. 1760. *Beschreibung des Hassle-Lands im Canton Bern*. Der Schweizerischen Gesellschaft in Bern Sammlungen von landwirthschaftlichen Dingen 4. Zürich: Bey Heidegger und Compagnie.

Sprüngli, J. 1762. *Topographische und ökonomische Beschreibungen von dem Hasslethal: Fortsetzung*. Abhandlungen und Beobachtungen durch die Ökonomische Gesellschaft zu Bern gesammelt 4. Bern: Ökonomische Gesellschaft zu Bern.

Statistisches Bureau des Eidg. Departement des Innern 1868. *Die Alpenwirthschaft in der Schweiz im Jahre 1864*. Zürich: Orell Füessli.

Stebler, F.G. 1903. *Alp- und Weidewirtschaft: Ein Handbuch für Viehzüchter und Alpwirte*. Berlin: Parey.

Storr, G.K. 1784. *Alpenreise vom Jahre 1781: Erster Theil*. Leipzig: In der Johann Gottfried Müllerischen Buchhandlung.

Storr, G.K. 1786. *Alpenreise vom Jahre 1781: Zweiter Theil*. Leipzig: In der Johann Gottfried Müllerischen Buchhandlung.

Stumpf, J. 1548. *Schwytzer Chronica*. Zürich: Christoffel Froschouer.

Taramarcaz, C. & Curdy, P. 2013. Là-haut dans la montagne . . . des îtres et des hommes: Inventaire des ruines d'alpage dans le Val de Bagnes. *Archäologie Schweiz*, 36(3):16–25.

Vischer, Daniel L. 2003. *Die Geschichte des Hochwasserschutzes in der Schweiz: Von den Anfängen bis ins 19. Jahrhundert*. Berichte des BWG, Serie Wasser. Biel.

Von Rütte, H. 1990. IVS Dok. BE 17: Meiringen – Obergesteln: Grimselpass. *Inventar historischer Verkehrswege der Schweiz. IVS Dokumentation*, 1–6.

Weiss, R. 1941. *Das Alpwesen Graubündens. Wirtschaft, Sachkultur, Recht, Älplerarbeit und Älplerleben*, Reprint der Originalausgabe (1992). Chur: Octopus-Verlag.

Wick, L., van Leeuwen, J.F.N., van der Knaap, W.O. & Lotter, A.F. 2003. Holocene vegetation development in the catchment of Sägistalsee (1935 m asl), a small lake in the Swiss Alps. *Journal of Paleolimnology*, 30(3):261–72.

Winckler, K. 2012. *Die Alpen im Frühmittelalter. Die Geschichte eines Raumes in den Jahren 500 bis 800*. Wien: Böhlau.

Wyss, J.R. 1816. *Reise in das Berner Oberland, Band 1*. Bern: Burgdorfer.

Wyss, J.R. 1817. *Reise in das Berner Oberland, Band 2*. Bern: Burgdorfer.

Zahler, H. 1909. Milch, Käse und Ziger im Ober-Simmental (Kt. Bern). *Schweizerisches Archiv für Volkskunde*, 13:1–31.

Zappa, F. 2008. *I segni visibili e invisibili del paesaggio rurale. Stein e Bétti, due alpi walser*. Aosta: Associazione culturale Augusta.

Zybach, A. 2008. "*Im indren Grund*". *Chronik von Innertkirchen*. Münsingen: Fischer.

CHAPTER 12

Short- and long-distance transhumant systems and the commons in post-classical archaeology
Case studies from southern Europe

ANNA MARIA STAGNO[*]

INTRODUCTION

The mountainous areas of the Mediterranean are characterized historically by seasonal movements of both people and animals. Both short- and long-range transhumance has played a fundamental role in this part of Europe. Long-distance transhumance could cover hundreds of kilometres and involve mountainous and coastal areas being used, respectively, as summer and winter pasturages. Short-range transhumance, by contrast, (referred to as 'monticazione' in Italian, 'estivage' in French and 'and ganaderia estante o travesía' in Spanish) served as a kind of vertical transhumance in which herd animals were moved from the valleys to mountainous grazing pastures over distances which did not exceed approximately 5 kilometres.

There are significant differences between these two types of seasonal movement. The first and most apparent of these is that long-distance transhumance mostly involved sheep and goats (although bovine transhumance has also been documented) while short-distance transhumance was mainly concerned with the movement of cattle. Second, in the case of long-distance transhumance, the 'professional' shepherds that followed flocks (and cattle or horses or suins herds) also required habitation facilities on-site in the seasonal pastures. However, within the monticazione system, herds were local and were taken daily from their sheds (which were often placed near the upper cultivation limits) to the grazing areas. This enabled the herders to return to their own homes every evening. Amongst the various forms of cattle farming, medium-range vertical transhumance has also been well documented in alpine regions. This type of animal husbandry involved several different grazing stages that related to the seasons. Beginning in May, the animals grazed in the pastures closest to the villages before moving to pasturage half way up the mountain. Later, the cattle were moved to their high-altitude summer pastures. This last pasturage area required an overnight presence by herders, as it was often placed at distances which were too great for a daily commute (Gaio, 2014; Mattone & Simbula, 2001).

The differences among these systems are reflected in the various methods of pasture organization, mountain stations, herder movements and economic circuits associated with these activities. It is also important to emphasize that all of these forms of farming contributed to the construction of reciprocal relationships between different social groups and settlements, as well as to transfers of fertility between lands that (in long-distance transhumance) were quite far apart. Fertility transfers helped to reconcile animal husbandry with agriculture (arable farming) by enabling agricultural specialization in areas that did not 'naturally' contain enough fertilizer for crops (Moreno, 1990: 243). In this sense, historical methods of organizing pastoral resources was not only crucial in defining diverse forms of access to and management of mountain resources (almost unanimously geared towards collective management) but also to the viability of cultivated valleys and coastal zones. For these reasons, transhumance was a vital component in the construction of rural landscapes, be they mountainous or coastal.

In recent years, post-classical archaeology has shown a new and steadily increasing interest in the study of mountainous areas and other spaces which have long been considered as 'marginal' and, therefore, almost completely devoid of archaeological interest. Within this context, archaeological investigations into pastoralism have become increasingly numerous as have larger research projects concerning a wide range of subjects both directly and indirectly related to this field. Most recently, such interests have been incorporated into more general discussions concerning the archaeology of common lands (hereafter 'commons'); the study of which is essential in order to understand organizational forms in and of mountainous areas and related settlement patterns (Lindholm et al., 2013; Oosthunizen, 2013; Stagno, 2016b). Such research is being developed through the adoption of increasingly multidisciplinary approaches that combine archaeological and historical research and, in many cases, with approaches from environmental archaeology and anthropology.

Beginning with a discussion of the first results of the multidisciplinary *Archimede* research project

© 2018 European Association of Archaeologists

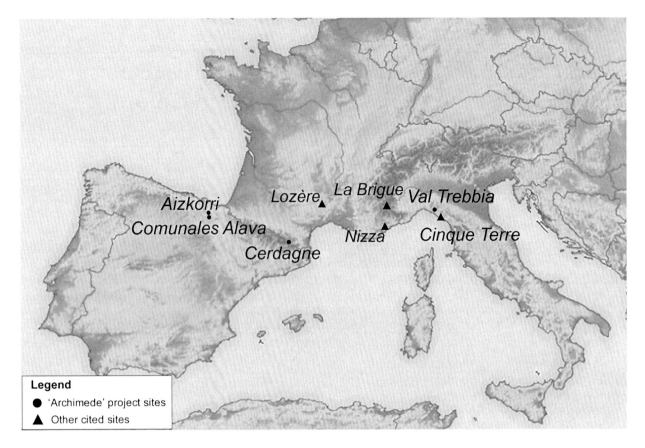

Figure 12.1. Map of the sites investigated by the 'Archimede' project (circles) which also designates the other sites detailed in the text (triangles)

(Archaeology of Commons: Cultural Heritage and Material Evidence of Disappearing Europe) – devoted to historical archaeological investigation of commons in the Basque Mountains, Ligurian Apennines and the French Pyrenees – this paper will discuss the problems associated with the archaeological study of short- and long-distance transhumant movements and the different possibilities that exist for distinguishing between them. Approached regressively, the overall objective of the *Archimede* project is to study the historical relationships between rights of access to commons and collective resources, local social groups and the environment. The common lands addressed in this article are those that were used by one or more communities (or local social groups) through a system of rules and customary rights that were often regulated by local or feudal rural statutes, at least until the end of the *Ancien Régime*[1]. The management histories of these areas developed through a long series of conflicts, through which rights were constructed and negotiated in turn (Moreno & Raggio, 1992). These lands took a variety of different forms (meadows, pastures, forests, wooded pastures and/or cultivated areas) which were managed in often very complex ways, that – at least from the medieval period – included multiple agro-sylvo-pastoral management practices which integrated the collection of firewood, grazing and temporary cultivation (Viader & Rendu, 2014). Moreno (1990) and Raggio (2007) have shown that the organization of grazing activities lay at the centre of these regulations and the rights of access to collective resources. Taking an archaeological approach to the exploration of the distinctiveness of different farming practices can provide valuable insights into diverse modes by which collective spaces were organized as well as to the transformations which took place over centuries and, consequently, to the forms of organization employed by the societies by which they were practiced (Fernández Mier et al., 2013).

This article seeks to connect common lands and seasonal settlements by following the various types of transhumant movement. The first section reflects on how the study of these movements can provide opportunities to 'spatialize' the relations between the various social groups involved and understand the ways in which movements were historically reconciled. The sections which follow present case studies that facilitate the discussion of possible indicators of vertical and horizontal transhumance practices. I conclude with a tentative list of archaeological indicators for different practices and the implications thereof in subsequent interpretations.

Transhumance as the Spatialization of Social Relationships

Historically, the organization of the two models of transhumance made different contributions to the establishment and development of physical spaces and to the relations between the social groups that used and inhabited them (Moreno & Raggio, 1990).

Short-distance transhumance (*monticazione*) is a clear example of the vertical exploitation of mountain resources, and of commons that could influence settlement patterns and present-day administrative boundaries (see Figure 12.2). Their form reflects the fact that these areas were not originally divided amongst multiple communities and settlements; they were only fixed within the administrative network following successive divisions that were the outcome of contestations and conflicts over common land (Tigrino et al., 2013). Long-distance transhumance resulted from social, economic and political differences between communities, even when they were separated by considerable geographic distances across state boundaries (and regardless of whether the movement was controlled by central institutions like the Dogana delle pecore di Foggia or the Mesta of Castilla). For this reason, the reconstruction of transhumance paths provides an important means of mapping relationships between diverse social groups. The existence of these pathways has been extensively studied in classical and proto-historical archaeology, and their reconstruction has highlighted that access to grazing resources in mountainous areas was closely linked to political and social factors, independent of geographical situation (Gabba & Pasquinucci, 1979; Delano Smith, 1979). Furthermore, the possibility of accessing pasturage could have been regulated by rental contracts or by reciprocal agreements that permitted access to grazing resources in communal and private pastures, a situation which has been well documented in the written sources and oral histories since the fourteenth century (Moreno, 1990; Conesa, 2012; Burri, this volume).

The variability is extremely wide and the reconstruction of pathways enables scholars to retrace different management strategies, and the tensions and conflicts concerning collective resources between social groups and individuals. For example, in the first half of the seventeenth century, the pastures and *bandite* of the municipality of Briga (Maritime Alps) were at the centre of a long series of trials in which the Briga community opposed a number of other parties (mostly senators

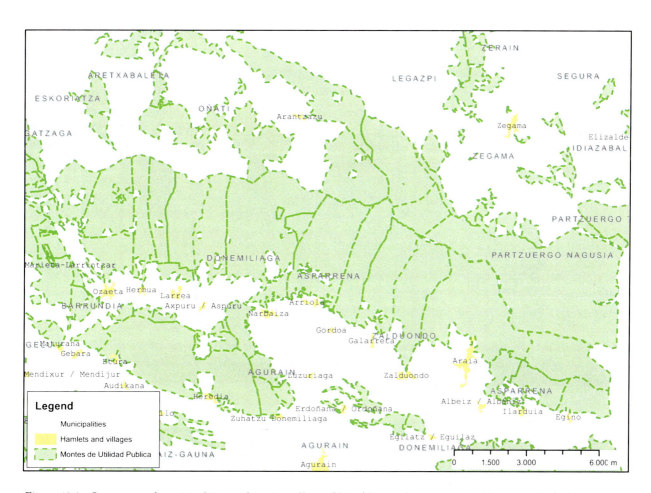

Figure 12.2. Commons and municipalities on the eastern Alevese Plain (the round areas correspond to preserved seles)

from Nice). As these senators had relatives in the area and had become creditors to the municipality, they exercised control over some land in the area for the period of time required for their debts to be paid (Palmero, 1992). As Briga and Nice were at opposite ends of an historical transhumance route, the creditors' interest in maintaining control over these lands by slowing the trial was linked to the possibility of continuing to exploit the pastures. Thus, the collection of proceeds from renting the land as pasture for transhumant flocks was in direct competition with local communities' use of the land. The acts which followed these conflicts – conflicts that also involved the community of Triora that shared part of the commons with Briga – show that there were 30 shepherds with 15,000 sheep in Triora during the summer of 1670. This trial led, in turn, to the sale of the common property that would finally become the private property of a few local families some 50 years later.

Another interesting case is documented in eastern Liguria. The rights to exploit collective resources in the coastal mountains of the Mesco-Bardellone Ridge (documented as the property of the *Magnifica Comunità of the Parish* and, therefore possession of the parish) historically belonged to social groups in the current Levanto, Monterosso and Pignone municipalities. However, even the parish of Brugnato in the mountainous Vara Valley enjoyed the rights to use these common lands that related directly to reciprocal agreements about transhumant movements made between mountain and coastal parishes (Pescini & Gabellieri, 2015).

In this, and many other cases, agreements were intended to exploit the fertilizing properties of manure when deposited in cultivated coastal areas. As such, they were related to the practice of selling 'fertilizing nights' – well documented in both coastal regions (like Provence and Cinque Terre; Maggi et al., 2006) and mountainous areas of southern Europe. These exchanges were regulated by specific agreements which dictated the amount of manure to be provided. The ethnographic reconstruction offered by the case of Lozère in the Massif Central makes it possible to shed light on their operation mechanisms. In this case, the manure supplied to each individual fund was established on the basis of the common grazing shares to which each person was entitled. In this case, the herds were enclosed within mobile fences every night (which served to collect the manure in one place). The shepherd secured room and board (in mobile huts that were property of the village) in return for the manure which collected in the pen overnight. It was the responsibility of the shepherd to move the manure to the various locations and to move his hut around the village with the help of the landowner (Brisebarre, 1992).

Traces of this practice can be found in pollen diagrams which record the presence of sub-species grown outside their habitats. Sheep not only transfer the fertility represented by their manure, that could be considered a voluntary environmental effect of transhumance movements, but also the pollen carried in their fleeces. This pollen is 'sown' along the routes traversed by the animals in question and might be regarded as an involuntary environmental effect of movement, as is the case with soil erosion. Therefore, pollen analysis can reveal the presence of species grown outside the local habitat.

The LASA group (Laboratory of Archaeology and Environmental History) at the University of Genoa conducted a series of studies in Cinque Terre on the history of the cultural landscapes which today are characterized by terraced vineyards and olive tree groves today. This study revealed a more complicated past; until the late nineteenth century, the area was involved in the seasonal movement of sheep and goats along transhumant routes between the coast and the mountains at the base of the Ligurian Apennines (c. Zignago) which might possibly have taken place since the Roman period (Figure 12.3). As suggested by the etymology of their toponyms, Zignago and Hibernatia are places of Latin origin and respectively may have served as mountain pastures in the summer and coastal pastures in the winter (Maggi et al., 2006). Pollen analysis in this area (at 300 m a.s.l.) revealed the presence of *calluna* (of the Ericaceae family) up to the nineteenth century. This is a species with an Atlantic distribution which cannot grow naturally so close to the sea. Today, *calluna* is only present within the main Cinque Terre watershed from 600 to 700 m a.s.l.; it does not reach the lower coastal slopes. The presence of *calluna* is possibly connected with transhumant pastoral practices and systems. Its disappearance within the pollen records likely echoes the abandonment of these practices in the late nineteenth century (Maggi et al., 2006). Therefore, the presence of mountain species in coastal areas is an historical effect of this particular husbandry practice which helps to explain historical processes of bio-diversification and could be considered an indirect marker of transhumant movement (Cevasco et al., 2015). Some useful information can also be gleaned by analysis of modern-day vegetation; it is this last which historical ecology seeks to identify and explore (for several examples see Cevasco, 2007: 138).

In the above example, it is interesting to note that until the end of the nineteenth century – thanks to the availability of local resources (grass and leaf fodder) – contributions of manure to the fertility of coastal terraces must have been due to the overwintering of thousands of sheep and goats in the terraced areas of the Cinque Terre. This allowed people in the area to specialize in olives and viticulture; the absence of grazing created a crisis for olive and grape growers. In fact, technical documents from the late nineteenth century reveal that the viticulture of the Cinque Terre often suffered from shortages of manure as a fertilizer (LASA, 2003: 85).

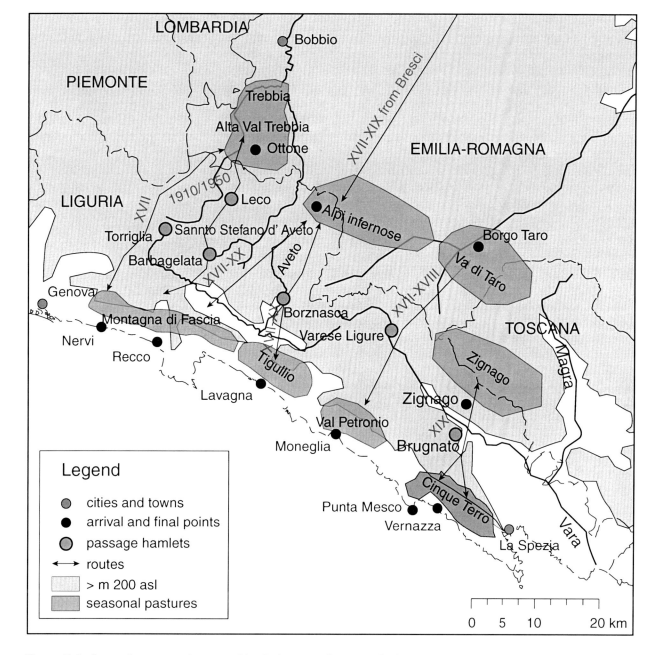

Figure 12.3. Seasonal movements in eastern Liguria (seventeenth–twentieth c.)
Source: From Moreno (1990), Moreno and Raggio (1990), Cevasco (2007)

Conciliating Transhumant Movements

Far from being systems and practices that developed in separate contexts, these types of transhumance often co-existed. It is for this reason that solutions were sought to reconcile these different movements. During the *Ancien Régime*, many local regulations and statutes concerning access rights to grazing lands were defined in order to reconcile these seasonal movements. Some communities, for example, excluded 'foreign' animals from their common pastures, while others made agreements which permitted their access and use (Raggio, 1995). However, many conflicts over access rights to collective lands involving different social actors are well documented since the medieval period; in many cases, they also left material evidence (such as usurpation acts) that can be investigated today.

In other cases, specific infrastructures were created in order to regulate these movements. This was the case, for example, with particular walls (*crèste*) which are found in an area in eastern Liguria between Nervi and Recco historically known as the Montagna di Fascia. Topped by cut shale slabs, the walls served to delineate local cattle farming areas and to prevent access by transhumant sheep. There were at least 4000 transhumant sheep on the Montagna di Fascia during the winter of 1820, from which seasonal movements would take place to the Apennine districts of Torriglia and Ottone – both being used as summer pastures for Genoese flocks and herds. Sheep grazing was distributed amongst pasture stations, particularly in chestnut, olive and mixed woodland groves where small houses and sheds were built to provide seasonal shelter for sheep, and partly in common wooded pasture. As attested in documents relating to conflicts over grazing rights between the eighteenth and nineteenth centuries, the Montagna di Fascia communities sought to reconcile transhumant sheep farming with the development of local cattle husbandry and to regulate the interaction between animals and the vegetation. The *crèste* were one of the solutions adopted in the winter pasture areas to limit the impact of livestock on the vegetation (Moreno, 1990: 87–106).

In the Basque mountains, especially in Gipuzkoa and Bizkaia, a type of separated land called '*seles*' is present in the collective lands that have undergone multiple management practices since at least the thirteenth century. These were created inside common lands and, since at least the eighteenth century, have had round forms and were defined by the presence of boundary stones (*mojones*). The *seles* were designed specifically for animal husbandry and breeding (Díaz de Durana & Fernández de Larrea, 2002) and were rented for long periods (50 years) to private entities with the possibility of renewal. One hypothesis links their creation to transhumance. In the Basque Mountains, the grazing of 'foreign' herds or flocks in the commons was historically permitted only during daylight hours (i.e. there were no possibilities for overnighting in common lands). Such a situation would not have been compatible with transhumant livestock. Such spaces could have allowed overnight stays (and the collection of manure) along the transhumance paths toward the summer and winter pasturing stations. Comparing the distribution of *seles* and transhumance routes could help clarify these spaces' function and the changes they underwent over the centuries. The location and ownership of *seles* left them open to conflict which could potentially have been of long duration (Díaz de Durana, 2001).

In this initial analysis, then, *crèste* and *seles* appear to give material indications of the ways in which people reconciled different types of contemporary transhumant movement in the landscape (Figure 12.4).

LONG- AND SHORT-DISTANCE TRANSHUMANT MOVEMENT IN BASQUE COUNTRY

As previously mentioned, discussion of the problems associated with the archaeological identification of different types of pasturing systems (both long- and short-distance transhumance) is central to this paper.

In order to better characterize these historical activities, it is important to identify indicators that would permit a more effective qualification of the function and socio-environments within which they took place. The research conducted by the *Archimede* project has made a number of contributions to discussions relating to the indicators of and relationships between different grazing activities and the strategies through which they were organized within a framework of collective use.

The areas investigated are located in Gipuzkoa (the Sierra de Aizkorri Plateau) and in the eastern Alevese Plain (the *comunales* of Zalduondo and the mountain municipalities lying between Salvatierra, Narbaiza (San Millán), Heredia (Barrundia) and Zuazo de San Millán (St. Millán).[2]

This area is of interest because, within an area of about 80 km^2, there was significant variability not only in terms of geomorphology and altitude, but also within the organization of common spaces (*comunales*, *montes comunes de vecinos y moradores*, *Parzonería*), which today are classified as the *Montes de Utilidad Pública* (Figure 12.5). It is known that these mountain municipalities are located along historical short- and long-range transhumance circuits and routes (Díaz de Durana & Fernández de Larrea, 2003; Alberdi, 2004) and that they were also used for the production of firewood and charcoal (Aragón Ruano, 2001; 2003). The plateaus of the Gipuzkoa slopes were the endpoints for summer transhumance routes that incorporated Bizkaia and Gipuzkoa, whilst the use of the Alava slopes was mainly related to a type of local livestock farming.

All of the surveyed areas are currently protected as 'Habitats of Community Interest' and the Aizkorri area is denominated as the 'Parque Natural de Aizkorri y Araratz'. These surveys made the reconstruction of the complex history of the changes in the management of these spaces possible. Once again, one must emphasize the role that the long history of rural and collective land use had in generating the cultural and natural landscapes that are today recognized, and subsequently protected, as our common heritage (Rotherham, 2013).

Methods

Archaeological investigations began with an analysis of the current organization and use of commons. The survey methodology adopted the topographic approach used by historical ecologists and rural archaeologists insomuch as it focused on the study of historical environmental resource management practices and the ways in which these had been developed by successive local social groups (Moreno, 1990; Cevasco, 2007; Stagno, 2016a). The surveys were enriched by the adoption of specific perspectives and approaches from agrarian archaeology, an approach that is based on the study of

Short- and long-distance transhumance 177

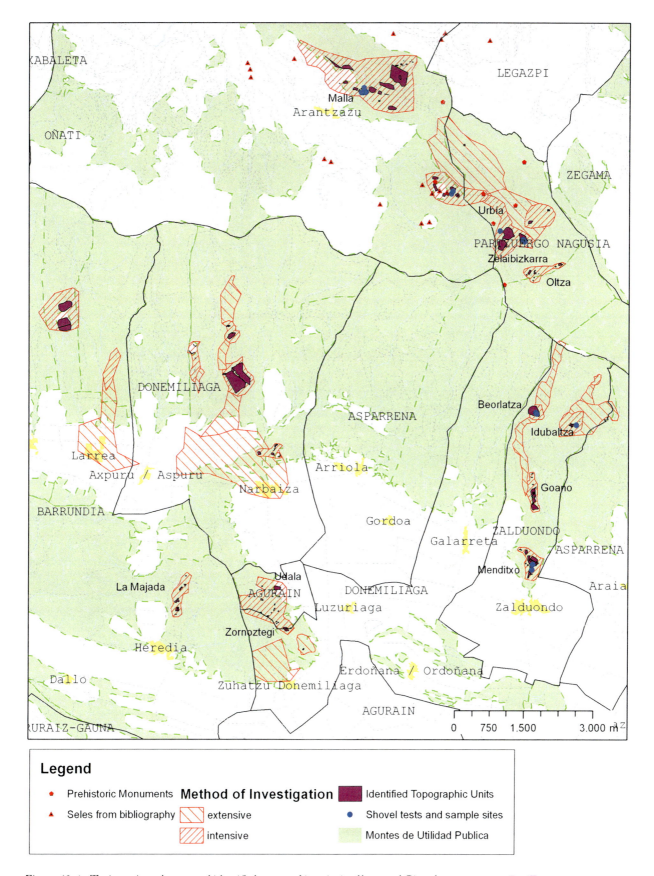

Figure 12.4. The investigated areas and identified topographic units in Alava and Gipuzkoa

agricultural systems and their links with settlements. In this way, it is more oriented towards the reconstruction of social structures (such as hierarchies and inequalities) in pre-industrial societies (Kirchner, 2010; Quirós Castillo, 2012; Fernández Mier, 2010). The investigations initially consisted of landscape archaeology and

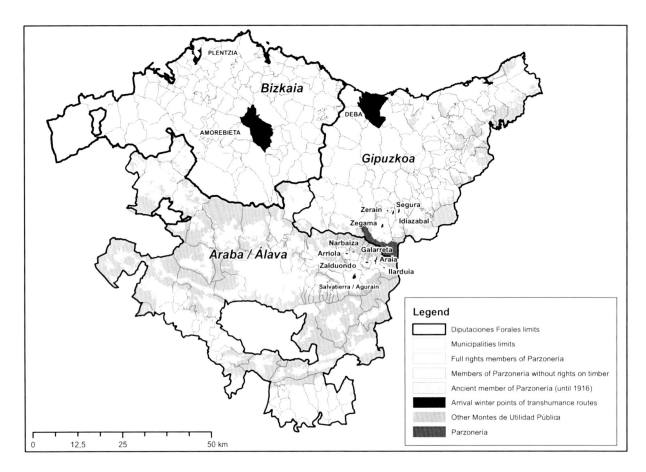

Figure 12.5. Hamlets involved with rights in the Parzonería General de Gipuzkoa and Alava and the location of the arrival points of a select few transhumance routes

historical ecology surveys as well as consultation with oral sources, small-scale excavations at sites which were selected in accordance with the survey results and archaeobotanical (anthracology, palynology, analysis of non-pollen palynomorphs, phytoliths and dendroecology) and physicochemical analyses.

Beginning with the analysis of the current situation and the identification of traces of past primary production (pastoral, forestry, agricultural), the objective of the research was to regressively explore these traces of past use. Such traces were namely those associated with cultivation, the production of fodder and charcoal, the presence of quarries, enclosures, seasonal settlements and wooded pastures (many of which are still recognizable by the presence of shredded [i.e. pruned] and pollarded trees). These traces are central to the identification of the different strategies used in the exploitation of environmental resources and are crucial components to creating an understanding of the role of conflict within these areas. The analysis of such traces, and of those derived from some specific local practices, such as *trasmochos* and *ipinabarres* (Aragón Ruano, 2013), provides the means for identifying changes in the different forms of individual appropriation and occupation of common lands and of their temporality (*sensu*; Ingold, 2000). Therefore, special attention was paid to the identification of elements that could assist the process of recognizing individual occupation sites in areas of collective land, the duration of their occupancy (i.e. temporary and permanent), their chronology and the functions they served (e.g. pastoral activities, cultivation, the production of fodder and coal and the quarrying of stone). In particular, distinct indicators of ownership were identified, such as rosaceae rows (particularly hawthorn), artefacts (enclosures, walls, seasonal settlement, boundary stones) and traces of the ancient *seles*. It is interesting to note that the value of hawthorn in claims of possession and its use in indicating the permanent appropriation of spaces by individuals is well testified not only in Basque Country (Agirre García et al., 2009; Azpiazu, 2011), but also in the Pyrenees and Ligurian Apennines.

Small test pits (0.7 x 1 m) were opened in selected sites (seasonal settlements, hypothetical temporary cultivation sites and charcoal kiln sites) at which sediments for archaeobotanical and physicochemical analysis were sampled. These investigations provided an idea of the chronology of individual traces in the current 'palimpsest', and helped understand changes in the management of spaces where traces were not conserved and visible at a superficial level (such as past changes in the use of the settlements and in agro/silvo/pastoral activities).

Cabañas, establos and *rebaños*: from transhumance to sedentary husbandry in Gipuzkoa

The area investigated in Sierra Aizkorri is located on a vast plateau characterized by grasslands that stretch from Oltza to Malla. Farming is still practiced here and is indeed favoured by the local administration, given its role in the maintenance of grass cover and controlling trees and shrubs (Aldezabal et al., 2015). For this reason, agronomists from the Diputación Foral de Gipuzkoa annually measure the quantity of livestock (sheep, cattle, horses and, to a much lesser extent, pigs) and their effects on the vegetation cover. The Oltza and Urbía area falls within the Parzonería General de Gipuzkoa y Alava of which the Oñati area has never been a part. Between 1747 and 1749, numerous documents can be found that relate to an attempt by Oñati to be recognized as a member of the general council of *parzoneros* and, therefore, the holders of procurement rights for the Urbía and Oltza pastures.[3]

The Parzonería is a particular management institution whose origins date to the medieval period. Historically, the Parzonería was sub-divided amongst the 11 surrounding *ayuntamientos* and *pueblos* (Figure 12.6). In the Urbía (and, to a lesser extent, the Oltza), there are a number of units that are inhabited during the summer season by shepherds grazing their sheep herds. In the Malla (an area outside the *Parzonería* that belongs to Oñati) the structures are concentrated in an area characterized by rocky outcroppings and cannot be inhabited, as they could only ever be used as the taverns, sheds and warehouses related to grazing in the pastures. In both cases, the buildings are the property of their respective municipalities (Partzurgoa and Oñati) and the hereditary rights of use continue as long as the individuals concerned are engaged in animal husbandry.[4] It is interesting to note that, until recent periods, the roofs of these structures could not be made of brick and only with more perishable materials, since the use of clay bricks would have correlated with individual ownership. The same prohibition, typical of many commons, is found in the rules established by Salvatierra to allow for the construction of *majadas* in its communal lands (Pozuelo Rodriguez, 2010: 622).

The Urbía area was historically part of transhumance routes that are still partially active today (Urzainki-Mikeleiz, 2007; Aragón Ruano, 2003). In this area, it was possible to interview a couple of the last shepherds who undertook transhumant movements over hundreds of kilometres.[5] Every spring, this shepherd transported the sheep from Amorebieta in Zegama in trucks, before making the assent to Urbía by foot. His uncle, by contrast, followed a route which departed from the northeast coast of Bizkaia at Plentzia, as had been the case since the 1970s. There are several nuclei of seasonal settlements in this area, which, according to the shepherd's story, relate to the different *pueblos* who exercised Parzonería use rights. Each of these

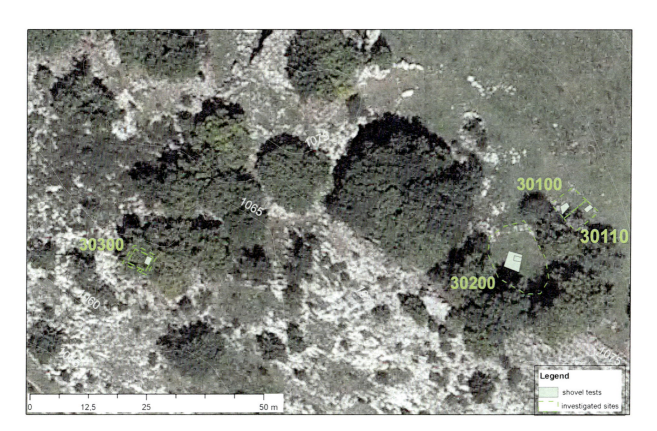

Figure 12.6. Sites and test-pit locations in Malla

pueblos had different reciprocity agreements with *pueblos* on the coast, representing opposite ends of winter transhumance routes. As such, the Zegama flocks wintered in Plentzia and spent the summer in Urbía; the Segura flocks wintered in Deba and spent the summer in Oltza. Archival documentation reveals historical modifications made to these agreements between the different social groups who exercised their use rights over grazing resources in these areas and their different transhumance paths (many of which can be traced back to at least the fourteenth century). Agreements were often reinforced by matrimonial strategies that linked different settlements. In the surroundings of Malla area, present structures (sheds and taverns) are used by people of the nearby hamlet of Arantzazu.

The whole of this area is recognized for its high archaeological value owing to the presence of numerous menhirs, tumuli and other prehistoric monuments (Altuna et al. 1990, 2002). Based on archaeological surveys in this area, three sites were identified (Malla, Urbía and Oltza) in which a number of multi-layered seasonal settlements were concentrated. The latter were created by cutting directly into the rock and, in many cases, were also associated with rock shelters and cave settlements (those in Urbía were partially studied by Gandiaga et al., 1989 and Ugalde et al., 1992–1993).

In the Malla, the smoothing and collapsing of the structures which occupy an area of about 4 hectares appear in some cases to have been obliterated by shredded and pollarded beech trees. This last is likely the remaining trace of a phase of historical wooded pasture. In the area, traces of abandoned terraces and other evidence for temporary cultivation (e.g. defined areas of hawthorn trees which are often in alignment) are also documented. In some cases, these alignments coincide with the boundaries of present *seles*, thereby demonstrating a very close relationship with phases of individual permanent appropriation. The test pits (Figure 12.7) were designed to verify the chronological relationships between structures and to characterize their precise functionality. Excavation was carried out on the interior and exterior of a rectangular-shaped structure (Sectors 30110 and 30100), probably an enclosure for sheep with traces of previous use phases (Sector 30200). The interior of another rectangular-shaped structure was subjected to test-pitting, showing that a current century-old shredded beech tree post-dated the structure's collapse (Sector 30300). The palynological analysis of samples was conducted in the profiles of test pits 30100, 30110 and 30200 as well as in the hypothesized temporary cultivation area defined by hawthorns trees just south of the settlements (UT 3007).

The archaeological sequence revealed a chronology that, despite obvious transformations, indicated continued use since at least the tenth century.[6] However, in some areas, traces of prehistoric use were also documented. Investigations revealed that the buildings had been seasonally inhabited around the thirteenth through fifteenth centuries (as evidenced by the presence of cooking and table ware fragments in the oldest layers), followed by a period of abandonment (definitive in the case of 30300) and subsequent re-use as sheds (30110 and 30200). This was followed by the definitive abandonment of the structures and their use as fenced enclosures (30100 and 30200) and, finally, their use simply as pasture. This change could indicate a modification in the use of the buildings from seasonal settlements with summer domestic use (possibly related to the use of the pastures for transhumance) to one that did not make provision for staying at the site (possibly related to a transition in the form of pasture connected to local transhumant livestock) according to a model resembling the present one. It seems likely that the growth in the formation of beech-wooded pasture took place during the second phase. As has already been intimated above, such growth can obliterate some older structures (such as 30300).

The presence of temporary cultivation areas could also be linked to this stage of use. Alternatively, the terraces (which will be investigated in the summer of 2016) could be linked to the earliest stages of the area's use and closely correlate with intense summer use. In this they were similar to the vegetable gardens documented in seasonal settlements at Urbía that were permanently inhabited during the summer months. This change could be related to changes in access rights to pastures, and maybe to changes in the social groups that used the area as summer pasture. It can be hypothesised that new modes of organisation in the collective spaces may have led to changes in farming systems. A *sel* in Malla, located between the seles of Iskista and Duru, is documented in a donation of 1439.[7] In the following centuries, the sel of Malla is no longer documented, whilst the other two continue to be detailed in the archival sources. In Gipuzkoa since the fourteenth century, conflicts concerning pasture access rights between the owner of the seles (i.e. those who use or rent them for the stabling herds during the night) and the local communities claiming exclusive usage of the common pastures are well documented. In this context, it is possible to suggest that the sel at Malla was sold (or given back) to the Oñati community, who owned the surrounding common-lands. Whilst archival analysis is still under way, it could nevertheless be proposed that the area of Malla was inside a *sel* until the fifteenth century, and used as summer farms by the 'professional' shepherds who lived there during the summer months, whilst the enclosures could be related to more the recent uses of the area in short distance transhumance systems as practiced by shepherds from Oñati and Arantzazu.

The transition from a structure with domestic use to a shed marks a conspicuous differentiation within the

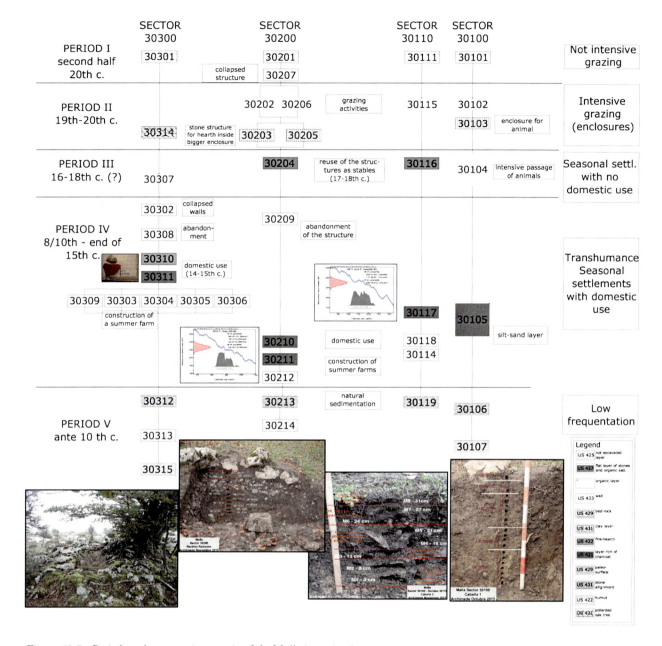

Figure 12.7. Periods and comparative matrix of the Malla investigations

buildings at Parzonería (where the presence of seasonal settlements with domestic use throughout the summer months continues to this day). In the Urbía area, seven 'hamlets' were identified that were composed of domestic structures in different states of preservation and which always neighboured current seasonal settlements. Throughout the area, traces of vegetable gardens and ancient wooded pastures were documented. A multi-layered soil profile (Profile 40000) was sampled and analyzed in order to characterize changes in the vegetation. In the area of Zelaibizkarra, the presence of a group of structures from the same period was documented. These structures also appeared to have been more recent than the other buildings investigated. In this area, two test pits were conducted in two structures (30400 and 400) in order to verify the chronology of the settlement and to characterize the nature of its expansion for comparison with documentary analysis. Based on the examination of a building and of a structure linked to the processing of ferrous materials (30400), both excavations confirmed a short and relatively recent history which possibly dated to the late nineteenth century. This would suggest, therefore, that the settlement might possibly have been built during the period in which demographic expansion in the area was at its maximum. From a methodological point of view, the survey would appear to confirm the relationship between the structures' states of preservation and their chronologies, as has been verified in other southern European mountainous areas (Le Couedic, 2010; Gassiot Balbé & García Casas 2014).

Transterminancia at Alava commons

The density of seasonal settlements in Aizkorri contrasts with that on the Alava side (where the presence and traces of structures are much more sporadic). However, the Alava slopes are more consistent with the traces of different stages of the use of non-settled spaces, as can be seen by the alternation of wooded pasture, woodland and areas of temporary and permanent cultivation.

Traces of wooded pastures, particularly featuring oaks, were consistently documented and temporary crops delineated by hawthorn were almost always identified within these areas. It has been also suggested that the temporal crops area corresponds to the intermediate zone between permanent crops and mountain woodlands (Pastor Díaz de Garayo, in press). In many cases, it is possible to suggest that the stages of temporary cultivation were followed by phases of permanent appropriation of the spaces, as shown by the construction of embankments (at Menditxo) and terraces (at Zornoztegi, La Majada, Udala and Menditxo).

Traces of settlements possibly related to seasonal use were only identified within the Zalduondo *comunales*, where two abandoned settlements (Beorlatza, UT 1302 and Idubaltza, UT 1213) and a multi-layered structure still in use (Goano, UT 1103) were documented. The two settlements were both located at about 1000 m a.s.l., respectively within and on the margins of mixed beech and oak woodlands. In both cases, traces of the production of charcoal and the oldest traces of pre-existing wooded pastures were testified by the presence of pollarded beech (at Idubaltza) and oak trees (at Beorlatza), the latter with specimens dating back at least four or five centuries (Figure 12.7). The transformation of ancient wooded pastures in forests related to charcoal production also suggests a change in the forms of exploitation of commons, most likely in their access rights (as already documented in the Ligurian Apennines by the end of the nineteenth century; Stagno et al., 2017).

A large rectangular enclosure housing at least two buildings was documented at Beorlatza. The enclosure appears to have been associated with the use of a wooded pasture (oak) and had already been abandoned when the beech woodland grew and the production of charcoal had begun. The test pits that were conducted (300 and 500) did not permit confirmation of the inhabitation of the structures and suggested that the settlement had only one, relatively recent, phase of use. At Beorlatza, archival documentation testified the existence of *majada* (pastoral sites for housing of livestock at night) in 1709 within a *robleda* which could indicate oak pasture.[8]

The site at Idubaltza is testified by both a structure and an area filled with an abundance of dumped ceramic material. The structure shows at least two occupation phases: the more recent is testified by an enclosure (perhaps from the first half of the twentieth century) built on the collapsed walls of an older building. The excavation was conducted outside the structure. The latter investigations permitted the collection of abundant pottery fragments (table and cooking wares) which dated between the fifteenth and seventeenth centuries as well as a significant quantity of tiles. It is possible to hypothesize that the materials found in the test pit came from an older structure (which potentially served a domestic purpose). In the same area, other traces of possible structures were identified which could suggest the presence of a settlement of a certain size, although the latter cannot be definitively linked with pastoral use.

At Goano (c. 800 m a.s.l.), a cattle shed showing at least three phases of use and for which the oldest characteristics potentially date to the seventeenth and eighteenth centuries was uncovered in an ancient (oak-) wooded pasture. Today, the structure is the property of the municipality of Zalduondo and is used to house cattle owned by the municipality's inhabitants when they overnight in the pasture. It is likely that the structure also had the same function in the past and was related to Skorta in the hamlet. Skorta was another shed that was intended for keeping the 'foreign' cattle that were in Zalduondo at sunset. These animals were seized and returned to the owners only after the payment of a fine.[9]

LOOKING FOR INDICATORS OF SHORT- AND LONG-DISTANCE TRANSHUMANT MOVEMENTS

In this paper I have discussed different forms of (short- and long- distance) transhumance and different ways to reconcile them in relation to the management of common lands. Further attempts were made to demonstrate how the archaeological evidence could serve to distinguish between short- and long-distance transhumance.

I have tried to discuss this topic through different sources and from different (albeit related) points of view with an eye to determining which kind of knowledge could best serve to interpret the archaeological evidence and to best characterize the environmental resources management practices related to those systems. Some examples helped me in this discussion.

Figure 12.8. Beorlatza: a. Charcoal kiln site. b. Ancient pollarded oak

The Briga example was useful as means to exemplify how different economic interests could be related to short- and long-distance transhumance movements and to show the strategies by which they were maintained as well as the local conflicts related thereto. The Mesco study helped to show that the existence of these strategies could be detected in the (present and past) vegetation and how this fact could suggest a complex articulation of society and its jurisdictional rules. The question of how to identify the markers of the different animal movements which could suggest different economic strategies is addressed also through the examples of *seles* and *crèste*. The presence of these features in different areas facilitated the conciliation of short- and long-distance transhumant movements. At the same time, they became the archaeological markers of the co-existence of these movements. From a certain point of view, the fact that different movement co-existed underscores the importance of the transfer of fertility and the organization of animal husbandry. This example helped to introduce the main question of the paper: the archaeological markers of husbandry and their social interpretation. The topic was discussed further via case studies in Basque Country. By this means this article made the attempt to demonstrate how the archaeological evidence could highlight transformations which not only suggest changes in the husbandry strategies, social relationships and economic circuits, but also reveal the complexity of the different models.

A survey conducted in the Ligurian Apennines on specific seasonal settlements, the function of which was linked to local mountain grazing between the seventeenth and twentieth centuries (and the location of which changed as a result of agricultural evolution), made it possible to develop ideas relating to the archaeology of *monticazione* (Stagno, 2016b). Research has suggested that a number of indicators could potentially be used to distinguish settlements related to *monticazione* from those related to long-distance transhumance. For example, structures related to *monticazione* do not contain permanent hearths or cooking wares since they were intended for temporary, daytime use. Furthermore, cheese production facilities which are well documented in seasonal settlements used in long-range transhumance are absent from *monticazione* structures. Milk was instead collected daily and brought down to the village (usually about 5 km away) to be made into cheese.

For the Basque Country, it has been noted that current spatial organization of the Alava area suggests mountain resources were exploited according to vertical models of movement – compatible with the practice of *ganaderia estante*. The archaeological evidence found to date appears to confirm such usage (which is still current) and suggests a possible relationship between local husbandry with temporary mountain cultivation (testified by vegetable enclosures) and the more consistent presence of wooded pastures. Moreover, temporary cultivation is absent in areas that are known to relate to long-distance transhumance, as in the case of Urbía (where instead gardens and fences are documented in well-defined spaces and neighbouring summer settlements). Current analysis and future investigations of the terracing at Malla (where the two models of exploitation were documented at different times) could provide confirmation of this hypothesis. Initial work has nonetheless highlighted the importance of using not just buildings to distinguish between pastoral systems, but also the organization and use of space around them (which in the case studies investigated here are all related to collective lands).

At the same time, fieldwork has shown that developing rigid models of pastoral systems is problematic. Some archaeological indicators of mountain pastoralism, such as enclosures for the collection of cattle and manure, are common to both long- and short-distance transhumance, and there are also differences amongst mountainous sites associated with short-distance local husbandry. While hay barns are characteristic of Ligurian *monticazione* settlements – hay saved on the terraces being stored before it was taken down to feed wintering cattle – they are not found in the Basque Country. Here, hay barns are only documented within the permanent settlements. This difference is an example of the variability which is encountered in the organization of space around mountainous pastoral sites in southern Europe.

It is important to emphasize that the two movements were related to two very different farming models. If short-distance transhumance was mainly linked to a type of local husbandry and was integrated into a single cycle with the function of fertility transfer (by manure), then long-distance transhumance is linked to broader economic cycles and fertility transfers over long ranges. Many models and variables can exist, and this is a first attempt to reflect on the possibility of serial archaeological indicators that could assist in the production of a better characterization of mountainous pastoral activities. In addition, such an approach can help to clarify how these different movements co-existed within various historical transformations and how these influenced the organization of collective lands and resources through continuous conflicts and negotiation processes.

ACKNOWLEDGEMENTS

This paper is based on the first results of a multidisciplinary research project called 'ARCHIMEDE – Archaeology of Commons: Cultural Heritage and Material Evidence of a Disappearing Europe' funded by the European Union, People – Seventh Framework Program (Marie Curie IEF, G.A. 630095). The project is led by the Research Group on Cultural Heritage and Landscape (ehu.eus/en/web/culturalheritage) of the University of the Basque Country (Spain) in collaboration with the Laboratory of Environmental Archaeology and History (www.lasa.unige.it) at the University of Genoa (Italy) and the Laboratory FRAMESPA-Terrae of the Université de Toulouse Jean Jaurès (http://framespa.univ-tlse2.fr/; Terrae: http://terrae.univ-tlse2.fr/). The investigations in Gipuzkoa were co-funded through the *Aizkorriko gune kalifikatuetan miaketa arkeologikoak/Prospecciones arqueológicasen espacios calificados de Aizkorri* project and were funded by the Diputación foral de Gipuzkoa (Spain).

Field surveys in the Basque Country were carried on with the collaboration of Carlos Tejerizo Garcia and Richard Santeramo of GIPyPAC and with students from the University of the Basque Country (Gonzalo Ibarzabal, Aitziber González García, Francisco Gómez Diez, Maialen Galdos Jauregi, Josu Santamarina) and a PhD student from the Archaeology Laboratory of Environmental Archaeology and History at the University of Genoa (Valentina Pescini). The sampling and laboratory analyses were conducted by researchers and PhD students from the University of the Basque Country: Begoña Hernández Beloqui (pollen), Marta Portillo (phytoliths), Amaya Echazarreta Gallego (NPPs) and Arantzazu Pérez Fernández (physicochemical analysis). The author is indebted to all those that assisted and contributed to this research.

NOTES

* Marie Curie Research Fellow, Grupo de investigación Patrimonio y Paisajes Culturales, Departamento de Geografía, Prehistoria y Arqueología, University of the Basque Country, UPV/EHU, Calle Tomás y Valiente sn, 01005, Vitoria-Gasteiz (Spain); Laboratorio di Archeologia e Storia Ambientale (Dafist-Distav), Università degli Studi di Genova; email: annamaria.stagno@ehu.eus

1 See Ingold (2008) for a general perspective and a critical reflection on the study history and Grossi (1977) for the historical-juridical issues. For a European overview, collective works such as Lana & Congost (2007), Rodgers et al. (2011), Alfani & Rao (2011), De Moor et al. (2002) are useful.

2 For a summary of the studies in this area, and more in the northwest of the Iberian Peninsula in general, with particular reference to the medieval period, see Fernández Mier and Quirós Castillo (2015) and Quirós Castillo (2011) (specifically on abandoned medieval villages studied in this area).

3 Archivo histórico Municipal de Salvatierra – Agurain, 0198, n° 25, 0199, n° 29.

4 Oral source: J.M. (70 years old) of Oñati interviewed at Zulatza (Oñati) in his *chabola*, at 16/06/2015.

5 Oral sources: F. (83 years old) and L. (65 years old) of Zegama interviewed at Lizarreta (Urbía) in the pastures on 18/06/2015.

6 AR15-bone - UE 30117: 900 ± 50 BP, INFN Labec – Florence, bone, Calibrated Age (95% level of probability) 1020 – 1225 AD; AR15 - UE 30212: 1260 ± 60 BP, INFN Labec – Florence, charcoal, Calibrated Age (95% level of probability) 655 – 895 AD.

7 *Cesión de la sexta parte de los bienes de Lope Ruiz de Lazarraga a favor de su hermana María de Lazarraga*, among which 35 seles (Archivo de la casa de Plaza-Lazarraga [Duque de Sotomayor]), Seles, Leg.1, Exp.3. I wish to thanks to Iosu Etxezarraga and Álvaro Aragón Ruano for the hint.

8 Archivo Histórico Municipal de Zalduondo, 10, 3.

9 Oral Source: Gustavo Fernando Fernández Villate (49 years old at 2015), Mayor of Zalduondo, interviewed in 05/10/2015, at Zalduondo.

REFERENCES

Agirre García, J., Moraza Barea, A. & Mujika Alustiza, J.A. 2009. Los elementos físicos como reivindicación del territorio y de sus frutos en los espacios de montaña. *Munibe Suplemento*, 32:286–313.

Alberdi, J.C. 2004. Usos ganaderos en espacios comunales: actividad básica en la sostenibilidad de los medios de la montaña basca. *Estudios Vascos*, 20:11–34.

Aldezabal A., Moragues L., Odriozola I. & Mijangos I. 2015. Impact of grazing abandonment on plant and soil microbial communities in an Atlantic mountain grassland. *Applied Soil Ecology* (November 2015). doi:10.1016/j.apsoil.2015.08.013 (accessed 15 December 2015).

Alfani, G. & Rao, R. eds. 2011. *La gestione delle risorse collettive. Italia settentrionale, secoli XII–XVIII*. Milano: Franco Angeli.

Altuna, J., Armendáriz, A., Barrio, L. Del, Etxeberria, F., Mariezkurrena, K., Peñalver, J. & Zumalabe, F. 1990. Carta Arqueológica de Gipuzkoa I. Megalitos. *Munibe (Antropologia-Arkeologia)* Supl. 7:1–508.

Altuna, J., Barrio, L. Del, & Mariezkurrena, K. 2002. Carta Arqueológica de Gipuzkoa. Megalitos. Nuevos descubrimientos 1990-2001. *Munibe (Antropologia-Arkeologia)* Supl. 15:1–38.

Aragón Ruano, Á. 2001. *Bosque guipuzcoano en la Edad Moderna: Aprovechamiento, ordenamiento legal y conflictividad*. Donostia: Aranzadi.

Aragón Ruano, Á. 2003. Gestión, uso y aprovechamiento de comunales y parzonerías en la Edad Moderna: el ejemplo de Entzia y Urbía. In: E. Pastor Díaz de Garayo, ed. *Sortaldeko Lautada historian zehar: gaurko tresnez baliatuz, joandako denborak argitu. La Llanada oriental a través de la historia: claves desde el presente para comprender nuestro pasado*. Vitoria-Gasteiz: Diputación Foral de Álava, pp. 81–91.

Aragón Ruano, Á. 2013. Guided Pollards and the Basque Woodland during the Early Modern Age. In: I.D. Rotherham, ed. *Cultural Severance and the Environment. The Ending of Traditional and Customary Practice on Commons and Landscapes Managed in Common*. Dordrecht: Springer, pp. 147–60.

Azpiazu, J.A. 2011. Los Bienes Comunales en el pasado y el presente del País Vasco. In: P. Nervi, ed. *Archivio Scialoja-Bolla. Annali di Studio sulla proprietà collettiva 1.2011*. Torino: Giuffré, pp. 65–89.

Brisebarre, A.-M. 1992. Pratiche pastorali collettive in Lozère: proprietà indivise e notti di concimazione. In: D. Moreno & O. Raggio, *Risorse collettive*, pp. 873–84.

Cevasco. R. 2007. *Memoria Verde. Nuovi spazi per la geografia*. Reggio Emilia: Diabasis.

Cevasco, R., Moreno, D. & Hearn, R. 2015. Biodiversification as an historical process: a plea for the application of historical ecology in bio-cultural diversity research. *Biodiversity and Conservation*, 24(12):3167–83.

Charbonnier, P., Couturier, P., Follain, A. & Fournier P. eds. 2007. *Espaces collectifs et utilisations collectives des campagnes du Moyen Age à nos jours*. Clermont Ferrand: Presses universitaires Blaise Pascal.

Conesa M. 2012. *D'herbe, de terre et de sang. La Cerdagne du XIVe au XIXe siècle*. Perpignan: Presses Universitaries de Perpignan.

Delano Smith, C. 1979. *Western Mediterranean Europe: A Historical Geography of Italy, Spain and Southern France since the Neolithic*. London: Academic Press.

De Moor, M., Shaw-Taylor, L. & Warde, P., eds. 2002. *The Management of Common Land in North West Europe, c. 1500–1850*. Turnhout: Brepols.

Díaz De Durana, J.R. 2001. Para una historia del monte y del bosque en la Guipuzcoa bajomedieval: los seles. Titularidad formas de cesión y de explotación. *Anuario de Estudios Medievales*, 31(1):49–73.

Díaz de Durana, J.R. & Fernández de Larrea, J.A. 2002. Economía ganadera y medio ambiente. Guipúzcoa y el Noreste de Navarra en la Baja Edad Media. *Historia Agraria*, 27:43–64.

Fernández Mier, M. 2010. Campos de cultivo en la Cordillera Cantábrica. La Agricultura en zonas de montaña. In: H. Kirchne, ed. *Por una arqueología agraria. Perspectivas de investigación sobre espacios de cultivo en las sociedades medievales hispánicas*. Oxford: British Archaeological Reports International Series, pp. 41–59.

Fernández Mier, M., López Gómez, P. & González Álvarez, D. 2013. Prácticas ganaderas en la cordillera cantábrica. Aproximación multidisciplinar al estudio de las áreas de pasto en la Edad Media. *Debates de Arqueología Medieval*, 3:167–219.

Fernández Mier, M. & Quirós Castillo J.A. 2015. El aprovechamiento de los espacios comunales en el noroeste de la Península Ibérica entre el período romano y medieval. *Il capitale culturale*, XII:689–718.

Gabba, E. & Pasquinucci, M. 1979. *Strutture agrarie e allevamento transumante nell'Italia Romana*. Pisa: Giardini.

Gaio, S. 2014. Archeologia e storia di un fienile della valle di Primiero (TN). Un approccio pluridisciplinare allo studio di un contesto insediativo rurale (sec. XV–XX). In: A.M. Stagno, ed. *Montagne incise. Pietre incise. Archeologia delle risorse nelle montagne europee. Archeologia Postmedievale, 17*, pp. 369–80.

Gandiaga, B., Ugalde, T. & Urteaga Artigas, M.M. 1989. Prospecciones arqueológicas en Urbía: yacimientos catalogados en las campañas de 1988 y 1989. *Kobie (serie paleoantropología)*, XVIII:123–66.

Gassiot Balbé, E. & García Casas, D. 2014. Histories d'ovelles i pastures. Arqueoiogia deis darrers segies de ramaderiaa l'alta muntanya. *L'arqueologia del món modern i contemporani*, 78:452–70.

Ingold, T. 2000. The temporality of the landscape. In: T. Ingold, ed. *The Perception of the Environment: Essays in Livelihood, Dwelling and Skill*. London: Routledge, pp. 189–208.

Ingold, A. 2008. Les sociétés d'irrigation: bien commun et action collective. *Entreprise et histoire*, 50(1):19–35.

Ingold, A. 2011. Écrire la nature. De l'histoire sociale à la question environnementale? *Annales. Histoire, Sciences Sociales*, 66:11–29.

Kirchner, H. ed. 2010. *Por una arqueología agraria. Perspectivas de investigación sobre espacios de cultivo en las sociedades medievales hispánicas*. Oxford: British Archaeological Reports International Series.

Lana Berasáin, J.M. & Congost Colomer, R. eds. 2007. *Campos cerrados, debates abiertos. Análisis histórico de la propiedad en Europa (siglos XVI–XIX)*. Pamplona: Universidad Pública de Navarra.

LASA. 2003. *Siti Lemmen e Cacinagora (Riomaggiore, SP). Studi e ricerche finalizzati all'identificazione delle dinamiche storiche dell'area, effetti delle pratiche agro-silvopastorali e dinamiche post-colturali della copertura vegetale*. Final Report. DipTeRis, DiSMeC, LASA, Università degli Studi di Genova.

Le Couedic, M. 2010. *Les pratiques pastorales d'altitude dans une perspective ethnoarchéologique. Cabanes, troupeaux et territoires pastoraux pyrénéens de la préhistoire à nos jours.* Unpublished PhD Thesis, Université François Rabelais de Tours.

Lindholm, K.J., Sandström, E. & Ekman, A.K. 2013. The archaeology of the commons. *Journal of Archaeology and Ancient History*, 10:2–49.

Maggi, R., De Pascale, A., Guido, M.A, Montanari, C. & Moreno, D. 2006. Per un'archeologia delle Cinque Terre. In: S. Musso & G. Franco, eds. *Guida agli interventi di recupero dell'edilizia diffusa nel Parco Nazionale delle Cinque Terre*, Venezia: Marsilio Editore, pp. 45–60.

Mattone, A. & Simbula P.F., eds. 2001. *La pastorizia mediterranea. Storia e diritto secoli XI–XX*. Roma: Carocci.

Moreno, D. 1990. *Dal documento al terreno. Storia e archeologia dei sistemi agro-silvo-pastorali*. Bologna: Il Mulino-Ricerche.

Moreno, D. 1993. Storia delle risorse ambientali e forme di appropriazione. In: F. Carletti, ed. *Demani civici e risorse ambientali*. Napoli: Jovene, pp. 61–76.

Moreno, D. & Raggio, O. 1990. The making and fall of an intensive pastoral land-use-system. Eastern Liguria, 16–19th centuries, in Archeologia della pastorizia nell'Europa meridionale. In: R. Maggi, R. Nisbet & R. Barker, eds. *Atti della Tavola Rotonda internazionale (Chiavari 22–24 settembre 1989), Rivista di Studi Liguri*, LVI:193–217.

Moreno, D. & Raggio, O. eds. 1992. Risorse collettive. *Quaderni Storici*, XXVII(3):613–924.

Oosthuizen, S. 2013. *Tradition and Transformation in Anglo-Saxon England: Archaeology, Common Rights and Landscape*. London: Bloomsbury Academic.

Palmero, B. 1992. Comunità, creditori e gestione del territorio. Il caso di Briga nel XVII secolo. In: D. Moreno & O. Raggio, eds. 1992. Risorse collettive. *Quaderni Storici*, XXVII(3):739–58.

Pastor Díaz de Garayo, E. in press. Aistra en el registro escrito: la historia de una comunidad. In: J.A. Quirós Castillo, ed. *Arqueología del campesinado medieval*. Aistra (Álava).

Pescini, V. & Gabellieri, N. eds. 2015. *Biografia di un paesaggio rurale Storia, geografia e archeologia ambientale per la riqualificazione di Case Lovara (promontorio del Mesco – La Spezia)*. Sestri Levante: Oltre Edizioni.

Pozuelo Rodriguez, F. 2010. *Fuentes documentales medievales del País Vasco 141, Archivo Municipal de Salvatierra-Agurain. Tomo IV (1501–1521). Apéndice 1259–1469*. Donostia: Eusko Ikaskuntza.

Quirós Castillo, J.A. 2011. Los paisajes altomedievales en el País Vasco, 500–900. De la desarticulación territorial a la emergencia de los condados. In: J.A. Quirós Castillo, ed. *Vasconia en la Alta Edad Media 450–1000*. Vitoria-Gasteiz: Universidad del País Vasco, pp. 29–54.

Quiròs Castillo, J.A., 2012. *Arqueología del campesinado medieval: la aldea de Zaballa*. Bilabo: Universidad del Pais Vasco.

Raggio, O. 1992. Forme e pratiche di appropriazione delle risorse. Casi di usurpazione delle comunaglie in Liguria. *Quaderni Storici*, 79:135–69.

Raggio, O. 1995. Norme e pratiche. Gli statuti campestri come fonti per una storia locale. *Quaderni Storici*, 88:155–94.

Raggio, O. 2007. Annotazioni su boschi, giurisdizioni e definizione delle risorse. In: M. Ambrosoli & F. Bianco, eds. *Comunità e questioni di confini in Italia settentrionale (XVI–XIX sec.)*. Milano: Franco Angeli, pp. 83–96.

Rendu, C. 2003. *La montagne d'Enveig, un estive pyrénéenne dans la longue durée*. Perpignan: Ed. Du Trabucaire.

Rodgers, C.P., Straughton, E.A., Winchester, A.J.L. & Pieraccini, M. 2011. *Contested Common Land: Environmental Governance Past and Present*. London: Earthscan.

Rotheram I.D., ed. 2013. *Cultural Severance and the Environment: The Ending of Traditional and Customary Practice on Commons and Landscapes Managed in Common*. Dordrecht: Springer.

Stagno, A.M. 2016a. Archaeology of Commons: a multidisciplinary approach to the reconstruction of multiple uses and conflicts on European uplands. In: *Third International Landscape Archaeology Conference 2014 Proceedings*, pp. 1–17. doi:10.5463/lac.2014.21

Stagno, A.M. 2016b. Seasonal settlements and husbandry resources in Ligurian Apennines (17th–20th centuries). In: J. Collis, M. Pearce & F. Nicolis, eds. *Summer farms: Seasonal Exploitation of the Uplands from Prehistory to the Present*. Sheffield Archaeological Monographs 16. Sheffield: J.R. Collis Publications, pp. 73–96.

Stagno, A.M. in press. *Lo spazio locale dell'archeologia rurale. Risorse ambientali e insediamenti (XIV–XX secolo)*. Firenze.

Stagno, A.M., Beltrametti, G., & Parola, C. 2017. Le charbonnage dans l'Apennin ligure (Italie): sites, pratiques, ressources (XIXème–XXème siècle). In: S. Paradise Grenouillet & S. Burri, eds. *Charbonnage, charbonniers, charbonnières. État des connaissances et perspectives de recherche*. Limoges, in press.

Tigrino, V., Beltrametti, G., Rocca, M. & Stagno, A.M. 2013. Terre collettive e insediamenti in alta val Trebbia (Appennino Ligure): la definizione della località tra Sette e Novecento. In: P. Nervi, ed. *Archivio Scialoja-Bolla. Annali del Centro studi e documentazione sui demani civici e le proprietà collettive 1. 2013*, Milano: Giuffré editore, pp. 105–56.

Ugalde, T., Urteaga Artigas, M.M. & Gandiaga, B. 1992–1993. Prospecciones arqueológicas en Urbía: yacimientos catalogados en las campañas de 1990 y 1991. *Kobie*, XX:57–85.

Urzainki Mikeleiz, M.A. 2007. *Parzonerías y parques naturales: comunidades de montes en Gipuzkoa: las Parzonerías*. Donostia-San Sebastián: Universidad de Deusto.

Viader, R. & Rendu, C., eds. 2014. *Cultures Temporaires et féodalité. Les cycles culturaux et l'appropriation du sol dans l'Europe Médiévale et Moderne*. Toulouse: Presses Universitaires du Mirail.

CHAPTER 13

Transhumance in the mountains of northern Tuscany (Italy)

MASSIMO DADÀ

INTRODUCTION

The "Da Canossa a Luni" project began in 2008, promoted by the University of Pisa and supported by various other institutions (the Superintendency for Archaeological Heritage in Tuscany and Emilia Romagna, the National Park of the Tuscan-Emilian Apennines, the provinces of Reggio Emilia and Massa Carrara and a variety of other municipalities). The project area is comprised of a transect that connects the Apennines of Reggio Emilia with the Tyrrhenian coast between Luni and Massa and which crosses the northern Apuan Alps, mostly within the historic region called Lunigiana (Figure 13.1). The main objective of the project involves the study of mobility (and particularly transhumance) within and between this mountainous region from late antiquity to the medieval period.

The project survey covered 1,148 hectares of the mountainous zone between Emilia Romagna and Tuscany (northern Italy) and allowed for the identification of the medieval hospice of San Lorenzo di Centocroci at which a third excavation season took place in 2015 (Dadà & Biggi, 2015a). Over the course of our research, we came to the realization that a very important aspect of it (which also, unfortunately, lacked preserved historical records) involved the pastoral activities linked to transhumance. Therefore, we began to revise the data we already had and attempted to gather those clues that were available about this practice in the medieval period.

This article is meant to report on research that is still ongoing and which, despite the difficulties and uncertainties involved in it, has nonetheless paved the way to a little-explored field of inquiry, adopting precise regressive analyses and the new examination of certain archaeological data.

SOME QUESTIONS ABOUT TRANSHUMANCE IN NORTHERN TUSCANY

Notes on the state of research

In recent years, transhumance has often been a subject of research. If one examines the Alps alone, Francesco Carrer outlined a number of outstanding questions (Carrer, 2013), while F. Cambi, G. De Venuto and R. Goffredo (2015) collected a number of essays in a book that takes into account the most recent research on pastoralism in Italy from the prehistoric to the medieval period. The recent publication of the e-book by Alessandra Martinelli (2014) offers a wide examination of transhumance in Tuscany from medieval times until today. The article therein by Lucia Giovannetti (2014) on the mountain near Lucca provides an exceptional attempt at researching transhumance through use of the material sources, among other things. By contrast, research of similar ilk in Tuscany can be better compared to pioneering attempts which draw necessarily generic interpretations. Such studies take little account of differences in time and space and also rely only seldom on excavation data. Even the important research conducted by Lina Pecini (2014) had to face up to a serious paucity of information which led the author to analyze and interpret the practice of transhumance across broad time spans (from the thirteenth to the twentieth century), comparing sources from very distant times.

Notes on discontinuity in the medieval period

The 'legend of the wildman' (variants of which can be found throughout Lunigiana), tells of a beastly, cave-dwelling creature who taught the locals how to make cheese, ricotta and butter. In Augusto C. Ambrosi's interpretation (1956), the folk-tale is seen as the transposition of a knowledge transfer that may have occurred between ethnic groups potentially with different physical traits and one, the new dominant population, which may have recently migrated to the area (Ferrando Cabona & Crusi, 1988: 57). The legend may, therefore, represent an echo of the distant origins of dairy conservation a *conditio sine qua non* for transhumance. In any case, the medieval historian must face the pressing matter of a potential 'secondary origin' for long-range transhumance (that is, the possible reintroduction of the practice following a presumed discontinuation during the early medieval period).

© 2018 European Association of Archaeologists

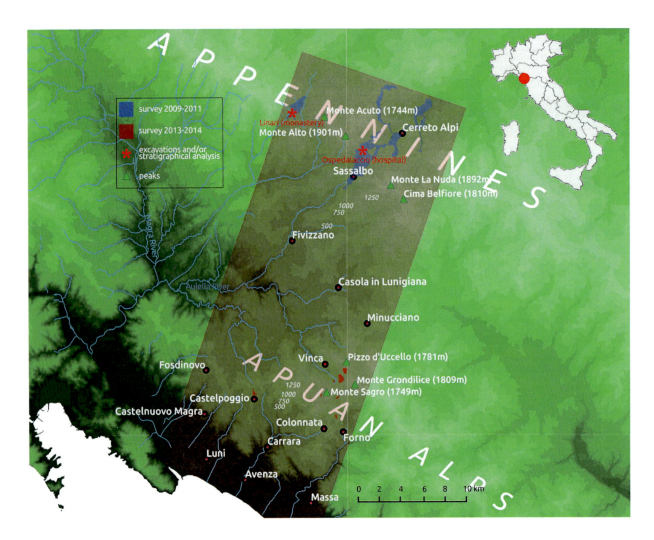

Figure 13.1. Map of the research area

The underestimation of transhumance in written and (especially) material records from Roman times to the medieval period – to which scholars have referred as "pastoral invisibility" (Carrer, 2013: 52) – both drives archaeologists to reflect upon the diagnostic indicators of pastoralism and to also guard historians from arguments *ex silentio*. In accordance with these considerations, Emilio Gabba expressed his conviction regarding the substantial continuity of transhumance during the medieval period (Gabba, 1985: 375). On the contrary, in his study on the Apennine region of Valva (Sulmona), Chris Wickham – suggested a rather abrupt decline (particularly during the Langobard age), at least in terms of long-range transhumance (Wickham, 1982: 54–57). Saverio Russo and Francesco Violante attribute this interruption to the uncertainty and precariousness of travel that resulted from the fragmentation of power during the early medieval period; they date the pivotal recovery of what they refer to as "great transhumance" to the twelfth century (Russo & Violante, 2009: 158–59).

While the first question we must answer regarding transhumance in the medieval period, therefore, regards the matter of its continuity, at the same time we must ask ourselves whether we can also presume that a certain degree of uniformity characterized the entire Apennine region or whether there was a great degree of variability in the practice throughout time and space. Such variability may also have had repercussions on those persons involved in horizontal transhumance; we know that it was often mountain people who relocated during the Contemporary Age (in what is called "reverse transhumance") (Dell'Omodarme, 1988: 947–48). However, for what concerns the medieval period and the Modern Age, this aspect would call for an exact inquiry which would take larger-scale economic, political and commercial changes into consideration.

Indeed, northern Tuscany was certainly subject to both horizontal and vertical transhumance (at least from the late medieval through to modern times; Pecini, 2014), suited as it is to housing large flocks, especially in the Apennine and Apuan regions. Even though marble extraction in the Apuan quarries had begun anew, it is not very surprising that Carrara's premier tax income during the fifteenth century derived from the transit of flocks through the passes that crossed the northernmost Apuan slopes leading to the Apennine pastures (Pelù, 1993: 120; Figure 13.2).

The Apennines and the Apuan Alps: so close and yet so different

Thus far, I have made little distinction when speaking of the Apuan Alps and the Apennines. Although they are geographically quite close, the two mountain ranges have extremely different geological, morphological and climactic features.

The rocky mass of the Apuan Alps occupies the far northwestern region of Tuscany and faces the Ligurian-Thyrrhenian Sea. Its unique lithology and harsh morphology cannot be found elsewhere in peninsular Italy and are, therefore, very different from the features of the nearby Apennine Range. As most of the rocks are of sedimentary origin (some, such as limestone and dolomite formed in marine environments), its rocks often underwent metamorphic processes leading to the formation of the famous white Carrara marble. Although the Apuan Alps are a modest range, at just below 2,000 m high, the technical definition of 'Alp' is due to the complex corrugation processes and the intensity of the erosion that determined the formation of the deep valleys and very steep, imposing cliffs. The presence of carbonate rocks and strong precipitation led to intense karstic activity producing wells and extensive caves (such as the Antro del Corchia's over 50 km of tunnels; Carmignani et al., 2001). From a climatic perspective, its proximity to the sea causes intense rains, creates particular conditions for the superficial freezing of its snowbanks and generally gives rise to conditions which vary hugely from mountainside to mountainside (Pizziolo, 1994).

The appearance of the Apennine Range is quite different from the Apuan Alps; the Appenines feature heftier mountains, high-altitude passes (few stand lower than 1,200 m) and peaks which rise above 2,000 meters in the oriental portion alone. In this particular segment, "the mountain chain – mostly formed of boulders from the Oligocene Era – presents itself as compact and solid, with parallel spurs jutting from it perpendicularly that form deep valleys carved by the millennial action of groundwater on the Lunigiana side" (Ferrarini et al., 1990: 22–23; translation by author). From the remarkable vantage point gained by standing atop the northern Apuan peaks, the change in the features of the range across the Cisa Pass is very evident: while to the east of the pass the range is rocky and imposing, the western side is grassier, its crests softer and peaks lower. The 2,122 m elevation of Mount Cusna descends to Nuda's 1,896 m and from Alpe di Succiso's 2,017 m and Orsaro's 1,831 m to Mount Molinatico's 1,549 m, Gottero's 1,640 m and Zuccone's 1,423 m.

Long-range transhumance

Transhumant livestock mostly consisted of sheep, although cattle, goats, horses and pigs were also driven in this way. Flocks from the Tuscan-Emilian

Figure 13.2. Pastures on the Apuan Alps: the huts of Sagro (top, background the Tyrrhenian Sea)

Apennines might spend winters in the Po Valley, while many shepherds from the coastal lowlands were also known to take their flocks to the mountain pastures of the Apennine Range. The most well-known transport route involves the long-range transhumance towards Maremma. This last is exceptionally well documented in both archival sources and in the song, poems and tales of folklore (Russo & Violante, 2009: 157).

It must certainly have been an impressive event. Every autumn, hundreds of flocks would descend from the cliffs of the Tuscan and perhaps even Ligurian Apennines, traveling along small paths that eventually led to junctions along the main routes. At these places, long caravans likely formed that would eventually crowd into the 'mandrie' (areas reserved for transhumant shepherds in which they could milk their flocks, make cheese and trade their products for warm food and shelter for themselves and their animals). After journeys that lasted several weeks and covered up to 300 km, the vast, flat Maremma landscape finally appeared. Unfortunately, it was also marshy and infested with malaria. The reverse journey was taken in springtime; shepherds were pushed to depart as early as possible so as to not hinder sowing, while they were simultaneously tempted to delay their departures as long as possible in order to avoid encountering the snow still on the mountain slopes.

According to the testimony of Renzo Ricci (who engaged in transhumance with his father from 1951 to 1969), shepherds from the Luni valleys traditionally set off on 25 May in groups made up of various flocks which were under the guidance of a leader (an expert shepherd) who was tasked with planning, guiding the caravan's journey and also managing the financial aspects linked to using the mountain pastures. Shepherds traveled with their entire families and carried almost everything that could be needed for mountain life with them (particularly the tools used for cheese-making and the products need to produce wool) (Pecini, 2014: 141). A few donkeys traveled with the sheep, as did a number of pigs which were then sold before heading back into the valley in September. It should be noted that the presence of pigs (*turmae porcorum*) is a recurring feature which appears throughout the late medieval sources.

Modern transhumance routes through Tuscany are well known (Marcaccini & Calzolai, 2003). The last shepherds who witnessed the practice first-hand (i.e. before its sudden disappearance in the 1960s) have provided detailed accounts of the paths they took and the travel time the journeys required. Those accounts have been transferred to a GIS by Massimiliano Grava (2014). This transhumance map for Tuscany features routes, stopovers and significant toponyms.

One such important toponym is the term 'mandria' (from the Latin 'mandra,' or 'flock'), the name given to some rest areas used by shepherds from at least the fourteenth century (Del Giudice, 1992: 51–52). Their locations had to consider how much land could be covered by flocks in one day as well as the situations of other (perhaps less-specialized) shelters. We know very little about the physical appearance of ancient *mandria* sites, even though some features must have been indispensable (e.g. an enclosure to protect flocks and to facilitate milking and a sheltered space to sleep, light fires and make cheese and other dairy products). From an archaeological standpoint, however, features like those are not valid diagnostic indicators.

Up to this point, we still face the same chronological vagueness that was lamented previously. Henceforth, we will attempt to draw more accurate and contextual interpretations using the Apennine Range and the Apuan Alps respectively.

TWO ATTEMPTS AT DRAWING THE MEDIEVAL PERIOD INTO FOCUS

The medieval hospice of Centocroci and its connection to transhumance

The mountain pass currently known as Ospedalaccio (1,270 meters above sea level) was known by the name Centocroci (*in Alpe de Centum Crucibus*) in medieval times. As previously noted (Manari, 2002: 36), the toponym is a corruption of *centrum crucis* (the 'centre of the cross') and refers to the intersection of the four roads from Sassalbo, Camporaghena, Valbona and Cerreto Alpi. In other words, if we draw back a little further, Centocroci was a point of connection between the Po Valley, the continental area of Italy and the Tyrrhenian coast and peninsular (Mediterranean) Italy.

Records of this pass and the hospice are few in number. In 781, an imperial degree issued by Charlemagne (Mühlbacher, 1906: 325) describes the border of the diocese of Reggio Emilia as passing "*in Centrocrucis*," a precise reference which nonetheless makes no mention of either a potential settlement or ecclesiastic building. The toponym's features, however, allow us to speculate that not only was the pass frequented, but that a four-way intersection stood there.

The presence of a road crossing over the Apennines is also attested by another decree issued by Charlemagne in 781 (Mühlbacher, 1906: 323) in which Apollinare, Bishop of Reggio Emilia received property from the royal treasury (*fisco regio*) within the area which would become Cerreto Alpi, bordering with the Serchia River and with a road ascending to the border with *Tuscia* (Tuscany). This was no doubt an Apennine crossing which quite probably represented one of the branches of the four-way 'cross'.

The existence of a hospice by the pass is only attested to a few centuries later; a 'San Lorenzo in Alpibus' is listed among the holdings of Canossa Abbey in 1116 in a bull issued by Pope Paschal II. In 1137, it came to the S. Prospero Monastery as part of a decree issued by Lothair II. It is listed in the first tithes of 1296–1297 as one institution in the Luni dioceses which was except from taxes, after which it disappears from written records (Salvatori, 2001: 211). Sixteenth-century documents conserved at the State Archive in Florence in the "Ancient Boundary Maps" collection as well as a pastoral visit by the bishop of Reggio Emilia in 1596 attest to the eventual abandonment and ruin of the hospice and the houses by which it was surrounded.

Other mountain pass hospices in this section of the Apennine range, such as Tea (Quirós & Castillo, 2000), Pietra Colice (Benente, 2008: 35–38) and Linari (Dadà, 2012: 106–13), were probably abandoned in a more or less sudden manner during the fifteenth century, as was with the hospital of Pontremoli (Dadà & Fornaciari, 2006). Clearly, we are faced with a profound change in the customs pertaining to the shelter and assistance of travelers. Our impression is that the phenomenon must have been a general one which might perhaps have occurred as a result of the "road revolution" of the thirteenth century and the more important role played by municipalities in road network management (Patitucci Uggeri, 2002, pp. 40–46). This reached the peripheral areas only very belatedly, thereby allowing the survival of customs tied to pre-existing power dynamics for long after the ruling had been made effective.

The project's excavation (under the direction of the author and with the cooperation of the national park, the University of Pisa and the Superintendency for Archaeological Heritage) uncovered a small apsed chapel (only 16 square meters) which probably dated to the thirteenth century. The chapel included an area at the front which may have been arcaded as well as some rooms which leaned against the south portion. A number of burials in the surrounding ground attest to its prolonged use as a burial ground. In fact, this last might even predate the chapel and suggests the presence of an older place of worship that has yet to be identified. To the north, a small room built with reclaimed stones attests to a later occupation phase which overlaps the previous cemetery and which necessitates a new or otherwise different conceptualization of the cemetery as such. Inside, a number of hearths occupy a clay floor throughout which the tracks of small poles can be easily seen.

The excavation also detailed the different phases at the site: a *denaro scodellato* coin struck during the reign of Otto I or Otto II (AD 973–1002) noticeably moves up the site's medieval occupation, while the association of Maiolica Arcaica and vacuolar ceramics date the final phases of the complex's lifespan between the fourteenth and fifteenth centuries.

Apparently, little can be said about the hospice's link to pastoralism and transhumance. However, an in-depth (and perhaps slightly audacious) reading of certain elements might shed light on this "pastoral invisibility".

As mentioned previously, archaeological analysis in Lunigiana has led to an historical and social interpretation of pastoral activities that is rather generic and poorly differentiated across time and space. Lacking precise archaeological indicators, it is useful to apply a regressive method to the uses of soil, settlements and landscape from restricted territories and even individual sites (Mannoni & Giannichedda, 1991: 304, 307).

As a result of these indications during the 2014 Landscape Archaeology conference in Rome, I argued that the origin of the mountain prairies reclaimed by forests during the mid-twentieth century generally dates back at least to the late medieval period. Through detailed regressive analysis, aerial photographs, cadastral documents, historic cartography and archival sources have been shown to support this conclusion.

In the Centocroci case, we know that the presence of vast surrounding prairies were described in the sixteenth century as '*prati dell'ospedale*,' or hospice fields. The use of such areas would have been contended by shepherds from the nearby villages of Camporaghena, Succiso and Cerreto. We also know that the surrounding houses seem to have formed a small village, whose occupation was quite probably seasonal. As previously mentioned, the excavation revealed a hut which was dated to the eleventh/twelfth century and which featured a low stone base with a wooden elevation and a small fireplace. A room to the north of the chapel was also discovered which was built with reclaimed stones after the abandonment of the cemetery which probably dates from the fourteenth or fifteenth century (Figure 13.3). Many fires were lit inside the room and containers tied to interconnected poles in the ground seem to have been placed above them.

The extreme scarcity of artefacts and the limited extent of the excavations allow little more to be said. In my opinion, it is necessary to draw inferences from the information at hand in order to face down the invisibility of past pastoral actions. We know that there was horizontal transhumance towards the Apennines in the late medieval period. We can also attest to the presence of meadows around the hospice in at least the early modern period and we have found multiple fireplaces in a room of a small, high-altitude seasonal village. Taking these pieces of information into account, therefore, I think it likely that they were linked to pastoral activity.

Does pastoral activity follow the site's use as a hospice without overlapping? Can the existence of a sort of mountain pasture village coagulating around a hospice

192 *Massimo Dadà*

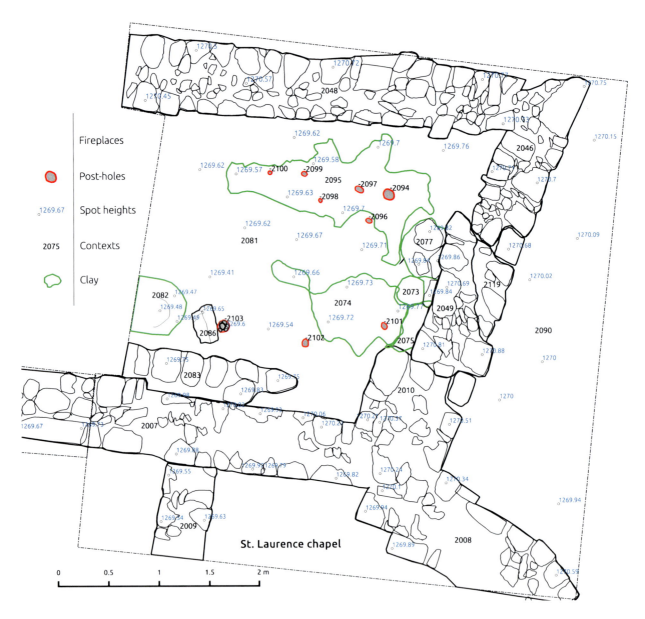

Figure 13.3. *Medieval hospice of Centocroci; lan of the northern room, probably used for pastoral activities in the fourteenth century*

be hypothesized, especially one whose nature was strongly linked to the sheltering of travelers, merchants and pilgrims? Did the hospital itself carry out a central function in transhumance instead or, more precisely, did it provide shelter for shepherds during the summer months? Such questions should surely be tackled in relation to other mountain pass hospices as well in an employment of the 'global approach' to the study of pastoral practices that was called for by Tiziano Mannoni and Enrico Giannichedda (1991: 307–10) some 25 years ago.

A versant-transhumance: the Vinca model

Vinca is a rather large medieval hamlet located in a generally steep valley at about 800 meters above sea level. It is surrounded by rocky peaks measuring up to 1,800 meters, which today feature a number of climbing routes that are well known among Italian practitioners. Its main economic activities during the late medieval period involved chestnut farming, some artisan activities (including the production of wool) and, especially, pastoralism. A memorandum from a meeting of Vinca's 'parliament' (in this case a council including the heads of each family) on 9 December 1576, testifies to the fact that many were absent, as they had left with their flocks. Of the 44 persons recorded absent, most were likely to have been shepherds (Boni & Ferrari, 2002: 165–66; Pecini, 2014: 144).

Today, the higher surrounding grassy slopes house hundreds of drystone huts: some isolated, others grouped in rather rarefied villages: the huts of Giovo, La Costa, Canal Busa, Sagro and Balzone. Although they were already present in the eighteenth century, these scattered villages grew noticeably during the nineteenth century. In the twentieth century, they were occupied by Vinca shepherds who moved their entire families to these tiny dwellings. During their occupancy, the inhabitants grew grain or potatoes in the nearby lands and also worked in the marble quarries. However, this occupation system cannot be applied retroactively, before high-altitude quarries began production in the late nineteenth century. The data attests to the existence of an extremely peculiar form of transhumance made possible by the particular features of the Apuan Alps and their proximity to the sea which dates far back in time.

The 'Comunalia' of Vinca (about 1,000 hectares of common pastures situated in a largely inaccessible rocky area) lays at the centre of a centuries-old dispute which began at least in the twelfth century and even saw the mediation of Nicolò Machiavelli in 1511. At the end of the fourteenth century, we know that people from Vinca brought their flocks to graze from November to March in the southern half of this area very close to Forno. The men from Forno grazed their flocks in the northern half from May to September (Baroni, 2001; Leverotti, 2001: 12–13, 66). This involved only very short-range transhumance from one part of the valley to the other, without any significant descents in altitude. It was made possible by the proximity of the sea insofar as the coastal climate proved beneficial in winter. This feature is not typical of a vertical transhumance, and I think it leads to a new category: a versant-transhumance which was probably widespread in the Apuan Alps (Figure 13.4).

Large terraced areas can be recognized around the pastoral villages which have the cadastral fragmentation typical of agricultural use and which can traditionally be contrasted with pastoralism. The case of the Giovo huts in the Vinca Valley suggests a system of coexistence; we know that flocks occupied the Forno mountainside from October to April. They probably reached the higher altitudes of the Vinca Valley in May in a place known as the 'Campo di Maggio' (i.e. May Field). We can assume, therefore, that from October to May the whole broad area below the Giovo Pass could be farmed with grains sown in autumn which would then be harvested in late spring. New crops would take their place in summer, finally allowing the flocks to fertilize the soil for the upcoming autumn sowing.

Our 2014 survey involved the area around Monte Sagro and allowed for the identification of more than 65 houses, all of which were made of drystone (Figure 13.5). Aerial photos of the same area from 1954 show woods, cultivated areas and pastures broadly comparable to Catasto Toscano in 1821. All the huts surveyed in the Vinca Valley which are mostly wooded at present were meadows in the first half of the twentieth century. The chronological analysis of these settlements allows us to date a progressive formation of higher-density areas after 1821. Previously, by contrast, individual buildings were more evenly distributed. Dating problems with these early buildings is especially due to little differentiation in the masonry techniques employed and to the absence of artefacts at the surface. After all, only stratigraphic excavations can provide more evidence for the medieval period.

CONCLUSION: WHAT WE DO AND DO NOT KNOW ABOUT MEDIEVAL TRANSHUMANCE IN NORTHERN TUSCANY

Given how much we know about modern and contemporary transhumance (especially from recent research), it is unfortunate that we do not know the extent to which that data is applicable to the medieval period. This is particularly notable with regards to the continuity or discontinuity of horizontal transhumance. Different existing interpretations are more likely to draw conclusions from specifically tailored archaeological surveys supported by archaeometric dating than from the written sources.

During this pioneering phase of archaeological research into medieval pastoralism, we must also tackle a great chronological uncertainty. In order to counterbalance the scarcity of older records, our search must begin in more recent times. It must, therefore, begin with those who personally witnessed transhumance during the mid-twentieth century. It is only from that point that researchers should approach the archival and cartographic sources of the modern era, etc., thereby attempting to connect the dots with what (little) we know about medieval times.

Although this trajectory relies on the supposed conservativeness of the pastoral world and/or on comparisons with records from other Italian regions, it nonetheless leaves a great chronological inaccuracy. As warned Mannoni and Giannichedda (1991), we run the risk of drawing generic and poorly differentiated interpretations that take little account of temporal and geographic variation and bounce between geographical determinism and the automatic transpositions of current practices in soil use, without a link to contemporary social and economic phenomena.

If not the central issue, then such shallow chronological knowledge is at least one of the main problems involved in the study of medieval transhumance in northern Tuscany. This state of affairs must be taken into account, especially when one considers the fact that the practice likely varied throughout time and space.

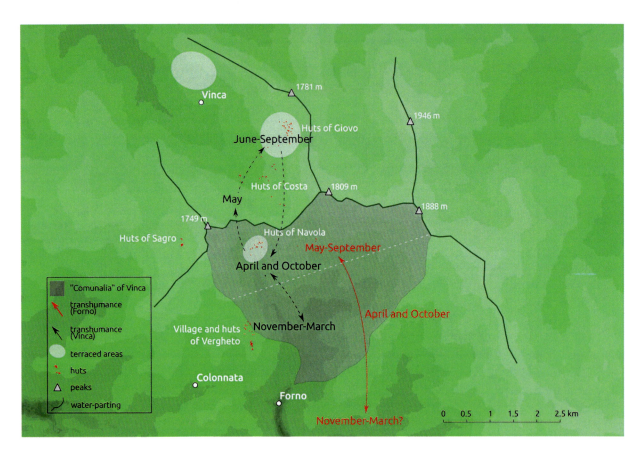

Figure 13.4. Map of the comunalia *of Vinca that shows fourteenth-century 'versant-transhumance'*

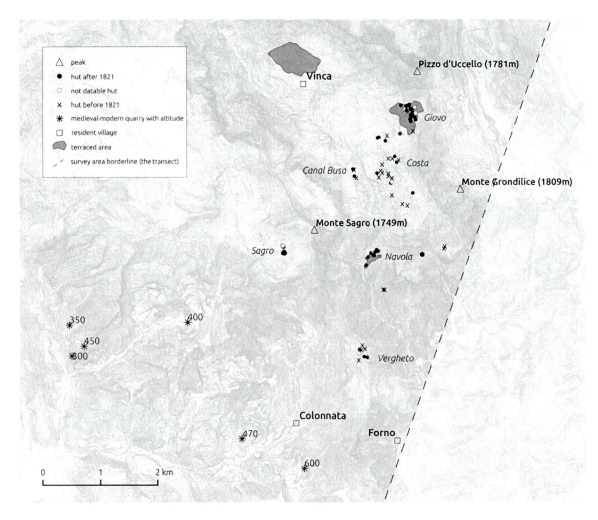

Figure 13.5. Pastoral huts around Monte Sagro

Generally, thirteenth to fifteenth-century records all attest to a consistent seasonal migration of flocks between the Apennine Range and the coastal plains. This seasonal migration then also carried on during the following centuries. We have no doubts about the existence of long- and short-range transhumance in northern Tuscany in the late medieval period, nor about the presence of locations for the sheltering of flocks. However, we face many uncertainties regarding the shepherds' provenance, the true import of the practice and about the very existence of high-altitude mountain pasture villages. Such doubts fade only from the fifteenth century onward (if not later). The Centocroci hospice may provide the first example of a pastoral settlement which may have featured a small communal workshop (the room north of the chapel). Unfortunately, the poor state of the evidence calls for cautious interpretation.

The Apuan Alps seem to pose an even more difficult case. While it is true that before the nineteenth century we must look to this mountain chain as a sort of suspended pastoral island (Dadà & Biggi, 2015b: 385–86), it is also true that seasonal migrations in the northern area seem to have been mostly carried out solely by local shepherds in what may be defined as short- or extremely short-range transhumance. Even Apuan shepherds practiced a form of versant-transhumance since medieval times, which in winter simply took advantage of the area's coastal exposure zones without significant descents in altitude. While probably not the only such case, the example from Vinca is well known because it regarded a clash between a community that had gradually developed a flourishing artisan activity (Forno) and a pastoral community (Vinca). It is around this settlement that many huts can be found whose existence from the nineteenth century onward was also linked to marble extraction, but which had previously been occupied solely by shepherds. Although some vague records date back to the sixteenth century, the information becomes more detailed from the eighteenth century onwards.

From interviews with the last first-hand witnesses we also know that the surrounding terraced fields were farmed in summer for the production of fodder, barley and rye. Were these cultures also employed in older times? Were those fields also sown in autumn and used for early harvest?

With the arrival of new funding, our research will next attempt to fine tune its archaeological investigations through on-site excavations aimed at analyzing every aspect of pastoral life and answering the many questions which remain. A particular area of focus will be on the chronological vagueness and the indeterminacy of the existing data (and the interpretations which are dependent upon them) which pose the foremost problem for the medieval period in this region of the world.

ACKNOWLEDGEMENTS

First, I wish to thank Sascha Biggi for his work on mobility in the Apennines. The "Da Canossa a Luni" project would not have been possible if not for the support and the funding provided by the National Park of the Tuscan-Emilian Apennines (Fausto Giovanelli, Giuseppe Vignali and Caterina Bertolini) and the cooperation of the Superintendency for Archaeological Heritage (Emanuela Paribeni), the University of Pisa (Letizia Gualandi) and SAP Società Archeologica (Agostino Favaro).

I would also like to express my gratitude to Stefano Di Meo for his work at the excavations at the hospice of Centocroci and to Dr. Marcella Giorgio, Dr. Antonio Fornaciari and Luca Parodi for their ongoing study about bones, pottery and coins.

Thanks also to Emma Pagano for the translation of this paper.

REFERENCES

Ambrosi, A.C. 1956. La leggenda dell'uomo selvatico in Lunigiana, abstract, *La Spezia.*

Baroni, F. 2001. Le questioni di confine: involontarie occasioni di conoscenza dei rapporti fra Stati. In *Carlo I Cybo Malaspina. Principe di Massa e Marchese di Carrara (1623–1662),* Atti del convegno di studi (Massa and Carrara, 8–11 November 2001). La Spezia: Luna Editore, pp. 115–27.

Benente, F. 2008. *San Nicolao di Pietra Colice. Introduzione agli scavi e all'area arche*ologica. Chiavari: Istituto Internazionale di Studi Liguri.

Boni, A. and Ferrari, B. 2002. *La Signoria di Firenze in Lunigiana: 1474, Statuti del comune medievale di Vinca,* Aulla: Centro Aullese di Ricerche e Studi Lunigianesi.

Cambi, F., De Venuto, G. & Goffredo, R. eds. 2015. *I pascoli, i campi, il mare. Paesaggi d'altura e di pianura in Italia dall'Età del Bronzo al Medioevo.* Bari: Edipuglia.

Carmignani, L., Conti, P., Disperati, L., Fantozzi P.L., Giglia, G. & Meccheri, M. 2001. *Carta geologica del Parco delle Alpi Apuane,* Seravezza: Parco Alpi Apuane.

Carrer, F. 2013. Archeologia della pastorizia nelle Alpi: nuovi dati e vecchi dubbi. *Preistoria alpina,* 47:49–56.

Dadà, M. 2012. *Archeologia dei monasteri in Lunigiana. Documenti e cultura materiale dalle origini al XII secolo,* Pisa: Pisa University Press.

Dadà, M. & Biggi, S. 2015a. Fivizzano (MS). Ospedale di Centocroci: le campagne 2010–2014. *Notiziario della Soprintendenza per i Beni Archeologici della Toscana,* 10:136–38.

Dadà, M. & Biggi, S. 2015b. Da Canossa a Luni. Archeologia della mobilità tra Appennino Tosco-Emiliano ed. Alpi Apuane. In P. Arthur & M.L. Imperiale, eds. *VII Congresso Nazionale di Archeologia Medievale (Lecce, 9–12 September 2015).* Firenze: All'Insegna del Giglio, pp. 384–88.

Dadà, M. & Fornaciari, A. 2006. L'ospedale medievale di San Giovanni a Pontremoli (Lunigiana, MS). *Archeologia Medievale,* 33:143–66.

Del Giudice, C.A. 1992. *Toponomastica storica della valle del Frigido (Massa di Lunigiana)*. Modena: Aedes Muratoriana.

Dell'Omodarme, O. 1988. La transumanza in Toscana nei secoli XVII e XVIII. *Mélanges de l'Ecole française de Rome. Moyen-age, Temps modernes*, 100(2):947–69.

Ferrando Cabona, I. & Crusi, E. 1988. *Storia dell'insediamento in Lunigiana. Alta valle Aulella*. Genova: SAGEP Editrice.

Ferrarini, E., Ronchieri, I. & Farina, A. 1990. L'ambiente. In: *La provincia di Massa-Carrara. Ambiente, storia, arte, tradizioni, economia*. Milano: Amilcare Pizzi Editore, pp. 11–42.

Gabba, E. 1985. La transumanza nell'Italia romana: evidenze e problemi. Qualche prospettiva per l'età altomedievale. In *L'uomo di fronte al mondo animale nell'Alto Medioevo*, Atti della XXXI Settimana di studio del Centro Italiano di Studi sull'Alto Medioevo (Spoleto, 7–13 aprile 1983). Spoleto: CISAM, pp. 373–89.

Giovannetti, L. 2014. Il paesaggio della memoria. In: A. Martinelli, ed. *Montagna e Maremma. Il paesaggio della transumanza in Toscana*. Pisa: Felici Editore. www.istosedizioni.com (accessed 20 January 2016).

Grava, M. 2014. *Nuova tecnologia per una pratica antica. La carta della transumanza*. In: A. Martinelli, ed. *Montagna e Maremma. Il paesaggio della transumanza in Toscana*. Pisa: Felici Editore. www.istosedizioni.com (accessed 20 January 2016).

Leverotti, F. 2001. *Massa di Lunigiana alla fine del Trecento. Ambiente, insediamenti, paesaggio, amministrazione*, Massa: Tipografia Grafica Apuana.

Manari, R.M. 2002. *Viabilità antica nella storia del crinale appenninico*, Reggio Emilia: Antiche Porte.

Mannoni, T. & Giannichedda, E. 1991. Alcuni dati archeologici sulla pastorizia nell'Appennino settentrionale tra protostoria e medioevo. In: R. Maggi, R. Nisbet & G. Barker, eds. *Atti della tavola rotonda internazionale Archeologia della pastorizia nell'Europa meridionale*. Bordighera: Istituto Internazionale di Studi Liguri, pp. 297–313.

Marcaccini, P. & Calzolai, L. 2003. *I percorsi della transumanza in Toscana*. Firenze: Polistampa.

Martinelli, A. ed. 2014. *Montagna e Maremma. Il paesaggio della transumanza in Toscana*. Pisa: Felici Editore. www.istosedizioni.com (accessed 20 January 2016).

Michelucci, M. (n.d.). L'istituto del campascuo e la sentenza del 1189 tra Vinca e Antona. www.demaniocivico.it/public/public/879.pdf (accessed 20 December 2015).

Mühlbacher, E. 1906. Pippini, Carlomanni & Caroli Magni Diplomata. In *Monumenta Germaniae Historica, Diplomata Karolinorum*, 1. Hannover: Hahnsche Buchhandlung.

Patitucci Uggeri, S. 2002. La viabilità di terra e d'acqua nell'Italia medievale. In: Patitucci Uggeri, S. ed. *La viabilità medievale in Italia. Contributo alla carta archeologica medievale*. Firenze: All'Insegna del Giglio, pp. 1–72.

Pecini, L. 2014. Transumanza e alpeggio in Lunigiana. Gestione degli spazi, fonti archivistiche e testimonianze orali. In: A. Martinelli, ed. *Montagna e Maremma. Il paesaggio della transumanza in Toscana*. Pisa: Felici Editore. www.istosedizioni.com (accessed 20 January 2016).

Pelù, P. 1993. Cenni sull'economia di Carrara e di Avenza nel Quattrocento. *Atti e memorie della Deputazione di storia patria per le antiche province modenesi*, 11(15):117–30.

Pizziolo, G. 1994. Le Apuane come sistema ambientale. I temi paesistici qualificanti. In: G. Pizziolo, ed. *I paesaggi della Alpi Apuane*. Firenze: Multigraphic, pp. 11–19.

Quiròs Castillo, J.A. ed. 2000. L'ospedale di Tea e l'archeologia delle strade nella valle del Serchio. Firenze: All'Insegna del Giglio.

Russo, S. & Violante, F. 2009. Dogane e transumanze nella penisola italiana tra XII e XVIII secolo. In M. Spedicato, ed. *Campi solcati. Studi in memoria di Lorenzo Palumbo*. Galatina: Edizioni Panico, pp. 157–72.

Salvatori, E. 2001. Presenze ospitaliere in Lunigiana. In *Atti del convegno Riviera di Levante tra Emilia e Toscana: un crocevia per l'ordine di San Giovanni (Rapallo-Chiavari, 9–12 september 1999)*. Genova: Istituto Internazionale di Studi Liguri, pp. 189–222.

Wickham, C. 1982. *Studi sulla società degli Appennini nell'Alto Medioevo. Contadini, signori e insediamento nel territorio di Valva (Sulmona)*. Bologna: CLUE.

CHAPTER 14

The role of marginal landscapes in understanding transhumance in southern Tuscany (twelfth–twentieth centuries AD)
A reverse perspective integrating ethnoarchaeological and historical approaches

EDOARDO VANNI AND DAVIDE CRISTOFERI

INTRODUCTION

Archaeological and historical studies of Mediterranean pastoralism have focused primarily on large-scale transhumance centred around a mountain-to-plain perspective. This particular concentration is the result of a variety of different conditions. First, pastoral practices have always been considered highly mobile. As a result, they are virtually impossible to identify in the archaeological record. Moreover, it is not easy to detect different kinds of pastoralism through written sources. The case study discussed in this chapter takes the long-term historical phenomenon of transhumance in southern Tuscany (1100–1950) as its subject. In so doing, it diverges from the traditional image of pastoralism which is present in the extant literature. It sets aside mountain-to-plain ideas and promotes the concept of integrated agro-sylvo-pastoral practices. Analysis of the archaeological records and ethnoarchaeological and historical data show us the decisive role played by marginal areas in the history of late medieval and early modern transhumance in southern Tuscany. Those landscape zones which are humid, including both lagoons and marshes are markedly instable. We argue that mobility and seasonality are key concepts in creating an understanding of transhumance as a socio-economic phenomenon.

In the study of Mediterranean pastoralism, great prominence has been given to long-distance (or horizontal) transhumance, as has been recorded in Italy for the late medieval and early modern periods (Braudel, 1949: 5–50; Volpe, 2006; Figure 14.1). Very little attention has been devoted to local, short-distance or vertical transhumance or farm-based pasturage (see debate in Corbier, 1999; Pasquinucci, 2004; Whittaker, 1988). In the historical period, almost every archaeological site is linked to some sort of agrarian practice. To reiterate, the present case study diverges from the traditional image of pastoralism presented by the literature, and focuses instead on agro-sylvo-pastoral activities and the role of marginal landscapes in the economic decision-making process.

In southern Tuscany, transhumant practices have been largely neglected by archaeological research (Cambi et al., 2015). This is due to a long tradition of studies that saw this area only through the lens of agrarian supply (Barker, 1988; 1989), first in order to explain the spread of the Etruscan civilization and, second, in terms of economic growth during the Roman period. The archaeological literature has traditionally regarded the land as a resource for the production of surplus destined for the market which was underpinned by slavery (for the most part) and free labour (in part). Although both hypothesized and greatly discussed in historical studies, the presence of transhumance in Italy in general and Tuscany in particular in the early medieval period has not been conclusively demonstrated due to a lack of clear sources (Gabba, 1985; Violante, 1995; Wickham, 1985). The argument which underlies the present work holds that transhumance and pastoral activities were left in the background of both historical and archaeological research. However, the fact that livestock and land were usually valued separately does not mean that they were not economically connected.

Archaeologically speaking, since pastoral practices can and did involve a high degree of mobility, multiple strategies must be used to reconstruct transhumance, especially when one wishes to utilize a reverse perspective (i.e. from mountains to plains, as is the case in the present study). Another factor to be considered is the visibility of pastoral sites and the fact that the routes which were utilized are virtually impossible to identify in the archaeological record (Forbes, 1995; Maggi et al., 1990; Nixon & Price, 2001).

Historically speaking, transhumance practices have usually been studied from a geo-anthropological or economic standpoint (Braudel, 1949; Calzolai & Marcaccini, 2003; Duclos & Pitte, 1994; Laffont, 2006; for Tuscany, Barsanti, 1987; Dell'Omodarme, 1988; Massaini, 2005). Either way, the study of large-scale transhumance has prevailed in the historiography at the expense of short-distance mobile pastoralism, as it is considered both more difficult to detect and less economically relevant. This approach has been greatly

© 2018 European Association of Archaeologists

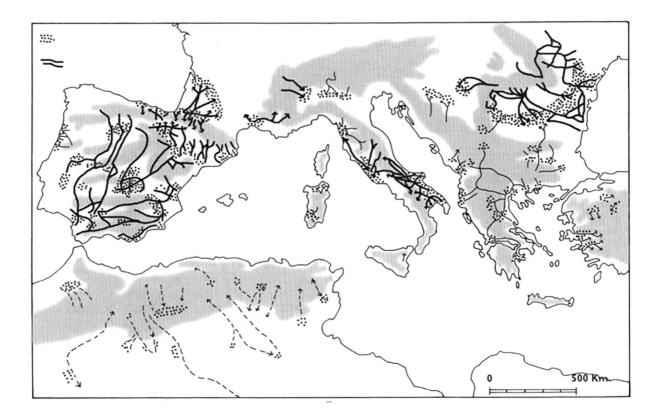

Figure 14.1. Mediterranean transhumance routes
Source: After Braudel (1949)

influenced by the availability of the written sources and the extent of the different pastoral phenomena.

We reckon that innovative multidisciplinary research strategies can increase our knowledge of different farming practices. Shifting the focus of historical research from customs records to other kind of sources (such as contracts, statutes or lawsuits in the records or even the evidence provided by archaeological or palaeobotanical investigations, etc.) could allow us to detect and understand short-distance transhumance and alternative farming practices. Traditional historical and archaeological studies must be integrated with the landscape in order to relate social and economic structures to site distribution and pastoral practices.

In this paper, we apply a multidisciplinary perspective as a means of reversing the traditional view of some historical phenomena. In part one Long-Distance Transhumance in Maremma (1100–1950), we employ the historical approach and examine the written sources in order to present a general outline of long-distance transhumance in the long term and some samples of late medieval local pastoralism. The second portion takes a more archaeological approach; by means of time-regression, we explain the relations between southern Tuscan settlements and marginal landscapes through the analysis of agro-sylvo-pastoral activities. The concluding remarks offer some suggestions to develop and widen this approach in future research.

Questions and Methodologies

The primary aim of this paper is to challenge current epistemological paradigms through the study of pastoralism in southern Tuscany (Figure 14.2). First of all, we reconsider the concept of marginal landscapes (e.g. humid environments, mountain areas, etc.) by evaluating their 'marginality' either in terms of economic and demographic potentiality or geographical 'liminality'. Second, we reduce the opposition between long-distance, politically driven transhumance and short-distance (or vertical) transhumance and subsistence. The present case study focuses on the interaction between different agro-sylvo-pastoral activities which are deeply embedded in a complex set of eco-cultural choices. In this regard, mobility is probably a more helpful concept by which to consider this kind of pastoralism in southern Tuscany. The micro-context is compensated by a long perspective and a global methodological approach. The local and topographic scale enables us to compare different evidence (archival, ethnographic and archaeological). Third, we question the presumed invisibility of pastoral activities in terms of the archaeological record and try to reverse the perspective taken by previous studies insofar as they tend to focus on the uplands at the expense of the lowlands.

To this end, we will make use of a series of different sources and approaches (historical ecology,

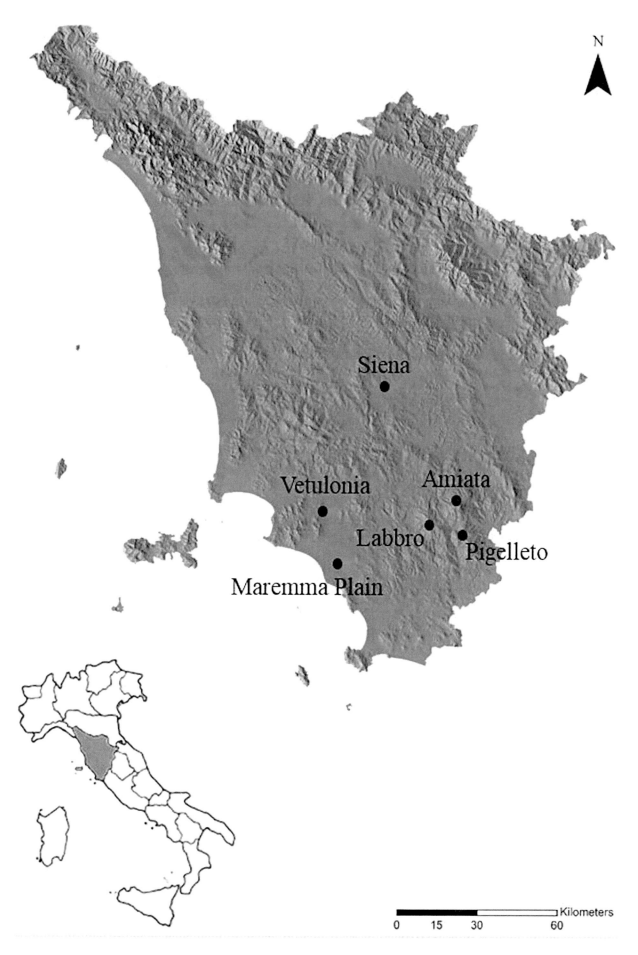

Figure 14.2. The study area showing the locations of sites quoted in the text (Tuscany, Italy)

palaeoebotanical sequences, archaeozoology, etc.), in order to investigate the exploitation of natural resources, environment transformations, mobility and agro-sylvo-pastoral practices. The production of new data requires different investigations and produces questions that need fresh answers. Archaeologically, we emphasize importance of re-evaluating settlement patterns and the need to re-examine some rural dwellings typical of pastoral activities (see Cevasco et al., 2008; Rendu, 2000).

The application of the regressive prospective suggests the presence of some possible historical continuity. We are quite certain that the practice of transhumance was a principle activity in this area from the late medieval period to the mid-nineteenth century. A comparison between the 1830 cadastre by Giovanni Inghirami under the reign of the Dukes of Lorena and that of 1929 by the fascist regime shows great variation in pasturage and fallow land. Approximately 70% of the Maremma Plain was used for pasturage in 1830. In 1929, by contrast, this sum had been reduced to 8% (Greppi, 2009: 119–20). During this timespan, the percentage of agrarian land remained mostly unchanged, while great importance was acquired by both woodland and agrarian land.

The ethnographic data tell us that the practice of winter pasturing in the Maremma Plain continued after the Second World War until the Agrarian Reform by the Central Italian State, after which stability definitively replaced mobility as a form of human landscape occupation. With regards to the ethnographic data, we are aware of the necessity of avoiding overly simplistic parallels between past and present practices. Nonetheless direct information about economic and cultural activities in the present can be morphologically significant for our understanding of similar behaviours in the past and constitutes a record for possible comparisons. In our case, the ethnographical enquiry involved five modern shepherds (called S1, S2, S3, S4 and S5; Vanni, 2014: 576–88) who were interviewed between 2012 and 2013. They were from different parts of the Apennines and used to go to Maremma in the winter with their flocks by means of various routes and in accordance with different timing and modalities. S1 and S2 were from the Tosco-Emilian Apennines (northeast), S3 and S4 were from the Casentino Apennines (west) and S5 was from the Garfagnana Apennines (north). At the time of their interview, all shepherds had been engaged as stationary farmers since at least the 1950s. We have utilized some of their testimonies in the text to further elucidate some points.

By means of our examination of the written sources (especially fourteenth- and fifteenth-century documents from the State Archive of Siena), we have explored the challenging relationship between Siena and its countryside at the end of the medieval period.

More specifically, this involved the careful review of the resolutions and statutes of the Sienese commune as well as those of the rural communities (Cristoferi, 2016: 66–84). In addition to long-distance transhumance from the Apennines to the plains, this work revealed a kind of mobile pastoralism strictly connected to the local commons system and to the region's agro-sylvo-pastoral economy. It was that very discovery that was the starting point for the reversed perspective we put forward in this paper. Together with classic long-distance transhumance, we emphasize some essential features of a poorly known and multi-faceted system of communal laws, requests for common rights, reports and conflict with state officials all laid out against a background of the necessity of verifying the connection of these various actions to environmental and economic change.

LONG-DISTANCE TRANSHUMANCE IN MAREMMA (1100–1950)

This section focuses on the development of long-distance transhumance over the long term by analyzing its relations with the settlement structures of Maremma and the expropriation of common lands through the development of Sienese customs. This line of inquiry has already received scholarly attention especially in relation to the modern period. Indeed, it is based on the development of Customs offices to manage transhumant sheep flocks from the late medieval period, as a result of the market revolution of Tuscany city-communes. Long-distance commercial transhumance was the main player in this revolution, in which marginal lands in northern (Apennines) and southern (Maremma) Tuscany were connected.

According to various sources, long-distance transhumance (200–250 km) developed in Tuscany from the end of the twelfth century, as was also the case in Spain and France (Gerbet, 2000: 163–82; Wickham, 1985: 400–455) and continued until the end of the World War II (Calzolai & Marcaccini, 2003). After AD 1100, the number and the quality of sources which discuss or otherwise relate to long-distance transhumance in Tuscany increase. If this development was connected to the growth in the production of written sources, it can also be read as a proof of a change in farming practices rather than simply to geographical and environmental factors (Cherubini, 1974: 129; Cristoferi, 2015: 122).

The economic and demographic growth of Tuscan cities, which formed one of the most urbanized region of Europe at the end of the thirteenth century led to an integration of market and labour demand between the marginal (and not intensively cultivated nor inhabited) areas and the cultivated countryside (Piccinni, 2006:

207–92; Wickham, 1990: 15–31). In this way, transhumance was boosted through capital and demand (for meat, wool, dairy products, draught oxen and leather, etc.) from the cities and their surrounding countryside. These demands were further facilitated through the availability of pastures, flocks and people at the areas around the borders of Tuscany (Collavini, 1998: 547; Wickham, 2001: 451–66). In consequence, great flocks of hundreds or thousands of sheep (as well as bovines) moved every year from the summer pastures on the Apennines and the inland valleys (Valdichiana, Valdorcia) to winter on the coastal plains of Maremma (from Pisa to Tuscania).

However, the situation in southern Tuscany worsened during the fourteenth-century crisis. The area's demographic, economic and environmental balance broke down as a result of various epidemics, floods, famines, wars and raids (Ginatempo, 1988; Cristoferi, 2016: 144–84). As a result, the commune of Siena (which already had started to exploit transhumance by gaining tolls and renting out Maremma pasturages) decided to reform its office for transhumance management in a public way in 1353 after the ravages of the Black Death. Marginal lands south of Siena which were empty of people but full of primary resources were transformed into farmland following the military advance of Siena. After this date, the commune of Siena began to own the majority of common lands (which may have covered over 50% of community territory) and the pasture rights from every seigneurial lord or rural community defeated and submitted (Cherubini, 1974: 231–312; Cristoferi, 2016: 334–401; Farinelli & Giorgi, 1998: 159–263).

The Sienese office which was known after 1366 as the 'Dogana dei Paschi' (lit. 'Customs of Pasturages') allowed anyone to use its new grazing lands during the winter after payment of a toll (which was established according to the number and race of the animals introduced). The Customs' development ended with the Statute of 1419 (see Cristoferi, 2015: 124–26; Imberciadori, 2002: 97–126). However, in the 1360s, its monopolistic aim was clear and its yearly revenues were high (around 18,000 gold florins in 1361–1362). In order to gain as much income as possible (especially after the fifteenth century), Customs officials made use of a short-term strategy in which they enabled the overgrazing of the pasturages (Cristoferi, 2015: 127–28). As a result of the expansion of pasturage land and the end of regional wars, this ensured the Customs' best economic returns since 1353. At the same time, this system also caused many environmental problems (such as the scarcity of grass) and conflicts between local and transhumant shepherds as well as between transhumant shepherds and Maremma peasants (Cristoferi, 2016: 62–73). In a nutshell, if Maremma had already been a somewhat marginal area before the formation of the Sienese Customs, the development of transhumance worsened the crisis in the region. At the same time, it also assured the necessary resources Siena required to develop over the centuries and to cope with its financial troubles (Cristoferi, 2016: 301–11). These prominent changes carried out by Siena are apparent in the exponential increase of archaeozoological remains of pertinent ovicaprids from the twelfth to fifteenth centuries (Ginatempo, 1987: 173–97; Tozzi, 1981: 56–63, 209–303; Salvadori, 2006: 177–180) in key sites along transhumance routes, such as Scarlino and Grosseto.

After the conquest of the Sienese Republic and the foundation of the Grand Duchy of Tuscany under the Medici (1555), the Customs system was further improved through a new Statute (1572), a greater regional integration of flock mobility and the increasing investment of the nobility and the royal family in transhumance and farming. As it predated the great crisis of the seventeenth century caused by epizootic diseases and by the rise in the price of cereals at this moment in time the Maremma had been even further emptied of people. This left some 350,000–400,000 head of sheep and cattle (Barsanti, 1987: 266–69). This marginal landscape became more and more central to the Tuscan economy. In 1778, in accordance with physiocratic ideals, Duke Peter Leopold of Lorena (1765–1790) abolished the two pillars of transhumance in Tuscany: most of the commons and feudal rights to Maremma pasturage and the Sienese Customs (Barsanti, 1987: 83–126). The aim was to replace the sheep, malaria and swampy lands with cereal fields and stable farming, thereby increasing the demographics and economic performance of the area (Barsanti & Rombai, 1986). Underdeveloped and under-populated, Maremma could no longer remain a marginal area.

Although abolition of common areas continued on into the nineteenth century, even if they were in crises, transhumance practices survived. If investments and the number of transhumant flocks went down, cattle-owner associations or both large and small as well as shepherds (which often belonged to the same communities) continued the practice of wintering in Maremma (Pontecorvo, 1932: 236–47; Zucchini, 1932: 136–43). These groups purchased or rented the pastures they needed from the private sector and, since the beginning of twentieth century, began to use the railways for their transport needs (Pasquini, 1905: 183–86). The general conditions of labour and market demand continued to support the economic viability of transhumance (although it eventually became residual) until the end of World War II (Calzolai & Marcaccini, 2003). Through the agrarian reforms of 1950s, southern Tuscany (as well Italy's other marginal and swampy regions) were reclaimed and devoted to intensive agriculture. Transhumance ended, and many shepherds became smallholders or stable breeders (Massaini, 2005).

Tracing Local Mobile Pastoralism Patterns in Late Medieval Maremma from The Written Sources

This section concentrates on different forms of mobile pastoralism. These various kinds of mobile pastoralism were practiced by the inhabitants of Maremma alongside hunting and fishing as well as salt work, woodcutting, mining and grain production, as has probably been the case since the Roman period (Vanni & Cambi, 2015 and references therein). Even upon the foundation of the Customs (1353), the mobility of men and animals in the region had probably been ongoing since the early medieval period. The distribution of hilltop villages founded during the early medieval period and their subsequent survival capacity was principally due to the exploitation of salt flats, forestry and animal husbandry and (albeit secondarily) to the control of the main transhumance routes. During the thirteenth century, new settlements were founded in order to regulate the movement of sheep (Cammarosano & Passeri, 1976). Paganico, Cinigiano, Roccalbegna and Manciano in the inland areas, Montemassi in the north and Pereta and Capalbio in the south developed as centres for the control of transhumant movement within the Customs system (Cristoferi, 2016: 346–73; Calzolai & Marcaccini, 2003; Vanni, 2014).

Farming was, therefore, just one more of a wide range of agro-sylvo-pastoral activities which were practiced more or less intensively (Cherubini, 1981b: 91–115; Pinto, 1982: 53–67) according to the main strategy and the resources that the local environment and the institutional structures allowed. In late medieval Maremma we can see the presence of the following (both outside and along the historical long-distance transhumance routes):

- short- and medium-distance transhumance, the former within the territory of the Sienese Customs (around 4500 km²), the latter from the Amiata Mountain and Orcia Valley area to the Grosseto Plain (around 50–60 km)
- local farming practices centred on the movements of the herds within a restricted community territory (around 10–20 km).

These practices were based on a variety of different kinds of animals which were allowed to graze on the common lands by agreement with seigneurial lords (before 1353) or Siena (after 1353). If Siena expropriated the commons during its conquest of Maremma, it also partially maintained them to safeguard the economic and fiscal sustainability of the new communities (Cristoferi, 2016: 346–402). However, Sienese concessions differed from one community to the other in accordance with the demographic, economic and strategic burden of each. Usually, Siena left the communities marginal or otherwise small grazing lands such as marshes, bush and woodland which were suitable for pastoral economy (Piccinni, 1990: 35–58).

Local shepherds exploited these pasture rights in their community territory alongside the Customs system and grazed both their own as well as foreign cattle (which they manage by means of a farm-share contract called a 'soccida' from the Latin 'socio' or 'shareholder'). In the late medieval period, Sienese and Florentine merchants and butchers began investing in cattle (Cherubini, 1981c: 311–35) as part of a system in which they farmed out the responsibility of raising the animals in exchange for half of the revenue obtained by the final sale of the products thereby produced (after one–five years). Using the pasturage right local shepherds were able to cut part of the expense presented by the Customs' tolls (generally by half) and also established a stable base for their activity (Lisini, 1895: resolution n. 88).

In accordance with the great seasonal variability of pastoral strategies, these features (Le Roy Ladurie, 1975: chapters four and five) suggest that some of the cases classified in the previous two typologies could have been (or could have developed into) normal transhumance movements according to Braudel's definition of long-distance transhumance (i.e. with the main base of said transhumance in the plain; Braudel, 1949: 5–50). In any case, these kinds of mobile pastoralism were managed by shepherds who might also have been peasants, hunters, woodcutters or wageworkers according to the seasons and to the prevailing economic and social context (Imberciadori, 2002: 237). As a result, this mobile pastoralism could have been semi-subsistent (i.e. engagement in mobile pastoralism was intended as a means of assuring the necessary funds and products required by the family in accordance with the demands of the market). In any case, we can observe a commercial survival economy in the first case (Thoen & Soens, 2015: 137–39). Both the animals themselves and the products produced from small flocks (of ten to twenty-five beasts) which were often owned by a farm-share contract could be sold on either the Sienese or another sub-regional market to secure the survival to a peasant's family.

Although they are focused on the fourteenth and fifteenth centuries, what follows are a few preliminary suggestions of ways in which we might improve our classifications of these systems (and to also better understand the system itself). Future research should focus on notarial documents, such as the soccida contracts drawn up between Siena, its territories and Maremma for a broader period of time. Once the institutional framework can be reconstructed, these kind of sources (which may contain precise and rich information about pastoral strategies) will allow us to carry out in-depth analysis of the different forms of local mobile pastoralism.

ECO-CULTURAL CHOICES FROM A MOUNTAINOUS MARGINAL LANDSCAPE

THE MONTE LABBRO ECOLOGICAL NICHE (MONTE AMIATA – TUSCANY)

From the perspective of historical ecology, landscape can be understood as the historical result of complex interactions between humans and nature (Balée, 2006; Grove & Rackham, 2001). Reconstructing the history of the vegetation through pollen analysis and modern analogues could not only tell us about human activities in general, but might also help us to recognize specific practices and strategies. Archaeobotanical research enables us to get a handle on the cultural transformations of land affected by even a prehistoric human presence. More specifically, the diffusion of some species or the recurrence of particular tree *taxa* in pollen diagrams has always been explained by the management of transhumance or pasturing in general (Malo & Suárez, 1995).

Change in land use over time is nicely illustrated by the data from the Monte Labbro ecological *niche* (see McClure, 2015) in the immediate surroundings of the volcanic massif of Mount Amiata (1900 m a.s.l.). From an ecological point of view, a relic population of lichens, mainly *Lobarion* (*Lobarion Pulmonaria, Nephroma laevigatum, Peltigera Collina*), in association with *Xanthorion* indicates specific transformations in the landscape in post-medieval times (Paoli & Loppi, 2001). In general the lichens are extremely representative for the reconstruction of past environments because of a series of features they require for growth (Öckinger et al., 2005). They are usually associated with old-growth forests because they depend on certain microhabitats not found in younger forests, or because they have poor dispersal capacity and, thus, need a long time for colonization (Sillett et al., 2000). The most important factor limiting the distribution of lichens is probably their poor long-range dispersal capacity. Nonetheless, it seems evident that some species are indicators of ecological continuity and long habitat persistence in peculiar places with high preservation quality. In some cases, the association of peculiar lichen *taxa* may be related to differently managed landscapes (orchards, coppices or grazing; see Gauslaa, 2005). A study conducted in central Italy on *Lobarion–Xanthorion* communities in a chestnut forest has shown that "[t]he occurrence of these lichen assemblages is related to the long- term turn coppicing, a management strategy less detrimental than short-rotation forestry" (Matteucci et al., 2012: 68). In our case, the lichens indicate the presence of an ancient and ecologically continuous forest both in relation to quality as well as the persistence of certain sylvo- pastoral practices. The *Xanthorion* communities tell us about the presence of dry stands with high level of direct and indirect solar radiation, while the *Lobarion* communities are mainly related to wooded glades with humid environments which are extremely rich in nitrogen. Probably an alternation of forest clearance, coppicing and pollarding provided optimal conditions for these species, thanks to the continuous canopy coverage which allowed constant and moderate direct solar radiation and high humidity rates at trunk level.

Contrary to what one would expect from this data, the environment around Monte Labbro is currently completely barren, probably because of the intense forest clearance practiced in the past for obtaining pastures (Frenzel & Weiss, 1994; Limbrey & Bell, 1982; Wickham, 1990). Although we are not in a position to date this activity with any certainty, the analysis of the aerial photographs available for the 1954–2013 period shows significant changes in cover vegetation.[1] In 1954, the Monte Labbro landscape consisted almost exclusively of meadows, pastures and open areas (around 90% of a total surface of c. 50 h). In 2013, however, only 10% of the surface presented such features, the rest of the area being completely covered by woods (except for the immediate vicinity of the peak, which is characterized by rocky slopes and shrubs. Historical maps show that the open landscape that was visible in 1954 had ancient origins. The considerable number of toponyms recorded in the 1822 cadastre (*Bandite, Prati, Sodi*, etc.) testifies to the prevalence of meadows and pastures and suggests that the husbandry phenomenon was deeply rooted in this landscape. In addition, around a hundred huts are marked on the land registry (*Capanna, Capanne*, etc.); in some cases, they are even listed with the names of the owners, e.g. *Capanna di Petruccioni* (Petruccioni's hut). Interestingly, the toponym *Ajaccio* frequently occurs in relation to these huts. Similar toponyms were noted by Pieri (1969) in a survey in southern Tuscany. Pieri derives *diaccio* (and similar forms) from *glaciem* ('ice'), suggesting a connection with mountain areas. This explanation, however, does not seem entirely convincing. First, many of these toponyms are found near the lagoons and rivers of the Maremma Plain. Second, and most importantly, *diaccio* may also derive from the vulgar Latin *jacium* (Devoto, 1969), which in turn relates to the Latin *jacere* 'to lay', differentiated with *di-* (or *dj-*). Possibly of medieval origin, these names (Diaccio, Addiaccio, Diaccialino, Diaccia Botrona, etc.) are particularly abundant in the hills surrounding the plain and do not seem to have anything to do with ice (a rare phenomenon in Maremma), but rather derive from the noun *addiaccio* (composed of *ad* and the vulgar latin *jacium*), indicating a shelter (or, occasionally, an enclosure) for shepherds and their flocks and generally referring to places shepherds grazed their animals (Firmati, 2002: 64).

Given this data, we can safely assume that the beginning of the nineteenth century was *a terminus post quem* for the forest clearance of Monte Labbro. Since the clearance was already both well established and crystallized by that time, we can speculate that it had actually begun long before that date in connection with transhumance practices and the exploitation of the resources of Amiata in general. It is possible that the authors of this forest clearance were the same shepherds that used to stay in this area for pasturing during the summer (as testified by the several huts and enclosures which are still clearly identifiable through archaeological remains and aerial photographs; see Figure 14.3). Ethnoarchaeological research has shown that shepherds used to clear woods as a means of obtaining open areas or branches for fodder (Barker, 1989; Cevasco, 2007; Desplanques, 1969; Moreno & Poggi, 1996; confirmed by S1 and S4). Interestingly, these sylvo-pastoral activities are confirmed by the presence of some hooked sickles sketched on rocks by modern shepherds in the Apennine area (Sani, 2011; Vanni, 2015a). Such sickles were used by shepherds for non- intensive forestry (leaves and twigs) and forest management for pasturage. In this system, shepherds and many others actors (such as charcoal-burners or woodcutters) were involved in a complex system of agro-sylvo-pastoral practices aimed at exploiting different kinds of resources.

Some transhumant modern shepherds interviewed over the course of the ethnographic enquiry provided further evidence for the possibility that these peculiar eco-cultural choices should be regarded as part of an integrated economy (Vanni, 2014: 558–88; especially S2, S3, S5). In their childhood, at least two shepherds used to spend the summers with their fathers' flocks around the Monte Labbro meadows. This lasted until the 1950s when the population of these mountain areas drastically decreased. As there was no longer a need to cut wood for charcoal or timber, thereby creating pastures for transhumant shepherds (S2 and S3), the practice ceased. In other words, it appears clear that there was a deep connection between mobility and settlement/demographic density. If we look at the history of settlement density, Amiata Mountain was one of the most populated districts of the Sienese countryside between the fourteenth and sixteenth centuries AD (Ascheri & Kurze, 1989; Cambi, 1996; Ginatempo, 1988). This was the long-term result of the settlement strategy begun by Lombard and, subsequently, maintained by the Aldobrandeschi family during the ninth and eleventh centuries in their construction of a series of fortified villages (Kurze & Citter, 1995; Nucciotti, 2006: 179–80), most of which survived the crisis of the thirteenth century (Wickham, 1989). This density was accompanied by the construction of a tight network of roads for the circulation of both men and goods. One crucial point of this network (itself not far from Monte Labbro) was represented by the weekly rural fair that took place at the church of *Lamula*, a real commercial *emporion* founded in the ninth century (Nucciotti, 2006: 186). The fair tradition and began in the second half of the twelfth century AD at the latest and was formed under the aegis of the Aldobrandeschi. When viewed from such an angle, the Amiata seems anything but marginal.

One of the fortified settlements mentioned above has been identified on the western slopes of Monte Labbro (Castel Vaiolo) at the beginning of the Trasubbie Valley (one of the most utilized historical transhumance routes). It was characterized by the remains of drystone fortifications and was occupied in the second half of the tenth century. This may suggest that the substantial

Figure 14.3. The compound enclosures of barren Monte Labbro

changes in land use practices began precisely around this period (Nucciotti, 2007). Although not particularly significant, the archaeological deposits are rich in ceramics and archaeobotanical remains. However, occupation at the site seems to have been short-lived and represents a sealed context characterized by sub-circular postholes cut directly into the rocky outcroppings. Soil sampling has permitted the discovery of a considerable amount of archaeobotanical remains. The further analysis of the material has revealed the presence of diverse varieties of cereals (barley and wheat) and legumes (beans – *vicia faba minor* and peas – *pisum sativum*). Furthermore, the discovery of a conspicuous quantity of toasted chestnuts demonstrates a precocious anthropization of the area which dates back to the tenth to eleventh century AD (Nucciotti, 2007: 669–70). It now seems clear that the spread of chestnut in the Italian peninsula was concomitant with the Roman culture, from about 2700 cal. BP (Di Pasquale et al., 2010). Nonetheless, the sylviculture of *Castanea* was not systematically practiced (Di Pasquale et al., 2010: 871). Where this was, in fact, the case, it was mainly for timber production, suggesting practices of coppice management alternating with pasturage. Relevant changes occurred in the early medieval period (see Buonincontri et al., 2015). Archaeobotanical data from the rural settlement of Miranduolo (close to Siena in Tuscany and occupied between the seventh and fourteenth century AD; see Valenti, 2011, 2012) indicates a drop in chestnut management for construction and firewood from mid-ninth century AD and the beginning of the exploitation of the chestnut trees with the express intent of producing nuts (Buonincontri et al., 2015). This practice eventually exhibited a veritable increase beginning in the fourteenth century AD (Di Pasquale, Buonincontri, et al., 2014). In addition to these landscape transformations we may imagine substantial changes in sylvo-pastoral practices, which had begun to specifically address the management of pastures made from chestnut trees (by pollarding), deciduous *Quercus* coppicing and (potentially) pig breeding.

Alongside the cultivation of chestnuts (one of the earliest examples as yet identified in Italy), open landscapes, wooded pastures and legume fields were likely to have already been present in the Monte Labbro area in this period. Unfortunately, legumes do not easily lend themselves to long-term storage and, consequently, did not represent an appropriate food resource for humans. Pliny the Elder testifies that *Vicia faba* was used during the Roman period for the production of bread flour during the religious feast of *Lemuralia* in honour of the dead. As the celebrations coincided with the maturation of the legumes (the beginning of May), the products were immediately consumed. Other authors, such as Varro and Columella considered the legumes ideal fodder for flocks, especially during the dry season (Varro. *Rust.* 2.2.16; Colum. 6.3.3).[2] Experimental research has

shown that legumes (*Vicia faba* and *Pisum sativum*; see Buttery & Gibson, 1990) are excellent nitrogen fixers with very high long-term trends in N2-fixing activity. In fact, they used to be cultivated as a means of encouraging pastures and increasing their quality and quantity (Denton et al., 2013; Peoples & Baldock, 2001). The beans and plants themselves can also be employed as fodder in alternating agro-pastoral regimes (Skerman et al., 1988). The cultivation of legumes is still practiced in some Mediterranean grazing areas to ensure fertility and fodder (Beck & Materon, 1988). In Italy, grazing systems in which legumes are related to pastoralism have been observed in Sardinia and Trentino (Safronova et al., 2012), particularly as a way to maintain and preserve marginal landscapes.

SYLVO-PASTORAL STRATEGIES IN THE PIGELLETO RESERVOIR

Another area where peculiar agro-sylvo-pastoral practices appear to have been common since the eighteenth century is that of the Pigelleto Reservoir not far from Monte Labbro. The site covers some 1,312 ha and reaches altitudes which range between 458 and 951 m a.s.l. A study of the phyto – associations of plants in this area (Miozzo & Montini, 2007) recognized a considerable amount of meadow pasture relics. Peculiar associations of *Bromus erectus* with *Centaureo bracteatae-Brometum* would be due to periodic human actions, such as mowing aimed at obtaining fodder (see Pierson & Mack, 1990: 531). The presence of other species is either the result of selective animal grazing (such as in the case of *Arrhenatherum elatius*, *Lolium perenne* and *Cynosurus cristatus*) or is a typical feature of abandoned pastures (*Phalaris coerulescens*). The aerial photographs available for the period between 1940–2010 confirm the massive presence of meadows and show a complex wooded pasture system composed by relic populations of *Abies Alba* (silver fir), *Fagus* (beech), *Carpinus* and *Castanea sativa* (chestnut). Field surveys have identified individual trees whose ages were estimated to be over 100. Except for the silver fir which seems autochthonous (Miozzo & Montini, 2007: 55–56), the other populations are connected to the eco-cultural choices which have characterized the area for centuries. We know that *Fagus* and *Carpinus* were mainly cultivated for their leaves and twigs which were used as winter fodder (Rasmussen, 1993; Haas et al., 1996; Hejcmanová et al., 2014; Moreno & Cevasco, 2013). By contrast, the cultivation of *Castanea sativa* was particularly precocious in this area and was exploited first and foremost for nuts and wood (Cherubini, 1981a; Krebs et al., 2004; Squatriti, 2013: 55–87). Nonetheless, the management of chestnut trees requires periodic pruning and a constant soil clearance in order to prevent excess vegetation from reducing the fecundity of the trees. Before the advent of agro-industrial machines, these needs were fulfilled by animal grazing. Experimental studies conducted in Mediterranean climatic zones have shown how the quality and efficiency of chestnut cultivation systems (species richness, protection against erosion and nut production) is encouraged by pasturing. At the same time, a significantly higher production of forage has been observed under the trees (Hadar et al., 1999; Gondard et al., 2006: 1136; Martins et al., 2011: 181–83).

The decline of *A. alba* was generally associated with "a marked opening of forests and the expansion of deciduous trees such as *Fagus* and *Quercus*" due to human activities (Vescovi et al., 2010: 36; see also Terhürne-Berson et al., 2004: 265). In Tuscany, the intensive use of *A. alba* or silver fir for carpentry and fuel probably dates back to the Bronze or Iron Age (Magny et al., 2007: 176) and certainly increased during the Roman period, when it was particularly sought out for shipbuilding (Di Pasquale, Allevato, et al., 2014: 1305). New and recent pollen sequences from central Italy (see Di Pasquale, Allevato, et al., 2014) have confirmed the role of human pressure in the decline of *A. alba* (Vescovi et al., 2010) and the comparatively low impact of climate change on the depletion of *A. alba* (Tinner et al., 2013). The extremely reduced modern distribution of *A. alba* gives us the slightest inkling of the strong impact presented by human activity during this period. In the context of our study, the cutting activities which began in eighth century BC heavily altered the natural state of the pre-existing woodlands and created the present landscape suitable for mobile pastoralism. Usually attributed to periods of intense mining and metalworking production the major deforestation of this area peaked in the Roman period (between the third century BC and third century AD). In this same timespan, the forest seems to have appreciably contracted, indicating a vegetation change to more open shrub (*macchia*) in which *Erica* was dominant (Di Pasquale, Buonincontri, et al., 2014: 1497–98). The presence of large senatorial and imperial estates (called '*latifundia*') in this part of Etruria based essentially on slave labour for extensive and/or specialized agro-pastoral activities (Carandini, 1985; Regoli, 2002) suggests that the development of *macchia* and the contraction of tree species was probably the effect of overgrazing or was caused by Rome's demands for lumber (Vanni, 2014: 388–402). A slight increase in the forest canopy between the eleventh and thirteenth centuries AD (no samples being available for the sixth–tenth centuries) indicates lower human pressure and a corresponding expansion of wooded pastures (Di Pasquale, Buonincontri, et al., 2014: 1499) due to the growth caused by extensive olive and chestnut cultivation (see Bergmeier et al., 2010: 3005; Cortonesi, 2005).

The exploitation of fir trees for the construction of public buildings was extraordinarily continuous over time. In the first half of the sixteenth century AD, fir timber from the Pigelleto Reservoir was used for the building of Pope Pious II's residence in Pienza (*Pii Secundi Pontificis Max. Commentarii*, 1584). In his autobiographical memories, Pious II described an intensively exploited cultural landscape insofar as he mentioned not only cultivated fields and vineyards, but also pastures and meadows. The widespread presence of chestnut and beech clearly trickle through the Pope's memoirs, especially his specific description of the suitability of cleared areas for the *pecuaria* (the Latin word for flocks). World War II marked a reduction of wooded pastures and an increase in the number of open fields and pastures. After the 1960s, there was a massive reforestation of the landscape at the expense of fields and meadows due to the decrease of population in the area. Some pastures which had undergone regular mowing in the previous decades seem to have survived exclusively around the relic silver fir populations (which are extremely reduced at present) and the sulphurous springs of the plateau.

The concentration of pastoral activities around hot springs must be considered in the light of said springs' healing properties. Treatment with sulphurous water was an important therapy for some epizootic diseases and the cattle illnesses which were a constant threat to farmers and shepherds alike (Frizell Santillo, 2004; e.g. Strabo. 6.3.9–10 about transhumance shepherds; S1 used to frequent the basin). The presence of sulphurous water in areas exploited for short-distance transhumance must, thus, have been an important factor which favoured the maintenance of herds (Vanni, 2015a). Therefore, the continued use of these sites must be reconsidered in the light of this peculiar healing practice. In the case of Poggetti Vecchi (near to the ancient lake of Prile), eighteenth-century sources testify to the practice of immersing flocks in the basin in order to cure them. The continuity of this practice was confirmed by interviews with modern shepherds in the context of the present research (Vanni, 2014: 576–88). At the location described, a basin for the storage of hot water was found together with black-glazed ware, a few pieces of marble and zoomorphic *ex-voto* (Curri, 1978: 200). The site probably represents a rural shrine near to a hot spring (rather than a thermal bath), an example of many of other such sites which have been well attested in Etruria during Etruscan and Roman times (Chellini, 2002: 81–186; Ciampoltrini, 1993). As B. Santillo Frizell recalled, "[m]any of the sacred places with particular healing waters were probably used for animals earlier than [they were] for humans." His statement underscores the immense importance held by domestic animals in ancient economies (Frizell Santillo, 2004). Approximately 2 km north of Poggetti is another hot spring to which the ancient maps refer as 'Caldanelle' (lit. 'hot springs'). At this location, hot water was collected by brick walls built in the fourteenth century (although similar constructions had probably been in use since at least the thirteenth century). During the medieval period, this particular hot spring fell under the jurisdiction of the Sienese Republic (as did other sulphurous sites along key travel routes between Sienna and Maremma Plain, such as Bagni di Petriolo (see Boisseuil, 2002). The use of mineral waters and sulphurous springs in particular has not been examined in previous studies of ancient pastoral economies, although it is a vast and complex subject, especially in the parts of the Mediterranean where transhumance was practiced.

The cadastre of 1822 show that the Pigelleto area is full of toponyms like *Ajaccio, Ajacci, Diaccino* or *Capanne dei Pompei* (Pompei's huts) that we discussed above as epiphenomena of pastoral practices. In addition to these, toponyms like *Carboniere, Carbonaia*, etc. (lit. 'charcoal burnings') are also marked on the map. To obtain charcoal, woodland had to be cleared and then burned for days in circular kilns built with perishable materials and covered with clay. A farm by the name of *Podere Pinza* appears on an 1822 land registry at the centre of a network of routes not far from a silver fir wood (whose structures are still detectable in the ground). A western path departed from the farm and suddenly stopped when it reached the *Pian dei Caprai* (Goat Shepherds' Plateau) where there are many abandoned meadows and pastures. The eastern path (called the '*Strada della Doganella*' (Customs path) acts as a clear reference to transhumant husbandry (Figure 14.4). The entire route is visible in historical maps: from Pinza farm it proceeded eastwards to a main road called the '*Via Dogana*' (Customs Road) which came from the eastern Apennines and bordered the Amiata Slopes via *Cassia* (the Roman road). Following the natural corridor formed by the Albegna and Fiora rivers basins, the *Via Dogana* continued to the main plains by the shores of the Thyrrenian Sea.

This route from the Apennines was used by transhumant shepherds and their big flocks as part of a wider network of long-distance and horizontal transhumance. However, the branch of this road that reaches the Pigelleto Plateau, and which, importantly, begins at the *Podere Dogana* (Customs farm, currently in ruin) was probably also frequented by shepherds practicing a short-distance and vertical transhumance between Maremma and Amiata (S2 and S3). Given its restricted extension (only the Pigelleto Plateau), it seems safe to assume that either the flocks were limited in size or the shepherds who converged there in the summer did not

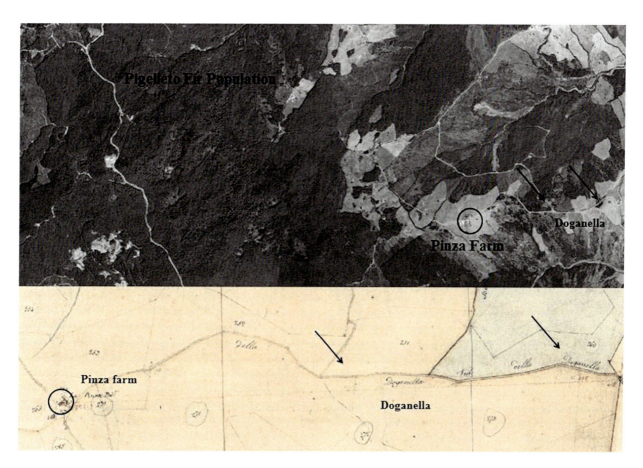

Figure 14.4. The Pigelleto Reservoir showing the customs road mentioned in the cadastre of AD 1822 (Doganella)

specialize exclusively in husbandry and transhumance, but instead also took part in other seasonal activities. These shepherds used micro-mobility in order to exploit various resources through different sylvo-pastoral subsistence techniques (forestry, temporary agriculture and pastoralism).

REVERSING THE PERSPECTIVE: PLAINS MARGINAL TO WHAT?

Since the identification of pastoral activities by archaeological investigation is difficult, many scholars tend to privilege the study of mountainous areas where the records are (in some ways) more easily discernible. This increased visibility in the mountains is principally due to the non-intensive exploitation of these marginal landscapes in comparison to the plains (where the survival of archaeological records is often compromised by demographic pressure and agro-industrial activity). In addition, plains have often been subjected to the transformations caused by the geo-pedological phenomena that are unknown in the mountains.

In the past, Maremma Plain was a complex environment generated by the interaction of marine shore regression, lagoons, lakes and the basin of the Ombrone River (Resti, 2009; for morphological and sedimental dynamics see Arnoldus-Huyzendveld, 2011; Bellotti et al., 2004; Biserni & van Geel, 2005). The millenary and fluctuating evolution of this system exhibits features comparable to those taking place in the main Mediterranean deltas (Arnoldus-Huyzendveld, 2007, 2011; Bellotti et al., 2004). According to the morpho-sedimentary model of the major Italian Tyrrhenian deltas – the Volturno, Tiber, Ombrone and Arno plains – as proposed by Bellotti, the Ombrone River mouth was first inside the lagoon and the sea level rose with a discontinuous and ever decreasing rhythm. Between 6000 and 3000 BP, the Ombrone reached the sea and the lagoon began to evolve into an unstable entity, with an increase in its sediments brought about by human activities (deforestation, agriculture, pastoralism, etc.). This instability decreased when the Prile Lake evolved into a salt lagoon (Citter, 1996: 13–23) which probably favoured the presence of pastures and *incultum* until the first millennium BC when open vegetation (mainly consisting of oaks) began to take over (Buonincontri et al., 2013). As for the Maremma Plain, we can reasonably suppose that its eventual transition to a salt lagoon must have taken place around the eighth century BC. During the medieval period, drainage was minimal and the lagoon turned into a swamp (Wickham, 2001; Figure 14.5).

The reconstruction of these wetlands is not a mere exercise in the creation of a virtual landscape; it is crucial for understanding the history of an area's population(s) and their practices (Van de Noort, 2008; Van de Noort & O'Sullivan, 2006). It reveals a certain degree of instability between humid and non-humid zones (which probably began very early, around the second half of the second century AD). This pattern of instability is generally considered suitable for *incultum* (non-cultivated areas). Archaeological and historical research, however, has demonstrated that *incultum* were intensively exploited by a multiplicity of different mobile strategies, such as forestry, fishing and pastoral practices (Burri, 2014: 10–15 for an alternative account). This has important implications for archaeological reconstruction.

The Italian humid zones were affected by the presence of endemic diseases (especially malaria; see Sallares, 2006, with bibliography therein). Malaria is spread by mosquitoes from the *Anopheles* family and is particularly rampant between June and October. As far as the ancient times are concerned, we are not in a position to assess the diffusion of malaria with any certainty, nor do we know exactly when the disease first made its appearance in the area. We do, however, have some indirect evidence from palaeopathology to the effect that malaria was present in Maremma at the beginning of the thirteenth century. In the city of Cosa, a significant percentage (around 52%) of the individuals buried in Forum II Cemetery (dated to AD 1010–1265) had been affected by porotic hyperostosis and talassemy, two pathologies typically associated with malaria (Fentress, 2003: 357–60). If we gather information from various contexts which are often considered separately, we may assume an earlier presence of malaria in the region. Similar pathologies have been identified in individuals buried in the *villa* of Settefinestre (dating from the second–third century AD) during phase of reoccupation. In this particular context, strontium and zinc analyses point to good nutrition at the site, arguably due to a high consumption of meat and dairy products (Mallegni & Fornaciari, 1985). In addition, the distribution of polyvisceral votives on terracotta dating from the Roman republican period also intimates an early presence of malaria in the area (Fabbri, 2004–2005). Since malaria notoriously affects the internal organs, the presence of these peculiar objects may well be related to this particular disease. A clear reference to tertian fever (as malaria is also known) was found in a recently discovered inscription at the Campetti sanctuary at Veii (near Rome) which has been dated to the first half of second century AD (Fusco, 2008–2009: 450–55). The rhythm of the malaria cycle corresponds with the rhythm of summer–winter/plain–mountain transhumance. The occurrence of malaria must, thus, have been decisive for settlement strategies and choices related to the development of a sylvo-pastoral lifestyle in the area. Considering the above, we can hypothesize that this

Figure 14.5. Prile Lagoon and other humid environments during the medieval period

correspondence was not at all coincidental; rather, we suggest that it was for precisely this reason that transhumance was adopted in the region. It was an adaptation to the presence of malaria. This may have been one crucial factor for the enormous success of the practice.

WETLANDS AND PASTORAL PRACTICES: WHERE DID THE SHEPHERDS LIVE?

Generally speaking, in terms of animal husbandry, marginal landscapes composed of marshes and lagoons are not completely separate as functional economic structures (Vanni, 2015a). Historical pictures, ancient maps and ethnographic studies testify to the fact that all shepherd villages in the Maremma area were placed along the rivers or around the lagoons (Figure 14.6). Evidence for this kind of settlement is archaeologically apparent as well; a series of huts were found along the slopes situated to the north of Prile Lagoon near to the Etruscan-Roman town of Vetulonia, a unique case within the Italian peninsula. In fact, until the present time, the material identification of modern pastoral huts has been restricted to mountainous areas (for the reasons listed above). By contrast, archaeological studies have mainly utilized archival pictures, historical maps and oral tradition (Brandt & Karlsonn, 2001). In our case, the field survey allowed for the identification of at least three sites (A, B, C). Although they were probably independent, they were not far from each other (Figure 14.7). Until the 1960s, all structures exhibited drystone bases (S1 and S5). Sites A and B are characterized

Figure 14.6. Historical photographs representing shepherds' villages (1865) and maps (1680–1699) with huts around Prile Lagoon

by the presence of partially preserved single elliptic drystone walls (measured with diameters varying between 4 to 5 m). They also exhibited the presence of large, flat rocks at the entrances and probably belonged to nuclear families (in this instance, usually composed of father and son; see Figure 14.8). The roof and, in part, the walls of these huts (of which we have no record) must have been made of perishable materials found in the surrounding area. The elliptical shape of the huts (entirely different from the circular ones recorded at Monte Labbro) was clearly designed to resist the windy winters of the plain. At present, no excavation has been possible. Therefore, the sites have not been dated. However, the current owner of the site declares that the huts were already present when he bought the estate in the fifties; the previous owner used the structures to shelter his flocks. Site C seems little more complex than the others in terms of its living phases and functional features. We can recognize at least four circular structures which do not belong to the same occupation phase. The two smaller huts exhibit the same kind of building features as are present at sites A and B, while the larger huts (10–15 m of diameter) seem to have both had two different occupation phases with clear traces

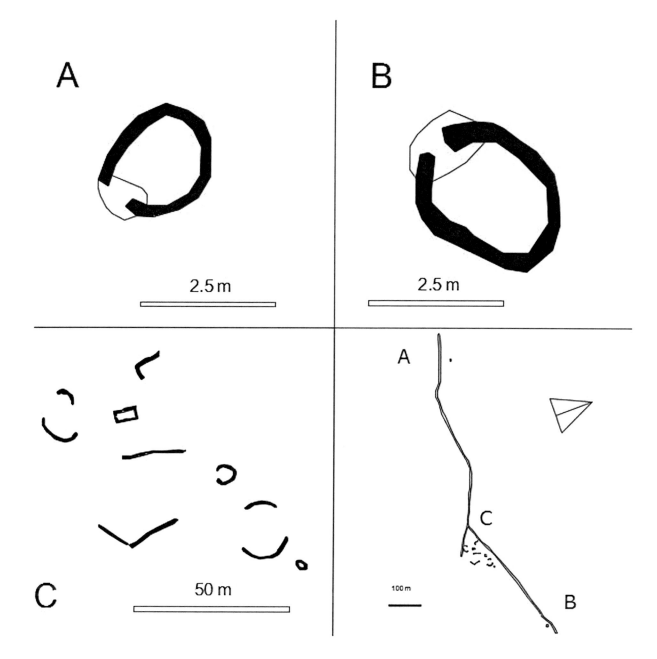

Figure 14.7. Modern huts near Vetulonia

of restoration and reuse. The foundations of rectangular structures are preserved around the huts. The latter are probably the remains of compound enclosures used to group the flocks together (they measure between 6 to 10 m in length). Site C exhibits characteristics of what historical sources called *Vergheria* (a village of shepherds in which more than one family lived).

In the first half of the last century at least some of these huts were sporadically inhabited by transhumant shepherds who returned to Maremma during the winter. Should it be required, these same persons would make restorations to the huts that would sometimes take three or four days to complete. In following winters, they usually tried to come back to the same place. If the shepherds were unlucky and the structures had collapsed or were already occupied, their best option was to look for abandoned houses or shelters. The underlying implication behind this practice suggests that the occupation of huts and pastoral practices in general were intermittent activities that required mobility, but that they are nonetheless neither completely immaterial nor undetectable in today's landscape. It must also be acknowledged that not all shepherds built new huts every year from perishable materials; some of them stayed in stable shelters built from bricks or roof tiles. In other words, what we are questioning is the supposed invisibility of pastoral dwellings. Our methodological response is to underline the role of specific archaeological records in order to detect pastoral activities. The fact that not all shepherds or seasonal workers habitually

Figure 14.8. Hut with foundations (site B)

constructed their own shelters, preferring instead to squat in pre-existent structures implies that reoccupation phases of rural houses should not necessarily be attributed to free-farmers. Once again the direct testimonies of the shepherds interviewed confirms the practice of the reoccupation of stable structures along rivers and lagoons and, possibly, in proximity of routes of passage (S1, S2 and S5). Furthermore, functionally linked to different actors and agro-pastoral systems, the socio-economic complexity of these kinds of settlements emerges from typological studies which reveal that, during the eighteenth and nineteenth centuries, the same hut-building techniques were used by both shepherds and charcoal workers (Vanni, 2014: 586–87) and some villages were intermittently occupied by charcoal workers and shepherds without any interruption.

Concluding Remarks

From our perspective, some archaeological and historical patterns call for careful re-evaluation. The small sites often found at a considerable distance from urban centres might have been interpreted as proof positive of the existence of a class of free peasant farmers. Should we take the context discussed here into account, it seems as if such sites were mixed insofar as they related in different ways with the more commercial urban centres over the long term.

Demography, risk and land capabilities should be taken into account as important variables in this regard. Archaeologists tend to often assume that fertile areas were reserved to agricultural activity, whereas pastoralism would be confined to marginal areas unfit for agriculture. Therefore, archaeological research in areas that appear suitable for agriculture usually focuses on this specific kind of activity, disregarding the possibility that pastoralism may also have been practiced in the same areas. If suitable land exists in terms of agrarian production, the soil must then also be suitable for pastoralism. However, for the late medieval and early modern period, different forms of capital investment and uses should be considered (and this not only in relation to large-scale transhumance).

Issues surrounding occupation continuity are not oriented towards agriculture alone. Those multifunctional sites which survived seem to have had a key role in increasing interest in the control of transhumance and salt resources from at least the thirteenth century. However, after they declined, a subsistence economy nonetheless survived them in accordance with the Sienese concessions and interests.

The presence of malaria was decisive for settlement strategies and for the development of a pastoral lifestyle in the context considered. This implies a new historical relationship between humid zones and mobility. Not only did winter pasturing abound in this kind of environment, but the practice of transhumance and permanent mobility was the best mode of life within such an environment.

Epistemologically, we need to mediate between sets of oppositions: ancient literary records *versus* material records, anthropological present (dynamic) *versus* archaeological evidence (static), transhumance *versus* fixed-based agro-pastoralism and mountains *versus* plains.

Ethnoarchaeological studies in combination with landscape archaeology have great potential for enabling a holistic understanding of pastoral economies on material, socio-economic and political terms (Bartosiewicz & Greenfield, 1995; Solinas, 1989–1990) and also challenging some previous assumptions. For instance, pastoralists have been always considered highly mobile; their sites have been assumed to be all but invisible. Rural sites with plentiful ceramic evidence and permanent structures (cut stone, roof tiles, etc.) have generally been ruled out as locations where one would expect to find shepherds.

Assuming a neat separation between cultivation and animal husbandry is extremely dangerous. Two generalized and highly misleading images must be challenged: 1) that pastoralism was a way of life and economic system that remained unchanged from the Neolithic until the nineteenth century AD and 2) that villages and households were settled by peasant-cultivators rather than transhumant shepherds.

The multiple strategies for understanding a multi-layered landscape as the historical product of human/nature interactions help us to overcome the overly simplistic debate between politico-institutional influences and the physical environment as an explanation for transhumance. Continuity does not concern the practice in itself but rather the network of natural resources and human choices.

Micro-mobility and seasonality seem to be the key concepts for understanding these phenomena (Vanni, 2015b). A pastorally centred agricultural regime, in turn, is suggestive of certain patterns of human occupation. Pastoralism requires mobility, "even in the absence of large-scale transhumance . . . all forms of pastoralism are based on people and animals' daily moving around the landscape, over cumulatively significant distances" (Vaccaro et al., 2013: 173–74).

Rather than routes of transhumance, it may be more useful to conceive of these paths in terms of *corridors* of mobility within which specific practices took place as an interface between different economic zones: corridors of memory for the preservation of historical heritage, corridors as markers between different economic and cultural zones and floral corridors as keys by which to interpret the ecology of the landscape.

Landscape is not a reified entity. It seems to us that we study and are part of a permanent and resilient landscape where practices and strategies for managing natural resources are continuously negotiated between human and nature. Marginal landscapes (such as humid zones or mountainous areas) are not empty historical and archaeological objects; they are instead at the centre of complex networks of economic and social choices.

ACKNOWLEDGEMENTS

We would like to thank the editors for their helpful advice as well as W. Ryckbosch, R. Giomi and M. Pieraccini for improving the English text in the initial draft. All errors are due to the authors themselves.

NOTES

1 Unless indicated otherwise, all aerial or satellite images and historical maps come from the open access archive provided by the Region of Tuscany (Project CASTORE, http://web.rete.toscana.it/castoreapp/). The historical maps refer to the land registry of 1822–1823. All the other images or photographs were made by E. Vanni.
2 For the editions of all ancient sources, see www.perseus.tufts.edu/

REFERENCES

Arnoldus-Huyzendveld, A. 2007. Le trasformazioni dell'ambiente naturale della pianura grossetana. Dati geologici e paleo – ambientali. In: C. Citter & A. Arnoldus – Huyzendveld, eds. *Archeologia urbana a Grosseto I. la città nel contesto geografico della Bassa Valle dell'Ombrone*. Firenze, All'Insegna del Giglio, pp. 41–61.

Arnoldus-Huyzendveld, A. 2011. Landscape development of the coastal plains of Rome and Grosseto between 20,000 and 3,000 years ago. In: M. van Leusen, G. Pizziolo & L. Sarti, eds. *Hidden Landscapes of Mediterranean Europe: Cultural and Methodological Biases in Pre- and Protohistoric Landscape Studies*. Proceedings of the International meeting Siena, Italy, May 25–27, 2007. British Archaeological Reports International Series 2320. Oxford: Archaeopress, pp. 161–69.

Ascheri, A. & Kurze, W. eds. 1989. *L'Amiata nel medioevo. Atti del convegno internazionale (Abbadia San Salvatore – Si, 29 maggio – 1 giugno 1986)*. Roma: Viella.

Balée, W. 2006. The research program of historical ecology. *Annual Review of Anthropology*, 35:75–98.

Barker, G. 1988. The archaeology of Etruscan countryside. *Antiquity*, 62:772–85.

Barker, G. 1989. The archaeology of Italian shepherd. *PCPS*, 215:1–19.

Barsanti, D. 1987. *Allevamento e transumanza in Toscana: pastori, bestiami e pascoli nei secoli XV–XIX*. Firenze: Edizioni Medicea.

Barsanti, D. & Rombai, L. 1986. *La guerra delle acque in Toscana. Storia delle bonifiche dai Medici alla Riforma Agraria*. Firenze: Edizioni Medicea.

Bartosiewicz, L. & Greenfield, H.J. 1995. *Transhumant Pastoralism in Southern Europe. Recent Perspectives from Archaeology History and Ethnology*. Budapest: Archeolingua.

Beck, D.P. & Materon, L.A. eds. 1988. *Nitrogen Fixation by Legumes in Mediterranean Agriculture*. Dordrecht: Martinus Nijhoff Publishers.

Bellotti, P., Caputo, C., Davoli, L., Evangelista, S., Garzanti, E., Pugliese, F. & Valeri, P. 2004. Morpho-sedimentary characteristics and Holocene evolution of the emergent part of the Ombrone River delta (southern Tuscany). *Geomorphology*, 61:71–90.

Bergmeier, E., Petermann, J. & Schröder, E. 2010. Geobotanical survey of wood-pasture habitats in Europe: diversity, threats and conservation. *Biodiversity and Conservation*, 19:2995–3014.

Biserni, G. & van Geel, B. 2005. Reconstruction of Holocene palaeoenvironment and sedimentation history of the Ombrone alluvial plain (South Tuscany, Italy). *Review of Palaeobotany and Palynology*, 136:16–28.

Boisseuil, D. 2002. *Le thermalisme en Toscane à la fin du Moyen âge. Les bains siennois de la fin du XIIIe siècle au début du XVIe siècle*. Roma: École française de Rome.

Brandt, R. & Karlsonn, L. eds. 2001. *From Huts to Houses. Transformations of Ancient Societies. Proceedings of an International Seminar organized by the Norwegian and Swedish Institutes in Rome, 21–24 September 1997*. Acta Instituti Romani Regni Sueciae, Series, 4/56. Uppsala: Astrom Editions.

Braudel, F. 1949. *La Méditerranée et le monde méditerranéen à l'époque de Philippe II*. Paris: Armand Colin.

Buonincontri, M., Allevato, E. & Di Pasquale, G. 2013. The problem of the alternating dominance of deciduous and evergreen vegetation: archaeo-anthracological data from northern Maremma. *Annali di Botanica*, 3:165–71.

Buonincontri, M., Saracino, A. & Di Pasquale, G. 2015. The transition of chestnut (*Castanea sativa* Miller) from timber to fruit tree: cultural and economic inferences in the Italian peninsula. *The Holocene*, 25(7):1111–23.

Burri, S. 2014. Reflections on the concept of marginal landscape through a study of late medieval *incultum* in Provence (South-eastern France), *Postclassical Archaeology*, 4:7–38.

Buttery, B.R. & Gibson, A.H. 1990. The effect of nitrate on the time course of nitrogen fixation and growth in *Pisum sativum* and *Vicia faba*. *Plant and Soil*, 127:143–46.

Calzolai, L. & Marcaccini, P. 2003. *I percorsi della transumanza in Toscana*. Firenze: Polistampa.

Cambi, F. 1996. *Carta archeologica della provincia di Siena. 2: Il Monte Amiata: Abbadia San Salvatore*. Siena: Nuova Immagine Editrice.

Cambi, F., Citter, C., Cristoferi, D., De Silva, M., Guarducci, A., Macchi, A., Pizziolo, G., Sarti, L., Vanni, E., Volante, N. & Zagli, A. 2015. A cross-disciplinary approach to the study of Transhumance as territorial identity factor in long term perspective: the TraTTo project –Southern Tuscany paths and pasturages from prehistory to the modern age. *Review of Historical Geography and Toponomastics*, 10(19–20):85–98.

Cammarosano, P. & Passeri, V. 1976. *I castelli del senese. Strutture fortificate dell'area senese – grossetana*. Siena: Monte dei Paschi di Siena.

Carandini, A. ed. 1985. *Settefinestre: una villa schiavistica nell'Etruria romana 3*. Modena: Panini.

Cevasco, R. 2007. *Memoria verde. Nuovi spazi per la geografia*. Reggio Emilia: Diabasis.

Cevasco, R., Moreno, D. & Stagno, A.M. 2008. Géographie historique et archéologie environnementale des bâtiments ruraux: quelques notes de terrain sur l'habitat animal dans un site des Apennins Ligures (Nord – Ouest de L'Italie) du XVII au XX siècle. In: J.-R. Trochet, ed. *Maisons paysannes en Europe occidentale, XV–XXI siècles*. Paris: Furet, pp. 71–79.

Chellini, R. 2002. *Acque sorgive salutari e sacre in Etruria*. British Archaeological Reports International Series 1067. Oxford: Archaeopress.

Cherubini, G. 1974. *Signori, contadini, borghesi. Ricerche sulla società italiana del Basso Medioevo*. Firenze: La Nuova Italia.

Cherubini, G. 1981a. La civiltà del castagno in Italia alla fine del medioevo. *Archeologia Medievale*, 8:247–80.

Cherubini, G. 1981b. *Risorse, paesaggio ed utilizzazione agricola del territorio della Toscana sudoccidentale nei secc. XIV–XV*. In: *Civiltà ed economia agricola in Toscana nei secc. XIV–XV: problemi della vita delle campagne del tardo medioevo*. Pistoia: Centro Italiano di Studi di Storia e d'Arte di Pistoia, pp. 91–115.

Cherubini, G. 1981c. *Le campagne italiane dall'XI al XV secolo*. Torino: UTET.

Ciampoltrini, G. 1993. Le terme pubbliche nelle città dell'Etruria centro-settentrionale fra I e II secolo d.C. *Studi Classici e Orientali*, 43:427–46.

Citter, C. ed. 1996. *Grosseto, Roselle e il Prile. Note per la storia di una città e del territorio circostante*. Mantova: Società Archeologica Padana.

Collavini, S.M. 1998. *"Honorabilis domus et spetiosissimus comitatus": gli Aldobrandeschi da conti a principi territoriali (secoli IX–XIII)*. Pisa: ETS.

Corbier, M. 1999. La transhumance: aperçus historiographiques et acquis récents. In: H. Hermon ed. *La question agraire à Roma. Droit romain et société, perception historiques et historiographiques*. Como: Edizioni New Press, pp. 37–56.

Cortonesi, A. 2005. L'olivo nell'Italia medievale. *Reti Medievali Rivista*, 6(2):2–29.

Cristoferi, D. 2015. *La costruzione della Dogana dei Paschi di Siena (1353–1419)*. In: I. Del Punta & M. Paperini, eds. *La Maremma al tempo di Arrigo. Società e a paesaggio nel Trecento: continuità e trasformazioni*. Livorno: Debatte Editore, pp. 121–31.

Cristoferi, D. 2016. "Il reame di Siena": la costruzione della Dogana dei Paschi e lo sviluppo della transumanza in Maremma (metà XIV-inizio XV secolo) (unpublished doctoral thesis, University of Siena).

Curri, C.B. 1978. Forma Italiae(5). *Vetulonia*. Firenze: Olschki Editore.

Dell'Omodarme, O. 1988. La transumanza in Toscana nei secoli XVII e XVIII. In: M. Massafra & G. Delille, eds. La transhumance dans les pays méditerranéens du XVe au XIX siècle. *Mélanges de l'école française de Rome*, 99(2):947–69.

Denton, M.D., Pearce, D.J. & Peoples, M.K. 2013. Nitrogen contribution from faba bean (*Vicia faba* L.) reliant on soil rhizobia or inoculation. *Plant and Soil*, 365:363–74.

Desplanques, H. 1969. *Campagne ombrienne. Contribution à l'étude des paysages ruraux en Italie centrale*. Paris: A. Colin.

Devoto, G. 1969. *Avviamento alla etimologia italiana, Dizionario etimologico*. Firenze: Le Monnier.

Di Pasquale, G., Allevato, E., Cocchiararo, A., Moser, D., Pacciarelli, M. & Saracino, A. 2014. Late Holocene persistence of *Abies alba* in low-mid altitude deciduous forests of central and southern Italy: new perspectives from charcoal data. *Journal of Vegetation Science*, 25:1299–1310.

Di Pasquale, G., Allevato, E., Russo Ermolli, E., Coubray, S., Lubritto, C., Marzaioli, F., Yoneda, M., Takeuchi, K., Kano, Y., Matsuyama, S. & De Simone, G.F. 2010. Reworking the idea of chestnut (*Castanea sativa* Mill.) cultivation in Roman times: New data from ancient Campania. *Plant Biosystems – An International Journal Dealing with All Aspects of Plant Biology*, 144(4):865–73.

Di Pasquale, G., Buonincontri, M., Allevato, E. & Saracino, A. 2014. Human-derived landscape changes on the northern Etruria coast (western Italy) between Roman times and the late Middle Ages. *The Holocene*, 24(11):1491–502.

Duclos, J.-C. & Pitte, A. eds. 1994. *L'homme et le mouton dans l'espace de la transhumance*. Grenoble: Glenat.

Fabbri, F. 2004–2005. Votivi anatomici fittili e culti delle acque nell'Etruria di età medio – e tardo – repubblicana. *Rassegna di Archeologia*, 21B:103–52.

Farinelli, R. & Giorgi, A. 1998. "Castellum reficere vel aedificare": il secondo incastellamento in area senese. Fenomeni di accentramento insediativo tra la metà del XII secolo e i primi decenni del XIII secolo. In: M. Marrocchi, ed. *Fortilizi e campi di battaglia nel Medioevo attorno a Siena*. Siena: Nuova Immagine Editrice, pp. 159–263.

Fentress, E. 2003. *Cosa V: An Intermittent Town, Excavations 1991–1997* (MAAR Suppl. Series II). Ann Arbor (MI): University of Michigan Press.

Firmati, M. 2002. New data from the Fortified Settlement of Ghiaccio Forte in the Albegna Valley. *Etruscan Studies. Journal of the Etruscan Foundation*, 1(9):63–75.

Forbes, H. 1995. The identification of pastoralist sites within the context of estate-based agriculture in Ancient Greece. *Annual of the British School at Athens*, 90:325–38.

Frenzel, B. & Weiss, M. eds. 1994. *Evaluation of Land Surfaces Cleared from Forests in the Mediterranean Region During the Time of the Roman Empire. Paläoklimaforschung/Palaeoclimate Research* 10. Stuttgart-Jena-New York: Gustav Fischer.

Fusco, U. 2008–2009. Iscrizioni votive ad Ercole, alle Fonti e a Diana dal sito di Campetti a Veio: ulteriori elementi per l'interpretazione archeologica. *Rendiconti della Pontificia Accademia Romana di Archeologia*, 81:443–500.

Gabba, E. 1985. La transumanza nell'Italia romana: evidenze e problemi, qualche prospettiva per l'età altomedievale. In: *L'Uomo di fronte al mondo animale nell'alto Medioevo*. Spoleto: CISAM, pp. 373–90.

Gauslaa, Y. 2005. Lichen palatability depends on investments in herbivore defence. *Oecologia*, 143:94–105.

Gerbet, M.-C. 2000. *Un élevage original au Moyen Âge. La péninsule Ibérique*. Paris: Atlantica-Séguier.

Ginatempo, M. 1987. Per la storia degli ecosistemi e dell'alimentazione medievali: recenti studi di archeozoologia in Italia. In: R. Francovich, ed. *Archeologia e storia del medioevo italiano*. Roma: Carocci Editore, pp. 173–97.

Ginatempo, M. 1988. *Crisi di un territorio: il popolamento della Toscana senese alla fine del Medioevo*. Firenze: Olschki Editore.

Gondard, H., Romane, F., Santa Regina, I. & Leonardi, S. 2006. Forest management and plant species diversity in chestnut stands of three Mediterranean areas. *Biodiversity and Conservation*, 15:1129–42.

Greppi, C. 2009. Il paesaggio agrario nell'Otto e Novecento. Popolazione e uso del suolo nelle fonti statistiche e catastali. In: G. Resti, ed. *Ombrone. Un fiume tra due terre*. Pisa: Pacini, pp. 113–29.

Haas, J.N., Karg, S. & Rasmussen, P. 1996. Beech leaves and twigs used as winter fodder: examples from historic and prehistoric times. *Environmental Archaeology*, 1:81–86.

Hadar, L., Noy-Meir, I. & Perevolotsky, A. 1999. The effect of shrub clearing and grazing on the composition of a Mediterranean plant community: functional groups versus species. *Journal of Vegetation Science*, 10:673–82.

Hejcmanová, P., Stejskalová, M. & Hejcman, M. 2014. Forage quality of leaf-fodder from the main broad-leaved woody species and its possible consequences for the Holocene development of forest vegetation in Central Europe. *Vegetation History and Archaeobotany*, 25:607–13.

Imberciadori, I. 2002. *Studi su Amiata e Maremma*, 2nd ed. Firenze: Accademia dei Georgofili.

Krebs, P., Conedera, M., Pradella, M., Torriani, D., Felber, M. & Tinner, W. 2004. Quaternary refugia of the sweet chestnut (*Castanea sativa* Mill.): an extended palynological approach. *Vegetation History and Archaeobotany*, 13:145–60.

Kurze, W. & Citter, C. 1995. La Toscana (= L'occupazione della Maremma toscana da parte dei Longobardi e la frontiera meridionale). In: G.P. Brogiolo, ed. *Città, castelli, campagne nei territori di frontiera (VI–VII sec.). V Seminario sul Tardoantico e l'Altomedioevo in Italia Centrosettentrionale (Montebarro-Galbiate, 9–10 giugno 1994)*. Mantova: Società Archeologica Padana, pp. 159–86.

Laffont, P.-Y. 2006. *Transhumance et estivage en Occident des origines aux enjeux actuels*. Toulouse: Presses Universitaires du Mirail.

Le Roy Ladurie, E. 1975. *Montaillou, village occitan de 1294 à 1324*. Paris: Gallimard.

Limbrey, S. & Bell, M. eds. 1982. *Archaeological Aspects of Woodland Ecology*. British Archaeological Reports International Series 146. Oxford: Archeopress.

Lisini, A. 1895. *Provvedimenti economici della Repubblica di Siena nel 1382: tratti da un testo a penna del senese R. Archivio di Stato*. Siena: Enrico Torrini.

Maggi, R., Nisbet, G. & Barker, G. eds. 1990. *Archeologia della pastorizia nell'Europa Meridionale*. Rivista di Studi Liguri, 56.

Magny, M., de Beaulieu, J.-L., Drescher-Schneider, R., Vanniere, B., Walter-Simonnet, A.-V., Miras, Y., Millet, L., Bossuet, G., Peyron, O., Brugiapaglia, E. & Leroux, A. 2007. Holocene climate changes in the central Mediterranean as recorded by lake-level fluctuations at Lake Accesa (Tuscany, Italy). *Quaternary Science Reviews*, 26:1736–58.

Mallegni, F. & Fornaciari, G. 1985. *Le ossa umane*. In: A. Carandini, ed. *Settefinestre: una villa schiavistica nell'Etruria romana 3*. Modena: Panini, pp. 275–77.

Malo, J.E. & Suárez, F. 1995. Herbivorous mammals as seed dispersers in a Mediterranean dehesa. *Oecologia*, 104:246–55.

Martins, A., Marques, G., Borges, O., Portela, E., Lousada, J., Raimundo, F. & Madeira, M. 2011. Management of chestnut plantations for a multifunctional land use under Mediterranean conditions: effects on productivity and sustainability. *Agroforest Systems*, 81:175–89.

Massaini, M. 2005. *Transumanza. Dal Casentino alla Maremma storie di uomini ed armenti lungo le antiche dogane*. Roma: Aldo Sara Editore.

Matteucci, M., Benesperi, R., Giordani, P., Piervittori, R. & Isocrono, D. 2012. Epiphytic lichen communities in chestnut stands in Central-North Italy. *Biologia*, 67(1):61–70.

McClure, S.B. 2015. The pastoral effect. *Current Anthropology*, 56(6):901–10.

Miozzo, M. & Montini, P. eds. 2007. *Conservazione di Abies alba in faggeta abetina nel Pigelleto-Monte Amiata*. Firenze: Regione Toscana.

Moreno, D. & Cevasco, R. 2013. Rural Landscapes: The Historical Roots of Biodiversity. In: M. Agnoletti, ed. *Italian Historical Rural Landscapes. Cultural Values for the Environment and Rural Development*. Dordrecht Heidelberg London New York: Springer, pp. 141–52.

Moreno, D. & Poggi, G. 1996. Storia delle risorse boschive nelle montagne mediterranee: modelli di interpretazione per le produzioni foraggere in regime consuetudinario. In: S. Cavaciocchi, ed. *L'uomo e la foresta. Secoli XIII–XVIII*. Firenze: Le Monnier, pp. 635–53.

Nixon, L. & Price, S. 2001. The diachronic analysis of pastoralism through comparative variables. *Annual of the British School at Athens*, 96:395–424.

Nucciotti, M. 2006. L'Amiata nel medioevo (secoli VIII–XIV): modi, tempi e luoghi della formazione di un paesaggio storico. In: Z. Ciuffoletti, ed. *Il parco minerario dell'Amiata. Il territorio e la sua storia, a cura di Zeffiro Ciuffoletti*. Arcidosso: Effigi Edizioni, pp. 161–98.

Nucciotti, M. 2007. Arcidosso (GR). Castel Vaiolo: archeologia di un insediamento rurale del X secolo. *Notiziario della Soprintendenza per i Beni Archeologici della Toscana*, 3:664–73.

Öckinger, E., Niklasson, M. & Nilsson, S.G. 2005. Is local distribution of the epiphytic lichen Lobaria pulmonaria limited by dispersal capacity or habitat quality? *Biodiversity and Conservation*, 14:759–73.

Paoli, L. & Loppi, S. 2001. Una raccolta di licheni dal Monte Labbro (Grosseto). *Atti Museo Storia Naturale Maremma*, 19:17–20.

Pasquini, G. 1905. L'organizzazione della transumanza dei greggi dal Casentino in Maremma. In: *Atti del Quinto Congresso degli allevatori di bestiame della Regione Toscana*. Firenze: Comizio Agrario di Firenze, pp. 183–86.

Pasquinucci, M. 2004. Montagna e pianura: transumanza e allevamento. In: M. Clavel-Levêque & E. Hermon, eds. *Espaces intégrés et ressources naturelles dans l'empire romain. Actes du colloque de l'Université de Laval-Québec (5–8 Mars 2003)*. Besançon: Institut des Sciences et Techniques de l'Antiquité, pp. 165–78.

Peoples, M.B. & Baldock, J.A. 2001. Nitrogen dynamics of pastures: nitrogen fixation inputs, the impact of legumes on soil nitrogen fertility, and the contributions of fixed nitrogen to Australian farming systems. *Australian Journal of Experimental Agriculture*, 41(3):327–46.

Piccinni, G. 1990. Ambiente, produzione e società della Valdorcia nel tardo medioevo. In: A. Cortonesi, ed. *La Val d'Orcia nel medioevo e nei primi secoli dell'età moderna*. Roma: Viella, pp. 31–58.

Piccinni, G. 2006. La politica agraria del comune di Siena. In: G. Piccinni & A. Cortonesi, eds. *Medioevo delle campagne. Rapporti di lavoro, politica agraria, protesta contadina*. Roma: Viella, pp. 207–92.

Pieri, S. 1969. *Toponomastica della Toscana meridionale (valli della Fiore, dell'Ombrone, della Cecina e fiumi minori) e dell'Arcipelago Toscano*. Siena: Accademia degli Intronati.

Pierson, E.A. & Mack, R.N. 1990. The population biology of *Bromus tectorum* in forests – effect of disturbance, grazing, and litter on seedling establishment and reproduction. *Oecologia*, 12:302–15.

Pii Secundi Pontificis Max. 1614. *Commentarii*. Roma: Ex typographia Dominici Basae.

Pinto, G. 1982. *La Toscana nel tardo medioevo. Ambiente, economia rurale, società*. Firenze: Sansoni.

Pontecorvo, G. 1932. *Le condizioni dell'economia rurale nell'Appennino toscano, II, Pratomagno e Appennino Casentinese*. Firenze: Tip. M. Ricci.

Rasmussen, P. 1993. Analysis of goat/sheep faeces from Egolzwil 3, Switzerland: evidence for branch and twig foddering of livestock in the Neolithic. *Journal of Archaeological Science*, 20:479–502.

Regoli, E. 2002. La Media e la Tarda Età Imperiale. In: A. Carandini & F. Cambi, eds. 2002. *Paesaggi d'Etruria. Valle dell'Albegna, Valle d'Oro, Valle del Chiarone, Valle del Tafone*. Roma: Edizioni di Storia e Letteratura, pp. 218–45.

Rendu, C. 2000. Fouiller des cabanes de bergers: Pour quoi faire? *Études rurales*, 153–54:151–76.

Resti, G. ed. 2009. *Ombrone. Un fiume tra due terre*. Pisa: Pacini.

Safronova, V.I., Piluzza, G., Zinovkina, N.Y., Kimeklis, A.K., Belimov, A.A. & Bullitta, S. 2012. Relationships between pasture legumes, rhizobacteria and nodule bacteria in heavy metal polluted mine waste of SW Sardinia. *Symbiosis*, 58(1):149–59.

Sallares, R. 2006. Role of environmental changes in the spread of malaria in Europe during the Holocene. *Quaternary International*, 150:21–27.

Sani, G. 2011. *Le rocce dei pennati. Sulle tracce delle rocce Sacre dei Liguri – Apuani nelle Alpi Apuane (Toscana nord occidentale)*. Empoli: Centro Arte Rupestre Toscano.

Frizell Santillo, B. 2004. Curing the flock. The use of healing waters in Roman pastoral economy. In: B. Santillo Frizell, ed. *PECUS. Man and Animal in Antiquity. Proceedings of the Conference at the Swedish Institute in Rome, September 9–12, 2002*. Roma: The Swedish Institute In Rome, pp. 80–93.

Sillett, S.C., McCune, B., Peck, J.E., Rambo, T.R. & Ruchty, A. 2000. Dispersal limitations of epiphytic lichens result in species dependent on old-growth forests. *Ecological Applications*, 10:789–99.

Skerman, P.J., Cameron, D.G. & Riveros, F. 1988. *Tropical forage legumes*, 2nd ed. Roma: FAO.

Solinas, P.G. ed. 1989–1990. *Pastori sardi in provincia di Siena. Vol. I: Demografia ed economia: profilo statistico; Vol. II: Il discorso lungo un viaggio. Brani di interviste sull'immigrazione sarda; Vol. III: Economia e strutture sociali*. Siena: Provincia di Siena.

Squatriti, P. 2013. *Landscape and Change in Early Medieval Italy Chestnuts, Economy, and Culture*. Cambridge: Cambridge University Press.

Terhürne-Berson, R., Litt, T. & Cheddadi, R. 2004. The spread of *Abies* throughout Europe since the last glacial period: combined macrofossil and pollen data. *Vegetation History and Archaeobotany*, 13:257–68.

Thoen, E. & Soens, T. 2015. The family or the farm: a Sophie's choice? The Late Medieval Crisis in Flanders. In: J. Grendel, ed. *Crisis in the Later Medieval period. Beyond the Postan – Duby Paradigm*. Turnhout: Brepols Publishers, pp. 130–238.

Tinner, W., Colombaroli, D., Heiri, O., Henne, P.D., Steinacher, M., Untenecker, J., Vescovi, E., Allen, J.R.M., Carraro, G. & Valsecchi, V. 2013. The past ecology of *Abies alba* provides new perspectives on future responses of silver fir forests to global warming. *Ecological Monographs*, 83:419–39.

Tozzi, C. 1981. L'alimentazione nella Maremma medievale. Due esempi di scavo. *Archeologia Medievale*, 1:299–303.

Vaccaro, E., Bowes, K., Ghisleni, M., Grey, C., Arnoldus-Huyzendveld, A., Cau Ontiveros, M.Á., Mercuri, A.M., Pecci, A., Rattigheri, E. & Rinaldi R. 2013. Excavating the Roman peasant II: excavations at Case Nuove, Cinigiano (GR). *Papers of the British School at Rome*, 81:129–79.

Valenti, M. 2011. Miranduolo (Chiusdino, SI). Campagna 2011. (FOLD&R Italy Series 241). http://www.fastionline.org/docs/FOLDER-it-2011-241.pdf. Accessed 7 May 2013.

Valenti, M. 2012. Villaggi e comunita` nella Toscana tra VII e X secolo: la ricerca archeologica. In: P. Galetti, ed. Paesaggi, Comunità, Villaggi. Fondazione Centro italiano di Studi sull'Alto Medioevo: Spoleto, pp. 477–504.

Van de Noort, R. 2008. The archaeology of wetland landscapes: method and theory at the beginning of the 21st century. In: B. David & J. Thomas, eds. *Handbook of Landscape Archaeology*. Walnut Creek: Left Coast Press, pp. 482–548.

Van de Noort, R. & O'Sullivan, A. 2006. *Rethinking Wetland Archaeology*. London: Duckworth.

Vanni, E. 2014. *Sistemi agro – silvo – pastorali in un contesto dell'Etruria costiera. Aspetti conservativi del paesaggio in una prospettiva di lunga durata* (unpublished doctoral thesis, University of Foggia).

Vanni, E. 2015a. The role of natural resources as electrification points for mobility. An archaeological perspective. In: XVIII *CIAC: Centro y periferia en el Mundo Clásico/ Centre and periphery in the ancient world S. 2. La Arqueología del paisaje. Los recursos naturales. Landscape Archaeology, Natural resources*. Mérida: Museo Nacional de Arte Romano, pp. 193–96.

Vanni, E. 2015b. Mobility as a proxy for defining cultures: reconsidering identity and transhumance from a long – run perspective. *Review of Historical Geography and Toponomastics*, 10(19–20):125–50.

Vanni, E. & Cambi, F. 2015. *Sale e Transumanza. Approvvigionamento e mobilità in Etruria costiera tra Bronzo Finale e Medioevo*. In: F. Cambi, G. De Venuto & R. Goffredo, eds. *I pascoli, i campi, il mare. Paesaggi d'altura e di pianura in Italia dall'Età del Bronzo al Medioevo, Storia e Archeologia Globale 2*. Bari: Insulae Diomedae, pp. 107–28.

Vescovi, E., Kaltenrieder, P. & Tinner, W. 2010. Late – Glacial and Holocene vegetation history of Pavullo nel Frignano (Northern Apennines, Italy). *Review of Palaeobotany and Palynology*, 160:32–45.

Violante, C. 1995. Una notizia di transumanza verso la Maremma nell'Alto Medioevo. In: I. Zilli, ed. *Fra spazio e tempo: studi in onore di Luigi De Rosa*. Napoli: Edizioni Scientifiche Italiane, pp. 805–7.

Wickham, C. 1985. Pastoralism and underdevelopment in the Early Medieval period. In: *L'uomo di fronte al mondo animale nell'Alto Medioevo*. Spoleto: Centro Italiano di Studi sull'Alto Medioevo, pp. 400–455.

Wickham, C. 1989. Paesaggi sepolti: insediamento e incastellamento sull'Amiata, 750–1250. In: M. Ascheri & W. Kurze, eds. *L'Amiata nel Medioevo*. Roma: Viella, pp. 101–38.

Wickham, C. 1990. La montagna e la città. L'Appennino toscano nel Medioevo. In: C. Greppi, ed. *Paesaggi dell'Appennino toscano*. Venezia: Marsilio, pp. 15–31.

Wickham, C. 2001. Paludi e miniere nella Maremma toscana, XI–XIII secolo. In: *Castrum 7: Zones côtières littorales dans le monde méditerranéen au Moyen Âge*. Roma-Madrid: École française de Rome – Casa de Velázquez, pp. 451–66.

Whittaker, C.R. ed. 1988. *Pastoral Economies in Classical Antiquity, (Cambridge Philological Society, Supplementary Volume 41)*. Cambridge: The Cambridge Philological Society.

Zucchini, M. 1932. *Le condizioni dell'economia rurale nell'Appennino toscano*, III, *Romagna, Toscana, Val di Sieve e Val di Bisenzio*. Firenze: Tip. M. Ricci.

CHAPTER 15

Transhumant herding systems in Iberia

MARGARITA FERNÁNDEZ MIER AND CATARINA TENTE

INTRODUCTION

The topic of medieval transhumance in the Iberian Peninsula inevitably brings to mind *La Mesta* (beginning in the thirteenth century, *La Mesta* referred to a complex system of transhumant long-distance paths which allowed shepherds to move large flocks of sheep either southwards to the rich winter commons in Southern Iberia or northwards to the summer pastures in the Cantabrian Mountains; Gerbet, 1991). In addition to the fact that it survived well into the nineteenth century, the importance of *La Mesta* has made it a centrepiece of medieval stockbreeding studies in Iberia (see Klein, 1920; Bishko, 1963).

Indeed, this very emphasis on the *Mesta* has upstaged research on alternative forms of transhumance and common land management. Furthermore, the study of the role of big, oligarchic owners has overshadowed those of small owners and town councils in the management of grazing areas and the heterogeneous nature of the conflicts generated by grazing rights.

From the 1970s onwards, Spanish and Portuguese historians shifted their approach by targeting pre-*Mestan* livestock-management strategies, stressing the agencies of large northern Benedictine monasteries and the knights of the town councils, both of which were the main actors in large-scale sheep breeding (Pastor, 1970). Medium-distance transhumant arrangements can be documented from the tenth century as they alternated between summer and winter pastures. In some cases (and after the profound reforms in the sixteenth century), these systems were preserved and maintained well into the twentieth and even twenty-first centuries (García Martínez, 1988, 2003). In recent years, the focus has shifted to common land management by local communities, including the examination of the guidelines used for a variety of ecological niches, governance of the grazing areas, identity-related issues and the processes involved in confrontation and social unrest (Aguadé Nieto, 1993; Escalona Monge, 2001; Fernández Conde, 2001; Fernández Mier et al., 2013).

Anthropological studies, still a novelty in this field, have emphasized transhumant circuits and the shepherd's way of life and material culture. These interests are linked to local hopes for tourist interest, visitor promotion and the rekindling of regionalism as all of those phenomena are based on the importance of herding and its associated communal practices (García Martín, 1994; Elías Pastor & Novoa Portela, 2003).

Even more recent still is the arrival of archaeological studies on the scene of transhumance investigation. A monograph issue of *Debates de Arqueología Medieval* (2013) was recently devoted to stockbreeding and outlined the main lines of investigation. It also included the novel perspectives presented by landscape archaeology and zooarchaeology.

Of special interest is the study of common lands (especially those in mountainous areas), particularly those commons which were used as pastures. Such an approach considers the importance of livestock in rural economies, thus overcoming the old paradigms which equated herding with primitivism while stressing peasants' and shepherds' agency as masters of their territory who were also capable of rationalizing the use of their lands (Fernández Mier & Quirós Castillo, 2015).

All the aforementioned approaches have furnished us with a more complex and nuanced view of transhumant herding. Among the varied new perspectives which have only recently been taken now into account are the role of peasant societies in the management of pastures in the medieval period (ninth to twelfth centuries) and the long clash between nobility, ecclesiastic elites, villagers and larger landowners over the control of the pastures.

In the light of this historiographic context, how can archaeology contribute to our understanding of medieval stockbreeding and the types of transhumant herding associated with it? Can archaeological research shed light on other aspects of Iberian transhumant cycles? As was explained above, archaeology has turned to cattle production only very recently; undoubtedly, this delay must have been partly caused by the ephemeral nature of most of the practice's by-products and the consequent lack of reliable archaeological material. However, the central role recently assumed by bioarchaeological perspectives as well as landscape archaeology has brought with it new and promising approaches to the complex issue of transhumant herding and its cyclic nature.

© 2018 European Association of Archaeologists

Ecosystems and Methodological Underpinnings of The Study of Transhumance

Two Iberian case studies provide good examples of the intricacies of studying transhumance systems: Cantabrian Mountains in northwest Spain and Estrela Mountain in central Portugal (see Figure 15.1).

The Cantabrian Mountains are abrupt and rugged, their orography being at the root of a compartmentalized geographic arrangement. Narrow fluvial valleys run along an oblique axis to the 80-mile-long mountain range, while some small secondary valleys run parallel to it. The differences in elevation are quite dramatic, they range from 300/400 m a.s.l. in the northern lowland riverbeds to peaks which clock in at well over 2000 m a.s.l; the summer pastures usually lie within a range of 1200 to 2000 m a.s.l.

These Cantabrian fluvial valleys typically present steep limestone slopes and summits (which are largely unsuitable for agriculture) although some terraces near the headwaters provide good grazing fields at the headwaters. From the Neolithic Revolution on, several types of transhumance have been practiced there: valley transhumance, short-distance transhumance, medium-distance transhumance (coast-to-mountains) and long-distance transhumance (from Southern Iberia to the Cantabrian Mountains).

Estrela Mountain, the highest elevation in mainland Portugal at 1992 m a.s.l., is a granitic mountain range at the headwaters of the Mondego River, which describes a curve from its northern to its western flank. The highly diversified climate conditions that characterize the region can be explained by the relative proximity of the Atlantic Ocean to the west and the Spanish *Meseta* to the east as well as its altitude. Altitudinal layering of the vegetation cover in Estrela Mountain can be split into three main zones: a basal section (up to 800/900 m a.s.l. and heavily Mediterraneanized and deeply altered by human intervention); a middle section (from 800/900 to 1300/1600 m a.s.l., corresponding to declining oak forests due to fires and the grazing) and an upper section (above 1300/1600 m a.s.l., where juniper came to dominance after the human-led destruction of its post-Würmian cover of pine and birch). Geologically, the region is characterized by granites and schists, often found under a thin cover of acidic soil. This is an important limitation regarding the preservation of organic material, such as human or faunal remains. Due to anthropogenic deforestation and subsequent soil erosion – a fact attested since Neolithic times in the region – fertile land is found mostly in lower areas, at the foot of mountains and in river valleys. In higher altitudes, outcroppings dominate the landscape. Estrela Mountain is one of the few Portuguese mountain

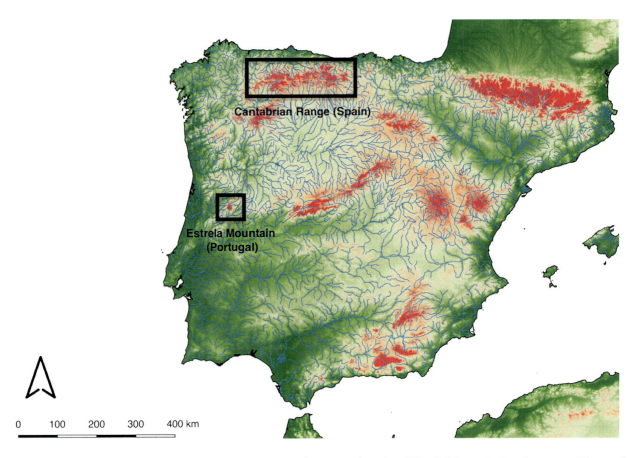

Figure 15.1. Iberian case-study area: Cantabrian Mountains (northwest Spain) and Estrela Mountain (northern-central Portugal)

ranges for which transhumance can be documented. The reference work for transhumance in the region was written in the 1930s by Orlando Ribeiro (1940–1941), who documented the seasonal movements of sheep, and sometimes goat, flocks from lowland villages.

From a methodological point of view, cross-disciplinary studies are an essential part of transhumance research and should also lead to a combined analysis of the data provided by written, toponymic, archaeological, ethnographic and palaeoenvironmental sources (López Gómez et al., 2016).

Documentary evidence is very succinct prior to the thirteenth century, and fourteenth and fifteenth century parchments are somewhat more explicit. It is only after the sixteenth century that there is an abundance of relevant written sources, although they have not yet been commonly utilized in connection with transhumance. There was a great increase in the number of references to pastures, both in the collections of ecclesiastical and common lordships and in the archives of the councils and local *juntas* (local administrative entities which managed several villages), and including also notarial certificates. A critical reading of these can certainly help us to understand how and to what extent herding put pressure on pasture lands and their management as well as how that pressure affected its main players and how alternative uses of the land could be implemented.

Our research teams have also used toponymy as a valuable source of information. Place names abound in our area of study and are remarkably resilient, a fact which facilitates the identification of the places mentioned in the documentary sources (especially after the twelfth century; Fernández Mier, 2006). A thorough comparison of present-day place names with the toponyms found in the documents[1] was combined with archaeological field surveys and excavations to help ascertain economic practices and their chronologies.

Livestock breeding systems in both Estrela Mountain and the Cantabrian Mountains can also be better understood through ethnographic and anthropological analyses. In both areas, transhumance has persisted into the twentieth century. Even though the liberal governments of the nineteenth century placed some pressure on communal land management, many mountain areas were able to keep or recover their traditional ownership systems, facilities and the material culture associated therewith by means of collective exploitation. Only in the 1960s did these traditions start to disappear *en masse* due to the dismantling and disintegration of rural environments in Spain and Portugal which resulted in an exodus towards industrial centres (Daugstad et al., 2014).

Nowadays, transhumance is just a residual practice. However, thorough field surveys and examination of the remaining buildings and tools, together with the documentary and archaeological sources, go a long way to clarify these practices.

Generally speaking, the written sources provide information on four main issues: pasture boundaries, social clashes caused by competition for grazing rights, ownership and management systems or pasture leasing (e.g. involving big landowners). In addition, descriptive and interpretive ethnographic accounts help us document building patterns (sheds, cabins, houses or livestock enclosures) and their traditional uses as they were recorded in oral testimonies. It is not uncommon for one pasture area to have undergone different types of transhumant exploitation at the same time. Naturally, this complicates the identification of their associated remains. In those cases, oral sources are especially relevant if we are to understand all the complexities inherent to transhumant systems.

Due to the resilience of some of their socio-economic traits and their belated conservation of these ancient practices, our two areas of study are particularly well suited to this cross-disciplinary and ethnographically informed approach (González Álvarez et al., 2016).

SHORT-DISTANCE TRANSHUMANCE AND PEASANT COMMUNITIES

Short-distance mountain transhumance involves the movement of flocks from villages to high-altitude pastures. This vertical movement can be undertaken just by a few shepherds, but in certain regions a two-settlement arrangement existed, in which a sizeable part of a village's population moved to communal dwellings in the mountains. In Portugal two types of housing units exist: *brandas* or estival mountain settlements situated over 1000 m a.s.l. and *inverneiras* (winter villages situated in the valleys). In the Cantabrian Mountains, the estival settlements are called *brañas* or *mayaos* and range between 600 and 1400 m a.s.l.

Still today, anthropological research on Estrela Mountain and the Cantabrian Mountains can document this system of valley transhumance, nowadays mainly oriented to cattle, with its movement of herds from lowland pastures in the vicinity of the villages (at the bottom of the valley or mid-slope) to the summer commons in the highlands. Although these communities currently specialize in cattle rearing, their use of agricultural land as a complement can be documented well into the twentieth century. The balance between livestock breeding and agriculture required wide compromises in the midst of these peasant communities, as well as the existence of some very precise statutes which held until the twentieth century. Many villages in the Cantabrian Mountains have kept the documents in which these statutes were encoded, sometimes as early as the fourteenth century; in other cases, we know about them only through oral accounts. There is an abundant bibliography on livestock breeding in the valleys, especially concerning the seventeenth, nineteenth and twentieth centuries (García Fernández, 1988; Rodríguez Gutiérrez, 1989; González Álvarez, 2013).

Short-distance or valley transhumance (2–5 km) in the Cantabrian Mountains (NW Spain)

Geographic, ethnographic and historical research has informed our understanding of cattle management. Our description of these practices relies on ethnographic accounts collected in two valleys located in the Cantabrian Mountains along the Pigüeña and Trubia rivers. Our main sources are oral surveys conducted in the 1990s, which we compare with a corpus of medieval records from the several landholders present in the area from the twelfth to the fifteenth centuries. Among these landowners were ecclesiastical powers (Balmonte Monastery and Oviedo Cathedral), secular lordships (the lords of Entragu from the sixteenth to nineteenth centuries) and the documents generated by the villages from the fifteenth century on which codified the rules for managing the commons (Álvarez Menéndez et al., 1990; Fernández Mier, 2006).

During the winter, livestock (mainly cattle and sheep) were kept in barns and were grazed on the meadows near the village. After the harvest, fields were also collectively used as pastures, which meant different months depending on the crop: August to March for spelt fields and only a fortnight in March in the case of corn.

Crops were cultivated in semi-collective enclosures. These were located in wide areas close to the village; each small division or enclosure (called *ería* or *sienra*) was exploited by a family. After the harvest, the remaining plant stubble was gathered collectively by all owners. The size of the herds allowed in the *erías* depended on the area they enclosed (García Fernández, 1988; Fernández Mier, 2010).

Halfway between the habitational areas and the high-altitude pastures lay the *morteras*, which were also semi-collective units used for the feeding of livestock. They were managed following the same principles as applied to the cultivated land. In this case, the aim was to gather hay for storage. This task was undertaken between April and July. In March/April and then in November/December, the herds were collectively allowed into the *morteras* as an intermediate stage before and after their stay in the high pastures. Most villages had more than one of these grass-producing *morteras* and they rotated their use in order to enhance their complementarity. When the herds were in these pastures, one individual was trusted by the community to take care of them, preventing them from going out of

bounds while also keeping alien livestock from entering the area (Bueida, 1991; Fernández Mier, 2013).

Orography dictates a wide variety of practices related to the uses and exploitation of these grazing fields in the different territories. Nevertheless, their main features remain constant throughout the Cantabrian Range. From the sixteenth century onwards, regulations of their use were amply dealt with by each village's ordinances. These established very precisely when the livestock were to be removed from upland areas (in order to allow for adequate resting periods for the pastures), on which days the herds were supposed to enter and leave them as well as the manner in which the repair of fencing systems should be managed (Álvarez Menéndez et al., 1990).

These semi-collective lands can still be located. While they are still a part of the local lore in some cases, in others, researchers can compare the place names as they appear in the written sources with those used today, or take into account the morphology of a particular place. They subsequently underwent a process of privatization; this can usually be traced through telltale signs such as partition of the plots into individual smallholdings and the building of cabins for shelter and for storing early-summer hay (García Martínez, 1988; Rodríguez Gutiérrez, 1989; Álvarez Menéndez et al., 1990).

During the summer months, livestock were transferred to the upland commons which belonged to each village or to a whole parish. Grazing rights were inherent to both native and non-native residents. Specific statutes regulated the size of the livestock that could be supported by the pastures and when they could enter and leave as well as different timelines for cattle, horses, sheep and goats (although the latter usually graze on lower-value pastures). There were also rules for the maintenance of paths, fencing, dangerous areas and the use of collective cabins, fountains and drinking troughs.

Brañas or *mayaos* are the names given to groups of huts or shelters situated in the upland pastures. Some of these are even protected, especially when located within the bounds of a national park. Their architectural diversity throughout the Cantabrian Mountains is remarkable. These buildings were used to protect newly born livestock and as shelter for the herdsmen who walked to and from the village at dawn and at dusk in order to milk the cows. A large number of *brañas* are still in use, although most of them have been almost completely abandoned. Archaeological excavations, through a wide variety of methodologies, have furnished us with ample information on the many activities developed in the *brañas* as well as the chronology. In the *braña* belonging to the village of Vigaña in the Pigüeña Valley, random survey pits compensated for the absence of archaeological information on the surface. These methods allowed for the gathering of data about prehistoric land use in the area, as well as tile making in the nineteenth and twentieth centuries (Fernández Mier et al., 2013).

We find a variety of constructive typologies in the *brañas*, from circular buildings with a false dome, used as a shelter for the livestock, to larger rectangular buildings with several rooms (Figure 15.2). The latter could be used for hay stocking and for sheltering both livestock and herdsmen. In addition to this, a variety of corrals, chapels, lodgings (near the main roads) and cold storages for milk. The archaeological cataloguing of this rich material heritage has only just begun. Although ethnographers have devoted a great deal of attention to it, they have generally limited themselves to the analysis of those buildings which are still standing and/or which were still in use until fairly recently (Graña García & López Álvarez, 2007).

Brañas enabled villagers to move a part of their daily activities to the uplands. Each family sent at least one of its members (especially in the early summer for the reaping); sometimes, they even farmed if it became necessary. The importance of this double life, up and down, is clearly seen in the fact that some *brañas* held their own festivals in the summer months, which gathered people from neighbouring villages and from those which shared grazing rights in the area.

From the sixteenth century onwards, there is abundant evidence for the regulations and codes which ensured a rational and multi-faceted use of all herding-related spaces. These prescriptions emanated from village councils which represented all the individuals in a village (Rodríguez Gutiérrez, 1989; Alvarez Menéndez et al., 1990). Unfortunately, these are not available for earlier centuries; therefore, understanding how these economic systems emerged and evolved in medieval times proves more difficult.

In addition to archaeological investigation in the Cantabrian Mountains, recent bioarchaeological research has unveiled evidence of major deforestation which appears to have started in Roman times. This process intensified in the fifth century and continued until the tenth century, leaving a largely treeless landscape with large grazing areas. In some cases, this was paired with intensive livestock breeding near the villages. In others, it appears to have been coupled with

Figure 15.2. Braña La Mesa *(Asturias, Spain). A* braña *used in short-distance transhumance situated in the highest pastures of the Cantabrian Mountains*

Source: © *Margarita Fernández Mier*

signs of cultivation. The data suggest a mixed economic system in which livestock breeding and cultivation were complementary, including pasture areas and meadows for hay production along with fields destined for crops and vegetables (Fernández Fernández, 2011). A coherent exploitation of a village's ecological niches could, thus, be achieved. In consequence, a village's location strongly predicted its economic specialization, with livestock becoming more relevant for higher villages (Fernández Mier & Quirós Castillo, 2015).

Similar economic arrangements can be found in some geographic areas adjacent to the northwest Iberia in which comparable transhumance-related buildings have been documented. A good example of this comes from the Aralar Range in the Basque Country, where such constructions have been documented from the sixth–seventh centuries. These Aralar *brañas* were gradually constructed by several generations of herdsmen. Their construction was contemporary with the consolidation of village networks in river valleys which points to a scenario in which fertile lowland areas and seasonal upland pastures combined in order to form a coherent economic system (Agirre et al., 2003a, b).

Another example comes from Galicia; the presence of cattle was documented in the sixth century. Some animals fell down a crevice while grazing and could not escape from it, thus hinting at extensive livestock breeding at that stage (Pérez-Rama et al., 2015).

An archaeological approach to pasture use in Estrela Mountain (Portugal)

Short-distance movements in Estrela Mountain are characterized by vertical displacements carried out by shepherds alone (rather than entire communities). This transhumant system does not imply the building of habitational structures or even well-defined settlements. Orlando Ribeiro's study of the region's pastoralism mentions the fact that around the month of April (and after the melting of the snow on the peaks), flocks would be moved to the highland pastures. Their owners would take turns sowing and taking care of the animals. When the weather was harsh, shepherds slept in mountain sheepfolds. However, moving the livestock to the mountains was less profitable than keeping them in the valleys. In this regard, Ribeiro (1940–1941: 251; translated from the Portuguese) writes:

> Here, the owners I interviewed during the separation of the different herds told me that sending flocks to the mountains was a custom that they always had done so, but also that if the flocks (sheep) stayed in the *Terra Chã* (literally, "the plain land") they would profit more

because they lost weight in the mountains; that flocks were also sent to the upland because the peasants could not take care of them during the intensive working period on the crops.

However, in some Portuguese regions, this kind of short-distance transhumance concerned entire communities rather than just the shepherds and their animals. A good example of this can be found at Castro do Laboreiro, where a larger segment of the community, composed by several families, moved along with the animals and settled in communal housing units near the mountain pastures. This implied, therefore, a twofold housing seasonal system in which the so-called *brandas* were the more permanent places located above 1000 m a.s.l. (at which families stayed from Easter to Christmas) and the *inverneiras* were the villages situated in the valleys (occupied during the winter months between December and March/April, when the snow covered the uplands; Lima, 1996: 12).

This twofold settlement system comprising *brandas* and *inverneiras* is documented only in the Peneda and Gerês mountains (Ribeiro, 1991a; Lima, 1996), which are located in the northernmost mountain ranges of the country, immediately south of the Galician border. Written or ethnographic records of such settlements are unknown in Estrela Mountain, a fact suggesting in a first moment of analysis that the herding system inherent to them was never practiced in the area. However, the discovery and study of an early medieval site – an enclosure named Soida, in the municipality of Celorico da Beira – led us to think otherwise or, at least, that some other ethnographically unrecorded system was there at play.

Indeed, this particular site is located on the top of an elongated promontory (around 1000 m a.s.l.) whose steep and irregular topography allowed for the building of only a few huts. Fieldwork carried out in 2006 and 2007 focussed on the enclosure and the domestic structures inside it. Initially interpreted as a fortification, the enclosure took the form of a thick stone wall (ca. 3 m wide) which was complemented by a palisade of indeterminate height. In the so-called Sectors II and III, the remains of two huts were identified and excavated. Whereas their superstructures should have been built with light, perishable materials, their infrastructures were solely composed by stone-structured hearths (see Figure 15.3). This site was abandoned by the end of the tenth century after a fire which completely destroyed it (Tente, 2010; Tente & Carvalho, 2011). In sum, Soida differs from the remaining coeval sites in the region which are either located in or near valley bottoms. Furthermore, activities witnessing a permanent occupation (such as storage, metalworking or grinding tools) are absent from the archaeological record, a fact which strongly intimates the possibility that Soida was a temporary habitation site.

Figure 15.3. Soida (Celorico da Beira). Archaeological site from the tenth century, Estrela Mountain
Source: © Catarina Tente

Unfortunately, on the basis of the available archaeological data alone, it is not possible to confirm if the entire Soida community moved to the mountains during the spring/summer season (as was documented in Peneda and Gerês) or if (perhaps, more likely) stock raising was a task which was carried out only by some families. Further research may bring the finding of similar sites in the highlands which would help us to test the interpretation of Soida as a *branda* settlement and, therefore, its relation to a specific (now extinct) strategy of pastoral exploitation of the mountain in medieval times. Considering the scarcity of the evidence obtained from the site, it is reasonable to think that only a segment of a major demographic unit moved to the uplands along with the herds, therefore differing in this particular aspect from the Peneda and Gerês ethnographically documented case studies.

It should also be noted that in the Peneda and Gerês examples, such seasonal movements were not motivated solely by pastoralism. They were part of a broader and more complex agrarian system involving arable crops and in which the herding of sheep, goats and cattle were also benefiting from it (Ribeiro, 1991b: 255). Under the hypothesis put forward above to explain the Soida case, in Estrela Mountain and its adjacent drainage basins, we might be dealing with an earlier economic system, an instance of medium-sized demographic scale between individual and communal types of mobility (i.e. a segment of a larger community). Interestingly, the ethnographic parallels to the huts identified in Soida are the transhumant shepherd huts (*choupanas*) dated in the Estrela Mountain from the first half of twentieth century (Oliveira et al., 1969). However, similar structures have also been identified in the archaeological record of some valley villages, such as São Gens and Penedo dos Mouros (Tente, 2012).

MIDDLE-DISTANCE TRANSHUMANCE

Middle-distance (60–90 km) transhumance in the Cantabrian Mountains

From the tenth century onwards, monasteries in northwest Iberia began to acquire pastures, *brañas* and grazing lands, and this trend intensified in the two following centuries (Escalona Monge, 2001). Two such examples can be found with the monasteries of Courias and Sahagún which dominate wide pasture areas which are both north and south of the Cantabrian Mountains respectively and which adamantly defended the borders of their estates. The written records emphasize the importance of the herding activities of the local elites as well as the monasteries, a fact which was confirmed by pollen analyses, pointing to an expansion of grazing land and a reduction in woodland area (Fernández Mier & Quirós Castillo, 2015).

The Monastery of Courias in Asturias offers an excellent example of this. Although the monastery already owned several *brañas* in the eleventh and twelfth centuries, it concomitantly began to effectuate a set of policies aimed at annexing more high-altitude lands in an obvious attempt to strengthen its power as a livestock owner. This emphasis on *brañas* and pastures shows clearly in the written record as a recurrent theme (García, 1980). The monastery's struggle to gain access to the upland pastures in the Cantabrian Mountains is thus quite apparent. The monks' focus was on cattle; their success brought about the consolidation of a supra-local ecclesiastical power nucleus between the twelfth and thirteenth centuries which controlled ample and well-defined domains and which furthermore were not subjected to partitions as was the case with hereditary lordships. Probably as early as the twelfth century, Courias configured a set of transhumant networks connecting the coast (or mid-mountain areas) with the highest parts of the Cantabrian Mountains. However, this hypothesis has yet to be verified; more archaeological research would be needed in order to ascertain the chronology of those transhumant systems.

Aside from the lands owned by the Church, a sizable part of the territory belonged to the Crown. Through the twelfth, thirteenth and fourteenth centuries, royal lands were re-organized in accordance with the founding of new towns (*burgos, villas* and *pueblas*). These new urban centres administered their surrounding areas (the *alfoz*) and established regular markets which channelled the economy of the whole region (Ruiz de la Peña, 1981). A new oligarchy emerged. Their attempts to seize land had a profound effect on the management of pastures; the process of the appropriation of grazing lands by town councils accelerated to the detriment of the commoners. These town councils (*concejos*) had great interest in pastoralism and pastures, as indicated by the privileges gained by some of their number in the fourteenth century and which allowed their herds to travel from the mountains to littoral regions. An easy example of these developments can be found in the case of the councils of Ponga and Amieva in Asturias. In 1395, they were granted free-grazing rights by King Henry III of Castile. The council of Casu acquired the same rights from King John II in 1447 (Ruiz de la Peña, 1977: 169–72). It is clear that a number of town councils had strong interests in herding and livestock rearing, which speaks of local oligarchies setting up complex economic networks which aimed at exploiting both lowland pastures (near the coast) in the winter

and high pastures (located in the mountain passes) in the summer. This arrangement mirrored that developed by monasteries during the fourteenth and fifteenth centuries.

After the thirteenth century, monastic orders gradually lost some of their power and their domains were transferred to a secular aristocratic class with a focus on livestock. This new group put great pressure on the ecclesiastical entities, town councils and villages in order to secure their access to estival grazing lands in the Cantabrian Mountains. The ensuing clash was in essence a fight for hegemony, with these secular noblemen trying to establish a speculative brand of stockbreeding which was in direct conflict with that practiced by peasant communities, relying on a combination of herding and agriculture (García Martínez, 1988; Fernández Mier et al., 2013; García Cañón, 2006).

In this context of social unrest and territorial disputes between monasteries, town councils and prominent aristocrats, new social groups emerged, namely the *vaqueiros de alzada* and the *pasiegos*, two communities which specialized in short-distance transhumance. Their identities became cemented between the sixteenth and eighteenth centuries. The *vaqueiros de alzada* live in central western Asturias and an adjacent area in the Leonese Mountains. *Vaqueiro* families have two dwellings for the winter and summer seasons, and move twice a year taking their animals and belongings with them, in a journey known as *alzada*. *Vaqueiros* spend winters in coastal or mid-mountain locations and summers in higher-altitude villages. The activities they perform in the latter are similar to those carried out by the local peasants who live in those upland areas year-round and which correspond to the valley transhumance described above. *Vaqueiro* settlements modify the landscape in distinct ways; their summer and winter villages (*brañas*) consist of true houses rather than simple cabins. Even more conspicuous is the parcelling out of lands that previously must have been commons (and have, thus, undergone a process of privatization; see Figure 15.4).

The *pasiegos* live in the Pas Mountains, in the provinces of Cantabria and Burgos. In the spring, *pasiego* families move to the summer pastures and stay there until autumn (De Terán, 1947). In this case there are several stages to their transhumant cycle, as the whole family moves from one hut to the next. Some families own as many as four huts, and they stay in all of them as they complete their yearly cycle. This movement is called *muda* (Corbera Millán, 2003, 2006, 2008).

Both systems (*alzada* and *muda*) originated within a context of intensified stockbreeding activity which began in the fourteenth century, a period marked by population growth and a rise in the demand for animal products. This brought about an important transformation of the landscape: including a generalization of hay

Figure 15.4. Moudreiros (Asturias, Spain). A winter vaqueiro *village or* braña de invierno
Source: © Margarita Fernández Mier

meadows and the intensification of pressure upon areas of extensive stockbreeding (which, nevertheless, did not disappear). This process has been styled as *la revolución de las cercas* (the fencing revolution) (García Martínez, 1988). There are abundant post-sixteenth-century sources recording these developments, which were complete by the eighteenth century, but some archaeological research is still needed if we are to understand all of their complexity. Some additional research on the fourteenth and fifteenth centuries could also help to explain the origins of these changes. The fact is that, while places of habitation date from the seventh and eighth centuries and (for the most part) still remain inhabited still today, their landscapes were considerably transformed after the fourteenth century. This phenomenon is especially evident in stockbreeding areas.

These forms of transhumance come with a rich legacy of material culture which has, in many cases, remained until today. Our team has already begun its investigation of this body of data from an archaeological standpoint (López Gómez, 2013; López Gómez et al., 2016).

Complementary transhumance systems in Estrela Mountain (Portugal)

There are two scales of ethnographically documented transhumance on Estrela Mountain. One short-distance system (described in the previous section) occurred in the summer when flocks went up to graze on mountain pastures. Another medium-distance system began with the first snowfall in November/December. Whereas some few animals returned from the uplands to graze on the pastures located around the valley villages, most were grouped in large herds and were grazed by herdsmen from the villages that were hired by the owners of the herds (Ribeiro, 1940–1941). These herds initiated a long way to faraway lands, encompassing journeys of more than 100 km each at the rate of 20 km per day. Different villages established different destinations for their flocks (Ribeiro, 1940–1941): the ones situated on the northeast slopes went to the Douro Valley, those that were located on the western slope went south to the lowlands of the Tagus Basin and, finally, the villages situated in the central area of Estrela Mountain chose the low Mondego Basin, more specifically, the fertile lands of the Coimbra (see Figure 15.5).

It is not yet possible to establish the historical origin of these transhumant movements. The oldest written references to mountain pastures go back to the first territorial charters endowed to the mountain villages of Folgosinho, Gouveia, Linhares, Seia and Manteigas. These documents allow us to conclude that these pastures were of considerable importance for local economies. Inaccurate border divisions in mountain areas were often a cause for conflict between these municipalities, occasionally even of a warlike nature, and entailing the dispute over communal pastures (Ribeiro, 1940–1941). It is likely that the systematic exploitation of these pasture lands and their integration into a transhumant system – either vertical or horizontal – goes back to sometime before the twelfth century, a time period when these practices seem to have already been well established. A clue may be found in the pollen studies carried out on Estrela Mountain. Indeed, palynological research in highland lagoons – at Charco da Candeeira and Lagoa Comprida, located at 1400 and 1600 m a.s.l., respectively – allowed the reconstruction of a bioclimatic model from the end of the Pleistocene to the present day. According to the results thereby obtained, there is evidence for an increase in deforestation during early medieval times, a fact that testifies to the systematic economic exploitation of the middle and upper sections of the mountain during this time period. The factors underlying this large-scale deforestation around AD 1000 are clearly identified: forest fires associated to the opening of plots for pasture and cereal agriculture. In consequence, spontaneous vegetal cover of oak, birch and willow forest was irrevocably replaced by heath. Thus, AD 1000 may have been the moment when the pastoral exploitation of the highlands became an intensive economic practice (Janssen & Woldringh, 1981; Van Der Brink & Janssen, 1985; Van der Knaap & Van Leeuwen, 1997).

These transhumant strategies in Estrela Mountain comprised until very recently two different geographical scales, as presented in this paper. Due to the fact that each complements the other, it is possible that they began at the same time. The preservation of such social and economic costumes is deeply rooted, and originated, in an ideology of communitarianism that characterized these farming communities until as recently as the 1970s.

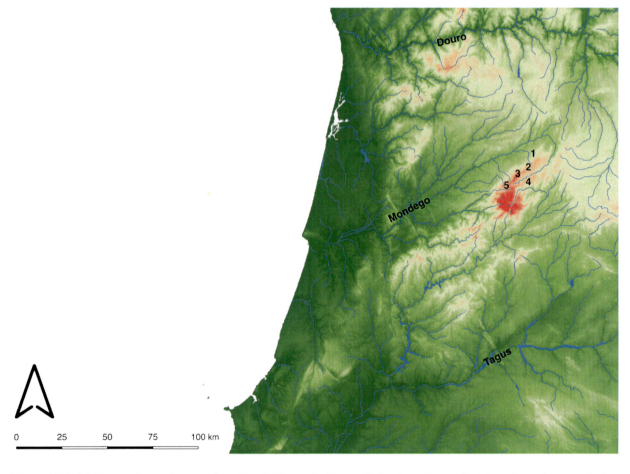

Figure 15.5. Medium-scale transhumance from Estrela Mountain (Portugal) showing villages of origin and transhumance destinations (middle of twentieth century). Villages of 1) Linhares, 2) Folgosinho, 3) Gouveia, 4) Manteigas, 5) and Seia on Estrela Mountain, all of which received formal Charters in the twelfth century.

LONG-DISTANCE TRANSHUMANCE

From the thirteenth century on a new form of transhumance appears in Iberia, adding yet more diversity to its medieval herding practices. Long-distance transhumance is also connected to the rise of *La Mesta*. The influence of *La Mesta* was uneven across Iberia; it barely affected areas within the present-day Portuguese borders; in the Cantabrian Mountains, it concerned most of the highest pastures.

The *Honrado Concejo de la Mesta* was established in the first half of the thirteenth century. Even from its inception it assembled a network of routes and regulated rights of passage and grazing for the *Mesta's* Merino sheep flocks. An effect of this was an intensification of ovine production (especially after the fifteenth century). Although the role of large landowners in the *Mesta* has often been highlighted, in medieval times, the *Mesta* grouped together a diverse body of livestock owners whose interests where not necessarily aligned. The *Concejo* (council) was strengthened during the Catholic Monarch's reign (fifteenth century) when it started to be presided by the chairman of the *Consejo Real*. Also under Isabella I and Ferdinand II it acquired greatly extended rights of way for its flocks, now no longer bound to Castile but extended to Aragon. From then on, the most important families from both kingdoms began to gain influence in the inner workings of the *Mesta*, a fact which brought about a process of the concentration of wealth in the seventeenth century as the oligarchy hoarded the rights to the use of grazing areas while they also profited from wool export to other European countries (Pascua Echegaray, 2007).

To date, research on *La Mesta* has focussed on its internal dynamics and its organization as an institution, the sociological aspects concerning its participants and, especially, its transhumance routes, from the most important *Cañadas Reales* to the secondary branches that led to specific places in Castile (Aitken, 1947; García Martín, 1991). Some attention has been also devoted to the *Casa de Ganaderos de Zaragoza*, in Aragon, which regulated grazing rights on the Crown's commons and even administered justice in both civil and criminal law within its area of influence (Fernández Otal, 1993).

The presence of Southern Iberia herds in our area of study can be traced back to the thirteenth century (Ruiz de la Peña, 1977), but it was during the fourteenth century when it became fully established, following the interests of the new landholding aristocrats who had gained control of the commons. The Earldom of Luna in León is an example of this: innumerable confrontations with the locals ensued the rarl's lease of ample extensions of land to big *Mesta* livestock owners. Some contemporary written sources give detailed account of these events, which severely harmed the local stocks

(García Cañón, 2006). The arrival of *Mestan* herds introduced a new stockbreeding model which was characterized by its speculative and market-oriented nature and was radically different from the small-scale subsistence level production practices of local peasants.

La Mesta's main material remains are the important livestock paths or *cañadas* which facilitated the movement of big herds. The *brañas* or huts used by *Mestan* shepherds are small and consist of only one room, as herds were kept in enclosures situated nearby (Figure 15.6). These huts (*chozos*) and their enclosures can often be documented in the same *brañas* used by local stockbreeders. Therefore, two different construction types occupied the same physical space at the same time while concomitantly retaining different functionalities (i.e. they were used by different social groups who practiced two different types of transhumance on disparate scales).

CONCLUSION

Thus, from the late thirteenth century and along into the fourteenth and fifteenth centuries, the Cantabrian Mountains became a place of confluence where several different systems were at work at the same time exploiting pasture lands: 1) transhumant stockbreeding as a complement to agriculture and non-transhumant stockbreeding in the villages, 2) short-distance transhumance involving a movement from the coast (or mid-mountain areas) to the uplands, undertaken by whole families specialized in livestock breeding; 3) market-oriented pastoralism or long-distance transhumance, involving the movement of big herds from Central and Southern Iberia.

These three models reflect the interests of the various social actors at play: local peasants and shepherds, *concejo* oligarchs, high-rank aristocrats and ecclesiastical entities. Their approaches to the exploitation of pastures were connected to different sets of economic orientations which were themselves manifested in the animal species they chose. Non-transhumant and short-distance transhumant livestock were in most cases cattle (although complemented with smaller species), while the big long-distance transhumant herds owned by important lordships were sheep flocks.

Consequently, pastures in the Cantabrian Mountains were in great demand, a fact which generated unrest when the interests of the different social groups clashed. The ensuing conflicts involved a process of appropriation, privatization and the parcelling out of grazing lands which had already begun in the thirteenth century. Over the course of the following centuries, this process caused rapid transformations in the landscape. As mentioned in our introduction to this complex

Figure 15.6. A chozo *for* Mesta *herds from the Cantabrian Mountains*
Source: © Margarita Fernández Mier

issue, exploitation of these pasture areas continued well into the twentieth century, when a slow but unstoppable decline began which would eventually lead to the demise of most stockbreeding traditions (Fernández Mier et al., 2013).

Iberia is one of the most mountainous areas in Europe. From prehistoric times, this fact has facilitated the deforestation of large highland areas for the purposes of pastoralism. During the medieval period, a variety of transhumant systems developed which involved not only different types of movement (short to long distance), but also different trade targets. These systems originated in the competing economic interests of the social groups aiming at controlling the pastures.

From small-scale valley transhumance to long-distance south/north transhumance not to mention intermediate arrangements, various modes of pasture exploitation have coexisted in Iberia which have generated a rich legacy of material culture whose archaeological analysis has only barely begun.

More multidisciplinary research is needed to further clarify the transhumance and the management of grazing lands. The existence of sufficient written sources as well as the survival of these practices into the twentieth century will undoubtedly make Iberia a suitable testing ground for such studies.

Note

1 This is especially the case with regards to minor toponymy. Also, this kind of research has to take into account the fact that while some toponyms may have endured, they might now refer to different places.

References

Agirre, J., Moraza, A. & Mujika, J.A. 2003a. Primeros vestigios de un modelo económico de ganadería estacional especializada. Los fondos de cabaña tumulares de Arrubi y Esnaurreta (Aralar). *Kobie*, 27:105–29.

Agirre, J., Moraza, A. & Mujika, J.A. 2003b. La transición entre dos modelos de ganadería estacional de montaña. El fondo de cabaña pastoril de Oidui (Sierra de Aralar). *Kobie*, 27:163–90.

Aguadé Nieto, S. 1993. *Ganadería y desarrollo agrario en Asturias durante la Edad Media (siglos IX–XIII)*, Barcelona: El Albir.

Aitken, R. 1947. Rutas de trashumancia en la Meseta Castellana. *Estudios Geográficos*, VIII:185–99.

Álvarez Menéndez, B., Fernández Hevia, J.M., Fernández Mier, M. & López Calvo, M.J. 1990. Espacio y propiedad en un territorio de montaña: la Tierra del Privilexu (Teberga). *Boletín del Instituto de Estudios Asturianos*, 133:145–214.

Bishko, C.J. 1963. The Castilian as Plainsman: The Medieval Ranching Frontier in La Mancha and Extremadura. In: A.R. Lewis & T.F. McGann, eds. *Second International Congress of Historians of the United States and Mexico*. Austin: University of Texas, pp. 47–69.

Bueida, E. 1991. El pueblu quirosán. Una unidá social. *Cultures*, 1:1–100.

Corbera Millán, M. 2003. Campesinos y montes en Cantabria: competencia y conflictos por los aprovechamientos entre los siglos XVII y XVIII (1650–1850). In: C. Varela Vázquez & J.S. García Marchante, eds. *Las relaciones entre las comunidades agrícolas y el monte: coloquio hispano-francés de geografía rural*. Cuenca: Universidad de Castilla-La Mancha, pp. 283–96.

Corbera Millán, M. 2006. Técnicas pastoriles y paisaje rural: origen y evolución de las praderías invernales en los valles del Nasa-Lamasón. *Ería*, 71:301–18.

Corbera Millán, M. 2008. El proceso de colonización y la construcción de paisaje en los Montes del Pas. *Ería*, 77:293–314.

Daugstad, K., Fernández Mier, M. & Peña Chocarro, L. 2014. Landscape of transhumance in Norway and Spain. Farmer's practices, perceptions, and value orientation. *Norwegian Journal of Geography*, 68:248–58.

Debates de Arqueología Medieval. 2013. Granada. http://www.arqueologiamedievaldebates.com/

De Terán, M. 1947. Vaqueros y cabañas en los Montes del Pas. *Estudios Geográficos*, 8:493–536.

Elías Pastor, L.V. & Novoa Portela, F. eds. 2003. *Un camino de ida y vuelta. La trashumancia en España*. Barcelona: Lunwerg.

Escalona Monge, J. 2001. Jerarquización social y organización del espacio: bosques y pastizales en la Sierra de Burgos (siglos X–XII). In: J. Gómez Pantoja, ed. *Los rebaños de Gerión*. Madrid: Casa de Velázquez, pp. 109–37.

Fernández Conde, F.J. 2001. Aspectos de la ganadería y del pastoreo en Asturias durante la primera Edad Media. In: J. Gómez Pantoja, ed. *Los rebaños de Gerión*. Madrid: Casa de Velázquez, pp. 139–57.

Fernández Fernández, J. 2011. *Estudios multiescalares sobre el Valle del Trubia (Asturias, España)*, Oviedo. http://hdl.handle.net/10651/12949. 30/11/2017

Fernández Mier, M. 2006. La toponimia como fuente para la historia rural. La territorialidad de la aldea feudal. *Territorio, Sociedad y Poder*, 1:35–42.

Fernández Mier, M. 2010. Campos de cultivo en la Cordillera Cantábrica. La agricultura en zonas de montaña. In: H. Kirchner, ed. *Por una arqueología agraria. Perspectivas de investigación sobre los espacios de cultivo en las sociedades medievales hispánicas*. British Archaeological Reports International Series 2062. Oxford: Archaeopress, pp. 41–59.

Fernández Mier, M. 2013. Arqueología agraria del Norte Peninsular. Líneas de investigación sobre un paisaje multifuncional. El ejemplo de Asturias. In: A. García Porras, ed. *Arqueología de la producción en época medieval*. Granada: Alhulia.

Fernández Mier, M., González Álvarez, D. & López Gómez, P. 2013. Prácticas ganaderas en la Cordillera Cantábrica. Aproximación multidisciplinar al estudio de las áreas de pasto en la Edad Media. *Debates de Arqueología Medieval*, 3:167–220.

Fernández Mier, M. & Quirós Castillo, J.A. 2015. El aprovechamiento de los espacios comunales en el noroeste de la Península Ibérica entre el período romano y el medieval, *Il capitale culturale*, XII: 695–723.

Fernández Otal, J.A. 1993. *La casa de ganaderos de Zaragoza. Derecho y trashumancia a fines del siglo XV*, Zaragoza: Institución Fernando el Católico.

García Cañón, P. 2006. *Concejos y señores. Historia de una lucha en la montaña occidental leonesa a fines de la Edad Media*. León: Universidad de León.

García Fernández, J. 1988. *Organización tradicional del espacio en Asturias*. Gijón: Silverio Cañada Editor.

García García, E. 1980. *San Juan Bautista de Corias: Historia de un señorío monástico asturiano (siglos X–XV)*. Oviedo: Universidad de Oviedo.

García Martín, P. 1991. *Cañadas. Cordeles y veredas*. Valladolid: Junta de Castilla y León.

García Martín, P. 1994. *Por los caminos de la trashumancia*. León: Junta de Castilla y León.

García Martínez, A. 1988. *Los vaqueiros de alzada de Asturias*. Oviedo: Principado de Asturias.

García Martínez, A. 2003. La trashumancia en Asturias. In: L.V. Elías Pastor & F. Novoa Portela, eds. *Un camino de ida y vuelta; la trashumancia en España*. Barcelona: Lunwerg D.L, pp. 95–107.

Gerbet, M.C. 1991. *L'elevage dans le royaune de Castille sous les Rois Catholiques (1454–1516)*. Madrid: Casa de Velázquez.

González Álvarez, D. 2013. Traditional pastoralism in the Asturian Mountains: an ethnoarchaeological view on mobility and settlement patterns. In: A. Lugli, A. Stoppiello & S. Biagetti, eds. *Ethnoarchaeology: Current Research and Field Methods. Conference Proceedings, Rome, Italy, 13th–14th May 2010*. Oxford: Archeopress, pp. 202–8.

González Álvarez, D., Fernández Mier, M. & López Gómez, P. 2016. An archaeological approach to the brañas: summer farms in the pastures of the Cantabrian Mountains (northern Spain). In: J. Collis, M. Pearce & F. Nicolis, eds. *Summer Farms. Seasonal Exploitation of the Uplands from Prehistory to the Present*. Sheffield Archaeological monographs 16. Sheffield: J.R. Collis Publications, pp. 203–19.

Graña García, A. & López Álvarez, J. 2007. *Los teitos en Asturias. Un estudio sobre la arquitectura con cubierta vegetal*. Gijón: FMCE and UP. Muséu del Pueblu d'Asturies and Ecomuseo de Somiedo.

Janssen, C.R. & Woldringh, R.E. 1981. A preliminary radiocarbon dated pollen sequence from Serra da Estrela, Portugal. *Finisterra*. XVI, 32:299–309.

Klein, J. 1920. *The Mesta. A Study in Spanish Economic History*. Cambridge: Cambridge University Press.

Lima, A.C.P.S. 1996. *Castro Laboreiro. Povoamento e organização de um território serrano*. Braga: Instituto da conservação da Natureza. Parque Nacional da Peneda-Gerês. Câmara Municipal de Melgaço.

López Gómez, P. 2013. Ganadería de alta montaña en la Edad Media: el caso de Cangas del Narcea, Asturias. *Arqueología y Territorio*, 9:185–99.

López Gómez, P., González Álvarez, D. & Fernández Mier, M. 2016. Los espacios ganaderos de alta montaña en la Cordillera Cantábrica: su registro arqueológico. In: A.

Malpica & G. García Contreras, eds. *Actas de las Jornadas "El registro arqueológico y la Arqueología medieval". XIII Jornadas de Arqueología Medieval de la Casa de los Tiros, Granada 12–14 de junio de 2012*. Granada: Universidad de Granada, pp. 399–421.

Oliveira, E., Galhano, F. & Pereira, B. 1969. *Construções Primitivas em Portugal*. Lisboa: Edições Dom Quixote.

Pascua Echegaray, P. 2007. Las otras comunidades: pastores y ganaderos en la Castilla medieval. In: A. Rodríguez, ed. *El lugar del campesino. En torno a la obra de Reyna Pastor*. Valencia: Universidad de Valencia, pp. 209–37.

Pastor, R. 1970. La lana en Castilla y León antes de la organización de la Mesta. *Moneda y Crédito*, 112:47–69.

Pérez-Rama, M., Vaqueiro Rodríguez, M. & Grandal d'Anglade, M. 2015. Indicios de pastoreo extensivo en el noroeste peninsular durante el dominio suevo. *Cuaderno Laboratorio Xeolóxico de Laxe*, 38:107–34.

Ribeiro, O. 1940–1941. Contribuição para o estudo do pastoreio na Serra da Estrela. *Revista da Faculdade de Letras*, VII (1–2):213–303.

Ribeiro, O. 1991a. *Portugal, o Mediterrâneo e o Atlântico*. 6ª ed. Lisboa: Livraria Sá da Costa Editora.

Ribeiro, O. 1991b. Brandas e inverneiras em Castro Laboreiro. *Opúsculos Geográficos IV. Vol. O Mundo Rural*. Lisboa: FCG, pp. 251–56.

Rodríguez Gutiérrez, F. 1989. *La organización agraria de la Montaña Central Asturiana*. Oviedo: Principado de Asturias.

Ruiz de la Peña, J.I. 1977. *Baja Edad Media. Historia de Asturias*. Gijón: Ayalga Ediciones.

Ruiz de la Peña, J.I. 1981. *Las polas asturianas en la Edad Media: Estudio y diplomatario*. Oviedo: Universidad de Oviedo.

Tente, C. 2010. *Arqueologia Medieval Cristã no Alto Mondego. Ocupação e exploração do território nos séculos V a XI*. PhD thesis presented to FCSH-UNL. Lisbon, photocopied.

Tente, C. 2012. Settlement and territory in the Upper Mondego Basin (Centre of Portugal) between the 5th century and the 11th century. *Archeologia Medievale*, XXXIX:385–98.

Tente, C. & Carvalho, A.F. 2011. The establishment of radiocarbon chronologies for early medieval sites: a case study from the upper Mondego Valley (Guarda, Portugal). *Munibe*, 62:461–68.

Van Der Brink, L.M. & Janssen, C.R. 1985. The effect of human activities during cultural phases on the development of mountain vegetation in the Serra da Estrela, Portugal. *Review of Paleobotany and Paliology*, 44:139–215.

Van Der Knaap, W.O. & Van Leeuwen, J.F.N. 1997. Late Glacial and early Holocene vegetation succession zonation, and climatic change in the Serra de Estrela, Portugal. *Review of Palaeobotany and Palynology*, 97:239–85.

CHAPTER 16

Transhumance dynamics in the Gredos Range (central Spain) during the last two millennia
Environmental and socio-political vectors of change

JOSÉ ANTONIO LÓPEZ-SÁEZ, ANTONIO BLANCO-GONZÁLEZ, DANIEL ABEL-SCHAAD, SANDRA ROBLES-LÓPEZ, REYES LUELMO-LAUTENSCHLAEGER, SEBASTIÁN PÉREZ-DÍAZ AND FRANCISCA ALBA-SÁNCHEZ

INTRODUCTION

Pastoral systems can be considered agrarian strategies that provide subsistence products while also facilitating adaptive processes to environmental conditions (Salzman, 2004: 2–3). Livestock raising in the Mediterranean Basin has shaped areas of high-quality farming and is also responsible for maintaining biodiversity, especially in mountain ecosystems and rural settings (Azcárate et al., 2013; Lozny, 2013). In the Iberian Peninsula, *transterminance* (i.e. the seasonal vertical movement of livestock be they bovines or ovicaprids from valley bottoms to relatively close upland ranges) was a major pastoralist custom at least since Roman times, and most likely in prehistory as well. The success of the system was the direct result of several factors, including its resilience and adaptability to highly unpredictable and fluctuating rainfall regimes in order to match the grazing pressure of livestock to the seasonal availability of pasturage (Ruiz & Ruiz, 1986; Blondel, 2006; Manzano Baena & Casas, 2010).

Beginning with the advent of the high medieval period (twelfth to thirteenth centuries), the movement of livestock was developed at an unprecedented scale which involved logistical arrangements which were both massive and expensive in order to accommodate the emerging economic sector as it integrated with the growing industrial production of early modern states. Horizontal (north–south) long-distance transhumance is a form of extensive semi-annual pastoralism whereby livestock is moved between fixed points in order to exploit the seasonal variability of grazing resources. In this way, it takes advantage of the northern highland pasturelands in summer and the southern dehesa landscapes in winter. This practice was protected by the Spanish Crowns (Castilian and Aragonese kingdoms) through successive tax concessions and pasturage privileges and its organization was managed at an almost pan-Iberian scale by the *Concejo de la Mesta* (Klein, 1920; Anes & García Sanz, 1994). Transhumance in Spain during the early modern period reached its peak as a key activity because of two local species of sheep: the *merina* variety (highly valued in Europe for

its wool) and the *churra* variety (which is raised principally for the production of mutton). Nearly 3.5 million transhumant sheep flocks covered distances of up to 700 km (Bilbao & Fernández de Pinedo, 1982) along a network of royal droveways (*cañadas reales*) that extended over c. 125,000 km and occupied some 420,000 ha (Klein, 1920: 34–39). The final goal of most such extensive stock raising activities was the provision of staples for the internal urban markets (the so-called *ferias* in Medina de Rioseco and Medina del Campo) and the international exportation of high-quality wool via the Cantabrian trade ports for the famous textile production centres of the Low Countries.

Unfortunately, nowadays there is little environmental evidence for the impact that the development of transhumance might have had on past ecosystems. However, the problem can be approached from a palaeopalynological angle (Buckland & Edwards, 1984). The palynological evidence for pastoral activities is predicated upon the identification of pollen from plant taxa indicative of pastureland (*Plantago lanceolata*, *P. major/media*, Chenopodiaceae, *Urtica dioica*, *Polygonum aviculare*) as well as coprophilous fungi ascospores from Sordariaceae as a proxy for the natural manuring of soil (Behre, 1981; López-Sáez & López-Merino, 2007).

Short-distance vertical movement of livestock (cattle and sheep) following cyclical routes (i.e. *transterminance*) has been traditionally practiced in the Gredos Range of Spain since the area was first permanently settled in medieval times, as has proven to be the case in other mountainous areas (Barrios, 1984; Martín-Viso & Blanco-González, 2016). Moreover, for several centuries, transhumant flocks crossed the Gredos Range by the royal drove roads of the *Mesta* in their semi-annual migration to southern pastures (Blanco-González et al., 2015). In mountain regions with long histories of human settlement (such as is the case for the Gredos Range) the effects of transhumance on the dynamics of Holocene forest landscapes prove fascinating research topics that have been addressed in previous studies (Abel-Schaad & López-Sáez, 2013; Abel-Schaad et al., 2014; López-Sáez et al., 2014). In fact, the introduction of domestic animals by man into a particular territory is

© 2018 European Association of Archaeologists

an important factor that helps to explain local vegetal extinctions and the transformation of woodlands. Such changes mainly occur only through natural fire cycles; therefore, the expansion of pioneer species – especially ones whose dormant buds 're-sprout' after the burning – can affect vegetal composition. The combination of recurrent fires and grazing can cause progressive deforestation in mountainous landscapes (Valbuena-Carabaña et al., 2010). This phenomenon had a great effect on the pine forests of the upper Gredos Range. In turn, this triggered the extinction of numerous local populations (Pardo & Gil, 2005; López-Sáez et al., 2014; López-Sáez, Abel-Schaad et al., 2016).

This article reviews the palaeoenvironmental evidence available from the Gredos Range for the last two millennia and compares it with relevant historical and archaeological data. The designation of this particular study area is due both to the historical importance of transhumance to the area's economy as well as to previous lack of information about vegetation/livestock dynamics within these grazing systems during the last millennia. In short, this paper aims to integrate the history of climatic and environmental change with the socio-economic, political and cultural developments that took place in this part of central Spain from the Roman period until the present day.

Geographical and Historical Setting

The Gredos Range is comprised of a chain of sunken and elevated blocks of granitic and metamorphic lithology within the Spanish Central System (Figure 16.1). It consists of a series of mountain blocks (or *sierras*) separated by the intramontane valleys or troughs which traditionally acted as natural corridors and are, therefore, the most suitable locations for permanent settlement (e.g. Tormes Valley and Alberche Valley). The climate in the Gredos Range is Mediterranean insofar as it includes a summer drought period lasting three–five months which is followed by heavy rainfall in the autumn and winter. The southern slopes (especially those along the Tiétar Valley) feature warmer and wetter conditions due to increased sunlight exposure and to predominantly humid and southwesterly winds which prevail there. Differences in altitude are very remarkable and range from over 1600 to above 550 m a.s.l. on the southern slopes and in the intramontane valleys. Deciduous forests of *Quercus pyrenaica* represent the predominant vegetation, with some forests of *Pinus sylvestris* and *Pinus nigra* along the timberline. By contrast, highland areas over 1600 m a.s.l. are occupied by broom shrub lands (*Cytisus oromediterraneus, Echinospartum ibericum*) or even heath (*Erica* species) and grass at the highest peaks.

Before its permanent colonization in the twelfth to thirteenth centuries (Barrios, 1984), this region was sparsely frequented by scattered herders who followed a semi-mobile way of life in which they occupied pastoral seasonal shelters (locally known as *majadas* and *tinaos*) as they followed their flocks. The high medieval period represents a turning point in the long-term process in which the highland landscapes were re-modelled. In 1250, the foundation of small, rural, nuclear villages in the main intra-mountainous valleys (such as Tormes and Alberche) marked a point of no return in the definitive sedentarization of previously dispersed and itinerant pastoralist communities. The passes of the Gredos Range (El Pico and Serranillos in the central part of the range) were necessary transit spots for transhumant herders and their large flocks as they crossed the Central System on their way from the Northern Meseta tablelands to the winter pasturelands of southern Spain. The villages in those highland settings were stopover and provisioning points along the seasonal routes which followed the *Mesta* royal droveways. This paper focuses on three of these north–south corridors in particular: the Cañada de La Plata in the westernmost area of the Central System, a droveway which essentially follows an old Roman highway from northwestern Iberia to Seville, the Cañada Real Leonesa Occidental which crosses the central section of Gredos Range through the Puerto del Pico Pass and the Cañada Leonesa Oriental which borders the oriental end of the Gredos Range and follows the Tiétar Valley on the range's southern slope (Figure 16.1).

Palynological Records and The Signature of Transhumance

Four humid zones (peat bogs) located between 1000 and 1700 m a.s.l. were investigated in the Gredos Range[1] by López-Merino et al. (2009); López-Sáez, López-Merino et al. (2009); López-Sáez, Alba-Sánchez et al. (2016); Abel-Schaad & López-Sáez (2013) and Luelmo-Lautenschlaeger (2015) in relation to said scholars' palynological research. As the pollen records thusly obtained were adjacent to mountain passes, they permit the identification of contemporary livestock activity. This paper discusses only the most complete and representative pollen records from the Gredos Range (Figure 16.2) in the form of synthetic curves summarizing fluctuations of taxa for which occurrences and/or variations might be interpreted as vegetation successions triggered by human activities. However, many other pollen records are known from these mountains (López-Sáez, López-Merino et al., 2010; López-Sáez et al., 2014; López-Sáez, Abel-Schaad et al., 2016) – including their lowland areas – which

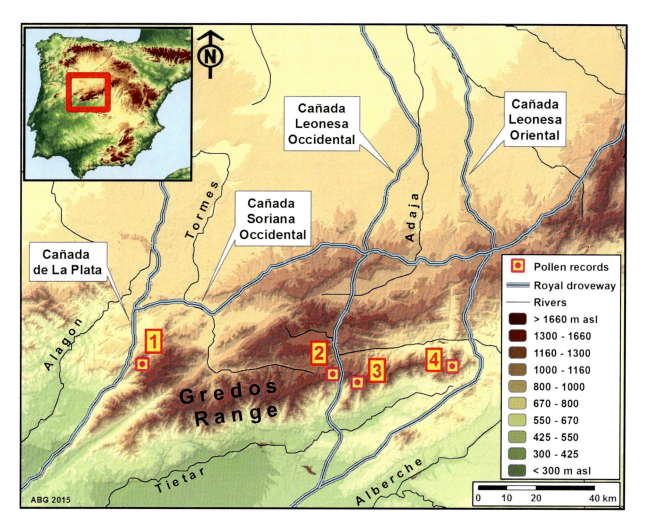

Figure 16.1. Location of the Gredos Range in central Iberia. Pollen cores mentioned in the text: 1) Peña Negra, 2) Puerto del Pico, 3) Serranillos, 4) Pozo de la Nieve.

will also be addressed in the discussion. Numerous ^{14}C dates and high-resolution palynological work (including the identification of non-pollen palynomorphs and micro-charcoal quantification) permitted the assessment of the development of ecosystems and the identification of man's occupation rhythm within the landscape. The study of microfossils other than pollen and the pteridophyte spores present in pollen slides (also called 'non-pollen palynomorphs' or 'NPP') have previously been useful in palaeoecological interpretation (van Geel, 2001). NPP are of diverse origins (and even include fungal spores, algal remains and various kinds of plant and animal fragments; López-Sáez et al., 1998, 2000). This has led to a classification system of NPP by morphological type which is identifiable through a series of codes developed at the University of Amsterdam. In this way, upon the identification of a NPP type, information from previous studies can be used for environmental interpretation. This procedure has been successfully applied in many palaeoecological and palaeoanthropological studies. Although NPP studies are scarce in the Spanish Central System, several surveys have been conducted in the Gredos Range (López-Sáez & López-Merino, 2007).

In the Spanish Mediterranean region, the combination of pollen and non-pollen palynomorphs together with measurements of charcoal particles have shed light on the influence of human activities on vegetation changes during the Holocene (Carrión et al., 2010, 2015). In order to understand the nature and extent of human impact on ancient vegetation, it is important that we define the major anthropogenic indicators recorded in pollen diagrams from the Gredos Range (Figure 16.2). These mainly include:

1) Agriculture: Primary anthropogenic indicators of agriculture such as *Cerealia* or *Secale* have been used in this study to assess changes in land use. Special attention needs to be paid to *Cerealia*, as the pollens of several wild grass taxa also demonstrate similar morphological features (Beug, 2004). This implies that such examples may not necessarily have come from cultivated fields, but could rather have originated from the local vegetation. Hence, records of

this pollen type should be considered with caution (local cultivation can be accepted when its values are ≥3%) and only in connection with the other anthropogenic indicators (López-Sáez et al., 2003; López-Sáez & López-Merino, 2005).

2) Arboriculture: *Castanea* and *Olea* should be noted when found in great abundance, especially in the post-Roman period (Conedera et al., 2004; López-Sáez, López-Merino et al., 2009).

3) Grazing pressure: Anthropozoogenous taxa (Chenopodiaceae, *Plantago lanceolata*, *Plantago major/media*, *Polygonum aviculare*, *Rumex* sp., *Urtica dioica*, *Hyosciamus niger*, *Solanum nigrum*, Rubiaceae) can be related to grazed pastures.

4) Coprophilous fungal ascospores (Sordariaceae: *Sordaria*, *Podospora*, *Sporormiella*, *Cercophora*) and *Riccia* spores are also important (Carrión, 2001; Carrión & Navarro, 2002; López-Sáez & López-Merino, 2007). Fossil ascospores of dung-related fungi can be used to assess the presence of past fauna, particularly herbivores: when the spores are documented in the fossil record with low percentages and can be found only sporadically, they indicate wild animals. However, when the spores are documented in a continuous manner and generally appear with high values, they are indicative of livestock (López-Sáez & López-Merino, 2007; Cugny et al., 2010).

Samples for pollen analysis were treated after the method established by Faegri and Iversen (1989). Sediment was dissolved in 10% KOH, carbonates were removed with 10% HCl, silicates diluted in concentrated HF and most organic material removed. Finally, samples were mounted in glycerine. In most cases, more than 500 grains were counted per sample. Pollen types were defined according to Reille (1999) and Beug (2004). Percentage pollen diagrams were plotted using the *Tilia* software (Grimm, 1992). Several groups of pastoral indicators (anthropozoogenous taxa and coprophilous fungi) were distinguished in the manner discussed above. The rate of human impact on vegetation may be inferred thanks to the nature and abundance of these anthropogenic indicators. These have been informed by earlier studies of current local pollen rain/vegetation/land-use relationships within different types of agricultural systems[2] (López-Sáez, Alba-Sánchez et al., 2010, 2013, 2015).

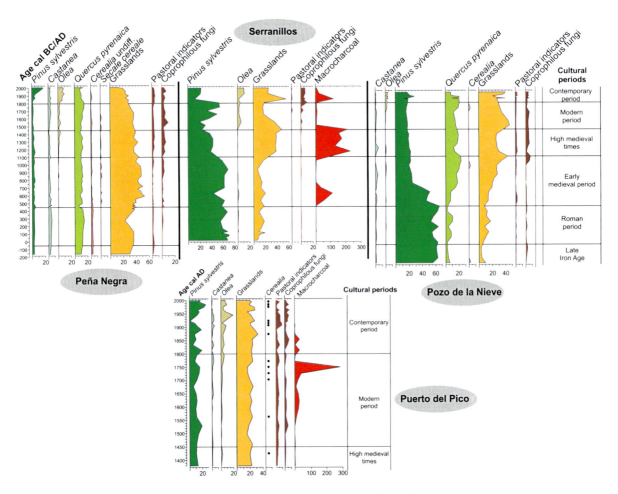

Figure 16.2. Synthetic pollen diagrams of four well-dated peat bogs from the Gredos Range

DISCUSSION

Roman period (~50 cal BC–cal AD 450)

The pollen date obtained from the Roman period (from the late first century BC to the middle fifth century AD) suggests the development of a heterogeneous landscape which contained not only variations in the rhythms of human impact, but also significant spatial variability. For instance, pollen diagrams from the lowland areas of the Gredos Range (i.e. Jerte at 1180 m a.s.l., Lanzahíta at 588 m a.s.l. or even Peña Negra at 1000 m a.s.l.; see Atienza, 1993; López-Sáez, López-Merino et al., 2010; Abel-Schaad & López-Sáez, 2013) show higher human pressure than those located at higher elevations (i.e. Serranillos at 1700 m a.s.l. or Pozo de la Nieve at 1450 m a.s.l.; López-Merino et al., 2009; López-Sáez, López-Merino et al., 2009; Luelmo-Lautenschlaeger, 2015). The fact that there are high levels of *Cerealia* pollen in Peña Negra, where the greatest human impact can be highlighted in the whole Gredos Range during this period is also worthy of note. This is probably related to the particular situation of this pollen record (at low altitude) which also provides evidence of a highly deforested landscape (*Pinus sylvestris* <5%, *Quercus pyrenaica* c. 10%) as well as the presence of the pastoral indicators and coprophilous fungi which would indicating the passage of herds through this area (Cañada de La Plata) in the late Roman period rather than a permanent local presence. In addition to the spread of grasslands required to supply the increasing numbers of livestock present, the western Gredos Range acted as a way of passage for herds through the communication network developed by Romans, who provided the first evidence of the movement of livestock over long distances (Gómez-Pantoja, 2004). In this sense, the Peña Negra pollen record clearly shows the transition from land use during the early phases of the Roman period (when the study area would have been a secondary cattle transfer zone) to a more intensive model during the late Roman period, as evidenced by the high values of coprophilous fungal spores indicating the further development of livestock grazing (Abel-Schaad & López-Sáez, 2013).

However, the high-altitude deposits (1400–2000 m a.s.l.) from the western Gredos Range show the minimum values of pine pollen while grasslands and heathlands spread. Although the records are poorly dated (López-Sáez et al., 2014), such patterns are shown by the pollen sequences from Garganta del Trampal, Dehesa de Navamuño, Garganta de la Solana, Barrera de las Corzas, El Quemal-Candelario, La Covatilla, Cuerpo de Hombre and Presa del Duque (Atienza, 1993; Ruiz-Zapata et al., 2011). This increased human impact is related to the intensification of livestock rearing, the extension of tree crops (*Castanea* is very well represented in Peña Negra) as well as the contribution of mining activities in the lowlands. By contrast, the landscape of the central and eastern Gredos Range appears to have scarcely been altered by human activities in high-altitude deposits (1400–1700 m.a.s.l.), such as Prado de las Zorras, Redondo, Puerto de Chía, Puerto de la Peña Negra, Navarredonda, Narrillos del Rebollar, Garganta de los Caballeros, Serranillos or Pozo de la Nieve (Andrade, 1994; Franco-Múgica et al., 1997; Dorado et al., 2001; López-Merino et al., 2009; Ruiz-Zapata et al., 2011; López-Sáez, López-Merino et al., 2009; López-Sáez et al., 2014; López-Sáez, Abel-Schaad, et al., 2016; Luelmo-Lautenschlaeger, 2015). Therefore, the greater accessibility of the western Gredos Range to a major urban centre might explain the attractiveness of this area for pastoral activity during the Roman period. In the central and eastern Gredos Range, the topographical context is quite different, as the high-altitude zones are less accessible.

Contrary to what has been observed in the eastern Spanish Central System (Ayllón, Guadarrama and Pela ranges) (Franco-Múgica et al., 1998, 2001; Gómez-González, Ruiz-Zapata, López-Sáez et al., 2009; Gómez-González, Ruiz-Zapata, Gil et al, 2009; Currás et al., 2012; López-Sáez et al., 2014), it seems that the central and eastern Gredos Range did not suffer the effects of extensive deforestation, especially at high altitudes. The data from the Serranillos and Pozo de la Nieve pollen records (Figure 16.1) suggests a phase of stability (or even decline) in human activity after the Late Iron Age with the development of important pine (*Pinus sylvestris* >60%) and oak (*Quercus pyrenaica*) forests (Figure 16.2). However, it is plausible that a generalized logging system was established as a means of supplying the local valleys with timber. In fact, from 50 cal BC, the incorporation of the Gredos Range into Roman rule is archaeologically evident. This is shown by the presence of late Republican imported commodities, coins and utensils in some of the later pre-Roman hillforts, (i.e. El Raso) and in early cities, such as *Avela* (modern-day Ávila) (Mariné, 1995; Blanco-González et al., 2015). The principle organization of the Roman countryside in the province of Lusitania occurred c. AD 50 under the Flavian dynasty. It consisted of the agrarian colonization of the more fertile lands through a web of scattered farmsteads and rural compounds and the foundation of the earliest aristocratic residential *villae* in these lowland landscapes (Blanco-González et al., 2009). If one considers the fact that the Gredos Range was only an access route during this period (it was part of a marginal territory which was sparsely populated due to its unsuitability for the development of urban centres; Mariné, 1995), it is easy to understand the low level of human impact on high-mountain ecosystems. Most of the population gathered in urban centres. The development of a strong network permitted long-distance livestock movements (Gómez-Pantoja, 2004). In any case, evidence of such movements through the mountain passes of Serranillos and Pozo de la Nieve are not apparent; the values of pastoral indicators and coprophilous fungi are low and sporadic (Figure 16.2). Both pollen sequences record the continued exploitation of pastures (as documented by asynchronous curves of pines and grasslands). What is remarkable is that this practice was initiated in prehistoric times (i.e. during the third millennium BC; López-Sáez, Blanco-González et al., 2009; López-Sáez et al., 2014).

Early medieval period (c. cal AD 450–1100)

In the transition between the later first millennium and the early second millennium, this region was a kind of no-man's land as it was outside the rule of any of the early states which competed for the tenure over the land. Therefore, until military and political possession (the so-called 'Re-conquest') and the subsequent permanent colonization of Gredos Range by the northern Christian kingdom around AD 1080, this mountain acted as a border between Muslim and Christian powers for several centuries (c. cal AD 711–1100) (Barrios, 1984; García-Oliva, 2007; Quirós-Castillo, 2011; Blanco-González et al., 2015). Since this fringe area was beyond the control of any state-like polity, there are no textual sources for this period. This can be coupled with the widespread lack of documentary sources in Western Europe before the eleventh century (Escalona, 2009; Martín-Viso, 2009; Quirós-Castillo, 2011; Vigil-Escalera, 2015). Moreover, archaeological remains in such inner, rural settings are not well studied. In addition, the material culture of the period has almost no distinctive diagnostic traits, due to the maintenance of items such as late *terra sigillata* (Samian tableware) pottery and the scarcity of imports (Vigil-Escalera, 2015: 101–48).

As a rule, the early medieval period is usually considered a period of decline in human activity or abandonment of many landscapes across much of Europe (Behre, 1988: 668–69). However, palaeoecological evidence from the early medieval period from within our study area suggests maintenance and even an expansion of agro-pastoral activities; this trend can also be seen in the Pyrenees (Galop, 1998). In fact, the Visigoth period (c. cal AD 450–711) was a phase which witnessed widespread deforestation in the Gredos Range (López-Sáez et al., 2014; López-Sáez, Abel-Schaad, et al., 2016). This was especially the case at low altitudes within subsistence patterns which were oriented around livestock, although farming did continue. This increase is likely related to the grazing activities (as seen in the high values of pastoral indicators and coprophilous fungi, Figure 16.2) which were intended to preserve upland pastures. Forests were cleared to obtain new pastures and new land was cultivated during a period in which there was a proliferation of the rural habitat and the land was exploited by a relatively free (i.e. independent peasantry; Escalona, 2009; Martín-Viso, 2009; Quirós-Castillo, 2011). These forest clearances were mainly executed by means of fire (see maximum of macro charcoal in Serranillos, Figure 16.2). At lower altitudes, the valley bottoms of the western Gredos Range and Tiétar Valley saw important changes in the composition of their vegetation at the beginning of the early medieval period with the expansion of grasslands, agricultural activities and the development and diversification of cultivated plants in the pollen records from Lanzahíta and Peña Negra (López-Sáez, López-Merino et al., 2010; Abel-Schaad & López Sáez, 2013). Rye (*Secale cereale*), a crop better adapted to low temperatures, as well as other cereals were intensively cultivated in these low-lying areas, especially in Peña Negra (Figure 16.2) which, once again, intimates the presence of increasing human pressure on mountain areas. Such expansions probably had a lot to do with forest clearance by fire in the foothills and middle-altitude slopes which would subsequently allow livestock to graze in areas that had previously been marginal. Rye had probably previously been grown in small-scale fields on well-oriented slopes in intramontane valleys. The floristic diversity of the arboreal taxa also increased with the establishment of orchards: *Castanea* and *Olea* emerged as ubiquitous cultivated trees in the valley bottoms. These species were probably very important in some places, such as at Peña Negra, Serranillos and Pozo de la Nieve (Figure 16.2). At higher altitudes, the rapid degradation of forests probably led to the establishment of management practices which were designed to maintain pine forests for sylvo-pastoral purposes. This observation provides essential background information against which it is easier to understand the importance of the customary know-how of these rural communities; their production strategies were very carefully balanced with local resources in a highly sensitive environment. At Serranillos, Narrillos del Rebollar and Navarredonda (Franco-Múgica et al., 1997; Dorado et al., 2001; López-Merino et al., 2009; López-Sáez, López-Merino et al., 2009) in the central Gredos Range, tree cover declined during this period (c. cal AD 650), although this occurred more gradually than in the eastern Gredos Range (Pozo de la Nieve) where pine populations decreased very sharply and permanently (*Pinus sylvestris* <30%; Figure 16.2) (Luelmo-Lautenschlaeger, 2015). The increases in pastoral indicators and coprophilous fungi in Pozo de la Nieve also suggest an intensification of pastoral activity in the eastern Gredos Range with the spread of grasslands. This activity may have been partly responsible for the decline in tree pollen as grazing animals put extra pressure on a fragile ecosystem.

At high-altitude sites (>1400 m a.s.l.) in the western areas of the Gredos Range, an initial phase of forest recovery is recorded at cal AD 700–950 in the pollen records of Garganta del Trampal, Dehesa de Navamuño, Cuerpo de Hombre and Presa del Duque (Atienza, 1993; Ruiz-Zapata et al., 2011) as a result of a decline in livestock raising and farming activities. At this time, heath and grasslands decreased in addition to other pastoral indicators and there was no evidence in the record of olive or sweet chestnut cultivation. Conversely, grasslands spread at low-altitude sites such as Peña Negra (Abel-Schaad & López-Sáez, 2013) by means of fire clearance of the woodlands in order to sustain a livestock population which nevertheless increased. This is demonstrated by increased values of both pastoral indicators and coprophilous fungi (Figure 16.2). A similar picture can be documented in the central and eastern Gredos Range at high-altitude sites (>1400 m a.s.l.), such as Hoyos del Espino, Ojos Albos, Puerto de Chía, Puerto de la Peña Negra, Navarredonda, Serranillos and Pozo de la Nieve c. cal AD 680–1010 which all exhibit the recovery of high mountain pine forests (Andrade, 1994; Franco-Múgica et al., 1997; Dorado et al., 2001; Blanco-González et al., 2009; López-Merino et al., 2009; Ruiz-Zapata et al., 2011; López-Sáez, López-Merino et al., 2009; Luelmo-Lautenschlaeger, 2015). These areas show little evidence of pastoral indicators, coprophilous fungi, olive cultivation and also have low values of charcoal concentration (Figure 16.2).

Unfortunately, early medieval archaeology in the region is still in its infancy due to its poor material evidence and important difficulties in the organization of systematic surveys (e.g. low visibility due to dense forest coverage, lack of diagnostic items and structural remains, the absence of textual references, etc.; Vigil-Escalera, 2015). Recent field surveys have succeeded in identifying the sort of rural settlements which were typical of this period (Quirós Castillo & Vigil-Escalera, 2006). Their outlines and structural features are known through several excavations of such farmsteads (Gómez-Gandullo, 2006; Díaz de la Torre et al., 2009; Vigil-Escalera, 2006, 2015: 258–62), although these kinds of rural settlements were founded at lower altitudes, often below 1200 m a.s.l. The historical data from this period (cal AD 711–1100) fully corroborate the evidence presented by the palynological data insofar as they describe an economic model based on livestock grazing and small subsistence crops managed by relatively self-sufficient peasants in the central and western areas of the Gredos Range which were sparsely populated (Franco-Moreno, 2005). Such activities were denser at middle altitudes (c. 900–1110 m a.s.l.) than they were in the valleys or at high altitudes (García-Oliva, 2007; Blanco-González et al., 2009). After this initial phase of forest recovery, forest clearance was continuous around the above-mentioned high-altitude deposits of the Gredos Range cal AD 950 which exhibited decreasing values of *Pinus sylvestris* in the Serranillos and Pozo de la Nieve pollen records (Figure 16.2). This could be to the result of seasonal exploitation of these areas within a transterminant-like strategy. Deposits located at lower altitudes showed a different pattern. Livestock intensification involved neither a broad clearance of forested areas, nor the use of fire. Interestingly, local pine and oak forests even exhibit a recovery. This was possible because of pasture management strategies (especially irrigation) in areas that had previously been deforested, like Peña Negra in the western Gredos Range (Abel-Schaad & López-Sáez, 2013). Fire and grazing indicators also leave a large signal too, especially between cal AD 1000–1100 (Figure 16.2) which point to a slightly more intense human pressure in Serranillos and Pozo de la Nieve which was probably related to the presence of northern Christian settlers. Crops slightly improved during this phase, helped as they were by the milder climatic conditions of Late Medieval Warm Episode (cal AD 950–1350). Sweet chestnut and (to a lesser extent) olive groves grew at almost all sites. The same was true of cereal crops, especially during the millennial transition period as was detected in the deposits of Peña Negra (where both *Cerealia* and *Secale cereale* increased in their percentages) and Pozo de la Nieve (Figure 16.2).

High medieval times (c. cal AD 1100–1450)

The underlying trend of expanding and intensifying agro-pastoral activities increased during the twelfth to fifteenth centuries under the strong pressure of feudal powers. From the political 'Re-conquest' and the demographic repopulation of the Gredos Range by AD 1080, it is clear that the urban councils had directed a process of intensification of the rural economy to some degree (Monsalvo, 2003). This trend was intended to supply urban markets and was based on the intensification and specialization of livestock husbandry. The widely available written documentation from this period speaks to the dynamism of relatively long-distance movements between urban centres on both sides of the mountain range and confirms the importance of such areas' demands for cereals, olive oil and wine (Barrios, 1984). Indeed, this was the 'golden age' of *La Mesta*, an organization founded in AD 1273 that provided important privileges to large livestock owners (Klein, 1920; Anes & García-Sanz, 1994). Large transhumant herds travelled through the livestock trails from wintering areas south of the Gredos Range to the northern summer ranges (Figure 16.1).

The permanent occupation of the intra-mountainous valleys by peasant communities settled in rural compounds (most of them still survive as villages today) led to a marked phase of forest clearance. In addition to these long-lasting nucleated villages, there was also a network of scattered pastoral buildings and some unsuccessful farmsteads which would eventually be deserted. These constructions were made using massive materials (stone-walled fences and thatched huts) and are, therefore, far more conspicuous than previous buildings which led to their growing recognition by archaeologists (e.g. González Calle, 2002; García Garcimartín, 2004). They were key in supporting the extensive agro-sylvan activities that significantly contributed to the shaping of the mountainous landscapes. Almost all pollen diagrams from high-altitude spots in the Gredos Range show the maximum extent of grasslands, the decline of pine forests and a clear rise in the levels of livestock indicators. This impact on the forests can partly be associated to transterminant flock movements – locally known as *de travesío* – and the seasonal exploitation of high-altitude areas. This was very apparent in the pollen records (Figure 16.2) which exhibited the now familiar increase of pastoral indicators (which testify to combined agrarian practices) and coprophilous fungi (as a clear signature of the occupation of these highlands by domestic flocks of cattle and sheep). The Pozo de la Nieve and Puerto del Pico pollen records are good examples of these facts (Luelmo-Lautenschlaeger, 2015; López-Sáez, Alba-Sánchez et al., 2016). However, some other pollen diagrams also indicate the passage of cattle through long-distance trail ports as evidenced by a lower presence of those livestock within a wider framework of increasing human pressure. This could have been the case at Serranillos (López-Merino et al., 2009). Besides this, the high concentration of macro charcoal related to the milder weather conditions of the Late Medieval Warm Episode (cal AD 950–1350) suggests an increase in fire-related forest clearance (Figure 16.2).

The full integration of the agro-pastoral landscapes of the Gredos Range into the late medieval productive economy is represented by the maximum extent of grasslands (Poaceae) in the highest altitude records and a marked specialization in certain crops (i.e. rye, other cereals, olives and sweet chestnuts) in the lower altitude niches close to the villages. The low-altitude deposit at Peña Negra is a good example of such an area.

Modern and Contemporary periods (c. cal AD 1450–2000)

During the early post-medieval or modern period (cal AD 1450–1800), the persistence of livestock is clearly

visible in most pollen sequences in the Gredos Range. The key development during this period is the intensification and expansion of long-distance transhumance. Whilst written sources suggest that this developed from 1273, the late and post-medieval periods certainly witnessed the extension and intensification of this system in our study area (López-Sáez et al., 2014). Pollen records show an increase of human pressure on the Gredos Mountains. The clearance of high mountain pine forests was conducted in order to obtain pastures, particularly by local farmers who kept their herds by means of transterminant movements. Only Navarredonda, Puerto del Pico and Serranillos (Franco-Múgica et al., 1997; López-Sáez, López-Merino et al., 2009; López-Sáez, Alba-Sánchez et al., 2016) remained as passages for transhumant livestock (indicated by continuous values of both pastoral indicators and coprophilous fungi, Figure 16.2), while Peña Negra, Garganta del Trampal, Dehesa de Navamuño and Presa del Duque (Atienza, 1993; Ruiz-Zapata et al., 2011; Abel-Schaad & López-Sáez, 2013) exhibited the signs of local pasture exploitation. Despite the deteriorating weather/climate conditions related to the Little Ice Age (cal AD 1350–1850), a new wave of systematic deforestation occurred in the sixteenth century (*Pinus sylvestris* <30% in Serranillos, Figure 16.2) along with continuous population growth and agricultural expansion (Mariné, 1995). At high altitudes, the continued development of vegetation was dominated by anthropogenic taxa/grasslands. Reduced tree cover was also apparent. Charcoal analyses indicate that fires occurred at 1395 m a.s.l. at Puerto del Pico at c. cal AD 1725–1750 and pastoral indicator species and coprophilous fungi suggest that this zone (close to the Cañada Leonesa Occidental; Figure 16.1) bore witness to some of the highest levels of anthropogenic activity (Figure 16.2). This was probably due to the elevated numbers of animals which visited the site, perhaps reflecting a change in wider pastoral practices (López-Sáez, Alba-Sánchez et al., 2016). The valley bottoms saw the continued development of a mixed farming economy with diversified agricultural practices, especially cereal crops (including rye) and olive orchards (particularly in Peña Negra, Serranillos and Pozo de la Nieve, Figure 16.2) as well as chestnut groves at some specific places (Peña Negra, Tiétar and Alberche valleys) (López-Sáez, Glais et al., 2016).

The centuries of the subsequent post-medieval or contemporary period (cal AD 1800–2000) witnessed substantial changes in vegetation. There was a generalized increase in tree cover in the study area. In most places, this was dominated by *Pinus* species, although in other *Olea* came to the forefront (Peña Negra, Pozo de la Nieve, Puerto del Pico). This phenomenon might represent the modern landscaping practices which occurred in low-lying areas from the nineteenth century onwards (Figure 16.2). Several afforestation plans completed the transformation of the landscape with massive pine plantations which, naturally, contributed to a broad increase of tree cover. The most important change in recent years has been the sudden rise of macro charcoal in Serranillos and Puerto del Pico (c. cal AD 1800–1875) which reflects local man-made fires (López-Merino et al., 2009; López-Sáez, Alba-Sánchez et al., 2016) and (sometimes) even the continuous emergence of pastoral indicators and coprophilous fungi throughout the Gredos Range or the disappearance of cultivated taxa (*Secale cereale* disappeared in Peña Negra while *Cerealia* did so in Pozo de la Nieve). The dissolution of *La Mesta* in 1836 and the successive liberal Confiscation Laws which turned the control of land-use to local stock-breeders (Ezquerra-Boticario & Gil-Sánchez, 2008) did not lighten livestock pressure on mountain areas at all, instead causing new clearances for new pasturage. This shift to increased local grazing activities is also reported from other pollen records from the Gredos Range (López-Sáez et al., 2014). Inasmuch as this period coincides with the final stages of the Little Ice Age and the subsequent gradual warming, it is possible that the warmer climatic conditions of cal AD 1850 increased the length of the high-altitude pastoral season and resulted in a more visible modification of the vegetation around the pollen records (Figure 16.2). The palynological evidence for the more recent past in the middle and high altitudes probably also suggests an increase in the extent and/or density of the forest (Peña Negra, Pozo de la Nieve, Puerto del Pico) which was linked with a decline in agricultural activity and biological revival.

CONCLUDING REMARKS

This chapter offers a synthetic overview of pastoral activities in the marginal and hostile environments of central Spain, focusing on the Gredos Range during the last two millennia. To this end, this paper dealt with the published historical evidence from the region in order to collate independent lines of evidence, including: on the one hand, the overarching historical process supported by the archaeological material and the written sources (from the eleventh century onwards) and, on the other, previously published and ongoing studies of several high-resolution palaeoenvironmental records. Transhumance was tremendously important for this study area, a fact which has not previously been integrated into the history of climatic fluctuations, environmental changes and the socio-political factors for this time. All in all, these interdependent vectors shaped the highland landscape. The high mountain scenery of the Gredos Range can only be understood based on the resilience and adaptive capacity of the transhumance which has been exercised in this massif in recent

millennia under changing climatic conditions and in different cultural settings.

During early medieval times, these settings played a major role in the dynamics of warfare, colonization and exploitation in inner Iberia. Despite important lacunae in the factual evidence (especially archaeological remains), our interdisciplinary approach has underlined a phenomenon of increasingly coupled human and animal pressure on high mountain resources which involved an aggressive agro-forestal expansion under cold and arid climatic conditions related to the initial Early Medieval Cold Episode (cal AD 450–950). These expansive strategies merely involved transterminance, that is, short-distance or vertical movement of herders with their flocks who led a semi-mobile lifestyle in which they sheltered in pastoral shelters. In short, no true transhumance was practiced at that time. The deforestation of upland pinewoods and oak forests and particularly the exploitation of the high mountain pasture were probably due to these seasonal activities. As far as ecological resilience is concerned, it is precisely in this period that the current high mountain landscapes of the Gredos Range are managed. The substantial increase in pastoral pressure and the recurring use of fire led to an unsustainable situation for the high mountain pine forests (>1400 m a.s.l.). These forests were no longer resilient to human impact. After this time period, they began to disappear. Even today, it is only a few scattered trees in the surroundings of the Puerto del Pico Pass which remain.

During the high medieval period and under the milder weather conditions of the Late Medieval Warm Period (cal AD 950–1350), forest clearance was also related to the vertical movements of flocks and the seasonal exploitation of high-altitude areas, described in the written records as mobile or *de travesío* flocks. Only from c. AD 1250 did long-distance transhumance become fully operative in this region, after the foundation of small, rural, nuclear settlements in the main intra-mountainous valleys (which represented the definitive sedentarization of previously dispersed, migrant herders). Meanwhile, agro-pastoral pressure increased in low-altitude settings due to the full integration of these landscapes into the feudal system and a marked specialization in certain crops (rye, olives and sweet chestnuts) in low-altitude areas. Under the weather conditions of the Little Ice Age, the area was caught up in the momentum of the system of *La Mesta* and the intensive pressure it placed on high mountain pine forests and their increased clearance for the creation of high-quality pastures. In sum, high-altitude mountain areas demonstrate the potential for evaluating the resilience and vulnerability of these settings and to trace the trajectories of land-use as a sensitive laboratory for studying medieval social practices and their signature on vegetation.

ACKNOWLEDGEMENTS

This work was funded by the HAR2013–43701-P project (Spanish Ministry of Economy and Competitiveness). We are grateful to Antonio López Andreu (R.I.P.) and Pilar Sáez Navas for their collaboration and assistance during fieldwork.

NOTES

1 These studies were part of the 'Socio-ecological dynamics, resilience and vulnerability in a mountain landscape: the Central System 9000 cal. BC–AD 1850' research project (HAR2013–43701-P). All pollen cores are noted in Figure 1.
2 For further information about the pollen data, refer to López-Merino et al. (2009), López-Sáez, López-Merino et al. (2009), López-Sáez, Alba-Sánchez, et al. (2016b), Abel-Schaad & López-Sáez (2013) and Luelmo-Lautenschlaeger (2015).

REFERENCES

Abel-Schaad, D. & López-Sáez, J.A. 2013. Vegetation changes in relation to fire history and human activities at the Peña Negra mire (Bejar Range, Iberian Central Mountain System, Spain) during the past 4,000 years. *Vegetation History and Archaeobotany*, 22:199–214.

Abel-Schaad, D., López-Sáez, J.A. & Pulido, F.J. 2014. Heathlands, fire and grazing. A paleoenvironmental view of Las Hurdes (Cáceres, Spain) history during the last 1200 years. *Forest Systems*, 23:247–58.

Andrade, A. 1994. *Dinámica de la vegetación durante los últimos 3.000 BP en las Sierras de la Paramera, La Serrota y Villafranca (Ávila) a partir del análisis polínico*. Unpublished PhD thesis, University of Alcalá de Henares.

Anes, G. & García Sanz, A. 1994. *Mesta, transhumancia y vida pastoril*. Valladolid: Junta de Castilla y León.

Atienza, M. 1993. Evolución del paisaje vegetal en las Sierras de Béjar y Francia durante el Holoceno, a partir del análisis polínico. Unpublished PhD thesis, University of Alcalá de Henares.

Azcárate, F.M., Seoane, J., Castro, S. & Peco, B. 2013. Drove roads: Keystone structures that promote ant diversity in Mediterranean forest landscapes. *Acta Oecologica*, 49:107–15.

Barrios, A. 1984. *Estructuras agrarias y de poder en Castilla. El ejemplo de Ávila (1085–1320)*. Ávila: Universidad de Salamanca.

Behre, K.E. 1981. The interpretation of anthropogenic indicators in pollen diagrams. *Pollen et Spores*, 23:225–45.

Behre, K.E. 1988. The role of man in vegetation history. In: B. Huntley & T. Webb, eds. *Vegetation History*. Dordrecht: Kluwer Academic Publishers, pp. 633–71.

Beug, H.J. 2004. *Leitfaden der Pollenbestimmung für Mitteleuropa und angrenzende Gebiete*. Stuttgart: Gustav Fisher Verlag.

Bilbao, L.M. & Fernández de Pinedo, E. 1982. Exportation des laines, transhumance et occupation de l'espace en Castille aux XVI, XVII et XVIIIèmes siècles. In: M.

Cattini, ed. *Migration, Population and Occupation of Land Before 1800*. Budapest: Akadémia Kiadó, pp. 36–48.

Blanco-González, A., López-Sáez, J.A., Alba, F., Abel, D. & Pérez, S. 2015. Medieval landscapes in the Spanish Central System (450–1350): a palaeoenvironmental and historical perspective. *Journal of Medieval Iberian Studies*, 7(1):1–17.

Blanco-González, A., López-Sáez, J.A. & López-Merino, L. 2009. Ocupación y uso del territorio en el sector centromeridional de la cuenca del Duero entre la Antigüedad y la Alta Edad Media (siglos I-XI D.C.) *Archivo Español de Arqueología*, 82:275–300.

Blondel, J. 2006. The 'design' of Mediterranean landscapes: a millennial story of human and ecological systems during the historic period. *Human Ecology*, 34:713–29.

Buckland, P.C. & Edwards, K.J. 1984. The longevity of pastoral episodes of clearance activity in pollen diagrams: the role of post-occupation grazing. *Journal of Biogeography*, 11:243–49.

Carrión, J.S. 2001. Pastoreo y vulnerabilidad de la vegetación en la alta montaña mediterránea durante el Holoceno. *Cuadernos de Geografía*, 70:7–22.

Carrión, J.S., Fernández, S., González-Sampériz, P., Gil-Romera, G., Badal, E., Carrión-Marco, Y., López-Merino, L., López-Sáez, J.A., Fierro, E. & Burjachs, F. 2010. Expected trends and surprises in the Lateglacial and Holocene vegetation history of the Iberian Peninsula and Balearic Islands. *Review of Palaeobotany and Palynology*, 162:458–75.

Carrión, J.S., Fernández, S., González-Sampériz, P., López-Merino, L., Peña, L., Burjachs, F., López-Sáez, J.A., García-Antón, M., Carrión Marco, Y., Uzquiano, P., Postigo, J.M., Barrón, E., Allué, E., Badal, E., Dupré, M., Fierro, E., Manzano, S., Munuera, M., Rubiales, J.M., García Amorena, I., Jiménez Moreno, G., Gil Romera, G., Leroy, S., García-Martínez, M.S., Montoya, E., Fletcher, W., Yll, E., Vieira, M., Rodríguez-Ariza, M.O., Anderson, S., Peñalba, C., Gil García, M.J., Pérez Sanz, A., Albert, R.M., Díez, M.J., Morales, C., Gómez Manzaneque, F., Parra, I., Ruiz Zapata, B., Riera, S., Zapata, L., Ejarque, A., Vegas, T., Rull, V., Scott, L., Andrade, A., Pérez Díaz, S., Abel Schaad, D., Moreno, E., Hernández-Mateo, L., Ochando, J., Pérez Navarro, M.A., Sánchez Baena, J.J., Riquelme, J.A., Iglesias, R., Franco, F., Chaín, C., Figueiral, I., Grau, E., Matos, M., Jiménez Espejo, F., Arribas, A., Garrido, G., Finlayson, G., Finlayson, C., Ruiz, M., Pérez Jordá, G. & Miras, Y. 2015. *Cinco millones de años de cambio florístico y vegetal en la Península Ibérica e Islas Baleares*. Madrid: Ministerio de Economía y Competitividad.

Carrión, J.S. & Navarro, C. 2002. Cryptogam spores and other non-pollen microfossils as sources of palaeoecological information: case-studies from Spain. *Annales Botanici Fennici*, 39:1–14.

Conedera, M., Krebs, P., Tinner, W., Pradella, M. & Torriani, D. 2004. The cultivation of *Castanea sativa* (Mill.) in Europe, from its origin to its diffusion on a continental scale. *Vegetation History and Archaeobotany*, 13:161–79.

Cugny, C., Mazier, F. & Galop, D. 2010. Modern and fossil non-pollen palynomorphs from the Basque mountains (western Pyrenees, France): the use of coprophilous fungi to reconstruct pastoral activity. *Vegetation History and Archaeobotany*, 19:391–408.

Currás, A., Zamora, L., Reed, J.M., García-Soto, E., Ferrero, S., Armengol, X., Mezquita-Joanes, F., Marqués, M.A., Riera, S. & Julià, R. 2012. Climate change and human impact in central Spain during Roman times: high-resolution multi-proxy analysis of a tufa lake record (Somolinos, 1280 m asl). *Catena*, 89:31–53.

Díaz de la Torre, J., Bores, M., Caballero, J. & Cabrera, B. 2009. El despoblado de San Cristóbal o Las Henrenes (Cillá, Ávila): Una aproximación al paso de la Edad Antigua a la Edad Media. In: I. Martín Viso, ed. *¿Tiempos oscuros? Territorios y sociedad en el centro de la Península Ibérica (siglos VII–X)*. Madrid: Sílex, pp. 159–80.

Dorado, M., Valdeolmillos, A. & Ruiz-Zapata, M.B. 2001. Actividad humana y dinámica de la vegetación en la Sierra de Ávila (Sistema Central Español) desde el Bronce Medio. *Polen*, 11:39–49.

Escalona, J. 2009. The early Castilian peasantry: an archaeological turn? *Journal of Medieval Iberian Studies*, 1(2):119–45.

Ezquerra-Boticario, F.J. & Gil-Sánchez, L. 2008. *La transformación histórica del paisaje forestal en Extremadura. Tercer Inventario Forestal Nacional 1997–2007*. Madrid: Ministerio de Medio Ambiente.

Faegri, K. & Iversen, J. 1989. *Textbook of Pollen Analysis*. Chichester: John Wiley.

Franco-Moreno, B. 2005. Distribución y asentamiento de tribus bereberes (Imazighen) en el territorio emeritense en época emiral (s. VIII–X). *Arqueología y Territorio Medieval*, 12:39–50.

Franco-Múgica, F., García-Antón, M., Maldonado, J., Morla, C. & Sainz-Ollero, H. 2001. Evolución de la vegetación en el sector septentrional del Macizo de Ayllón (Sistema Central). Análisis polínico de la turbera de Pelagallinas. *Anales del Jardín Botánico de Madrid*, 59:113–24.

Franco-Múgica, F., García-Antón, M. & Sainz-Ollero, H. 1997. Impacto antrópico y dinámica de la vegetación durante los últimos 2000 años BP en la vertiente septentrional de la Sierra de Gredos: Navarredonda (Ávila, España). *Revue de Paléobiologie*, 16:29–45.

Franco-Múgica, F., García-Antón, M. & Sainz-Ollero, H. 1998. Vegetation dynamics and human impact in the Sierra de Guadarrama, Central System, Spain. *The Holocene*, 8:69–82.

Galop, D. 1998. *La forêt, l'homme et le troupeau dans les Pyrénées. 6000 ans d'histoire de l'environnement entre Garonne et Méditerranée*. Toulouse: Geode, Laboratoire d'Ecologie Terrestre.

García Garcimartín, H. 2004. *El Valle del Alberche en la Baja Edad Media (s. XII–XV)*. Ávila: Diputación de Ávila.

García-Oliva, M.D. 2007. Un espacio sin poder: la Transierra extremeña durante la época musulmana. *Studia Historica, Historia Medieval*, 25:89–120.

Gómez-Gandullo, J.A. 2006. Avance sobre las excavaciones arqueológicas en el yacimiento de épocavisigoda de La Legoriza, San Martín del Castañar (Salamanca). In: J. Morín, ed. *La investigación arqueológica de la época visigoda en la Comunidad de Madrid*. Madrid: Comunidad de Madrid, pp. 216–35.

Gómez-González, C., Ruiz-Zapata, B., Gil, M.J., López-Sáez, J.A., Santiesteban, J., Mediavilla, R., Domínguez, F. & Vera, S. 2009. Evolución del paisaje vegetal durante los últimos 1.680 años BP en el Macizo de Peñalara (Sierra de Guadarrama, Madrid). *Revista Española de Micropaleontología*, 41:75–89.

Gómez-González, C., Ruiz-Zapata, M.B., López-Sáez, J.A. & Gil-García, M.J. 2009. Aportaciones de la palinología en la reconstrucción del impacto ganadero, en los alrededores de Rascafría (Madrid), durante el Holoceno reciente. In: A. Romero, F. Belmonte, F. Alonso &

F. López, eds. *Advances in Studies on Desertification. Topic 5: Impact of Livestock and Agriculture in Terrestrial Ecosystems*. Murcia: Universidad de Murcia, pp. 693–96.

Gómez-Pantoja, J. 2004. *Pecora consectari*: transhumance in Roman Spain. In: B. Santillo Frizell, ed. *Pecus: Man and Animal in Antiquity*. Rome: The Swedish Institute in Rome, pp. 94–102.

González Calle, J.A. 2002. *Despoblados en la comarca de El Barco de Ávila (Baja Edad Media y Edad Moderna)*. Ávila: Diputación de Ávila.

Grimm, E.C. 1992. *Tilia, version 2*. Springfield: Illinois State Museum.

Klein, J. 1920. *La Mesta: A Study in Spanish Economy History, 1273–1836*. Harvard: Harvard University Press.

López-Merino, L., López-Sáez, J.A., Alba-Sánchez, F., Pérez-Díaz, S. & Carrión, J.S. 2009. 2000 years of pastoralism and fire shaping high-altitude vegetation of Sierra de Gredos in central Spain. *Review of Palaeobotany and Palynology*, 158:42–51.

López-Sáez, J.A., Abel-Schaad, D., Pérez-Díaz, S., Blanco-González, A., Alba-Sánchez, F., Dorado, M., Ruiz-Zapata, B., Gil, M.J., Gómez, C. & Franco-Múgica, F. 2014. Vegetation history, climate and human impact in the Spanish Central System over the last 9,000 years. *Quaternary International*, 353:98–122.

López-Sáez, J.A., Abel-Schaad, D., Robles-López, S., Pérez-Díaz, S., Alba-Sánchez, F. & Nieto-Lugilde, D. 2016. Landscape dynamics and human impact on high-mountain woodlands in the western Spanish Central System during the last three millennia. *Journal of Archaeological Science: Reports*, 9:203–18.

López-Sáez, J.A., Alba-Sánchez, F., López-Merino, L. & Pérez-Díaz, S. 2010. Modern pollen analysis: a reliable tool for discriminating *Quercus rotundifolia* communities in Central Spain. *Phytocoenologia*, 40:57–72.

López-Sáez, J.A., Alba-Sánchez, F., Robles-López, S., Pérez-Díaz, S., Abel-Schaad, D., Sabariego-Ruiz, S. & Glais, A. 2016. Exploring seven hundred years of transhumance, climate dynamic, fire and human activity through a historical mountain pass in central Spain. *Journal of Mountain Science*, 13:1139–53.

López-Sáez, J.A., Alba-Sánchez, F., Sánchez-Mata, D., Abel-Schaad, D., Gavilán, R. & Pérez-Díaz, S. 2015. A palynological approach to the study of *Quercus pyrenaica* forest communities in the Spanish Central System. *Phytocoenologia*, 45:107–24.

López-Sáez, J.A., Blanco-González, A., López-Merino, L., Ruiz-Zapata, M.B., Dorado, M., Pérez-Díaz, S., Valdeolmillos, A. & Burjachs, F. 2009. Landscape and climatic changes during the end of the late prehistory in the Amblés Valley (Ávila, central Spain), from 1200 to 400 cal BC. *Quaternary International*, 200:90–101.

López-Sáez, J.A., Glais, A., Robles-López, S., Alba-Sánchez, F., Pérez-Díaz, S., Abel-Schaad, D. & Luelmo-Lautenschlaeger, R. 2016. Unraveling the naturalness of sweet chestnut forests (*Castanea sativa* Mill.) in central Spain. *Vegetation History and Archaeobotany*, http://doi:10.1007/s00334–016–0575-x

López-Sáez, J.A., López-García, P. & Burjachs, F. 2003. Arqueopalinología: Síntesis Crítica. *Polen*, 12:5–35.

López-Sáez, J.A. & López-Merino, L. 2005. Precisiones metodológicas acerca de los indicios paleopalinológicos de agricultura en la Prehistoria de la Península Ibérica. *Portugalia*, 26:53–64.

López-Sáez, J.A. & López-Merino, L. 2007. Coprophilous fungi as a source of information of anthropic activities during the prehistory in the Amblés Valley (Ávila, Spain): the archaeopalynological record. *Revista Española de Micropaleontología*, 39:103–16.

López-Sáez, J.A., López-Merino, L., Alba-Sánchez, F. & Pérez-Díaz, S. 2009. Contribución paleoambiental al estudio de la trashumancia en el sector abulense de la Sierra de Gredos. *Hispania*, 231:9–38.

López-Sáez, J.A., López-Merino, L., Alba-Sánchez, F., Pérez-Díaz, S., Abel-Schaad, D. & Carrión, J.S. 2010. Late Holocene ecological history of *Pinus pinaster* forests in the Sierra de Gredos of central Spain. *Plant Ecology*, 206:195–209.

López-Sáez, J.A., Sánchez-Mata, D., Alba-Sánchez, F., Abel-Schaad, D., Gavilán, R. & Pérez-Díaz, S. 2013. Discrimination of Scots pine forests in the Iberian Central System (*Pinus sylvestris* var. *iberica*) by means of pollen analysis. Phytosociological considerations. *Lazaroa*, 34:191–208.

López-Sáez, J.A., van Geel, B., Farbos-Texier, S. & Diot, M.F. 1998. Remarques paléoécologiques à propos de quelques palynomorphes non-polliniques provenant de sédiments quaternaires en France. *Revue de Paléobiologie*, 17:445–59.

López-Sáez, J.A., van Geel, B. & Martín, M. 2000. Aplicación de los microfósiles no polínicos en Palinología Arqueológica. In: V. Oliveira, ed. *Contributos das Ciências e das Technologias para a Arqueologia da Península Ibérica*. Porto: Adecap, pp. 11–20.

Lozny, L.R. ed. 2013. *Continuity and Change in Cultural Adaptation to Mountain Environments. From Prehistory to Contemporary Threats*. New York: Springer.

Luelmo-Lautenschlaeger, R. 2015. *Dinámicas socioecológicas en el Valle de Iruelas (Sierra de Gredos, Ávila) durante el Holoceno reciente*. Unpublished MA thesis, University Autónoma de Madrid.

Manzano Baena, P. & Casas, R. 2010. Past, present and future of transhumance in Spain: nomadism in a developed country. *Pastoralism*, 1:72–90.

Mariné, M. 1995. El patrimonio arqueológico de la Sierra de Gredos. In: M.A. Troitiño, ed. *Gredos: territorio, sociedad y cultura*. Ávila: Diputación de Ávila, pp. 19–48.

Martín Viso, I. 2009. Espacios sin Estado: Los territorios occidentales entre el Duero y el Sistema Central (siglos VIII–IX). In: I. Martín Viso, ed. *¿Tiempos oscuros? Territorios y sociedad en el centro de la Península Ibérica (siglos VII–X)*. Madrid: Sílex, pp. 107–35.

Martín-Viso, I. & Blanco-González, A. 2016. Ancestral Memories and Early Medieval Landscapes: The Case of Sierra de Ávila (Spain). *Early Medieval Europe*, 24(4):393–422.

Monsalvo, J.M. 2003. Frontera pionera, monarquía en expansión y formación de los concejos de villa y tierra. Relaciones de poder en el realengo concejil entre el Duero y el Tajo (c. 1072–c. 1222). *Arqueología y Territorio Medieval*, 10:45–126.

Pardo, F. & Gil, L. 2005. The impact of traditional land use on woodlands: a case study in the Spanish Central System. *Journal of Historical Geography*, 31:390–408.

Quirós Castillo, J.A. 2011. Early Medieval Landscapes in North-West Spain: Local Powers and Communities, Fifth-Tenth Centuries. *Early Medieval Europe*, 19(3):285–311.

Quirós Castillo, J.A. & Vigil-Escalera, A. 2006. Networks of peasant villages between Toledo and Velegia Alabense, Northwestern Spain (V–Xth centuries). *Archeologia Medievale*, 33:79–130.

Reille, M. 1999. *Pollen et spores d'Europe et d'Afrique du Nord, 2nd edn*. Marseille: Laboratoire de Botanique Historique et Palynologie.

Ruiz, M. & Ruiz, J.P. 1986. Ecological history of Transhumance in Spain. *Biological Conservation*, 37:73–86.

Ruiz-Zapata, M.B., Carrasco, R.M., Gil-García, M.J., Pedraza, J., Razola, L., Domínguez-Villar, D. & Gallardo, J.L. 2011. Dinámica de la vegetación durante el Holoceno en la Sierra de Gredos (Sistema Central Español). *Boletín de la Real Sociedad Española de Historia Natural (Sección Geología)*, 105:109–23.

Salzman, P.C. 2004. *Pastoralists, Equality, Hierarchy, and the State*. Boulder: Westview.

Valbuena-Carabaña, M., López de Heredia, U., Fuentes-Utrilla, P., González-Doncel, I. & Gil, L. 2010. Historical and recent changes in the Spanish forests: a socio-economic process. *Review of Palaeobotany and Palynology*, 162:492–506.

van Geel, B. 2001. Non-pollen palynomorphs. In: J.P. Smol, H.J.B. Birks & W.M. Last, eds. *Tracking Environmental Change Using Lake Sediments, vol. 3, Terrestrial, Algal, and Siliceous Indicators*. Dordrecht: Kluwer, pp. 99–119.

Vigil-Escalera, A. 2006. El modelo de poblamiento rural en la Meseta y algunas cuestiones de visibilidad arqueológica. In: J. López Quiroga, ed. *Galia e Hispania en el contetxto de la presencia germánica (ss. V–VII). Balance y perspectivas*. BAR IS 1534, pp. 89–108.

Vigil-Escalera, A. 2015. *Los primeros paisajes altomedievales en el interior de Hispania. Registros campesinos del siglo quinto d.C.* Bilbao: Universidad del País Vasco.

CHAPTER 17

Ovine pastoralism and mobility systems in Romania
An ethnoarchaeological approach

ROBIN BRIGAND, OLIVIER WELLER, FELIX ADRIAN TENCARIU, MARIUS ALEXIANU, ANDREI ASĂNDULESEI

INTRODUCTION

Whenever one studies sedentism and the development of unequal society, one must also address territories and the forms and rhythms of settlement. In the Carpathian hinterlands, the quality, abundance and relative availability of mineral and agropastoral resources were important criteria in the location and establishment of settlement. Stretching broadly from the Danube to the Prut on one side and to the Tisza and the Pannonian Plain on the other is a key area for examining the genesis and development of the European Neolithic. It allows scholars to trace the diffusion and expansion of the first colonization front from Southeast Europe in the early sixth millennium BC. By the second half of the fifth millennium, these areas witnessed an intense and standardized production of high value objects (copper, gold, etc.) which spread within the major cultural groups (e.g. in Moldavia, the Cucuteni cultural complex of approx. 4600–3500 BC).

In the Romanian part of Moldavia a Franco-Romanian team has been conducting research on land occupation and the dynamics of the site networks for the past 15 years.[1] By means of solid databases, spatial analyses, paleoenvironmental studies and ethnoarchaeological surveys, we have tried to understand and trace the settlement choices made by Neolithic and Chalcolithic communities (ca. 6000–3500 BC). Furthermore, we have tried to characterize the forms of resource use (particularly salt) whose exploitation seems to have been one of the key elements behind the development of the first agro-pastoral communities.

When considering the territorial organization of a prehistoric community, a purely archaeological approach is both overly influenced by the fragmentary nature of the data and by the haphazard nature of the discoveries that have been made to date. These problems are aggrandized by the very few systematic surveys which have been carried out in this area. In this context, how can we highlight new habitat configurations based on the specialization, complementarity and seasonality of production? In instances such as this one, it may, therefore, be useful to adopt an actualist's approach. In this way, one might enrich archaeological interpretations by providing reference data which may clarify ancient mechanisms and the temporality of settlement and land use. This study of the pastoral societies of Romania (which still remain very traditional) provides a frame of reference for territorial practices which can enrich how we read the ways in which ancient societies organized and managed space.

After a review of relevant archaeological problems, we will establish how the socio-economic structures specific to Romania constitute a relevant laboratory for an ethnoarchaeological approach to pastoralism. The characteristics of sheep husbandry in Romania will be addressed in two different stages. First, we will address the issue of specialized and highly mobile husbandry in plain or hilly areas; second, we will discuss the nature and dynamics of the seasonal ebb and flow of movements in areas of high elevation. Subsequently, we will discuss the role of salt in the seasonal movement of people and herds before considering long-distance transhumance in Romania as a whole.

ARCHAEOLOGICAL BACKGROUND

Towards the end of the sixth and especially during the fifth millennium BC, there was an evolution of both social and economic needs in Central and Eastern Europe. This can be observed through the density and diversification of settlement patterns as well as an increasing exploitation of natural resources strictly correlated to the expansion of exchange networks. This transfer of ideas and objects occurred in the context of the assertion of major cultural groups in a largely amended social and economic framework. Various approaches allow us to establish the place of animal husbandry in the economies of recent prehistory.

1) Geography of ancient settlements. In Moldavia, the geography of the Neolithic period (sixth millennium BC) manifests foremost as clustered habitats along valley floors and on low terraces. However, with the advent of the early fifth millennium, there appeared a new territorial organization in which the population became more dispersed. Settlers favoured hillfronts

© 2018 European Association of Archaeologists

and high terraces overlooking large rivers (Figure 17.1). Many secondary occupations have been documented (especially near salt springs) (Brigand & Weller, 2015; Weller et al., 2015). It was also during the first four centuries of the fifth millennium BC that evidence for salt production is the greatest in relation to the small density of the population. Produced since the earliest Neolithic (Dumitroaia, 1994; Ursulescu, 1977; Weller & Dumitroaia, 2005), for the first time salt became the centre of specific territorial strategies that seem to have been based on hierarchized population with more specialized functions.

Some of the signs marking the broader socio-economic and technological changes occurring in Europe in the fifth millennium BC included extensive land use, the intensification of salt exploitation, the arrival of the first pyrometallurgical innovations and extended exchange networks. From around 4500 BC, the intense and standardized production of massive copper objects emerged among the major cultural groups of the Carpathian-Danubian area. It was a time of social as well as territorial complexity: both more numerous and more strongly hierarchized, settlement sites were established in a variety of ecosystems with very diverse potential. Changes in the nature (permanent villages, fortified or open settlements or even small, farmhouse-like satellites) and pattern (a population dispersal related to different ecological niches) of settlements also indicate

Figure 17.1. *1) High terrace Chalcolithic settlement (Dealul Pandele) and sheepfold without a dairy (Zmeu, Lungani, Iași); 2) Brine supply at Hălăbutoaia salt spring (Țolici, Petricani, Neamț); 3) View of Hălăbutoaia salt spring (in the background) and the salt exploitation site (with archaeological remains which date from the Neolithic to the Middle Ages).*
Source: Images by R. Brigand 1) and O. Weller 2), 3)

changes in their means of production, which was then based on the increased mobility of the domestic units and a specialization of production (Lazarovici & Lazarovici, 2003). This mobility manifested as pendulatory occupation between stages of abandonment and exploitation, and these states alternated with each other regularly. Documented by modest material remains without architectural elements, the satellite sites denote seasonal occupation connected to agricultural, pastoral and salt-working activities.

The findings are random and rely overly much on a limited number of surveys. Secondary occupation sites are excavated very seldomly and cannot be compared with the well-documented studies which have been completed on the major sites. In situations such as these, how can we assess the animal husbandry taking place in these new, more intensive forms of land use and environmental anthropization? Let us turn instead to the knowledge gleaned from paleoenvironmental and faunistic markers.

2) Paleoenvironmental approaches. The excavations carried out in collaboration with the Museum of History and Archaeology from Piatra Neamţ around the salt spring from Lunca (*Poiana Slatinei*, Neamţ County) reveal the existence of relationships between salt-producing activities and animal husbandry. The Neolithic hearths at Lunca revealed the use of different kinds of wood (ash, hazel, oak, elm, etc.). This indicates that the fuel was selected from an environment which contained oak, ash and elm (Weller et al., 2008). The question is whether the selection of the wood can be related to the techniques used for evaporating saline water. Two hypotheses have been advanced: a salt-production technique in which brine was sprayed over a glowing pyre or the use of those same tree species for the evaporation of salt and for feeding livestock, as the practice of tree pruning by livestock has been demonstrated since the Neolithic (e.g. Thiébault, 2005). This geographical proximity between salt production and foddering activities is interesting in that it suggests synchronous seasonal activities. These are doubly important as they are still part of the current landscape (pruning, salt production and animal husbandry; see Figure 17.1).

Around Ţolici salt spring (*Hălăbutoaia*, Neamţ County), the palynological sondages produced evidence of anthropization related to animal husbandry. The pollen of weeds, plants and mushrooms specific to well-trodden places and pastures has been attested since the early Neolithic (Danu et al., 2010). Only in the last stages of the third millennium BC did the first cereal pollens appear. These surveys suggest, therefore, early pastoral exploitation which presumably was associated with the opening of the environment and the search of fuel for the production of salt which was subsequently followed by a more lasting presence underlined by the agricultural production evidence.

The precocity of pastoral occupation has also been documented in Transylvania, at 239 m above sea level, where taxa indicating agricultural activities have been recorded as early as 7000 cal. BP. Pastoral taxa, however, have been recorded from 8000 cal. BP (Feurdean et al., 2015). Around Bisoca (and its abundant salt deposits), the first discrete evidence of anthropic presence, probably pastoral (*plantago lanceolata*), are attested between 7200 cal. BP and 6750 cal. BP and that at an altitude of 890 m a.s.l. It was only between 5600 and 3400 cal. BP that the first signs of agricultural activity left their mark (Tanţău et al., 2009: 168).

3) The skeletal remains. Study of the faunal remains allow us to restore the importance of the cattle and ovicaprid herds to their rightful place in the economy of prehistoric communities. By studying the composition of livestock in terms of age and gender, archaeozoologists acquire relevant clues about the type of production that was undertaken. However, few sheep/goats slaughter profiles have been made for the Romanian Neolithic or Chalcolithic. Nevertheless, work in Dobrudja has made some progress, especially as it is in this steppe region that sheep were often the best represented (Bejenaru & Stanc, 2013) in contrast to other regions of Romania (which were dominated by cattle).

In the southeast, recent research has highlighted a tendency for the standardization of sheep husbandry practices for the optimization of meat production in the second half of the fifth millennium and the first centuries of the fourth millennium BC (Bréhard & Bălăşescu, 2012). The development of farming techniques relied on a web of complementary sites integrated into a network of relationships between a main facility (the tell) and a series of specialized peripheral sites. The amplitude of this pastoral system remains difficult to establish, as such seasonal sites are still poorly known. Although difficult to transfer elsewhere because of the specificity of the organization of the habitat in southeast Romania, the settlement model suggested by this study is exciting because it underlies the temporal and spatial complexity of the modalities of pastoral exploitation.

THE ROMANIAN LABORATORY

Little data is available for reconstructing the seasonal movements of herds and men in the Romanian Carpathians on account of the great disparity of the archaeological research that has been done there. Specifically, archaeological data is extremely rare for alpine and sub-alpine sectors (aside from the exploratory research on life patterns in Romanian high-altitude areas carried out by J. Nandriş and G. Lazarovici; see Lazarovici & Kalmar Maxim, 1987; Lazarovici & Ardeţ, 2015; Nandriş, 1987, 2015). In Moldavia, the Chalcolithic occupation of the mountains are only observed up to an elevation of 500 m (and that in conjunction with salt springs) and this data comes only from rescue excavations (the building of the Bicaz Lake dam on the Bistriţa River; see Nicolăescu-Plopşor & Petrescu-Dîmboviţa, 1959). In the karst landscape of Banat, the caves used during the Neolithic were at similar altitudes (Luca, 2005). However, we know little of the activities that took place there (and even less is known about any relations between the mountains and the plains at this time).

In other contexts, it is possible to observe early settlement at high elevations marked by seasonal movements on a regional level: Neolithic sheepfolds have been found in the French Alps and Pyrenees above 1500 m a.s.l. and even near to 2000 m a.s.l. (e.g. Rendu, 2003; Thiébault, 2005). If few clues are available for the moment, we expect that future research will stimulate archaeology along the Carpathian chain through which we will better understand the dynamics of seasonal movements between the plains and the heights.

Conversely, ethnohistorical and ethnoarchaeological approaches are more advanced. Those of J. Nandriş (1987), M. Alexianu et al. (1992, 2007, 2011) have demonstrated that the ancient practices were surprisingly long lasting; even the technological innovations stimulated by the opening of Romania towards Europe made little headway. Indeed, in an era of market liberalization, Romania remains one of the few countries in Europe where small-scale farming remains the predominant socio-economic activity in rural regions. This is reflected in the persistence of the family farm (*gospodărie*), a small, family-based unit of agricultural production founded on an economy of subsistence and exchange. This system of production relies on traditional forms of mutual support and the organization of collective work. These form the basis of the village-based communitarianism that H.H. Stahl (1969) identified as the descendant of older social structures. In his major work, *Les anciennes communautés villageoises roumaines, asservissement et pénétration capitaliste*, Stahl did not hesitate to assert that

> the village community is, above all else, a means of shared economic exploitation of a collective holding using very rudimentary pastoral and agricultural techniques, regulated by a system of social relationships that are directly derived from ancient tribal organizations, the traces of which survive precisely because the processes of production are so little developed.
>
> (Stahl, 1969: 50)

Undermined by the establishment of communism and the collectivization of land from 1948 onwards, it was only after 1989 that the old system of family-based self-sufficiency re-emerged (Lagneaux, 2007).

This underscores the importance of examining the issue of pastoralism as a means of further exploring the strong sense of community and identity which characterizes Romanian rural culture (Figure 17.2). The carrying out of activities associated with animal husbandry (particularly the rearing of sheep) underpins rural communities' ways of life, whether through the organization of pastures, the preparation and movement of herds to the mountains in the summer or the production and distribution of products such as milk, wool and meat. The economic and social implications of pastoral activities have been the focus of a long scientific tradition. This was particularly the case among geographers interested in the modalities of upland pasture exploitation. For example, one could cite the work of de Martonne (1902, 1904) who is credited as being the first to highlight the importance of pastoralism in the southern Romanian Carpathians. Romanian researchers subsequently developed several avenues of research, such as the study of the various pastoral typologies, the techniques used in the construction of sheepfolds and the forms of social organization associated with herd management. In the seminal works of Vuia (1924), Herseni (1936), Morariu (1942) and Dunăre (1956), we see that particular attention was paid to defining categories that could be used to illustrate the different forms of land occupation and their timeframes in various areas (modelled in Figure 17.3). A synopsis of the various types of pastoralism recorded between past and present in the Carpathians is presented which focuses on ovine-based pastoralism.

LOCAL/AGRICULTURAL PASTORALISM

This first clearly distinct type of pastoralism has proven to be the most common surviving form of pastoralism in the hill regions and plains of Romania. It is the one with the closest analogies to ancient, daily animal husbandry which would exploit the diverse potential of the various soils alongside agricultural activities.

The distinctiveness of local pastoralism lies in its close association with agricultural activities: the flock (which sometimes includes goats and pigs as well as sheep) does not leave the territory of the village until after the autumn harvest, when restrictions on pastures are lifted and when any common graze-able lands can be accessed (subject to agreement with the landowners and/or the local authorities). During the summer grazing period and within the confines of the village territory, each flock is led to pasture on rented lands (communal or private) which have not been planted (meadows, harvested fields, headlands, mown meadows, fallow land and waste ground) or which will not be planted with winter wheat until the autumn. Thus, this

Ovine pastoralism and mobility systems 249

Figure 17.2. The study area in Romania (stars): the Moldavian Plain and foothills and the southern Carpathians. Views of a number of sheepfolds examined as part of the study: 1) Crivești (Strunga, Iași), 2) Boureni (Bălțați, Iași), 3) Țolici (Petricani, Neamț), 4) Roșiile-Parâng (Petrila, Hunedoara), 5) Scărița-Parâng (Petroșani, Hunedoara), 6) Băsești (Pârjol, Bacău).
Source: Images R. Brigand 1), 2); O. Weller 3), 6) and A. Lucet 4), 5)

form of pastoralism ensures the rational and systematic fertilization of all fields within the communal territory. Several sub-types have been identified, both through our fieldwork and through previously published data.

1) The ewes spend the entire summer outside the village (albeit within the village territory), which necessitates the presence of one or more ewe pens (particularly for separating the ewes from suckling lambs) and a dairy for the production of milk products (Figure 17.4, no. 1). This common configuration assures that the activity remains, to a certain extent, independent, with the preparation of milk products being carried out on-site by the shepherds themselves (Dunăre, 1984: 85).

2) More rarely, we encounter a local sheepfold that includes a resting and milking pen, but which lacks an associated dairy, as milk products are produced in the village itself, i.e. at the owner's farm using milk which is collected two or three times a day (Figure 17.4, no. 2). This arrangement means that the shepherds are only involved in the tending and milking of the flock at some times of the day (often with the help of the owners).

Figure 17.3. *Models of the various types of pastoralism (nineteenth–twentieth centuries)*
Source: After R. Vuia (1980)

3) Another situation, described by Iordache (1986: 62) exists in which the pastures are situated close to the village. This requires the shepherd to bring the herd to the owners' houses so that each owner milks his sheep on the farm. In such situations, the family farm must be equipped with a milking pen and a sheep shed. The production of milk products is, therefore, carried out within the farmyard and the shepherd is only responsible for tending the sheep during the daytime.

Depending on the region and the customs of the villagers, the shepherd may only be responsible for watching over the flock while it is grazing, the ewes being brought back to the village and picked by their owners for the night. This situation (which closely resembles that which Dunăre terms sedentary husbandry) is common for dairy cattle. The cows are returned to the village each evening and reclaimed by their owners who look after the milking and stabling of the animals for the night.

The Carpatho-Balkan form of local/agricultural pastoralism is based on a high level of mobility in order to better meet both agricultural demands and to best avoid the infections associated with over-trodden pens (Figure 17.3). It requires lightweight pastoral equipment (milking pen and corridor and well as a resting pen and shelter) that can be rapidly dismantled and reassembled within the space of a few hours. In former times the equipment was loaded on sledges. However, in more modern times it generally tends to be transported on horse-drawn carts. The process of fertilizing agricultural land is no longer as important a consideration as it was prior to the collectivization of the land. In fact, herds are prohibited on private land although they are tolerated in autumn on certain arable lands after the harvest. Shepherds sometimes come to arrangements with landowners provided that the latter own some of the animals within the flock. Indeed, while regular movement (*mutare*) of equipment and facilities still occurs, it takes place mainly for sanitary reasons today. For this reason, it occurs within a limited space (Figure 17.4, no. 2). A characteristic feature of local pastoralism is the *prepeleag* (*prepeleac, sărciner*) (e.g. Iordache, 1986: 79), the trunk of a dead tree whose trimmed branches are used to hang dairy utensils in order to keep them out of the reach of dogs. Usually fixed in the ground at the entrance to the sheepfold, the *prepeleac* is a strong marker of identity in the context of local pastoralism. Although more rare, they also occur at the entrances to stone shelters in the alpine zones of the southern, eastern and northern Carpathians (Vuia, 1980: 245).

Mountain Pastoralism and Seasonal Movements

It is clear that the poor soils and short growing season of mountainous areas do not favour agricultural activity. In the Carpathians (as well as other areas), sheep and goat husbandry is widespread because the issue of feeding the flocks can be solved by over summering the animals in upland pastures.

Just as is the case in other parts of Eastern and Southeast Europe, there are few archaeological traces

Figure 17.4 .1). A seasonal sheepfold with facilities for the preparation of milk products (Țolici, Petricani, Neamț; image R. Brigand), 2) A WorldView2 panchromatic image (October 15th, 2010, image courtesy of the Digital Globe Foundation) of the summering of a sheepfold without a dairy (four locations) located to the west of Valea Oii (Bălțați, Iași). Right, the prepeleag, *a symbol of local mobile pastoralism*
Source: After Iordache (1986: 80)

in Romania that can allow us to recreate the dynamics of alpine land occupation. The first seasonal movement from village to the first elevations very likely took place for the Chalcolithic of the Carpathian-Danubian area in a manner similar to what has been observed in southern France. It likely involved pastoral settlement that was nonetheless limited to the elevations that were accessible to shepherds and their flocks within the space of a single day (Brochier, 2005). In this regard, the marginal position of certain caves occupied during the Neolithic and the Chalcolithic and the carstic domain of southwestern Romania (Banat) is relevant, particularly when the toponymy clearly indicates a recent use of these shelters (e.g. *Peștera Oilor*, lit. 'the cave of sheep', Luca, 2005: 20). The research carried out by the team of the Highland Zone Ethnoarchaeology Project (Nandriș, 2015) greatly advances the field by systematically registering the pastoral structures of the Cerna Văr Massif (Lazarovici et al., 2015). Several forms of this practice have been recorded by ethnographic investigations:

1) The first of these can be categorized as pendular pastoralism: It involves an annual pastoral movement undertaken every summer between the home village and mountain pastures. Thus, every spring, the flocks leave the village and make their way to the high pastures which they reach as soon as the snow melts. The climb may be punctuated by planned stops at intermediate sheepfolds. These sheepfolds are generally located in meadows below the alpine forest level. Starting in the beginning of June, these stops also take place beyond that level. The descent which follows in the autumn is also undertaken in a gradual manner (starting from the first of September onwards). Autumn is passed in the post-harvest stubble of cultivated fields, in meadows where regrowth is exploited and then in post-harvest corn fields. Following the first cold snap, some shepherds choose to undertake short-distance movements (limited to the valleys and plains within a 100 km radius) before returning home for Christmas. Others opt for long-distance transhumance to the Danubian Plain and Moldova. This slow progression towards mountain pastures is dictated on the one hand by the melting of the snow cover and, on the other, by the arrival of winter. Movement nonetheless remains closely tied to the rhythms of agricultural production, a fact which led R. Vuia (1980: 253–71) to label the system as one of agricultural pastoralism with high-altitude grazing in the summer. According to Vuia (1980: 272–99), it should be distinguished from pastoralism linked

to haymaking in the intermediate spaces between the village and the mountains.

2) This second form of mobility involves stops in the sub-alpine hay-producing areas, even if that means spending part of the winter in the zones where large quantities of hay are stored. In such instances, we are dealing with the type of bi-pendular pastoralism described by Dunăre (1977; 1984: 59). Following the autumn descent in which the flocks approach their home village, the animals and their charges leave once again to overwinter in proximity to the summer pasture areas with the caveat that they stay at the edges of the forest and in the clearings. In other words, they remain in those areas where hay had been harvested and stored. Dunăre describes the way in which bi-pendular pastoralism provides farmers with a means to fertilize their land, be it agricultural land close to the village (in spring and autumn), alpine pasture (during the summer) or sub-alpine hay meadows (in spring, autumn and, especially, winter). It is precisely this exploitation of sub-alpine hay meadows that provides the manure for orchards at lower altitudes (Dunăre, 1984: 60). Attested since the fifteenth century, Dunăre (1969; 1977) has observed the same constituent elements (based on overwintering in the sub-alpine hay-producing zones) throughout haymaking areas. This is, for example, the preferred solution in the eastern Carpathians where the temporary occupation sites used during spring and autumn haymaking are also used for the overwintering of flocks (Vlăduțiu, 1973: 236).

Forest grazing has been strictly forbidden since 1996 (Mertens & Huband, 2004: 161). Nevertheless, shepherds continue to use forest roads and, on occasion, penetrate the forest in times of prolonged bad weather, particularly in inaccessible mountain areas. Although rich grass can be found in these areas, its regrowth is slow which means that an area of forest grazing can only be exploited once every two to three weeks. While forest plants have excellent nutritive value, their rarity and limited vigour mean that shepherds prefer to exploit forest grazing only occasionally or at the end of the summer when milk production has dropped. Another problem associated with the exploitation of forest grazing is the increased risk of predation (particularly by bears). The slow progress of the flock as it files along tortuous forest paths as well as the slower intervention of the guard dogs means that bears can more easily launch an attack from upslope, break the line and snatch a ewe or a lamb.[2]

PASTORAL ARCHITECTURE

The architecture associated with the summering of flocks outside the village is very rudimentary and reflects ecological specificities (Figure 17.2). Despite certain regional variations, a similar model is found throughout the lowland and hill zones. This model is articulated around the various elements which make up the sheepfold (Figure 17.5): a site for the production and storage of milk products (stână, dairy; celar, cellar or store), the enclosure (holding pen) and milking pen (strungă, comarnic), the receiving and resting pen and the shepherd's hut (colibă: located close to the enclosures). The terminology used varies from region to region. For example, the resting- and holding pens associated with the sheepfold/dairy (stână) are referred to as staur (staul, staor, etc.) in the Banat and in Transylvania, while coșa is the preferred term in southeast Transylvania. Other terms used occasionally throughout the Transylvanian region are mreajă, țarc and seci. In Moldavia, the most commonly used terms are târlă and ocol while the term arcaci is also found in the southwest and is probably of Dobrogean origin (Iordache, 1986: 64).[3]

The strungă (the area where ewes are milked) forms the junction between the pre-milking pen (holding pen) and the resting pen. The term is sometimes also applied to the pre-milking pen itself. Situated on a slight slope so as to facilitate the flow of water and animal urine, and to dissuade animals from re-entering, the milking pen is composed of a sloping roof made of branches, reeds or planks supported by four forked posts. Composed of one or more gates and commonly referred to as a comarnic, such shelters open onto the resting pen. The latter is generally larger and is delimited by a wattle fence, planks or (more commonly) by a structure built of slender tree trunks c. 10 cm in diameter. In the lowlands, part of the pen is usually protected from the prevailing winds by a palisade of reeds. When the sheepfold is located close to a village, a pig pen often adjoins the resting pen, particularly when the majority of the flock belongs to a single shepherd. Blocks of rock salt (industrial salt is used in areas lacking natural salt outcroppings) are placed in the resting pen, supported on forked sticks set in the ground (crivală) or placed on a wooden tray. The salt can also be placed outside the pens and around the sheepfold (e.g. Vuia, 1980: 295).

Strictly speaking, the dairy is where cheese is made and stored. The structure is extremely rudimentary: the roof is generally singularly pitched (only rarely double-pitched) and the building is usually composed of one or two rooms measuring 4–5 m². A storeroom is always present; it is there that the curd (caș) is stored on ventilated shelves after being drained and shaped. The second room is the place where cheese is actually made: it generally contains the draining table (crintă) and (in the corner) the hearth used to boil the whey in the preparation of urdă. More often than not, the dairy consists of a single space – sometimes partly buried and made of clay or wood-based materials (bordei) (Figure 17.2, no. 1). The draining area and hearth are located outside under a veranda-like structure. One sheepfold we

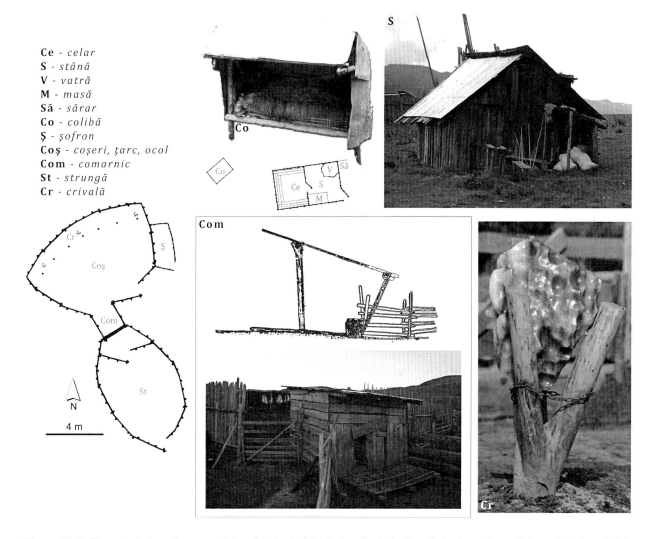

Figure 17.5. The typical plan of a seasonal sheepfold in the Moldavian foothills. Ce – Cellar/store, S – milk house, V – hearth, M – draining board, Să – reserve of rock salt, Co – cabin, Ş – pig pen, Coş – resting pen, Com – milking pen, St – pre-milking pen/milking area, Cr – salt stand

Source: Images O. Weller and R. Brigand. Drawing of the milking pen after Vuia (1980: 285)

visited was situated close to a salt outcrop which exhibited a specific area used for storing salt throughout the summer period. (Figure 17.5). However, the shepherds' sleeping quarters is never located in the cheese preparation area. The most common form of sleeping accommodation consists of a small cabin (*colibă*) measuring c. 2 × 1.5 m, composed of a single-pitched roof supported on four forked posts with three walls (of planks or wattle) a fourth side open oriented towards the holding pen(s). It is situated as close as possible to the flock and even today exhibits very little regional differentiation. A number of variants (invariably very rudimentary and temporary in nature) are described in the ethnographic literature (e.g. Iordache, 1986: 68–76).

Unlike the lightweight structures associated with local/agricultural pastoralism in which the sheepfold and pens are re-built every year, high mountain grazing involves more durable structures located at the upper edge of the forest. Quadrangular in plan, the dairies are built of tree trunks (sometimes squared) which are then assembled using either corner notches or angular corner posts. Although roof may be double-pitched, it usually has three or four pitches. An open space in the gable, protected by the projecting roof, allows air and smoke to pass. Traditionally clad using strips of wood nailed to each other (*şindrele*), modern roofs are generally clad with metal sheeting. Cheese storage is located at the far end of the dairy (i.e. opposite the entrance). In the Parâng Massif of the southern Carpathians as well as elsewhere in Romania, interviews conducted by the shepherd M. Jura and our field survey team have shown that the sheepfold/dairy never includes separate structures for the production and storage of dairy products. A sturdy shelter adjoining an abandoned sheepfold (Figure 17.2, no. 5) has been noted in the southern Carpathians area. However, this structure was used to separate lambs from their mothers at night, thereby preventing them from suckling and also providing protection from nocturnal predators.

Although the interior of the dairy is sometimes divided by a wooden partition, it is most usually composed of a single room with a central post from which a pot hanger is suspended. The hearth is usually protected by stone slabs close to one of the walls. The area closest to the door is furnished with long benches which acted as tables and bunks for the persons who lived and worked there. Normally, shepherds sleep close to the flock in a cabin (*colibă*) or shelter which might be under a rock or put together from wood, foliage and plastic. As mentioned above, this is always open towards the flock. Other components of the sheepfold include the holding pen and the milking pen which closely resemble those found in the lowlands in that they are both situated on a slight slope so that water does not stagnate and so that the ewes cannot easily force their way through. On the far side of the gate, a wooden platform is often installed so that the area is kept mudfree and so that the ewes stumble if they attempt to escape while being milked. The resting pen may contain the pre-milking pen and the shepherd's shelter (as is attested to in the southern Carpathians by both our field surveys and the historiography).

SPATIAL PATTERNS

We should also point out a number of spatial patterns that allow us to determine certain constants governing the situation of local sheepfolds in the Romanian Carpathians: a preference for an eastern orientation (in order to benefit from the first light of day), sloping ground and, in particular, an ecotone location which allows for access to a number of different ecosystems (wetland areas and high plateau wasteland, saline environments and water resources e.g.). These natural causes also imply coherence between current pastoral phenomena and the factors which affected Chalcolithic settlement. Although it was most likely not linear, this geographical continuity is the very basis of the ethnoarchaeological approach. It allows a better understanding of the behaviours and material processes entailed by the exploitation of some ecological niches (Nandris, 1987). This, however, does not extend to mountainous areas, as there is no extant documentation of pastoral settlements there in recent prehistory (it has not yet been specifically researched). The settlement context in the plains is rather similar due to specific constraints. Studying these spatial patterns can effectively improve our understanding of the choices made by the first agro-pastoral societies.

The highest and most hostile pastures are often reserved for sheep (that is to say, for castrated males and sterile ewes). No longer in use today, the pastoral buildings in these high altitudes are built of stone and are small in size as they are intended to provide shelter for the shepherd during the summer grazing of the pastures (Figure 17.6). In such situations, the sheep were not penned at night. Instead, they slept in the open (which made it more difficult to protect them from predators). However, in some cases, the exploitation of high pastures was facilitated by the construction of rudimentary enclosures using stone or wood when proximity to the forest allowed it. Circular or (less frequently) quadrangular in plan, they were sometimes built up against a boulder or rock face. The cabins (*cotroană*) are found throughout grazing areas and usually depended on a principal sheepfold for food and salt supplies. For example, no fewer than ten of these small structures have been recorded in the glacial cirque at the foot of the northern slope of Parâng. While all were not necessarily in use at the same time (some are archaeological structures), they nonetheless represent a well thoughtout settlement strategy for the alpine pastures. This is confirmed by our informants. They recall that the even dispersal of flocks throughout the pastures led to the fertilization of the soil and, thus, a more rapid regrowth.

All of the shepherds in alpine areas interviewed by our team mentioned the absence of pre-established circuits, although they did recall a single, strong guiding principle: the foraging resources in an area should never be exhausted, but should rather be grazed sparingly. Thus, for example, the pastures situated around the sheepfold are generally abundant and of good quality due to heavy grazing by the flock in the morning and evening: animal manure and trampling results in rapid regrowth. This is, in fact, the best-maintained area of pasture, as it may have to be used as a reserve in the case of severe weather. The summits and steep slopes beyond the last rocky barriers are only occasionally and briefly grazed, as grass is rare there and grows slowly because of the harsh conditions.

De Martonne (1904: 229) noted that "there was no better study area than the Parâng Massif for investigating the organization of pastoral life". As we have seen above, these spaces still retain dense pastoral populations which allow for the creation of a number of invaluable ethnographic observations. These areas are also of interest because they offer the opportunity to identify spatial patterns associated with well-defined places (like the stone cabins that appear at pasturage sites or livestock watering holes). Other notable fixed points that structure the movements of the flocks are the stone saltholder (*săruri* or *sănuni*) on which the shepherd spreads salt for the flock once or twice a week in dry weather.[4] In the glacial cirque on the north side of Parâng, three salt distribution points have been observed: each consists of three or four slabs on which the salt is placed. They are situated on gently sloping ground close to waterways in resting areas where the flock gathers to ruminate during the hottest hours of the day. In alpine

Figure 17.6. High mountain pastures, North Parâng zănoaga. Top left, a drawing of a cotroană 1) View of a resting area in the glacial cirque on the north side of Parâng, 2) a rehabilitated cotroană, 3–4) ancient temporary shelters, 5) stone salt-holder.
Source: Top left drawing after Iordache (1986: 84). Images A. Lucet 1), 4) and R. Brigand 2), 3), 5)

zones in particular is a preference for coherent pastoral units: the sheepfold is usually situated in the lower third of the mountain pasture a short distance from the forest edge. This recurrent configuration allows the shepherd to benefit from an effective subdivision of the fold site which is well spread out over the slope. High-altitude temporary shelters (which are often with an overnight pen) allow for the better management of the pastoral resources of the summer grassland.

Ethnoarchaeology of Salt and Pastoralism

One aspect that has interested us in recent years is the relation between the exploitation of salt rock and ovine pastoralism in landscapes where this important mineral is still largely available. It is an undeniable fact that common salt is one of the essential nutrients necessary for human consumption just as it is for livestock. Salt has an important regulatory function for the health and normal development of the body (be it human or animal). We also know that wild animals meet their mineral needs (including that for sodium chloride) by movements that allow them to ingest the necessary salt from halophyte plants, mineral waters and plants rich in sodium chloride. Once such movements are constrained, they must be met artificially. Insufficient intake can lead to a loss of appetite and weight, decrease in lactation and (in the case of severe deprivation) to damage of the central nervous system and even death (Berger, 1993: 5, 23; McDonald et al., 2011: 117: Suttle, 2010: 183–84). Usually, a sheep will consume around 9–10 g of salt per day at a salt lick (National Research Council, 1985: 11; Pugh, 2014). A simple calculation shows that approximately a ton of salt is needed per year for a herd of 200–300 sheep. This remains the same in spite of the fact that in Moldavia it was observed that the amount of salt offered to sheep varies according to flock and shepherd. Several informants concur that a quantity representing approximately 0.5 kg per animal was usually laid out once a week, but never on Sundays or *post* days (fasting days in the Orthodox religious calendar).

The projects which concentrated specifically on the ethnoarchaeology of salt projects have primarily focused on the salt springs and on building a repository of current or sub-current and non-industrial practices for the use and exploitation of salt springs, salt rock outcroppings and even salty soils (Alexianu, 2013).

1) Use of natural brine. It is difficult to gain a handle on the relationship between the exploitation of natural brine and animal husbandry despite recurrent observations of sheepfolds near salt springs in the numerous surveys that have been carried out. Farmers and shepherds habitually buy salt blocks from various sources (stores, traveling salesmen and even online), or, more rarely, they acquire salt first-hand by exploiting naturally occurring brine. In addition to the uses of brine in the alimentation of the shepherds, two examples for animal husbandry have also been documented.

The first of these is very common in areas close to the salt springs and involves sprinkling the fodder (in the barn or directly over the haystacks) with the brine in order to make it more palatable and to prevent mold growth. The second, more original use involves the crystallization of the brine in the sheepfold. In the 1940s and 1950s, the shepherds located less than 200 m from the salt spring at Țolici, boiled pans of brine on a flat space of land near the sheepfold (Alexianu et al., 2007: 142). How this igneous salt was distributed to flocks was unclear, although it is assumed that it was delivered on flat stones, directly on the ground or possibly mixed with the fodder. This last method is found among transhumant shepherds in the Danubian Plain, some of which favour crushed salt to blocks for its ease of transportation.

As is the case elsewhere, salt is widely used as a bactericide and preservative. With respect to cheese, the *caș* (drained and shaped curd) prepared in the sheepfold becomes cheese only after it is salted in the village. After it has been cut into slices, it is stored in a container and salted using thick layers of salt or by immersion in brine. Other alternatives exist depending on the shelf life desired. For instance, a kind of cheese called *brânză frământată* (lit. 'kneaded cheese') is made from crushed curds mixed with salt. Intended for winter consumption, it was kept in small containers protected from the air by a layer of beech leaves and a clay seal.

2) Salt mountains/cliffs. The extensive investigation conducted by the French-Romanian team from 2011 around the salt mountains from the extra-Carpathian areas of Romania (more accurately in the southeastern parts) identified several kinds of practices. These involved the relationship between salt harvesting (modes of exploitation, persons involved, ways of transportation, etc.) and the ovine pastoralism observed in the areas surrounding several salt outcroppings of the Moldavian sub-Carpathians. In this area, important tectonic dynamics associated with slope erosion processes contribute to the outcropping of salt core (Figure 17.7). Within these areas, local and pendulatory pastoralism can be founded, both of which are closely related to salt exploitation (Alexianu et al., 2015: 51; Brigand et al., 2015). According to our informants, acquiring salt for the animals is usually done twice a year: in early spring (for consumption over the warm season) and in late autumn (for the winter months). In most cases, the shepherds gather the salt themselves. They use common tools (spades, pickaxes, hammers and chocks) and transport it to the sheepfold in wains (*căruță*) (500–600 kg at once) or with horses with two large sacks placed on the saddle. Rock salt blocks are almost exclusively destined for animal (especially bovine or ovid) consumption.

Salt extraction is accomplished via tool kits used exclusively for salt digging (spades, chisels, sledge hammers, adzes, pickaxes, etc.) on vertical cliff faces. The process involves the removal of blocks of various sizes (from 2–3 kg to several dozens, depending on the thickness of the salt level). There is also a mention of an extraction method in chambers which measure 2–2.50 m in deep and 1–1.50 m in wide which is completed without supports. Such instances are different from the mining exploitation at Valea Sării, where a horizontal extraction from 5 to 10 m deep involved pine supports. After its removal, the salt is transported in a similar fashion to the mountain pastures when the flocks leave the village. Sometimes, if the initial amount of salt is finished during the summer, the shepherds make an additional trip to the outcropping (sometimes up to 50 km).

Besides the subsistence form of salt supply managed by the shepherds, we also had the unique opportunity to come across a form of unofficial specialization in salt excavation. As *huscari* in the eastern Carpathians (a name which refers to those persons who produce salt from the water of salt springs; Alexianu et al., 2011: 14), several informants are denizens of the community of salt diggers. Aside from their daily agricultural occupations, these villagers excavate salt from the outcroppings upon solicitation. As who produced *huscă* often operate within a barter system, one of the salt diggers interviewed took payment especially in agricultural products (barley, wheat, corn, sunflower seeds, etc.).

In such cases, we are dealing with half-time specialists, a category of individuals much more numerous and active in the recent and probably the distant

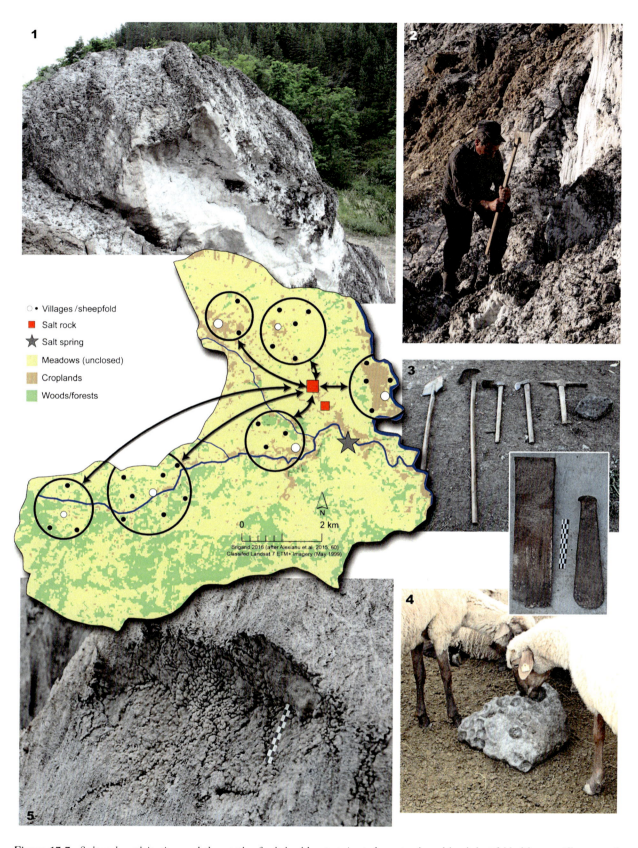

Figure 17.7. Salt rock exploitation and the supply of salt boulders to private homesteads and local sheepfolds (the map illustrates the commune of Vrâncioaia). 1), 2), 5) Salt rock exploitation and cutting tracks at Paltin, Tulnici and Jitia (Vrancea), 3) the tools used for quarrying and processing of the salt rock, 4) salt lick blocks placed on the ground in the resting pen

Source: Images O. Weller 1), 3), 5); R. Brigand 2); F. Tencariu 4)

past. As salt is very cheap these days in addition to be easily procurable, the hard work of manually extracting it is no longer profitable. Once brought to the sheepfolds, salt is kept away from humidity in small storage sheds, on shelves, wood boxes or simply under the bed in the shepherd's hut. Recording these nearly extinct practices is invaluable, as it identifies the significant role of salt exploitation by village communities, particularly by pastoral communities engaged in over summering in semi-mountainous areas in the Carpathian hinterlands. The pastoral calendar has been closely associated with specific movements linked to the procurement of rock salt, both at the time of the summer ascent and prior to overwintering in the village. Also, the modes of exploitations, quantities, tool kits, ways of transportation, trade and barter, etc. are elements which have been preserved almost unaltered for centuries that could provide hints to creating an understanding of human mobility determined by the need for salt from the historic and even prehistoric past.

3) Salt soils. Another area of research worthy of greater attention concerns the exploitation of saline soils by sheep farmers. These are well known by both flocks and their shepherds. While salted soil attracts the animals, it causes intestinal injuries which are likely to be fatal when mixed with earth. In certain contexts which have exceptionally dense saline soils, salt-enriched water sources (which are in contact with the mineralized strata) are used for watering animals within the artificial drinking troughs which are dug in the earth (Figure 17.8, no. 2). In these cases, the shepherd does not need to provide extra salt. However, in plain areas

Figure 17.8. Salted soils and pastoralism in the Moldavian Plain. 1) A view on the sărătura *(the former salt spring in the background),* Arcaci *(Valea Oii, Iași). Several Chalcolithic sites have been documented at the back on the hillside, 2) Drinking trough for sheep herds dug in salty soil, 3) Shepherd from* Valea Sărată.

Source: Images R. Brigand 1), 2) and F. Picard 3)

which were strongly affected by communist collectivization, such rudimentary practices aimed at meeting the physiological needs of the herd have not been extensively studied. The spatial relationship between salt and pastoral use of the land is all the more obvious when toponyms from the shepherd's vocabulary refer to areas with mineralized soils and salted waters (*Arcaci, Oituz, Strunga*, etc.) The fact that valleys enjoying a strong pastoral activity (such as the *Valea Oii*, literally the 'valley of the sheep') and a high density in salted soils were also the most densely populated ones in the fourth and fifth millennia BC is an important issue for further ethnoarchaeological and paleoenvironmental studies (Ursulescu, 2015; Brigand & Weller, 2016).

In this context, the dialectic between salt and the needs of sheep husbandry requires closer examination, not only at a local scale but also at a regional one in order to identify the significant role of salt exploitation by village communities (particularly by pastoral communities engaged in over summering in semi-mountainous areas in the Carpathian hinterlands).

LONG-DISTANCE TRANSHUMANCE

A much written-about form of pastoralism involves the overwintering of flocks and shepherds (principally from the southern Carpathians) in the milder grasslands of the Wallachian, Transylvanian and Banat plains in the case of short-distance transhumance (regional and/or inner-valley) and in the Danubian or coastal grasslands in the case of long-distance transhumance (extra-regional) (e.g. de Martonne, 1904; Constantinescu-Mirceşti, 1976; Butură, 1978; Vuia, 1980). Dunăre (1977, 1984) unambiguously identifies an economic origin for long-distance transhumance in Romania during the eighteenth and nineteenth centuries. A well-documented growth in the wool textile industry throughout Romania and in the southern Carpathians, particularly around the towns of Braşov, Azuga, Caransebeş, Cisnădie and Timişoara resulted in a high degree of specialization in sheep-rearing. The numbers of sheep being kept very rapidly outstripped the carrying capacities of the areas concerned.

Indeed, livestock owners in the southern Carpathians and their hinterlands – villages to the south of Sibiu (*poienari*), in Burzenland and Sacele (*bârsani, mocani*), in Bran to the south of Braşov (*brăneni*), Sebeş (*mărgineni*) or from the south Carpathians (*ungureni*) – whose main activity was sheep-rearing and who also possessed several hundred animals (often over 1500), were forced to seek grazing opportunities which lay at considerable distances (Figure 17.9). This dynamic is attested to by cases in which Transylvanian flocks of 2000 to 3000 animals are recorded in the remotest parts of the southern and eastern Carpathians. This is also shown by those cases in which transhumant flocks overwintered on the plains of Muntenia, Moldavia and Dobrogea and even further afield in the Hungarian, Slovakian and Moravian plains or even to the east of Moldova in the Ukraine, the Crimea and the Caucasian Plains (Lupaş et al., 2009). The presence of Transylvanian shepherds has also been recorded between Turkey and Greece in the region of Adrianopole (Dunăre, 1984: 62).

Estimates suggest that between 1 and 2.5 million transhumant sheep crossed the Danube in the direction of Dobrogea every year in the mid-nineteenth century (Constantinescu-Mirceşti, 1976). Further calculations suggest that an additional 1 million transhumant sheep from the Carpathians overwintered in the Crimea and some 300 flocks were recorded near the Dniepr Delta with certain flocks traveling as far as the Volga, the Astrakan and the foothills of the Caucasus (Maruşca, 2012: 254). These dizzying figures give an idea of the scale of long-distance Transylvanian transhumance as it spread throughout all areas of Eastern and Southeast Europe, at least during its apogee in the eighteenth century and the first half of the nineteenth century.

All of the informants who provided information regarding transhumance were involved in the practice between 1950 and 2000, a watershed date after which economic, legislative and sanitary conditions led to the gradual disappearance of both long-distance and short-distance transhumance (for a recent overview, see: Huband et al., 2010; Juler, 2014). Up until this date, transhumance routes and mobility systems appear to have remained close to the historical model. Thus, for example, in the 1980s, a particular sheep farmer from Costeşti in the Moldavian Plain might have joined forces with three or four other shepherds (forming a combined flock of 400 to 450 animals) to pass the summer months in the eastern Carpathians before overwintering on the Prut Plain or venturing as far as Botoşani or the Siret Plain. In the southern Carpathians, we should envisage flocks of 2000 to 3000 animals which moved towards the western plains of Oradea and Timişoara and even to the Hungarian lowlands or towards the southern plains of Calafat and the Bărăgan and on to Bulgaria. In such cases, we have noted the existence of certain informal arrangements (particularly in the case of winter pastures). Thus, a flock from Petroşani in the southern Carpathians would migrate regularly over five years on lands farmed by a Calafat (Banat) agricultural co-operative who, in return for money, allowed the ewes to graze waste lands and non-cultivated areas. As soon as the snows arrived and grass was buried under a thick covering, the animals would be transported back to their home village by rail where they would then be redistributed among their owners. When a return home in winter was involved, the system might be described as 'reduced transhumance'.

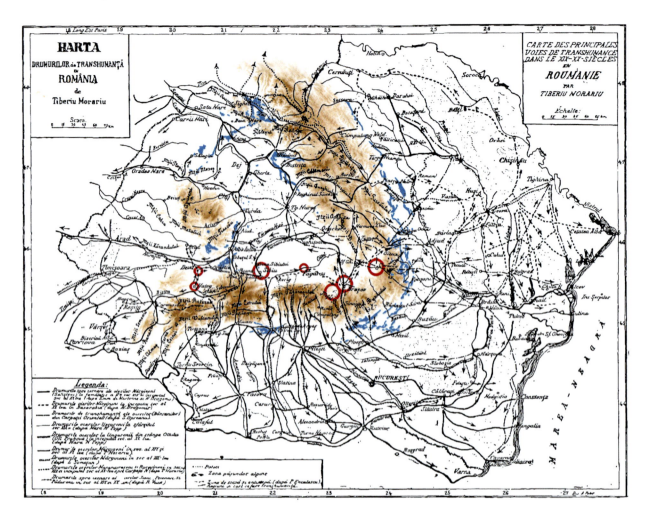

Figure 17.9. Transhumance routes overlap mountain relief and the geology of salt (in blue). The centres of long-distance Romanian transhumance (in the nineteenth and twentieth centuries) are indicated by red dots
Source: After T. Morariu (1942)

Small-scale reverse transhumance occurs when sheep are brought to low-lying areas where they can exploit early grass growth before the summer climb to high pastures.

Conclusion

Our actualist approach aims to enrich archaeological interpretations by providing reference data which may clarify ancient mechanisms of settlement and exploitation of the environment. This is a fundamental approach as it permits the recording of a part of cultural heritage that has been irremediably altered and which will soon disappear altogether. Therefore, there is a great degree of urgency in documenting this information as quickly as possible. We believe that it will enrich the ways in which we read the spaces occupied by past societies. In the region of the Romanian Carpathians, despite extremely rich ethnographic records and the research avenues opened by J. Nandriş, archaeologists have still not seized on this area. This is remarkable for many reasons. First of all, although it faces rapid change, it is evident that the principal traits of traditional pastoralism as described by the Vidalian geographer de Martonne in the early twentieth centuries still exists today. This is the opportunity to contribute to the creation of a reference corpus on the pastoral practices of Romania which will, in turn, allow us to structure our knowledge concerning the forms and rhythms of spatial settlement by taking account of new variables in accordance with a procedure which involves the modelling of territorial strategies. Thus, it should be emphasized that this research highlights several mechanisms of environmental occupation and exploitation.

1) It is difficult to transpose the great transhumance such as the one we have documented for the contemporary period to ancient societies, let alone to those of recent prehistory. It seems more pertinent to consider movements similar to those observable around the Carpathians today: they are small in amplitude, rarely go outside of the home valley and are often limited to areas which are accessible within a day's walk. Limited

to the communal territory or to the immediate land-forms, this local pastoralism is characterized by very high mobility meant to optimize the exploitation of the pastures. In the mountains, a multitude of temporary shelters (usually dependent on a principal sheepfold located at the forest edge) allowed for a rational exploitation of the various alpine sectors.

2) Salt, and especially rock salt, was integrated into the pastoral territories' resources, at least on a local scale. It is difficult to progress with such analyses at a regional level as the evidence is more tenuous. The results for such a phenomenon on a local scale nevertheless allow us to hypothesize that salt was an important resource in relation to pastoral settlement. Because of the way it was exploited, it was also likely to have been an important marker of summer pasturing or wintering routes. Similarly, it could explain seasonal movements of wide amplitude, which would coincide with transhumance routes and salt roads, the salt-producing activities taking place especially during summering. Is a profusion of salt related to recurrent transhumance routes? One might examine Ocna Sibiului (Sibiu mines), Piatra Neamț, Bacău, Târgu Ocna and Râmnicu Sărat, the salted lakes area of the northern Black Sea, etc.

3) These results address archaeological problems on several levels. First, the high degree of mobility that was present in addition to agricultural activities evoke the agropastoral farmhouses evidenced by the archaeological data. The latter are scattered across the territory and are marked by cycles of abandonment and reuse, far from the synchronous image apparent from the archaeological inventories. Our work assumes that pastoral structures (either with or without cheese production) likely existed at the margins of Neolithic settlements, especially during the fifth and fourth millennia BC, when specialized production slowly began to appear. Thus, this research opens up to an ethnoarchaeological investigation of the exploitation techniques which might have been used. This includes documenting dairy and cheese production as well as the social investment required in addition to its operational chain: curdling milk (by naturally acidic brine or rennet collected from a suckling lamb), cheese making and preservation. Another important aspect of the research concerns building techniques. In similar ecological conditions, the variety of construction methods and materials used allow us to highlight practices which have seldom been observed by archaeologists.

Although we know that ethnographic data should be approached with caution, we do not propose to mechanically transpose our observations to the Neolithic or Chalcolithic periods; the current or sub-current forms of pastoralism are not living fossils of the prehistoric ones, but are rather the result of historical and environmental processes. Nevertheless, researching present-day societies can lead us to reformulate certain questions related to the Neolithic and the development of complex economies. For example, the investigation of the important role of salt in the process of dairy and cheese production – as a coagulant, bactericide, conservation, in the processing of the hides, etc. – can allow us to clarify the choices made by the first agropastoralists with respect to the exploitation of available resources. This dialectic between pastoral activity and salt exploitation is rich in perspectives and allows for the painting of a new picture of population movement in prehistoric Europe.

ACKNOWLEDGEMENTS

This research is supported by the French Foreign Office (DGMDP-DPMA), the CNRS and the University of Panthéon-Sorbonne. It has also benefitted from a Fleishmann Grant from the French Society of Ethnology and from close collaboration with the Alexandru I. Cuza University of Iaşi and the ArheoInvest interdisciplinary platform. The study is also supported by a grant of the CNCS-UEFISCDI, project number PN-III-P4-ID-PCE-2016-0759 within PNCDI III. The French-Spanish network on Pyrenean pastoralism *DEPART* was a great source of encouragement for our fieldwork in the Carpathians. The kind contributions of F. Picard, A. Lucet and M. Jura are gratefully acknowledged as are those of the informants who have given generously of their time and who have provided a huge body of valuable information.

NOTES

1 The research was carried out within the framework of a French-Romanian collaboration conducted in Romania through two CNCS (Romanian National Research Council) research projects (2007–2010; 2011–2016) managed by M. Alexianu (for a presentation of the ethnoarchaeological goals and the most recent results, see Alexianu et al., 2012) and an archaeological campaign by the French Ministry of Foreign Affairs overseen by O. Weller (2004–2015).

2 However, it should be noted that overwintering in forest areas was once permitted. We know, for example, that at the end of the eighteenth century overwintering in forests was taxed at the rate of one of every ten ewes with the additional condition that the shepherds could only trim trees and were forbidden from actually felling them (Butură, 1978: 223). During the communist period (and up to quite recently, as a matter of fact), shepherds found using forest pastures generally came to informal arrangements with the forest wardens. Usually they got away with paying a tax of one or two ewes from a flock of 100.

3 It is well known that linguists have shown particular interest in the pastoral phenomenon in Eastern and Southeast Europe, particularly because of the clear similarities in

pastoral terminology found throughout the Carpathians and the Balkans. It is one of the main arguments used to support the idea of a shared cultural origin for a pastoral civilization which was spread through the migration of Wallachian shepherds of Romanian origin. Between the thirteenth and sixteenth centuries these shepherds moved throughout the Carpathian-Balkan region disseminating summer grazing techniques to the native populations (Kopczynska-Jaworska, 1963: 81). For example, one might compare the similarities between the following words *stână* (Romanian), *esztena* or *sztina* (Hungarian), *staniska* (Slovkian), *stan* (Serbian) and *stena* (Bulgarian). Likewise, the terms *strungă*, *colibă* and *coșar* occur throughout the Carpathian-Balkan region (Vuia, 1980).

4 Unlike low-lying areas and the foothill zones, shepherds here prefer non-compacted coarse salt and, to a lesser extent, rock salt (both of which are difficult to transport using pack-donkeys in steeply sloping areas). Salt supplies are procured from a principal sheepfold or village. The salt is placed in a sheepskin bag, which is salted and turned inside out (*burduf*) and which is also used for preserving cheese. It is then placed on a stone and is often ground to a finer consistency on the spot (Ionescu, 1977: 45; Iordache, 1986: 93).

References

Alexianu, M. 2013. The saturated model: a first application in world and Romanian ethnoarchaeology. In: A. Marciniak & N. Yulman, eds. *Contesting Ethnoarchaeologies. Traditions, Theories, Prospects.* New York: Springer, pp. 211–26.

Alexianu, M., Dumitroaia, G. & Monah, D. 1992. Exploatarea surselor de apă sărată din Moldova: o abordare etnoarheologică. *Thraco-Dacica*, 13(1–2):159–67.

Alexianu, M., Tencariu, F.A., Asăndulesei, A., Weller, O., Brigand, R., Sandu, I., Romanescu, G., Curcă, R.-G., Caliniuc, Ș. & Asăndulesei, M. 2015. The salt from Alghianu beck (Vrancea County, Romania): a multifaceted ethnoarchaeological approach. In: R. Brigand & O. Weller, eds. *Archaeology of Salt. Approaching an Invisible Past.* Leiden: Sidestone, pp. 47–63.

Alexianu, M., Weller, O. & Brigand, R. 2007. *Izvoarele de apă sărată din Moldova subcarpatică.* Iași: Demiurg.

Alexianu, M., Weller, O. & Brigand, R. 2012. EthnosalRo: an ethnoarchaeological project on Romanian salt. *The European Archaeologist*, 38:17–22.

Alexianu, M., Weller, O., Brigand, R., Curcă, R.-G., Cotiugă, V. & Moga, I. 2011. Salt springs in today's rural world. An ethnoarchaeological approach in Moldavia (Romania). In: M. Alexianu, O. Weller & R.-G. Curcă, eds. *Archaeology and Anthropology of Salt: A Diachronic Approach. Proceedings of the International Colloquium.* BAR IS 2198. Oxford: Archaeopress, pp. 7–24.

Bejenaru, L. & Stanc, S. 2013. *Arheozoologia Neoliticului din estul și sud-estul României.* Iași: Ed. Univ.

Berger, L. 1993. *Salt and Trace Minerals for Livestock, Poultry and Other Animals.* Alexandria: Salt Institute.

Bréhard, S. & Bălășescu, A. 2012, What's behind the tell phenomenon? An archaeozoological approach of Eneolithic sites in Romania. *Journal of Archaeological Science*, 39(10):3167–83.

Brigand, R. & Weller, O. 2015. Spatial analysis for salt archaeology. A case study from Moldavian Neolithic.

In: R. Brigand & O. Weller, eds. *Archaeology of Salt: Approaching an Invisible Past.* Leiden: Sidestone, pp. 157–179.

Brigand, R. & Weller, O. 2016. Sel et peuplement néo/énéolithique à l'épreuve de l'analyse spatiale: le cas de la Moldavie (Roumanie). In: G. Dumitroaia, C. Preoteasa & C.-D. Nicola, eds. *Cucuteni Culture Within the Neo-Eneolithic Context. Cucuteni 130.* BMA 24. Piatra-Neamț: Ed. Constantin Matasă, pp. 291–325.

Brigand, R., Weller, O. & Alexianu, M. 2015. A new technique for salt block preparation at Coza (Tulnici, Vrancea County, Romania). In: M. Alexianu, R.-G. Curcă & V. Cotiugă, eds. *Salt Effect. Second Arheoinvest Symposium. From the Ethnoarchaeology to the Anthropology of Salt.* BAR IS 2760. Oxford: Archaeopress, pp. 223–27.

Brochier, J.-L. 2005. Des hommes et des bêtes: une approche naturaliste de l'histoire et des pratiques de l'élevage. In: J. Guilaine, ed. *Populations néolithiques et environnements.* Paris: Errance, pp. 137–54.

Butură, V. 1978. *Etnografia poporului român. Cultura materială.* Cluj-Napoca: Ed. Dacia.

Constantinescu-Mircești, C. 1976. *Păstoritul transhumant și implicațiile lui in Transilvania și Țara Românească in secolele XVIII–XIX.* Bucharest: Ed. Academy of the Socialist Republic of Romania.

Danu, M., Gauthier, E. & Weller, O. 2010. Human impact and vegetation history on salt spring exploitation (Hălăbutoaia, Țolici, Petricani, Neamț, Romania). *International Journal of Conservation Science*, 1(3):167–73.

Dumitroaia, G. 1994. Depunerile neo-eneolitice de la Lunca și Oglinzi, județul Neamț. *Memoria Antiquitatis*, 19:7–82.

Dunăre, N. 1956. Problema cercetării etnografice a păstoritului. *Studii și cercetări de istorie*, 7(1–4):173–76.

Dunăre, N. 1969. Păstoritul de pendulare dublă pe teritoriul României. *Anuarul Muzeului Etnografic al Transilvaniei*, 1965–1967:115–38.

Dunăre, N. 1977. L'élevage bi-pendulaire dans les zones de fenaisons de l'Europe. *Apulum*, 15:763–67.

Dunăre, N. 1984. Types traditionnels de vie pastorale dans les régions carpatiques de pâturages et de fenaisons (Roumanie, Ukraine, Pologne, Tchécoslovaquie, Hongrie). In: *L'élevage et la vie pastorale dans les montagnes de l'Europe au moyen âge et à l'époque moderne.* Clermont-Ferrand: Institute of Studies of the Massif Central, pp. 55–67.

Feurdean, A., Marinova, E., Nielsen, A.B., Liakka, J., Veres, D., Hutchinson, S.M., Braun, M., Timar-Gabor, A., Astalos, C., Mosburgger, V. & Hickler, T. 2015. Origin of the forest steppe and exceptional grassland diversity in Transylvania (central-eastern Europe). *Journal of Biogeography*, 42(5):951–63.

Herseni, T. 1936. L'organisation pastorale en Roumanie. In: *Omagiu Profesorului D. Gusti, XXV de ani de invățământ universitar.* Bucharest: Arhiva pentru știința și reforma socială, 13, pp. 242–56.

Huband, S., McCracken, D.I., Mertens, A. 2010. Long and short distance transhumant pastoralism in Romania: past and present drivers of change. *Pastoralism: Research, Policy and Practice*, 1(1):55–71.

Ionescu, C.D. 1977. *Prin Munții Mehedinților.* Craiova: Ed. Scrisul Românesc.

Iordache, G. 1986. *Ocupații tradiționale pe teritoriul României.* Craiova: Ed. Scrisul Românesc.

Juler, J. 2014. După coada oilor: long-distance transhumance and its survival in Romania. *Pastoralism: Research, Policy and Practice*, 4(4). https://doi.org/10.1186/2041-7136-4-4

Kopczynska-Jaworska, J. 1963. La vie pastorale dans les Carpathes. *Etudes rurales*, 9:80–89.

Lagneaux, S. 2007. Terre à terre. L'identité rurale roumaine en friche. Approche anthropologique. In: C. Bessière, E. Doidy, O. Jacquet, G. Laferte, J. Mischi, N. Renahy & Y. Sencébé, eds. *Les mondes ruraux à l'épreuve des sciences sociales*. Versailles: Ed. Quae, pp. 501–12.

Lazarovici, G. & Ardeţ, A. eds. 2015. *Ţara Gugulanilor. Studii de etnoarheologie, etnografie şi etnoistorie*. Cluj-Napoca: Ed. Mega.

Lazarovici, G. & Kalmar Maxim, Z. 1987. Săpături arheologice de salvare şi cercetări etnoarheologice în munţii Petrindului în anul 1986. *Acta MN*, 24–5:949–96.

Lazarovici, G. & Lazarovici, C.-M. 2003. *The Neo-Eneolithic Architecture in Banat, Transylvania and Moldavia*. In: D.V. Grammenos, ed. *Recent Research in the Prehistory of the Balkans*. Publications of the Archaeological Institute of Northern Greece 3. Thessaloniki: Archaeological Institute, pp. 369–486.

Lazarovici, G., Nandriş, J. & Maxim, Z. 2015. Cerna Văr – Piatra Ilişovei. Generalităti. In: G. Lazarovici & A. Ardeţ, eds. 2015. *Ţara Gugulanilor. Studii de etnoarheologie, etnografie şi etnoistorie*. Cluj-Napoca: Ed. Mega, pp. 153–92.

Luca, S.A. 2005. *Descoperiri din Banat*. Bucharest: Ed. Economică.

Lupaş, T., Petruţiu, N.S., Jianu, N., Achim, A., Călugăruţoiu, S., Muntean, I., Muntean, P., Apolzan, S., Dragomir, Z., Dădârlat, D.A., Dârdea, I., Şchiopu, N., Alexa, A., Iuga, I., Nan, I., Mihu, I. & Nistor, M. 2009. *Oierii mărgineni in Crimeea şi Sudul Rusiei*. Sibiu: Ed. Salgo.

Martonne (de), E. 1902. *La Valachie. Essai de monographie géographique*. Paris: Armand Colin.

Martonne (de), E. 1904. La vie pastorale et la transhumance dans les Karpates méridionales. Leur importance géographique et historique. In: *Zu Friedrich Ratzels Gedächtnis*. Leipzig: Dr. Seele & Co., pp. 227–45.

Maruşca, T. 2012. *Recurs la tradiţia satului. Opinii agrosilvopastorale*. Braşov: Ed. Universităţii Transilvania.

McDonald, P., Greenhalgh, J.F.D., Morgan, C.A., Edwards, R., Sinclair, L. & Wilkinson, R. 2011. *Animal nutrition*. Harlow: Pearson.

Mertens, A. & Huband, S. 2004. Romanian transhumance, the past, the present and future scenarios. In: R.G.H. Bunce, M. Pérez-Soba, R.H.G. Jongman, A. Gómez Sal, F. Herzog & I. Austad, eds. *Transhumance and Biodiversity in European Mountains*, Report of the EU-FP5 project TRANSHUMOUNT (EVK2-CT-2002–80017). Wageningen: Alterra, pp. 155–70.

Morariu, T. 1942. Păstoritul în Alpii francezi şi în Carpaţi. *Sociologia Românească*, 4(7–12):375–92.

Nandriş, J. 1987. Romanian ethnoarchaeology and the emergence and development of Cucuteni in the European context. In: M. Petrescu-Dîmboviţa, V. Chirica & D. Monah, eds. *La civilisation de Cucuteni en contexte international*. Iaşi: BAI, pp. 201–22.

Nandriş, J. 2015. Ethnoarchaeological attitudes. An introduction to the aims and methods of the Highland Zone Comparative Ethnoarchaeology Project. In: G. Lazarovici & A. Ardeţ, eds. 2015. *Ţara Gugulanilor. Studii de etnoarheologie, etnografie şi etnoistorie*. Cluj-Napoca: Ed. Mega, pp. 29–31.

National Research Council 1985. *Nutrient Requirements of Sheep*. Washington: National Academy Press.

Nicolăescu-Plopşor, C.S. & Petrescu-Dîmboviţa, M. 1959. Principalele rezultate ale cercetărilor arheologice de la Bicaz. *Materiale si cercetări arheologice*, 5:45–60.

Pugh, D.G. 2014. Nutritional Requirements of Sheep. In: Susan E. Aiello, ed. *Merck Veterinary Manual*. Eleventh edition. N.p., Jan. 2014. www.merckvetmanual.com.

Rendu, C. 2003. *La montagne d'Enveig. Une estive pyrénéenne dans la longue durée*. Perpignan: Ed. Trabucaire.

Stahl, H. 1969. *Les anciennes communautés villageoises roumaines, asservissement et pénétration capitaliste*. Bucharest-Paris: Ed. Académie de la République Socialiste de Roumanie-CNRS.

Suttle, N.F. 2010. *Mineral Nutrition of Livestock*. Wallingford: Cabi Publishing.

Tanţău, I., Reille, M., de Beaulieu, J.-L., Fărcaş, S. & Brewer, S. 2009. Holocene vegetation history in Romanian Subcarpathians. *Quaternary Research*, 72:164–73.

Thiébault, S. 2005. L'homme, la végétation et la montagne au Néolithique. In: J. Guilaine, ed. *Populations néolithiques et environnements*. Paris: Errance, pp. 243–57.

Ursulescu, N. 1977. Exploatarea sării din saramură în neoliticul timpuriu, în lumina descoperirilor de la Solca (jud. Suceava). *Studii şi Cercetări de Istorie Veche*, 28(3):307–17.

Ursulescu, N. 2015. The role of salt supply in the location of Neolithic and Eneolithic settlements in Moldavia (Romania). In: M. Alexianu, R.-G. Curcă & V. Cotiugă, eds. *Salt Effect. Second Arheoinvest Symposium. From the Ethnoarchaeology to the Anthropology of Salt*. BAR IS 2760. Oxford: Archaeopress, pp. 121–24.

Vlăduţiu, I. 1973. Creşterea animalelor în zona Bicaz, In: *Etnografia văii Bistriţei*, Piatra Neamţ: Bicaz research group of the Socialist Republic of Romania, pp. 177–245.

Vuia, R. 1924. Câteva observaţii şi constatării asupra păstoritului şi asupra tipurilor de case la români. *Lucrările Institutului de geografie al Universităţii din Cluj*, 1:323–32.

Vuia, R. 1980. Tipuri de păstorit la români (sec. XIX – începutul sec. XX). In: M. Pop & I. Şerb, eds. *R. Vuia. Antologie*. Studii de etnografie şi folclor, II. Bucharest: Minerva, pp. 207–362.

Weller, O., Brigand, R., Dumitroaia, G., Garvăn, D. & Munteanu, R. 2015. A pinch of salt in the prehistoric Eastern Carpathian Mountains (Romania). In: M. Alexianu, R.-G. Curcă & V. Cotiugă, eds. *Salt Effect. Second Arheoinvest Symposium. From the Ethnoarchaeology to the Anthropology of Salt*. BAR IS 2760. Oxford: Archaeopress, pp. 125–33.

Weller, O. & Dumitroaia, G. 2005. The earliest salt production in the world: an early Neolithic exploitation in *Poiana Slatinei*-Lunca, Romania. *Antiquity*, 79 (306). www.antiquity.ac.uk/projgall/weller/.

Weller, O., Dumitroaia, G., Sordoillet, D., Dufraisse A., Gauthier, E. & Munteanu, R. 2008. Première exploitation de sel en Europe: techniques et gestion de l'exploitation de la source salée de Poiana Slatinei à Lunca (Neamţ, Romania). In: O. Weller, A. Dufraisse & P. Pétrequin, eds. *Sel, eau et forêt. D'hier à aujourd'hui*. Cahiers de la MSH Ledoux 12. Besançon: Presses Universitaires de Franche-Comté, pp. 205–30.

Index

Pages in italics indicate figures on the corresponding pages.

actor network theories (ANT) 5
Afforestable Land Survey (ALS), Scotland 62
Alexianu, M. 248
Alpine transhumance 4; *see also* Oberhasli, Bernese Alps,
  Switzerland; southern France
Alps (France) *see* southern France
Alpwirtschaft 157
Alva commons 182
Ambrosi, Augusto C. 187
Ancien Régime see Mediterranean transhumance
An Cnoc Buí *see* South Connemara, Ireland
Ängersjö, Dalarna 18
animal pens, Bernese Alps 159
Anonymous Life of St Cuthbert, The 110
Apennines *see* Tuscany (northern), Italy
Apuan Alps *see* Tuscany (northern), Italy
archaeology 6–7, 30; approach to pasture use in Estrela
  Mountain, Portugal 224–5, *225*; ethnoarchaeology of salt
  and pastoralism in Romania 255–9, *257–88*; evidence for
  transhumance in Newfoundland 46–50; field definition
  and data of Scotland 61–6; multistage agricultural
  systems, Bernese Alps 157–62; of Romania 245–7, *246*
Archimede project *see* Mediterranean transhumance
Auvergne region, France: animal husbandry importance in
  129; conclusions on 132–3; differences between Cantal
  and Sancy Mountains in 129–32, *130–2*; end of medieval
  period and beginning of specialised breeding in 124–7,
  125–6; introduction to 121; mid-fifteenth through
  nineteenth centuries as golden age of the shepherd in
  127–9, *128*; permanent settlement during medieval
  period in *123*, 123–4; research methodology 121–3

Backasätern shieling 23–4, 33, 40
Barnard, H. 4
Barrowman, Chris 78
Beorlatza 182, *183*
Bernese Alps, Switzerland *see* Oberhasli, Bernese Alps,
  Switzerland
Bhiliscleitir, Scotland 75–8; archaeological methodology
  78–80; archaeological results 80–2; discussion on
  ephemeral occupation surfaces 88–91; structure 10 82–7;
  structure 11 87–8
Big Mussel Pond, Newfoundland 48–50
Bil, Albert 60–1, 75
Blache, J. 9
Black Death 22
Blair, John 110
booleying 93, 101–2
boundary objects 3, 4
Bouyssou, L. 125
Braña La Mesa, Spain *223*, 223–4
Branigan, K. 75
Braudel, F. 4, 7
Bresc, H. 138
Brigand, Robin 6, 8
Browne, C. R. 95

Bullock, P. 80
Burren Beo Trust 11
Burri, Sylvain 7

cabañas of Gipuzkoa *179*, 179–82, *181*
Cabouret, Michel 16, 17, 18
Calvert, George 44
Cambi, F. 187
Campbell, Mary 76, 82
Camp Shiel, Scotland 68, *69*
Cañadas Reales 229
Cantabrian Mountains, Portugal *220*, 220–1; middle-
  distance transhumance 225–7, *227*; short-distance or
  valley transhumance in 222–4, *223*
Cantal, France *see* Auvergne region, France
Carna peninsula *see* South Connemara, Ireland
Carrer, Francesco 145, 187
Casa de Ganaderos de Zaragoza 229
Centocroci hospice 190–3, *192*
Charlemagne 190
Common Agricultural Policy (CAP) 10
commons and collective practices 8–9
Coste, P. 144
Coulet, N. 139, 147
Cribb, R. 4
Cristoferi, Davide 6, 9

Dalby Parish, Värmland County, Sweden
  30–3
Davies, A. L. 72
Davies, E. 4
Debates de Arqueologia Medieval 219
de Tregoz, John 114
De Venuto, G. 187
Discovery and Excavation in Scotland (DES) 62
Dodgshon, Robert 60
Domesday Book 110, 113, 117
Donnelly, William 65
du Lac-d'En-Haut, France *123*
Dunăre, N. 248, 252

EAA Glasgow 1–2, 5, 11
Edramucky, Scotland 68
Emanuelsson, Marie 18
England 109; first phase of medieval transhumance in
  110–13, *112*; second phase of medieval transhumance
  in 113–14; summary of development of transhumance
  in 115; third phase of medieval transhumance in
  114–15; towards a long-term perspective on 117–18;
  transhumance as developing practice in 109–15;
  transhumance as social practice in 116–17; transhumance
  as transformative practice in 115–16
establos of Gipuzkoa *179*, 179–82, *181*
Estrela Mountain, Portugal 224–5, *225*; complementary
  transhumance systems in 227–8, *228*
ethnoarchaeology of salt and pastoralism 255–9, *257–88*

ethnography: of shielings in Scandinavia 15–16; of South Connemara, Ireland 94–5
Everitt, Alan 110, 113

Faegri, K. 236
Fau, L. 127
First Edition Survey Project (FESP) 62
Foster, P. 75
Fournier, G. 125, 130
Fox, H. S. A. 116, 117
France: Auvergne region (*see* Auvergne region, France); south-eastern (*see* southern France)
Frizell Santillo, B. 206

Gabba, Emilio 188
Galaty, J. G. 4
Gammelvallen, Ängersjö 17
Gardiner, Mark 1, 9
Gaulton, Barry C. 6
Giannichedda, E. 193
Giddens, A. 5
Giovannetti, Lucia 187
Gipuzkoa *179*, 179–82, *181*
Gleannán *see* South Connemara, Ireland
Goano 182
Goffredo, R. 187
Gräfjellprosjektet, Hedmark County, Norway 33–6
granges 114
Grava, Massimilano 190
Gredos Range, Spain: conclusions on 241; early medieval period 238–9; geographical and historical setting 234; high medieval times 239–40; introduction to 233–4; modern and contemporary periods 240–1; palynological records and the signature of transhumance in 234–6, *235–6*; Roman period 237–8
Griesemer, J. R. 3

Harrison, John 60
Henry III, King (Castile) 226
heritage of transhumance 10–11
Herlandsetra Nedre, Norway 37
Herlandsetra (ovre), Norway 37, 39
Herseni, T. 248
Hooke, D. 113
Hougen, Bjørn 16, 20

Iberia: archaeological approach to pasture use in Estrela Mountain 224–5, *225*; complementary transhumance systems in Estrela Mountain 227–8, *228*; conclusions on 229–30, *230*; ecosystems and methodological underpinnings of study of transhumance in *220*, 220–1; introduction to 219; long-distance transhumance in 229; middle-distance transhumance in Cantabrian Mountains of 225–7, *227*; short-distance or valley transhumance in Cantabrian Mountains of 222–4, *223*; short-distance transhumance and peasant communities in 221–2
Innertkirchen BE, Switzerland *160*, 160–3
Innertkirchen BE, Zum See, Switzerland *161*, 161–2
intersectionailty 5
Iordache, G. 250

Ireland *see* South Connemara, Ireland
Isle of Lewis *See* Bhiliscleitir, Scotland
Italy *see* Mediterranean transhumance; Tuscany (northern), Italy; Tuscany (southern), Italy
Iversen, J. 236

John II, King (Castile) 226
Johnson, D. L. 3, 4
Jones, Glanville 109–10, 117

Khazanov, Anatoly 3
Kiltryie, Scotland 69, *70*, *70–1*
Kupiec, P. 6

Lacapell-Barrès Mountains site 127, *128*
La Mesta 4, 9, 219, 229; *see also* Iberia
Lancaster, Roger de 114
landscape palimpsest 9–10
Larsson, Jesper 18
Late Medieval Agrarian Crisis 16, 18, 24–5
Lawers Burn, Scotland 68–9, *70*
Lothair II 191
Luick, R. 4

MacDonald, Catriona 76
MacLeod, Anne 76
MacSween, Malcolm 67
maids, shieling 20–1, *22*
Mannoni, T. 193
Maremma plain 200–2; *see also* Tuscany (southern), Italy
marginal landscapes: eco-cultural choices from mountainous 203–5, *204*; reversing the perspective on 208–9, *209*
Martinelli, Alessandra 187
Martonne, E. de 248, 254
material culture in Newfoundland 53–4
Mediterranean transhumance 4; archaeological methods 176–8; cabañas, establos, and rebaños *179*, 179–82, *181*; conciliating transhumant movements 175–6, *177*; introduction to 171–2, *172*; long- and short-distance transhumance movement in Basque Country 176–82, *178–9*, *181*; looking for indicators of short- and long-distance 182–4; as spatialisation of social relationships *173*, 173–4; transterminancia, Alava commons 182; *see also* Tuscany (northern), Italy; Tuscany (southern), Italy
Melgårdssetern, Norway 34, *35*, 39, 40
Milek, K. 6
milk processing in Oberhasli, Switzerland 166
mobility 7–8
Moldavia 245, 247–8; *see also* Romania
Monastery of Courias 226
Montagne de la Vèze, France 127
Monte Labbro Ecological Niche 203–5, *204*
Monte Sagro 193, *194*
monticazione settlements 183–4
Morariu, T. 248
morphology of summer dwellings of South Connemara, Ireland 97–101, *99–101*
Morrison, Dan 76

Moudreiros, Spain 226, *227*
mountain pastoralism and seasonal movements in Romania 250–2, *251*

Nandris, J. 248
National Folklore Commission, Ireland 95
neo-traditional organisations 25
Ness Archaeological Landscape Survey 78
Newfoundland 43, 55; archaeological evidence for transhumance in 46–50; Big Mussel Pond 48–50; brief introduction to 43–4; conclusions on winter housing and European transhumance based on 54–5; discussion of winter houses in 50–1; historical evidence for transhumance in 44–6; material culture in 53–4; spatial organisation of winter communities in 51–2, *53*; Sunnyside 1 46–8
new ruralism movements 25
non-pastoral transhumance 55
northern Tuscany, Italy *see* Tuscany (northern), Italy

Oberhasli, Bernese Alps, Switzerland: *Alpwirtschaft* as part of multistage agricultural systems in 157; animal pens 159; archaeological sites 157–62; building remains *158*, 158–9; conclusions on 166–8; cultural and historical context of Alpine summer farming infrastructure in 163–6, *164*; delimitation of alpine regions in 165; ethnographic sources 163; extant alpine huts 163; historical pictorial sources 162–3; historical written sources 162; Innertkirchen BE *160*, 160–3; Innertkirchen BE, Zum See *161*, 161–2; introduction to 155; milk processing in 166; non-archaeological sources 162–3; pasture walls 159; prospection results 157; raising livestock in 165–6; rock-shelter structures 159; settlement structure 160–2; transport topography and land expansion in Oberhasli 155–7, *156*; wild hay production in 166
Oosthuizen, S. 116–17
Ostrom, Elinor 8
Otto I (emperor) 191
Otto II (emperor) 191
Oxford English Dictionary 1

Pailherols, France 127
palaeobotany 6–7, 17, 30; Scotland 66–7
palimpsest, landscape 9
pastoral architecture of Romania 252–4, *253*; ethnoarchaeology of salt and 255–9, *257–88*
pastoralism 1–2, 11; local/agricultural Romanian 248–50, *249–50*; mountain, Romanian 250–2, *251*; non-pastoral transhumance and 55; overview of transhumance and 3–4; semi-nomadic 3; wetlands and 209–12, *210–12*
pasture walls, Bernese Alps 159
Pecini, Lina 187
Peebles Archaeology Society 68
Pigelleto Reservoir, Tuscany 205–8, *207*
Pious II, Pope 206
place-names of Scotland 61
Portugal *see* Iberia
post-colonialism 5
praxeology 5
Provence, France *see* southern France

Rackham, Oliver 115–16
Raven, J. 75
rebaños, Gipuzkoa *179*, 179–82, *181*
Reckwitz, A. 6
Rendu, C. 7
resistance to social structure in South Connemara, Ireland 101–2
Ribeiro, Orlando 224
Ricci, Renzo 190
rock-shelter structures, Bernese Alps 159
Rødseter, Norway 35–6, 39
Romania: archaeological background of 245–7, *246*; conclusions on 260–1; ethnoarchaeology of salt and pastoralism in 255–9, *257–88*; introduction to 245; as laboratory 247–8; local/agricultural pastoralism 248–50, *249–50*; long-distance transhumance in 259–60, *260*; mountain pastoralism and seasonal movements in 250–2, *251*; pastoral architecture of 252–4, *253*; spatial patterns in 254–5, *255*
Ross, Alasdair 59
Russo, Saverio 188

salt and pastoralism in Romania 255–9, *257–88*
St. Clément, France 127, *128*
Sancy, France *see* Auvergne region, France
Sandnes, Jørn 16
Scheuchzer, Johann Jakob 157
Sclafert, T. 138
Scotland: archaeological field definition and data of 61–6; archaeological methodology 78–80; archaeological results 80–2; architecture of shielding huts of 63; Bhiliscleitir structure 10 82–7; Bhiliscleitir structure 11 87–8; conclusions and discussion 71–2; discussion on ephemeral occupation surfaces 88–91; documentation on 59–61; evidence of function of huts of *64*, 65; excavations of shieling huts of 67–9, *70–1*; introduction to 59; morphology of groups of huts of 66; Ordnance Survey (OS) 61–2; paleo-environmental proxy evidence 66–7; place-names of 61; recent archaeological surveys in upland 75; site of Bhiliscleitir in 75–8; size of groups of huts of 65–6; size of huts of 63
semi-nomadic pastoralism 3
shielings, Scandinavian 15, 25–6; academic study of 29; age, origin and content 29–30; Backasätern 23–4, 33, 40; Dalby Parish, Värmland County, Sweden 30–3; farm, and outland use as innovation package 18–20; future for 25; Gräfjellprosjektet, Hedmark County, Norway 33–6; Herlandsetra (ovre), Norway 37, 39; Herlandsetra Nedre, Norway 37; long-term use of flexible 38–40; mapped as relict 15–16; in medieval and modern times 21–5; Melgärdsetern, Norway 34, *35*, 39, 40; new methods and emergence of new history of 16–18; Rødseter, Norway 35–6, 39; shieling maids and 20–1, *22*; Søndre Veseterstulen, Norway 37–8; Sorgärdsvollen, Norway 34–5, 39; Vesetra, Norway 37–8, *39*; Vestfold County, Norway 36–8
shielings, Scottish: archaeological methods 78–80; archaeological results 80–2; architecture of 63; Bhiliscleitir site 75–80; evidence of function of *64*, 65; excavations of 67–9, *70–1*; morphology of groups of 66; size of 63; size of groups of 65–6; structure 10 82–7

Smith, Philip E. L. 43, 55
social practice theories 5
social structures of transhumance 8–9
Soida, Estrela Mountain 224–5, *225*
Søndre Veseterstulen, Norway 37–8
Sørgårdsvallen, Norway 34–5, 39
South Connemara, Ireland: conclusions on 105–6; division of space at transhumant settlements of 102–5; introduction to 93–4; morphology of summer dwellings in 97–101, *99–101*; resistance to social structure in 101–2; study-area and ethnographic evidence for transhumance in 94–5; transhumant settlement in 95–7
Southern Alps, France *see* southern France
southern Europe *see* Mediterranean transhumance
southern France: conclusions on 147–9, *148*; doubts and the first evidence of seasonal pastoral migration between Provence and the southern Alps, AD 1100–1300 137–9, *138*; forms of seasonal pastoral migration organisation in 141–3, *142–3*; introduction to transhumance in 135–6, *137*; migration routes 143–4; road and daily life on summer and winter pastures in 141–7, *142–3*, *145–6*; shepherd's lifestyle and activities on pastures 144–7, *145–6*; summer ascending migration of flocks from Provence to the southern Alps in 138–9; winter grazing of Alpine herds in 137, *138*; wintering and summering migration flows from AD 1300–1500 139–41, *140–1*
southern Tuscany, Italy *see* Tuscany (southern), Italy
Spain *see* Gredos Range, Spain; Iberia
spatialisation and spatial patterns: organisation of winter communities in Newfoundland 51–2, *53*; in Romania 254–5, *255*; of social relationships in southern Europe *173*, 173–4
Stahl, H. H. 248
Star, S. L. 3
Stoops, G. 80
Sunnyside 1, Newfoundland 46–8
Sussex Downs, England 111, *111*
Switzerland *see* Oberhasli, Bernese Alps, Switzerland
Sylvo-Pastoral strategies in the Pigelleto Reservoir 205–8, *207*

Tipping, R. 66, 72
Torrin, Isle of Skye 68
transhumance: archaeological evidence in Newfoundland 46–50; as boundary object 3, 4; Centocroci hospice and 190–3, *192*; complementary systems in Estrela Mountain, Portugal 227–8, *228*; defining 1–3; as developing practice in medieval England 109–15; division of space and 102–5; ecosystems and methodological underpinnings of study of Iberian *220*, 220–1; first phase of medieval English 110–13, *112*; Gredos Range palynological records and signature of 234–6, *235–6*; heritage from the past for the future 10–11; historical evidence in Newfoundland 44–6; importance in south-eastern France 135–7, *138*; landscape palimpsest and 9–10; long-distance, in Iberia 229; long-distance, in Romania 259–60, *260*; long-range, in northern Tuscany 189–90; looking for indicators of short- and long-distance 182–4; in Maremma, Tuscany 200–2; middle-distance Cantabrian Mountains 225–7,

227; mobility and its meaning in 7–8; movements conciliation in southern Europe 175–6, *177*; new methodological approaches and new encounters with 6–7; non-pastoral 55; overview of pastoralism and 3–4; peasant communities and short-distance Iberian 221–2; second phase of medieval English 113–14; settlement in the Carna Peninsula, Ireland 95–7; as social practice in England 116–17; social structures of 8–9; as spatialisation of social relationships in the Mediterranean region *173*, 173–4; study-area and ethnographic evidence in South Conmemara, Ireland 94–5; theoretical perspectives on historical European 4–6; third phase of medieval English 114–15; as transformative practice in England 115–16; Vinca model 192–3, *194*; winter housing and 54–5
transterminancia, Alava commons 182
Tuscany (northern), Italy: Apennines and Apuan Alps of 189, *189*; Centocroci hospice 190–3, *192*; conclusions on 193, 195; introduction to 187, *188*; long-range transhumance in 189–90; notes on discontinuity in the medieval period in 187–9; questions about transhumance in 187–90; two attempts at drawing the medieval period into focus in 190–3, *192*; versant-transhumance Vinca model of 192–3, *194*
Tuscany (southern), Italy: conclusions on 212–13; eco-cultural choices from mountainous marginal landscape of 203–5, *204*; introduction to 197–8, *198*; long-distance transhumance in Maremma 200–2; Monte Labbro Ecological Niche 203–5, *204*; questions and methodologies 198–200, *199*; reversing the perspective on plains marginal landscapes in 208–9, *209*; Sylvo-Pastoral strategies in the Pigelleto Reservoir 205–8, *207*; tracing local mobile pastoralism patterns in late medieval 202; wetlands and pastoral practices 209–12, *210–12*

Vanni, Edoardo 6, 9
Värmland County, Sweden 18, 30–3
Venovcevs, Anatolijs 6
Vera, Frans 115
Vesetra, Norway 37–8, *39*
Vestfold County, Norway 36–8
Vinca model 192–3, *194*
Violante, Francesco 188
Vuia, R. 248, 251

Wager, Sarah 115
Warner, Peter 117
Welinder, Stig 2
Wendrich, W. 4
wetlands, Tuscany 209–12, *210–12*
Whyte, Ian 113
Wildgoose, Martin 68
wild hay production in Oberhasli, Switzerland 166
Winchester, A. 61
winter housing, Newfoundland *see* Newfoundland
Witney, K. P. 110
Wrathmell, Stuart 110–11

Zalduondo, Italy 182